United States

Faithful and Fearless

Faithful and Fearless
MAJOR HOWARD EGAN

EARLY MORMONISM and the
PIONEERING of the AMERICAN WEST

WILLIAM G. HARTLEY

Faithful and Fearless: Major Howard Egan, Early Mormonism, and the Pioneering of the American West

Copyright © 2017 Howard Egan Biography LLC

All rights reserved. This book or any portion thereof may not be reproduced or used in any manner whatsoever without the express written permission of the publisher, Howard Egan Biography LLC, except for the use of brief quotations in a book review.

The views herein expressed are the responsibility of the author.

Book layout and cover design by Pictures and Stories, Inc.

Printed in the United States of America
Book Printers of Utah, Inc.

First Printing, 2017

ISBN 978-0-9986960-1-0
Library of Congress Control Number: 2017956160

Howard Egan Biography LLC
1975 East Woodside Drive
Holladay, Utah 84124

For orders or questions, please use the following email address: majorhowardeganbiography@gmail.com

For additional information, please visit the following website:
www.majorhowardegan.com

∽

"Egan is a man who attends to his duty strictly

and will never be taken or caught by surprise nor will never

be seen running from danger."

Sheriff H.G. Ferris, Hancock County, Illinois

∽

Contents

Preface XV

1 Ireland Could Not Hold Them 1
The Egans of the Meelaghans 1
Ireland 3
Tullamore, Kings County 4
Social Conditions during Howard's Boyhood 6
Anne's Death and the Decision to Emigrate 8
The Atlantic Crossing 11
Young Howard, Ships, and the Sea 12
The Egan Connection to Ireland 13

2 Montreal Orphan Who Became a Sailor 14
In French-Speaking Montreal 14
A Land in Need of Workers 17
Two Seasons: Winter and Summer 18
More Egan Deaths 19
Howard's Years as a Sailor 21
A Sailor's Life 22

3 Salem, Tamson Parshley, and Mormonism 26
The Seaport of Salem 26
The Newlywed Egans 28
Tamson's New Hampshire Heritage 30
Firstborn Howard Ransom Egan 32
Howard and Rope Making 32
"I Have…Many People in This City Whom I Will Gather Out" 34
Converts Howard and Tamson 37

4 Rope Maker and Policeman in Nauvoo 38
Crossing "the States" in 1842 38
The Founding of Nauvoo 39
Newcomers in a "River City" 39
The Egans' Home 42
Howard's "Nauvoo Rope Manufactory" 42
Tamson and Domestic Life in Nauvoo 44
Shops, Stores, Services, and Trades 46
Rising Temple Walls 48
Sunday Meetings 48
Joseph Smith as Prophet-Teacher 49
The Nauvoo Legion 50
Nauvoo's Masonic Lodge 51
Howard of the Lineage of Judah 52
James Monroe 53
One of the Forty Policemen 53
Electioneering for Joseph Smith for President 56

5 The Martyrdom and Nauvoo's Final Two Years 59
The Martyrdom 59
The "Mantle of Joseph" Meeting 61
In the Seventeenth Quorum of Seventies Presidency 61
Police Work 64
Repeal of the Nauvoo City Charter 64
Hired as a Constable 65
Protecting Brigham Young 66
The "Old Police," the "New Police," and the "City of Joseph" .. 67
Howard, Hosea Stout, and Police Work 68
Howard's Ten-day Patrol Outside Nauvoo 71
A Man To Be Relied On 73
Decision to Leave Illinois 73

6 Temple Blessings and Evacuation Plans 74
Finishing the Temple 74
Eyes on the West 75
Decision to Abandon Nauvoo 76
Exodus Explained in the October Conference 77
Preparations for Spring Departures 78
Studying Explorer Fremont's Reports 81
Howard's Ropes 81
Temple Ordinances Before Leaving 82
The Egans' Plural Marriages 83
Adopted into Heber C. Kimball's Family 85
"To Make an Early Start West" 86
Sugar Creek Encampment 88
Egan Sites in Today's Nauvoo 90

7 Captain Egan and the Iowa Trek 92
Difficult First Fifty Miles 92
Richardson's Point Camp, March 7–18 94
Crossing the Chariton River 95
Counting on Good Traders 96
Howard a Captain of Fifty. 96
More Trade Trips 97
"The Most Severe Time We Have Had" 98
"No Toil Nor Labor Fear" 99
Garden Grove, April 24 to May 12 100
Family Moves Ahead Without Howard 101
Mount Pisgah, May 18 to June 1. 102
To the Council Bluffs Region 103
Trade Trips Down River 105
Waiting beside the Missouri 106
A Battalion and a Halt for Winter 107
The Land Agreement 108

8 Dangerous Secret Assignment 109
Crossing the Missouri River. 109
Battalion Leadership Schism 110
Dangerous Secret Errand. 111
To Fort Leavenworth 112
Onto the Santa Fe Trail. 113
Finding the Battalion at the Arkansas River 114
Causing Command Trouble 116
Accompanying the Battalion to Santa Fe 118
Soliciting Battalion Money 120
Dangerous Return Trip. 122
Mission Accomplished 123

9 First Winter At Winter Quarters. 125
A Month of Hard Labor 125
Doubtful Story About a Nauvoo Cannon 129
Howard's First Trading Trip from Winter Quarters 129
A Revelation Directing the Move West 132
Trading Trips Two, Three, Four, and Five 132
Sickness and Death at Winter Quarters 134
Tamson and Domestic Life 134
Absences at a Cost. 135

10 Captain of Ten in the 1847 Pioneer Company 137
When Was the Destination Selected? 137
Creating the Select Company 138
From Winter Quarters to the Platte. 139

  241 Pounds of Bacon 142
  Along the "Platte River Road" 143
  Difficult Loup Fork River Crossing 144
  Into the High Plains Region 145
  Measuring Distance. 148
  Up along the North Platte River 150
  Landmarks 151

11 Reaching the Great Salt Lake Valley 154

  Fort Laramie 154
  Dangerous Upper Platte Crossing 156
  The Sweetwater, Independence Rock, and Devil's Gate 158
  Waters Flowing to the Pacific. 160
  Fort Bridger in Mexican Territory 162
  The Hasting's Road and Donner Trail 163
  The Great Salt Lake Valley at Last 165
  Howard's Reaction to the Valley 167

12 Starting a Settlement and Retracing the Trail 168

  A Single and Welcome Day of Rest 168
  Laying Out a Settlement 169
  Tree with a Hornets' Nest 171
  Covenanting through Rebaptism 172
  Building Homes and a Fort 172
  Beginning the Return Trip 175
  A Captain of Ten Again. 176
  Meeting the "Big Company" from Winter Quarters 176
  Indian Raiders Steal Horses 178
  Resupplies from Winter Quarters. 179
  Family Reunion. 180
  Important December Meeting across the Missouri. 180
  Six Day Seventies' Jubilee 181
  Preparing to Close Down Winter Quarters 181
  Winter Quarters Postscript 183

13 Taking Tamson and the Boys West 184

  April 1848 Conference 184
  In Kimball's Second Division 184
  Wounded in the Elkhorn Gunfight 186
  Along the Platte's North Side 189
  Camp Captain for Mississippi Saints. 191
  Crossing to the Oregon Trail. 192
  Drought, Feed Shortages, and Dust 193
  Cattle Death Zone 195
  Completing the Journey 197

14 Kanesville Mail, Nancy, and Utah Freight................200
- Three Weeks in Great Salt Lake City 200
- Fast Mail Carrier to Council Bluffs 201
- Wintering in the Kanesville Area 202
- Outfitting the Egan Freight Company......................... 204
- Boulware's Ferry.. 206
- Following the "Old Fort Kearney Trail" 206
- Joining the Oregon Trail and Constant Traffic............... 208
- Along the Platte, Then Fording the South Platte 210
- To the Upper North Platte Crossing 211
- Avoiding a Robbery Near South Pass.......................... 212
- Needing Help from the Valley................................ 213
- Arriving Home to a New Home 213
- The Family During Howard's Absence 214
- A New Baby and an Additional Wife........................... 216

15 By a New Southern Route to the Gold Fields 217
- News about Gold in California 217
- Mormons and the Gold Rush 218
- The Need for a Southern Wagon Route......................... 219
- Gold Mining Missionaries 220
- The 1849 Southern Trail Companies........................... 220
- Why Did Howard Go?.. 221
- The Route... 222
- Winter Travel the Length of Utah 222
- Across Southern Nevada Deserts 224
- To Cajon Pass and California Ranches 226
- Heading for the Sierra Nevada's Gold Regions 227
- A Pack Train and Egan's Wagon Company 229
- Traveling Up El Camino Real 229
- Mission San Buenaventura and Beach Travel 231
- From Mission St. Ines to Mission San Juan Baptista.......... 232
- Supplies and Instructions at San Jose....................... 233
- The Northern and Southern Gold Regions 234
- Across Pacheco Pass and the San Joaquin River 235

16 Running a Trading Post and Assisting Apostles 237
- Searching Where to Prospect................................. 237
- Setting up a Trading Post and Prospecting................... 238
- Buying Trips to Stockton.................................... 242
- Assisting the Apostles 243
- Health and Business Troubles 246
- Leaving California via Carson Pass.......................... 248
- The California Trail along the Humboldt River 249
- Taking the Salt Lake Cutoff................................. 250
- Troubled Homecoming 251

17 The "Mountain Justice" Killing of James Monroe 252
- A Homecoming Heartbreak 252
- Paramour James Monroe. 253
- Work for Uncles John and Enoch Reese, Merchants. 254
- Decision to Seek Justice. 256
- Monroe's Appeal to Brigham Young 259
- Howard Confronts and Kills Monroe 260
- Back Home. 262

18 A Jury Trial and Acquittal 263
- Grand Jury Investigation and Findings 263
- George A. Smith's "Mountain Common Law" Defense. 266
- Judge Zerubbabel Snow's Charge to the Jury 269
- "Not Guilty". 271
- Support for Defending Family Honor 271
- Family Repercussions. 273
- Loss of the Plural Wives. 273
- Monroe's Son William. 274

19 City, Family, and Cattle Drives 276
- Residents in Great Salt Lake City 276
- A Tannery Business. 278
- Nineteenth Ward Members 279
- Willie's Boyhood. 279
- Utah and Church Developments 280
- Costly Fire 281
- Selling Cattle in California for Livingston & Kinkead 282
- Howard's Near-Death Freezing and Crippling. 285
- Difficulties on the California Trail 286
- Failed Shortcut 287
- Howard's "Fearful Fall" 289
- An 1854 Cattle Drive 290
- "Tecumsee" 290
- "Cautious Kindness". 291

20 The "Ten Days Bet" and the New Egan Trail 292
- Operating out of "Sloughhouse" and Putah 293
- Prior Attempts to Find a Central Route to California. 295
- Scouting the 1855 Egan Trail 296
- Howard's Historic Ten (Eleven) Day Trip to Sacramento 298
- Three Months of Cattle Business in California 302

21 Famine, Handcarts, Reformation, and Fort Limhi 303
- Drought and Grasshoppers 303
- A Cattle-Killing Winter 305
- The Famine of 1856 306
- A Gap in Howard's Record 307
- Helping Handcart Emigrants 307
- The "Mormon Reformation" 308
- With President Young's Caravan to Fort Limhi 309

22 Difficult Assignments During the "Utah War" 313
- A Federal Territory or a Theocracy? 313
- The United States Army's "Utah Expedition" 314
- Nauvoo Legion Readiness 315
- Defensive Actions to Protect the Territory 317
- Camp Scott and "Johnston's Army" 318
- Mormons' Echo Canyon Defenses 319
- Winter Lull and Spring War Preparations 319
- Howard Brings Ammunition from California 320
- Preparations for a Spring Invasion 321
- Thomas L. Kane's Peace Mission 322
- Kane's Peace Negotiations 323
- Escorting Colonel Kane Across the Plains 324
- From Florence to Philadelphia 326
- With Thomas and Elizabeth Kane in Philadelphia 326
- Egans Join the "Move South" 328
- Peace Settlement and a Presidential Pardon 329
- Camp Floyd Army Post 330
- Historian MacKinnon's Assessment of Howard's Utah War Service 331

23 Howard and the Chorpenning Western Mail 333
- A Bird with Poorly Flapping Wings 333
- George Chorpenning and the "West Wing" Mail 334
- Family News from Canada 335
- Rivalries on the "East Wing" 335
- Butterfield Overland Mail Competition on a Southern Route 336
- Chorpenning Shifts to the Egan Route 336
- Indian Doctor Cures Howard's Snow Blindness 339
- Creating a Stagecoach Route on the Egan Trail 339
- A Cutoff Avoiding the Forty Mile Desert 341
- Distracting an Annoying Indian 341
- Capt. Simpson's Refinements of Egan's Route 343
- The Egan-Simpson Road 347

  Howard's Road Improvements 348
  Gosiutes, Deep Creek, and the Indian Farm 349
  Chorpenning's Express Company Failure. 350
  Frustrations About Not Being Paid 352

24 A "Ramrod" for the Pony Express 354
  Why the Pony Express? 354
  Ramrod Howard: One of Five District Superintendents 356
  The Mail Relay System 357
  Historic First Pony Express Ride 358
  Howard Carries the First Pony Express Mail to Salt Lake City 359
  Riders and Horses 360
  Mail and Postage. 362
  The Stations Howard Supervised. 363
  "Paiute War" and Costly Damage to Howard's Line 367
  Range Boys. 371

25 Pony Express, Egan Adventures, and the Telegraph 372
  Soldiers Help Quell the Violence. 373
  Traveler Burton's Descriptions of Howard's Operations. 374
  Civil War Shifts Butterfield to the Central Route 376
  Egan Family Pony Express Stories 379
  Near-Ambush in Egan Canyon 380
  Reprimand for Taking a Shortcut 381
  Circle Ride in a Snowstorm 382
  Continuous Ride of 330 Miles 383
  Riding Out an Attack 383
  Fatal Horse Fall 383
  Saving Nick Wilson's Life 384
  Ras's Wedding in Between Rides 384
  Telegraph Terminates the Pony Express. 385
  Pony Express Legacies. 387

26 Overland Stagecoach Supervisor. 389
  Ex-Sailor on the Desert Sea 389
  Stagecoach Mail Starts on the West Wing 390
  The Concord Stagecoach. 391
  Supervisors, Conductors, Drivers, and Station Hands 393
  Butterfield Overland Mail Moves to the Central Route 394
  Overland Mail Operations, 1861–1862 394
  Appointed Overland Stagecoach Superintendent 395
  Passengers and "Hard Traveling" 397
  Ransom's Three Days Without Food. 398
  Desert Pirates 399

	Col. Connor Establishes Camp Douglas	400
	Bear River Massacre	401
	The Gosiute Indian War in 1863	402
	Near-Killing of Ransom at Deep Creek	403
	Stagecoach Driver Killed Near Eight Mile Station	403
	Howard Drives a Stagecoach After the Driver Is Killed	404
	Killings and Arson at Canyon Station	405
	The 1863 Gosiute Peace Treaty	406
	Wells Fargo's "Grand Consolidation"	406
	The "Golden Spike" Forces Stagecoach Relocations	409

27 The 1860s, Deep Creek Ranch, and the Family 411

- Family Changes 411
- Deep Creek Valley 412
- Egan Station and the Ranch 413
- Egan Stories About Deep Creek 416
- Treasurer Rumfield's Visit 418
- William Egan's Recollections 419
- Young Ranch Hands 421
- Ruby Valley Store and Farm 423
- Military Officer in the Short "Morrisite War" 424
- Third District Court Deputy Clerk 426
- Old Indian Left to Die 427
- Wagon Train Ruins and Skeletons 427
- Tamson's Family Letters 428
- Ras's Mission to England, 1868–1869 429
- Stagecoach Supervisor Out of a Job 430

28 Miner, Missionary, City Life, and Final Days 432

- Prospector 432
- The *Egan Ledge* Claim 433
- Helping Direct the Clifton Mining District 433
- Howard's Mining Claims 435
- "Living Is Very Hard" 436
- Exit from Ranching and Mining 437
- Disposing of the Ranch 438
- Amazing Spiritual Outpouring Among Native Americans 439
- Howard's Gosiute Mission 441
- At Home in Salt Lake City 442
- Nineteenth Ward United Order Soap Factory 443
- Policeman, Deputy Sheriff, and Guard Work 444
- Nursing Fatally Ill Brigham Young 445
- Guard Duty at Brigham Young's Grave 447
- Howard's Death on March 16, 1878 448
- Nineteenth Ward Funeral 450

29 Tamson, the Family, and Publishing "Pioneering the West" ... 452
- Widow Tamson 452
- Postscripts About Howard's Former Wives 454
- The Egan Sons 455
- Howard Egan's Hundredth Birthday Reunion 459
- Plans to Publish Howard's Diaries 461
- Book Contract with Skelton Publishing Company 461
- Howard R.'s Additions of "Thrilling Experiences" 462
- Printing and Delays 463
- *Pioneering the West* is Born 463
- The Egan Papers at Yale University 465

30 Major Howard Egan: The Man And His Legacy 466
- Impressive Presence 466
- Storyteller with a Sense of Humor 468
- Dependable Toughness 468
- What Kind of Mormon? 471
- Pioneering the Untamed West 473
- Businessman 474
- Livestock Skills 475
- Literate 475
- Comfortable Being Away 476
- Sense of Fairness and Generosity 476
- Cautious Compassion for Native Americans 477
- His Place in the History of the American West 479
- His Place in Mormon History 480
- Monuments, Markers, Namings, and Events 481

Notes 487

Bibliography 569

Index 597

About the Author 619

Preface

Howard Egan (1815–1878) is one of the American West's outstanding frontiersmen and developers. He is best known for being one of the original 1847 Mormon Pioneers and for his involvement with the Pony Express. But he also had participated in a host of other exceptional experiences as an Irish immigrant, Canadian orphan, sailor, Salem rope maker, policeman, Nauvoo Legion major, homeless refugee, Santa Fe Trail secret agent, twice wagon train captain, gold rush trading post operator, avenger of his wife's seducer, cattle drover, explorer and discoverer of a vital western trail, recipient of dangerous Utah War assignments, Pony Express rider and district manager, overland mail stagecoach driver and superintendent, desert rancher and merchant, friend of Native Americans, silver miner, deputy sheriff, and guard to Joseph Smith and Brigham Young.

In activities of The Church of Jesus Christ of Latter-day Saints (the Mormon Church), Major Egan belonged to a small circle of fearless and dependable men, including Porter Rockwell, Hosea Stout, and Lot Smith, upon whom leaders counted to fill difficult assignments. He was well regarded by contemporaries. His three diaries are vital sources of history about the American West. His Egan name still designates a canyon, a mountain range, and other geographic features in the Great Basin region.

Yet, despite his significant accomplishments and contributions, Egan lacks a scholarly biography. In 1917 his sons published *Pioneering the West*, an invaluable collection of Egan-related documents and materials, but not a biography. J. Raman Drake's 1956 thesis "Howard Egan: Frontiersman, Pioneer, and Express Rider" is a useful but limited survey, now outdated. James D. Martin's 110-page *The Story of Major Howard Egan*, published in 2000, has good wheat, bothersome chaff, and can't be relied upon because it lacks documentation.

When Howard Egan descendant Robert Sloan and his wife Janet asked me to write a book-length history of Egan, I was an associate professor of history at Brigham Young University, affiliated with the Smith Institute for LDS Church History. The Sloans and I agreed the Egan history should be thorough, honest, accurate, and that it must be a history my academic colleagues could respect and that the general public—including Egan descendants—would enjoy reading.

Research about Howard Egan begins with *Pioneering the West*. Now a classic in western literature, *Pioneering the West* presents stories and recollections by three Egan sons about Howard Egan, the Pony Express, stagecoaching, and Native Americans. It contains edited versions of Howard Egan's 1847, 1849–50, and 1855 original diaries, along with other of his writings and documents. At Yale University, in the Beinecke Library's Western Americana collection, I researched the original Howard Egan diaries and papers, upon which *Pioneering the West* is based. Comparing those with *Pioneering the West*'s transcriptions, my research assistant Kristina Skousen and I found the differences to be too minor to justify making new transcriptions.

The Sloans shared with me extensive binders and files of Egan materials they've collected for decades. Help, too, came from other individuals, including genealogist Maryan Egan-Baker for research about Egans in Ireland and Canada; Barbara Ann Aye in Ottawa for Canadian research; Sandra Day for Parshley research in New Hampshire; and Elayne Stanton Allebest for Egan-Ireland insights. I searched and extracted from scores of relevant books, monographs, and articles dealing with the Gold Rush, overland trails, Pony Express, stagecoaching, Egan's associates, Ireland, Canada, Salem, Utah, Nevada, California, and early Mormonism.

Primary sources I consulted, other than the Egan family's materials, are records from the LDS Church Historical Department, the Utah State Archives, the Utah Historical Society Library, special collections and library holdings at Brigham Young University and the University of Utah, the National Archives, the Library and Archives of Canada in Ottawa, the Salem Public Library, the New England Historic Genealogical Society in Boston, Yale's Beinecke Library, the Huntington Library in San Marino, the California State History Library in Sacramento, and the Bancroft Library at University of California, Berkeley. I am grateful for the help that the staffs at these libraries and repositories gave me. Documents and data on the internet also proved increasingly useful, as archives constantly added more and more primary materials.

I felt the "power of place" when visiting Egan-related sites in Massachusetts, New Hampshire, Nauvoo, Iowa, Utah, along the Mormon Battalion's route to Santa Fe, the Mormon Trail from Nauvoo to Utah, the Pony Express trail in Utah and Nevada, gold rush sites in the Sierras, Carson Pass, and the California Trail in Nevada.

The Howard Egan story told here has gaps. Most regrettable is that a paucity of records makes us short-shrift Egan's experiences in Montreal, his years as a sailor, his gold-rush work operating the Salt Lake Trading Company, and his wife Tamson's life story. Egan descendants and leading databases present conflicting genealogical information not always easy to unscramble, and therefore the genealogy presented in this book is what Janet Sloan and I feel is the best. Instead of including an appendix containing Egan genealogical data, we refer readers to what is posted on the website majorhowardegan.com.

I am responsible for the book's structure, facts, and interpretations, and the balancing act regarding how much or how little to say about particular matters and episodes. For example, among some historians Egan is best known for killing James Monroe, and the trial that followed, so I devote two chapters to those events. Also, because few adults today are well-versed regarding Mormon and western U. S. history during Howard Egan's time period, I've provided more historical context than my historian colleagues might want.

My narrative cautiously uses such introductory terms as "perhaps," "possibly," "most certainly," "very likely," and "no doubt," in situations where such seem justifiable. For clarity's sake, we refer to Egan son Howard Ransom Egan as "Ransom" until father Howard's death, after which we use "Howard R." We designate son Richard Erastus Egan as "Ras," which is what his mother called him. When dealing with Howard's wife Nancy Redden and her brother Jackson, although some sources spell the name *Redding*, records closest to the family in the Nauvoo period spell it *Redden*, which is the spelling we use. And, although *Goshute* is the favored spelling now for that Native American group, we use *Gosiute*, a spelling common in Howard Egan's day.

The chapters' endnotes, all of which are in short form, are in one section in the back of the book. The full citations are spelled out in the bibliography.

Several Egan descendants helped with final production work. John Howard and Jeanette Egan provided hundreds of hours proofing and critiquing; John descends from Howard Egan's son Richard Erastus or Erastus. Catherine Sloan Blake, also a descendant through Erastus, directed the selection, obtainment, and positioning of pictures and illustrations. David Sloan, likewise an Erastus descendant, oversaw the production of the maps, designed by Janis Chan. Catherine and David also did proofreading, as did their mother Janet L. Sloan, whose husband Robert C. Sloan was a descendant of Erastus. Three grandchildren of Robert and Janet—Daniel Sloan, Sarah Sloan, and John Newton—were also proofreaders for the book. Elayne Allebest, part of son Howard Ransom's posterity, helped review early chapters.

Tom and Alison Taylor of Pictures and Stories, Inc. directed the design and print production. We are grateful to Brigham Young University's Smith Institute and BYU's Charles Redd Center for Western Studies for their support, and to history colleagues Ron Esplin, Bill MacKinnon, Will Bagley, Ron Barney, Jesse Petersen, Ron Walker, Brian Cannon, Ted Moore, and Mike Shamo for suggestions and encouragement.

Here, then, is a biographical history of Major Howard Egan. We invite readers to tag along with Egan while he engages in exciting, dangerous, and dynamic developments in early Mormonism and the early American West. ◆

∼ 1 ∼

Ireland Could Not Hold Them

Unlike arid Great Basin regions in the American West where Howard Egan's name is linked, he started life on a lush green island surrounded by sea. He was born on June 15, 1815 in the Meelaghans, a townland near the town of Tullamore in Ireland's center. Eight years later, Howard's widower father moved his family to Lower Canada, breaking a string of Egan generations who resided in Ireland. Howard never saw his emerald homeland again.

The Egans of the Meelaghans

Howard's beginnings were pure Irish. In Irish history the Egans are "an ancient Irish family." Egans migrated to southern Eire far back in the fourteenth century. "As well as being known for their expertise in areas such as law and history, the family of Mac Aodhagain or Mac Egan were noted for their musical skills. Some of them also established a reputation for their poetical skill." Although the Mac Egans made valiant efforts to preserve their property, England's Cromwellian government took away nearly all of their landed possessions after the rebellion of 1641. By then, diverse spellings of the name appeared "as hard-pressed clerks grappled with the difficulties of writing down unfamiliar Irish words and surnames in Latin and English forms." Variants included Aodhagain or Mhic Aodhagain, M'Egaine, J'Heagan, Heagan, Keegan, O'Egan, and MacEgan. In Celtic myth the name meant fire or fire-god. Decorating their ancient Egan crest is the motto "Fortitude and Prudence."[1]

When Howard was born, his father, Howard Egan Sr., was about thirty-three, and his mother, Anne Meath, perhaps twenty-eight. Howard Egan Sr.'s parents were Bernard and Betty (or Betsy) Egan—her maiden name is not known. They both were born in Ireland in the 1760s and lived in the Meelaghans in Kings County (now Offaly County). Howard Egan Sr. was born in 1782 in the Meelaghans. He and Anne Meath married around 1805 in Kings County.[2] She was born about 1778.

Egan Family Cottage where Howard Egan, Sr. and Howard Egan, Jr. were born, Pioneering the West

The Meelaghans is a townland, a small geographical division of land like a farm or a cluster of cottages and outbuildings. Kings or Offaly County contains 1,128 townlands—including the Meelaghans—which average 406 acres each.[3] If asked by an outsider where they were from, a resident of the Meelaghans would give the name of the nearest town, Tullamore, located three miles to the northwest. In the county, the Meelaghans were in the civil parish of Geashill, and in the Geashill Barony.

Howard Egan Sr. began life in the humble cottage that his grandfather Bernard Egan built in the Meelaghans. Howard Jr. was born there as well. Land records show that Bernard Egan's farm was occupied in 1800 by William Egan, the oldest son, and was then "re-let" to both William and his brother Howard Egan (Sr.). William died in 1812. In 1813 the tenancy was in the names of Howard and third oldest brother Edward Egan.[4] As of 2017 the cottage was still there. It matches the photograph dated about 1900 and published with Howard Jr.'s story in *Pioneering the West*. Even though Bernard had built the cottage, he didn't own the land it stood on. Rather, he leased it from British aristocracy. Every acre in the Geashill Barony belonged to Lord Edward, Second Earl Digby.[5]

Howard and Anne Meath Egan's children and their years of birth are:

Eliza	1806	Howard	1815
Mary	1807	Anne	1817
Catherine	1808	Richard	1819
Bernard (Barney)	1810	Margaret (Gretta)	1822
John	1812	Evelina	1822

All were born in the Meelaghans. They belonged to the Killeigh Parish of the Church of Ireland.[6] Because Killeigh Parish's registers did not start until 1808, the Egan parents' marriage and the births of their first three children are not found in church records. The records do document Howard Jr.'s infant baptism on September 20, 1815. Also listed are the baptisms of his siblings Bernard (Barney), John, Richard, Evelina, and Margaret (Gretta).[7]

Killeigh Parish Church, Tullamore, Ireland, Egan Family Archives

Ireland

To mention Ireland conjures up thoughts of St. Patrick's Day, leprechauns, the Blarney Stone, shamrocks, and lucky clovers. Dublin, Belfast, Kilkenny, Londonderry, and Limerick are some of the most well-known places in Ireland. Ireland has also been associated with bitter feuding between Irish Catholics and Protestants, bad blood that dates back decades before Howard Jr. was born. Ireland is the twentieth largest island on the earth, some 304 miles long and 172 miles wide. Great Britain is to its east, fourteen miles away at its closest. A mild but changeable oceanic climate blesses Ireland with lush vegetation.

The popular perception is "Irish-Catholics." Protestant Irish, like the Egans, were the exceptions. Catholicism came early to Ireland. St. Patrick is generally recognized as the island's patron saint. The *Chronicle of Ireland* records that in 431 A.D. Bishop Palladius arrived on a mission from Pope Celestine I to minister to the Irish "already believing in Christ." The same chronicle records that Saint Patrick, likewise a bishop, arrived the following year. There is debate about the missions of the two, but the consensus is that both took place, and that the older Druid tradition in Ireland collapsed in the face of the new religion. During the Reformation, England turned Protestant. In the 1690s a system of Protestant English rule took root in Ireland, unfavorable to its Catholic majority and likewise to Irish Protestants, who resented English rule. In 1801 Ireland became part of the "United Kingdom of Great Britain and Ireland."[8] In his boyhood days, being among the Protestant minority, Howard Jr. probably heard his share of anti-Catholic sentiment.

Tullamore, Kings County

Howard spent his boyhood in the heart of Ireland. In 1556 an act of the Irish parliament created King's County, named after Philip, then king of Ireland. The county, a bit south of Ireland's dead-center, comprises a flat landscape. Nearly half of the county is bog, mountain, or waste. The soil is generally not very fertile, but Tullamore, occupying a central position in the county, is in a very fertile agricultural district situated along the Tullamore River.[9] The town is about fifty miles west-by-south from Dublin. Tullamore means "big mound" or "hill," a reference to Hip Hill, a mound near town.[10]

During the seventeenth century Tullamore was a wee village with perhaps 400 people. It grew at a moderate pace in the eighteenth century, adding a military barrack, church, tannery, and linen factory.[11] When Howard Egan Sr. was about age three, a failed attempt to launch a hot air balloon caused a fire that burned about 100 houses—one-third of the town, which then consisted almost wholly of thatched cabins. After the fire, Tullamore experienced "significant economic growth," fostered by the coming of the Grand Canal in 1798 that linked Tullamore to Dublin.[12] Landlord Charles William Bury helped rebuild the town in a better configuration than before the fire, and helped erect a town hall and a new church, St. Catherine's, which opened in 1815, the year Howard Jr. was born.[13]

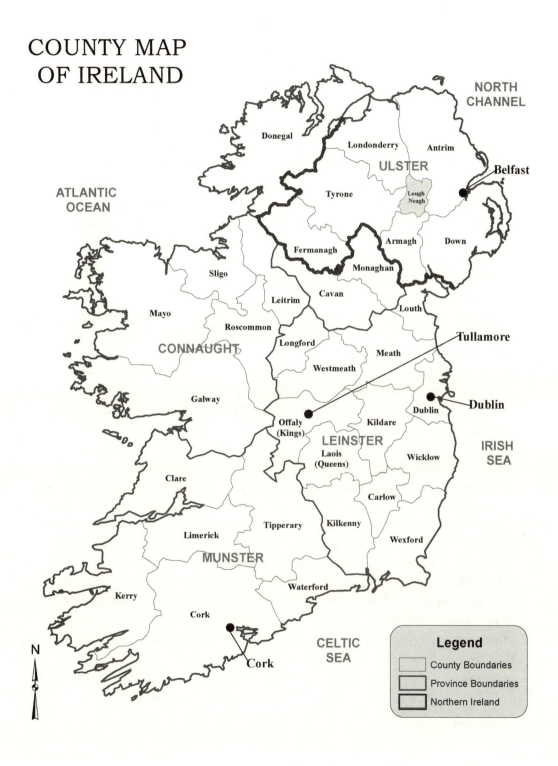

Social Conditions during Howard's Boyhood

Based on the Egans' cottage and lease situation, we presume the family was poor, lived humbly at a survival level, and struggled to have adequate food and clothing. Tullamore residents and those on the outskirts, like the Egans, raised cattle, grew hops, barley, and potatoes, and extracted peat. Bogs supplied a never-ending quantity of peat for fuel. A table of prices for 1811 in King's County identifies common items Howard and Anne would have purchased for their family: hay, coal, beef, mutton, eggs, bacon, turkey, wheat, flour, milk, shoes, whiskey, ale, and cheese. Also listed were "labor costs" for carpenters, harvest laborers, day labor of children, mowing grass per acre, thresher per day, plough with two horses per day, saddle horse per day, and shoeing a horse.[14]

A description written two decades after the Egans emigrated told of living conditions in King's County, which likely were similar to what they experienced. Farm sizes on average were twelve to seventeen acres. Considerable tracts of bog were reclaimed each year. Chief crops were wheat and potatoes, except near the bogs and mountains where oats were the principal crop. "The houses of the small farmers are very mean, and the peasant's cabins are throughout miserably poor, in a few instances weather-proof, and mostly thatched with straw." The food was potatoes, milk, and oatmeal. "Though illiterate, the people are very anxious to have their children instructed, as is evident from the number of small schools in all parts…They speak English every where," and rarely did someone speak Irish. Clothing of the coarsest material was manufactured at home.[15]

Two major events jolted the world in 1815, Howard's birth year, both of which impacted the Egans in subsequent years. The first was the end of the Napoleonic Wars, which brought peace but hard economic adjustments to Europe, including Ireland. A "slump in agricultural prices" hurt Irish agriculture. Howard Sr., like many Irish farmers, very likely suffered income losses caused by the post-war depression. Between 1815 and 1825, wheat prices on the Dublin market fell by a third and "had profound effects on the Irish farming community." For many small farmers "there was really no further economy that they could make, and accordingly they either fell heavily into debt or else lost their hold on the land."[16]

In 1815, too, the most powerful volcanic eruption of the nineteenth century created a climatic catastrophe. Mt. Tambora, a volcano in the East Indies, erupted in April, blowing off its top one-third. The huge amount of dust blasted into the upper atmosphere caused destructive weather events. The earth's northern hemisphere suffered through a "volcanic winter and summer," such that 1816 became known as "the year without a summer." Cool temperatures and heavy rains caused harvest failures in Britain and Ireland. Then, like one domino knocking down the next, failure of the wheat, oat, and potato harvest caused a famine, the famine caused malnutrition, and the malnutrition contributed to a typhus epidemic between 1816 and 1819 that killed 400,000 Irish.[17]

Other than the dates of Howard Jr.'s birth and baptism, little is known specifically about him as a boy. He probably knew that north of Tullamore is a gravel ridge known as the Arden Hills. South are the Slieve Bloom Mountains. On the east and west are flat bog lands, relieved only on the eastern side by the stump of an extinct volcano known as "Croghan Hill." A traveler's guide published in 1819, when Howard Jr. was four, said that Tullamore was a neat, regularly built town, with "stately streets" and "handsome dwellings."[18] It observed that a linen manufactory had been introduced, that "barracks are spacious and handsome," and the market-house functioned well. "The Grand Canal runs down by the town," and "the Church is adorned with a lofty steeple."[19]

In 1821 Tullamore had a population of 5,444.[20] The British government conducted a survey between 1818 and 1820 of social conditions in the Egans' Killeigh Parish, which is helpful for us to understand their living situation. Parish priest Fr. James Kinsella recorded the findings. They show that a good number of deserted children, widows, aged, and infirm had no means of support. The ordinary diet for the poor was "potatoes only, sometimes milk." In general, the condition of the poorer classes had "much deteriorated" since the end of the Napoleonic wars.[21]

The year 1822 saw great scarcity and famine.[22] When Sir Walter Scott traveled to Ireland about that time, he was appalled by the condition of the peasants in the countryside. "Their poverty has not been exaggerated," he wrote, "it is on the extreme verge of human misery."[23] Such hard and desperate times for Irish peasants forced thousands to emigrate, including the Howard Egan family.[24]

It's possible that young Howard Jr. received some schooling in Ireland. During the time Fr. James Dowling was the priest in Killeigh Parish, a school report of the diocese, called "Parochial Schools Returns for 1824," was drawn up, the year after the Egans emigrated.[25] It showed that the parish had "hedge" or rural schools, which were simple buildings with roofs covered with straw. Parents paid to have their children taught spelling, writing, and "figures." The two area schools closest to the Egan cottage were in the Meelaghans and about a mile away at Annaharvey. Both were Catholic schools, but included Protestant children as well. John Bayham taught at a lime-and-stone Protestant school in Killeigh, within three miles of the Egans, where, in 1824, he taught twelve male and eight female students.[26] Perhaps young Egans attended one of these schools. By the time Howard was in his thirties he wrote and spelled well, but where and how he learned to do so is not known.

Anne's Death and the Decision to Emigrate

In 1822 the Egan family increased by two, with the birth of twins Margaret (Gretta) and Evelina. The cottage was crowded. Early the next year, death struck the family a terrible blow. On February 15, 1823, mother Anne died in the Meelaghans.[27] Howard Sr. was now a widower with ten children, ranging in age from infant to seventeen years. With so many children, he faced a dismaying future. Howard Jr. was seven years old when he lost his mother. "It appears that after the death of his wife Howard [Sr.] got into rather poor circumstances, and was obliged to sell his part of [his lease to] the farm to a man by name of Watson and then went to Canada."[28]

Although *Pioneering the West*, the earliest history written about Howard Egan Jr., indicates that the family emigrated in 1823, some Egan researchers have suggested that the migration took place in 1825.[29] Their case makes two claims. First, it argues that the Egans were part of an historic emigration program spearheaded by Peter Robinson that brought more than 2,500 Irish to Canada in two ships in 1823 and nine ships in 1825.[30] Second, a roster of passengers aboard an 1825 St. Lawrence steamboat, the *Chambly*, lists a "Thomas Howard Agan." Of course, "Agan" well could be a variant spelling of Egan. This Thomas Howard Agan was accompanied by seven others and two children, meaning ten people in the group, which is the number in Howard Egan Sr.'s emigrating family. Also, the list doesn't mention a wife, which would have been noted had a wife been present, just as our Howard had no wife with him. Therefore, this Thomas Howard Agan, some assume, could be our Howard Egan Sr., meaning the Egan family emigrated in 1825, not 1823. The Canadian national archives has lists of passengers on the St. Lawrence Steamboat Company's steamers from Quebec to Montreal for all the years between 1819 and 1835, and our Howard Egan family is not on the 1823 passenger lists.[31] This absence also supports the idea that the man named "Agan" on the *Chambly* could be Howard Sr. Additionally, three Egan children died in Canada almost at the same time, in June and July of 1825, within weeks of when they could have arrived in Montreal. Those deaths perhaps were due to a disease they contracted onboard ship.

However, the Robinson program, the *Chambly* list, and the 1825 date are problematic notions. The first problem is that Robinson's official reports make very clear that he recruited from the baronies of Cork and neighboring counties "from the South of Ireland." Cork is about one hundred miles from where the Egans lived.

Another problem is that Robinson's program insisted that emigrants be paupers. The prime reason why the British government approved Robinson's program was to find out if such a sponsored migration would uplift the downtrodden masses by giving them land grants to develop farms in Upper Canada (not Lower Canada where

Emigrants at Cork Quay, Illustrated London News,
May 10, 1851, National Archives

Quebec and Montreal are). "I confined myself strictly to the selection of persons of no capital whatever," Robinson said, "and who might more properly be called paupers." His instructions that those chosen to go should be without the means of supporting themselves in Ireland "were scrupulously adhered to." He enlisted only those "unable to obtain an honest livelyhood at home or to pay their passage to Canada." The Egans were poor, but not paupers.

Furthermore, Robinson designed his plan specifically for Catholics, though he made a few exceptions. "In every town or village from which emigrants were expected, I called upon the Roman Catholic priest, as well as the more respectable inhabitants," Robinson explained. "Several priests entered into the [recruiting] matter with much zeal." [32]

Based on what Robinson's program sought to accomplish, the Egans weren't qualified. They lived far away from Cork. They were not Catholics. And, Howard Sr., though poor, was not a pauper—he had lease rights he could sell. Many Irish, not part of Robinson's program, emigrated in those same years by other means, on other emigrant ships.[33]

Another problem is the Agan family's make-up, as listed on the *Chambly*'s June 7, 1825 roster. True, the number in the group, ten, fits the Egans, and the man's middle name, Howard, is suggestive. Also, the year 1825 seems like a better emigration year than 1823, given that in 1823 the youngest Egan was an infant or toddler. However, not easy to dismiss is *Pioneering the West*'s statement about Howard, that "after the death of his mother, when about eight years of age, 1823, with his father and eight other children, he left Ireland."[34] Howard himself must have provided that date. He was eight years old in 1823, and ten in 1825, so he was old enough to have a knowledge of the correct year, if not from his own awareness then from his siblings with whom he associated for several years after the emigration.

Also, the name Thomas Howard Agan is enigmatic. Yes, Agan could be a variant spelling of Egan, but the first name Thomas, without other corroboration, is foreign to our Howard Egan. Equally troublesome, the *Chambly* passenger list, the heart of the circumstantial case, says the Thomas Howard Agan group included only two children under age twelve.[35] But in 1825, Howard Sr. had four children under age twelve, not two: Howard, ten; Anne, eight; Richard, five; and Evelina, three. Likewise, it needs noting that the *Chambly* left Quebec for Montreal on June 7, 1825, which was *before* any of Robinson's nine ships arrived in Quebec.[36] So, any proposal to change the Egans' emigration date to 1823 from 1825 needs a firmer foundation.

A report about the 1823 Irish emigrants underscored that "when the times became depressed and their means were diminishing, they were glad to embrace any opportunity that would afford a better prospect; and reports were circulated that in [North] America they would better their condition."[37] Howard Sr. fit that description. Studies show that Irish emigration back then "normally occurred shortly before marriage became probable, and close to the moment when household control was transferred from one generation to another."[38] He then had three daughters reaching marriage age—seventeen, sixteen, and fifteen. Additionally, his own small acreage could not accommodate being divided in the near future into parcels big enough for his four sons. Work opportunities for his children were scarce.

So, for "push" and "pull" reasons, the Egans headed for Canada, where the Irish were welcome. Canada was part of the British Empire, and people in the British Isles were "free to go" to other British-controlled lands without restrictions.[39] Shipping between the British Isles and Canada was common and available. Had Howard Sr. and his family been dirt-poor, they could not have crossed the Atlantic: emigrants needed monetary resources to pay for the move, or some kind of subsidy. Howard Sr. had to make arrangements to sell his equipment and animals. As noted below, he sold his tenant farm rights to a man named Watson, a transaction that perhaps let him pay off obligations and afford ship passage.

The Egans left Ireland between two major waves of Irish immigration that history books emphasize: one that followed Napoleon's defeat in Europe in 1815 and peaked in 1819, and another during the 1830s.[40]

The Atlantic Crossing

When Howard Sr. and his large family left their Meelaghans cottage, they didn't take with them one of the twin daughters, Margaret, also called Gretta. She stayed, probably in the care of deceased mother Anne's sister, Aunt Mary. Howard then took his nine other children to a port and boarded a ship. The closest seaport was Dublin, sixty-eight miles away, connected to Tullamore by the Grand Canal. No official immigration record or passenger ship lists have been found that document when and how the Egans crossed the Atlantic Ocean. The Egans could have sailed in 1823 on the brig *Alexander* that left Dublin on April 19, with 142 settlers heading to Quebec, or on the brig *John and Mary*, which sailed from Dublin on April 30, taking 164 settlers to Quebec.[41] Since it wasn't until 1824 that steamships first connected the British Isles with Canada, the Egans traveled as sailing ship passengers.[42] Irish who emigrated to Canada before 1824 journeyed on "timber ships," which unloaded in the British Isles and then headed back to North American ports.

For the westward voyage, the sailing ships were fitted with plank berths below deck, huge water casks, and iron-strapped-brick cooking devices on deck, all of which were dismantled at the journey's end so the ships could be loaded again with timber cargoes.[43] Such sailing vessels were small, carrying less than three hundred passengers, and were subject to great up, down, and sideways shoves by strong waves or wind.

The sea journey required between six and eight weeks. It was risky, the chief

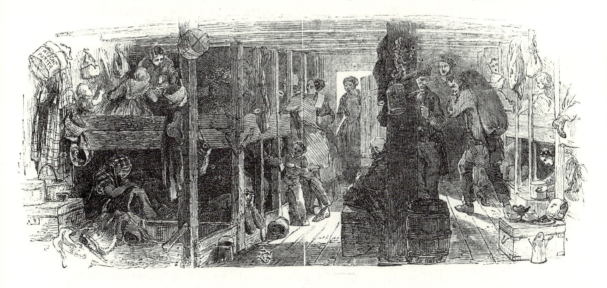

Emigrants Between Decks, Illustrated London News,
May 10, 1851, National Archives

dangers being fire, disease, storms, and icebergs. Passengers did not travel in comfort. Seasickness was common. Quarters below deck in steerage were crowded, damp, dark, smelly, and unclean, and became near-suffocating when hatches had to be closed during storms. Food was poor and often poorly cooked. Limited water for cooking and drinking meant that little laundry could be done, or personal hygiene taken care of. The behavior of fellow passengers often caused difficulties.

The Egans' route, determined by prevailing winds and ocean currents, was northwesterly across the broad blue-green North Atlantic into frigid waters by the Sea of Labrador, where dangerous white icebergs often drifted into the sailing zones. Then the ship sailed southwesterly, entering the damp, foggy Grand Banks off the coast of Newfoundland, an island guarding the mouth or gulf of the St. Lawrence River. Perhaps the Egans' ship stopped at a port in the Gulf of St. Lawrence for food and water, placing them within the British Empire again. When the ship sailed into the Gulf they entered Lower Canada, the shorelines on both sides being part of the province of Quebec.

The St. Lawrence River below the city of Quebec is regarded as an arm of the sea that is called the Gulf of St. Lawrence.[44] As the Egans discovered, sailing ships entering the Gulf faced a difficult navigational challenge caused by "racing currents" in the 350 miles of the broad lower stretches before reaching Quebec.[45] From the Gulf the Egans' vessel moved southwesterly into the thirty-five-mile wide mouth of the St. Lawrence. That river, eight-hundred miles long, flows down to the Atlantic from Lake Ontario, one of the Great Lakes. The Egans saw settlements along the river's edge. Their sailing ship stopped at Quebec to unload passengers and cargo.[46] From there, paddle-wheeling steamboats with names like *Lady Sherbrooke* and *New Swiftsure* took the passengers upriver to Montreal in thirty-six hours.[47]

During the Egans' 180 mile journey upriver to Montreal, their steamboat entered a narrow river containing "tortuous channels and shallows," including the shallow Lake St. Peters (St. Pierre), through which the river flowed just below Montreal. Among an emigrant group six years earlier the passengers' eyes were entirely closed by mosquito bites.[48] To dock at Montreal's wharf, boats had to pass St. Helen's Island and deal with the St. Mary's current, which rushes into the St. Lawrence at the upriver end of Montreal, making boat maneuvers "dangerous: within the port of Montreal."[49]

Young Howard, Ships, and the Sea

An eight-year-old boy is impressionable. So, for young Howard, sailing across the Atlantic must have felt adventurous. Perhaps it made a lasting and favorable impression on him, because a few years later he became a sailor. Emigrant children were fascinated by the captain and crew who operated the ship; how sailors furled and unfurled the white sails, the system of ropes, masts, pulleys, and rope riggings that supported the sails, how the ship responded to currents and winds, the creaking and groaning of ship timbers and masts, the flapping of sails and flags, the shrieks of circling sea birds, the sightings from deck of silvery fish, dark green seaweed, and distant ship silhouettes, and the anticipation of sighting land. Had Howard's Atlantic crossing been a bad experience for him, he probably would not have become a sailor himself.

Howard's adventure in crossing the Atlantic Ocean proved to be the first of many exciting experiences he'd enjoy during the next half century of his life.

The Egan Connection to Ireland

After Howard's family left Ireland, Egan relatives continued to live on the Meelaghans property.[50] Father Howard's brother, Edward, stayed on his part of the Egan property. In 1898, Howard Egan Jr.'s son, Richard Erastus, made contact with Uncle Edward's branch of the family, who told him that Howard Sr. sold his part of the Meelaghans farm to a man by the name of Watson. In time, Edward Egan's son William obtained that part of the farm from Mr. Watson. As of 1900, William's son Edward Egan, a poet, said he himself was living in the old thatched house where Howard Jr. was born. Poet Egan also said that when he was younger, John Egan—Howard Sr.'s brother and Howard Jr.'s uncle—lived with his (the poet's) family, and told him memories of senior Howard Egan before he moved his family to Canada.[51]

This Edward Egan gained fame in Ireland as a poet and fiction writer. He was born on August 9, 1858, and died in 1940.[52] Educated locally, he spent a brief period in Australia, then returned home about 1890. He became a regular contributor of verse and prose in the 1890s, and was popular up to the 1930s. His booklet, *Kings County Couplets*, was published in 1892 and had a great run not only in the county but all over the Midlands and in Dublin. His short stories earned him accolades, and it was said "the aroma of Ireland exhales from his every page."[53] After 1900, Egan relatives in Canada kept in contact with Edward, as did Howard Jr.'s son, Richard Erastus.

Even though Howard Jr. spent but eight years in Ireland, his descendants have felt pride in the Irish connection provided by Howard and his Egan name. Attracted by Ireland's mystique, some have researched Irish genealogy records, visited his homeland, inspected his boyhood home in Meelaghans, and attended MacEgan clan gatherings in Ireland. ◆

～ 2 ～

Montreal Orphan Who Became a Sailor

While the Egans' steamboat on the St. Lawrence River approached Montreal, Howard Sr. and his children peered anxiously at the city soon to be their home. One newcomer about that same time said the boat-deck view of Montreal was "quite imposing" because of the large number of buildings with tin roofs, spires, and steeples glittering in the sun, and the mountain rising to the left of the city. Impressive, too, was the island of St. Helena in the harbor, the surges in the nearby St. Mary's rapids, and the tall-masted ships and river craft clogging the waterfront, including rafts loaded with lumber.[1] Up close, though, the city seemed uninviting. The landing place lacked decent wharfs, and residents dumped their garbage nearby. Boats generally anchored by the shore where crews, with great difficulty, unloaded cargo onto the beach.[2] Passengers walked on planks from ship to shore.[3]

In French-Speaking Montreal

The Egans stepped ashore as strangers in a foreign land. It's not known if anyone they knew met them, if father Howard had any job possibilities, or if they had housing lined up. The Egans, Irish and Protestant, now started life anew in French-speaking Montreal in the Catholic-dominated Province of Quebec.[4]

Back in the 1600s French explorers claimed this part of Canada. In 1608, traders established a post at Quebec, and in 1642 settled at Montreal. French settlers came in small numbers. During the French and Indian War (1754–1760) the British captured the city of Quebec. Losing that war, France, in the Treaty of Paris in 1763, surrendered the region to the British. However, the French language, names, and culture continued to dominate the region, and such continues to this day.

During the American Revolution, English-speaking Loyalists fled from the beleaguered colonies northward into Canada. Tensions soon arose between the French and the English parts of Canada, producing the Constitutional Act in 1791. It divided

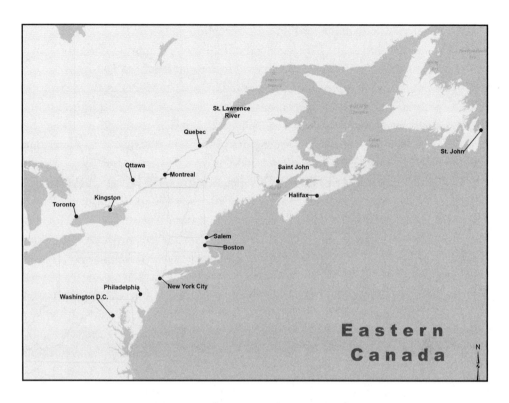

Quebec into English-speaking, Protestant Upper Canada (today's province of Ontario), and French-speaking, Catholic Lower Canada, including Quebec Province.[5]

A family story suggests that at some point the Egans moved from Montreal "farther up the river" to a place near a town named something like Callander, but confirming evidence hasn't been found.[6] Records confirm the Egans were Montreal residents in 1825.

The city, occupying an island about thirty miles long and nine miles wide, was named after Mount Royal, which stood immediately west of what was then downtown Montreal. The triple-peaked mount protected the city from west winds that blew at times "with a violence seldom surpassed."[7] Montreal's activities bunched along the river in Lower Town and up the slight rise into Upper Town.

Street names reflected the French and Catholic shapings of the city: Bonsecours Street bounded Montreal on the northeast, St. James Street on the northwest. Notre Dame Street, up along the slope but paralleling the river, was Montreal's main avenue. That, and St. Paul Street, had flagstone pavement, but other streets were dirt. City streets were "inconveniently narrow" and, when muddy or knee-deep in snow, bothersome to pedestrians. Water pooled because the streets lacked gutters. Animals roamed freely, pigs being the most common.[8] When the Egans walked or rode after sunset they saw night watchmen walking their rounds, some lighting oil street lamps. A town crier frequently passed through the main streets shouting out community announcements.

The Egans found imposing government facilities up from the Landing Place: a large, plain courthouse; a jail that housed not only criminals but debtors; the governor's house; stone barracks that could accommodate one thousand troops; and the Champ de Mars, a military parade ground and public park. Travelers' descriptions about the time when the Egans arrived agree that the city's buildings of dark-colored limestone with massive iron shutters looked and felt gloomy. Older houses resembled those in ancient French cities. The city's landmarks included the older Notre Dame Roman Catholic Church, the newer and more stylish Protestant English Episcopal Parish Church on Notre Dame Street, the Montreal Bank, and the Mansion House Hotel. A memorial statue of Lord Nelson, a naval hero in Britain's recent war with Napoleon, stood atop a seventy-five foot monument at the top of New Market Street. The city contained several nunneries.[9]

The Egans encountered many new types of people. A count in 1816—seven years before the Egans arrived—showed that Montreal had 16,000 residents, of whom 10,000 were French-speaking and Roman Catholic, 1,500 were English and chiefly Anglican, 2,000 were Scottish and mostly Presbyterian, 1,500 were Americans, whom locals considered irreligious, and only 1,000 were Irish. Half of the Irish were Roman Catholic and half Protestant.[10] Protestants from Tipperary, Ireland, who settled in Quebec supported the United Church of England and Ireland, or Anglican church. So did the Egans.[11]

Nelson's Monument, courtesy McCord Museum of Montreal

A Land in Need of Workers

By 1823, when the Egans arrived, Canada's main export items were pot ashes and pearl ashes, grain, flour, timber for masts and spars, square timber, staves, lumber, and such items as flax-seed, butter, lard, soap, candles, grease, tallow, ale, essence of spruce, hemp, and castoreum.[12] Canada needed workers, so it welcomed immigrants. But, as an 1817 Irish newcomer discovered, "it is very hard to do business here without speaking French."[13] Despite language problems, father Howard and probably the older children found jobs. Between 1825 and 1828, Montreal records show that Howard Sr. was a "laborer."[14] The Egans found lodging and fed and clothed themselves.

They came at a good time, economically. The years of 1823–1824 brought increased prosperity in Montreal. In 1824, the city built a permanent town wharf two hundred feet long, which improved the dock facilities.[15] The year 1825 was a boom year.[16] Market days were Tuesdays and Fridays, when farmers brought meat, vegetables, poultry, eggs, butter, and other produce to sell at New Market and at Old Market, the main marketplace because of nearby drinking establishments. Shops were small and few, and—lacking display windows—the merchants often sold their goods outdoors. "For the benefit of the farmers who could not read," many shops had signs above their doors that bore symbols or pictures of the main enterprise, such as a boot or a drinking cup. Fish markets sold fish caught locally, except during wintertime when sleighs brought fish to town from Boston, packed frozen in snow. The Egans, who used peat for fuel in Ireland, now burned wood.[17] For currency the Egans handled a mix of British, French, Spanish, Portuguese, and United States coins.

Bonsecour Market Scene in Winter, *courtesy McCord Museum of Montreal*

Perhaps young Howard knew about a new rope manufactory that opened in 1825. The rope-walk, where the strands were twisted together, powered by a steam engine, was twelve hundred feet long and housed in a two-story stone building. The firm employed between thirty-six and fifty people.[18] By 1832, Howard's older brother John was a rope maker in Montreal.[19] Howard would be a rope maker in Salem, Massachusetts and later in Nauvoo, Illinois.

With Howard Sr. working to provide for the family, the older sisters served as substitute mothers to the younger siblings. It's likely the younger children received some schooling.

Two Seasons: Winter and Summer

In contrast to Ireland's mild climate, Montreal had two distinct and intense seasons: winter and summer. Winters brought an "immense quantity of snow," and temperatures plummeted into the minus thirties, frigid conditions that the Egans learned to endure. The St. Lawrence River usually froze over, and navigation closed from about November 25, when the buoys were removed from the channel, until April 25. Between January and April, men laid out roads on the frozen St. Lawrence River, on which sleighs slid into town from the countryside. In winter "but little is doing."[20] Most Montreal houses had running water from the Montreal Water Works reservoir; water flowed through cast iron pipes deeply buried beneath the city streets to protect them from freezing.[21]

St. James Street, *courtesy McCord Museum of Montreal*

In spring when river ice thawed, business began to bustle, even though melting snows made country roads impassable and city streets slush and mud. St. Lawrence shipping restarted, and the Montreal harbor came alive with boats and rafts of timber, staves, and lumber intended for the Montreal market. In the summers, temperatures soared into the nineties. As summer dragged along, business began to be sluggish, because Montreal by then had been resupplied and its goods shipped. Summers meant plagues of houseflies and mosquitoes. Then in the fall, with the cooling of the weather, business resurrected because the city had to be resupplied before the river iced over for the winter.[22]

More Egan Deaths

Two years after the Egans arrived—and when Howard was about ten years old—one of his brothers and two of his sisters died, all within a one-month period. Evelina, the two-year-old twin, died on June 30, 1825. Next was Anne, two years younger than Howard, who died on July 20 in the General Hospital. Then Bernard or Barney, five years older than Howard, died on July 27 at age fifteen. What caused their deaths so close together isn't known, but an outbreak of a contagious disease is suspect. Then, culminating the Egan tragedies, father Howard died on August 5, 1828.[23] Young Howard now had no parents. Well could he have said what the poet Edward Egan penned years later: "Thus I was left in early youth to fight life's stern battle unaided and alone, with none to guide my youthful steps."[24]

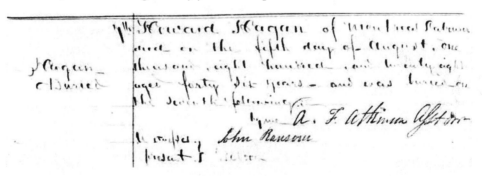

Death certificate of Howard Hagan (Egan), August 5, 1828

The surviving children of Howard and Anne Egan, now orphans, had to fend for themselves and take care of each other. They were Eliza, about twenty-two; Mary, about twenty-one; Catherine, nineteen; John, sixteen; Howard, thirteen; and Richard, about nine. Five of the six children, including Howard, were old enough to find income-producing work.

What impact did so many family deaths have on young Howard? What happens in the heart, mind, and soul of a boy who loses his mother when he is eight, three siblings when he is ten, and his father when he is thirteen? Some young people in similar situations become hardened or afraid to love someone, or insecure about themselves. Some become afraid of death, while others devalue life and adopt reckless lifestyles. Did Howard vent his grief, or hold it in? Did he feel cheated by life, or did the deaths make him more religious and more grateful for life's blessings? These are questions we can't answer. But what is certain is that the losses forced young Howard to become independent in life earlier than he expected. They contributed to character traits he exhibited by age twenty-seven, such as enterprise and self-reliance, concerns about religion, respect for authority, admiration for his siblings, a desire to have a family, and perhaps a propensity for alcohol.

Catherine. At age nineteen, third-oldest Egan child Catherine married John Ransom in Montreal. The Anglican Christ Church records say John, a bachelor, and Catherine, a "spinster," were married "by the publication of banns" on June 22, 1828.[25] Father Howard died three months after their wedding. Because Howard Jr. looked up to John Ransom, in 1840 he and his wife gave their firstborn the middle name of Ransom. It's possible Howard, who was then thirteen, lived with Catherine and John Ransom for a time before he became a sailor.

Eliza. According to the Montreal Anglican Christ Church records, on April 29, 1830, oldest sister Eliza married.[26] Her husband was Henry Benallack, who was born in Cornwall, England, on August 6, 1805. Both the bride and groom resided in Montreal.

Mary. Mary Egan and Adam Higgins (born July 1802), both of Montreal, married on July 3, 1833. She was twenty-six, Adam thirty-one. Witnesses were her brother John Egan and her brother-in-law Henry Benallack.[27] When Mary died years later, her death was recorded by Montreal's Congregational Church of Zion.[28]

John's Death. Early death snatched yet another of Howard's siblings. Anglican Christ Church Cathedral records say that John Egan of Montreal, a rope maker, died on April 22, 1832, when nineteen years old.[29] That year cholera swept through Montreal, killing almost two thousand. However, the outbreak started five weeks after John died.[30]

Richard. The last of the Egan orphans to marry was Richard. He and Maria Stuart (Stewart), both of Montreal, wed on November 8, 1841. Rector John Bethune, of Montreal's Christ Church Parish, performed the ceremony.[31]

Howard's Years as a Sailor

Howard became a sailor. Four documents make that case. In William M. Egan's introduction to *Pioneering the West*, he states that "Howard went to sea and followed the life of a sailor until grown when he settled in Salem, Massachusetts." William learned that information directly from Howard.[32] A second source is John D. Lee. Late in 1846, Lee recorded in his diary a statement Howard made during Lee and Howard's trip to collect Mormon Battalion pay (see Chapter 8). Near Cimarron Springs in present-day Kansas, Battalion men took sides against their own officers during a heated argument. Lee offered his opinions. Then Howard was invited to speak. He said that "he had been on board of a man of war for 3 years & has seen the time that all wanting to throw every officer over board was for some one to give the word."[33]

Howard's 1847 diary (see Chapters 10 and 11) provides further evidence. During his daily travels by covered wagon train across the prairies and plains, he constantly noted the wind velocity and directions, matters a former sailor would pay close attention to, but which his fellow diarists only mentioned slightly. Then, as additional evidence, Howard's stepson William tells that at age twelve, when he was helping at the Egans' Deep Creek Ranch, "Father would call us in the morning to get and milk the cows and used to say we should answer by our feet striking floor as the sailors did. He had been an old sailor."[34]

Egan family folklore contains an unsubstantiated story that Howard wore a gold earring in one ear from his sailor days.[35]

Man-of-War H.M.S. Victory, *the oldest surviving man-of-war in existence, docked at Portsmouth, England, Library of Congress Prints and Photographs Division*

A Sailor's Life

Port Montreal serviced boats and ships plying the Great Lakes, the St. Lawrence River, and even the Atlantic. Howard saw opportunities to become a sailor or seaman. As noted, he followed the "life of a sailor until grown," meaning he started at a young age. If he became a sailor when he was fifteen, a typical starting age for sailors back then, that would be in 1830. He spent three years aboard a man-of-war ship. We know that by 1839 he was working ashore in Salem, Massachusetts and not sailing anymore. That leaves up to about six years unaccounted for. It's possible those were sailing years for him, in the navy or otherwise.

A man-of-war back then was a naval sailing ship heavily armed for battle duty. Canada had no navy, so Howard may have served in the British navy. From England to Canada, from India to Australia, the British dominions enjoyed maritime protection provided by Britain's Royal Navy, the world's finest sea power.[36] At times the navy advertised in Montreal for men, as shown by an 1817 advertisement for pursers—men good at arithmetic and handwriting—for His Majesty's Ship *Champlain*, a vessel in a flotilla of British ships working in Lake Ontario and other Great Lakes.[37] Howard's country of birth was officially the "United Kingdom of Great Britain and Ireland," so perhaps Howard felt willing to serve under the British flag.

Heaving the Lead, *artist J. A. Atkinson, 1807, Anne S. K. Brown Military Collection, courtesy Brown University Library*

The British navy's practice of impressment—the act of taking men into a navy by force with or without notice—ceased after 1814, near the end of the Napoleonic Wars. Howard was therefore not forced into service but instead enlisted. The man-of-war was the largest ship built in the great age of sail. As "ships of the line," they were designed to engage in "line warfare," a naval tactic where two columns of opposing ships would try to outmaneuver each other to bring their largest cannons into range of the enemy.[38] The navy had man-of-war vessels operating in Lake Ontario, with a naval headquarters in Kingston, at the lake's east end and at the beginning of the St. Lawrence River. During the 1830s there was not yet a standard Royal Navy uniform.[39]

It's perhaps impossible to visualize anything but romanticized images of the type of work and lifestyle that Howard and other sailors of that long-gone era adopted. As one historian cautions: "We cannot eat their food, nor see with their eyes, nor sleep in the bunks of their recastle; only rarely may we see the machinery that was central to their working lives."[40] However, some aspects of the sailors' life back then seem certain. Smooth sailing came and went because the vulnerable sailing ships faced seasonal changes in weather, unpredictable winds, unexpected storms, thick fogs, shifting currents, and floating dangers. Ship parts and mechanisms sometimes broke or malfunctioned. Leaks and fires could be fatal. If Howard's cruises took him into the Great Lakes or out through the Gulf of St. Lawrence and along the Canadian maritime provinces, he dealt at times with turbulent, unpredictable waters and weather. "The sailor was the only human being who worked and lived in a place that was in motion."[41]

Three years, Howard said, is how long he served on the man-of-war. It seems likely that after those years he found work on non-naval crafts. Opportunity was there. "New merchant ships were being built in every shipyard of the lower provinces," a naval officer said regarding the 1830s, which meant that "merchant seamen were in great demand." The agents for the shipbuilders "made a practice of bribing the seamen of naval vessels to desert for service on their ships." The navy expected that "many seamen on a man-of-war would desert to seek work on merchant vessels, whenever the opportunity offered."[42] A host of North American non-naval sailors worked in and out of northeast Atlantic ports. Merchants owned many of the commercial vessels, hiring ship captains to operate the trade runs, but a number of ship masters owned their own vessels. Cargo-carrying coastal schooners hired crews as needed, paying them wages by the voyage.[43]

Sailors, as a class, were "working men who got wet." Often they were sons of farmers and of fishermen, part of the lesser-educated "working class." Stereotypes portray nineteenth century sailors as the roughest types of men, drunken and violent ruffians, uncivilized, "misfits living in a world of their own," although many did not fit that image. Seafaring attracted men escaping poverty or legal problems, as well as those "with ambition to see the world, to acquire skills, and to share warm comradeship that they saw and envied in sailors." Most crewmen were very young men but nevertheless experienced workers. Teenagers served most often as cooks or ordinary seamen.[44] Seafaring took young men into an exclusive brotherhood of Neptune's disciples, among men who shared a "secret," like members of a fraternal order.

Sailing for three years or more, Howard came to know how a ship worked, from bow to stern. He knew ship parts, such as the forecastle, poop deck, quarter deck, mizzen mast, yard-arms, and sails like topgallant and spanker and spinnaker, and the buntline and halyards that raised sails. He knew about pulleys, knots, knives, sewing canvas, loading and unloading cargo, and using limited space effectively. Most of the sailors' craft could be learned without literacy, but sailors had incentives and opportunities to read and write. While at sea, Howard had downtime when he could develop reading and writing abilities.

An essential lesson sailors imbibed early and well was to obey orders and follow the chain of command. Crews learned teamwork and how to function as a unit so that the common enterprise could succeed. But, almost contradictorily, they had to become self-reliant and able to take care of themselves in any circumstance. Toughness was a virtue, one that came to characterize Howard's later life on land. As one sailor's poem asserted, "In the struggle for power or the scramble for self, Let this be your motto, rely on yourself."[45] Howard exemplified in his post-sailing years a number of the traits that young sailors had to develop:

> Size up other men's leadership abilities, including captains and officers
> Become used to the society of men engaged in difficult missions
> Be accustomed to the lonely life, cut off from contact with family and friends
> Get along without many personal possessions
> Survive on simple diets, mainly of dried, pickled, or salted foods
> Perform hard physical labor for long periods of time
> Struggle against and survive great challenges caused by nature, accidents, and malfunctions
> Associate with extremely tough, crude, and dangerous men
> Be among men who drank heavily and who in port, if not at sea, became drunk
> Defend themselves and revenge wrongs done them
> Share with other sailors songs, tall tales, and storytelling

Regarding that last trait, the records show that "at sea, men made their own entertainment." In forecastles during watches below "the yarns go round and round and you are not counted a sailor if you can't keep your end up." The yarn was one way that men came to know each other, a part of a "ritual of affirming ties with the brotherhood of men."[46] Two ingredients in Howard's adulthood, as our later chapters show, were humor and telling stories.

Most sailors had a "home port." Perhaps Howard's was Montreal. Whether it was or not, Howard probably returned home whenever he could to see his remaining siblings and in-laws.[47] In the mid to late 1830s, Howard quit being a sailor. He took up residency in Salem, Massachusetts. Never again did he visit Canada or any of his siblings. However—as explained in Chapter 29—long after Howard's death his son Ras, pursuing family genealogy, located and visited Egan cousins in Canada and established a bridge between them and the generation of western Egans.

After sailors left their ever-in-motion lives on water, they often found that the skills acquired at sea served them well on land. One logical adaptation that Howard made on land, after long experience with ships' ropes, was to become a rope maker.[48] ♦

~ 3 ~

Salem, Tamson Parshley, and Mormonism

Howard left Ireland about age eight, became an orphan at thirteen, and married at twenty-four. That means he lived eleven years from the time his father died in Montreal in 1828 until he married Tamson Parshley in Salem, Massachusetts late in 1839. He spent at least three of those years, probably more, being a sailor. We don't know why or when Howard became a resident of Salem, although a good guess is that he was on a ship that docked there and arranged to quit sailing and live there in 1838. A life sketch written by his son Erastus said that Howard, "until he married," worked for a Mr. Chisholm in Salem at ropemaking.[1]

The Seaport of Salem

Salem, fifteen miles northeast of Boston, is best known for a witch hysteria outbreak in the 1690s, when the town's pious elders and judges had twenty men and women executed for supposedly being witches. Today's tourists flock to see the witch museum, witch graves, and reenactments of a witch trial. Also well-visited is the Salem Maritime National Historic Site's wharfs, warehouses, customs house, and replicated 1797 square-rigged sailing ship *Friendship*. The site celebrates the port's two centuries of rich maritime history during the nostalgic era of tall sailing ships, in which Howard participated. It stands just a few short blocks from where Howard and Tamson once lived, and where Howard helped operate a rope-walk on South Street. Also a tourist draw is the "House of Seven Gables," featured in author Nathaniel Hawthorne's 1851 novel by that title. The seaside mansion was prominent while Howard lived in Salem, but with less than seven gables.

Salem sits at the mouth of the Naumkeag River on Massachusetts Bay, and juts out between Salem Harbor and Beverly Harbor. First settled by Europeans in 1626, for the next two centuries its harbor, boats, and businessmen developed a flourishing trade. They shipped codfish, timber, rum, and other goods along the North American

*House of Seven Gables, Salem, Massachusetts,
New York Public Library Digital Collection*

coast, south to the West Indies, and to ports across the Atlantic. By 1790 Salem was the sixth largest city in the new American nation, and a world-famous seaport. The port reached its prime between the end of the Revolutionary War and the War of 1812.[2]

As of 1837, Salem had 14,985 residents. A directory that year identifies thirty-three individuals or firms engaged in the rope, twine, line, or cordage occupations, and Howard's name is not among them, nor is he listed as a resident. However, a line and twine factory operated at 18 South Street.[3] Sources say that in 1842, by which time Howard had married Tamson Parshley, he was a rope maker and lived at 16 South, next door to the factory.[4] Of possible connection to Tamson is a person in the rope business named Darling Huntress, living on South Essex Street. Tamson had relatives named Huntress (see below), including a great-grandmother, Tamsin Huntress, for whom she probably was named.[5]

A history published in 1839, the year when Howard and Tamson married, said Salem's numerous streets were filled with "well built houses, many of them elegant," and the city had eight banks, six insurance companies, six newspapers (three weekly and three twice a week), and manufacturers for such products as alum, saltpeter, white lead, and India rubber. Its sixteen churches included eight Congregational (four of which were Unitarian), two Baptist, one Episcopal, one Friends, one Christian, one Universalist, one Catholic, one Methodist, and a " Seamen's Bethel."[6]

The Newlywed Egans

On November 24, 1839, Howard Egan and Tamson Parshley published their intent to marry.[7] How they met isn't known but it was presumably in Salem.

Tamson was born to Richard Parshley Jr. and Mary Caverly in Barnstead, New Hampshire.[8] Although her birth date has been questioned, best evidence shows she was born on July 27, 1824.[9] Barnstead is about seventy miles northwest of Salem. In that day, children commonly left home at today's high school ages to become apprentices, hired hands, live-in domestic help, or care-givers for relatives needing assistance. Several Parshleys lived in Salem in the 1830s and 1840s, almost all of them related to Tamson's uncle and aunt, Paul and Lydia Parshley.[10] Because Aunt Lydia died in 1834 and left several minor children, it's possible that Tamson at some point went to Salem to help with the motherless children.

Tamson Parshley, 1865, Egan Family Archives

A week after publishing their intent to marry, Howard Egan and Tamson Parshley married, on December 1, 1839.[11] Reverend Matthew Hale Smith performed the ceremony.[12] He served as the minister of the First Universalist Church in Salem from 1838 to 1840.[13] The groom was twenty-four years old, the bride fifteen.

Our generation winces to read about girls in the nineteenth century marrying when in their young teens, like Tamson did at fifteen, but such was not unusual back then. Not until the twentieth century did a separate life category called adolescence or "teenager" emerge, a "time-out" period before youths assumed adult responsibilities. The later creation of high schools and mandatory attendance laws produced that new life stage. Before then, children received limited schooling. Youths moved within a fluid timetable geared to maturity and family circumstance. When physically able, boys and girls moved into adult work and were treated like adults no matter how old they were. Older boys and girls, as soon as they could, were expected to move out from the ever-growing family.[14]

When Tamson and Howard wed, Howard had no relatives in New England. His siblings were in Canada. Tamson had family close by, some in Salem. Her parents and siblings lived in and around Barnstead, seventy miles distant, and she had uncles, aunts, and cousins in Barrington, half that distance away.

A story still circulates, and brings smiles among Howard and Tamson's descendants, that Howard "deceived Tamson about his nationality" because he discovered she didn't like the Irish. Therefore, he told her he was born in Montreal, not Ireland.[15] According to another version, well after Howard's death his son Richard Erastus visited Montreal, learned from Egan relatives there that they were from Ireland, and told Tamson. That news made her pace the kitchen, alternately pushing her fist into each hand and exclaiming, "Damn that man; Damn that man."[16] Yet a third variant says Howard, on his death-bed, confessed to Tamson "his Irish birth," and "Tamson reportedly told him that she would not forgive him in this life nor in the life to come."[17] A fourth account says that "Howard discovered in time that this young English girl did not like the Irish," so he "arose to the occasion by changing the pronunciation of his name to make it sound French Canadian and changed the place of his birth to Montreal."[18] Howard's patriarchal blessing record in Nauvoo gives Tullamore, Ireland, as his birthplace, but his death record in Salt Lake City says he was born in Montreal, Canada, which accords with the Irish-denial legend.

If in fact Howard hid his Irish beginnings from Tamson, grounds existed for him to do that. At that time, Irish Catholics and cheap Irish labor caused anti-Irish sentiment to bubble in America. The year 1834 was termed the "Great Riot Year," in part because riots broke out between Irish and American work teams at canal and railroad construction sites in Maryland and New York. Boston experienced an anti-Catholic (Irish) "Charlestown Convent" riot. In New York City, a municipal election riot pitted Irish against Americans. A national anti-Catholic political party, the "Know-Nothing Party," formed. Irish men sometimes were stereotyped as alcoholics and termed "white Negroes" in a derogatory manner. Newspaper cartoons and drawings used a prehistoric apelike image to depict Irish faces.[19]

Howard, according to *Pioneering the West*, became a naturalized citizen of the United States in October 1841.[20] Citizenship then required five years of residency, so, for Howard, that five years would have begun in 1836 or earlier. He could have established residency while still working as a sailor. His naturalization and citizenship papers haven't been located.

Tamson's New Hampshire Heritage

Tamson had New Hampshire ancestors named Caverlys, Huntresses, Drews, Danielsons, and Parshleys. New Hampshire lands were settled within three years of when the Pilgrims landed at Plymouth. Initially part of the Massachusetts colony, New Hampshire became a British province in 1679, and was one of the thirteen colonies that founded the United States of America. Most early settlers came from England and reached New Hampshire from Connecticut or western Massachusetts. Two New Hampshire locations in particular, Barrington and Barnstead, are where Tamson's immediate relatives lived.

Caverly Roots. Tamson's mother was Mary Caverly. The Caverly families in America are of Scotch and English origin. The Caverly name first appears on record in America in 1680—Philip Caverly in Portsmouth, New Hampshire.[21] Tamson's ancestor Moses Caverly settled in Barrington in 1746. Tamson's mother, Mary Caverly, was born in 1792 in Barrington Township. She married Richard Parshley Jr. in 1814.[22]

Tamson's birthplace, Barnstead, is about eighteen miles northwest of Barrington. Settlement began in Barnstead in 1767.[23] Many of Barnstead's first settlers came from Barnstable, Massachusetts, and Hempstead, New York, so the town's name took part of both places' names, *Barn* and *stead*. Located in New Hampshire's Lakes Region, Barnstead capitalized on soil that was good for grazing and "easy and productive." By 1830, during Tamson's girlhood, the township included a few small villages, 2,047 residents, 2,500 sheep, and several ponds or lakes.[24]

Parshley Family Line. Tamson's father was Richard Parshley, Jr. His father, Richard Parshley, Sr., was born in 1752 in Barrington to parents named John Parshley and Tamsin Huntress (note the name Tamsin). Richard Sr. and four of his brothers had served in New Hampshire regiments during the Revolutionary War and fought at the Battle of Bunker Hill.[25] Richard Sr. was a joiner by trade. Tamson's father Richard Jr. was the fifth of eleven children born to Richard Parshley Sr. and Anna Sloper, all in Barrington. Grandfather Parshley died in 1828, when Tamson was not yet four, so she never really knew him. Grandmother Anna Sloper Parshley died on December 6, 1837, when Tamson was thirteen, so Tamson probably had some contact with her.

Tamson's Parents and Siblings. Tamson's father, Richard Parshley Jr., married Mary Caverly on January 31, 1814, at Barrington.[26] By trade he was a tailor. Tamson and her seven siblings all were born in Barnstead between 1812 and 1833—Tamson in 1824.[27] Her parents lived a long time after she and Howard married in 1839; father Richard died in 1857 and mother Mary in 1880. Tamson's Parshley and Caverly aunts, uncles, and cousins lived close enough for her to associate with them during her childhood and youth, and later in Salem.

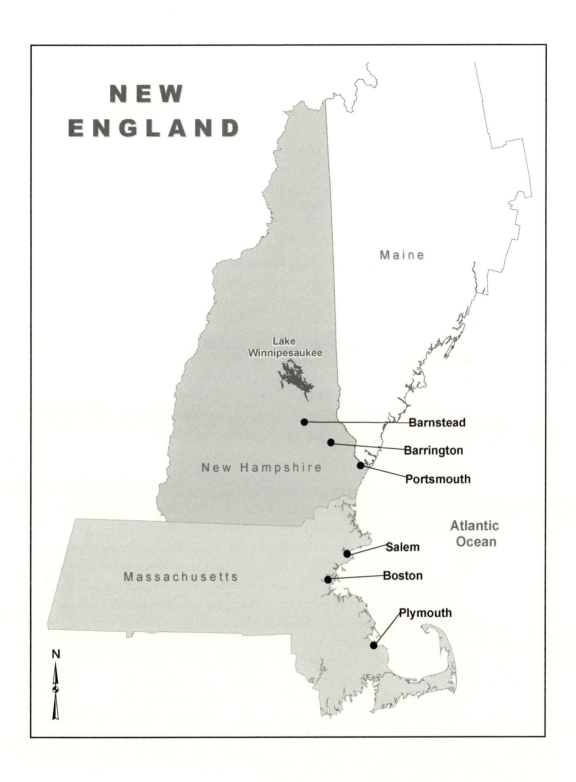

Firstborn Howard Ransom Egan

On April 12, 1840, Tamson gave birth to her and Howard's first child, Howard Ransom Egan. The naming honored his father and his Montreal uncle John Ransom, who had married Howard's sister Catherine. Given short distances, it's likely Tamson's mother and other relatives came to Salem to assist her during and after the delivery. Howard Ransom's birthplace has always been listed as Salem, but local birth records do not list him. Perhaps Tamson went to New Hampshire to be among relatives for the birth. He was born with one deformed foot. For years he had to wear a shoe specifically designed for that foot.[28]

Why Howard Egan's name isn't found in the Massachusetts and New Hampshire 1840 censuses is a mystery. One explanation could be that Howard and Tamson were visiting in New Hampshire when the census was taken, and they, not being in residence, weren't listed.

Howard and Rope Making

Howard "worked for a Mr. Chisholm at Rope Making."[29] A Salem directory for 1842 lists "Howard Egan, ropemaker, 16 South."[30] A line and twine operation was located next door at 18 South Street, so Howard, very likely, worked there. The directory contains this advertisement for Chisholm's products:

> Joseph Chisholm manufacturers and offers for sale, Lines, Marline, twines and Cords; as cod lines, log, deep sea, clothes and other lines of various descriptions. Bed cords and ropes, made from Russia and Manila hemp and flax. Factory, 18 South Street, opposite Harbour Street or N. Pond Street.[31]

Salem had several rope-walks manufacturing rope products. A rope-walk was a long, straight, narrow lane, or a covered pathway, running one to two thousand feet long. Most rope-walks were set up outdoors, but sometimes had wooden shelters. For practical purposes a rope-walk needed to be sheltered, and long rope-walk buildings were distinctive structures in some communities.[32]

As a sailor, Howard developed expertise regarding rope types and qualities. Ships had sails, and sails required ropes long and short, fat and thin. Massive ropes raised and lowered anchors and secured ships to wharfs. Ropes tied sails to yards and booms. Riggings served as rope ladders for sailors. Crews lowered cargoes into the holds and pulled them up with ropes. The Friendship, a replica 1797 three-masted cargo vessel at Salem's Maritime National Historic Site, has an amazing fifty-five miles of rope in its riggings.[33]

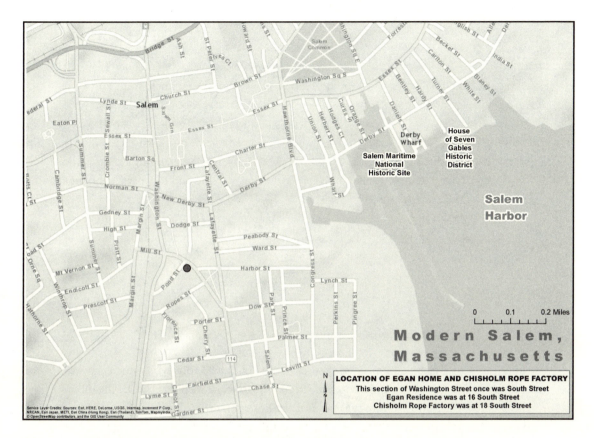

Howard learned and mastered the four basic steps of rope making: (1) preparing the *fiber*, (2) spinning the fibers together to form *yarns*, (3) twisting the *yarns* in bunches to form *strands*, and (4) winding the *strands* to become *rope*. It was a process similar to spinning wool, but on a grander scale.

The process, rather simple in operation, is hard to explain. Most rope at the time was made from hemp, which was a major cash crop for farmers in Massachusetts and nearby. Salem also imported it. Today, hemp growing is widely banned because of hemp's close relationship to marijuana. Hemp plants grow to be fifteen feet tall. Rope was made from fibers peeled from the tall, upright hemp stem. Hemp fibers are very strong. Raw hemp fibers first had to be hatcheled (straightened or combed just like combing our hair in the morning) using boards forested with metal spikes. The separated fibers then were taken by a spinner who would wrap a bundle around his waist, twist some strands onto a rotating hook and, while the hook-on-a-wheel turned and he walked backwards, twist or "spin" up to one thousand feet of *yarn* in about a quarter hour. This length of *yarn* then would be wound onto bobbins and taken to the rope-walk. The rope-walk required two workers, one at each end. At one end, the

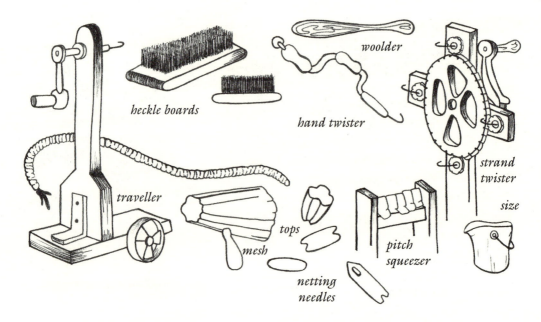

Tools Used in Rope Making, drawing by Eden Sloan, 2017

rope-walk had a jack, which had three hooks that could be rotated. At the opposite end was a carriage with a single, rotatable hook. An assistant would crank the handle of the jack so that the *yarns* were twisted into *strands* by the rotation of the three hooks on the jack. Twisting caused the lengths to contract, so that the carriage had to move up along the rope-walk, under the control of the rope maker. Then, the hook on the carriage rotated in order to twist the strands into the *rope*. The rope maker controlled the production by continually pushing back its formation point to give a tight structure. Meanwhile, the assistant continued to rotate the crank "to make up for the loss of twist in the strands." The final *rope* was about two-thirds the length of the *yarns* used.[34]

The finished rope was treated with very hot pine pitch to make it water resistant, especially for use at sea, and "the combination of dried hemp and the open flames of the tarring vats was very risky."[35]

Howard carried his rope making skills, and perhaps some apparatus, with him when the Egans moved to Nauvoo, where he set up his own rope-walk and manufactured ropes and cords (see Chapter 4).

"I Have…Many People in This City Whom I Will Gather Out"

On August 10, 1841, Joseph Smith, President of The Church of Jesus Christ of Latter-day Saints, instructed a leadership council in Nauvoo, Illinois, that missionaries should be sent to Salem.[36] A conference selected Benjamin Winchester and Erastus Snow to go.[37] Elder Snow had been in the eastern states with his young family for a year, and expected to return to Nauvoo that fall. Hyrum Smith, of the Church's First Presidency, did not pressure Elder Snow but did give him a copy of a five-year-old revelation to read.

That revelation came when Hyrum, Joseph Smith, and Oliver Cowdery had visited Salem in 1836. The three had spent a month preaching and going house to house, with little success. While puzzling over the residents' indifference, Joseph Smith received a revelation, which is now Doctrine and Covenants 111. In it the Lord affirmed that "I have much treasure in this city for you, for the benefit of Zion, and many people in this city, whom I will gather out in due time for the benefit of Zion, through your instrumentality." Further, "wealth pertaining to gold and silver shall be yours...There are more treasures than one for you in this city."[38] No evidence shows that Howard was in Salem when Joseph Smith visited there in 1836, but Tamson might have been.

Elder Snow, hoping to return to Nauvoo, prayed about the matter. "I felt willing to do the will of the Lord; I prayed earnestly to know His will, and His spirit continually whispered to go to Salem." Nevertheless, he tried the apostolic "casting of lots" to decide the matter. On one paper he wrote "Nauvoo" and on another "Salem." Then, he prayed earnestly that God would show him "by the ballot" where he should go. Twice in succession he drew the one marked Salem. So, he wrapped up his assignments in New Jersey, and, on September 3, 1841, the Snow family and Elder Winchester arrived in Salem, "strangers and alone."[39]

Erastus Snow, LDS Church History Library Daguerreotype Collection

They found lodging, then hired the Masonic Hall by the month. They advertised their mission in the newspapers. Beginning on September 6, they had good attendance at their meetings. In mid-September they wrote, published, and distributed 2,500 copies of an eight page "Address" to the citizens.[40] Elder Winchester returned to Philadelphia. Elder Snow held "assemblies" four nights a week, and during the day preached in Salem and nearby places.[41] On October 10 he wrote from Northbridge, Massachusetts, that he had labored in Salem for nearly four weeks:

> Truth is rapidly gaining ground and prejudice wearing away, and considering the circumstances under which I commenced there, the overwhelming tide of public opinion, the multitude of falsehood in circulation, the entire ignorance of the real character and principles of the Latter Day Saints which there prevailed, the number of chapels, churches and priests, the superstition of the people, and considering, too, that Salem is the place where witches formerly performed such wonders for which they lost their lives, I think the prospects are very flattering.[42]

Elder Snow preached three times on Sundays at the Masonic Hall, and, during the week, in private residences. In Salem, the Reverend Mr. A. G. Commings, a Christian Baptist minister, openly opposed Elder Snow by publishing a newspaper called the *Genius of Christianity*, which poured out wrath upon Mormons and Mormonism. His antagonism produced a public debate between him and Elder Snow at the Mechanics Hall. Several hundred attended. For six evenings the debate lasted, and each night the excitement grew. Snow felt that "public feeling continued to turn against my opponent, for his arguments were chiefly epithets and insults." Because of the debates, many investigated the Mormon doctrines. Attendance at Snow's preaching meetings increased. Most who came were "those that stood aloof from all societies."[43] Elder Snow's sympathetic and kindly personality, as well as his skill expounding scriptures, drew people to him.[44]

On November 8, 1841, Elder Snow performed his first baptisms. By the month's end, the Masonic Hall was too small to handle the crowds his preaching drew. He hired the Lyceum, which held six hundred. He preached, too, in Lynn and Marblehead, and in homes in Salem. Seventeen more accepted baptism. In answer to anti-Mormon tirades printed in Boston and Salem newspapers, he wrote articles in the *Salem Observer*, the *Advertiser*, and the *Argus*. Saints rented the Masonic hall once again and put extra seats in it. In February 1842 Snow baptized twenty-one.[45] On February 4 he wrote a summary to Hyrum Smith and William Law:

> Though I advertized in the papers, and circulated gratis, a large quantity of our addresses through the city, yet it was a long time before I could get people to take notice of me more than to come and hear and go away again…Had I not known that Jesus had many sheep in this city, I think I should have been disheartened and not tarried to reap where I had sown, for this is the only place in which I ever preached so long without baptizing.

He said he hadn't baptized anyone until late in November, but now his converts numbered thirty-six. "Those baptized are respectable and good livers, but not wealthy, though quite a number own property here in the city." He observed that some of his converts "begin to have a spirit of gathering, but as yet I have not encouraged it."[46]

Converts Howard and Tamson

Howard and Tamson Egan were among the treasures the revelation said Salem would yield. As an infant, Howard had been baptized in the Irish Protestant Church. When the Egans relocated to Catholic Montreal, they affiliated to some degree with Anglican doctrine and practices. Howard, faced with the deaths of his parents and siblings, must have struggled with questions about life's purposes and what happens to one's soul after death. By 1842 he had religious concerns, which Elder Snow's preaching addressed. During Tamson's growing-up years in New Hampshire, her family's denomination likely was Congregational. It's not known how Howard and Tamson became interested in Elder Snow's message and converted. The exact dates of Howard and Tamson's baptisms aren't known either, but they probably took place in February or March 1842.

Whoever baptized Tamson, probably Elder Snow, had to exercise great care immersing her because she was seven or eight months pregnant. When she gave birth to a baby boy on March 29, 1842, she and Howard named him Richard Erastus Egan. The name Richard was for Tamson's father and grandfather, and the Erastus name honored Elder Erastus Snow. A month later, Elder Snow's wife also gave birth to a son.

Earlier, on March 5, 1842, Elder Snow organized the Salem Branch with a membership of fifty-three drawn from Marblehead, Lynn, and Salem; the Egans belonged to that branch.[47] The Nathaniel Ashby family of Salem were among Snow's earliest converts. Nathaniel was the first in his household to hear Elder Snow preach, and he convinced his wife Susan to go and listen. Elder Snow baptized the couple, as well as their oldest son and daughter.[48] The Snows lived with the Ashbys for about two years.[49]

On May 1, 1842, Elder Snow baptized the moderator of the Commings-Snow debates, Hyrum K. Bryant, who had been a follower of Commings. At a conference held on May 25 the Salem Branch reported it had seventy-nine members. A month later it had ninety.[50]

"I have much treasure for you," the revelation had instructed Joseph Smith in 1836, "and many people in this city, whom I will gather out in due time for the benefit of Zion." In partial fulfillment, Elder Snow's missionary labors in Salem and nearby areas produced 120 baptisms, including the Egans. The next step, as the revelation specified, was that converts needed to gather with the Church to benefit Zion, which meant moving to Nauvoo and helping build it up. Accordingly, after their baptisms, Howard and Tamson gained the "spirit of gathering." They gave up their lodging, Howard quit his job, and the four Egans set out for Nauvoo to live among the Latter-day Saints. ◆

~ 4 ~

Rope Maker and Policeman in Nauvoo

To convert requires change. Most faiths let converts continue to live where they are, but Mormonism, when the Egans embraced it, expected its new adherents to uproot and gather together to build a Zion society where believers could practice their religion openly and be tutored by their leader and prophet, Joseph Smith. For the newly baptized Egans, that place was Nauvoo, Illinois. As a Mormon center, Nauvoo started from scratch in 1839 and ended in 1846.[1] For four of those seven years, the Egans lived there. They participated in and experienced many historic Mormon developments, including construction of the Nauvoo Temple, Nauvoo Legion activities, the introduction of new doctrines, the martyrdom of Joseph and Hyrum Smith, and, finally, a forced exodus of about fifteen thousand Saints including the Egans.

Crossing "the States" in 1842

Until Howard moved his family about 1,500 miles to Nauvoo in 1842, his nautical miles far exceeded land miles he'd traveled. Their route from Salem probably followed that taken by other Salem converts. Railroads then were few, but travelers made good use of America's excellent canal systems that connected with lakes and rivers. On October 14, 1843, the Nathaniel Ashby family left Salem for Nauvoo. They first went to Boston, where they boarded a train that carried them due west to Albany, New York. From there, Erie Canal boats pulled by horses or mules conveyed them to Buffalo. Next, a Great Lakes steamer paddle-wheeled them across Lake Erie to Cleveland, Ohio. From Cleveland they headed eastward, perhaps by stagecoach, to Wheeling, where they boarded an Ohio River steamer. Riverboats carried them down the Ohio River, past Cincinnati and Louisville to Cairo, Illinois, and then north up the Mississippi River to St. Louis and to Nauvoo. The Ashbys arrived on November 3, after a twenty-day journey.[2] During 1842 the Egans made a trip similar to the Ashby family's.

They would have waited for warm weather for the sake of little Howard Ransom and Richard Erastus, and for waterways to be ice-free. For Howard and Tamson, traveling nearly three weeks with a two-year-old and an infant, and transferring baggage from train to boat to stagecoach to boat, required strength and patience. Theirs was the opposite of a pleasure trip.

The Founding of Nauvoo

When the Egans stepped ashore at Nauvoo, the rising city was barely three years old. Back in 1838, friction in Missouri between Mormons and their neighbors produced a brief "Mormon War," causing Governor Lilburn Boggs to order the Saints "exterminated or driven from the state." That winter, five thousand to seven thousand property-stripped refugees found safety in and around Quincy, Illinois. When Joseph Smith, after months in Missouri jails, reached Quincy in May 1839, he arranged for the Church to purchase land eighty miles upriver in a place called Commerce in Hancock County, Illinois. This swampy hamlet consisted of six houses clustered on the edge of a great bend of the Mississippi River. Joseph Smith instructed his followers to relocate there.

Through hard labor, a host of constantly arriving Saints drained off swamp areas, hacked down bushes and trees, laid out streets, and erected log cabins and frame homes. They named the settlement Nauvoo. On bluffs that overlooked the burgeoning lowland neighborhoods, workers scratched out another grid of streets and house lots to create "Upper Nauvoo." When the Egans arrived in 1842, they saw near the bluff's crown the beginnings of walls for a temple. Gazing west from the bluffs, they beheld below them the sweeping mile-and-a-half-wide Mississippi River and its islands. They saw across the river the small town of Montrose, Iowa Territory, where Saints also were settling. Then, east from the temple site, the Egans viewed extensive prairie where LDS farmers were turning sod-land into productive farms.

About 130 miles southeast, in Illinois's capital city of Springfield, Abraham Lincoln was a young, little-known attorney practicing law. The Egans would have heard little about him but a lot about Illinois Congressman Stephen A. Douglas. John Tyler was President of the United States, while Secretary of State Daniel Webster from Massachusetts and southern senators Henry Clay and John Calhoun were national political "giants" at the time.

Newcomers in a "River City"

The Egans reached Nauvoo during the summer or fall of 1842.[3] Howard and Tamson had been married less than four years. He was twenty-seven, she seventeen or

View of Nauvoo from Montrose, Iowa, *artist A. Henry Lewis,
Classified Photograph Collection, courtesy Utah State Historical Society*

eighteen, and both boys under age three. As newcomers, the Egans became "fellow citizens with the Saints" but knew practically no one. Nauvoo's population then stood at about five thousand. The Egans heard a variety of English accents spoken by New Englanders, Canadians, southerners, and people from the British Isles. Howard's speech probably sounded more British than anything.

In Howard and Tamson's eyes, Nauvoo presented quite a contrast to old seaport Salem. Salem had cobbled streets lined with prim wood and stone residences and business houses, some more than a century old, while Nauvoo consisted of log cabins and small wood-framed houses, a few brick homes, several hurriedly-built shops, and dirt streets. Joseph Smith, being Church president and city mayor, was Nauvoo's most important resident, but he lived in a two-story log and frame house by the river.[4] Salem faced the sea; Nauvoo nestled by a broad river.

Unlike Salem's complex of docks and piers, Nauvoo's four river landings barely qualified as such. Smoke-puffing riverboats came and went. For example, between March 7 and 11, 1843, eleven steamboats arrived. Eight headed upriver and three downriver, and another passed without stopping.[5] Barges, canoes, dugouts, flat-boats, keelboats and log skiffs plied the nearby currents.[6] From the river, muffled bells and shrill whistles announced boat arrivals. The Mississippi was the interstate highway of its day. Emigrants and store goods reached Nauvoo mostly by boat from St. Louis, 190 miles downriver. At least twice Howard would travel by boat downriver to fill Church assignments (see Chapters 5 and 6). Ferryboats and small craft regularly crossed the river to Montrose.[7]

If Howard and Tamson, as Salemites, developed tastes for Atlantic cod or lobster or herring, Nauvoo fisherman reeled in walleye pike, bass, catfish, and perch. Because of the river, residents suffered from mosquitoes, gnats, and other pesky river-bred bugs. During Nauvoo's hot and humid summers, malaria felled not a few residents.

Early in 1843, newcomer John Needham said that the city covered four miles "laid out in lots and streets in nice order," and each house had a quarter, half, or full acre of land attached to it, "which makes the houses appear scattered for two square miles." But, "in the center, near the temple, they are quite close like other towns." Needham was "surprised to find so many good brick-built houses." Two or three areas of the city "have a very business-like appearance with having different kinds of shops." Streets were "not yet paved," making them dusty in dry weather and "in wet weather unpleasant."[8]

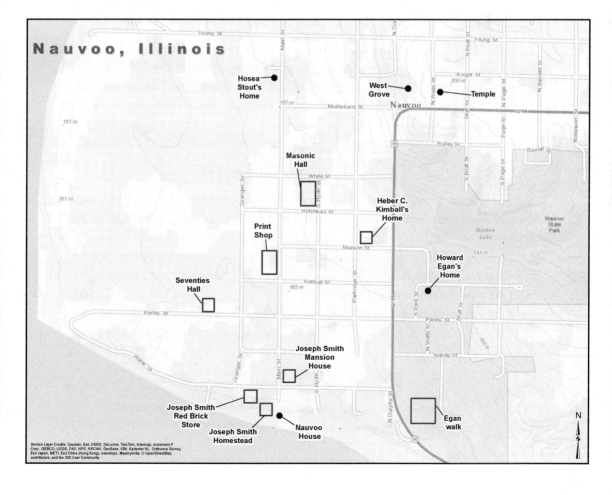

The Egans' Home

Nauvoo's streets intersected at right angles and bore names of leading Mormons, such as Kimball, Sidney, Partridge, and Hyde. Parley Street was the primary east-west street, Main Street the north-south one. The Egans lived at the city's south end, inland four blocks from the river. The 1842 tax records list them as tenants or renters on lot 2 in block 9 of the Hibbard Addition. Tax records the next year say the Egans still were tenants living "between Hibbard 12–2 and Barnett 7–2."[9] On July 10, 1843, George Alley purchased part of lot 2 in block 9 of the Hibbard Addition and intended, the records say, to convey the east half to Howard Egan. On today's street map, the Egans' residence site would be two blocks east of Durphey Street (north-south Highway 96) and between east-west running Parley and Kimball streets (Kimball now ends at Durphey and doesn't continue east). So the site is not accessible by current streets, and all the houses once in their neighborhood are long gone. They lived about four blocks north of Howard's rope-walk (see below).

"I remember the house we lived in," son Howard Ransom said. "There was two rooms facing the street with a hall between. We lived in the left hand room, another family lived in the right hand room. I don't remember of ever going in there. There was a flight of stairs in the hall that led to two rooms above." The Egans planned to build a house, which they didn't finish, or at least never lived in. "One day I was with Mother," Ransom recalled, "when she showed me the foundation of a house and said, 'They were going to build our home there, then it wouldn't be so far to the factory,'" meaning Howard's rope-walk.[10]

Howard's "Nauvoo Rope Manufactory"

How well or poorly the Egans prospered in Nauvoo can't be determined. One notable characteristic of Nauvooers was poverty. Too little money was available for investment, industry, or trade, so the economy struggled. As Joseph Smith phrased it when inviting Saints to gather to the city, "Let all that will, come, and partake of the poverty of Nauvoo freely."[11]

Residents needed ropes for wagons, winches, boats, household beds, crates, laundry lines, and livestock, among other uses, so Howard set up a rope making operation. "Nauvoo Rope Manufactory," announced his ad in the *Nauvoo Neighbor* newspaper issue of April 26, 1843:

> The subscriber wishes to inform the citizens of Nauvoo and the surrounding country, that he has established a rope manufactory in this city, where he intends to manufacture Cordage of every description, bed cords, clotheslines, rope lines, etc. which he will sell at St. Louis prices. Intends keeping an assortment of

the above mentioned articles constantly on hand. Any persons wishing to purchase will do well to examine his stock before purchasing elsewhere. All orders promptly attended to. Howard Egan

Howard located his rope-walk in block 20 of the Hibbard Addition, four blocks south of the Egan home. It was two blocks east of Durphey Street between what then were east-west Water and Lumber Streets. The site now is not accessible by streets, and no buildings stand there.[12] Howard's rope-walk site is a block or two east of a bend in Highway 96 as it exits Nauvoo. Joseph Smith's family lived roughly four blocks west and one block north of Howard's rope-walk.[13]

Nearly two years after he opened his business, the *Nauvoo Neighbor* on February 19, 1845 carried an announcement that Egan's rope business had become the Egan and Sanders' manufactory.[14] The business used Howard's rope-walk and produced "cordage of all descriptions, twine, chalk lines, etc. which they will sell at St. Louis prices." They intended to manufacture from the "best materials" in the "best manner," to "be sold at the lowest prices." They offered "St. Louis wages" as payment for hemp, a main ingredient in ropes. Hemp grew abundantly in the area. Ransom penned a fine description of father Howard at work in his rope-walk:

> Father had a rope factory down close to the river where mother used to go with his dinner and often took me with her. I remember of seeing Father with a big arm-full of hemp backing down the walk as he was spinning out the twine to make ropes of, and at other times he and another man would be throwing hemp over a hetchel [comb], and dragging it back to free it of sticks or dirt and make it ready for spinning. At one time I saw him as he finished a large and long rope, there were three strands each composed of many small ones. The three strands were each hooked on one turning hook, and a man far down the walk had the three strands fastened to a hook called a looper. This was in a belt the man wore about his waist, so he could lean back and keep the cords tight and off the ground.
>
> ...father had a conical shaped block of wood and had three grooves in it in his hands. In each groove laid one of the strands, and as they would twist enough to suit him he would back down towards the lower end. I was following him down the walk when he gave me a scare by turning to face the man and putting one hand to the side of his mouth, yelled out at the top of his voice, "slack up on that looper." The man was pulling too hard I suppose.
>
> I remember of seeing posts that had arms across the top with pegs sticking up like rake teeth to hold twine separate as twisted. I don't know how far apart these posts were, but it seemed to me they were about two or three rods [32 to 48 feet], and as high as a man could reach. The factory was very long but not enough when Father had to make sea cables, so he placed a good many posts beyond the lower end of the walk. Some of them were on the sand bar, but as I saw them then, there were a few standing in the river.

For rope products not made on demand, Howard must have had a place to store inventory. Suggestive that Howard had warehouse space is a police mention on May 26, 1845 that thieves broke into a warehouse at Nauvoo's upper landing and stole goods belonging to "Bryant and Egan." It's not known if the Egan was Howard or someone else.[15]

Early in March 1845, the Twelve Apostles decided to buy canvas and rope so they could erect a massive tent tabernacle at the west entrance of the temple. Joseph Smith, before he died, had initiated the project. The elliptical tabernacle, to run north and south, was expected to seat as many as ten thousand people in seats rising like an amphitheater. Elder Orson Hyde headed east and raised funds to buy four thousand yards of canvas and appropriate fixtures. He collected fourteen hundred dollars and bought canvas, which he shipped from New York by mid-September.

Because the tabernacle needed lots of rope, leaders turned to Howard. "Elder Egan is gone to St. Louis to buy about 125 dollars worth of hemp," Brigham Young recorded on June 27, 1845, "to make cords for it [the tabernacle]." Leaders wanted the tabernacle reared and ready by fall. Workmen cleared ground for it. In August, Howard delivered to the Church thirteen coils of half-inch rope weighing 493 pounds, three coils of three-inch rope, and a coil of three-fourths-inch rope, for which his business was paid close to $120.00.[16] But then, during September, Church leaders suddenly halted the tabernacle project. Under anti-Mormon duress they decided the Saints must leave Illinois by the next spring (see Chapter 5). So the tabernacle canvas found use as wagon covers, and people packing up and equipping wagons found Howard's cords very useful.[17]

Nauvoo tithing records for 1843 and 1844 show that Howard regularly paid tithing, but not in cash. His contributions were in labor and rope products. Tithing records show that he donated 596 pounds of rope, five dozen bed cords, and a thousand feet of twine. Rope was valued at between ten and twelve cents per pound, bed cords at twenty to twenty-five cents each, and twine at fifty cents per hundred feet.[18] That Howard paid his tithes in ropes, cords, and twine means that most of his income from rope sales came not as money. Apparently his customers bartered with him, paying him with goods and services, not cash.

Tamson and Domestic Life in Nauvoo

Records tell little about Tamson's life in Nauvoo. Certainly she was busy with her two small boys and housework—cooking, washing dishes, doing laundry, sewing, gardening, shopping, making clothes, and handling sicknesses. Son Ransom was in Nauvoo from ages two to six, and his recorded memories of Nauvoo do not include any schooling. For half of 1843 and three months in 1844, Tamson was pregnant with Charles John Egan, who was born on March 28, 1844. His two names might be for Tamson's younger brother, Charles Parshley, and Howard's older brother, John. Baby Charles's brothers were ages four and two. Little Charles died on October 7, 1844, at nearly eight months old, from inflammation of the brain.[19] He is buried in what today is called the Pioneer Cemetery east of town on Parley Street. Once again Howard lost a loved one to premature death.

Joseph Smith organized the Nauvoo Female Relief Society of Nauvoo on March 17, 1842, in the "lodge room" above his Red Brick Store.[20] The society, with Joseph's wife Emma as president, was created to encourage women "to provoke the brethren to good works in looking to the wants of the poor" and to correct the morals and strengthen the virtues of the community.[21] At its membership peak the Society enrolled more than 1,300 LDS sisters.[22] Membership rolls do not show Tamson's name. Possibly, being so young a wife and mother, she felt a bit out of place and didn't join.

Information about other Nauvoo homemakers suggests how Tamson spent some of her time.[23] On their house lots most families cultivated "a neat garden" that provided in season an abundance of corn, potatoes, beans, melons, lettuce, onions, and radishes for their own use or trade.[24] Many residents kept a cow for milk and butter-making cream, chickens for eggs and meat, and perhaps a pig or two. Nauvooers had an abundance of meat—beef, ham, bacon, and sausage. During summer and fall, when gardens and orchards matured, fresh vegetables and fruit could be had in good supply, but not during the rest of the year. Farms on Nauvoo's outskirts yielded corn, wheat, oats, rye, and potatoes in abundance. Households had no refrigeration, so women preserved fruit by canning in bottles and jars using corks, and preserved meats by smoking, salting, or drying. Home-baked bread was a staple, as were breakfast griddle cakes made of cornmeal or buckwheat. Stores

Nauvoo 1846, LDS Church History Library

provided flour and eggs. Sugar was scarce, so honey and molasses served for sweeteners. In 1845, Irene Hascall Pomeroy told relatives the foods that mattered most to her were flour, butter, eggs, sugar, molasses, pork, milk, corn, and potatoes.[25]

Most homes had a table and a few chairs. Walls were usually whitewashed rather than painted. Wood floors had rag rugs or factory-made carpets. Fireplaces or cast iron stoves cooked the food, warmed water, and heated the house.[26] For fuel, residents used wood, probably purchased. Friction matches had come into vogue by then. Tamson's housework entailed scrubbing grates, hearths, and floors, constantly attending fires, trimming candle or lamp wicks, and carrying water in and out. Water for cooking and cleaning came from wells or cisterns that collected rainwater. Water from wells, highly suffused with lime, left clothes grayish, but rainwater, being soft, was ideal for washing clothes and bodies. Tamson probably scrubbed a lot of laundry on a washboard, which she dried on clotheslines—ropes that Howard had manufactured. No doubt she made some clothes for her family, and occasionally hired a seamstress.

For light at night, residents used lard-oil lamps and candles. In fact, because few people owned clocks, some evening meetings' starting time was simply "at early candlelight." Family members often shared bedrooms and sometimes even shared beds. It is very likely that the Egans slept on lattice-rope beds made with cords Howard manufactured. Warming pans helped heat beds on cold nights. Bathing? It was believed a best practice to wash with cold water every day and take one warm bath weekly. Each household had a tub used for laundry and bathing. The river became a common place for men and boys to bathe. Citizens made do with chamber pots and commodes, and with small outdoor privies located away from the house.[27]

Shops, Stores, Services, and Trades

Nauvoo was a "walking city." Carriages, wagons, horses, and mules were in short supply. For his rope business, Howard might have acquired a wagon or cart and a horse or mule or two. Walking allowed people to become acquainted with each other, including prominent civic and church leaders. Even Joseph Smith became well-known to residents on a first-name basis. People addressed him not as "President Smith" but as "Brother Joseph." He was ten years older than Howard.

By 1845, Nauvoo had more than 300 businesses, ranging from doctors and lawyers to hat makers and undertakers.[28] Upper Nauvoo's businesses grouped along Mulholland Street, and Lower Nauvoo's around Main Street. Farmers sold their produce at a licensed farmers market on Main Street, a quarter mile north of the river. General merchandise was sold in more than two dozen crammed and cramped general stores and in several drug stores.[29] Joseph Smith's "Red Brick" store was on Water Street,

Joseph Smith's Red Brick Store, rebuilt, courtesy Kenneth Mays

five blocks west of the Egans' home.[30] As a policeman, Howard came to know almost all the businesses in town.

Major industries scarcely existed, but the city had small-scale grist and lumber mills as well as brick making, soap making, a comb factory, a match factory, tanneries, and the Nauvoo Coach and Carriage Manufactory. Blacksmiths and silversmiths were available. City craftsmen produced boots and shoes, pottery, and wood items like chairs, doors, window sashes, and barrels. Nauvoo even had breweries. The City Council banned "spirituous liquors," but beer was not considered liquor. Beer was the Coca-Cola of its day, even thought to benefit health. Society then believed that drinking too much water, which often tasted odd or even awful, posed health problems. Nauvoo leaders put a stamp of approval on the Nauvoo Brewery and allowed each ward to have a beer retailer.[31]

Nauvoo had no banks. Money, if and when Howard or Tamson had any, included American, Spanish, and English coins, and paper currencies printed by cities, states, and private banks. Nauvoo issued city scrip. Church tithing scrip circulated. Such a babel of bank notes made counterfeit bills easy to pass. They posed serious problems for policemen like Howard.[32]

Rising Temple Walls

Week by week, temple construction dominated the city's life. Each morning the Egans heard a bell at the temple site toll at 7:00 a.m. to announce the start of another day. It tolled again at noon and 1:00 p.m. and a last time at 6:00 p.m.

What purpose the temple would serve only became clear gradually. Joseph Smith first taught the doctrine of baptism for the dead in October 1840. On January 19, 1841, he received a revelation, now Doctrine and Covenants section 124, wherein the Lord instructed the Saints to "build a house to my name, for the Most High to dwell therein," where "the fulness of the priesthood" would be restored, and where "I may reveal mine ordinances." The temple must have a baptismal font "that they, my saints, may be baptized for those who are dead." However, until the font was ready, baptisms took place elsewhere. Saints, using lists they assembled of deceased relatives and friends, went to the Mississippi River and were baptized as proxies on their behalf.

Hundreds found employment at the temple site. As "temple tithing," men and older boys were expected to donate each tenth day of labor to working on the temple, so Howard did his share. Very likely workmen used Egan ropes at the construction site.[33]

Sunday Meetings

Unusual for a religious capital, Nauvoo didn't have even one chapel or church. Sunday church meetings, open for the entire membership, were held outdoors, weather permitting, in one of three groves in Upper Nauvoo. One grove stood immediately west of the temple, one four blocks east, and another in a hollow south of Mulholland Street. At the more popular "West Grove" a portable stand stood front and center, with plank benches arranged in a circular fashion around it. The Egans and other attendees sat on the benches, or on tree stumps, the ground, or their wagons. On Sundays, according to James Palmer,

> The Saints assembled in a grove near the sight [sic] of the Temple where was erected a Stand or platform for the speakers and it was nearly always filled by our leading officers....The prophet did not always address the meetings but when he did all ears ware [sic] opened and the most profound silence was observed, and those that spoke in his presents [sic] no matter what subject allowed themselves to be corrected if needed, which was done by him in a kind and christian-like manner.[34]

During winter, Saints met in larger private homes for worship and prayer meetings. After the Masonic Hall and Seventies Hall were built, some Sunday meetings took place there.

When the Egans first came to Nauvoo, the Church's First Presidency consisted of Joseph Smith, Hyrum Smith, and William Law. Members of the Quorum of the Twelve Apostles, who comprised the second level of Church leadership, included Brigham Young, Heber C. Kimball, Lyman Wight, William Smith, John E. Page, John Taylor, Wilford Woodruff, George A. Smith, and Willard Richards. William Marks was the Nauvoo Stake President.[35]

The concept of wards as local Church units began not from a specific revelation but from city practicality. For governing purposes, many larger cities in America created political subunits called wards. Traditionally, municipal wards sent representatives to the city council, conducted elections, and provided city services. Nauvoo was divided into three municipal wards and then, in 1842, into ten wards. Church authorities saw these civil divisions as useful to assist the poor and needy, so a bishop was assigned to each municipal ward to monitor and care for the poor, but not to hold Sunday meetings. From these beginnings, it became Church practice for local ecclesiastical units to be wards headed by bishops.[36]

The Egans resided in the Third Ward in the city's southeastern section. Elders, priests, teachers, and deacons quorums were stake quorums. Wards had none.[37] Continuing a custom started in Kirtland, the Church had monthly (sometimes less) fast days on a Thursday, which members kept by fasting and praying and by attending a general or a ward meeting.[38] On May 15, 1845, for example, "all works were stopped. Meetings were held in the several wards and donations made to the Bishops for the poor, enough was contributed to supply the wants of the poor until harvest."[39]

Joseph Smith as Prophet-Teacher

Like most new converts the Egans wanted to see, meet, and hear Joseph Smith. Some recorded their impressions. One was English immigrant James Palmer, who reached Nauvoo in 1842 and rejoiced, saying: "I am in a location where I can be instructed more fully in the principles of eternal life by the Prophet Joseph Smith and the Twelve Apostles of the Church of Christ."[40] In mid-1843, John Needham penned his first impressions of the prophet for Millennial Star readers in England, saying: "Joseph Smith is a great man, a man of principle, a straight forward man; no saintish long-faced fellow, but quite the reverse. Indeed some stumble because he is such a straight forward, plain spoken, cheerful man, but that makes me love him the more." Needham had "seen and been in the company of Joseph, and heard him speak several times. I love him, and believe him to be a Prophet of God."[41] Unfortunately, Howard and Tamson either did not record their impressions of the young prophet or that record has been lost.

Joseph Smith took advantage of the general Sunday outdoor church meetings to preach and teach. His time in Missouri jails provided him "time for prayer and contemplation," and "to ponder his course, to synthesize ideas, to formulate goals, and to communicate in an unhurried manner with the Lord."[42] These spiritual deepenings gave rise in Nauvoo to Joseph Smith assuming, more than before, the role of prophet-teacher, whereby he "introduced many uniquely Latter-day Saint teachings, doctrines not only new to the Prophet's Christian contemporaries outside the Church, but mostly not taught to the Latter-day Saints prior to 1839."[43]

These new teachings became central doctrines and practices in Mormonism: celestial marriage, plural marriage, pre-mortal existence, proxy ordinances for the dead, temple endowments, the plurality of gods, the materiality of spirit, and God being an exalted man.[44] On April 7, 1844, during a Church conference, a vast crowd heard Joseph Smith preach outdoors what is now well-known as the "King Follett Discourse." He honored a deceased Mormon elder named King Follett, then elaborated on several profound doctrines of the Restoration, including that the intelligence of man is eternal, that God is an exalted man, and that man has the potential to become like God.[45]

While doctrines expanded, Church members individually made personal decisions about accepting or rejecting them. The Egans, as the next two years showed, embraced the new teachings and participated in new temple ordinances and ceremonies that were introduced (see Chapter 6).

The Nauvoo Legion

Howard was a major in the Nauvoo Legion. Late in 1840, the state of Illinois chartered Nauvoo as a city. The charter allowed for a military organization known as the Nauvoo Legion, a unit of the Illinois state militia, answerable to both the mayor and the governor. By appointment from the governor, Joseph Smith commanded the Legion with the rank of lieutenant-general. The Legion consisted of two brigades—one of horse troops and one of foot soldiers.[46] State law required every able-bodied male resident between the ages of eighteen and forty-five to be in a militia unit, so Nauvoo males belonged to the Legion.[47] The men received military instruction, drills, and discipline in order to be ready "to execute the laws," to act as escorts, and to enhance public parades and ceremonies.[48]

Howard's adopted son William, born six years after the Egans left Nauvoo, understood that his father was a major in the Nauvoo Legion; hence, he was called "Major Howard Egan."[49] Howard had naval experience, which made him a valuable man to have in the Legion. Due to a "failure to preserve muster rolls and recruitment records," no roster exists of the Legion's entire membership, which numbered approximately 3,000 men. Howard's name does not appear on the incomplete lists of the Legion's officers and privates. The Legion had a six-tier organization, running top to bottom from commander-in-chief to division, brigade, regiment, battalion, and company. A major, like Howard, had command of a battalion, or perhaps a company.[50]

The Legion participated prominently in the social and ceremonial life of Nauvoo. Its drills and parades impressed onlookers, non-Mormons as much as Mormons. In May 1843 the Legion practiced military maneuvers on its parade ground east of Joseph Smith's farm on the prairie, which drew much attention. It's likely Howard participated. After that event, General Smith said that "in point of discipline, uniform, appearance, and a knowledge of military tactics" the Legion was "the pride of Illinois."[51]

Lieutenant General Joseph Smith, Nauvoo Legion, Utah Historical Society

Nauvoo's Masonic Lodge

Howard joined Nauvoo's Masonic Order. During the Joseph Smith era, fraternal lodges enjoyed widespread popularity in America. Many Mormon men, including Hyrum Smith and Heber C. Kimball, had been Masons prior to converting. Some of the city's Masons arranged for Illinois Grandmaster Abraham Jonas to install a lodge in Nauvoo on March 15, 1842 (before the Egans arrived). During the installation ceremonies Joseph Smith officiated as Grand Chaplain. That evening, with the Masons assembled in his Red Brick Store office, the Prophet received the first degree of Freemasonry. Lodge members then commenced weekly early morning meetings; Joseph Smith attended only a few lodge meetings.[52]

Lodge records note that rope maker Howard Egan was accepted into membership on June 1, 1843, and that he attended lodge meetings regularly.[53] Masonry was, and is, "a religious and philosophical brotherhood" that provides sociability, mutual help, instruction, and rituals purportedly centuries old.[54] Lodge brothers taught tolerance and charity, and shared a genuine religious brotherhood and concern for one another. Members could advance through various degrees of Masonry, which required rituals involving secret signs and routines.[55] Joseph Smith let a lodge be established, but only if membership was not limited and exclusive, as was the case in nearly all Masonic lodges. As a result, nearly half of Nauvoo's men became Masons. The lodge's roster lists 1,529 names.[56]

Needing a large place to meet, the lodge built the Masonic Hall, which Hyrum Smith dedicated on April 5, 1844. Howard attended lodge meetings there. In addition to hosting Masonic activities, the three-story building served as a community cultural hall where concerts, musicals, and dramas were performed.[57] The Nauvoo police force, including Howard, often met there. Illinois Masonic politics caused the Nauvoo Lodge to be severed from the Grand Lodge, but it continued until April 10, 1845, when Brigham Young advised that it suspend activity.[58] Visitors to today's Nauvoo enjoy cultural performances in the replicated Masonic Hall, now called the "Cultural Hall," near the corner of Main and White Streets.

Howard of the Lineage of Judah

On September 23, 1843, Howard received a patriarchal blessing under the hands of Church Patriarch Hyrum Smith, the Prophet's brother. The blessing book lists Howard's birthplace as Tullamore, Ireland. "You are of the lineage of David of the Tribe of Judah," the blessing pronounced. Mormons of Jewish descent were and are extremely rare. Howard was promised "an inheritance in Zion," and that his posterity "had the right to and blessings of the priesthood from generation to generation." Howard was assured that he would "be blessed in your temporal associations and in your habitations and your days and years shall be given unto you according to your faith and the desires of your heart." Howard, the patriarch pronounced, would "have your name written together with acts in the archives and Chronicles of your brethren, as also perpetuated by your posterity,"[59] which this book seeks to do.

Patriarch Smith also blessed Tamson. He declared she was of the seed of Ephraim. The blessing said she would have times when her heart would be "sorrowful, perplexity and grief will be your tribulations," but "you shall have consolation and comfort" and "communion with the Spirit." She would have days and years multiplied upon her head "unto three Score years and ten if your faith fail not to continue."[60] She lived ten years beyond that time frame.

James Monroe

A Pennsylvania convert named James Madison Monroe arrived in Nauvoo about the same time the Egans did. He found work as one of Nauvoo's school teachers.[61] He said he became "on terms of greatest friendship" with Howard and Tamson. Being born on January 9, 1823, he was not quite two years older than Tamson. A bachelor, he had romantic feelings towards her. That friendship terminated, and, Monroe later said, "we lived as distant neighbors only."[62] But in Utah in 1850, he took advantage of Tamson while Howard was absent in California, which resulted in deadly consequences for Monroe (see Chapter 17).

One of the Forty Policemen

Salem, with its sailors and pubs and harbor riffraff, dared not be without policemen. But Nauvoo, a religious haven, at first needed nothing more than a constable or two. But as population rose, commerce grew and crime increased. Boats, stagecoaches, and horses brought in visitors, including a fair share of thieves, swindlers, seducers, and counterfeiters. Some of these ne'er-do-wells faked religious conversion in order to blend in, while secretly committing crimes for which the Mormon people received blame. "Undesirables" occasionally came from Missouri, intending to capture, arrest, kidnap, or take hostage Joseph Smith and other Church leaders. Responding to rising crime, the City Council passed ordinances in May 1842 and January 1843 calling for a "Night Watch."[63] By the end of 1843 Howard was one of the Night Watch force.[64] No doubt he was enlisted because he was trustworthy, reliable, and an ex-sailor able to deal with rough types of people.

In early December 1843, residents of Nauvoo's second and third wards petitioned the City Council for better protection. Responding, the Council passed an ordinance on December 12 authorizing the mayor

> ...to select and have in readiness for every emergency forty policemen, to be at his disposal in maintaining the peace and dignity of the citizens, and enforcing the ordinances of the said city, for ferreting out thieves and bringing them to justice, and to act as daily and nightly watchmen, and be under the pay of said city.

Nauvoo Legion officer Jonathan Dunham became captain of the police, or High Policeman, and Hosea Stout the vice-captain. The officer staff included Jesse Harmon and John D. Lee. Howard became one of the forty.[65] It's likely that police were chosen partly because of where they lived, thereby giving the force a familiarity with the city's many neighborhoods. Howard had served on the just phased-out city Night Watch. For that work, on January 8, 1844, Mayor Joseph Smith authorized him to be paid:

> This may certify that Howard Egan, has done Sixteen days duty as a policeman.[verified by] Jonathan Dunham, H.P. The City Treasurer will pay Howard Egan Sixteen dollars for services done as City Watch, out of any monies in the Treasury not otherwise appropriated. Nauvoo. January the 8th 1844. [signed] Joseph Smith, Mayor.[66]

On December 29, 1843, the City Council swore in the new police force. The men pledged to support federal and state laws and city ordinances. Did Howard get to wear a badge? We don't know. As first assignments, the police had to see that all dead animals and critters were removed, ensure that all houses were kept orderly, stop boys from fighting, prevent children from floating off on the ice, and "correct anything out of order, like a father."[67]

The police should expect that thieves had crept into the Church, Joseph Smith instructed, but they must not use thieves to catch thieves as was done in other places. Be forbearing until compelled to strike, he urged, and then "do it decently and in good order" and "break the yoke so that it cannot be mended." Let Missourians alone, he warned: "let us keep cool as a cucumber in a frosty morning. Say nothing about Missouri. Soft words turn away wrath." Study the city's ordinances, the mayor continued, "and ferret out all brothels and disorderly conduct, and if a transgressor resists cuff his ears, if any one lifts a weapon, presents a pistol, etc. take his life if needs be. Take care of your own lives. Let no horse be taken away, or anything stolen." He promised he'd pay double the amount of any bribe offered a policeman if the officer reported it to him. But then the prophet-mayor made a statement that jerked the police to attention. He said he believed that his life was more in danger "from some little doe head of a fool" in Nauvoo than from enemies abroad. He feared that a Brutus, someone close to him, might betray him. Then, not separating his city job from his prophetic calling, he blessed the policemen.[68]

Police captain Dunham's records show that on December 31, Howard, in one of his first police assignments, did guard duty with five other men supervised by sergeant Josiah Arnold.[69]

But word spread like wildfire that Joseph suspected a Brutus among the inner circle. Like whacking a hornet's nest, it triggered speculations about who the Brutus was. On January 3, 1844, the City Council called a special meeting with the police. Councilman Hyrum Smith reported that William Law, Joseph Smith's second counselor in the First Presidency, had complained to him that Eli Norton had told Law that the police had been sworn secretly by the mayor to put Law out of the way within three months. Chief Dunham, he claimed, had warned Brother Law to be careful of his personal safety.

In response, Mayor Smith polled the police, asking if any had heard him privately tell them to harm Brother Law. None had. Mayor Smith reminded the police that their primary duty was to stop thieves. "If you see a man stealing and you have told him to stand 3 times, and warned him that he is a dead man if he does not stand, and he runs, shoot off his leg." But, he affirmed, no enemy of Mormonism should be harmed unless he draws weapons on the police. Needing to hear Eli Norton's side of the story, Marshal John P. Greene brought him to the meeting. Norton said that statements policeman Daniel Carns made had suggested that Law was the doe-head. Carns explained his remarks, saying that "by the covenant we have made at Baptism we are bound to protect each other in righteousness." Mayor Smith emphasized that no accused man should be meddled with without a proper trial and testimonies offered. The Council spent most of the day examining Carns and Norton. Then, police were sworn in and questioned by William Law and the city aldermen. At the end, Law shook hands with Joseph Smith. Then the police and Council heard him pledge to stand by Joseph to the death. Sadly, Law did turn against Joseph Smith, and three months later was excommunicated on April 18.[70]

On January 5, 1844, another rumored threat produced another City Council special session dealing with the police. There, Nauvoo Stake President William Marks charged that several men had told him that he, Marks, and Brother Law were considered Joseph's enemies, and one policeman threatened that if either man came in his way "they might be popped over." The policeman was Warren Smith. Joseph Smith told all present that he never gave instructions publicly or secretly that any leaders who were disaffecting should be harmed, that he "never could bring my feelings to take revenge on my enemies." After the hearing, Brother Law and others who felt threatened accepted the Council's findings that the police were not spreading such stories. The Council gave the police a vote of confidence and thanks. Joseph Smith suspected that these rumors came from "those who do not want a police; they want to prowl in the streets at pleasure without interruption."[71]

Because Howard and nine other police had missed that January 5 hearing, they appeared before the Council on January 13 and were sworn to tell the whole truth regarding "the matter between William Law, and William Marks and the City Council." Howard and the rest testified they had received no private instructions from the Mayor. After that, the "Brutus" cauldron simmered down. But that excitement, which welcomed Howard to the police force, clearly warned that Joseph Smith's life might be in danger.[72]

On dates unknown, Howard was one of those picked to guard the home of Joseph Smith, who is purported to have said he "felt safe when Howard Egan was on guard."[73]

In terms of "regular" crime, on March 29 someone robbed a store of fifteen hundred dollars in cash and property. Police didn't have time to get involved because unknown men took a black man they suspected, named Chisem, into the woods and tied, stripped, and inhumanly beat him until he nearly died. One involved was charged for that assault and fined, and an accessory acquitted. "Lynch law will not do in Nauvoo," the *Nauvoo Neighbor* vented.[74]

Police pay became an ongoing, unsettled issue. On April 13, 1844, Mayor Smith proposed the City Council consider paying the police. He wanted each city ward to hold a public meeting to see if the people would pay the police. If not, then the Council should. The Council requested the marshal to set up ward meetings to promote the donations, but the idea fizzled.[75] On June 8 the council learned that the marshal had borrowed funds to help the police. Howard, it appears, had done fourteen weeks of part time police work without pay.

Electioneering for Joseph Smith for President

On January 29, 1844, the Twelve and others decided to support Joseph Smith to run as an independent candidate for the presidency of the United States. Because the state of Missouri had trampled the Saints' civil rights and refused to compensate the Saints for losses, Joseph Smith felt the federal government should have the power to intervene in states if necessary to protect victims of mob violence. National presidential candidates sidestepped the issue, knowing how adamantly southern states, bent on protecting slavery, pushed the states' rights issue. After seeking opinions from the national political parties' potential candidates for president, Joseph Smith could not support any of them. So, he chose to run himself. This would allow him to advocate his views of government and to publicize that the Saints deserved redress for their severe losses in Missouri.[76]

On February 8, 1844, his political platform became public and circulated as a booklet titled *View of the Powers and Policy of the Government of the United States*. It proposed that the president be given full power to send an army to suppress mobs within a state to quell "domestic violence," even without the state's permission. It called for the abolition of slavery by purchasing slaves with revenue from federal land sales. It proposed prison reform; a national bank; the annexation of Texas, Oregon, and California; free trade; sailors' rights; and national unity as opposed to political parties' factionalism.[77]

To launch a nationwide campaign for Joseph Smith, calls went out during the Church's April 1844 general conference for volunteers to "preach the Gospel and electioneer." On April 15, leaders set a schedule for public political conferences in every state, which members of the Twelve and the electioneers would attend. Campaign directors assigned between two and twenty-seven electioneering missionaries per state. Willard Snow and Howard Egan were selected as numbers one and two out of thirteen elders sent to New Hampshire. Snow was the son of Erastus Snow, who had taught the Egans in Salem. Leaders scheduled New Hampshire's conference for Peterborough on July 13 and 14.[78] Presumably, Howard filled his assignment. Available records neither confirm nor refute this.

Some 340 missionaries carrying the Prophet's political tract were assigned to all twenty-six states and Wisconsin Territory.[79] On May 17, Joseph Smith and Sidney Rigdon were officially nominated as the "National Reform Party" candidates for president and vice-president at a convention in the Red Brick Store's assembly room. Soon after the convention, many if not most of the electioneering elders headed out. The Prophet, deluged with sticky problems at home, did not personally hit the campaign trail. A new group overseeing Church temporal affairs, the Council of Fifty, orchestrated the campaign and planned for a national convention to be held in Baltimore on July 13.[80] Meanwhile, Senator Henry Clay of Kentucky became the Whig Party's candidate for president, James K. Polk of Tennessee became the Democratic Party's, and James G. Birney of Kentucky became the Liberty Party's.

Brigham Young counseled the electioneers, some of whom were able spokesmen, some not, "to take care of yourselves, be wise, be humble, and you will prosper," and to "magnify your calling, keep yourselves pure and innocent, and your path shall be clear as the horizon. Go humbly and prayerfully, trusting and believing in God, and what you desire to do you will accomplish. Cease not to ask the Father what you shall do, and He will give you the Spirit."[81] He further instructed:

> These Elders...will appoint conferences in all places in their several states where opportunities present, and will attend all the conferences, or send experienced and able Elders, who will preach the truth in righteousness, and present before the people "General Smith's Views of the Powers and Policy of the General Government," and seek diligently to get up electors who will go for him for the Presidency. All the Elders will be faithful in preaching the Gospel in its simplicity and beauty, in all meekness, humility, long-suffering and prayerfulness.[82]

Electioneers left Nauvoo on different dates. On May 21 a contingent of one hundred boarded the steamer *Osprey* for St. Louis, bound for their assigned states.[83] They traveled without purse or scrip, so, where possible, they tried to locate members of the Church to help them with lodging and food. Many, assigned to their native states, visited family relations.[84] Because Tamson was from New Hampshire, possibly Howard visited some of her Parshley and Caverly kinfolk. A study of the electioneers indicates they sometimes endured hunger, fatigue, illness, and rudeness, although on the whole their campaigns didn't become rowdy or violent. Some were "severely opposed," denied permission to rent halls, or were "pelted with old tobacco chews and other filth."[85]

Politicking provided proselytizing opportunities, so the electioneers preached nearly daily. Several baptized converts.[86] The men held conferences at which they campaigned for Joseph Smith and read from his *Views*, but they also obtained up-to-date information about the branches. "The campaign provided a way to organize and account for the many branches of the Church scattered across the United States," and the campaigners "probably did as much to strengthen the existing church as they did to garner votes."[87]

This mission gave Howard first-hand insights into how politics in America worked, and to experience what it's like to be a proselytizing missionary. In public and private he had to stand up for and promote Joseph Smith in two ways: as a presidential candidate and as a modern-day prophet and church leader. But Howard never would see Joseph Smith again. The leader's martyrdom on June 27, 1844 ended the campaigning and brought the electioneers home.

Meanwhile, Democrat James K. Polk won the presidential election. ◆

~ 5 ~

The Martyrdom and Nauvoo's Final Two Years

While Howard and the electioneering missionaries campaigned throughout the United States, anger erupted back home when the Nauvoo City Council destroyed the *Nauvoo Expositor* printing office. Joseph Smith, facing a crisis, on June 10 wrote to the electioneering Twelve to come home immediately: Brigham Young in Boston; Heber C. Kimball and Orson Pratt in Washington D.C.; Orson Hyde and William Smith in Philadelphia; Parley P. Pratt in New York City; Wilford Woodruff in Portage, New York; George A. Smith in Peterborough, New Hampshire (near where Howard was laboring); John E. Page in Pittsburgh; and Lyman Wight in Baltimore.[1] The prophet would be killed before the leading elders returned, and Nauvoo's future seemed uncertain.

The Martyrdom

On June 27, 1844, mobs murdered Joseph Smith and his brother Hyrum. Word took two weeks or more to reach some of the electioneering missionaries. Stunned, they headed home. Whether Elders Egan and Snow held the scheduled July 13–14 conference in Peterborough isn't known. During their returns, some encountered hostile locals and threats. Fortunately, electioneering had taken the Twelve away from Nauvoo and out of harm's way when the murders took place.[2]

Howard returned home. Tamson and others updated him about the *Expositor* uproar that had precipitated the martyrdom. He learned that back on June 7, Church dissenters, including William Law, earlier suspected of being a "Brutus," published the first issue of the *Nauvoo Expositor*. It declared Joseph Smith "pernicious and diabolical," and accused him of teaching "heretical and damnable doctrines." The publishers said that "we are earnestly seeking to explode the vicious principles of Joseph Smith"

Nauvoo Expositor, June 7, 1844

and are "striking a blow at tyranny." They urged the Illinois Legislature to cancel the Nauvoo Charter.[3]

An enraged Nauvoo City Council met on June 10. Believing the "opposition party" was publishing inflammatory material "to raise a mob on us and take the spoil of us as they did in Missouri," they called the *Nauvoo Expositor* "a greater nuisance than a dead carcase[sic]." After reviewing the Illinois constitution and Blackstone's *Commentaries on the Laws of England*, the Council voted to suppress the newspaper as a public nuisance. Members of the Nauvoo Legion and some police then destroyed the *Expositor*'s printing press.[4]

The demolition infuriated the *Expositor* backers, and it heated anti-Mormons' tempers to red-hot. On June 17, fears of mob activity caused Mayor Smith to order the Nauvoo Legion activated. As the Legion's commander, Joseph Smith then declared martial law. On June 19, he ordered picket guards positioned on all roads into Nauvoo and an inner guard posted on all city streets and alleys.[5] State authorities intervened by having Joseph Smith arrested on charges of causing a riot, meaning the *Expositor* action, and for treason for declaring martial law without the governor's permission. He was taken to and imprisoned in Carthage, the county seat, where a mob later surrounded the jail and shot and killed him and Hyrum.[6]

Nauvoo residents, Howard was told, had reacted with a mix of shock, disbelief, anger, sorrow, worry, confusion, and fear. James Palmer recalled the tense mood:

> Our people determined to protect themselves against mob violence and armed themselves as best they could. And the Nauvoo Legion was ordered out on muster and put in readiness for protection and to allways act on the defencive [sic]. We were told to place our guns and amonition [sic] where we could put our hand upon it the darkest night that ever was, and be ready to run at the tap of the drum.[7]

On June 29, from 8:00 a.m. to 5:00 p.m., "many thousands" solemnly passed through the Mansion House to view Joseph and Hyrum's bodies lying in state. Possibly Tamson and the boys attended the viewing. Howard had not yet returned from electioneering. Saints agonized that murderers had killed two of the "best men that ever lived on the earth."[8] Revenge simmered, but apostles Willard Richards and John Taylor, survivors of the Carthage jail attack, called for inaction, watching and waiting for the absent apostles to return. Mourning and numbness replaced retaliation.

The "Mantle of Joseph" Meeting

As fast as possible the Twelve returned from the eastern states. The Saints felt uncertainty about who now should be in charge of the Church. On August 8, at a decision meeting in the East Grove, members listened to Sidney Rigdon, once Joseph's counselor in the First Presidency, claim a "guardianship" for the Church.[9] By then Howard was back home. After a noon break, the meeting resumed, and President Young arose and presented the case for the Twelve being Joseph's proper successors. Howard and Tamson both were there when one of the great mystical moments in Latter-day Saint history occurred. "When President Young arose to address the congregation," the account closest to the event reads, "his Voice was the Voice of Brother Joseph and his face appeared as Joseph's face & Should I not have seen his face but herd [sic] his Voice I should have declared that it was Joseph."[10]

Howard shared his witness in a letter to Jesse C. Little in New Hampshire, and, in December, Little repeated Howard's comments to Brigham Young: "He [Egan] said if a man had been blinded he would hardly have known if it were not Joseph."[11] Years later, Tamson's son William heard her say that she "saw Brigham Young look like Joseph and speak in his voice" at that meeting.[12] Many others recalled that Brigham Young's voice and appearance altered, giving assurance that he was Joseph Smith's successor.[13] The congregation then voted in favor of the Twelve leading the church.

Nevertheless, some members didn't accept that decision.[14] Factions formed. Some followed Rigdon, others believed recent convert James J. Strang's claims that he'd been appointed to succeed Joseph Smith. Emma Smith felt that the leadership role should transfer to her son Joseph Smith III. However, the majority of Saints, including the Egans, embraced the Twelve's leadership.

With Joseph Smith dead, anti-Mormon activists expected the Church to collapse and members to scatter. They waited for it to happen. Therefore, for the year following the martyrdom, Nauvoo remained relatively calm and free from outside threats.

In the Seventeenth Quorum of Seventies Presidency

Late in 1844, Howard was ordained to the office of a Seventy, which then had a different function in the Church than today. It was a missionary calling. What priesthood office he held before that, if any, isn't recorded. His ordination was part of an unexpected mass ordination of Seventies that marked a sharp redirection in Church doctrine and practice. Back on February 28, 1835, Joseph Smith, based on an unrecorded revelation "showing the order of the Seventy," organized a First Quorum of Seventy. Not only was the seventy-man membership an unusual number, but its seven presidents were a clear departure from the typical president-and-two-counselors form. The seventies differed from other priesthood quorums, according to Doctrine and Covenants Section 107, because their calling was to be "traveling ministers" and "especial witnesses unto the Gentiles and in all the world." They served under the direction of the Twelve.[15]

By 1839 a second and third quorum of seventies had been organized.[16] The seven presidents of the First Quorum, who served as the First Council of the Seventy, oversaw all the seventies quorums. Then, during the April 1844 general conference, Joseph Smith had announced a "great, grand, and glorious revelation" that surprised the Saints. Earlier revelations had commissioned the Church to establish a Zion society in Jackson County, Missouri. Efforts to do so failed. But now, the revelation pronounced, not just Jackson County but "the whole of the Americas is Zion itself from north to south." As Joseph Smith explained:

> I have received instructions from the Lord that from henceforth wherever the Elders of Israel shall build up churches and branches unto the Lord throughout the States, there shall be a stake of Zion. In the great cities, as Boston, New York, &c., there shall be stakes...this work shall commence after the washing, anointings and endowments have been performed here.[17]

At a general conference three months after his death, the Twelve instituted a two-pronged plan to create stakes throughout the United States. They assigned eighty-five high priests, by name, to go out and preside over branches, also termed stakes, in all the congressional districts in the United States. These high priests were "to go and settle down" with their families and build up stakes as large as Nauvoo's. As a second prong, during the next months the Twelve expanded the number of seventies quorums from three to thirty-four, drawing in "all those elders who are under the age of thirty-five, and also all the priests, teachers, deacons, and members, who are recommended to be ordained." Priests, teachers, and deacons in those days were adults, not youth.[18] Seventies would preach and baptize and raise up branches, meaning stakes, over which the high priests would preside. At the conference where the plan was announced, about sixty brethren were ordained high priests and 430 as seventies. By the time the conference closed, a twelfth seventies quorum had been created.[19]

New quorums kept forming. On January 12, 1845, the Seventeenth Quorum was organized. Howard was called as one of its seven presidents. Daniel Repsher served as

Replica, Nauvoo Seventies Hall, courtesy Kenneth Mays

its senior president. The quorum's enrollment record lists Howard as age twenty-nine, a rope maker, from Lower Canada.[20] In this new calling Howard fully expected to soon become a proselytizing missionary. Nine months previously he had done missionary work while electioneering in New England. However, leaders decided that the high priests and seventies must receive the temple endowment before departing. "There has been but few elders sent out since the death of the prophet," Nauvooer Sally Murdock wrote in August 1845, "but when the seventies receive their endeument [sic] they will go forth with power to all the nations kindreds tongues and people of the earth."[21]

Meanwhile, seventies quorums took turns meeting in the new Seventies Hall on the northeast corner of Bain and Parley streets (where a reconstructed version now stands). Workmen completed the original two-story, brick structure late in July 1844, and Brigham Young dedicated it that December. The first floor contained a chapel for meetings and the training of missionaries. The second floor held offices and a large hall that housed a museum and a library. Howard attended several of his quorum's meetings in that fine building, where the members sang hymns, prayed, and "testified of their faith."[22] Perhaps Howard and Tamson attended some lectures, lyceum presentations, or traveling displays held there.

Howard's mission call never came. Before the plan could be implemented for high priests and seventies to saturate the United States, anti-Mormon pressures in Hancock County forced the Saints to abandon Nauvoo and seek refuge in the unsettled west.

Police Work

After the two Smith murders, Howard and Tamson had cause to wonder how safe the Mormon people were. Trouble, they saw, came from disaffected Mormons living in the city and from anti-Mormon activists beyond Nauvoo's neighborhoods. Howard and other Nauvoo police tried to keep abreast of lawbreaking in Nauvoo and of crime and trouble in nearby areas that might spill into Nauvoo. The Nauvoo Legion, too, stayed alert. Latter-day Saints lived in several smaller settlements near Nauvoo: Ramus (Macedonia), Fountain Green, La Harpe, Bear Creek, Green Plains, Yelrome (Morley's Settlement), Carthage, and Warsaw. The Twelve felt responsible for the safety of members in those places and those across the river in Iowa Territory.

Adding to confusion following the murders, the Nauvoo police force threatened to quit because of no pay. On July 13, 1844, two weeks after the martyrdom, the pay issue came to a head. Councilman William W. Phelps told the City Council that the police were important and that the marshal wanted Council authority to provide the police with food. No ordinances regulated police pay. On August 10, twenty-one petitioned the city to be paid. By then, Howard, back from electioneering, was doing police work again. Policemen Hosea Stout and Daniel Carn affirmed that the police were willing to watch the city, in shifts, but that they "wanted to live" while doing so.[23]

On September 14, 1844, police chief Dunham unsettled citizens by saying the police were about to be broken up. Elder John Taylor pleaded they not be, saying the police must be sustained because "they are willing to go any length for the safety of the city."[24] On January 11, 1845, more than two dozen police petitioned the City Council to be paid half of the penalties recovered from breakers of city ordinances. The council vetoed this proposal, not wanting to financially incentivize arrests. The council also didn't want to make police work a church calling for fear of interfering with Church presiding officers. That same day, the council passed an ordinance authorizing the mayor to enlarge the police force to five hundred men, "provided the service of such Policemen shall not be chargeable to This City."[25] Every time the issue of police compensation came up, someone said there must be an ordinance covering it, and "each time they realize there isn't such an ordinance, they nevertheless end up doing nothing about it."[26]

Repeal of the Nauvoo City Charter

On August 5, 1844, Hancock County held elections. Because of Nauvoo voters, most county offices went to candidates who were not anti-Mormon. Non-Mormon Minor Deming became sheriff, rankling anti-Mormons who felt he'd be friendly with the Mormons. Their ire, plus accusations that Nauvoo harbored criminals, led state legislators to push to repeal the Nauvoo Charter and end the "sovereignty within a sovereignty" it created.[27]

Responding to charges that Nauvoo didn't punish crimes and criminals, Brigham Young in January 1845 rebuked Nauvoo's civic authorities and city parents for failing to maintain law and order. He exhorted city officials to put down "thieving, swearing, gambling, bogus-making, retailing spirituous liquors, bad houses, and all abominations practiced in our midst by our enemies who…publish that these things are practices by us."[28] He launched a campaign to change Illinois public opinion and to increase police crackdowns.

First, he sent men into counties on both sides of the river to publicly correct misrepresentations. Then, the City Council issued public denials that any criminals had been harbored. It blamed anti-Mormon newspapers for false accusations, and voted to bolster the city police by up to five hundred part-time officers. A Hancock County deputy sheriff discovered that a theft ring operating thirty miles inland was funneling contraband through six agents in Nauvoo and then on to a holding depot ten miles inside Iowa. His investigation found that, public opinion to the contrary, none of the culprits was a Latter-day Saint.[29]

When the legislature met for its 1844–1845 term, it gave heated consideration to repealing the liberal Nauvoo Charter. The Senate passed the repeal on December 19, the House on January 24. "The tide of popular passion and frenzy was too strong to be resisted," said Illinois's attorney general Josiah Lamborn.[30]

Hired as a Constable

Word of the legislature's repeal measure reached Nauvooers on January 29, 1845. No charter meant no City Council, no municipal courts, no legal government other than the county, and no police.[31] However, Nauvoo city elections already were underway with nominees selected, so the city council voted on January 30 to proceed with the voting, in case Governor Ford vetoed the charter-repeal bill. In the February 3 election, 850 voted and approved the nominees. Despite having no legality, newly elected city officials took office, including mayor Orson Spencer. Albert P. Rockwood became the city marshal.[32]

Important for Howard, the Council agreed that the city needed "an active standing police," so they voted that a police supervisor be assigned to each ward. They also appointed four constables: Howard Egan to keep the peace in the city's Third Ward, Benjamin Boyce the First Ward, E. J. Sabine the Second Ward, and Daniel M. Repsher the Fourth Ward. These were paid positions, so the Egan household began to receive some compensation for Howard's police work. Said Captain Stout: "I was much pleased with the good feeling manifested towards the old Police by the Council, who seemed willing to extend the hand of patronage to us after we had spent the winter thus far without any remuneration, and kept up the guard to the satisfaction of the Twelve and other authorities."[33] Brigham Young instructed Howard and the other constables "to search out the very characters & have their eyes about them." The Council assigned the constables also to be the fire wardens in their wards.

Apostle Willard Richards on February 19 personally tried to pay the police forty dollars for guarding him and others of the Twelve. The police declined his offer, saying it was their Church duty to guard the Twelve and the Temple.[34] They deemed it "sufficient remuneration for us from the Twelve, to be thought worthy to be entrusted with your lives; & consequently the salvation of the Church."[35]

Protecting Brigham Young

On the evening of February 25, 1845, police worried that suspicious characters in town planned to collect a company of "mobocrats" and waylay Brigham Young, Heber C. Kimball, and others returning from Macedonia, twenty-five miles inland. Duly alarmed, police captain Stout ordered all the police who could to procure horses and, "armed for defense," gather at police headquarters immediately. They did. But then word came that the brethren were not coming to Nauvoo that night. Stout decided to take seven men anyway, including Howard, and ride to Macedonia to be sure all was right. The patrol left at 9:00 p.m., and had a pleasant moonlit ride. Muddy roads fatigued the horses. They reached Benjamin Johnson's home in Macedonia at half past 2:00 a.m. Brigham Young, awakened, told them he'd been impressed the evening before that something was wrong, so he had not left Macedonia as planned. The posse, including Howard, after putting up and feeding their horses, "all laid down and took a short sleep."

Brigham Young, Frederick Piercy sketch,
Route from Liverpool to Great Salt Lake Valley

After breakfast the next morning, Young's group and Stout's men started for Nauvoo. Twenty-three men from Macedonia accompanied them through the timber about seven miles. There the big posse halted. Then, for the men's amusement, Howard recited a humorous sermon at Brigham Young's request. Young then gave the Macedonia riders counsel and blessed them, and they rode back. While the Stout and Young groups approached Nauvoo, rain and snow made the ride disagreeable. Stout, Howard, and other guards escorted Elders Young and Kimball and the others to their several homes. "So," Stout recorded, "the designs of our enemies were frustrated."[36]

This episode shows that Howard had a reputation for telling entertaining stories. Helen Mar Kimball recalled that young people always anticipated the times when John Kay and Howard guarded the Brigham Young home because

> ...they were very entertaining—Egan with his interesting yarns and anecdotes, and the singing by John Kay, it would be useless for us to try to describe, but suffice it to say, his voice (a baritone) was most magnificent,...and many an evening we were thus entertained, as we circled around...and the hours flew by so swiftly that midnight was often there before we knew it.[37]

The "Old Police," the "New Police," and the "City of Joseph"

Finally accepting the Charter's repeal, the Nauvoo City Council met for the last time on March 8, 1845.[38] After the repeal, the Twelve worried about police protection. For two years the city police, with backup from the Nauvoo Legion, had kept the peace.[39] However, thanks to having no charter, "the town was soon over-run with all manner of ruffians from the mob camp around about," said William B. Pace, one of the Old Police. Wandle Mace said that parties disembarked from steamboats, caused trouble in the city, then returned to the boat "well knowing we had no law to protect us since the city charter was taken away."[40]

A favorite story in Mormon lore describes an unofficial band of Nauvoo males who intimidated strangers by following them around while whistling and whittling on wood with "significant knives." In several instances, strangers were "whistled and whittled" out of town. The whistlers did not molest the suspicious persons in any way, or even talk to them, but simply followed them "whittling and whistling as they went."[41]

On March 14, 1845, the Old Police met at the Masonic Hall to reorganize and function as "new police" under Stephen Markham. According to Hosea Stout, "it was concluded to organize the whole community of Saints in this County into Quorums of 12 deacons [who then were adults] and have a Bishop at their head and they could thus administer in the lesser offices of the Church and preserve order without a charter."[42] On March 24 the Twelve met at the Concert Hall and ordained bishops "who were directed to set apart deacons in their wards to attend to all things needful and especially to watch; being without any city organization, we deemed it prudent to organize the priesthood more strictly that the peace and good order hitherto sustained by the city might still be preserved." These deacons would be the "New Police."[43] Not a legal entity under state law, it was an interim agency under church officers. These quorums of "New Police" patrolled the streets in rotation day and night and served as bodyguards for church leaders. After the bishops deployed the deacons, residents saw on each street corner a guard standing watch from sunset to dawn, assigned to report any suspicious activity.[44]

On April 5, because anti-Mormons threatened to break up general conference the next day, the police met at their headquarters and planned a defense. The conference went off quietly. By then "great peace and union prevailed among all the Saints." The conference approved that the community, governed now by ecclesiastical mandates, be called not Nauvoo but the "City of Joseph."[45] On April 12 the Old Police hosted the Twelve and their families at a party in the Masonic Hall.[46]

A big change came on April 16, 1845, when the Church, acting under an Illinois law regarding towns (not cities), organized a new town. By law the town could include only one square mile. Old Nauvoo would have needed fourteen such towns to cover its expanse.[47] Five trustees became the City of Joseph's administrators: Alphaeus Cutler, Orson Spencer, Charles C. Rich, Theodore Turley, and David Fullmer. These trustees appointed Stout to be captain of the town's police force, and designated that the Old Police serve with him. They allowed the deacons, or New Police, to continue as an emergency defense force, which in reality acted as a "thinly veiled militia" under Nauvoo Legion general Charles C. Rich. Howard and the Old Police's main jobs now were to protect the nearly completed temple from sabotage and to safeguard the Twelve.[48]

On Sunday, April 27, an apostate attended the worship service held at one of the stands, whereupon "a company of boys assembled to whistle him out of town." Stout stopped them, but later that day learned the man "had been whistled out immediately after the meeting."[49] Old Police like Howard must have smiled when the whistlers and whittlers convinced an undesirable to skedaddle. On May 6 the Twelve met with the Old Police at the Masonic Hall "to make preparations to prevent any surprises by the mob."[50]

Howard, Hosea Stout, and Police Work

Police captain Stout's detailed diary documents that he and Howard patrolled, attended meetings, and enjoyed socials together. Just about every evening Stout met with the police assigned to that night's duty. On May 19, 1845, for example, Stout said he was "with Egan" and met with the police just before dark. On May 25, a Sunday, after the general church meeting, Stout "went on the flat and met with the police and at dark patroled with Egan, Daniels, Kay, and other policeman, on the flat, and upper landing, and was out all night." The next day Stout learned that during the night someone broke into a warehouse at the upper landing and stole "Bryants & Egans" goods.[51] If those were Howard's goods, they probably were rope products. Police stayed on the lookout for the stolen goods. At dark Stout "met in Council" with four apostles and five policemen, including Howard. Next morning the same men met again and "we remained there all day" until the evening police meeting.

Hosea Stout, 1860, LDS Church History Library

On May 30 Stout "went from the temple to see Br. Egan." On June 19 Stout met with Egan and two other police "to do some business in temporal matters." Later, Stout went to see Brigham Young, "who gave us instructions about the police and, after having some talk with Egan and Harmon," went home at about 11:00 o'clock. The next day Stout met with the police "as usual," went to consult with Brigham Young, and then patrolled with Howard and four others until midnight on a warm, still, rainy night. The next day Stout "went up to the upper landing with Egan." Rain on Sunday, June 22, broke up the public worship service, so Stout met with the police in the Seventies Hall and then "patrolled until day light in company with Egan" and others. During June, Stout met almost daily with the police, sometimes with Howard in attendance. On July 1 a concert was held for the police in the Masonic Hall. The Twelve attended. "We had an entertaining time," Stout said, enjoying "as much beer, wine, cakes &c as we could eat or drink."[52] The festivities began at 10:00 a.m. and lasted until 6:00 p.m.

On July 18, 1845, Stout met with the police at the Masonic Hall, then went home at dark "accompanied by Brs Egan and Shumway." After supper he and Howard patrolled Lower Nauvoo until nearly midnight. Stout recorded that Tamson's birthday produced a delightful feast and fine music. On the morning of July 29 Stout and Andrew Lytle went "to the flat and went to see Egan and Kay." After an evening meeting with police, Stout attended Tamson's twenty-first birthday party (indicating she was born in 1824, not 1825) held in the Egans' home.[53] "Br. Egan came with a buggy after me to go to a small party at his house to celebrate his wife's birth day. I went, we had a most agreeable entertainment and had a very delicious Supper well served up, plenty of wine & beer & other good drinks." (As noted in Chapter Four, beer and wine were acceptable then because they were not considered liquor.) It was a fine social:

> The feast was mostly entertained with music, (i.e.), three violins bass viol and horn, with occasional Singing and agreeable conversation. Br William Clayton, Wm Pitt, Hutchison, Smithie & Kay were the musicians. We continued untill about half past twelve o'clock at night when we dismissed and went away. I have been to but few such agreeable parties in my life where a few were assembled together with the same good feelings of friendship. All seemed of one heart & partook of the enjoyment of the good things and comforts of [life] with the dignaty which bespoke that they knew how to appreciate the blessings of God in the way that he designed we should. May they all have many more such good & happy nights.[54]

On the morning on August 6, Stout met with several police at the Masonic Hall, where Brigham Young gave them "a charge," after which "we all seemed to be of one heart and mind." Stout then went to the upper landing with Howard and Brother Kay, then down to the river where Howard and Kay crossed on a ferry. Stout mentions Howard again in his September 4 entry, when he, Howard, and two others patrolled until nearly midnight. On September 7 the police set up a picket guard outside the city "as the mob was threatening again." The next day Stout visited a store, a tailor, and then went to the rope works "to see Br Egan but did not see him."

Word reached Nauvoo on September 11 that arsonists were burning buildings at Morley's Settlement, twenty-six miles south of Nauvoo. "What will be next God only knows," Stout journalized. Nauvoo buzzed with talk about military and police readiness. Church leaders decided to "let the mob burn for the time being the houses of the Saints, and not make war on them." The city sent hundreds of teams to evacuate Saints from Morley's and other settlements being torched. Sunday, September 14, after the general church service at the stand, leaders held a business meeting. Anyone not in good fellowship was not allowed to attend, and, Stout said, "police in keeping them away had to flog three who were determined to stay." Leaders in that meeting decided to post a guard below, or south of, the city to prevent persons from going into or out of the city who were "trying to make a difficulty." The Nauvoo Legion was "put in immediate readiness for defense." Those were uncertain and dangerous days.

On September 17, those attending a meeting at the temple "decided that there be a guard kept night & day around the Temple and that no stranger be allowed to come within the Square on the Temple Lot." They agreed that "there be 4 large lanterns… placed about 25 feet from each corner of the Temple to keep a light by night for the convenience of the guard." Temple guards were posted, and the Legion was given "shoot to kill" orders. Tolling the temple bell would be the signal for men to rush to the parade ground armed and equipped.[55]

Howard's Ten-day Patrol Outside Nauvoo

On September 18, Stout received orders from Nauvoo Legion General Charles C. Rich to send twenty well-armed men in three wagons to Camp Creek about ten miles east-northeast of Nauvoo. Stout sent men "from the 1st and 4 regiments under the command of Howard Egan of the old Police. This was done from reports brought in that the mob were about to commit their depredations on that settlement." Brigham Young assumed the position of commanding general of Mormon forces, with authority above that of the Legion generals and the county sheriff, to direct the defense efforts. A committee negotiated with "the Mob Party," who promised peace that winter only if the Saints agreed to leave the state by April 1.[56]

General Rich received a note from "Captain" Egan, who was at Camp Creek. It said that most of the mob was moving due south towards Carthage to set fires there. "Captain Egan has spies out watching them and the remainder of his force concealed in the bushes ready for immediate action," Rich said, while Howard awaited further orders.[57] On September 21 "Capt. Egan," at Camp Creek, wrote a note to "Gen. B. Young" in Nauvoo:

> Dear Sir. Yours of the 19th came to hand this day. I have just returned from an excursion through the timber near Pontusuc [Pontoosuc] where I heard there was a force collecting [.] I have not Made any Discovery as yet[,] a number of the Mob has left there homes & taken a large lot of provisions with them the[y] swear the[y] will take to the bushes and shoot every Dam Mormon that passes on the Road[.] I keep a gard on two of the most traveled roads from the South. I have been campeled to send a man home that is sick and I thought I would write this, these few lines to let you know what we are doing. Yours, Howard Egan[58]

On September 21, Young was handed Howard's note. That day Stout heard orders to recall "the out post guards," so he told Captain Egan to return from Camp Creek. The next day, part of Howard's company arrived, but Howard and five others stayed "to make observations, Egan to be home at daybreak." On September 23, Libbeus T. Coon wrote from Camp Creek that four men left by Captain Egan wished to be relieved, "if consistent with Capt. Egan's will." Howard by then was heading back to

Mob Burning Morley's Settlement, *artist C.C.A. Christensen,
Scenes from Mormon History Collection, courtesy LDS Church History Library*

Nauvoo. The Camp Creek Saints were told to move to Nauvoo.[59] The next day dozens of men were sent from Nauvoo to help Mormons in the other settlements move their "goods, grain, and families" into Nauvoo. About a hundred wagons became involved in that evacuation effort.[60]

On September 26, according to Stout's diary, Brigham Young called the Mormon militia men together and gave instructions. He wanted teams constantly bringing in grain, corn, straw, and rails. Stout described how Young then reviewed a proclamation of intent that he and the other leaders had just issued. He quoted Young:

> "I never intend to winter in the United States except on a visit, we do not owe this country a single Sermon. We calculated to go all the while for I do not intend to stay in such an Hell of Hole and if this bee your mind signify it by saying Hie"–which was loudly responded to by the assembly…"They are as corrupt as Hell from the president down clean through the priest, and the people are all as corrupt as the Devil. I will leave them and God grant I may live to get to some place of peace, health and safety."

Before the meeting broke up, "at 11 o clock Capt Egan left with his company for Carthage" fifteen miles southeast of Nauvoo. The next day, General Rich sent six horsemen "to the relief of Capt Egan" stationed at Carthage.[61] On September 28, Illinois state militia general John J. Hardin and his troops took control of Carthage and, in Captain Egan's presence, said he wanted no organized military forces operating in Hancock County except those under his command. That day Stout dispatched two wagons to meet "Capt Egan and his troops who were on the road from Carthage a foot." That evening "Capt Egan & troops arrived and reports the number of troops now in Carthage under the command of Gen Hardin of the Illinois volunteers to be about 320 men who are sent by the Governor to maintain & be the efficient arms of the Law as he published in his general Orders to Hancock county."[62]

A Man To Be Relied On

Howard proved through his police service, his Nauvoo Legion position, and then this patrol duty that he carried out dangerous duties well and had a level of toughness and courage the Church could, and would, count on in future difficult situations. Responding to Howard's patrol work, Hancock County deputy sheriff H. G. Ferris sent this praise about Howard to Sheriff Jacob Backenstos:

> The men here under the command of Egan have acted nobly, been faithful and attentive to duty and truly deserve praise. They could not have done better. Egan is a man who attends to his duty strictly and will never be taken or caught by surprise nor will never be seen running from danger.[63]

Decision to Leave Illinois

The Twelve concluded that the time had come to find a new home for the Saints. During the first days in October, they promised anti-Mormon factions, the citizens in nearby counties, and Governor Thomas Ford that the Mormons would leave the next spring. That pledge ended the anti-Mormon raids and pacified both sides. Spring was only seven months away, hardly enough time to organize and carry out a mass evacuation of close to 17,000 people.[64] But in January, renewed anti-Mormon threats forced the Twelve and about 2,500 others, including the Egans, to leave in February. They left in the middle of winter, a full two months ahead of schedule. ✦

~ 6 ~

Temple Blessings and Evacuation Plans

In Nauvoo during 1845, a driving issue, a crucial crusade, was to complete the temple. Leaders felt adamant that members, particularly the seventies (including Howard) and the high priests assigned to duties throughout the United States, needed to receive ordinances available only in the temple. At the temple site, construction work progressed at a good pace, which seemed to signal that the Saints would stay in Nauvoo indefinitely. Late in 1845 Howard and Tamson entered the nearly-finished temple and became endowed, sealed in celestial marriage, accepted Nancy Redden as a plural wife, and were adopted into Apostle Heber C. Kimball's family.

By the year's end, anti-Mormon hostilities and government denials of proper protection caused Church leaders and members to agree to forsake Nauvoo within months and relocate westward, outside of what was then the United States. During February 1846, the Egans packed up and pulled out of Nauvoo, and became part of Brigham Young's advance company of evacuees. Eight months later, Nauvoo stood nearly deserted, bereft of its Mormon citizenry, while less-than-holy hands desecrated the stately temple.

Finishing the Temple

Shock from Joseph Smith's murder in 1844 halted construction at the temple site for two weeks before resuming. During the next year, masonry teams finished the sixty-foot-high walls. On May 24, 1845, Nauvooers gathered for a stirring capstone ceremony celebrating the completion of the temple walls. When the last stone was laid, shouts of "Hosannah to God and the Lamb" rended the air.[1]

Workers in the basement replaced the wooden baptismal font and oxen with ones carved from stone. Son Ransom recalled that when he was about age six Tamson led him by the hand up to the temple and showed him "the large baptismal font that was supported on the backs of twelve stone oxen. There were four on the side where we stood, one at each corner, and two between them just as natural as life."[2] Howard's papers include a certificate that entitled him to the privilege of the font, "having paid property and labor tithing in full."[3] Howard had posthumous baptisms performed in the font in behalf of his deceased father Howard and mother Anne, his brothers Bernard and John, and his sister Anne.[4]

Eyes on the West

After Lewis and Clark explored to the Pacific in 1804–1806 and reported about the extent and resources of the vast Louisiana Purchase, Americans felt fascinated by those western regions. The idea of relocating Mormons to the West had long percolated. During the 1830s Church leaders tried to establish the Gospel among the "Lamanites" beyond the Missouri River.[5] By the late 1830s a spirit of "Manifest Destiny" tempted the United States to acquire the new Republic of Texas, Upper California, and Oregon. Joseph Smith felt the nation should "grasp all the territory we can."[6] According to Anson Call, President Smith prophesied while in Montrose, Iowa on August 6, 1842, saying that the Saints would be driven to, and become a "mighty people" in, the midst of the Rocky Mountains.[7] Also in 1842, Joseph Smith proposed a "Great Western Measure" to investigate unoccupied western locations for Saints to settle.[8]

During 1843 and 1844, the *Nauvoo Neighbor* published more than a dozen articles dealing with the West, including highlights from explorer John C. Fremont's report about his first western expedition, excerpts from Lansford Hastings's *The Emigrants' Guide to Oregon and California*, and a report about Charles Wilkes's California explorations.[9] Howard most likely read some of the newspaper reports, and certainly heard of them, leading him to wonder about the vast, unsettled land.

On January 12, 1844, Joseph Smith requested the Twelve to send a company "to explore Oregon and California, and select a site for a new city for the Saints," and to preach wherever they could. Fourteen men were called to the journey. He asked a newly created Council of Fifty to direct the Church's temporal projects, including ones in the West.[10] Nine apostles sat on that Council. In March, the Fifty discussed how best "to secure a resting place in the mountains, or some uninhabited region, where we can enjoy the liberty of conscience." There's no indication their thinking was to find a replacement for Nauvoo; rather, that resting place would be in addition to Nauvoo. Two weeks later they drafted a petition to Congress seeking authorization to raise a large army to promote American interests in the West. That April (1844) is when Joseph Smith made his startling pronouncement that Zion now meant the whole of the Americas.[11]

> **UPPER CALIFORNIA**
> *by John Taylor, April 1845*
>
> *The Upper California,*
> *O that's the land for me!*
> *It lies between the mountains*
> *and the great Pacific Sea:*
> *The saints can be supported there,*
> *And taste the sweets of liberty*
> *In Upper California—*
> *Oh that's the land for me.*
> *Oh, that's the land for me.*
> *Oh, that's, &c.*
>
> *We'll go and lift our standard,*
> *we'll go there and be free:*
> *We'll go to California*
> *and have our Jubilee,—*
> *A land that blooms with beauty rare,*
> *a land of joy and liberty,*
> *With flocks and herds abounding—*
> *Oh, that's the land for me!*
> *Oh, that's, &c.*

Song mentioned in Howard's journal [15]

After Joseph Smith's death, the Twelve and the Fifty kept eyes on the West. Late in 1844, Council member James Emmet led a company, despite the Twelve's objections, across Iowa and established Camp Vermillion among Sioux Indians in the southeastern tip of today's South Dakota.[12] Council member Apostle Lyman Wight led about 150 Saints, then cutting timber for Nauvoo in the Wisconsin pineries, to Texas and founded a settlement near Austin.[13] Those ventures were not secrets to Nauvooers.

During March and April of 1845, the Twelve and the Fifty discussed ways to explore the west, particularly Upper California. That spring, Oneida Indian convert Lewis Dana and other LDS emissaries met with tribes in the middle Missouri River region, gaining approvals for Mormon settlements among them.[14] By May 1845 the Twelve had sent letters to President James K. Polk and state governors asking them to provide the Saints with a place of safety. A few responses came, all negative, but suggested Texas or unsettled regions in the west as an alternative.[16]

Decision to Abandon Nauvoo

In the summer of 1845 the Twelve, feeling the heated pulse of anti-Mormon sentiment in the region, decided the Saints must pull out of Nauvoo and relocate somewhere in the West. In the face of anti-Mormon violence between September 16 and 24, 1845, which sent Howard and other militiamen out on defensive patrols, Church leaders promised that the Saints would leave Illinois the next spring. They pledged that Mormon farmers would not plant any winter wheat. But, this agreement required that raids stop and Saints be allowed to peacefully prepare to leave. When Mormons pleaded that to afford the move they needed to sell property, cattle, and furniture at fair prices, locals answered that the exodus better happen no matter what sold or didn't sell.[17]

Such a forced evacuation of the population of a thriving city was un-American, unprecedented in American history, and tragic. On a smaller scale, upset and covetous Americans in Missouri had employed violence twice to deprive Mormon farmers and shopkeepers of life, liberty, and property. But for Illinois citizens and elected officials to condone and even fuel the forced departure of what amounted to about 15,000 people stains that state's history. Their trashing of Mormon rights had found a model of sorts in President Andrew Jackson and other national leaders' forced relocation of Native American tribes. A Hancock County resident years later said Nauvoo at its peak had some 1,200 hand-hewn cabins, "most of them whitewashed inside," 200 to 300 good substantial brick houses, and 300 to 500 frame houses.[18] For residents who had labored for years to turn swamps and prairie land into Illinois's second-largest city, and set up farms and businesses, this expulsion felt criminal. Among many of the victims, bitterness and resentments toward legal systems, government officials, and anti-Mormons endured for the rest of their lives and produced retributions in Utah.

Exodus Explained in the October Conference

The Church held a general conference October 6–8, 1845, inside the Nauvoo Temple, even though construction was not finished. Thousands attended, and as a seventies quorum presidency member Howard no doubt was among them. Perhaps Tamson too. Authorities instructed about the need to evacuate and head west for the Rocky Mountains.[19] Elder Parley Pratt explained why, after such an outlay and expense to buy lands, build houses, and erect the temple, Saints needed to leave. "We want a country where we have room to expand," he said. "The people must enlarge in numbers and extend their borders; they cannot always live in one city, nor in one county." The Twelve, Elder Heber C. Kimball said, "want to take you to a land, where a white man's foot never trod, nor a lion's whelps, nor the devil's; and there we can enjoy it, with no one to molest and make us afraid." With sarcasm he added that "we are not accounted as white people, and we don't want to live among them. I had rather live with the buffalo in the wilderness." Prone to prophesying, he predicted correctly that "in five years we will be as well again off as we are now."

Apostle George A. Smith raised a vital matter. "When we were to leave Missouri," he reminded, "the saints entered into a covenant not to cease their exertions until every saint who wished to go was removed, which was done." He wanted "to see the same principle carried out now, that every man will give all to help to take the poor; and every honest industrious member who wants to go." President Brigham Young "moved that we take all the saints with us, to the extent of our ability, that is, our influence and property." The motion carried unanimously. This Nauvoo Covenant motivated President Young from then until his death in 1877, and shaped the Church's emigration policy for decades.[20]

Elder Smith informed the congregation that some exodus companies already were being organized, but people need not rush for assignments because "the Twelve will take care to have proper captains appointed in due time." Some Nauvooers begged to travel in the Twelve's company, so Elder Kimball explained that "we calculate you are all going in the first company, both old and young, rich and poor; for there will be but one company."[21]

Hopefully Howard and Tamson, being converts only recently, heard Mother Lucy Mack Smith's talk at that conference, in which she recalled the Smith family's hardships, trials, privations, persecutions, and sufferings during the eighteen years since son Joseph received the golden plates. At times her testimony "melted those who heard her to tears." Near the conference's end, President Young stated what today would be called a concise "mission statement" for the Church: "we are determined also to use every means in our power to do all that Joseph told us."

When the conference ended, Howard and Tamson assumed they had until spring, six months, to obtain wagons and ox teams, load up months' worth of food and supplies, pay and collect debts, stay healthy, and sell or trade anything they could.

Preparations for Spring Departures

Soon after the conference, attendee Irene Pomeroy wrote a letter saying that "The Church as a body intend removing in the spring...they have their arrangements made. They are going in companies consisting of one hundred families each, every company a half a mile apart, every wagon two rods apart. They make calculations for twenty-five hundred families."[22] On October 11, Brigham Young appointed captains for twenty-five companies of one hundred wagons each. Each captain recruited people for his company. Perhaps Howard's police friend Hosea Stout, captain of the twenty-fourth company, enlisted the Egans. Young requested that each company build its own wagons.[23] Nauvoo itself had close to 11,500 residents, and counting Saints living nearby in Illinois and Iowa, about 17,000 Saints could join the migration if they chose to.[24]

A planning committee calculated what each "family" of five adults needed to take on a trip that might be two thousand miles to the west coast and could last four or five months.[25] That detailed list exceeded what most Nauvooers could round up, but it served as a guideline for people like the Egans. It said that each family needed one good strong wagon, well covered, with three good yokes of oxen, two or more cows, at least one good beef cow, and some sheep if they had any. For food the family needed one

Lions Camp April 19th 1846

An account of the property belonging to the persons of the second ten in the fourth fifty.

Howard E. Kimball six in family, one waggon 3 horses, waggon and 2 horses belonging to Philander Cotrin in care of President Hawes 100 lbs of crackes, 15 lbs of sugar 15 lbs of salt 10.00$ worth of cordage 20 lbs of flax 1 chest 1 trunk 2 beds and bedding 1 sett of Tea things, sundry cooking utencils, one watch worth $10.00, one fifteen shooter 1 saddle.

John Hay ten in family, one horse, one cow, one bed and bedding, one watch worth 10.00$ one clock, two rifles, one fifteen shooter, some iron and steel with a variety of tools weighing from four to five hundred weight, 40 lbs of flour ½ bushel meal, ½ bushel beans, one bag of biscuits, 2 chests, one saddle and bridle

William P. Kimball 3 in family, 1 horse 1 waggon, 1 clock, one watch, 1 bed and bedding 1 rifle.

Edward M. Kimball 4 in family, one horse, one cow, one bed and bedding, 10 lbs salt one peck of beans one rifle and one waggon.

Jacob F. H. Young 4 in family one waggon belonging to B. Young, 2 horses belonging to Sterling Davies, 2 beds and bedding 10 lbs of flour, one rifle.

Edward P. Dusett 4 in family one cow two beds and bedding, ten pounds of flour one

Camp of Israel Reports, April 19, 1846. LDS Church History Library

thousand pounds of flour or other bread stuff and good sacks to put it in, a bushel of beans, one hundred pounds of sugar, a few pounds of dried beef or bacon, ten pounds of dried apples, five of dried peaches, twenty of dried pumpkin, and some pepper and mustard. Two families should have between them a five-gallon keg of alcohol. They should take up to five hundred pounds of clothing and bedding, and a good tent and furniture. They needed ten to fifty pounds of seeds, farm and other tools, cooking and eating utensils, nails, a good rifle or musket per man, goods to trade with Indians, and "a little iron and steel." Wagons must not exceed two thousand pounds without passengers, or 2,800 pounds with passengers.[26]

A final destination was not announced. Rumored possibilities included California and Vancouver Island. "If going to the coast," the recommendations explained, "it is not necessary to carry seed wheat, oats, or grass, nor are cattle and sheep absolutely necessary except to live on while upon the journey, as the country abounds in both cattle and sheep." Each company of one hundred families or wagons needed a few horses, ropes and pulley blocks for crossing rivers, two ferry boats, a fish net, and fish hooks and lines for each family. This published list, Howard knew, would skyrocket buyer demand for rope, cords, and twine.

Families bought and bartered for tools, clothing, bedding, medicines, oxen, rifles, boxes, barrels, ropes, harnesses, foodstuffs, and seeds. Howard's ropes gave him good barter material. People struggled to collect and pay debts. Nauvoo became "one vast mechanic shop, as nearly every family was engaged in making wagons. Our parlor was used as a paint shop in which to paint wagons," recalled Bathsheba Smith, and "all were making preparations to leave." Every available space from the shop to the parlor was used to assemble boxes, covers, wheels, and harnesses. Reports on November 23 said 3,285 families were organized for the trek.[27] By then the Saints were doing their all to prepare, as this November 30 description shows:

> Every hundred have established one or more wagon shops. Wheelwrights, carpenters and cabinet makers are nearly all busy; nearly all foreman wagon makers, and many not mechanics, are at work in every part of the town, preparing timber for making wagons. The timber is cut and brought into the city green; hub, spoke and fellow timber boiled in salt and water, and other parts kiln dried. Shops are established at the Nauvoo House, Masonic Hall, Arsenal. Nearly every shop in town is employed in making wagons. Teams are sent to all parts of the country to purchase iron. Blacksmiths are at work night and day and all hands are busily engaged getting ready for our departure westward as soon as possible…for a general exodus in the spring.[28]

Church trustees advertised to buy cattle for the upcoming journey: "The undersigned wish to purchase one thousand yoke of cattle, from four to eight years old, for the removal of The Church of Jesus Christ of Latter-day Saints. A ready market will be found for all the working cattle and mules that may be brought in." Over 20,000 acres of good farming lands "some of which are highly improved" were offered in exchange for "goods, cash, oxen, cows, sheep, wagons, etc."[29] It struck outsiders as odd that Saints, while laboring vigorously to finish the temple, at the same time constructed wagons they would use to leave the temple behind.

Studying Explorer Fremont's Reports

The Twelve studied any reports they could find about routes to and places in the West. They took particular interest in Congress's March 1845 publication of government explorer John C. Fremont's reports of his 1842 and 1843–44 expeditions. His detailed travel notes included maps by Charles Preutt. On the first exploration, Fremont surveyed the Platte River "up to the head of the Sweetwater." During the second trip, he made a circuit that included boating on Great Salt Lake and examining Utah Lake.

On December 20, 1845, in the temple, Elder Franklin D. Richards read part of Fremont's account to Brigham Young and others of the Twelve, and on the 27th apostle Parley Pratt read from Lansford Hastings's *The Emigrants' Guide to Oregon and California*. On December 29 Pratt read from Fremont's journal to Elders Young and Kimball.[30] On December 31 those two elders examined maps "with reference to selecting a location for the Saints west of the Rocky Mountains," and read other travel reports.[31] Because the Egans became part of Elder Kimball's family by priesthood adoption (see "Adopted into Heber C. Kimball's Family" on page 85), Kimball likely shared some of Fremont's and Hastings's information with Howard.

Howard's Ropes

During December and January and up until February 2, Howard delivered to the Church large quantities of rope, twine, and lines needed for the exodus. His bill of charges to Bishop Newel K. Whitney shows these deliveries, for which he was "paid in full" nearly 400 dollars on February 3, 1846:[32]

120 lbs	tent cord	8.25 lbs	packing
280 lbs	tent cord	397 lbs	rope
5.5 lbs	sewing twine	275.5 lbs	rope
24.5 lbs	seine twine	9 dozen	fishing lines
59 lbs	match rope	18 lbs	sewing twine
125 lbs	Pam rope	- - - -	Fishing lines
14 lbs	sewing twine	- - - -	Wagon lines
62 lbs	seine twine	1	bed cord

Howard kept his rope-walk operating right up until the exodus began, to help supply the wagon companies. But his business, like others in the city, faced closure rather than sale, because who would buy a business whose customer base was moving away? There's no evidence he took west with him any of his rope-making apparatus.

Temple Ordinances Before Leaving

To provide Saints with temple blessings before their wilderness journey, leaders rushed sections of the temple to completion and then provided washing, anointing, endowment, and sealing ordinances between late December 1845 and early February 1846.

Nauvoo Temple, *artist C.R. Savage, courtesy Perry Special Collections, BYU*

Before Joseph Smith died he had introduced about sixty people to the temple rites in temporary rooms, including the assembly room above his store. After his death the apostles had endowed another fifteen people. On November 30, 1845, President Young dedicated the temple's attic rooms for temple ordinances. The work of endowing members commenced on December 10. Nearly every day and some nights, the rites and ordinances were administered, and in total 5,583 men and women received them before the last company went through the temple on February 8, 1846. "For most Saints, the endowment represented spiritual power and protection to endure the trials ahead as they left their homes and started anew."[33]

Although many seventies, by quorums, helped administer the temple ordinances, Howard was not an officiator.[34] According to the Nauvoo Temple Endowment Register, Howard and Tamson Egan received their temple washings, anointings, and endowments on December 16, 1845. More than fifty people received the ordinances that day.[35] For temple garments, to be worn underneath their clothing, Tamson either hand-made hers and Howard's or had someone else sew them.

The Egans' Plural Marriages

In 1831, while making an inspired revision of the Old Testament, Joseph Smith pondered biblical passages indicating that revered patriarchs and prophets of old were polygamists. He questioned that practice and inquired of the Lord about marriage in general and about plurality of wives in particular. In response he received a life-changing revelation. Because he had inquired, the revelation said, Joseph needed to prepare his heart to receive and accept the Lord's law regarding marriage. The revelation explained that unless performed by divine authority and sealed by the Holy Ghost, all contracts made by mortals were null and void in the afterlife. Thus, marriage contracts became null and void after death unless sealed by divine authority. By this revelation, Joseph Smith received authority, like the ancient apostle Peter, that whatever he sealed on earth would be sealed in heaven, including marriages he performed.

Further, the revelation explained that Abraham, Isaac, Jacob, Moses, David, Solomon "as also many others of my servants, from the beginning of creation until this time" had more wives than one, and "in nothing did they sin save in those things which they received not of me." The revelation taught that under certain conditions a man might be authorized to be sealed to more than one wife.[36] The revelation made clear that the Church would be required one day to live the law, and that he, Joseph Smith, must live it himself.[37] Joseph hesitated to obey this 'higher law,' knowing how deeply having plural wives would offend Christians cut from the same monogamous cloth as he was.

However, Joseph took his first plural wife in 1835, and another in Nauvoo in 1841 or 1842.[38] He never made public the revelation or his efforts to obey, but in 1842 he taught the celestial marriage doctrine privately to Brigham Young, Sidney Rigdon, Heber C. Kimball, Parley Pratt, Orson Pratt, and Willard Richards. On July 12, 1843, he dictated the marriage revelation to clerk William Clayton who put it into writing for the first time. Not until 1852 did the Church publish the revelation, officially making it public. Today the revelation is section 132 in the Doctrine and Covenants.[39]

Selected men and women who accepted Joseph's private instructions to them about plural marriage, who believed it was revealed doctrine, "did so only after intense personal struggles. Most resolved their concerns through a spiritual witness. They accepted participation as a religious duty."[40] In every recorded case in Nauvoo "the initial attitude toward entering plural marriage was negative." The act of accepting plural marriage was a courageous act of loyalty because entering into it "caused considerable anguish."[41] No doubt Howard and Tamson experienced a soul-distressing process before embracing the practice.

It appears that Howard married Catherine Clawson in 1844. In 1869, apostle George A. Smith wrote a letter to Joseph Smith III, president of the Reorganized Church, a Mormon off-shoot group, trying to convince him that both Joseph and Hyrum Smith had performed plural marriage ceremonies before they were killed. As proof, Elder George A. Smith listed several such marriages, including the sealing of Catherine Clawson to Howard Egan by Hyrum Smith in 1844. "Egan had a wife at this time," Smith emphasized.[42] His source of that information was Mary Ellen (Abel) Kimball. On August 6, 1869, Mary Ellen gave a sworn statement to Salt Lake County notary public James Jack, saying that in 1844 she witnessed the marriage of Catherine Clawson to Howard Egan, who had a wife already, performed by Church Patriarch Hyrum Smith.[43]

Catherine Reese was born on January 27, 1804 in New York City. She was eleven years older than Howard and had been married before, to Zephaniah Clawson on January 8, 1824. They had six children. Zephaniah disappeared and was believed to have died in a steamboat explosion on the Ohio river. Nothing more is known about her marriage to Howard. She went west in 1848 using the Clawson name, divorced Howard, and married Brigham Young in 1855.[44]

On January 23, 1846, in the Nauvoo Temple, Howard was sealed to Tamson Parshley, turning their civil marriage into an eternal, celestial one. That same day Howard also was sealed to Nancy A. Redden. Her name sometimes was spelled "Redding."[45] Nancy was part of a Redden family from Hiram, Portage County, Ohio, where she was born in 1826. Her parents were George Grant Redden and Adelia Higley. When she became Howard's bride she was nineteen and Tamson twenty-one.

Nancy had received the endowment rites on December 25, 1845. Howard would take Nancy to Utah in his 1849 wagon company, not in 1848 when he and Tamson went west. Nancy's brother Return Jackson Redden, like Howard, was a tough and fearless man who served as a private detective and body guard for Joseph Smith. He and Howard both would travel in the Camp of Israel's Iowa crossing in 1846 and in the history-making 1847 Pioneer company.[46]

Adopted into Heber C. Kimball's Family

Also in the temple, on February 1, 1846, Howard was sealed and adopted into the family of Heber C. Kimball, with Brigham Young officiating.[47] This was according to a "Law of Adoption" that the Church practiced first in Nauvoo and then for a half-century afterwards.

Aware that there could be no salvation of the family outside the priesthood, many Latter-day Saints were directed by Brigham Young and other Church leaders to be "adopted" or sealed to faithful Church leaders instead of to their own parents, many of whom had either roundly rejected the gospel or clung to their own religious beliefs. Consequently, thousands were "adopted" into the families of Brigham Young, John Taylor, Wilford Woodruff, Willard Richards, and other early apostles and prominent leaders. This practice continued until 1894.[48]

Elder Kimball adopted the Egans and nine other men and their families.[49] The adoptions were intended to form a circle or small tribe of people dependent on one another for their physical and spiritual welfare. Some adoptees added the adopter's surname to theirs, hence John D. Lee, adopted into Brigham Young's family, sometimes called himself John D. Lee Young.[50] At least once Howard used the Kimball name: during the Camp of Israel's Iowa crossing, a list of officers involved in the reorganizings in late March 1846 near the Chariton encampment shows "Howard E Kimball" as one of the captains. Howard often referred to Heber C. Kimball as "Father" and one of Kimball's wives, probably first wife Vilate, as "Mother."[51]

Heber C. Kimball, Frederick Piercy sketch, Route from Liverpool to Great Salt Lake Valley

"To Make an Early Start West"

In late January 1846, LDS leaders heard troubling rumors that plans were afoot to destroy the temple and to arrest and kill Church leaders, that Illinois Governor Thomas Ford was sending troops into Nauvoo, and that anti-Mormons were organizing to steal the LDS wagons "to prevent us from moving west" in order to prosecute and persecute the Mormons.[52] To make matters worse, federal courts became involved in pursuing charges against Church leaders for supposed counterfeiting going on in the area. Governor Ford warned, perhaps as a ruse to scare the Saints into leaving, that the United States would send a federal army in the spring to block the exodus on grounds it was a crime for armed Americans to "invade" a foreign territory like the Great Basin or California, which belonged to Mexico, or Oregon, which the British claimed.[53]

Troubled by such threats, the Twelve felt they must halt the temple ordinance work so they themselves could leave quickly, not only for their own safety but to preserve the Saints not yet ready to go. On January 11 the Twelve and the Fifty arranged "to make an early start west." Two days later they received reports about those "who were prepared to start west immediately, should the persecutions of the enemies compel them to do so." A total of 140 horses and seventy wagons were "ready for immediate service."[54] On January 18 the company captains met again in the Temple's attic story and agreed that their safety depended on leaders departing from Nauvoo "before their enemies shall intercept and prevent their going."[55]

By January 20 the situation seemed so alarming that the "High Council of the Church" issued a circular letter to members and "all whom it may concern."[56] It said that leaders intended "to send out into the western country from this place, some time in March, a company of pioneers, consisting mostly of young, hardy men, with some families." Those called would need to be furnished with "an ample outfit," a printing press, farming utensils of all kinds, mill irons, "bottling cloths," grains, and seeds of all kinds. "The object of this early move is to put in a spring crop, to build houses, and to prepare for the reception of families who will start so soon as grass shall be sufficiently grown to sustain teams and stock." These advance people were "to proceed west until they find a good place to make a crop, in some good valley in the neighborhood of the Rocky Mountains where they will infringe upon no one." They'd make a resting place there until a permanent location could be found.[57] "I hope we will find a place," Brigham Young said in a January 24 business meeting, "where no self-righteous neighbors can say that we are obnoxious to them."[58]

On January 29 "a number of the governor's troops were prowling around Nauvoo."[59] Suspicious and worried, Church leaders on February 2 decided "it was imperatively necessary to start as soon as possible." President Young counseled the leaders to "procure boats and hold them in readiness to convey wagons and teams over the river, and let everything for the journey be in readiness so that when a family was called to go, everything necessary might be put into the wagon within four hours, at least." Young worried that "if we are here many days…our way will be hedged up. Our enemies have resolved to intercept us when we start." That afternoon he met with captains of the hundreds and fifties and gained their consent for some early departures.[60] With good weather on February 4, Charles Shumway ferried wagons across the river and camped inland seven miles beside Sugar Creek. This started the first phase of departures, the ahead-of-schedule "Winter Exodus." In the original plan for twenty-five companies of one hundred wagons, Shumway had been captain of the thirteenth company. William C. Staines drove one of the Shumway teams.[61] In Nauvoo on Sunday, February 8, Brigham Young "addressed the Saints in the grove and informed them that the company going west would start during the week across the river." He and Elders Kimball, Parley Pratt, John Taylor, and Orson Hyde preached farewell sermons.[62]

During the rest of February, wagon after wagon ferried across the Mississippi to the Montrose side, and drove to the Sugar Creek encampment. Nauvoo police supervised much of the river crossing. Stout had his men gather flatboats, lighters, and skiffs into a small fleet, and then they worked night and day crossing the saints.[63] Howard, being one of the police, almost certainly assisted with the ferrying. On February 9 Lorenzo Snow and his family of seven camped at Sugar Creek with two wagons and a tent. "There were a hundred families gathered in there before us," he said.[64] On February 10 the Twelve placed Elder Joseph Young, the senior president of the Seventies, in charge of the big body of Saints who would stay in Nauvoo until spring. He also received responsibility to complete and dedicate the temple.[65]

It seems certain that before the Egans left, Howard and Tamson spent time urgently buying, selling, trading, discarding, and packing a minimum cargo into precious wagon space. "Our wagons were perfectly crowded," said one Nauvooer, with "as much as seemed we could possibly get along with."[66] The Egans loaded in food that would not spoil easily: items like salted ham, bacon, dried beef, dried beans, dried corn, crackers, flour, corn meal, salt, and sugar. They would not see potatoes or carrots or most vegetables again for a long time. Very likely their wagon carried an extra supply of Howard's ropes, cords, and twine.

To close their home's front door for the last time, to take final gazes at Howard's rope-walk, and to give farewell glances at familiar buildings and streets, must have triggered some emotions in the Egans' hearts. Then, with a bowed canvas top attached to their wagon and two teams of oxen or horses hitched, they steered towards one of Nauvoo's boat landings. Ransom Egan, age six at the time, later described the river crossing:

> I well remember the Mormon Exodus and of sitting in a covered wagon with Mother and brother Erastus, and this is the first I remember of him. The wagon was standing on the bank of the Mississippi river with the front end facing the water. There was another wagon close by. I had seen two wagons on a flat boat leave the shore and go out of sight. Mother said we could go next when the boat came back. I did not see it for I had gone to sleep, but the next morning when I opened my eyes it was raining, and peeping out of the front end of the wagon I could see that Mother and quite a large crowd of people were standing by a large fire that had been built against a stump just in the edge of the forest. The Mississippi river was just back of us. We had been brought over in the night.[67]

Diaries kept by people who departed in February record a good weather history for that month. February 10 and 11 were the only days when rain fell. The other days were clear or too cold for rain. Therefore, Tamson and the sleeping boys probably crossed the river on the 10th or 11th, no doubt with Howard's help. It seems unlikely that Howard left Tamson alone to drive their wagon the seven muddy miles to the Sugar Creek Camp. On February 15, Brigham Young crossed the river with his family of fifty and fifteen wagons, accompanied by Willard Richards and family, and George A. Smith. "The roads were very bad." They arrived at the Sugar Creek camp about 8:00 p.m. The Nauvoo brass band also crossed that day.[68]

Howard, as a Kimball adoptee, was under obligation to travel with Elder Kimball's group. Kimball's large family of plural wives, children, foster children, and some of his adopted sons and their families arrived at the Sugar Creek camp on February 17.[69] Wife Nancy's brother Return Jackson Redden was, like the Egans, in the Winter Exodus group, so Nancy might have traveled with him.[70]

Sugar Creek Encampment

An ever-arriving flow of wagons expanded the campground located by the St. Francisville Road bridge over Sugar Creek. Campers braved falling temperatures and some snowstorms. Campfires burned constantly. When Orson Pratt reached camp on February 14, he found people "suffering considerably from the storm and cold." "It is very cold," Patty Sessions wrote two days later, "the wind blows, one can hardly get to the fire for the smoke and we have no tent." Helen Mar Whitney recalled that "the youthful portion" held dances by the log fire "to amuse ourselves" and because "it was impossible to keep warm without exercise."[71]

Despite cold, snow, and camp difficulties, many Saints felt glad to be leaving behind mobs and unfair courts and hostile government officials. Perhaps Howard and Tamson shared some of future apostle Lorenzo Snow's Sugar Creek Camp sentiments:

Mormon Exodus from Nauvoo, artist Lynn Fausett,
Classified Photograph Collection, courtesy Utah State Historical Society

Tho' we suffered some from the wether, yet we felt greatly to rejoice in having accomplished this much towards freeing ourselves from the land of Gentile oppression, and we felt as tho' we could breath more freely and speak one with another upon those things where in God had made us free with less carefulness than we had hitherto done.[72]

Brigham Young urgently wanted to get the trek started, so on February 17, he assembled the brethren at Sugar Creek and, standing on a wagon, cried out, "Attention! The whole Camp of Israel." He explained that the camp had not yet moved on because they needed Bishop Newel K. Whitney and clerk William Clayton to arrive with wagons transporting needed Church property. He then issued rules and regulations. He ordered a camp census. To organize for the journey, he instructed that families be grouped into companies of tens, fifties, and hundreds.

On February 18 he and a few others returned to Nauvoo by ferry to hurry-up the needed wagons. But then the weather worsened, snow fell, and temperatures dropped below freezing. In camp, meanwhile, men built huge fires. People huddled in tents, wagons, and carriages. On February 22 Young left Nauvoo and recrossed the river in a flat-bottomed rowboat, dodging dangerous floating ice. The river didn't freeze over until February 24. Before the ice sheet formed, eighty percent or more of the people who would go in Young's company had already crossed, and were organized for the trek. On the 24th, temperatures plunged to twelve degrees below zero. The next day, Charles C. Rich was perhaps the first person to walk from Nauvoo across the ice. Because of the ice avenue, a few hundred latecomers joined the encampment. But the ice irked President Young, because it allowed people to go back and forth to Nauvoo, disrupting camp operations.[73]

On February 25, despite freezing temperatures, Bishop George Miller with about sixteen wagons and thirty to forty men started out on the westward trek, going five miles. Called the Pioneer Company, they went ahead of the Camp of Israel to locate the best route, improve roads and bridges, select campsites, and stockpile firewood.[74] But the bitter cold conditions prevented any others from starting. On February 27 Brother Clayton finally arrived with some of the long-awaited Church wagons. Bishop Whitney arrived the next day.

Finally, on March 1 the Camp of Israel pulled out of the Sugar Creek Camp and moved five miles. By then Howard, Tamson, Ransom, and Erastus had been camping in their wagon or in a tent for more than two weeks. While Tamson had done everything possible to keep her boys warm and dry, Howard had chopped wood, fed campfires, and kept their livestock from freezing. Breaking camp on March 1 did not come soon enough.

In total, Brigham Young's "Camp of Israel" contained between 2,000 and 2,500 Saints and 400 wagons when it finally started.[75] It's a common but incorrect belief that most of the Church members left in winter with Brigham Young. His was merely an advance company. Five times its numbers waited and left in spring, on schedule. Those spring departures were disorganized because "many of the previously-appointed company captains abandoned their assignments for spring and were allowed to join with the vanguard Company of the Twelve."[76]

Brigham Young's Camp of Israel, instead of being small and orderly, "became a swollen, unwieldy amalgam." It contained too many Saints who were poorly supplied and outfitted, which caused the Twelve constant difficulties for the next three months.[77]

Egan Sites in Today's Nauvoo

For the next three months a covered wagon and a tent would serve as the Egans' home, one on the move, often daily. None of them ever set foot again in Nauvoo. In time their home disappeared, as did Howard's rope-walk. However, Egan descendants today can find in restored Nauvoo several buildings and sites linked to the Egans' experiences: the Temple Site with its now-replicated temple, the restored Masonic or Cultural Hall, the replicated Seventies Hall, Joseph Smith's restored Mansion House, his replicated Red Brick Store on Water Street, the restored homes of Heber C. Kimball and Brigham Young, the Hosea Stout home site marker, the Old Nauvoo Burial Grounds two miles east on Parley Street where son Charles was laid to rest, and, of course, the ever-majestic Mississippi River. ◆

~ 7 ~

Captain Egan and the Iowa Trek

March 1846 found the Egans traveling with two thousand or more homeless refugees in a long, disjointed Camp of Israel wagon train, smacked by winter conditions, and making slow progress along muddy and crude rural roads. Hopes slowly died that at least part of the caravan could reach the Rocky Mountains by fall. Being the advance group, its primary tasks were to locate a travel route for themselves, and, of vital importance, find a new gathering place for the thousands soon to depart from Nauvoo. Much of the uprooted Church's future depended upon how well this lead company, headed by senior apostle Brigham Young, succeeded.

Diaries and recollections document well the Camp of Israel's Iowa crossing. Their mentions of Howard, particularly those by William Clayton and Horace K. Whitney, make this chapter possible.[1] During the wagon train's 320-mile crossing of southern Iowa Territory for nearly four months, Howard shouldered two leadership tasks.[2] In late March the Twelve restructured the plodding expedition into six companies of fifty wagons and assigned Howard to captain the Fourth Fifty. And, because spring grazing grass didn't grow until mid-April, the Twelve sent men out to work for and trade with locals for cattle feed, and also for foodstuffs and livestock. By the time the Camp of Israel reached the Missouri River in mid-June, Captain Egan was one of its principal traders.

Difficult First Fifty Miles

Winter-chilled wagons finally rolled out from the snowy Sugar Creek on March 1. Traveling just ahead of the caravan, Bishop George Miller led a hundred-man unit, called the "pioneers," assigned to prepare the road ahead by trimming trees and bushes and filling in low spots, and to prepare campsites and firewood. In the lead of the wagon train itself was the Nauvoo band of musicians. For the first hundred miles the company would pass through four sparsely settled Iowa counties, using existing roads.

After their first on-the-road encampment, the train rolled almost straight west through four inches of snow and over "several tedious hills" to the ice-edged Des Moines River.[3] They then turned north along the river's east bank and passed through the small town of Farmington where, Lorenzo Snow noted, they "excited great curiosity among the Gentiles." Residents thought the parade of Mormon refugees curious but enjoyed bargain-trades for Mormon household goods. Mormons traded horses for teams of oxen.[4] Oxen, slower than horses, could pull heavier loads, were gentler to manage, and could browse better.

From Farmington the procession followed a muddy road into Bonaparte Mills, a tiny mill-town, where some stopped to get grain ground. At Bonaparte the long train forded the two-foot-deep Des Moines River from the north shore, on an underwater natural rock ledge.[5] Then, on a "very bad road up the bluff" they veered west and passed two miles south of another river village, Keosauqua, which was Van Buren County's barely settled county seat. Next, the company crossed several miles of rolling prairie, dotted with de-leafed oak trees, and "under better cultivation than any we had seen since leaving Montrose."[6]

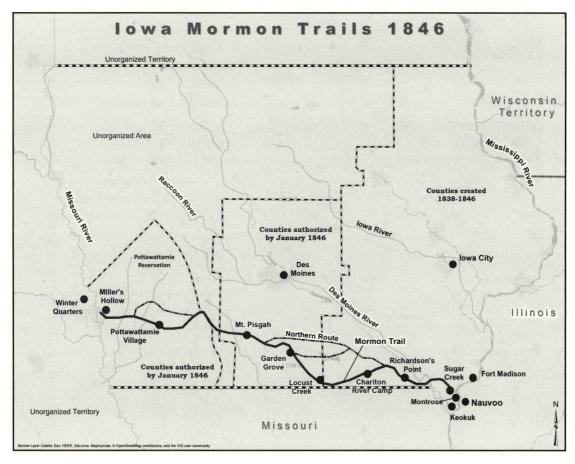

Richardson's Point Camp, March 7–18

The first documentation of the Egans' location during this Iowa crossing came at the Richardson's Point encampment ten miles from Keosauqua and fifty-five miles from Nauvoo. There, a city of tents popped up, "laid out in the form of a half hollow square fronting east and south, on a beautiful level."[7] This encampment lasted eleven days. Here, Brigham Young tried to bring better order to the migration. He assigned wagons into companies of fifty families each, one being Heber C. Kimball's fifty, which probably included the Egans. Mormon laborers obtained corn at low prices in exchange for "making rails, roofing houses, and building barns, etc. in which the brethren are daily engaged."[8]

The Richardson's Point stop gave Tamson and the boys consecutive days of camping in one place without packing up each morning and unpacking at night. They spent their days walking in yellow dry prairie grasses and "intolerable" mud, and breathing smoke from crackling hickory and oak log fires. It's safe to envision Howard, out with an axe and team, cutting and hauling tree limbs and bush branches for firewood. "Johnny cakes," meaning pancakes, became daily fare for most. Those who brought along cows–the Egans didn't—had milk and butter. Not being near a sizeable stream, campers did little laundry.[9]

William Pitt's Brass Band, artist
Dale Kilbourn © Intellectual Reserve, Inc.

Keosauqua residents invited the Nauvoo band to perform in town. So, with President Young's permission, the musicians gave two performances for hire in the courthouse (which is still the county courthouse today). On March 17, when musicians Clayton, William Pitt, J. F. Hutchinson, and James Smithies did a third concert there, Howard went with them. To our knowledge not a musician, his role probably was to provide security.[10]

Crossing the Chariton River

The next morning, March 19, cold and windy, the big procession resumed on a "public road."[11] After following the Fox River northwesterly and passing near the village of Bloomfield, the companies turned sharply southwest, encountering mud holes and sloughs. On March 22 the wagons carefully negotiated a difficult crossing of the Chariton River. Men lowered wagons by ropes, perhaps some made by Howard, down eastern slopes. Then the teams pulled wagons for four miles across very low bottomland that included the Chariton River, "a muddy looking stream about 4 rods wide, two feet deep, with a stony bottom, and steep banks on either side."[12] After fording, they struggled up steep bluffs, sometimes double-teaming.[13] During that difficult day, Howard and Tamson and the children could have complained strongly about living in wet clothes and muddy shoes or boots.

Fording the River, Classified Photo Collection, Utah State Historical Society

Atop the slope, in white oak timber, a vast camp took shape. "We filled the ridge with our tents & waggons for perhaps half a mile," Hosea Stout said.[14] Tents lined each side of the road.

The first wagons halted for nine days and waited for ones behind to catch up. Rain, hail, and snow plagued the place, causing diarist Eliza R. Snow to write on March 25, "the oak ridge on which we are encamped being of a clay soil, the mud of our street & about our fires, in our tents &c. is indescribable."[15]

Counting on Good Traders

The campers lacked corn for their teams, and grass wasn't growing yet, so trade with locals became essential. Howard was one of those sent out to trade. His rope business taught him how to make trade deals and negotiate purchase prices. In Nauvoo he'd traded to get hemp from local farmers, and he sold much rope by trading with customers who lacked cash. On March 25, despite a northwest wind and snow falling until afternoon, Howard went "into the country" to buy corn along with other men, driving wagons to "fetch it." When it was near dusk Howard and the teams returned with "a considerable amount of corn bought at twenty cents per bushel."[16]

Howard reported to President Young that another Mormon trader, Thomas L. Williams, went to the seller after Howard made the deal, and offered the seller five cents more per bushel in cash, seeking to outbid Howard. The next morning Young lectured all captains in front of his tent concerning the folly of one brother overbidding another to buy corn. "I said I wished I could see the man that followed Egan yesterday and overbid him, that I might kick him out of this Camp." Right after the meeting, Young sent Howard out again to find more corn.[17]

Howard a Captain of Fifty

The Twelve found it impossible to keep four hundred or more wagons moving forward at a reasonable pace. Here and there along the line, people had unfit wagons, unsuitable teams, not enough livestock feed, and inadequate clothing, and showed themselves unsuited to camping. Young complained that back at Sugar Creek he'd found fifty teams loaded with families "that neither God, man, nor the devil cared about their going," and eight hundred men reporting for the trip "without a fortnight's provisions."[18] Incessant rains stymied progress. Saints had traveled only about one hundred miles from Nauvoo. The line of their wagons became too stretched out. The company divisions set up at Sugar Creek and restructured at Richardson's Point proved unworkable because of storms, bad roads, break-downs, and people returning to Nauvoo. By then, nearly a hundred of the camp's approximately five hundred wagons had gone back.[19] Organizational changes had to be made.

On March 27, at Parley P. Pratt's camp six miles west of the Chariton Camp, a council reorganized the companies. In the new structure Brigham Young became "President over the whole camp of Israel," with Howard's friend William Clayton as the camp clerk. Company captains changed. Companies now bore numbers instead of being named for their captains. Ezra T. Benson became captain of the First Hundred, meaning wagons, with Albert P. Rockwood and Stephen Markham his sub-captains over fifty wagons each. John Smith took charge of the Second Hundred, and used John Harvey as one of his captains of fifty, and "Howard Egan Kimball" became the captain of his other fifty. Captain Egan's unit was designated the Fourth Fifty. Samuel Bent served as president of the Third Hundred, with Charles C. Rich and John Chrismas his captains of fifties. Heber C. Kimball, Brigham Young's right hand man, traveled in Egan's fifty and became its president, George H. Hales the clerk, Peter Haws contracting commissary, and Orson B. Adams distributing commissary.[20]

Howard, to manage the roughly fifty wagons in his contingent, counted on his sub-captains of ten to keep the people in each of the tens moving. Among the first instructions he passed along were that people in his fifty were not to set fire to the prairies or woods; to hunt without receiving orders to do so; or to carry guns, swords, and pistols in sight of others.[21]

Camp of Israel Reports 1846, LDS Church History Library

More Trade Trips

At March's end, Lorenzo Snow observed that "the country is thinly settled and we were much troubled to get corn to supply the whole Camp." Unable to graze, cattle were allowed to browse on tree limbs, twigs, and shoots. Many fed their teams dried corn and cornmeal from food reserves intended for humans.[22] On March 29, Howard and other captains went through the camp and inventoried wagons and teams belonging to Bishop Evans in Nauvoo. Later that day he reported on a just concluded buying trip during which he purchased 110 bushels of corn at twenty cents per bushel.[23] He missed a council meeting on March 30 because he was away on yet another corn-buying trip. He returned about 9:00 p.m. with thirty-four bushels.[24] That day William Clayton's diary mentioned that Jackson Redden, Nancy's brother, sold a horse for oxen. Several horse-for-oxen trades occurred about that time.

On April 1 the companies finally hitched up and moved out of the Chariton camp.[25] On Sunday, April 5, Elder Kimball arranged for his captains of ten to conduct sacrament meetings for their members. This was the first time the sacrament ordinance was provided since the Saints left Nauvoo.[26] Elder Kimball informed the Egan fifty that they needed to obtain corn, available ten miles away, because no corn would be found anywhere for the next fifty miles.[27] Captain Egan and his commissary, Peter Haws, went through the camp asking for money donations with which to buy corn. Haws obtained $31.45 and Egan $23.00.[28] Howard left the next morning and would be gone for two days.

If he used his own wagon, then Tamson and the boys traveled with someone else while he was gone. If he used a wagon that Elder Kimball provided, then Tamson probably drove the Egan wagon, or else one of the Kimball males did. After Howard left, the lead Camp of Israel companies crossed the east and middle forks of Locust Creek and encamped fairly close together.[29] Tamson had almost sole charge of the children.[30] She found herself in a camp made "very disagreeable and muddy" by rain. Her tent and others in the Egan fifty, except two, blew down during "a perfect gale with heavy rain, hail, lightning and thunder" that evening. Next morning, after a cold night, the ground was frozen stiff. Transparent-white skins of ice covered the prairie's many puddles of water. That day was fair, but mud and pools made roads impassable. Many in camp lacked food. The next day, April 8, leaders decided they must find a better campsite, so Tamson's group spent all day traveling only a quarter of a mile west. Some wagons could barely move through the mud, even with triple teams dragging them.[31]

On April 8, Captain Egan and the food wagons returned, bringing fifty-seven bushels of corn.[32] Most of the other company's wagons came back empty, so they envied the corn that did come in.[33] Elder Parley Pratt and his company pulled up and reported they'd had no corn since the morning before and could not obtain any. Even Howard's fifty felt pinched because his resupply could only provide them five ears of feed every three days.[34]

"The Most Severe Time We Have Had"

On April 9, Howard's fifty pushed ahead on bad roads amid heavy rains. By evening the teams were entirely worn down. Several outfits, stuck in the mud, made men labor until after dark bringing them in. Quite a number of wagons stayed back on the prairie overnight. Heavy rains doused the evening fires, and some people had little for supper because food wagons had not caught up. Clayton called this day "the most severe time we have had." In one Mormon camp "the mud and the water in and around our tents were ancle [sic] deep."[35]

That situation might be the one recalled by Ransom. His memory "was of some man unhitching the team from the wagon and putting it ahead of another team on another wagon and going off out of sight," at a place where "it was raining all the time and water all over the ground except here and there a small point sticking up above the water. The land must have sunk, and how we got out of it I don't know, but now I think it was there or there abouts that Mother and I got our start of rheumatism."[36]

The next morning, gales blew down the tents. "It rains and blows very badly," Clayton wrote, "and is very severe on our women and teams."[37] Teamsters suffered most. The camp's corn shortage debilitated the livestock. On April 11 Captain Egan and Clayton rode out to help extract Jacob Peart's wagon from a slough and "it took five yoke of oxen and twelve men to draw it out," Clayton wrote. The day was fair and "very cold." Men sent twelve yoke of oxen back to help out two wagons, which did not reach camp until late at night.[38]

"No Toil Nor Labor Fear"

On April 12, a Sunday, Howard and Clayton attended a captains' meeting, where President Young announced an unexpected change in their route. Back at Richardson's Point, Church leaders had decided to follow existing roads westward into and across the northern edge of Missouri to Banks Ferry, fifty-five miles upriver from St. Joseph, close to present day Oregon, Missouri. There they would cross the Missouri River and link up with the Oregon Trail.[39] But Young now canceled that plan and ordered the Camp of Israel to turn northwesterly. That would keep them from passing into Missouri settlements hostile to Mormons and head them toward a region called "the Council Bluffs" along the Missouri River, where Omaha, Nebraska and Council Bluffs, Iowa are now. This change meant they would leave existing roads behind and blaze a new route through "unsettled prairies." Young said they would soon establish rest settlements with cabins and farmland where those improperly outfitted could be left behind.[40]

William Clayton
Engraved Portrait Collection,
LDS Church History Library

The Egans, Claytons, and others broke camp on April 13 at noon and moved four miles and up a difficult ascent to be near President Young's camp at Locust Creek. Even when employing eight extra yoke of oxen, they still had to leave three wagons behind. On April 14, Howard and Clayton rode back to assist the missing wagons, and then went hunting. They "saw only squirrels and I got five of them," Clayton said.[41]

On April 15, Howard unknowingly witnessed music history be made. Clayton rejoiced to hear news of the birth of his son in Nauvoo, which inspired his musician's mind. "This morning I wrote a new song," he recorded in his journal, a hymn he titled "All Is Well." It expressed the general feelings of the faithful and hard-pressed pioneers, and helped them to "gird up their loins" and "fresh courage take," and even in the face of death to "shout praises to our God" because "All is well." Clayton adapted his lyrics to an old English tune, "All is well, all is well." This hymn soon became the anthem for Mormon pioneers, "Come, Come, Ye Saints."[42] That evening Clayton played in the band, then hosted a "social christening" at his tent. Among his ten guests were Howard Egan and Jackson Redden.[43]

Garden Grove, April 24 to May 12

Blessed grass finally sprouted. Orson Pratt rejoiced on April 15 that "scanty grass" had started to show itself. Livestock now could graze. The next day Howard's company moved seven miles and formed a camp on a beautiful prairie. "There is some little grass for our cattle here," Clayton wrote. Men in the Egan fifty moved the big herd of camp cattle a mile to the southeast, with guards, to keep them from rambling through tents and wagons. Then, Howard, Jackson Redden, John Kay, and Peter Haws went hunting.

At a council meeting held on April 18 at the Pleasant Point encampment, men were selected to go into the countryside selling, trading, and to labor. Also, the Twelve wanted to pick well-supplied men to form a company to push ahead and "go over the mountains," so they had captains of ten inventory all properties that people in their companies possessed.[44] Their lists are very revealing about what the travelers carried in their wagons: flour, crackers, meal, meat, salt, sugar, coffee, tea, beds, quilts, cloth, matches, candles, clocks, wheat, seed corn, plows, hoes, axes, carpenter tools, stoves, rifles, muskets, shot guns, bowie knives, powder, and lead caps.

The inventory for Howard's ten, the second ten in the fourth fifty, lacks details that other tens' ledgers contain. It does show that Howard had six in his family. These would be Howard, Tamson, Ransom, Erastus, Nancy, and someone we can't identify. The Egans had one wagon and three horses. Howard also was caring for another person's wagon and two horses. The Egans' spartan belongings included one hundred pounds of crackers, fifteen pounds of sugar, fifteen pounds of salt, twenty pounds of flax, one chest, one trunk, two beds and bedding, a set of "tea things," sundry cooking utensils, one watch, one fifteen shooter rifle, one saddle, and cordage worth ten dollars. Nancy's brother Jackson Redden, in that same ten, had thirteen in his family, two wagons, two horses, nine oxen, three cows, three rifles, two pistols, five beds, and one set of harnesses.[45]

Five days and two campsites later, forward wagons found "good grass and much of it." During another day's travel, Clayton said, "grass looks green and cattle have filled themselves well." They encountered rattlesnakes. Late on April 24 Clayton "went to hunt a camping spot with Egan." They met some women "who told us Grand River was only a mile ahead and that the other companies were required to go down there. We started and soon arrived at the main body of the camp." They liked the location. "The ground here is rich, timber good, and the prospects good for heavy crops," Clayton noted, and "wild onions grow in abundance."[46] Leaders ordered that a farming settlement be formed, which soon was named Garden Grove.

Men started plowing, planting, digging a well, and chopping wood. Grass was about eight inches high and trees had leafed out.[47] Eliza R. Snow termed it a "plantation" where farms would be created to assist the poor.[48] Ransom considered Garden Grove "a most beautiful place." At first the wagons parked in a row side by side, he said, with room to pass between them. Men built a bowery, a roof of brush piled atop a pole framework, and the wagon tongues were tied to it "making a long shady lane." He and some other boys went with men who collected brush for the top of the bowery. In a grove on the lower ground that lacked underbrush, "there was a nice grass sod all over, under the trees, making it a boy's paradise play-ground." He and the boys "wanted to run to the edge of the timber" but the men made them stay in sight, "saying there was lots of wild animals in there." When the men had their loads of brush ready, they made the boys return to camp with them.[49]

Brigham Young, hoping to send ahead a select group of men, properly outfitted, no families, for the mountains, requested the captains to inventory and determine how many men could be outfitted for the mountain expedition. On the evening of April 28 he met again with company officers, including Howard, and reviewed their reports and rosters. But, before anyone could go ahead, Garden Grove had to be established. The council appointed one hundred men to make fence rails, forty-eight to build houses, twelve to dig wells, ten to build a bridge, and the others to start plowing.[50]

Family Moves Ahead Without Howard

The Saints spent a busy, rainy three weeks at Garden Grove, from April 24 to May 12. On April 27, the camp urgently formed trading expeditions to go south across the

Missouri border. Clayton spent part of four days "packing up china and crockery to be sent by Egan" and "preparing for Egan to start trading. He has gone with Jackson Redding and has taken $288.00 of church property besides two span of horses and harness and near $60.00 of mine." How long this buying and trading trip took Howard isn't known, but he's not mentioned in records again for about a month.

When the Camp of Israel resumed its journey on May 12, it was smaller. It left behind about five hundred people to develop Garden Grove. Clayton and others held back briefly. On May 15 he selected a campsite across the Grand River from Garden Grove. Some men there went back "for the other wagons," Clayton said, which arrived about 6 p.m., and among these was Howard's family, without him: "Reddings have come here also, and Sister Egan with one or two others." It's possible this "Sister Egan" was Nancy. By then Garden Grove looked like a cabin settlement, for "many houses have been built, wells dug, extensive farms fenced, and the whole place assumes the appearance of having been occupied for years."[51]

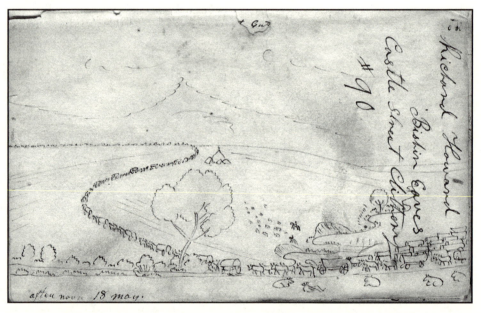

Mount Pisgah, Peter O. Hansen sketch, LDS Church History Library

Mount Pisgah, May 18 to June 1

The Camp of Israel reached the middle fork of the Grand River on May 18 and stopped to establish Mt. Pisgah, a second farming settlement for those not equipped to go farther west. By then, families began arriving from Nauvoo, the first of the "spring exodus" hordes. They had taken better routes north of where Young's caravan had traveled. They came in three weeks, compared to the ten weeks Young's company had spent.[52]

Leaders tried but failed to borrow wagons and teams from the Pisgah campers to enable the Twelve and the proposed select company to push ahead for the Rockies that season. On May 21, when a motion was made to help outfit the mountain crew, "a part voted in favor, and a part did not vote either way."[53] On May 22 President Young assembled the Saints and asked all those who lacked proper outfits for the western push to leave the meeting. Most did. Those who remained agreed to go west if allowed. In subsequent days, individuals asked Young if they should leave their families behind at Pisgah or plan to continue west with the Camp of Israel.

May 25 and 26 saw much rain. Clayton did not reach Mt. Pisgah until May 26, where, apparently, the Egan family already had stopped. It seems likely that Tamson took advantage of the stopover at Mt. Pisgah to do laundry. Women washed clothes in buckets or tubs, using water from the river or from wells the men had dug.[54] Women's work included constantly caring for their children, milking cows, sewing clothes, patching clothing, cleaning mud and dirt from tents and wagons, cooking meals over campfires or on portable stoves, washing dishes, scouring cooking pans, and borrowing or trading for items the family needed. Women's visits with one another helped buoy up their spirits.[55] On May 31 Clayton recorded that he'd heard Howard was near, returning from a trading trip. Two days later Howard showed up and rejoined his family.

To the Council Bluffs Region

Young's Camp of Israel, reduced in size at Garden Grove and Mt. Pisgah but reinforced by arrivals from Nauvoo, now numbered more than five hundred wagons. Some groups newly arrived from Nauvoo continued to travel together. Existing companies of fifties and tens in the Camp of Israel let newcomers from Nauvoo fill in their vacancies.[56] Howard, Tamson, Ransom, and Erastus continued to travel with Heber C. Kimball's wagons.[57] The Camp of Israel resumed its trek towards the Council Bluffs on June 1. It made good progress, moving six to twelve miles per day. On June 6 the Kimball and Young fifties camped together, forming a circle, and called the place "Ring town."[58] The next day they held a Sunday meeting. In President Young's counsel, he instructed women regarding their roles in their families:

> I instructed the Sisters to keep themselves and tents clean, and not to dictate those over them, it was their duty to raise all the children they could lawfully, and rear them up in the name of the Lord, watching over them and keeping them from playing with ungodly children, or from falling into danger, or exposing

themselves to sickness; and when they raised them up to deliver them to their husband's business, they should be careful of his feelings, and seek his interest, and men should be kind and affectionate to their wives, not abusing or exposing them to hardships.⁵⁹

He instructed that the wagons travel by tens. Travel resumed on June 8. The wagon procession passed the main village of Pottawattamie Indians, later called Indiantown, located a mile west of present Lewis, Iowa.⁶⁰ John D. Lee said the village had fifty wigwams, and that "some few lots of grounds were enclosed by Pole fenses & tilled by the squaws." This Indian village life should have piqued sharp interest in young Erastus and Ransom, if not the Egan adults. Beyond the village, the wagons crossed with difficulty two branches of the Nishnabotna River.⁶¹

That day, Captain John Pack started a fight with Howard. It livened up the day's travel and gave gossips something new to talk about. Captain Pack wanted to pass Howard and travel in front of him, which Howard didn't want him doing. "Brother P being jealous of Br. E for him being ahead of him with his wagon," Peter Hansen Kimball wrote, "struck his [Howard's] oxen to drive them out off the road which made Br. E. angry." Howard "struck Br. J. P. often several strick from both sides, in his eye, so bad that he fell down and still he struck him." Another diarist recorded that Brother Pack "smote" Howard's team with a stick three times until Howard "with a blow of his fist brought him to the earth then kicked him." John D. Lee, commenting on the altercation, said, "This, however, can alone be attributed to the weakness & depravity of mortal man—for they were doubtless both good men." Horace K. Whitney called the altercation "a trifling difficulty" between Egan and Pack "about the right of place." The next day, during the noon stop, a court was held regarding the fight "and the matter was settled between them." This fight shows that ex-sailor and ex-policeman Howard would defend himself when he thought someone mistreated him or his team.⁶²

John Pack, Engraved Portrait Collection, LDS Church History Library

On June 13 Heber C. Kimball's companies, including the Egans, first saw the

Missouri River. "From our stopping place," Horace K. Whitney said, "we can perceive the Missouri River" and beheld "a swampy wet bottom intervening" between them and the river. They viewed, too, "the grand and lofty hills on the opposite side of the Missouri River, their pinnacles wildly jutting up and reaching far above the surrounding scenery." They camped some two miles from the river. A tiny settlement down river a ways was called Point aux Poules, or Traders Point. It included the residence of Indian Agent Robert B. Mitchell and a branch of the American Fur Company operated by Peter A. Sarpy.[63] The inhabitants were mostly French, mixed-race, and Indians, and conversations were in English, French, or Indian.[64] Howard, who heard French spoken in his boyhood Canada, once again was among people speaking French.

With wagons constantly arriving, families soon created a line of camps from the Missouri River back along the trail nine miles, forming what became called the "Grand Encampment." By June 21, Brother Amos Fielding counted no less than 910 wagons between Council Bluffs and three days' distance back, which meant about four to five thousand people.[65] Camps in the hills and vales found wood, water, and wild strawberries, but they badly needed food and lots of supplies, which Sarpy's post could not provide them.

Trade Trips Down River

Down river, accessible by existing roads along the east bank of the Missouri River, were Missouri towns and farms. Elder Kimball wasted no time sending Howard and other agents sixty miles or more into Atchison County, Missouri. Early on June 15, Howard and others "went out into the country to day for the purpose of trading." Two days later the Kimball Company again sent "a number of hands with teams" down to Missouri "to get Wheat, flour, corn &c. for Bro. K." Howard served as the "principal agent" for the Kimball traders. Several other trading groups made similar round trips, which required nearly three weeks. In Missouri, Howard contracted for the corn and wheat. Before returning, the traders had to thresh some of the wheat and take it to a mill to be ground into flour. They had to "shell out" corn. They also obtained and hauled back seed wheat, and bought some cattle.[66]

A week before the traders arrived back, Elder Kimball sent Daniel Davis and John Davenport down to help haul back the purchases. With that help, the loaded wagons returned to the Mormon encampments on or near July 7. The fact that Howard's traders were successful shouldn't be taken for granted. Apostle John Taylor's two traders returned the day before "without bringing wheat or corn or trading their horses for cattle, leaving Taylor's company suffering for want of provisions."[67]

Waiting beside the Missouri

Near present-day Council Bluffs, Tamson, the boys, and Nancy briefly summer-camped and rested as part of the Grand Encampment. To outsiders, like Thomas L. Kane—a well-connected Pennsylvanian who came to help recruit a battalion of Mormons for Mexican War service—the temporary Mormon encampments were a sight to behold. Kane saw miles of bottomlands north and east of Point aux Poules, which was

> ...crowded with covered carts and wagons; and each one of the Council Bluff hills opposite was crowned with its own great camp, gay with bright white canvas, and alive with the busy stir of swarming occupants. In the clear blue morning air, the smoke streamed up from more than a thousand cooking fires. Countless roads and bypaths checkered all manner of geometric figures on the hillsides. Herd boys were dozing upon the slopes; sheep and horses, cows and oxen, were feeding around them, and other herds in the luxuriant meadow of the then swollen river. From a single point I counted four thousand head of cattle in view at one time. As I approached the camps, it seemed to me the children there were to prove still more numerous.[68]

Maybe the Egans were part of that scene. "It was the appearance of their women," Kane discovered, that showed that "Mormons had been bred to other lives." Although "their ears were pierced and bore the loop-marks" of jewelry, the women were without earrings, finger-rings, necklaces or brooches which had been sold or traded during the trek across Iowa. Their clothes proved their poverty was recent, he said, noting among them "the neatly darned white stocking, and clean bright petticoat, the artistically clear-starched collar and chemisette, the something faded, only because too well washed, lawn or gingham gown." In the camps he found "women in greater force" than laundresses along the Seine River in France, "washing and rinsing all manner of white muslins, red flannels and parti-colored calicoes, and hanging them to bleach."[69] If Tamson and Nancy were not in that picture, their daily labors probably matched it.

At this last camp before crossing the fast-flowing Missouri River, the Egans could feel fortunate that, despite exposure and meager diets for four winter and spring months, none in their family had died. Howard's police associate and friend Hosea Stout had buried two little boys along the way.

On the swift Missouri River's eastern shore, diligent Mormon workmen built a ferry boat and launched it on June 29. The Egans waited their turn, along with five thousand or more others, to be ferried. But, even if or when the mass of homeless Saints got across the river, what next? The Twelve didn't know. The people lacked food, the Church lacked money, and the land on the west side of the Missouri was Indian land. Then, like a blessing from the blue, Army Captain James Allen arrived from Ft.

Leavenworth, and—because of the newly declared war with Mexico—he provided the Twelve a workable location option.

A Battalion and a Halt for Winter

A myth, almost dead but still twitching, is that the United States government wronged the Mormons by demanding that a battalion of their men serve Mexican War duty. In fact, President James K. Polk only with reluctance allowed the battalion to be recruited as a favor to the uprooted Mormons. Back when Church leaders first decided to move the Saints west, they urged Eastern States mission president Jesse C. Little to lobby the federal government for any kind of assistance possible. Brother Little arrived in Washington D.C. a week after the United States declared war on Mexico. He contacted President James K. Polk. There was no shortage of men to serve in the war. Because war plans called for General Stephen Watts Kearny to take an American force to California, President Polk authorized Kearny "to receive into service as volunteers a few hundred Mormons who are now on their way to California, with a view to conciliate them, attach them to our country, and prevent them from taking part against us." On June 3 orders reached General Kearny to muster in Mormon volunteers.[70] On June 19, Kearny gave Captain James Allen orders to recruit four or five companies of Mormon volunteers.[71] He authorized Allen to offer them pay, rations, and allowances for a one year enlistment. The battalion would go to Fort Leavenworth, be supplied, and then follow General Kearny's route to Santa Fe.

Captain Allen and three dragoons (cavalry men) rode to Council Bluffs and on July 1 gave Brigham Young the enlistment offer. Mr. Kane arrived soon after that and assured the Mormons the enlistment was a good opportunity. Timing was inopportune because President Young himself was seeking to recruit two hundred to five hundred men to send ahead immediately towards the Rocky Mountains. Because Young drove a hard bargain, Captain Allen allowed the Church and its refugees three big benefits. First, Allen gave permission for the Mormon refugees to locate on Indian lands on both sides of the river, without government interference, until they could prosecute their journey.[72] Second, five hundred Mormon men, as soldiers, would be moved west at government expense and be allowed to keep their arms. And, third, the men's pay and clothing allowances would provide cash needed by their families and the Church. This enlistment opportunity, Young said, was "from above, for our good."[73]

In late July Captain Allen marched nearly five hundred Mormon recruits 180 miles down along the Missouri River to Ft. Leavenworth. There, they outfitted and began their long infantry march to Santa Fe. Meanwhile, thousands of the displaced and poorly provisioned Saints prepared to survive a winter near the Missouri River.

The Land Agreement

On debatable authority, Captain Allen put into writing that he gave "permission to a portion of the Mormon people to reside for a time on the Pottawatomie lands, obtained from the Indians on my request, and fully approved by me." He added that "such of the Mormon people as may desire to avail themselves of this privilege are hereby authorized to do so, during the pleasure of the United States."[74] That agreement, along with the assent of Indian chiefs, was sent to President Polk, the secretary of state, and the Department of Indian Affairs at St. Louis. "If their continuance is really to be temporary and for such length of time only as will enable them to supply their wants and procure the necessary means, for proceeding on their journey," the St. Louis agency concluded, "the government will interpose no objections."

The agency recognized that the Mormons' lack of provisions and the near approach of winter would expose them to much suffering, "if not starvation and death." But, it pointed out that their stay on the Indian lands must not interfere with the government's "Indian removal" then underway, or with Iowa's efforts to obtain statehood that year. The agency hoped that the Mormons would "resume their journey in the spring, or at such period as the season for traveling will justify." Government agents should "impress upon them the necessity of leaving at the earliest moment their necessities and convenience will justify."[75] Based on these agreements, the Saints developed and lived at Winter Quarters for two years, and made many small settlements in southwestern Iowa Territory. ◆

~ 8 ~

Dangerous Secret Assignment

In July 1846 the Twelve's hopes to place that year a small, advanced, select group of men in or beyond the Rocky Mountains suffered setbacks. For that expedition to happen, Saints must quickly cross the Missouri River and have sufficient manpower both for the mountain company and to care for the main body of Saints left behind. However, the river crossing took longer than expected, and the enlistment of five hundred men in the Mormon Battalion removed badly needed manpower. Therefore, the expedition didn't take place that year. The Twelve searched for places where thousands of Mormon refugees could prepare winter quarters for themselves.

Meanwhile, for a top secret errand they needed done, they recruited two trusted and fearless men they knew they could count on, John D. Lee and Howard.

John D. Lee, 1875, Portrait Collection, LDS Church History Library

Crossing the Missouri River

On July 8 the Egans ferried across the Missouri River as part of Heber C. Kimball's wagon company. Peter Hansen, who wrote Kimball's daily diary, documented the crossing, which took place near the present-day South Omaha bridge. Men herded the cows to the river and swam them across, he said. Late that day and even after nightfall, aided by "fine moonlight," the Kimball wagons crossed. "We have put on a boat and that is capable of holding only 3 wagons at a time," Hansen observed; "the current is quite favorable, setting in almost to the opposite shore, where there is quite an eddy."[1] On July 9 they parked four miles inland on open prairie, where heavy rains made life miserable. The next day they moved to what became the Cold Spring Camp.[2] They would stay there briefly and then move northward to Cutler's Park, where leaders expected to create living quarters for the winter.

On July 12, a Sunday, the refugees' distinguished guest from Philadelphia, Thomas L. Kane, spoke to Elder Kimball's encampment. He impressed them.[3] It is very likely Howard personally met Kane during that visit. Fate would decree twelve years later that Howard escort and guard Kane during the Utah War (see Chapter 22). Kane had come to help enlist five companies for the Mormon Battalion.[4] Two days later, Kimball's journal notes, "100 men are yet wanting to complete their recruiting list."[5] Gradually the fifth company filled up.

As of July 16, the Kimball camp contained twenty-two wagons and twenty-four tents. A week later the wagon count had shrunk to thirteen. Its cattle inventory included Egan oxen. During the last two weeks of July, Howard performed guard duty for at least four nights. By July's end, Hansen noted in Kimball's diary that "our camp is increasing fast." On August 6, the camp gave the fourteen guards each a number, so that assignments could be rotated. Howard became number thirteen. That day the Brigham Young Company camped next to the Kimball Company. Three days later this location was named Cutler's Park.[6]

Battalion Leadership Schism

Much is written about the Mormon Battalion and its epic march of nearly two thousand miles from Council Bluffs to San Diego and its army roles there.[7] Before the recruits left, Brigham Young counseled them, particularly the officers, not to use common medicines but to rely on priesthood blessings and herbal medicines. Young's agreement with recruiter Allen was that, should Allen later be unable to serve, Captain Jefferson Hunt of Company A, a Mormon officer, would take his place. "Young's words and religious points established in his followers' minds that ecclesiastical authority was more important than military discipline and authority," a stance which soon produced conflict within the Battalion.[8]

After marching the enlistees to Ft. Leavenworth for outfitting, Captain Allen appointed Dr. George B. Sanderson to accompany the unit. Allen, in return for recruiting the battalion, advanced in rank to lieutenant-colonel. For two weeks the men received equipment, allowances for uniforms, army indoctrination, and minor training. Rather than buying uniforms, the soldiers sent back to the Church and their families their army clothing allowance money of forty-two dollars. From the uniform fund,

President Young expected close to $21,000. However, when a delegation rounded up the enlistees' clothing money, they received only $5,192.[9]

Because Col. Allen fell ill, he ordered the battalion to march without him toward the Santa Fe Trail to follow General Kearny's Army of the West, of which they were part. Allen placed Captain Jefferson Hunt in temporary command. After a short shakedown march, the battalion received upsetting word that Allen had died on August 23. Fort Leavenworth officers sent Lt. James Pace of Company E, who'd been with Col. Allen, back up to the bluffs to inform Brigham Young of the commander's death. In line with Col. Allen's dying suggestion, Major Clifton Wharton, the commanding officer at Fort Leavenworth, approved that Lieutenant Andrew Jackson Smith take temporary command of the Battalion until General Kearny could be contacted.

On August 29, Lt. Smith, Dr. Sanderson, and others reached the Battalion. Smith took temporary command. He met with the Mormon officers. He told them that as a regular army officer he knew "the proper procedures for the procurement of provisions, requisitions, manning rosters, pay and allowances, drill, tactics, and training." And he'd been on the route to Santa Fe before. Captain Hunt and other Mormon officers listened, then agreed to accept Smith's leadership. However, some officers and many of the men didn't. They knew that Capt. Allen had promised Brigham Young that, if the command changed, a Mormon officer would succeed him. Technically, not one of the Mormon officers had received commission certificates. They had no formal standing in the Army. Even Smith lacked written orders to take command.[10] Dissent about leadership festered.

Dangerous Secret Errand

A month after the Mormon recruits marched off, Lt. Pace arrived back in the Mormon camps unexpectedly. He reached Cutler's Park on August 26, bringing news that Battalion commander Allen had died. President Young consulted with Col. Kane, still in camp, and then wrote letters to Army officers for Lt. Pace to carry back to the Battalion. Young's instruction was that the Battalion, based on Captain Allen's instructions, could and should appoint their own commander, preferably senior Mormon officer Jefferson Hunt.[11]

The small amount of uniform money the Battalion men had sent from Ft. Leavenworth disappointed President Young. He felt urgent need to receive the next Battalion donation: the soldiers' paychecks they'd receive after a month of service. Therefore, very hush-hush, President Young selected John D. Lee and Howard to accompany Lt. Pace back to the Battalion to pick up the first paychecks. Pace was one of Lee's adopted sons.[12] "Their mission was kept a profound secret in the breast of about 2 or 3 persons," Young said later.[13] Historian Juanita Brooks, in her biography of Lee, said Howard was a good choice for the mission because he "was a stranger to fear."[14] Because they'd be transporting money, the success of their trip and their very lives depended on secrecy. Lee said he was not allowed to tell his wives where he was going or how long he'd be gone. Likewise, Tamson didn't know where Howard was headed, only that once again he'd be away on some kind of Church assignment.[15]

According to Lee's diary, on August 26 President Young came to Lee's tent and "told me he had a Dangerous though Responsible Mission for me to perform which was to follow up the Mormon Battalion to receive payment." Young made Lee a promise: "Go & god will bless you & you shall have whatever you need for your Family—I will send 1 or 2 men with you—you will take a light wagon & a span of mules–that will travel 40 miles per day."[16] He appointed Howard to go with Lee.

To camouflage the purpose of Lee and Howard's departure, President Young allowed Lt. Pace to leave ahead of them on August 28, to visit his family back at Garden Grove. Then, on August 30, after Sunday meetings at Cutler's Park, Young, Heber C. Kimball, and Willard Richards, along with Bishop Newel K. Whitney, rode out on the prairie in President Young's carriage and met Lee and Howard, "who were with a waggon & span of mules." Finding they had forgotten Elder Richards's dog (Trip), both Richards and Young rode back for it and returned about 4:00 p.m. Trip became a watch dog to guard the wagon when Lee, Howard, and Pace slept at night. Young, Kimball, Richards, and Whitney "blessed us & in the Name of the Lord, said we should go & prosper & return in safety," Lee said, a blessing that came to pass. With Howard handling the reins, he and Lee drove down to the ferry on the Missouri River.[17]

The following account of their errand to the Battalion is drawn from John D. Lee's diary, without note citations, unless otherwise indicated.[18] Lee and Howard were cut from the same kind of sturdy cloth. They had both been orphaned at young ages and forced to make their own ways in the world before adulthood. Lee's diary entry for their departure day terms Howard "my helper, Friend & assistant," but during this trip together Howard found he could not support some of Lee's extreme behavior, which caused Lee to dislike him. Lee's diary of the trip, and accounts by some Battalion members, reveal Lee to be, as his biographer noted, "officious and dictatorial."[19]

To Fort Leavenworth

On August 31, Lee and Howard crossed the Missouri River to the east side, bought some food items, including three watermelons, and headed south. They reached St. Joseph on September 3. Lt. Pace arrived in town that day and joined them. Pace and Howard then bought provisions to supply the trio until they overtook the Battalion.

That night, LDS families helped them make a wagon cover and sacks for mule feed.[20]

On a dark, foggy morning, September 5, the three passed through Weston, Missouri, five miles above Ft. Leavenworth. They found a traffic jam of about fifty wagons waiting to ferry across. Lt. Pace showed the ferry operator his army "passport," so the man let them cross without waiting. The Battalion had departed three weeks earlier. Post Commander Wharton told the trio to stay until the next morning so they could carry U.S. mail with them. Fort Leavenworth, Lee noted, had a four-acre, well-shaded, "handsome" green, around which were four lines of structures—three of brick buildings and one of stables. This large military installation probably drew ex-naval sailor Howard's close attention.

Onto the Santa Fe Trail

The next day, Howard, Lee, and Pace headed out. At the Kaw River they paid Shawnee and Delaware Indians one dollar to be ferried across. They came to the Oregon Trail, bore right, and nine miles later turned onto the Santa Fe Trail. They passed thirty provision wagons. The war put a lot of supply vehicles on the trails to Mexico. After traveling twenty-six miles one rainy day, they camped on the prairie. They hobbled their team and "let them to grass after feeding them corn and oats, as we fed them grain 3 times per day." They prayed together, then Howard and Lee slept "in our little wagon," which allowed them only to lie on their sides with no room to turn over.

On September 8 and 9, travel tedium caused the trio to name streams after themselves—Lee's Creek, Pace's Creek, and Howard's Creek. By then they "seldom took time to cook." On the ninth, while descending a hill to a stream with Howard driving and the mules in a "sweeping trot," the wagon "ran over some rocks, throwing the weight on the lowere [left] hind wheel as it pitched down into a rut & broke the axle tree." This accident delayed them at least a day-and-a-half. Upon reaching Council Grove, they viewed the last good grove of trees that travelers westbound on the Santa Fe Trail would see: ash, black walnut, burr and black oak, chestnut oak, sycamore, elm, hickory, and others.[21] "At this grove is a blacksmith shop employed by the government," Lee wrote. On September 10 "we tried to get them to repair our carriage as Government property but they refused unless we would show U S on our mules or an order from Head Quarters." So, with wood so abundant, "we all went to work built a new axle tree and shod one of the mules." Lt. Pace found a letter waiting there for him from the Battalion, which told about its progress. Lee estimated the unit was about two hundred miles ahead of them. "Bro. Egan & myself washed from head to foot in the pure waters of Neosha." They changed clothes and Howard laundered a shirt and garment for himself and Lee. Hearing dire warnings about Indian depredations ahead, they decided to travel carefully, camp in the open, and try to camp with other traveling groups.

Finding the Battalion at the Arkansas River

With the wagon repaired, they left Council Grove by 6:00 p.m. and traveled until 2:00 a.m. By then they were on lands belonging to the Sac Nation. During the night their dog "made a tremendous to do," causing Lee to grab his fifteen-shooter rifle and check the camp perimeter. He saw a black bear try to attack Trip. Lee emptied his gun on the bear with no effect, but while he reloaded, the bear "eloped."[22] On September 11, the three left early and moved across prairie belonging to the Kaw Nation. After ten miles, at Lost Spring, they heard reports from travelers of new Indian troubles. Rains made the road soft. "Heavy wheeling," Lee called it. By September 12, the men

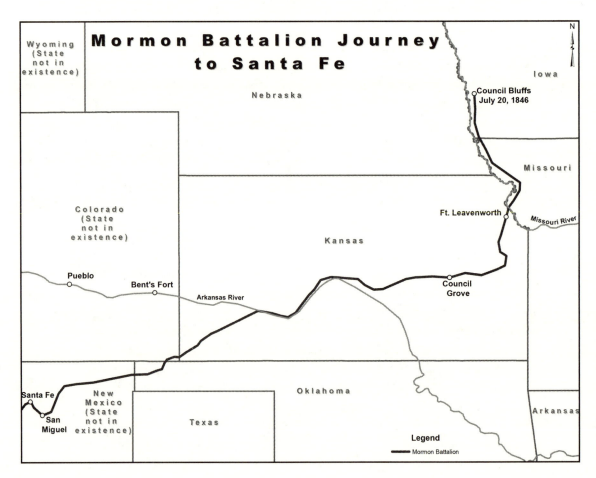

and dog, now on Pawnee lands, daily saw broken down government wagons and the remains of dead oxen that were victims of heat and thirst. "No gopher hills or humps to be seen," Lee said, describing the flat plain they next crossed. They camped by the Little Arkansas River, where they traded bacon for flour with another company.

Moving up the Arkansas River on September 13, they saw herds of buffalo. That night they dined on buffalo meat with army sutlers (suppliers) assigned to provision the Mormon Battalion. Seven miles later the trio camped. They now enjoyed "better pulling" because they'd put Lt. Pace's "fine horse" into the harness, replacing their worn out mules. They awoke the next morning surrounded by buffalo grazing less than three hundred yards away. That day they moved from Pawnee into Comanche territory. They passed a Spanish trading company heading for Missouri. Then, to their surprise, they met horsemen and three or four wagons who were Mormons from Mississippi. These strangers were coming from the west, from a winter encampment at Fort Pueblo up the Arkansas River. They "seemed overjoyed" to learn where the main Mormon encampments were. Lee promised them he would inform President Young about the Mississippi Saints' winter location and have Young send them instructions.

That evening, Howard, Pace, and Lee stopped with a company of thirty wagons carrying provisions for the army at Santa Fe. Invited to hunt buffalo, Lee and Pace rode off and shot two, then brought to camp two hundred pounds from one hump. Near dark the three drove hard to catch up with the provision company, "not feeling verry [sic] safe as we were liable to fall in the hands of the natives & be massacred with out having any means of defence as we had shot all our charges." The next day they again had to repair the hind axletree, then they drove thirty miles and camped near the Arkansas River. But they parked hundreds of yards off the road to prevent nearby Comanche Indians from seeing them. Next day, they drove sixty miles, going up the Arkansas River, which then was about a half mile wide. They frequently saw buffalo, antelope, and prairie dogs.

Finally, on the morning of September 17, they spotted the Mormon Battalion and an army regiment on the other side of the Arkansas River. Excited to see his comrades, Lt. Pace rode over and rejoined his unit. The soldiers had just started a fifty-mile crossing of the Cimarron Desert. Being messengers from the Camp of Israel, Pace, Lee, and Howard excited the march-weary men, as did the mail they brought.

Causing Command Trouble

Lee flaunted his authority from Brigham Young. Although a civilian, he demanded that the Battalion stop immediately to receive the decisions and orders he carried from the Church leaders. He was shocked that the Mormon officers had accepted Lt. A. J. Smith to command the unit. "Did the Battalion men vote on that?" Lee asked ranking captain Jefferson Hunt. No, Hunt said, they had nothing to do with the appointment. In total disbelief, Lee became adamant that Hunt immediately take command, as Brigham Young had ordered.

On the day before the trio arrived, Lt. Smith had split off from the Battalion a sick detachment, which Captain Nelson Higgins led up the Arkansas River towards Bent's Fort and Pueblo. Because Brigham Young's ground rules said that the Battalion must be kept intact, many soldiers in the Battalion resented the split-up. Also, Lee, Pace, and Howard caught an ear-full of gripes from enlisted men about Dr. Sanderson, who, with Lt. Smith's approval, forced them to take medicine against their wills and against Brigham Young's instructions. Pvt. Alva Phelps had died the day before, immediately after ingesting medicine the doctor forced him to take. Dr. Sanderson gained the nickname of "Dr. Death." Lee and Howard saw for themselves that sick men, unable to march, were being treated harshly. Out of sympathy, Lee and Howard put three or four sick soldiers in their little wagon, overloading it.

For three days an angry John D. Lee locked horns with the Army officers about the command and the doctor issues, almost causing a mutiny. Lee insisted the unit stop doing forced marches and be given a day or two of rest. Lt. Smith ignored Lee's requests. Later that day Lee asked Lt. Smith and Captain Hunt to ride in his wagon. They complied, whereupon Lee tongue-lashed the lieutenant. "When I came up with the Bat. & saw the suffering & oppression of these Soldiers," Lee accused, "my blood boiled in my veins to such an extent that I could scarce refrain from taking my Sword In hand & rid[d]ing them of such Tyrants." He warned Lt. Smith that if he saw more mistreatment of sick men he might "cut your infernal throats." He told Smith to conduct himself like his predecessor had done, showing respect for the men and their beliefs.

Lee warned that the enlistees felt ready to revolt and might not be kept restrained. He said if Smith and the doctor tried to cram medicine down him against his will he'd "cut their cursed throats," and hinted that in two minutes the battalion could rebel and take "your sweet life."[23]

Lee, one military historian assessed, was "out of control and out of mind," and as a civilian had no business interfering with military matters.[24] Captain Hunt, furious at Lee's disrespect toward the commander, jumped out of the wagon. Lee, after his tirade, expected Lt. Smith to challenge him to a duel, but Smith simply walked away.[25]

On September 18 the Battalion marched across twenty-four miles of the Cimarron Desert on Cheyenne Indian lands. They camped by the north fork of the Cimarron River in a vast wasteland parched by the sun. Soldiers had to drink a "filthy gruel of buffalo urine, bugs, and rain water left standing in mud holes."[26] That evening Lee read to some of the men parts of Brigham Young's letters. One letter opposed medicine, one said the command should devolve upon Jefferson Hunt, and a third instructed the men to turn their pay over to Lee to take back to the Bluffs. Lee riled many of the men toward rebellion and mutiny.[27] He then lectured the Mormon officers for not asserting rights Captain Allen had guaranteed them. Some officers accused back that Lee had no right to abuse Lt. Smith whom *they* had appointed commander.

Because Lee and Howard "expect to start back tomorrow," some men hurriedly wrote letters for them to take with them.[28] On September 19 the Battalion reached the Cimarron Springs about 11:00 a.m. and stopped for a day. Captain Hunt requested the soldiers' pay, but paymaster Jeremiah Cloud informed him that he lacked the funds to issue pay. He said that payments would be made at Santa Fe individually to each soldier, not in a lump sum check.[29] Disappointed by that news, Lee proposed a plan. Without notifying Lt. Smith, he and Howard would rush ahead of the Battalion to Santa Fe. He'd show General Kearny the original instructions that said the Battalion should choose their own commander, then pick up the Battalion's pay, and return with the General's decision.[30] They didn't go.

In the evening on September 20, during which day the Battalion finished the desert crossing, the Mormon officers met with Lee and Howard. They pointed out that Lee "came here & assumed the right to dictate this Bat. & even went so far as to light on our commander & Seargon whom we have appointed & abuse them which we considered to be an insult, & and that he was out of his place." Captain Jesse Hunter tried to convince Lee of his error, which "seemed to infuriate him still more, and he declared that no man had it in his power to stop his mouth."[31] Captain Hunt then arose and asserted he, not Lee, was the senior officer in camp and was the only one to advise the men. The Mormon captains agreed that Lee was out of line. They forbid him to go ahead to Santa Fe to lobby. Hunt chastised Lee and Howard because "bro Lee & Egan [had] been stirring up the Bat to revault, that they had no right to council this Bat., that he (Lee) must be put down."

Captain Hunt, trying to calm things, said he had good feelings toward Pace, Howard, and Lee, and would pay their portion for their board while they were with the Battalion headed to Santa Fe. Lee said he did not want Howard's name brought into question because Howard had had nothing to say, for or against, so he, not Howard, was to blame for the turmoil. The officers invited Howard to speak because "he had not said anything either way." Howard then said that "the reason he was silent was because he saw that they did not want any council. So he thought that in as much as they had burned their backsides they might sit on the Blisters." He then drew a comparison to an experience he'd had at sea:

> He had been on board of a man of war for 3 years & has seen the time that all was wanting to throw every officer over board was for some one to give the word & this was the situation that we found the Bat in when we came; So I evaded answering the question of the brethren & told them to be united that the times would be better &c.[32]

Howard's sailing days taught him that absolute authority rested with the officers, whose words were law, and discussion usually was not allowed. This was especially true on a man-of-war ship.

Captain Hunt ordered Lee to desist arguing, or else "harsher measures would need to be taken." After this, "all public mutinous language was stopped." The next day, September 21, Captain Hunt informed Lt. Smith that he, Smith, had full command and "had the right [to] give Lee, Pace & Egan their orders, telling if they did not hold their peace that they would be put under guard."[33]

Accompanying the Battalion to Santa Fe

During late September the Battalion marched into what is now New Mexico, covering less than twenty miles per day on average. On October 2, in response to orders from General Kearny, the Battalion divided in order to allow a strong part of it to go faster and reach Santa Fe in time for Kearny's deadline for them of October 10. This separation made Lee and others feel that, once again, the Mormon officers had betrayed the Twelve's counsel. "Every thing looks like a determination to go contrary to council in evry movement," Levi Hancock wrote in his diary; "some cryed, some ware mad & some prayed, some swore, some ware for taking the sword [and] settle the despute on the ground."[34]

On October 5 the advanced group, accompanied by Lee and Howard, camped near the Mexican village of Las Vegas. Howard saw there some five hundred houses made of sun dried bricks, his first exposure to adobe as a building material. Lee disliked the local people, considering them dirty, indolent, and uncivilized. He wrote that they grew corn, onions, peppers, "watered all the stuff they raise," and had large herds of cattle, sheep, goats, mules, and some horses. Howard saw how irrigating worked. Two days later this Battalion segment moved through San Miguel, where locals sold them corn, peppers, squash, apples, melons, and whiskey. On October 8 they received word that General Kearny, already on his way to California, had appointed Captain Philip St.

George Cooke to take command of the Battalion and lead it to California. With Kearny gone from Santa Fe and Cooke appointed, Lee saw no possibility for the Battalion to install their own commander.

The next day, October 9, Howard's part of the Battalion marched "in military order" into Santa Fe where they were greeted by "a salute fired on our entering." They saw a "town full of soldiers" with a huge American flag flying over the city that had just recently surrendered to General Kearny. In command was General Alexander Doniphan, who once had defended Joseph Smith in Missouri. Doniphan "received us with peculiar friendship," Lee wrote. In the city of some three thousand people, Howard noticed that none of the buildings was higher than one story except the cathedral, a dwelling house, and an old chapel. Santa Fe had six Catholic churches. By the town square stood the Mexican governor's residence. Houses generally were built of sun dried adobe bricks and had flat roofs. Irrigation made possible the valley's farms, gardens, and orchards. Levi Hancock called this "the poorest looking place I know of, mud houses that do not look as well as the Mormon brickyards did in Nauvoo unburned."[35]

Santa Fe Plaza, *artist Gerald Cassidy, New Mexico Museum of Art*

Soliciting Battalion Money

On October 10, Lee lobbied with General Doniphan's staff for the Battalion to be paid. He was told the soldiers would receive pay for a month-and-a-half and officers for two-and-a-half months, all in checks, except for some currency for clothing. That day Lee and Howard shopped at the city's stores. Women and girls sold pine nuts, apples, peaches, pears, large grapes, bread, onions, boiled corn, and melons. Some Battalion men went on a "spree," enjoying the local liquor. On October 11 the men in Company D received their wages, but many didn't donate them for Lee and Howard to take back to the Twelve.

That same day Lee and Howard, along with Captains Hunt, Hunter, and James Brown, and Lieutenant Lorenzo Clark visited the Battalion's new commander, who now was a lieutenant-colonel. Cooke received them with much courtesy. The men conversed freely. They read General Kearny's letter.[36] Cooke, thirty-seven years old, had graduated from West Point in 1827. He informed his guests that California had fallen to United States forces three months before. Only able-bodied men would go on, and those ill or unable would be sent to Pueblo for the winter.

Lt. Col. Philip St. George Cooke, Utah State Historical Society

The next day, October 12, while Lee worked to prepare for his and Howard's return to the Bluffs, Howard "was walking about to the groceres with some of the officers," unconcerned about helping Lee. This bothered Lee. The Battalion's slower division arrived that day. On October 13, Captain Hunt urged the Battalion men to send all the pay they could to the "Poor of Israel" and to donate to assist Howard and Lee to return there. The soldiers seemed agreeable. Hunt and other Mormon officers, worried that Lee, when back with Brigham Young, might distort their leadership decisions, wrote a letter to Young and entrusted it to Howard. He was not to deliver it unless Lee disparaged their position.[37]

On the fifteenth, officers received their pay in government drafts, not currency.[38]

That day three-fourths of the Battalion and most of its officers attended a ball in the city organized by Spaniards and Missourians. Each man paid two dollars per head. Lee opposed the party and felt that those who attended disgraced the priesthood by mingling with Missourians, prostitutes, and "children of darkness." Mormon soldiers spent a thousand dollars "foolishly," Lee complained, while the poor of Israel needed that money.

Two valuable gold watches disappeared that night, apparently stolen. The next day, searchers found nothing. Lee, who disliked Howard for not supporting his cause against Army officers, suspected that Roswell Stevens and Howard stole the watch belonging to Dr. Sanderson, but offered no evidence.[39] The next day Lee spent much time making out a roll of the Battalion members and "regulating" their checks to be taken to the Mormon Camps. Before supper Lee loaded items into his return wagon, filed a bill to be paid for the materials, and accepted about one hundred letters to take back. Levi Hancock gave Lee and Howard his Battalion diary to deliver to his wife Clarissa.[40] Lee received presents from the men, several of whom helped him with whatever he asked for.

On October 16 and 17 Major Jeremiah Cloud finished paying the Battalion enlistees.[41] The next day the Mormon commissioned officers sent a letter to Brigham Young and the Council, saying, "We are sorry that we cannot send you any more money at this time owing to the volunteers getting but one month and a half's pay."[42] Henry Standage wrote a long letter to his wife and mother, sent eight dollars to his wife, and one dollar to the Twelve. Levi Hancock sent almost fifteen dollars "to Headquarters, for my family."[43] LDS Battalion officers asked Lee how much money the men donated. "The Brethren drew but little money but out of that they were liberal," is what Lee recorded in his diary. Lee's biographer said Lee and Egan obtained over twelve hundred dollars, which would be roughly $38,000 in 2015 dollars.[44]

Col. Cooke organized a second sick detachment under Captain James Brown of twenty women and children and eighty-six men. They were sent to join Captain Higgins's earlier sick detachment at Pueblo. Once again, the unit saw a separation.

For safety reasons Lee wanted two men to accompany him and Howard back to the Bluffs. He enlisted one, Roswell Stevens, who was on the list of the soldiers being detached and sent to Pueblo. Then he recruited Lt. Samuel Gully, the Battalion's quartermaster, who was about to be reduced in rank. Gully resigned from the service so he could go with Lee and Howard. Gully was one of Lee's sons by the priesthood Law of Adoption.[45]

On October 19 the Battalion started to move out, heading south. Howard and Lee remained in Santa Fe. Lee helped Gully wrap up his commissary affairs. Lee felt that Howard was apt to drink too much if he were in a drinking crowd, which happened that night. "Bro Egan remained in the city around grog shops till after midnight," Lee wrote. During the night Howard disappeared, and was found lying in the middle of the street, flat on his back, his hat and shoes off. Lee carried him to the wagon, put him to bed, and thanked the Lord that Howard had not been robbed or even murdered.

Dangerous Return Trip

The next day, October 20, Howard attempted to ride a mule Lee had obtained, but it bounded like an antelope and threw Howard twice. He then led the mule three miles away to secret it from the army, which tried to commandeer all available mules in good condition. Lee had obtained the mule honestly and saw no reason to lose it. At 4:00 p.m. Lee, Howard, and Gully left town and started their long return trek on the Santa Fe Trail. Stevens left earlier, on the eighteenth. The three were barely on their way when little dog "Trip" warned them in time to scare off three would-be robbers.

The next day they caught up with Captain Brown's sick detachment. One day more and they located Stevens. For the rest of October, which had some severely cold days, they passed and visited briefly with several trading parties and government wagon trains. They traveled sometimes forty miles a day, or more. On October 30 they camped at the Cimarron River where they were joined by Norris Colbourn, "a good and generous trader" in charge of twenty-six wagons. Seeing they were wet and exposed, he gave them a bottle of "spirits," and prepared them a rich supper of chocolate, biscuits, butter, cheese, beef, pork, and pepper sauce. He gave Lee a box of sardines and four pounds of cheese, and next morning sent down to the four a "boiler" full of hot chocolate.

Lee called October 31 "Trip's Defeat" day. During the daytime six large wolves overpowered and killed the little dog. That evening an incredibly cold wind forced the men to blanket the poorest of the mules and, using ropes and wagon covers and pins, "we succeeded in getting in a comfortable shelter where we slept till morning." In early November they moved carefully through Indian country again. On November 2 they left the Arkansas River and "made our way as sly as possible." Travelers told them terrible accounts of white parties being attacked and robbed. In order to camp safely in the open they traveled a hundred mile stretch on November 2, 3, and 4 without water.

In the morning on November 5 they discovered five mules that Indians had stolen from Santa Fe traders two days earlier. "This certainly was ram caught in the thicket as 3 of our mules were about past traveling," said Lee. "The 5 mules just made us a change all round, which when we had done we thanked the Lord for this peculiar manifestation of his good will & went on our way rejoicing." Later that day, some young Indians visited the quartet and received food and small presents. Lee told one he'd give him two yards of calico if he'd "shoot me a buffalo." The Indian did. "We took from the animal the tongue, & about 50 lbs of the best," said Lee.

On November 7, finally out of Indian danger, they "made up a fire, baked bread, boiled a Buffalo's tongue for the morrow." The next day Lee drove off at 5:00 a.m. and "left Bro Gully & Egan to look up 2 of our mules." Five miles later Howard and Gully caught up with Lee. By then Lee believed, and wrote in his diary, that God had favored their journey because some companies just ahead of them had Indian troubles, and difficulties with mud and rain, but he and his companions did not.

They passed through Council Grove on November 9. Four days later they reached Fort Leavenworth, delivered mail, and crossed the Missouri River. Gully and Howard went ahead to arrange lodgings. At Weston the four men learned that at the Mormon encampments at the Bluffs "all was going well." The next day they reached St. Joseph where Howard and Gully lodged with Jacob Peart, who had been in Howard's fifty when it crossed Iowa. On November 15 the men spent the day trading in St. Joseph. Howard, using Battalion funds they were entitled to tap, purchased food and items needed by his family. Brother John Gheen gave them three bottles of Madeira wine and Lee a bottle of brandy. For the next three days Howard and his three companions drove up the east side of the Missouri River.

Mission Accomplished

On November 20 the four arrived home. Their trip had taken eighty-three days. Instead of finding a wagon campground near Cold Springs or at Cutler's Park, they drove into a sizeable log-cabin city named Winter Quarters. They saw buildings and streets tightly laid out along a bluff overlooking the Missouri River, some twelve miles north of the main Mormon ferry. Howard had not seen his family for twelve weeks. He found Tamson and the children waiting for workmen to finish a cabin that they had started for the Egans. Where plural wife Nancy Redden was living right then isn't known.

Even though Lee and Howard had been unable to carry out their assignment fully, they turned over twelve hundred dollars to Brigham Young. At Sunday meetings the next day President Young praised their mission. The two men had gone to the army for money, he announced, and "they have now returned in safety." Because of the infusion of Battalion pay, he proclaimed that "there has been a mericle wrought in Israel." It had been essential, he explained, that their mission be kept a secret. "Had their mission been public property the Mo's [Missourians] would have followed them, robed [robbed] and likely have killd them. Their journey was an arduous one and a dangerous one." He vowed to pay them for their services from moneys they had brought back. At the meeting, when their names were read, many people flocked to the stand to pick up nearly seventy-two packages and about 280 letters which Howard and the others brought back from the Battalion.[46]

That evening Lee and Howard met in council with Elders Young, Kimball, George A. Smith, Wilford Woodruff, Amasa Lyman, and Orson Pratt. Lee gave them a history of the Santa Fe trip. While he told about the oppression of the Battalion soldiers by Lt. A. J. Smith and "Dr. Death," Pres. Young "could no longer keep his seat" and pointedly asked Lee why Lee did not "take off his head," meaning the doctor's. After the meeting, Lee gave President Young $1,277 in Battalion checks. Privately, Lee told Young about "the conduct of my partner," meaning Howard, to which President Young replied that such was "nothing more than what he expected."[47] What that meant isn't clear.

Possibly, Howard received a hundred dollars for his mission. President Young offered that amount to both men. Lee declined to be paid because he considered the mission to be church service, voluntarily donated. On November 25, Lee "was at Howard Egan's and effected a settlement" involving the mules, goods the men bought for their families while at St. Joseph, and perhaps money.[48]

Howard had helped make a small miracle happen by bringing back Battalion money. He had filled a mission more important in ways than a proselytizing mission. He became something of a hero, deservedly. But for him to achieve this, his family had to be heroic, too. His absence deprived Tamson and the children and Nancy of his labor and companionship. They had difficult times without him and his help. Howard returned to them barely before harsh winter and outbreaks of scurvy permeated Winter Quarters. They probably expected he'd now be there for them when they needed him.

But Howard's short and long absences on church errands over the previous eight months were becoming a norm for him. Once again he couldn't stay with his family. As had happened while he led his company of fifty across Iowa earlier that year, the Saints' needed goods from Missouri in order to survive. So, for his family, the Kimball clan, and Winter Quarters Saints, Howard made more trading trips into Missouri, five to be exact, this time under winter conditions. ◆

~ 9 ~

First Winter At Winter Quarters

While Howard spent three months to retrieve Battalion money, Heber C. Kimball's extended family took some care of Tamson and the boys at Winter Quarters. Starting a cabin for her is one example. Horace K. Whitney recorded on November 6 that "another new house was started yesterday for Smithies and Egan." However, two weeks later when Howard returned, it wasn't finished, and he found Tamson and the children living out of a tent. Second wife Nancy probably stayed with Redden relatives.

The Twelve picked the site for Winter Quarters on September 11, 1846, during Howard and John D. Lee's absence. The site was fairly flat ground on the second bluff from the Missouri River, with brooks at the north and the south ends.[1] When Howard arrived, the settlement covered more than six hundred acres on terrain sloping gently toward the river. Fourteen streets intersected at right angles, and forty or more town blocks contained 594 lots. A full size block could contain twenty houses for 150 to 300 people. Residents lived in tents, dugouts, and log homes being erected as quickly as possible. Most log cabins were single room buildings, measuring twelve-by-twelve or twelve-by-eighteen feet, with room height of about seven feet up to the board-and-dirt covered roofs.[2]

A Month of Hard Labor

Four days after Howard arrived home, he and others "engaged in cutting and drawing wood from the bottom close by." The next day "the boys put up the logs of 2 more houses to-day thus making the 9th building," Horace Whitney noted, "one of which is intended for Bro. Howard Egan." Two days later Howard helped a crew load up poles from beyond the settlement site.[3]

On Sunday, November 29, Elder Kimball called his family together, which included the Egans, and gave them fatherly instructions. He spoke concerning evils going on among the people, "one thing being too much after strong drink." Drinking was not uncommon at Winter Quarters, and liquor was available there. Elder Kimball urged his listeners to honor their parents, including him, and to not hurt others' feelings.⁴

Howard spent the next day "drawing stone from the river," probably for a millrace being constructed.⁵ He started December putting up logs for a house for a Brother Wallace. On December 2 and 3, two "cold days," he and two others built a fence for a sheep yard. The next day he and William Kimball "drove a lot of sheep down here to our yard, which they took from Father Lott's sheep-yard." On December 5 Howard, William, and Horace branded fifty sheep on the forehead with the mark, "H.C.K." That day light snow fell, the first of the season.⁶

*Horace K. Whitney,
Portrait Collection,
LDS Church History Library*

Nine months of not living under a roof ended for the Egans on December 7. Howard, William, Horace, and George Rhodes "engaged in cutting and drawing 5 loads of wood," Horace wrote, and "this evening, after returning from work, Bro. Egan moved into his house."⁷

Before November, the community's wagons and teams had been stockpiling hay, carving out streets, and hauling logs and poles for cabins and fencing. After that, leaders sent as many wagons as possible to bring back food, goods, and supplies from Missouri, before winter might block such errands. On November 2 eight teams started for St. Joseph, 140 miles south. Another eighteen teams left the next day, sent for goods in St. Joseph ordered from St. Louis by Bishop Newel K. Whitney. On November 22, the day when Howard, Lee, Stevens, and Gully arrived back from the Battalion venture, so did "a number of teams" loaded with goods. Traders made constant trips for supplies. Arriving loads went into a newly constructed storehouse to be inventoried and organized. On December 8 the "bishop's storehouse" opened for business.⁸ It carried a full line of foodstuffs, textiles, household and hardware goods, various herbal medicines, and some books. It became the most popular place in town. Residents bought items by exchanging used goods, or on credit, or in return for labor credits.⁹ Howard's upcoming buying trips to Missouri each would earn him labor credits he and Tamson and his family could spend at Bishop Whitney's store.

In the early morning hours of December 9, six gunshots and a terrible outcry from dogs and Indians alarmed Winter Quarters residents. Sioux Indians attacked

Omaha Chief Big Head and his family, who were camped a little north of town. The Omahas fled into Winter Quarters for protection. Big Head and two others who were severely wounded were brought into town and attended to by the Mormons. That day, Howard left camp to cross the Missouri River to Council Point, to bring back a cow.[10] On December 10, herders drove cattle to herd grounds on rush bottoms forty miles upriver from Winter Quarters and took along an Egan cow, perhaps the one Howard had just brought in. The next day Howard and three others "engaged in drawing wood from the island," meaning drift wood.[11]

Six-year-old son Howard Ransom had an accident. According to Apostle Kimball's journal entry for December 13, "Yesterday it happened to Br Egands son Howard that he got the ends of two of his fingers cut off by Levy Gean [Gheen] who was playing with a hatchet."[12] Ransom and Levi were peeling bark off a "slippery elm log." Playing with the hatchet, Ransom said, Levi "cut off my two middle fingers of my right hand at the first joint. One finger was hanging by a little piece of skin." Ransom ran to the cabin, crying. Tamson wanted to cut the skin holding the finger, but Ransom begged her to stop. She put the finger on again and used splints and bandages. Three days later Tamson noticed the attached piece had mended, but in a twisted angle. For the rest of his life Ransom was "missing one finger and had another twisted at a funny angle."[13]

With friend Horace Whitney, Howard attended Sunday church services at the "Stand" on December 13.[14] Howard next labored at stable-building. On Monday, Horace noted, "Wm, H. Egan, G. Rhodes and myself went down on the bottom for the purpose of obtaining logs for a stable, but not finding them, we returned, bringing two loads of wood instead—afterwards we split a number of logs we already had." On Wednesday some men cleaned out an old storehouse to disassemble it, then used its logs to build the stable. Saturday found Kimball, Howard, and Smithies "yet engaged" in building the stable. Monday, December 21, the same three finished roofing on the stable.[15]

Mild weather had helped Winter Quarters develop quickly. Heber C. Kimball's priesthood-adopted son Peter Hansen said the settlement "looks quite beautifull to view from the hills, allthough it is log and sod houses and good many huts." Its main building was a Council House constructed of cottonwood logs.[16] Willard Richards's eight-sided house, its roof covered with dirt, was a curiosity. People called it by various names: the Octagon, potato heap, apple heap, coal pit, round house, or The Doctor's Den.[17] By Christmas, Elder Kimball's hired hands and his children and adopted sons had built for themselves and others twenty-five houses.[18]

A municipal or high council governed Winter Quarters. It divided the city into twenty-two wards, each with a bishop to look after the needy and the wives of the Mormon Battalion soldiers. The Egans lived in the Twentieth Ward, which included city block forty at the far north end of the city and north to Turkey Creek.[19] The council appointed Hosea Stout to command the police force of up to two dozen men. Howard, formerly one of Stout's policemen in Nauvoo, was not one of them.[20]

A December census showed that Winter Quarters had 583 cabins and 83 sod houses. It had two main streets running northward for some fourteen blocks, with perhaps fourteen cross streets. Each block covered five acres and contained twenty house lots measuring 72 by 165 feet. Houses sat near the streets. Outhouses were supposed to be at the back edge of a house's back lot. That census identified 3,483 people, with 757 men compared to 2,736 women and children. The settlement contained 814 wagons, 145 horses, 29 mules, 388 yoke of oxen, and 463 cows. Some 386 people were sick, including 117 men. A total of 138 men were absent, apparently on work or trading assignments. Healthy manpower in town stood in short supply.[21]

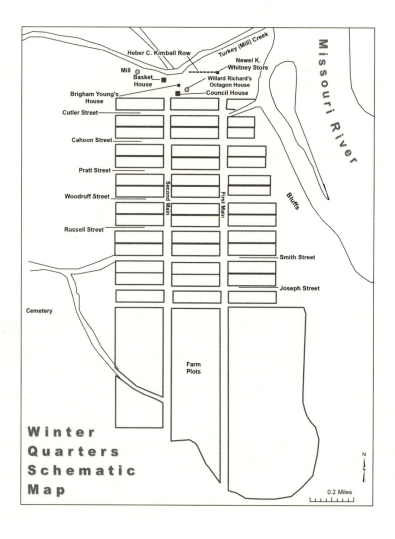

Winter Quarters, *artist C.C.A. Christensen, courtesy Museum of Art, BYU*

Doubtful Story About a Nauvoo Cannon

In 1908 the *Deseret News* published a tale about "Old Sow," a cannon Howard purportedly helped transport in the fall of 1846. Once stationed at New Orleans, the story goes, the cannon became outdated and sold as scrap iron. It ended up at Nauvoo, was buried, and, the article asserts, "in the fall of 1846 Major Howard Egan took the gun from Nauvoo to Winter Quarters." There, men hid it under river ice, after which it came to Utah with the 1847 Pioneers. However, Howard's schedule, as tracked below, had no room for him to make a visit to Nauvoo, hence the story lacks credibility.[22] Mormon folklore hosts a variety of stories about cannons named "Old Sow," such that, as one researcher warns, "it would appear the cannon known as the 'Old Sow' has bred a large litter of piglets and an equal number of stories to go with them."[23]

Howard's First Trading Trip from Winter Quarters

Appetites shrank food supplies, so the Kimball family sent Howard, their principal trading agent during the Iowa crossing, to Missouri on a purchasing trip. This was the first of five such trips he'd make, with little time in between each one.

On December 24 Howard and Daniel Davis, who also was a Kimball adoptee, prepared for the buying trip. Howard spent Christmas, a beautiful springlike day, with his family. Perhaps he and Tamson attended "a little party" at Father Kimball's, "which passed off finely under the direction of O. P. Rockwell."[24] Two days later Howard and Davis started for Missouri, each driving a wagon. Our account of their trip is based on Davis's diary, unless otherwise documented.[25]

They crossed the Missouri River. In Howard's wagon he transported a Brother Dayton and two ladies to Council Point. Between there and St. Joseph, Howard and Davis would cross a number of creeks and small rivers that flowed into the Missouri. Howard had been on that route three times before: once in June on a trade mission, again in September heading for Fort Leavenworth, and then just five weeks before while returning from the Battalion assignment. Familiar with the roads, he also knew Mormons living along the way.

When they camped near the Keg Creek crossing, Howard and Davis made a pledge to one another. "Brother Howard and I agreed to go on a temperance trip," Davis wrote, "and not drink any strong drink until we did return to camp." A few days later, they "joined in prayer and we agreed to unite in prayer morning and evening when convenient in our absence." After arriving in St. Joseph, Howard and Davis stayed with Church members Jacob and Mrs. Peart, whom Howard had last seen six weeks before. Howard visited stores and priced beans, sugar, and coffee, and he bought flour and meat and other items. He and Davis "got Sister Peart to cook us some victuals."

Daniel Davis, Historical Marker, Davis County, Utah

Awakening to a new year, 1847, on January 1, Howard and Davis faced cold and snow. They didn't do much by way of trading. They bought soap and arranged to buy one hundred pounds of saleratus (baking soda) and three sacks of salt at $2.50 per sack. On January 2 they left the Pearts at noon to start for home, through three-inch deep snow. Howard and Davis traveled for five miles, then stopped and bought some honey and butter. The next day they purchased almost ten pounds of butter from a Brother Lee. They reached Savannah, and at Tootle's store bought 24.5 bushels of wheat. They picked up other goods they'd selected a few days earlier, then resumed their journey. Howard went ahead and bought items from a Mr. Croton. Davis's wagon, heavily

St. Joseph, Missouri, *engraving, courtesy Missouri History Museum, St. Louis*

loaded, couldn't keep up with Howard's. "I got stuck," Davis said, "and had to get help." He overtook Howard after dark.

On January 5, they crossed the Nodaway on Lackey's ferry. That evening snow and cold wind blew in from the north. When Howard checked the next morning, he found one of his mules frozen to death. He and Davis didn't travel that day or the next because "it was so cold." They tried to "hire a horse to go home but did not succeed." Back at Winter Quarters, meanwhile, his family experienced "the coldest and most severe" weather of the season. "We could chop wood at the door scarcely 5 minutes without freezing," Horace Whitney said.[26]

On January 12, Howard and Davis reached the Missouri River ferry site, but were unable to cross their teams and wagons on the ice. They arrived at Heber C. Kimball's at sundown and "found our friends all well through the goodness and mercy of our God." Their trip, marked with rain, mud, snow, and intense cold, had taken them eighteen days.

From Smith and Donnell merchants in St. Joseph, M. Tootle & Company in Savannah, and other sellers, Howard and Davis had purchased more than $130 worth of commodities. They brought home 75 pounds of soap, 2 barrels of sugar, 12 dozen buttons, 6 bolts of cloth, 1 sack of coffee, 5 pounds of pepper, 24 bushels of wheat, 2 blue blankets, a half bushel of onions, 21.5 pounds of tobacco, 21 gallons of honey, a barrel, and other items.[27] Tobacco served as a gift or barter item when dealing with Indians.[28]

The next day Howard unpacked and spent time with his family. Horace Whitney noted that "this evening had quite a convivial party at Bro. Smithies" consisting of all the male members of the Kimball family. Nine attended, including Horace, William Kimball, and probably Howard. Father Kimball came for about an hour.[29]

A Revelation Directing the Move West

On January 14, 1847, Brigham Young presented to the Twelve an instruction revealed to him called "the Word and Will of the Lord concerning the Camp of Israel in their journeyings to the West." The Twelve shared it with priesthood members the next Sunday. It placed the trek under the Twelve's direction, not the Council of Fifty's, and required Saints to covenant to keep the commandments and statutes of the Lord. It gave practical direction for organizing companies and for caring for the poor, widows, orphans, and Battalion families. This revelation was "the first one that has been penned since Joseph was killed," Elder Kimball noted.[30] Based on that document, the Twelve fine-tuned plans for an initial pioneer company to head west in April and they instructed how Winter Quarters should be managed during the pioneers' absence.[31]

That same day, Elder Kimball, probably to explain the document, met with Howard, Davis, Horace Whitney, and William Kimball "and gave us some instructions," Davis said, "concerning our present and future good."[32] Saints in Winter Quarters and nearby settlements were invigorated by the new guidelines, and helped the pioneer company get staffed and supplied.

Trading Trips Two, Three, Four, and Five

Elder Kimball, knowing he'd leave in the pioneer company, made efforts to organize his large family and leave it as well supplied as possible while he was gone. But, at night on January 18, a house fire slightly interrupted his efforts. About 10:00 p.m. fire was discovered under the hearth in Father Kimball's room. Just in time, men removed contents from a chest near the fireplace. Horace Whitney said that "we took down the better part of the chimney in order to get at the fire, which we put out and rebuilt the chimney." Daniel Davis noted that "Father and I, Howard, Horace, Smithies, and King was up til four in the morning" dealing with the fire.[33]

Trip Two. The next day, January 19, Howard started on his second trading mission into Missouri. He had been home for one week. He should have felt dog-tired from the night-time fire struggle. George Rhodes accompanied him this time. Howard and Rhodes drove two wagons using two horses and four mules. Two other men with a team went along. This trip lasted eleven days. Howard and Rhodes returned on January 30. Accompanying them was Merritt Rockwell, another young man in the Kimball circle.[34] They pulled into Winter Quarters and deposited two barrels of flour, 24 bushels of meal, a sack of salt, twenty plugs of tobacco, ten pounds of butter, and corn.[35]

Trip Three. After three days at home, Howard and Rhodes left on February 3 on another buying trip. This one required twelve days. They and Merritt Rockwell returned on February 15 with ten barrels of flour, 24 bushels of ground corn, 2.5 bushels of potatoes, 42 pounds of tobacco, one gross of matches, two kegs of lard, a set of spinning wheel irons, and four papers of tacks.[36]

On the Road Again,
Library of Congress Prints and Photographs Division

Trip Four. Howard once again had but three days at home, barely time to change clothes and visit with his family. He set off on February 18 with George Rhodes. The next day a snowstorm and north winds attacked the bluffs region. Much snow fell that week. On February 26, Winter Quarters folks enjoyed "first rate sleighing."[37] While Howard was gone, both Elders Young and Kimball concentrated on getting the pioneer company organized to head west in April. In a February 17 letter, Elder Kimball told about the two grand divisions, one the Camp of Israel wagon company and the other for Winter Quarters, both with subdivisions into units of fifties and tens, all under the direction of the Twelve. "We have now already organized somewhere between twelve and fifteen hundred men," he said.[38]

After an eighteen-day absence, Howard and George Rhodes returned on March 6. Jacob Frazier, another of Kimball's adopted sons, was with them.[39]

Trip Five. The Kimball family network still needed food for those leaving in a month, including Howard, and for those like Tamson and the children who would stay home. So on March 9, again with but three days rest, Howard headed back to

Missouri. Weather then was "tolerable fair." Merritt Rockwell and Jacob Frazier went with him. This trip was shorter, requiring only eight days. The men returned on March 17 with a load of corn.[40]

Sickness and Death at Winter Quarters

Stories are plentiful about sickness and death at Winter Quarters during its first nine months, from August through April. An estimated four hundred died. Infants and children suffered the most. Dietary deficiencies caused most of the deaths. Scurvy, also called "black-leg" or "black-canker," took an ominous toll.[41] On March 18 Horace Whitney wrote:

> There is a disease, called by the folks here, the 'black-leg,' getting quite prevalent in the camp. It commences with a sharp pain in the ancles—swells, and finally, the leg gets almost black, and in many cases it proves fatal—There have a great many died, within the last month—It is caused, in great measure, by the want of vegetable food—and having to eat salt food.[42]

A sexton's partial list of burials up to May 1847 identified 286 of the deceased, but many burials did not get reported. Twenty-two of sixty-two babies that midwife Patty Sessions delivered died shortly afterwards. "Mormon women faced pregnancy and childbirth," historian Maureen Ursenbach Beecher observed, "knowing the chances of their child's not surviving infancy."[43] Among these women facing childbirth were both Tamson and Nancy, who at least by March knew they were pregnant.

Tamson and Domestic Life

Ransom said that the Egans' "log hut was neatly arranged and papered and hung with pictures and otherwise decorated" by Tamson.[44] Possibly the interior resembled that of another resident whose cabin furniture "consists of sacks, barrels, chests, trunks and two wood bedsteads with curtains from eaves to floor; my chest for a table."[45] To manage the Egan household, Tamson developed a routine of chores in cramped space. Mary Haskin Parker Richards, a friend of Tamson, described household tasks tackled by women in Winter Quarters.[46] Almost daily, Mary fixed breakfast, dinner, and supper. She baked bread once or twice a week. She also made pies, sweet cakes, and corn bread, and stewed apples. Indoor cooking made the cabin smoky. After the meals, washing dishes and pots was a time consuming task, given a lack of readily available water. During a harsh January cold spell, Mary once "had only wood enough to make one fire," so she fixed breakfast and then bundled up for the rest of the day. Perhaps Tamson, like Mary, spent time sewing, knitting, or braiding. Women washed the wooden cabin floors or swept the carpet remnants that covered dirt floors. They washed clothes about once a week. Some laundered in the Missouri River, others just outside the cabin or tent. Clothes hung outside to dry sometimes froze.[47]

Tamson was part of a female network in which women associated together and provided mutual support and assistance. The "ritual of visiting" mattered.[48] As an example, while Howard was absent between February 3 and 15, Tamson interacted with women friends and neighbors. She shared her home a few times with young Mary Richards, whose husband was on a mission in England. Mary's journal indicates she "slept the night with Sister Egan" on February 8, 9, 10, and 12.[49]

Mary Haskin Parker Richards, courtesy Maurine Ward

Polygamous families had to resolve the question of shared domiciles. Where second wife Nancy Redden Egan lived during this period is uncertain. Perhaps she lodged with some Redden family members. Her brother Jackson Redden, like Howard, was part of the Kimball team of male workers although not an adoptee. Sister wives proved to be good sources of companionship and support in some households, particularly when the husband was absent. Lacking evidence otherwise, we assume Tamson and Nancy were friends.[50]

Absences at a Cost

Winter Quarters proved to be sickly and deadly for its poorly housed and malnourished residents. But sickness and death would have been far more pervasive had not Howard and dozens of other men like him made strenuous trading and buying trips that brought in badly needed food and supplies. What those men did and endured is borderline heroic. Howard spent a total of sixty-seven days, during winter, on five purchasing trips. He camped out nearly every night. He carried money he needed to defend. He looked for and selected places where he could buy goods. He priced items, negotiated, made purchases, loaded those into his wagons, and did his best to protect his cargoes from rain, snow, and mud. Road conditions made driving difficult at times. Bumps and jarrings made him adjust his loads. He stayed prepared to guard his cargo day and night from robbers and animal predators.

These trips challenged him physically, mentally, and emotionally, if not spiritually. He dealt with loneliness. He wondered constantly how his family members were while he was away. He knew he was vulnerable to accidents, health setbacks, or robbers, such that he might not make it back home again. He knew full well that many at Winter Quarters depended on him.

The flip side to his valiant errands is that his absences placed difficult physical and emotional demands on Tamson and Nancy. And what about the Egan boys, who by mid-March were ages seven and five? His absences made the wives' and children's days and nights, already difficult, more so. True, Howard served his Church and his people, but he was an absentee husband and father. The calendar shows there were 199 days between Howard's departure on the Battalion errand on August 30 and when he returned from his last buying trip on March 17. He was away 156 of those 199 days, or nearly 80 percent of the time. Put another way, in eight months he had spent but six weeks at home.

His periods of absenteeism didn't stop; they increased. Three weeks after his last buying trip, he left early in April with the 1847 Pioneer Company. This time he would be gone from Tamson, Ransom, Erastus, and Nancy for eight straight months. And, compounding the situation for Tamson and Nancy, they were both four months pregnant when he left and would give birth in August, long before he'd return home again. ◆

~ 10 ~

Captain of Ten in the 1847 Pioneer Company

Men in Brigham Young's 1847 Mormon Pioneer Company, including Howard, comprise an honor roll in Mormon history. They are listed on historical monuments and plaques. Volumes containing all of their life sketches have been published. Their trek is celebrated in books, articles, songs, pageants, plays, paintings, parades, wagon train reenactments, movies, TV documentaries, and sermons, by plaques and grave markers, and by descendants and ancestral organizations.[1] In Utah, the Twenty-fourth of July is a state holiday honoring that pioneer band. A U.S. commemorative postage stamp honors them, and the federal government has made the company's route a protected national historic trail. United States and western history textbooks tell about the event. Even Brigham Young's attributed phrase at journey's end, "This is the Place," appears in collections of famous quotations.

Along with the 1843 Marcus Whitman wagon train to Oregon and the 1846 Donner Party to California, their venture ranks as one of the three most important "crossing the plains" stories in the history of the American West. Not only did Captain Egan's labors help the venture succeed, but his diary is one of the best records we have of the historic trek.[2] The story told here and in the next chapter generously summarizes and quotes from his diary, such that quotations not otherwise documented are from his record.

When Was the Destination Selected?

The 1847 Mormon Pioneer Company's journey was more for confirmation than exploration. Brigham Young had seen in vision the new gathering place and knew he'd recognize it when he saw it.[3] Back in Kirtland, Ohio, in 1834, Joseph Smith had said that "this Church will fill North and South America—it will fill the world ... It will fill the Rocky Mountains."[4] Joseph Smith's "Rocky Mountain Prophecy" in 1842 was not news to hundreds who already had heard him proclaim the idea.[5] In an April 1844 conference, a participant, speaking at the Prophet's urging, emphasized the expected establishment of a Zion "at the tops of the mountains and all nations shall flow unto it," referencing Old Testament prophecies from the prophets Isaiah and Micah.[6] One month before leaving Nauvoo, President Young reminded his associates that it was essential that "the House of the Lord should be reared in the Tops of the Mountains" and the "Banner of liberty" wave over the valleys within. "I know where the spot is," he said.[7]

Letters from Winter Quarters placed the expected destination "west of the Rocky Mountains, and within the basin of the Great Salt Lake or Bear River Valley," or as "the country east of the Utah and Salt Lakes and West of the Rocky Mountains."[8] The pioneer company chose to follow trails that could best take them to the vicinity of the Great Salt Lake.

Creating the Select Company

Brigham Young, in accord with the January "Word and Will of the Lord" revelation, organized a handpicked company of 144 men. Three women and two children also went.[9] Harriet Young, wife of Brigham Young's brother Lorenzo, suffered from asthma and declared she'd die if she stayed at Winter Quarters. Lorenzo wouldn't go without her, so Brigham Young reluctantly let her go. Harriet insisted on taking two children with her. Because she couldn't travel as a lone woman in that party of men, one of Brigham Young's wives went along, Clara, who was Harriet's daughter by a previous marriage. Norwegian Ellen Sanders Kimball, a wife of Heber C. Kimball, also joined them.[10]

Seven of the twelve apostles went: Young, Kimball, Orson Pratt, George A. Smith, Willard Richards, Amasa Lyman, and Erastus Snow. Young served as company president and superior captain, and he directed that the recruits be organized under captains and sub-captains. The captains of roughly a hundred (meaning men, not wagons) were Stephen Markham and Albert P. Rockwood. The five captains of fifty were Tarlton Lewis, Addison Everett, James Case, John Pack, and Shadrack Roundy. President Young appointed Howard, or "Captain Egan" as he was known during the Iowa crossing, to be one of fourteen captains of ten.[11] In Captain Egan's ten were Elder Kimball and his wife Ellen, and Hosea Cushing, Edson Whipple, Robert Baird, Philo Johnson, William A. King, George V. Billings, Thomas P. Cloward, and good friend William Clayton. Howard, Cushing, King, and Billings were adopted sons of Kimball.

Compared with overland trail wagon companies before and after, this one was unique. It was led by the top leadership of a religious organization. It prepared a route with trails and bridges for the thousands that would follow. Its members intended to find a settlement site, then send back half of the group to take family members there. The twelve dozen men in the company felt commitments to the cause that enabled them to weather disagreements. Wallace Stegner termed them "picked men, well-supplied, well-armed, and well-led," who "lost more days to the Sabbath than to any hazards of the trail." "Their story is not a story of hardship," he added, "it is a story of organization, foresight, and discipline."[12]

From Winter Quarters to the Platte

By March 30, 1847, Elder Kimball had six wagons loaded and ready to start from Winter Quarters. He handpicked Howard and Howard's brother-in-law Jack Redden to be two of twelve men in his wagons.[13] Kimball's first four wagons rolled three miles to an assembly spot. On April 8 Howard left Winter Quarters, driving a wagon pulled by two horses. That day he started a diary, perhaps inspired by his diarist friends William Clayton, Horace K. Whitney, and Daniel Davis. On the first page he wrote, "Journal Kept by Howard Egan on the Pioneer Expedition to the westward, commencing Thursday, April the 8th 1847." His first entry reads: "We started for the west to find a home for the Latter-day Saints, and went out as far as the Haystacks, about three

Howard Egan's Diary, April 17 1847, Beinecke Library, Yale University

miles, where the rest of the boys had already preceded us. Brigham Young's camp was about four miles ahead." Written in ink, his entries show that he knew how to write, spell adequately, and express himself well, although his handwriting in the little book is small and cramped and often hard to read.

Howard's first serious travel day was Friday, April 9. The assembled wagon train moved ten miles. Some reached the dangerous Elkhorn River on Saturday and started ferrying wagons across. Howard drove there the next day. The men ferried the company's seventy-two wagons across, using a cottonwood log raft "drawn by cattle with ropes on either side." Disembarking, the wagons jostled down the shoreline a mile and camped. Near this location, about a year later, an Indian would shoot Howard through the wrist (see Chapter 13). Father Kimball told his company they should not hunt or fish that evening because the Sabbath "was a day set apart for the service of the Lord and not for trivial amusements."

On April 12, the wagons camped by the broad, shallow, sluggish Platte River. This river would be their companion and a water source for the next several weeks. Later, travelers joked the Platte was "a mile wide and an inch deep, too thin to plow, too thick to drink."[14] The river "much surprised me," Howard said, "it being larger than I had anticipated." Clayton said the river was about a half mile wide.[15] That evening, four men familiar with the route ahead rode forward to survey it. One was Jack Redden.[16]

Brigham Young's Pioneer Company was not finding its way in the wilderness. Rather, they followed rough trails that meandered along the north side of the Platte up to Fort John, also called Fort Laramie, in present-day Wyoming. This Platte River

Giving Chase to Buffaloes, *artist F.N. Wilson*

Road at first was an Indian trail, then a route used by fur trappers and traders, and had also served as an alternate trail by some Oregon-bound wagons.[17] The Mormons brought with them general maps of the north side route, and they "picked up trail savvy as they moved along."[18] Young's company improved the route. Subsequent Mormon wagon trains would wear it into even better shape, and gold seekers bound for California in and after 1849 would pack down the road so well that it seemed paved in places. Because Mormons used and improved that route the most, it became known as the "Mormon Trail."[19]

While encamped by the Platte for five days, men fixed wagons and the leaders revised travel procedures. Three blacksmiths fired up forges, set wagon tires, and shoed horses. Howard took his wagon box off its wheels and running gears so that wheelwright Charles Harper could install two new axeltrees.[20] Jack Redden and the other scouts returned. They reported the route ahead was "unfavorable" because of a low, flat bottom that was uncrossable in wet weather, and rain seemed imminent.

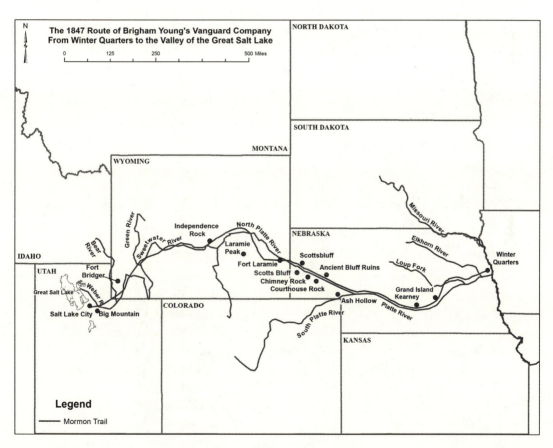

Howard's two horses "strayed away," so he borrowed Redden's horse, rode back towards the Elkhorn, and found one of them. Still a horse shy, he took William King with him early the next day to search. Ten miles from camp they found Howard's other horse. When some leaders, who had gone to Winter Quarters, returned, "we commenced to rig up our wagons," Howard said. President Young instructed the men to take care of their teams, to "cease all music, dancing and lightmindedness," and to pray. Hearing rumors that Indians might raid them, he promised that "if we were faithful and obeyed counsel the Lord would bless us and we should pass through safe."

241 Pounds of Bacon

On April 16, leaders created two divisions, which were hundreds with seventy-two men in each, led by Captains Rockwood and Markham. A system of night guards was spelled out, and a military regiment formed. "Each captain was to command his own ten in case of an attack from the Indians." Each ten camped together at night and formed one "mess" or eating group. "I thank the Lord for the privilege of being one of the number and enjoying the society of my father Heber," Howard noted.

During most of the trek the pioneers honored the Sabbath by not traveling. "Today, being the day set apart by Almighty God for His people to rest," Howard wrote on April 18, "we do not intend to travel." Light snow and cold winds cancelled church services. About sundown President Young gave the captains a set of rules and regulations, which Howard summarized:

> At eight o'clock and thirty minutes the bugle would sound and all should retire to their wagons and bow before the Lord and offer up their supplications before going to bed, and all fires should be put out; also the bugle sound at 5 o'clock in the morning when all would arise and offer up their thanks to the Lord, & at 7 oclock be ready to start. All spare hands were to walk by the off side of their waggons with their rifles loaded.

The rules also said the travelers must have their noon meals already cooked "so as not to detain the camp for cooking." At night, wagons would be drawn in a circle inside of which horses could be secured. Bedtime was 9:00 p.m. and all fires must be extinguished by then. The camp was "to travel in close order," and no one could leave camp without orders from his captain of ten. "Every man is to have his gun and pistol in perfect order," protect it from moisture, and keep it where "he can lay hold of it at a moment's warning."

Howard recorded that the Camp of Israel contained seventy-two wagons, which meant two men per wagon. It had sixty-six oxen, eighty-nine horses, fifty-two mules, nineteen cows, and a large leather boat hauled on wagon running gears. According to his inventory of his own ten, it consisted of six wagons pulled by horses, mules, and oxen. For food, flour was their staple, used to make pancakes and biscuits. They brought 1,228 pounds of flour, 125 pounds of sea-biscuits, 296 pounds of dried beans, and 241 pounds of bacon. They carried twenty-five pounds of dried beef, or beef jerky, and 825 pounds of beef that was not jerked—but in what state isn't said. They also hauled forty pounds of codfish, either dried or canned. One wagon carried the Kimballs' two-hundred pound bag of salt. Some of their nineteen cows provided them with milk.

For livestock feed, the six Kimball wagons carried 2,869 pounds of corn, ten bushels of oats, and 3.5 bushels of bran. For crops in their new homeland, they brought forty pounds of rape (an herb of the mustard family good for forage for sheep and hogs), fifty pounds of garden seeds, seventy-one pounds of unidentified seeds, and three hundred pounds of buckwheat. Their camping and traveling equipment consisted of one tent, two saddles, sixteen pounds of iron for horse and mule shoes and wagon wheel rims and parts, sixteen pounds of nails, six pair of double harnesses, one side of harness leather, and fifteen pounds of sole leather for shoes and boots. For ammunition they carried twenty pounds of lead and twenty-five pounds of powder. The tools they brought were two saws, six axes, five log chains, two plows, three hoes, and one spade, crowbar, scythe, and a tool chest. Howard's long list fails to note some essentials they must have brought, such as ropes, extra canvas, a hammer, matches, pots, pans, kettles, eating utensils, buckets, needles, thread, coffee, tea, sugar, saleratus or baking soda, bullet molds, and medicinal alcohol.

Along the "Platte River Road"

On April 19, the wagons traveled two abreast.[21] That afternoon four riders brought them mail from Winter Quarters. Howard received a letter from Jacob Frazier, a Kimball adopted son, and learned "that my family was all well, which I thank the Lord for." The next morning he fixed "a first-rate breakfast of our wild fowls," referring to a duck and two snipes Charles Harper shot the day before. Howard's entry didn't mention the impressive six-acre prairie dog village they rolled past.[22] During the day some fisherman using the leather boat and nets caught about two hundred carp and other fish. Howard cooked "a large buffalo fish" for supper.[23] President Young "came into our wagon," Howard noted, "and ate supper with Father Kimball." Pawnees had camped eight miles away, so a night patrol went on guard.

At 10:00 p.m. Howard wrote a letter to Tamson.[24] "My dear companion Tamson," it starts, "I never in my life had such feelings while away from home as I have on this trip." Yes, he "delighted to be in the society of my Father Heber where I can receive instruction and counsel from his lips." And yes, "My health has been very good since I left home." And yes, "we are all getting along first rate" because "the roads are very good and it is a beautiful country." But, "Tamson I feel sorrowful when I reflect upon your situation for I know your feeling when I am away from you." He was grateful that Heber C. Kimball's wife, not named but probably Vilate, was being "a kind and generous hearted mother" to her. He counseled Tamson to be humble and prayerful, to put away vanity and lightmindedness, and to pray for him and their children. "We shall all see each others faces and enjoy each others society again," he assured. "Give my love to Nancy," he added, "and my mother [Mrs. Kimball] and William [Kimball] and all the family." An eastbound traveler took his letter to Winter Quarters.

Howard drove one of the mule-team wagons on April 21. That day the company encountered a large party of Pawnee Indians, then came to the Pawnee village. The Mormons offered gifts, but too few, which displeased the Indians. They told the wagon travelers they couldn't go forward. The pioneers ignored that ultimatum, but that night posted two large shifts of fifty guards each. Howard stood guard until 10:00 p.m. on a "bitter cold night."

Difficult Loup Fork River Crossing

The Loup Fork River flows into the Platte River and blocked their way. To cross it, the company had to find a fording place. On April 22 Howard said they traveled along the Loup Fork and "stopped at the old Missionary station that was vacated last summer." In June 1846 Sioux Indians had raided, sacked, and burned a Pawnee Indian village and the Presbyterian mission station nearby.[25] "There is quite a large farm fenced in and some very good buildings on it," Howard noted. President Young forbade anyone taking anything off of the premises.

Early on April 23 scouts looked for and found a fording spot four miles up river. Meanwhile, Howard said, "Sister Ellen [Kimball] and myself took the opportunity to wash [launder]."[26] The day was hot. About 3:00 p.m., Howard reached the ford. One empty wagon managed to cross, so Orson Pratt drove his partially unloaded wagon into the river. Halfway across it stuck, so "four or five of us waded out to his assistance," Howard said. "The water in some places was waist deep." Brigham Young off-loaded items from his wagon into the leather boat. "We took the valuable part of his load and put it on board." Then one of President Young's horses fell down, and "with difficulty we saved them," Howard said, meaning the team. "We loosened them from the wagon and hauled it over by hand." Two more wagons crossed, and then President Young terminated fording efforts until morning.

Howard went with Young and others up the river and camped. After dark, Young and the captains met "to council which was the best way to cross the river." They decided to build a raft to float goods across, so that the lightened, empty wagons could ford. They assigned Stephen Markham to find a better fording place "and stake it out, and drive all the loose cattle over" to pack down the river bottom sand. The next morning Howard went with Elder Kimball, Lorenzo Young, and George Woodard to look for a place for crossing, but failed. They returned to camp only to find that wagons had already started to cross there.

"We took half the load out of some of our wagons and doubled our teams and crossed without any difficulty," Howard said. "Brother Kimball marched in the water with the rest of us." By 4:00 p.m. all of the wagons had forded. They traveled three miles down the shoreline and camped by a small lake with "plenty of sunfish in it. Brother Clayton caught a mess for us and they were first-rate," said Howard. He cleaned and cooked them for supper.[27] "All hands were tired working, crossing the river," and Howard felt to "thank the Lord the morrow is a day of rest." That Captain Egan regularly cooked for his ten implies he had cooking skills they appreciated.

Into the High Plains Region

Early Monday morning, April 26, guards fired at Indians they discovered crawling toward the wagons. The Indians disappeared, so by 8:00 the camp started. By fording the Loup Fork where they did, the pioneers had no trail to follow, so the scouts picked out places the wagons could navigate. They headed southward, and rejoined the Platte River on April 28, ending their Loup Fork detour. For the next five weeks they would travel up "the endless Platte Valley," gradually leaving the prairies and entering the high plains.[28]

By then they had crossed the ninety-eighth meridian west, the line where the High Plains begin and extend west to the Rocky Mountains. This region then was termed the "Great Desert" or "Great American Desert."[29] For westbound travelers, prairie grasses gave way to short, curled "buffalo grass." This became buffalo country. Semi-arid, the region lacked trees. Lips chapped and wood shrank and cracked. Travelers crossed fewer streams and found little firewood. They encountered strong winds.

On April's last day, the Camp of Israel traveled sixteen miles despite winds that blew "tremendously strong from the north and very cold." Because he'd been a sailor, Howard paid attention to wind. His diary during April had mentioned wind from the west, high winds, wind was north, wind blew up from the north, wind northwest, high winds from the south, winds from the southwest, wind northeast, wind south, and wind southwest.[30]

Their campsite that evening lacked water and wood. But, being in buffalo country, "we picked up some dry buffalo dung, which made a very good fire," Howard wrote, "and we dug a well and found plenty of water." Buffalo dung, or "buffalo chips," were the flat, dried excrement of the buffalo, composed of grass "masticated and digested, and dried in the sun…They burn fiercely and cook quite as well as wood."[31] It required the equivalent of three baskets full of buffalo chips to cook a meal. For a fire pit, cooks dug a trench about six inches wide, ten inches deep, and two feet long, such that it had an air draft. One traveler said they lighted a wisp of dry grass and placed it at the bottom of the trench, then fed the flame with "finely pulverized dry chips, which readily ignited." Others used gunpowder as fire-starters. Cooks like Howard filled their "fireplace" with broken chips and rested the cooking utensils on small rocks placed around the trench. The fire gave off "intense heat…but little smoke and only slight odor."[32]

May 1 became buffalo day. The pioneers spotted three on the bluffs, and then a large herd up ahead. Only five or six men, including Howard, had seen buffalo before. Historian Stegner observed that buffalo were, for travelers, a "universal provider and basic resource, giver of meat and thread and glue and leather, food and house and fire."[33] Mormon hunters went to work. Not knowing techniques of buffalo hunting, at first they had only modest success, killing one bull, three cows, and six calves. Elder Kimball joined the chase, taking with him "Egan's fifteen shooter" rifle.[34] He shot one buffalo and helped kill two others. George Billings drove a Kimball wagon out with two other teams to retrieve buffalo meat for Egan's ten. "The meat is very sweet," Clayton wrote, "and as tender as veal."[35]

Next morning, a Sunday, Howard helped "cut up a quarter of a buffalo cow and salted it down." He'd had previous experience with buffalo while on the Battalion errand. Levi Jackman said that "our Camp this morning had the appearance of a meat market. all hands ware busy fixing there Beef for Cooking and drying. and making roaps of the hide."[36] By nightfall, Howard said, "all hands were employed putting up racks to dry the buffalo meat." This was a Sabbath emergency situation—not a case of an ox in the mire but of buffalo meat that would spoil if not cured, meat that the company badly needed.

On May 4, fearing an Indian attack, the captains ordered that the wagons roll four abreast. About noon, eastbound traders were spotted across the Platte. So, some fifty-four Mormons, Howard among them, wrote letters to send with the strangers to Winter Quarters. "I finished writing the letter I commenced some time since," Howard recorded, "and sent it to my wife." He told Tamson that his health was "pretty good," and "Thank the Lord we are now in buffalo country and have killed a number of them and we are now traveling 5 wagons abreast of each other as there is Indians all around us." He estimated he was 250 miles from Winter Quarters. He admitted he felt homesick:

Wagons Abreast, *Classified Photograph Collection,* Utah State Historical Society

    I want you should write to me the first chance you get you don't know how I feel when I see others read letters and know body thinks enough of me to write. Think of me separated from my family in the wilderness and how cheering one word would be to me but never mind Tamson thers no mallice at heart we will live and do better...Pray for me for I do not forget you night or morning.

    He ended the letter "Goodby my dear, think of me."[37]

    Even though Young's caravan could have traveled better on the more broken in Oregon Trail on the south side of the Platte, he opted to stay on the north side. They improved that trail so that future LDS emigrants could avoid extensive contact and campsite competition with non-Mormon travelers on the south side. That afternoon, during a halt to let their cattle graze, the men practiced military drills. Later, they camped by a creek on a prairie "burned nearly all over." On May 5 they made good progress until their scouts stopped them "in consequence of the prairie being on fire ahead." They had not been out of sight of buffalo all day, passing thousands of them.[38] "Last night the Lord sent a light shower," Howard's entry on May 6 reads, "which put the fire out and made it perfectly safe to travel." Where grass had not burned, the feed was still "very scarce, as the numerous herds of buffalo eat it close to the ground."

On May 8 the prairie on both sides of the river was "literally covered with buffalo." The pioneers camped by the river where "feed is very scarce and very little wood. We have to use buffalo chips to cook with." Howard made his ten a little happier the next day, Sunday, because he "went to the south end of the island and washed myself and changed my clothes." That's his first mention of taking a bath. The weather then turned unpleasant:

> The evening was cold, with strong wind from the northwest. President Young ate supper with H. C. Kimball. Ellen tried to bake some bread, but could not, the wind blew so. I have to sleep on a chest in the front part of the wagon, crossways, and cannot stretch myself nor keep the clothes over me. It was so cold tonight, and the wind blowing in the wagon, so I went to bed with Brothers King and Cushing.

Even though Howard arose at 4:00 the next day, that night's sleep proved to be "the best night's rest I have had for some time." Before daylight he "made a fire and put the bread down to bake, then went to Brother [Philo] Johnson's wagon to write up my journal, as I have not much time to do it during the day or evening. I have to catch most of the [writing] time after taking care of my horses." But, "when the weather gets warmer, I hope I shall be able to write some early in the mornings." He attributed his "not writing much" to having "so little time." He admitted he copied from Clayton's diary. "Brother Clayton has kindly let me have his journal to take minutes from until I can get time to keep up every day."

Measuring Distance

On May 10 the company left behind the last stands of trees and timber. They now were 316 miles from Winter Quarters. For the next twenty-one days they would fuel their campfires with driftwood, sticks, and buffalo chips.[39] Each ten took turns leading the train "so as to divide the chore of breaking the road."[40] For several days they'd had "to make a new road," Clayton said.[41] "Our Ten took the lead today," Howard recorded for May 11, "which brought my wagon first." That evening he "felt quite sick, having a very bad cold." The company had just passed the confluence of the South and North Platte rivers, near the present-day city of North Platte. They headed up the north side of the North Platte. On May 13 Howard felt better "and I thank the Lord for it."

Odometer with graduating cogs

To measure distances they traveled each day, William Clayton, still in Howard's ten, counted revolutions of a wheel with a rag tied to it. Needing a better system, he created an odometer.[42] In his May 14 writings, Howard paid tribute to Clayton for inventing a machine "to tell the distance we travel. It is simple yet is ingenious." This odometer, with its system of graduating cogs, is mentioned in most histories of the 1847 pioneers. Using Orson Pratt and William Clayton's ideas, experienced mechanic Appleton Harmon constructed it. "I have understood that Brother

Clayton, The Latter-day Saints' Emigration Guide

Harmon claims to be the inventor, too," Howard wrote, "which I know to be a positive falsehood. He, Brother Harmon, knew nothing about the first principles of it, neither did he know how to do the work only as Brother Clayton told him from time to time." Clayton attached the odometer to an axle on one of the Kimball wagons.[43] Each night he recorded how many miles the odometer had counted that day.

Clayton helped Howard to know, and sometimes record, the daily mileages and names of trail sites, based on the odometer readings and on explorer John C. Fremont's maps of the Platte valley. Clayton carefully measured and named sites and stopping places with the intent of writing a trail guidebook for travelers. His *The Latter-day Saints' Emigrants' Guide*, published the next year, became a standard reference book for trail emigrants.[44]

Up Along the North Platte River

May 15 was cloudy and cold with strong north winds. "I baked some bread and fried some antelope meat," cook Howard said, "made some coffee and had a very good breakfast, all cooked with wet buffalo chips," which "are not a very good substitute for wood."[45] Wagons that day zigzagged up and over sandy bluffs, buffeted by rain and wind. "My wagon being heavily loaded," Howard said, "Brother Kimball told me to take the mules Brother Johnson worked ahead of his cattle and put them before my horses." The next day, Sunday, Howard received a portion of a butchered buffalo for his ten. "This forenoon my time was principally occupied baking bread and drying beef." A bugle blast brought the brethren together for an afternoon meeting. Four men spoke. Howard summarized Elder Kimball's talk, then commented, "the Spirit of the Lord rested upon him and he spoke with power, which cheered my soul." Regarding his own diary, Howard added: "I have the pleasure this evening of writing by the light of a candle made by Brother Edson Whipple out of buffalo tallow, and it burns beautifully."

On May 17 the wagon train camped a half mile from the Platte. "Brother [George W.] Harris and myself went down to the river and brought up a keg of water," Howard noted. Hunters brought in more buffalo meat, which was divided equally among the companies. The next day, President Young barred more hunting because the camp had more meat on hand than they could use. He criticized "the spirit of the hunter" who killed animals for the love of killing.[46]

May 19 dawned cloudy, the ground wet from nighttime rains. Worrying about items left out in the rain, Howard went out to cover them, and instead found reason to praise his brother-in-law:

> I got up to put the harness under the wagons, H. C. Kimball's saddle and other things which would get damaged by rain, when I discovered Brother Jackson Redding, who was captain of the guard, going around with some of his men picking up the harness and other things and putting them under cover. Captain Redding is a faithful, praiseworthy man, and a man who works for the good of the camp.

Howard also lauded Elder Kimball: "Brother Kimball has rode so much ahead to look out the way for the camp he has almost broke himself down and is pretty near sick, but his ambition and the care he has for the camp keeps him up." Rains cut their progress to eight miles that day. On May 20 they moved about sixteen miles. Across the Platte they could see Ash Hollow, a favorite Oregon Trail campsite. "The day has been quite warm and some of our teams lagged a little," Howard wrote on May 21, "Brother Cushing drove my team this afternoon while I rode in Brother Kings wagon and drove some for him."

On Sunday, May 23, the company stayed in camp. That "very fine and pleasant morning," Clayton recorded, "Brother Egan commenced washing very early on the banks of the river. He kindly volunteered to wash my dirty clothing which I accepted as a favor."[47] This was payback, perhaps, for using Clayton's diary. At noon the campers had what Howard termed "a first-rate meeting." President Young "gave us some glorious instructions, which done my soul good." Howard's entry the next day mentions a visit that Sioux Indians paid to their camp:

> They all crossed the river on their ponies, some of them singing. They were thirty-five in number. Some of them were women. They were all well dressed and behaved themselves better than any Indians I have ever seen before. Four of their chiefs came down to the camp. Colonels Markham and [Henry G.] Sherwood showed them around the camp. They took some provisions to those who were encamped up the river, and gave the chiefs their supper at the camp. The brethren put up a tent for the head chief and his squaw to sleep in.

Landmarks

Howard began seeing picturesque bluffs that wind and rain had carved to appear like buildings, earning them names like Courthouse Rock and Jail Rock. By midday on May 26 the pioneers passed towering Chimney Rock, an imposing overland trail landmark on the south side of the Platte. Its narrow rock shaft rose straight up from a rounded base. Science-minded Orson Pratt estimated it to be 260 feet tall. "We had traveled forty-one and a half miles since it was first seen with the naked eye," Howard wrote, underscoring how the high plains' dry, clear atmosphere let people see farther

Chimney Rock, Frederick Piercy sketch,
Route from Liverpool to Great Salt Lake Valley

than was possible in lower elevations. The next day, traveling through what Clayton called "scenery truly delightful beyond imagination," they passed another formation called Scott's Bluff and by wind-carved rock facings that resembled buildings and towers. At Scott's Bluff, Pratt determined the North Platte River to be 792 yards wide.[48] When bad weather on May 28 made the company stay put, Howard and Luke Johnson took the leather boat upriver about three miles to search for firewood. They retrieved "tolerably plenty" of driftwood, which that night fed flickering Mormon cook fires.

Because behavior backslid, especially during evening hours, President Young received a revelation to call the company to repentance.[49] On May 29, a Saturday, while the pioneers camped where the Nebraska-Wyoming border is now, President Young held a meeting. He chastised the attenders for too much evening dancing and card playing, quarreling, crudeness, gambling, levity, loud laughter, yelling, put-downs, and profanity, and for unholy attitudes that permeated camp life. He found not enough praying and good reading. What bothered him most was that irreligious actions and attitudes came from baptized, covenanted men, not from outsiders. He feared such behavior could sink the entire western settlement effort, and he didn't want the fault to be his. His repentance call resonated. Camp behavior improved markedly. Howard wrote the next day that men conducted themselves peaceably and "seem to have profited by the instructions."

On May 31 a "good hard road" led them to the first timber, hence decent firewood, in three weeks. They now had been on the road for fifty-six days. On travel days they had averaged about twelve miles per day; fifty-six days meant they had spent exactly one-half of the 111 days it finally took them to reach their Great Salt Lake Valley destination. The first half of their trek across prairie and then plains had gone well. One day more, and they would reach another major milepost on the western trails, Fort Laramie—which would mark their entry point into a mountainous region with new types of terrain and vegetation that would pose new challenges for the men, the teams, and the livestock. ♦

~ 11 ~

Reaching the Great Salt Lake Valley

Sailors long at sea welcomed ports. That's the same excitement overland trail travelers felt when they reached Fort Laramie. For Howard and the Mormon caravan, Fort Laramie was the only trading post or even settlement they would see during the first half of their westward journey. The Camp of Israel stopped near the post on June 1, 1847. "We have come this far without accidents, except the loss of two horses stolen by the Indians, and two killed," Howard wrote. "The Lord has blessed and prospered us on our journey, and the camp enjoys better health than they did when they left Winter Quarters."[1] Fort Laramie offered them a limited but welcome resupply place and news about activity on the trails behind and before them.

Fort Laramie

While doing business in the vicinity of the fort, four matters attracted the Mormons' attention. First, the trading post. There, they bought some high-priced supplies. Howard was not among those who went into the fort. At the post some of the Mormon traders learned news about travel circumstances ahead, the Rocky Mountains, the Great Basin, and the Bear River Valley. Some of that information came from three men, recently returned from the Sweetwater River area. They said that snow there stood two feet deep. To this news Howard wrote, facetiously, "it is evident that we are early enough for the feed," meaning travelers hadn't yet been able to overgraze the area's spring vegetation. Fortunately, finding pigweeds near the fort helped the pioneers have some "greens," after suffering a constant lack of fresh vegetables.[2]

Second, to their surprise they found other Saints already at the fort. "Six wagons, which are a part of the Mississippi Company that wintered at Pueblo, are here," Howard wrote on June 1. The group had been waiting for two weeks for the pioneer company to arrive. Third, word came that six or seven hundred wagon companies from St. Joseph soon would overtake them. Rumor said that perhaps two thousand wagons

Fort Laramie, *artist William Henry Jackson,*
courtesy Perry Special Collections, Lee Library, BYU

altogether would be rolling toward Oregon and California that season.[3] That meant the Mormons could have company for the next three hundred miles or so.

Fourth, travelers could not easily travel along the North Platte's east side so they had to cross the river to the west side and travel on the Oregon Trail. Orson Pratt estimated the North Platte at that point was 108 yards wide. Frenchman James Bordeaux, in charge of the fort, offered to ferry the Mormons with a "very good flat boat" for eighteen dollars, or twenty-five cents a wagon, or to rent the boat for fifteen dollars. Brigham Young rented it.

On June 3 the big ferrying effort began. The first wagon crossed in fifteen minutes. An upriver wind made the crossing easier, Howard said. By 5:00 p.m. the Camp of Israel's First Division had crossed. John S. Higbee then supervised the Second Division's crossing, Howard's division, at the rate of one wagon every eleven minutes. By 7:00 p.m., rains stopped the ferrying, leaving fifteen wagons yet to cross. Strong arms finished the task the next day, June 4.

The Pueblo contingent joined the Second Division, adding to it nine men, five women, and three children.[4] Howard listed them by name in his diary. Most had the surnames Crow or Threlkill. The Pioneer Company now consisted of 161 souls, even after a handful rode back to assist other Saints coming from Pueblo. Livestock numbered some three hundred head. That afternoon, the wagons, to descend a steep hill, "had to lock our wheels for the first time for six weeks," Howard said.

On June 5 the caravan rumbled up a steep bluff where a rocky road "shakes our wagons very much." Midday, they stopped at a large, natural warm spring. Pulling up the steep bluffs west of today's Guernsey, Wyoming, their wagon wheels helped grind ruts still visible in the soft rock.[5] Sunday evening, June 6, the Mormons camped between two Missouri companies of seventeen and eleven wagons. The next day, with towering Laramie Peak visible in the far distance to their left, the Mormon company leap-frogged three Missouri wagon companies. Howard called his ten's location that night, which was along Horse Shoe Creek amid ash and cottonwood trees, the most pleasant campground since they left Winter Quarters.[6]

Because the Oregon Trail headed a bit inland from the North Platte, the wagon train left and didn't rejoin the river for four days. On June 10, Clayton fished in nearby Deer Creek and "caught twenty-four with a hook and line, that would weigh sixteen pounds," which, early the next morning, Howard cleaned and fried. "We had a first rate breakfast."

Dangerous Upper Platte Crossing

Sunday, June 13, the pioneers were camped near where Casper, Wyoming now is, within a mile of the "Upper Crossing" of the Platte. At a 9:00 a.m. meeting, Howard said, "some of the brethren freed their minds" by voicing complaints. This caused Elder Kimball to exhort them "above all things to avoid everything that would tend to a division." Captains of tens met and tried to figure out how to get their dozens of wagons across the swift, deep North Platte. Provisions could not cross in the wagons, which meant wagons must cross empty and horses must be swam across unhitched. The leadership decided to convey the wagons' provisions in the leather boat they'd been hauling, and then to ferry the empty wagons on rafts.

After the captains' meeting, Howard and five or six other mounted riders forced their horses to swim across the river. When on the north side, the men constructed a raft from "pine and fir rails."[7] Others went up a mountainside to cut poles. That very warm day felt like summer, and "the ground here is covered with crickets," Howard noticed.

This North Platte crossing cost Howard several days of hard work in, on, and along the dangerous, deep river, and impaired his health. He strained harder during those days than perhaps any other five days of the trek. He spent June 14 at a ferrying site, three miles upriver from today's Casper, where the North Platte was a hundred yards wide and fifteen feet deep. That morning, while the First Division floated provisions over in the leather boat, Howard and men in the Second Division tried to transport their provisions on a raft. But, because of the strong current, they quit after floating two loads across.

Trying another method, they stretched a rope across the river, no easy task, then lashed two wagons together, fastened the rope to them, and tried to pull the conjoined wagons across. But, when wheels struck sand on the far side, the strong current rolled the wagons, one over the other, "breaking the bows, and loosening the irons." Needing a better plan, they tied four wagons together in a square, with poles lashed to the perimeter, forming a ring or boom. As before, they tried to drag that cluster over. "They all got over safe" although one wagon turned on its side when a side pole broke.

They lacked enough poles and ropes to repeat that method, so, Howard said, "we thought we would try one wagon alone," floating it across aided by the rope, with a man riding in its upper side to serve as weight to keep it from turning over. "I volunteered to go across in it," Howard said, being a former sailor who knew how to swim.

> Soon after we pushed off, Brother [Andrew] Gibbons jumped in the river and caught hold of the end of the wagon. When we got out about the middle of the river, the wagon began to fill with water, and roll from one side to the other, and then turned over on the side. I got on the upper side and hung on for a short time, when it rolled over leaving me off. I saw that I was in danger of being caught in the wheels or the bows, and I swam off, but one of the wheels struck my leg and bruised it some. I struck out for the shore with my cap in one hand. The wagon rolled over a number of times and was hauled ashore. It received no damage, except the bows were broken.

Trial and error convinced these challenged men that their first plan, rafting one wagon at a time, was the safest way, even though, Howard said, "it is very slow, and will take three or four days." The men used cattle on the other side to pull the ropes attached to the raft. Strong winds blowing downstream, from the southwest, plus the strong current, caused the men to move the raft a mile upriver from the crossing site. They loaded one wagon at a time at that launching site. Rain, hail, and gale winds disrupted the afternoon efforts. The river rose. "After toiling all day nearly up to our armpits in the water, we got over eleven wagons in the afternoon, making twenty-three during the day," Howard reported.

The next day, June 15, men built two more rafts. Winds blowing downstream continued, making it "very hard work to cross with the rafts." Twenty wagons made it. That day, leaders decided that once the trek could resume they'd leave about ten men behind to build a boat and operate a ferry to earn money from non-Mormon wagon companies. That day marked Howard's thirty-second birthday.

Next morning, at Brother Kimball's request, Howard rounded up a wagon and six mules for a special venture. With this outfit, and another from the First Division, he and nineteen others went searching for logs to chop into canoes. They returned that night with two partly finished canoes, twenty-five feet long. On that cold and windy day, Howard suffered: "My health is not very good, having worked in the water for two days, and in the course of it I caught cold, and have pains in my bowels."

But, rather than rest on June 17, he worked. "We hauled our three wagons down to the river," Howard said. They unloaded Brother William King's wagon and took his cargo across in the leather boat. They floated part of Kimball's load "on the large raft, Brother [Hans C.] Hansen and myself pulling it over" using mules or horses. Shortly after noon, all of the Mormon wagons had been conveyed to the north shore. However, cold water and wind-driven currents prevented the men from swimming the horses across. "This after noon it grew cold so that over Coats was worn," Levi Jackman said.[8]

An Oregon company arrived, and the Mormons agreed to ferry them across if paid a dollar-fifty per wagon. "The brethren suffered much working in the water, for it is very cold," Howard said. Some men continued to carve out the cottonwood trunks for the needed canoes. Others spent the night ferrying wagons for non-Mormons. Next morning, Howard said, "we went across the river early, and swam our horses over." This completed their crossing of the North Platte.

The company, instead of resuming its trail journey, waited while teams finished the boat, to turn it into an income-producing ferry. Workmen placed cross planks from one canoe to the other, six feet apart, then fastened planks running lengthwise, and added a rudder and oars. That afternoon they successfully launched the ferry. It carried a common size wagon, still loaded. For helping non-Mormon wagons cross, LDS ferrymen were paid in provisions valued at four hundred dollars, which were shared among the tens. Howard said his "camp" received flour and meal sufficient to last them "about twenty-three days."

The Sweetwater, Independence Rock, and Devil's Gate

On June 19, trail travel resumed. They left the Platte River, which they had followed for six weeks and about six hundred miles, and headed westward for a three-day crossing of broken, barren, sagebrush-covered land that lacked streams and timber. These fifty miles were perhaps "the worst stretch of trail between the Missouri and the Salt Lake Valley."[9] "We have to use the sage roots for cooking," Howard wrote on June 20, "as it grows wild in abundance in this region." They crossed rough ridges and an avenue of high rocks, and passed minor streams, a spring at Willow Creek, poisonous water holes, and strange "saleratus lakes" encrusted with white bicarbonate of soda.[10] Some riders spotted a few buffalo. By noon on June 21 they descended down to the gentle, meandering Sweetwater River. "The water tastes good," Howard noted. This river now became their new life-giving, long-term travel companion, much like the Platte had been. "On the banks of the river there is plenty of good grass but destitute of wood," Clayton wrote, "The only chance for fuel appears to be the wild sage and other small shrubbery."¹¹ The landscape, with hills and ridges and masses of granite rock, destitute of vegetation, seemed to Howard to be "very wild and desolate as well as romantic."

Independence Rock, *artist William Henry Jackson, courtesy Perry Special Collections, Lee Library, BYU*

After resting, the travelers and teams moved a half mile along the Sweetwater to Independence Rock, another of the trail's prominent landmarks. Howard didn't say if he climbed up onto it, like so many travelers felt compelled to do. He called it a "barren mass of bare granite" measuring four hundred yards long, eighty wide and one hundred yards in "perpendicular height." Perhaps he saw the hundreds of names of overland travelers, male and female, painted on the rock. Wilford Woodruff said the names were written in red, black, and yellow paint.¹²

After the next mile, the wagon train crossed the Sweetwater "without difficulty." They camped close to a giant cut in towering rocks called Devil's Gate, another spectacular trail landmark. Howard explored this wonder:

> I went to view the Devil's Gate, and while ascending the rocks I fell in with some of the brethren, and we went up in company. When we arrived at the top of the rock we found it perpendicular. The river runs between two high rocky ridges, which were measured by Brother Pratt and found to be 399 feet 6.5 inches [tall] and about 200 yards long. The river has a channel of about three

rods in width through the pass, which increases its swiftness, and it dashes furiously against the huge fragments of rocks, which has fell from the mountains, and the roaring can be heard a long distance. It has truly a romantic appearance, and the view over the surrounding country is sublime.

Devil's Gate, *Frederick Piercy sketch,*
Route from Liverpool to the Great Salt Lake Valley

During June's final days, the pioneers traveled along and near the Sweetwater, crossing it several times. Often the road was sandy, the landscape barren. Hunters found antelope but no buffalo. The Mormons interacted with some Oregon-bound wagon parties, each group sometimes helping the other with repairs or blacksmithing. During one long day they traveled eighteen miles, another day twenty-five. One day some of the men chopped ice from a strange turf-covered ice spring. On June 26 campers awoke to find "every thing Covered with frost and Ice in the water pails," Jackman said. At their noon stop, "the Snow lay in heaps under the north side of the bluffs ... 5 or 6 ft deep," he said, with green grass close by it and "dandelions in full bloom." So were a few strawberries and gooseberries.[13]

Waters Flowing to the Pacific

The caravan ascended slowly the gently sloped South Pass, which topped at 7,412 feet above sea level.[14] This saddle, which is not steep, narrow, or very noticeable, provided travelers a not-too-difficult way to cross the spine of America, the Continental

Divide, the dividing ridge that separates the waters of the Atlantic and Pacific. The Camp of Israel crossed the pass on June 27. Appropriately, the first campsite on the west side of the pass bore the name "Pacific Springs." Howard recorded that "we have the satisfaction of seeing the currents run west instead of east." They now were in Oregon Territory, he observed, and no longer in "Indian Territories."

At Pacific Springs eleven eastbound riders met them, leading pack mules loaded with furs and skins. One in the group was mountain man Moses "Black" Harris. He was the first man with whom the pioneers talked who had been to the Great Salt Lake. He advised against the Bear River and Salt Lake valleys as settlement sites. Many in Young's company traded goods with Harris for buckskin and for buckskin shirts, pants, and jackets. "I tried to trade with him," Howard said, but found the prices too high.

June 27 was also the third anniversary of the murder of Joseph Smith. This caused some in the company to be reminded why they were in the middle of the wilderness and how important their mission was to find a safe haven for the homeless believers in Mormonism.[15]

On June 28 the Oregon Trail forked. They were 297 miles beyond Fort Laramie. The north fork was the Sublette Cutoff, opened in 1844, that headed for Oregon. Taking the south fork, they soon came to and forded the Little Sandy, a modest stream. Howard's health had been "very poor" for two days and he suffered "with a very severe headache, but feel a little better this evening. As I had not washed my clothing for some time, I was under the necessity of washing this evening, and did not get through until after dark." Many others were ill, too. That evening mountain man Jim Bridger and two others, bound for Fort Laramie, came into their camp. Bridger, who'd been a trapper and guide in the mountains for a quarter century, was the first white man to discover the Great Salt Lake, back in 1824–25.

Leaders questioned Bridger about their destination region, and the frontiersman gave them "very imperfect and irregular" information, said Clayton. Howard, after washing his clothes, went to Bridger's camp. "From his appearance and conversation," Howard observed, "I should not take him to be a man of truth." Bridger contradicted Harris's reports about the Bear River area, but Howard felt "he spoke not knowing about the place."

During the last day of June, a hot day, several men felt too ill to drive their teams. "The brethren are all taken alike, with violent pains in the head and back and a very hot fever," Howard commented; "Some think it is caused by using the salaratus that was picked up on the lakes." Possibly they suffered from Rocky Mountain Spotted Fever, transmitted by wood ticks. Whatever the disease, it produced pain in the head, back, joints, and bones, hot flashes, chills, and sometimes delirium.[16] For these sufferers, riding in jolting wagons felt like torture.[17]

The caravan reached the Green River, "about as wide as the Platte," in present southwestern Wyoming. Each division assigned men to construct a raft, which they finished after dark. At division-president Kimball's request, Howard baptized George Billings for his health, who was running a very high fever. "He got relief immediately," Howard noted. (Baptizing the sick was an LDS healing ordinance rather common at the time.)[18] That afternoon Elder Samuel Brannan arrived in camp from California. He was the leader of Saints who had sailed from New York aboard the ship *Brooklyn* to Yerba Buena—today's San Francisco. He reported the *Brooklyn* Saints' circumstances to President Young, and tried hard to persuade the Pioneer Company to go to the Pacific coast and settle there.

Fort Bridger in Mexican Territory

For three days, rafts ferried wagons across the Green River. On Sunday, July 4, a dozen Mormon Battalion men from their wintering post at Pueblo caught up with them. Possibly Howard had met some of them during his trip with the Battalion to Santa Fe. To formally welcome them, Brigham Young lined them up, spoke a few words, and then led his company in shouts of "Glory to God" and "hosannah."[19] From the new arrivals they learned that the rest of the Pueblo group, some 140 Battalion people, were eight days behind them.

Once across the Green, Wilford Woodruff rejoiced that they now were "in California," meaning Mexico.[20] The ferrying had harmed Howard. "My health is very poor, for I have taken cold from working in the water, which has brought on the mountain fever again. It is a distressing complaint, and I took a lobelia emetic this evening, and H. C. Kimball administered to me, which relieved me some." He spent a "very sick" night.

During the next two days the wagons crossed the Ham's Fork River once and the Black's Fork River three times, the last one at a location where beautiful blue and red flowers, wild flax, and wild currants grew abundantly.[21] On July 7 they passed Indian lodges, crossed a grassy, brook-riddled valley floor, and arrived at Fort Bridger, located some 397 miles from Fort Laramie and sitting at an elevation of almost seven thousand feet. They camped a half-mile beyond the post. Grass was "much higher at this place than we have generally seen it," Howard noted. The whole region "seems to be filled with rapid streams."

Jim Bridger and Louis Vasquez had built Fort Bridger in 1843. A trading post, it primarily served trappers, Indians, and Oregon-bound emigrants. Howard copied Clayton's descriptions of the fort:

> Bridger's Fort is composed of two log houses, about forty feet long each, and joined by a pen for horses, about ten feet high, and constructed by placing poles upright in the ground close together. There are several Indian lodges close

by, and a full crop of young children, playing around the doors. The Indians are said to be the Snake tribe.

On July 8, Brother Kimball sent Howard, one of his best traders, to the fort. "I traded off two rifles, one belonging to Brother [Edson] Whipple and one to Brother G. Billings, for nineteen buck skins and three elk skins and some other articles for making moccasins."

The Hasting's Road and Donner Trail

At Fort Bridger the Mormon wagon train left the Oregon Trail, which at that point turned northward towards Fort Hall (near present-day Pocatello, Idaho). After breaking camp on July 9, a warm and dusty day, the dozens of trail-worn and dusty wagons journeyed thirteen miles on a rough track called the Hastings Road, which was not on their maps. This was the trail blazed and taken by the Donner Party the year before. "This route is but dimly seen, as only a few wagons passed over it last season," Orson Pratt noted.[22] The next day, Howard said, they "began to ascend the dividing ridge between the waters of the Colorado [River] and the great Basin," up a mountain "very high, and the ascent is very steep." At 7,700 feet, the Bear River Divide was 615 feet higher than South Pass.[23] Dealing with rugged mountains made some in the company wonder if Saints could survive in such a wilderness.[24]

So Great a Cause, *Clark Kelley Price, used with permission from the artist*

That evening the pioneers camped south of where Evanston, Wyoming now is. A mountaineer named Miles Goodyear visited them. He told them about his small trading post, Fort Buenaventura, near the Great Salt Lake, where the city of Ogden is now. Next morning, Porter Rockwell and others went with Mr. Goodyear "to look out the road. After dark the brethren were called together to decide which road they would take, as there are two roads. They decided to take the right hand road."

On July 12, the wagons crossed the Bear River, "a very rapid stream about six rods wide and two feet deep," and rolled by "The Needles." This impressive upshoot of towering tapioca-textured rocks is on the modern-day Utah-Wyoming border. By then Brigham Young was too ill to go on. So, while the caravan rolled ahead another seven miles and camped, eight wagons, including Howard's, stayed behind with sickly President Young. The next day, Elder Kimball and Howard rode ahead to communicate with the main group. Kimball, as the second in command of the entire train, ordered Orson Pratt to form an advance party of twenty-three wagons and forty-two men to "hunt out the road," meaning the Donner Trail. Jack Redden joined that advance group. Kimball and Howard then returned to Young's group. The Camp of Israel now had three components: an advance group that scouted and fixed the trail, the main body, and the rear contingent with Brigham Young and others who were sick.

The sick group spent a wait-in-camp day on July 14. Howard hiked with Lorenzo Dow Young and Apostles Kimball and Benson "on the top of a high mountain," meaning up into "The Needles." There, they "offered our prayers to the Almighty God in behalf of the sick and for our dear families." The next day, with pale and emaciated Brigham Young riding more comfortably in Wilford Woodruff's carriage, the group moved ahead, passed Cache Cave, entered Echo Canyon, and rejoined the main company.[25]

Today, Echo Canyon's floor contains transcontinental railroad tracks and highway I-80, but back then the canyon's tight floor, winding river, and thick brush made wagon travel awful. The company traveled down the canyon on July 16, crossing the Weber River several times and moving through willow thickets and across small hills. "We had a bad road for the sick to travel on," Wilford Woodruff wrote, "and Brother Brigham was worn out and worse at night."[26] Currant and elderberry bushes and flowers grew in profusion in the canyon. "The mountains seem to increase in height," Clayton said, "and come so near together as to barely leave room for a crooked road...It seems strange that a road could ever have been made through." When Howard looked upward, he saw red cliffs "towering some hundreds of feet above our heads." He heard echoes. "The rattling of wagons resembles carpenters hammering at boards inside the highest rocks," Clayton noted. "A rifle shot resembles a sharp crack of thunder and echoes back and for some time."[27] Thus the canyon's name.

On July 17, after exiting Echo Canyon and while camped by the Weber River, near where the town of Henefer is today, Howard and eight others hiked to the top of a very high mountain. They dressed in temple clothes and prayed for President Young and others who were sick. After prayers "they reverted to little boys" and rolled large rocks off the mountain, watching them fall and smash into pieces below. That evening, Howard went ahead with Elder Kimball and George A. Smith to explore, returning long after dark.[28] The encampment devoted Sunday, July 18, to resting, worship, and prayers. Bishops broke bread and administered the sacrament. Elder Kimball and others preached, which "done my soul good," Howard said.

On Monday morning, forty-one wagons in the main party moved southward, following Pratt's advance group's improved trail, while fifteen wagons stayed behind with President Young. However, Elders Kimball, Woodruff, and George A. Smith, along with Howard, rode ahead and checked on the main group, then returned.[29]

The Great Salt Lake Valley at Last

"President Young's health continues to improve, and it was thought best to travel in the cool of the morning, so we started at 5:30." So begins Howard's diary notation for July 20. Meanwhile, Pratt's advance company labored hard, clearing the Donner track of thick willows, rocks, and brush. They passed over Hogsback Summit and moved downhill to what Pratt called Canyon Creek, about where East Canyon Reservoir now is, and past two canyons leading toward and up Big Mountain. The main company, led by Willard Richards and George A. Smith, moved a day behind Pratt's group. Young's group, with Howard, lagged behind.

Brigham Young sent instructions ahead to the Pratt group to "bear toward the region of the Salt Lake" and there select a camp "regardless of a future location." Because of the lateness of the season, there was extreme need to find a tillable spot and begin planting immediately.[30] Accordingly, Pratt's party wended down into the Great Salt Lake Valley, explored it, and then, on July 22, selected a place to camp and plant.

Meanwhile, Howard's rear group moved into present-day's East Canyon on July 20, halted the next day, and then on July 22 proceeded ahead. During the next day they ascended the narrow, rough, rocky, brushy, wooded, steep ravine that leads to "the summit," meaning a saddle pass near the top of Big Mountain. That crest is about 7,250 feet above sea level.[31] President Young later said that while on the summit he directed Elder Woodruff to turn the carriage half way round "so I could view a portion of the Salt Lake Valley." At first gaze the "Spirit of Light rested on me and hovered over the valley, and I felt that there the Saints would find protection and safety."[32]

The final thirty-five miles down the steep western side of Big Mountain, up and then over Little Mountain, and down Emigration Canyon "were by far the most difficult of the journey," one historian explained:

> At times the groves of aspen, poplar, willow, shrub oak, and balsam were so thick there was 'scarce room' to pass through. And where the timber had been cleared, the path was so cluttered with stumps that it kept every teamster busy clearing them away. Boulders loomed everywhere out of the dense brush … their wagons descended 4,000 feet in two days.[33]

After crossing Big Mountain, Howard's rear company had to "chain both wheels" to slow their wagons' descents. During their July 23 afternoon stop at Birch Springs, they received word that both the advance and the main companies were in the Great Salt Lake Valley and found the valley soil to be "very rich and fertile." Howard's group with Brigham Young ended the day down near the mouth of Emigration Canyon. They made their final trail encampment. "The day has been the hottest we have experienced since we left Winter Quarters," Howard noted, "there was not a breath of air in the ravine, and the dust was almost suffocating."

He started their final day, July 24, by helping search for missing horses. Then, after he returned to the wagons, he and Horace Whitney rode ahead. Howard's diary entry that day reads:

> The road was rough and uneven, winding along a narrow ravine, crossing the small stream, which we last encamped on, about fifteen or twenty times. We then left the ravine and turned to the right and ascended a very steep pitch [near where "This Is the Place Monument" now stands], where we beheld the great valley of the Salt Lake spreading out before us.

This overlook is the same place where, Wilford Woodruff later recalled, President Young arose from his carriage bed and surveyed the valley and "while gazing on the scene before us he was enwrapped in vision for several minutes. He had seen the valley before in vision, and upon that occasion he saw the future glory of Zion and of Israel, as

Erastus Snow and Orson Pratt,
This is the Place Monument,
This is the Place Heritage Park

they would be, planted in the valleys of these mountains. When the vision had passed, he said, 'It is enough. This is the right place. Drive on.'"[34] Historians have long questioned if Young's statement atop Big Mountain and this one are both about the same experience, with Young or Woodruff mixing up where it actually happened. Perhaps they were two experiences, perhaps one.[35]

Howard's Reaction to the Valley

After Howard's eyes had scanned from that prominence the vast Great Salt Lake Valley, his mind and soul contemplated what it promised. He wrote on July 24:

> My heart felt truly glad, and I rejoiced at having the privilege of beholding this extensive and beautiful valley that may yet become a home for the Saints. From this point we could see the blue waters of the Salt Lake. By ascending one of the ridges at the mouth of this canyon, the view over the valley is at once pleasing and interesting.

He saw potential in the desert-like landscape. "Throughout the whole extent of the valley can be seen very many green patches of rich looking grass, which no doubt lays on the banks of creeks and streams."[36]

By noon Young's cluster of the rear caught up with the others, which had stopped about where the Salt Lake City and County Building now stands at Fourth South and State Street. Howard saw men plowing and planting potatoes, and others damming a creek soon to be named City Creek. Looking at the snow-capped mountains surrounding him, Howard's military mind decided that "this is the most safe and secure place the Saints could possibly locate themselves in. Nature has fortified this place on all sides, with only a few narrow passes, which could be made impregnable without much difficulty." He felt that "the saints have reason to rejoice and thank the Lord for this goodly land unpopulated by the Gentiles." Those words sound like a benediction for the pioneers' long 111-day journey west and an invocation for the new life Howard and the Saints would create in that isolated wilderness.

The travel-worn pioneer company had done its job. They had found a new location where the Saints could gather.[37] They were outside of the United States, in a section of Mexican Territory then called California that Mexican authorities never visited. They knew, because vast numbers of people from Winter Quarters already had headed onto the trail and could reach that spot within a few weeks, that it was urgent to set up farms and a settlement. Summer shadows and heat, if not a calendar, warned them they had arrived late in the planting season. Therefore, among the first items they pulled from their wagons were plows, shovels, and seeds. ◆

~ 12 ~

Starting a Settlement and Retracing the Trail

After such a long journey, six dozen well-worn wagons and thirteen dozen trail-weary souls deserved a rest. They got it, but only one Sabbath day's worth. Then, like a construction crew today arriving at a new town site, they started building a settlement for thousands soon to arrive. That meant roads, housing, fences, orchards, and farms. The desolate, dusty, cricket-infested floor of the Great Salt Lake Valley invited serious upgrades. Howard's insightful diary records information about the pioneers' first weeks of labor and his activities through September.

Their makeshift camps indelibly stamped into history two important beginnings. First, the tents and parked wagons marked the terminus of the Mormon Trail, defining its entire length. For the next two decades that trail would serve as a national highway for thousands going to Utah and California. Second, the camps marked the start of what became a major metropolis, Salt Lake City, the first of hundreds of Mormon settlements in the intermountain west and beyond.

A Single and Welcome Day of Rest

On Sunday morning, July 25, a bugle blast at 10:00 a.m. called the campers to a meeting. There, Elders Kimball, George A. Smith, and Ezra T. Benson spoke, "mostly expressing their feeling of gratification for the prospects of this country, each being highly satisfied with the soil."[1] Afterwards, Elder Kimball handed Howard a list of fourteen men to invite to a nearby willow grove. Howard kept minutes of that 1:00 p.m. meeting. "Most of you here present have been adopted into my family," the apostle told the group, "and your interest is my interest." He asked them "to be prudent and take care of your horses and cattle, and everything entrusted to your care." He and Brigham Young planned to ride out the next day to find a better settlement site "if, indeed, such can be found." He instructed the men to plant all the seeds they thought could mature, particularly buckwheat, peach stones, apple seeds, turnips, and cabbage, and he assigned four men to make buckskin clothing, shoes, and hats "as soon as possible." He wanted all to work together and "banish all peevishness from among your midst." Then, ending the hour-long meeting, he praised "his boys" for being faithful to their duties during the trek west.

Horace K. Whitney recorded bits of Kimball's counsel Howard didn't. Kimball asked that the men build an enclosure for night use for cattle and horses "for there are plenty of Indians in the vicinity." He urged them to keep the Sabbath day holy "whether others do or not," and to hunt, fish, or explore on a weekday and not on the Lord's day. Be willing to work, he urged, whether in a family or a church capacity. "Remember me and my family in your prayers," Kimball requested.[2]

Laying Out a Settlement

Monday morning, July 26, a bugle call announced the entire group of campers' first full work day in their wilderness setting. "We put up our tent this morning," Howard wrote, to shade the men doing work on clothes and shoes. Others plowed, worked on the road coming into the valley, and, in nearby canyons, cut trees for logs. A few did exploring. The valley, Howard said, had high mountains on its east, many with "white on the tops and crevices with snow." A range to the west meant the valley spanned twenty-five to thirty miles. To the northwest, the Great Salt Lake seemed to him to be about thirty miles across.[3]

That day Brigham Young, although weak from his illness, insisted that he go to the top of a knob-shaped prominence at the valley's north end. According to Apostle George A. Smith, Brigham Young had a vision in Nauvoo after Joseph Smith's death in which Joseph showed him a mountain on which stood a flag, an ensign. "Build under the point where the colors fall," Joseph said, "and you will prosper and have peace."[4] Young understood he was to lead the Church members west and that the peak he saw in vision would be the sign they had reached their appointed destination. Based on that forecast, a party consisting of Brigham Young, Heber C. Kimball, Willard Richards, Ezra T. Benson, George A. Smith, Wilford

Ensign Peak

Woodruff, Albert Carrington, William Clayton, Lorenzo Dow Young, and perhaps Parley P. Pratt climbed to the top. They concluded the hill was "a good place to raise an ensign" and named it Ensign Peak or Hill.[5] From its summit they used Elder Kimball's spyglass to survey the region, and, Howard heard later that day, "they appeared delighted with the view of the surrounding country." Young identified down below them a location where the temple should be built. Folklore to the contrary, the group didn't raise "an ensign" to the nations, and didn't fly an American flag or any flag. Rather, it appears that they merely waved, symbolically, a large yellow bandana from the summit.[6]

On July 27, Howard's first assignment was to move three Kimball wagons northwest for three-quarters of a mile. That's where Brigham Young's wagons were going, on the banks of what soon was named City Creek. Howard helped haul the Kimball main tent there as well as a wagon for Elder Benson. That day Elder Kimball kept an ox team and a four-mule team plowing "and is going to start another four mule Team." For the general encampment, Howard observed, "there are five prairie teams kept constantly plowing and three teams harrowing."

Jackson Redden/Redding

Horace Whitney presented Howard with a new diary book on July 27. Howard's first entry in it is dated July 28. It says that he and Jack Redden harnessed a mule and broke him to the plow. Next, they hauled poles with which to frame a bowery to shade the Kimball wagons. That afternoon, Young designated the site for a temple block, located "between the forks of City Creek." Howard, the ex-sailor who knew salt water well, was intrigued by Brigham Young's report that evening about the salt lake being so salty that "a man could not sink in it, if he should try." At that meeting, "it was moved and seconded that we should locate in this valley for the present, and lay out a city," Howard wrote, "which was carried without a dissenting voice."[7]

Thursday, July 29, Howard and two others sowed seeds "in a garden spot" about three miles from camp. More Mississippi Saints and Battalion members from Pueblo arrived that day. In the evening Elder Kimball, Edson Whipple, and Howard went for a walk and had "a very pleasant evening's conversation, then joined in prayer, and returned to camp about 11 p.m." The next day Howard, Jack Redden, and two others planted more seeds in the garden plot. "We have put in a few of almost all kinds of seeds," Howard said. Exciting for Howard that day, he received a new pair of buckskin pants that Robert Baird made for him, "which are the neatest and best fit I ever had." By late July Howard's friend Horace Whitney was borrowing Howard's diary from which to copy information into his own.

Based on available records, Howard had not been a farmer or farm hand before, so it's possible he now was learning the basics of farming. On Saturday, July 31, Howard with others sowed turnips, buckwheat, oats, and other seeds. By then the pioneers had plowed and mostly planted about fifty acres. Howard noted that "we have sowed for Brother Kimball's family three acres of buckwheat, one acre of corn, one acre of oats, half an acre of turnips, one-fourth acre of different kinds of seeds, and one bushel of potatoes." While some pioneers plowed and planted, others erected shelters. Lacking an abundance of wood, the men listened to suggestions from Battalion men who had wintered at Pueblo, and perhaps from Howard, about trying "the Spanish mode of building houses" of adobe bricks. Workers opened an adobe yard where water and dirt and straw were mixed together well and shaped into large bricks they set out to dry.

During most of August, Howard worked among trees up in the cooler canyons. His main work assignment day after day was to go seven or eight miles from camp and cut and stack loads of logs and poles. On August 4, Howard and Jack drove up what is now called Emigration Canyon, where they cut down and brought back two cedar trees for use in making bedsteads and pails. "We had quite a hard time of it, the road being almost impassable," Howard wrote, because rainstorms raised streams that wiped out the pioneers' bridges. Also that day Howard and others cut and brought back three loads of good logs for a planned storehouse. Howard retrieved balsam fir tree logs one day, and poles for a horse corral the next.

Tree with a Hornets' Nest

One of Howard's favorite stories involves a tree with a hornets' nest.[8] During one canyon trip he spotted what looked like a good tree to log. He hiked to it and whacked it with his ax, stirring up a nest of hornets. He ran down the hill to out-race a string of angry attackers. A few days later he and others went up that same canyon. The lead man turned off the road and said he was going to get that tree because "it's dead easy, it will roll right down the road." "You better not," Howard warned. "Wait a few days 'til I get out what I have chopped and then I will help you. That tree will make two good loads." No, the man said, he'd deal with it by himself. Howard and the other teamsters drove farther up, then watched. The man chopped a few times, then suddenly leaped aside, grabbed his coat, and flew down the road. When he came back up to where Howard was he said, "Darn you Egan, why didn't you tell me there was hornets near that tree?" "You never asked me, and I told you I would help you get it and so I will." "No you won't," he replied, while displaying his hornet stings.

A few days later, Howard revisited the tree early in the morning before the hornets were active. He placed dry grass and twigs on the nest, set it on fire, and listened to "the buzzing song of death of the enemy" above the crackling flames. Howard and his ax then transformed the tree into two good loads of logs, ready to be sawed. When he brought them down, he told the stung man they were part of the hornet tree. "How did you manage it?" "Oh easy," Howard joked, "This morning when it was cool I was afraid the poor things might suffer, so I gave them a little fire to warm up in. I think they were satisfied, for not one came out to complain." "Well, by jinks," the man said, "you had a joke on the hornets as well as on me."

Covenanting through Rebaptism

On August 7, the pioneers finished the valley's very first log building, a blacksmith shop, which they roofed with bush branches. Then, as part of a solemn ceremony to recommit themselves to building the Kingdom of God in this new place, Howard and more than fifty others in Kimball's entourage met at a small dam on what is now City Creek, where they were rebaptized.[9] Howard helped members of the Twelve do the baptizing. President Young and Elders Woodruff, Smith, Lyman, and Orson Pratt reconfirmed those baptized. Young's history says that a total of 289 pioneers were "rebaptized and renewed their covenant to serve the Lord."[10] That included the Twelve the evening before.

Building Homes and a Fort

On August 9 Howard, friend Horace, and others "went up the pass about six miles from here" and brought back four loads of poles to the adobe yard, where men were making bricks for houses. That evening Elder Kimball took some of his "sons" for a walk, probably Howard among them, told them of his plans for them to have house lots, discussed details about the return trip to Winter Quarters, and then prayed with them.[11] When Howard and Horace brought down loads once again the next day, they "found Brother Kimball, J. Redding, A. Gibbons and G. Billings engaged in laying the basement of a row of log buildings" to be part of a fort.

A little boy, Milton Therlkill, drowned behind the creek dam on August 11 and was buried the next day. This was the Mormons' first death in the valley. By then clusters of men were heading back towards Winter Quarters. Meanwhile, crews assigned to boil down lake water were starting to bring loads of pure salt to the camp.

On August 12 Howard had no idea that Tamson gave birth to a son she named Horace Adelbert. The first name might have been in honor of the Egans' friend Horace

Old Fort, *artist Paul D. Forster, used with permission from the artist*

K. Whitney. By August 13 Kimball's row of buildings, consisting of five houses, was five logs high, Howard noted. Adjoining those were house foundations for the Twelve. Seventeen homes were under construction.[12] Men built the houses so as to form a fort on a ten-acre plot, where Salt Lake City's Pioneer Park is now located at 300 South and 300 West. The houses were built of adobe and some wood. They were roughly fourteen by sixteen feet in size and their backsides formed a wall. A year later Howard would move Tamson and the boys into this fort, which by then had much expanded.

Before noon on August 16, Howard hunted for cattle. Then, because William King had just repaired William Clayton's odometer, Howard and Jack Redden rode out with Clayton to the warm springs to test it. The odometer worked. It counted one-and-a-half miles. A big group started east on August 17, consisting of 59 men and 32 wagons. Men leaving from the Kimball group were Brothers Clayton, Redden, Baird, and Thomas Cloward. The next day Howard, Elder Kimball, and four others went ten miles "up the pass" to where the outbounders were camped. Brother Kimball gave instructions to those leaving. Then, back at camp that evening, Elder Kimball called "most of his boys" together and let them pick house lots. Horace Whitney recorded these on the city plat map. Howard noted that, with Clayton gone, Horace became the recorder for Elder Kimball's journal.

On August 18 Howard worked for the first time, with the "rest of the boys," at the adobe yard and helped construct buildings. A day later he and Hosea Cushing hauled gravel for use on house roofs. That day Hans C. Hansen started making Howard a buckskin coat. Two days later, workmen were putting the finishing stages on Elder Kimball's houses–one man made a door, others covered the tops of some rooms, and another sawed lumber at a sawpit for floorboards. Howard, about set to leave the valley, recorded some of the progress the pioneers had made thus far:

> The laying out of the city is now completed. It is composed of 135 blocks, each containing ten acres, which is subdivided into eight lots, each containing one and one-fourth acres. The streets are eight rods wide. There are three public squares (including the adobie yard) in different parts of the city. The Temple block, like the rest contains ten acres.

Because nearly all the Kimballs' rooms were roofed, and the floor nearly finished in Ellen Kimball's room, Howard helped Elder Kimball move his wagons and personal effects "down to the stockade." On August 21, Howard and Cushing spent some time in the afternoon packing, unpacking, replacing, and carrying Kimball's belongings into the house.[13]

At an August 22 conference, Brigham Young issued instructions to those staying in the valley. Attenders voted in favor of several things: that workmen build a common fence around the farm area; that the settlement be named Great Salt Lake City of the Great Basin, North America; that the main river be called the Western Jordan; that nearby creeks be named City Creek, Mill Creek, Red Butte Creek, Canyon Creek, and Big Canyon Creek; and that Joseph Smith's uncle John Smith be president of the settlement as soon as he arrived. "Raise all you can," was one parting instruction; another was "live in the stockade until we come back." Elder Kimball urged all to "throw away selfishness for it is of hell." Then, he offered a sentiment that many of the men must have shared: "I wish to God we did not have to return. If I had my family here, I would give anything I have. This is a paradise to me."[14]

The next day Ellen Kimball moved into her room. She was four months pregnant. On August 24 Howard finally got to go to the Great Salt Lake. "We had a fine bath in its waters," he said, "and staid all night on the shore." The next day "we busied ourselves this afternoon in getting up the horses cutting grass for them, that we may hitch them up for all night in order to be ready with the rest to make an early start." That day Nancy, back at Winter Quarters, gave birth to a baby girl, Helen Jeanette Egan.

Beginning the Return Trip

During the morning of August 26, a number of those going back left the Valley, but not in one caravan. Howard finished up some business and then rode out and caught up with a cluster of wagons on the other side of Big Mountain. This began his journey back to his family. The Pioneer Company had accomplished its mission to find and start a new gathering place for the Saints. "We have accomplished more this year," Wilford Woodruff wrote, "than can be found on record concerning an equal number of men in the same time since the days of Adam."

> We have travelled with heavily laden wagons more than a thousand miles, over rough roads, mountains, and canons, searching out a land, a resting-place for the saints. We have laid out a city two miles square, and built a fort of hewn timber drawn seven miles from the mountains, and of sun-dried bricks or adobes, surrounding ten acres of ground, forty rods of which are covered with blockhouses, besides planting about ten acres of corn and vegetables. All this we have done in a single month.[15]

In his diary Howard only recorded details about his return trip up to September 7. Those in the Kimball wagons were Elder Kimball, Howard, Hosea Cushing, William King, George Billings, Andrew Gibbons, Carlos Murray, Ralph Douglass, Abel M. Sargant, William Ferril, Albert Sharp, Thurston Lawson, and Edwin Holden. Howard said he cooked for the mess group that included Elder Kimball. When the apostle recalled this trip a year later, he underscored how little food they took with them. "Brother H. Egan and I started from the valley with 14 pounds of flour," he said, "and that served us till we got to Laramie; then we got 10 pounds more" for the rest of the journey to Winter Quarters.[16]

On August 29 this contingent met westbound rider Ezra Benson who brought word that nine wagon trains of Saints from Winter Quarters had passed Fort Laramie and had reached the Sweetwater, totaling 566 wagons and 1,200 to 1,500 people. "He brought a number of papers and letters," Howard noted. "I received one from my wife dated 14th June, leaving them all well, which rejoiced my heart. I thank my Heavenly Father that He has blessed them with health and strength, and I pray God that He may preserve them from evil and from sickness and death, that we may enjoy each others society again."[17]

A Captain of Ten Again

On August 30 Howard said the men in his company were a mix of pioneers and Battalion men, totaling 103. The company had 36 wagons, 42 horses, and 35 mules. That evening President Young appointed captains and sub-groups. Stephen Markham became a senior captain, with Barnabus Adams and Joseph Matthews as captains of fifty. Howard was assigned to be one of the eight captains of ten. At 5:00 p.m. on August 31 the wagon train reached Fort Bridger, but Howard, William King and a few others, who had ridden ahead, arrived earlier. Howard's company arrived minus a horse, causing him and two others, who also had lost a horse, to ride back and search. They found the missing horses about 11:30 that night. It being cold, they made a fire "to warm ourselves," and let their mounts feed for half an hour, then started back. They reached camp "a little before sunrise." They breakfasted, then laid down to sleep while their horses grazed. The wagon train moved on without them. Brother Porter awoke them at 10:00 a.m., after which they rode on horseback until they caught up with the train that afternoon. Howard got into a wagon and moved on with the train, while the other men rested the horses. He noted that the streams and rivers seemed low compared to when he had crossed them in July.

Meeting the "Big Company" from Winter Quarters

The nine companies coming from Winter Quarters were termed the "Emigration Camp," who would become settlers in the location the pioneers had found. Numbering 1,448 people, with almost 600 wagons, they were under the general supervision of apostles Parley P. Pratt and John Taylor, as well as Joseph Smith's uncle John Smith.[18] Late in August their forward companies began to meet up with the returnees from the Valley. At the Big Sandy River on September 3, Brigham Young's wagons met Daniel Spencer's train of about fifty wagons, and learned that Apostle Parley P. Pratt's company was about six miles back. That evening, as would happen each time the returnees met westbound Saints, Presidents Young and Kimball and other leaders addressed the newcomers and told them about the valley. "Some of our company here met with their families," Howard said. Those who did turned around to go west with them.

The next day, the Young train reached Parley P. Pratt's company of seventy or eighty wagons, who had stayed in camp to receive the visit. "I saw many old friends," Howard noted. He took supper with Samuel Moore and his wife. Sister Moore became an angel for Howard because she "washed some clothes for me." The next day, September 5, the Young Company camped at Pacific Springs, where they found the Smoot and Wallace wagon trains. "Soon after we arrived Brother [Charles] Rich's company came up," and in it were more of Elder Kimball's wagons. Once again "a number of the brethren met their families and turned back." On September 7, when cold wind and snow whipped the Young train, they met up with Apostle John Taylor's company of one hundred wagons, on the banks of the Sweetwater. That group, knowing the

Crossing the Sweetwater, *artist Bryan Taylor, used with permission from the artist*

Young party would camp with them, put together a grand supper, "which was done in style," Howard noted. Howard's diary ends with that entry, even though the diary book has more blank pages. Our account for the rest of Howard's return trip depends on Horace K. Whitney's journal.[19]

The Young company met more wagon trains the next day. The morning of September 9 shocked the camp. Men discovered forty to fifty horses missing, stolen by Indians. Mounted men rode off in pursuit, but found few of the horses. Brigham Young, Heber Kimball, and others who up until then had been traveling on horseback now had to dismount, donate their horses to be in wagon teams, and become wagon passengers.[20]

Horace mentioned that on September 12 Howard and William King spent the day unsuccessfully looking for George Grant's missing horse. "They reported that they had seen 8 Indians at a distance, who were probably following the camp with intention of stealing horses." Hunters that evening killed three buffalo, "which furnished the camp with plenty of meat."[21]

Four days later the returning pioneers forded the North Platte near their former ferrying place. They found the river quite shallow, the water scarcely coming up to their wagon beds.²²

Indian Raiders Steal Horses

"Indians! Indians!" guards screamed about 8:00 a.m. on September 21. In less than a minute the bluffs and timbers were lined with mounted warriors charging at full speed upon the guards, horses, and the camp, firing guns. They shot at two or three of the guards and tried but failed to carry off one. In camp Brother Kimball and others sprang into their saddles armed with guns and pistols and rode out to head off the horses that Indians were driving away. They succeeded in collecting all of the animals except eleven. Soon after that, about two hundred Sioux appeared, and charged. The Pioneers fired a volley that broke the attack. The Indians broke and fled, and the brethren gave chase. Then, the chief and President Young recognized each other, having met weeks earlier on the Platte River, and the fighting ceased. The chief promised to return the horses. The wagon train moved about a half mile and camped in the open. Some of the stolen horses were brought into camp that afternoon. Elder Kimball visited the Indian's camp that evening, smoked the peace pipe with their leading men, and, through his efforts, more of the horses were recovered and returned to their owners.²³

The company rolled by Fort Laramie on September 24. Young, Kimball, and a few others visited the post, where Mr. Bordeaux, the proprietor, told them that "the chance of recovering our horses was rather a dull one."²⁴ The company moved on, traveling once again on the Mormon Trail. On September 27, Horace Whitney noted, Brigham Young organized the companies of tens "in a military capacity" because of the Indian dangers. Howard, Major Egan, became one of the military captains. Next day, west of Scott's Bluff, the newly organized military companies assembled and presented their arms for inspection. An inventory was taken of the guns and ammunition each man had.

Howard's son Ransom recalled a story Howard told him, which probably took place during this stretch of Indian danger in late September and early October.²⁵ Howard said that at one camp the men drove their livestock onto a point formed by a horseshoe curve in the Platte River, then parked their wagons in the neck of the horseshoe to block the animals in. With that kind of a corral, few guards were needed. Two hours before daylight Howard heard the "rumbling sound of many animals running." He jumped out of bed, put on his boots, "buckled on his belt which carried his Colts pistol and knife, grabbed his hat," and ran to head off the escaping livestock. "It was so dark that you could not see your hand a foot from your face." At top speed Howard "ran up against a naked Indian breast to breast. He knew it was an Indian, for he felt his naked skin." They both jumped back, no damage done.

In the blackness Howard dropped down as low as possible but still on his feet with his gun in one hand and the knife in the other. "He listened for the slightest rustle of grass, not wanting to fire at random for fear of getting an arrow in return." After waiting and hearing nothing, he sidestepped for about a rod. Hearing the animals running, "he placed his left hand on his breast holding his hunting knife point forward, made a dash ahead, determined that if he ran up against his friend again there would be something doing." He ran in that posture until he saw glistenings off the river, into which he had almost run. He figured out that the animals had not escaped but were running in a circle. At daylight he returned to camp. He saw no Indians but did see their tracks. A count proved that no animals were gone. The wagon train moved on.

Resupplies from Winter Quarters

On September 30 the company passed Chimney Rock, the high plains sentinel. By October 3 buffalo meat had become a necessity, Horace said, "most of the camp depending solely upon that for subsistence, being entirely destitute of flour & other provisions." Men on foot went ahead to overtake the ox train company that had left the valley before them, wanting to make them stop and help pull the Brigham Young Company's loads. However, horsemen from Winter Quarters brought better help—two wagons loaded with provisions and grain for Young's division.[26]

Six days before reaching "home," Howard wrote to Tamson and sent the letter ahead. He told her he welcomed "the opportunity to write a few lines to you for your comfort and to inform you of my good health." Using humor, he jokingly described his letter-writing position, spoofing Tamson's own evening routine: "It is now about sundown and I am writing in the grass, and I have not yet washed the dishes, and the children are crying, so you must excuse my short letter." He wrote that "it rejoices my heart to hear that you are well and in good spirits. Knowing your situation when I left I have been very anxious to hear from you, and I thank the Lord that you have been preserved with our little ones."

He mentioned the Indian problems at South Pass, which delayed his company, and then, expressing his desire for a good home-cooked meal, he told about his food situation. "Most of the brethren have been living on game for some time. Bro. Kimball and myself started from the Valley with 17 lbs. of flour. I have been under the necessity of putting father Kimball on a 1/2 of a pound of provision per day, yet he was cheerful all the time." He asked Tamson to thank Mary Kimball for some food she had sent out to them, brought by the relief party, which "came at a time when it was wanting."

"This day we have crossed the Loup Fork," Howard added, "a very dangerous stream to cross. I have had, with some others, to work in the cold water up to my waist for 3 or 4 hours." He concluded his letter warmly: "We are now about 160 miles from you and long to see My Dear Tamson and my little children. Remember me to Nancy and Mother and all the folks. May the Lord God of Israel bless and preserve you that we may enjoy each other's society again." He signed the letter: "I remain as ever and forever your affectionate companion, Howard Egan."[27]

Family Reunion

On Sunday, October 31, after a day of hard traveling, the Young Company drove into Winter Quarters "in order." People lined the street "to shake hands as we drove along. Each one drove to his own home."[28] This was a triumphant return, for the pioneers' expedition had been successful. Howard was happy to be home, and no doubt Tamson, Ransom, Erastus, and Nancy were glad for his safe return. For the first time he met his two children born during his absence: Tamson's eleven-week-old infant son Horace Adelbert and Nancy's nine-week-old daughter Helen Jeanette. Helen was Howard's first daughter.

The returners "found on our arrival that the brethren at winter quarters had been also greatly blessed in there [sic] labours in tilling the earth that it had brought forth abundance of corn Buckwheat turnips & other vegitables & the city was full of Hay & surrounded with corn."[29]

They'd had "a good crop of beans and some potatoes and plenty of garden," no apples or peaches, but "other kinds of fruit in abundance such as strawberries and rasberries and plumbs and grapes."[30] The settlement had "plenty of hay" and turnips and potatoes "in abundance."[31]

In December 1847 the Twelve, busily engaged in Winter Quarters for a second winter, sent an official "General Epistle" addressed to Mormons throughout the world. It said that the Winter Quarters Saints' "hearts and all their labors are towards the setting sun." It stated that the Church's primary purpose in the Great Salt Lake Valley was to build a new temple and establish "a place of peace, a city of rest, a habitation for the oppressed of every clime, even for those that love their neighbor as they do themselves, and who are willing to do as they would be done unto....The kingdom which we are establishing is not of this world, but is the kingdom of the Great God."[32]

Important December Meeting across the Missouri

The Twelve held a historic conference at Christmastime. In preparation for it, Saints across the Missouri River at Miller's Hollow hastily constructed a large cottonwood log tabernacle. Then, between December 24 and 27, Church members from up and down the Missouri River Valley gathered there. Very likely Howard, close as he was to Elder Kimball, attended. For more than two years the Twelve, collectively as a quorum, had served as the presidency of the Church. But at this conference the main business was a call for reconstituting the three-man First Presidency. Attenders approved the change, voting by priesthood quorums in turn. Senior Apostle Brigham Young became the new Church President, and chose as his counselors Elder Kimball and Apostle Willard Richards.[33]

The conference's action received a confirming vote at the Church's next annual conference held at Kanesville (Miller's Hollow's new name) on April 6, 1848. Similar sustaining votes took place in a general conference in England on August 14, 1848, and at the October general conference in Great Salt Lake City.[34]

Six Day Seventies' Jubilee

It seems likely that Howard, a seventy, participated in a big "seventies' jubilee" held on January 16–21, 1848 in the log tabernacle. This event featured six days of worship, talks, singing, celebrating, dancing, band numbers, and other amusements. Wilford Woodruff observed that the wagons parked around the tabernacle "looked like a large emigration camp," and that "the Saints enjoyed themselves thoroughly."[35]

During that celebration, on January 18, about 1,750 Saints signed two petitions. One petition urged the Iowa legislature to make the Pottawattamie tract of land, which included Miller's Hollow, a county. The other asked the nation's postmaster general to establish a post office in their area.[36] "There being no post office within forty or fifty miles of said Tabernacle," the petition enjoined, "the public good requires a convenient office."[37] Among names on the post office petition are Howard, Howard R., Richard E., and Harris [Horace] A. Egan. In a few months Kanesville—as the settlement became called in honor of Col. Thomas L. Kane—received a post office.

Preparing to Close Down Winter Quarters

By agreement with the government, the Saints had to leave Winter Quarters by the summer in 1848. Facing the shutdown, residents had two options: head for the Great Salt Lake Valley if well-enough supplied or move across the river into Iowa Territory. Winter blocked communications between Winter Quarters and Great Salt Lake Valley, which left the Egans and most everyone wondering how well the Valley settlement people were surviving a winter in the mountains. Would the Valley actually be ready for a big emigration from Winter Quarters?

Before the Winter Quarters' westbound masses could leave, Howard and other

The Kanesville Log Tabernacle, 2017, James E. Hartley, used with permission from the artist

men worked to supply them with food and with feed for the livestock. On March 25 Daniel Davis noted that Howard helped him unload some sixty bushels of "pounded out" corn that Davis had brought in from "the farm." On March 29 Howard took four mules and crossed the river to go once again on a buying and trading mission down to St. Joseph, his sixth such trip. On April 9, Davis, who also was on a purchasing trip, saw Howard near the town of Savannah, Missouri. Two days later, at Savannah, he loaded Howard's wagon and another man's wagon with wheat. Near the Nodaway River, Davis went to get wheat ground at Holister's Mill but "had to wait by the request of Bro. Egan." On April 18, nearing home, Davis stopped at Jesse Harmon's and ate dinner with Howard. Howard returned to Winter Quarters and after some time at home left again on April 29, to get flour in St. Joseph, his seventh trading trip.[38]

Howard, Tamson, and the boys packed up to head west. They would travel as part of the Kimball family group, anxious to start a new home in the Great Salt Lake Valley that fall. Why Nancy and her baby Helen Jeanette didn't go west with them isn't known. Wagon space probably posed a problem. Nancy moved over to the Kanesville area and lived with her Redden relatives. Howard would return to be with her and his daughter later that year, and they'd go west with him in 1849.

Winter Quarters Postscript

Winter Quarters existed for only two years, but its suffering and tragedies carved a lasting niche in LDS and western history. Today, thousands visit the site each summer, somewhat like a sacred pilgrimage, to see where homeless Saints driven from Nauvoo in 1846 rode out a terrible and deadly first winter. Several hundred died, many from scurvy. Winter Quarters had a better second winter, and the Egans lived through that one, too. After the Saints evacuated in the spring of 1848, the cabins and the wooden grave-markers disappeared within a decade or two. In the mid-1850s a town named Florence grew up there, which became a Mormon Trail outfitting place for almost a decade. Florence now is part of northern Omaha. The Winter Quarters cemetery has been restored, adorned with memorial plaques, a statue, and new markers placed on some graves. On its east side is the outstanding Mormon Trail Center at Historic Winter Quarters. Adding to the sacredness of the historic grounds is the Winter Quarters Nebraska Temple, which opened in 2001. ◆

~ 13 ~

Taking Tamson and the Boys West

Excitement permeated Winter Quarters during its second and final year. Residents fully understood government orders saying Winter Quarters had to terminate in 1848, so they eagerly listened whenever a returnee from Great Salt Lake Valley described the new gathering place. As happened two years before, residents again did their best to prepare wagons, teams, livestock, and provisions for a year of travel and settlement building. Those unable to head west were told to cross the Missouri River and set up temporary cabins and farms on the Iowa side. Howard's family would do both. He'd take Tamson and the boys to the Valley; Nancy and Helen would move to Iowa, to wait for Howard to return for them.

April 1848 Conference

With Winter Quarters soon to be vacated, Saints flocked to a Church general conference held across the river in the Kanesville Tabernacle on April 6, 7, and 8. Much conference business related to the imminent uprootings. The First Presidency, in order to lead the emigration west that year, needed and appealed for wagons and teams, either as donations or on loan. Also, by vote, the conference changed the name of Miller's Hollow, the tabernacle city, to Kanesville, in honor of Thomas L. Kane. Attenders sustained officers for a stake headquartered in Kanesville. Elder Orson Hyde became the Iowa presiding officer, assisted by a high council, bishops, and quorum presidents. A committee was appointed to select settlement locations in Pottawattamie County for the hundreds soon to pour in from Winter Quarters.[1]

In Kimball's Second Division

On May 9, 1848, the Missouri River steamer *Mandan* arrived from St. Louis with 108 emigrants and much freight ordered by those heading west. The next day "the town was all hurry and bustle" as men unloaded the boat. "The town is now full of goods," Hosea Stout noted on May 12.[2] Apparently the *Mandan* was the riverboat that so impressed eight-year-old Ransom Egan:

> How well I remember the excitement of us boys when we saw the smoke of a steamboat rising over the trees that were on a point of land just where the river made a great bend below the town. The boat was coming up stream and made a great cloud of smoke. It came in and passed between our shore and the island that lay opposite the town, then stopped at the next point above for wood. It was about a mile away. Some of the boys went up there to get a closer view, but I was afraid I would get my jacket dusted if I went, so refused to go with them.[3]

A dozen days later, John D. Lee noted that "every effort is Making by the Saints for their removal west & such as cannot go West are crossing to the east side of the river."[4] High water required that they use ferries to cross the Missouri. During the next week, wagon after wagon bound for Utah rolled out to rendezvous at the Elkhorn River ferry, almost thirty miles west. Near there, Brigham Young and Heber C. Kimball created two big wagon companies. Young led Division One and Kimball led Division Two, in which the Egans traveled. A month later Willard Richards would lead a Division Three, the year's last.

Elder Kimball's Second Division incorporated 662 people and 226 wagons. He traveled in the first fifty and with its first company of ten, as did the Egans and several of the Kimball "boys," including Howard's friends William H. Kimball, Daniel Davis, and George Rhodes. A company roster lists Howard, Tamson, and the three boys. But, curiously, after Tamson's name and before the boys' names, is the name of Mary A. Tuttle, age eighteen. Apparently Mary Ann, whom Howard would marry the next year, traveled with the Egans to assist Tamson with the children. The Egans' outfit consisted of one wagon, four oxen, one cow, and two pigs.[5]

Kimball's Second Division was different than the 1847 Pioneer Company, and not just in size. Instead of selected men with good wagons and horse and mule teams, this company contained hundreds of women and children, wagons pulled primarily by oxen, many worn out wagons, some wagons hitched to family cows never before harnessed, and many inexperienced drivers, including women and children. "Our teams are weak and our loads are heavy," Elder Kimball admitted in mid-June.[6] Accidents, spilled loads, stuck wagons, and broken wagon parts became common. Because Howard often had to help Elder Kimball deal with wagon train problems, Tamson often drove the ox team. Normally, the "driver" didn't sit in the wagon seat but walked to the left of the lead oxen.

On June 2 the Second Division's wagons ferried the fifty-foot wide Elkhorn River on a log raft. Cattle swam across. The captains then formed a large campground just below the crossing. That afternoon Elder Kimball dispatched Howard back to Winter Quarters to attend to business items and to urge Mary Fielding Smith "to come on as speedily as possible." Mary was the martyred Hyrum Smith's widow. She lacked a good team. Howard arranged for Cornelius Lott to drive two yoke of oxen to her to help out.[7]

The next day Tamson did some washing by the Elkhorn.[8] Herdsmen collected bellowing cattle and drove them two miles down along the river to graze. On Sunday, June 4, Saints assembled for a preaching and prayer service near Elder Kimball's wagon. Monday, instead of traveling, the people hid under wagon covers and tents seeking protection from pouring rain. By then, Howard had returned to his family.

Wounded in the Elkhorn Gunfight

"Throughout their migrating period," Mormon Trail expert Stanley Kimball noted, "Mormons had little trouble with Indians."[9] One exception involved Howard. Unless otherwise documented, the following account draws from the author's published article about the skirmish.[10] On Tuesday morning, June 6, before the cattle could be brought to camp and hitched to wagons, Indians, apparently Omaha or Otoe, raided the herd and stole several animals. A herdsman rushed to camp, sounding an alarm. Elder Kimball dispatched his son William H. and Howard on horseback, and also sent more than ten footmen to try to rescue the cattle. Apparently Peter Conover had charge of the footmen. Two more riders, Thomas Ricks and Willis Bartholomew, joined Howard and William. The four horsemen "proceeded at a rapid pace" about six miles down the river's east side. Hearing shots fired, they feared for themselves and the footmen.

The riders rode past and missed the Indians, then turned back and suddenly saw them. The Indians had killed John Pack's ox, butchered it, and were hauling the raw meat away. Both sides surprised each other. Indians pointed rifles at the horsemen. The Mormons fired first and the Indians returned fire. Howard spotted an Indian about twenty feet away aim his rifle at William Kimball. Howard fired his six-shooter and "the shot took effect. The Indian reeled & fell, which lowered his hand so as to cause the [fired] ball to take effect in the Horse's hip on which Wm. sat." "A Ball & 2 Buckshot" tore into Thomas Ricks's lower back and knocked him to the ground, almost lifeless. That left three in the saddle, badly outnumbered. "Egan with the other shot from his 6-shooter brought another Indian to the ground." He fired again and "brought another Indian to the ground, when a large Ball struck Egan on the right arm, Just above the wrist, which mangled the Leaders [tendons] So as to render it useless from further Servise."[11] Howard dropped his pistol and couldn't retrieve it. At the same time another ball hit Howard's horse in the neck, causing it to turn towards camp, almost throwing Howard to the ground.

Wounded and unarmed, Howard with Kimball and Bartholomew retreated. They left a motionless, bleeding Tom Ricks on the ground. The Indians fled. When the Mormons looked back, they saw an Indian moving towards Ricks and feared a scalping. But the Indian picked up a pistol, possibly Howard's, and followed the others down river. Apparently Howard, Kimball, and Bartholomew met up with the footmen, so they all headed for the battle site to retrieve Ricks. "Bro. Egan said his wrist pained him so," Bartholomew said, "that he must have it tied up, as he was getting faint. We then stopped and tied up his wrist."[12] Kimball wrapped a handkerchief around Howard's wound to try to stop the bleeding.

They put Ricks on a buffalo robe stretcher and headed quickly for camp. When a large group of Indians threatened them, both sides shouted and blustered. Men pulled Ricks into the timber for protection. Then, Conover sent two men to find a place to cross the river to seek safety. While the horsemen and footmen gained the west shore, Kimball helped Howard stay on his horse. Both of their horses had wounds. They then took a circuitous route towards the bluff to avoid riding in timber and to let Howard ride more smoothly. Howard became "very faint with loss of blood," so Kimball couldn't take him across the river on horseback or on foot. Meeting up with wagons belonging to Martin H. Peck and others heading for the camp, Howard climbed into a wagon, which conveyed him to the ferry. Someone sent for Dr. John Bernhisel, who came and worked on Howard's wounds.[13] They ferried Howard across and helped him walk to his family.

Thomas Ricks, Engraved Portrait Collection, LDS Church History Library

Dr. John M. Bernhisel, Engraved Portrait Collection, LDS Church History Library

Son Ransom had not seen his father all morning. He recalled that, earlier, "the campers heard that men had saved the stock but that a couple of the men had been wounded." The Egans didn't know Howard was one of them:

> Before noon, as I was sitting in the front of the wagon, I saw two men holding Father up and leading him towards our wagon from the ferry. His arms were hanging down and his chin was on his breast. I heard the men say that the Indians had shot him through the wrist. He had swam the Horn River that way, and had lost so much blood he could not do it again, so they had to bring him around by the ferry.

Dr. Bernhisel found no broken bones, but Howard's wound was serious. Son Ransom said that "Father had been shot in the wrist of his right hand, and the bullet cut every cord of the thumb and fingers in the course, but broke no bones."[14] Accounts written at the time say the ball hit in Howard's arm "above the wrist," so if the wound was in that area, and no bones were broken, it passed between the radius and ulna.

A carriage brought badly wounded Ricks to camp about 2:00 p.m. When news first had reached the camp that Ricks had been shot, his father, Joel Ricks, drove off in a light spring wagon with Thomas Whittle and a boy to find him. They didn't. Foolish to be there without guards, they were surrounded by twenty to thirty Indians, who threatened them, ransacked their wagon, stole items, and then turned them loose. Indians made signs to Brother Ricks informing him that in the skirmish four Indians had been killed and three wounded.

Meanwhile, at camp, Tom Ricks gasped for life. Elder Kimball and others blessed him. He seemed to rally. He survived. Camp leaders feared that Indians might attack the camp, so, taking precautions, they moved away from the timber where Indians could sneak up on them. By 3:00 p.m. the wagons had been hitched up, hurriedly loaded, and started moving two miles to the west. The small company bringing Mary Fielding Smith from Winter Quarters had not reached the Elkhorn by noon as expected. So, while the new encampment was forming, Elder Kimball sent ten footmen, well-armed, to find Mary Smith's group.

Meanwhile, Indians found and chased Doctor Jesse Brailey. When one aimed a rifle at him the doctor aimed his umbrella back, causing the Indian to flee. Three miles east of the Elkhorn, the footmen found the Mary Smith group and escorted them and their fifteen wagons to the ferry and to the new camp by about 5:00 p.m. That evening the Kimball Company wagons formed into a tight corral and posted extra guards. Apparently searchers found and brought back some of the stolen cattle.

Howard's being shot started the Egans' trek west in a frightful way. But the wound was a blessing for young son Ransom, who had not seen much of his father thus far in the journey. "I now could see him every day," the boy recalled, "and watched Dr.

Bernhisel dress the wound and trim the ends of the cords with a pair of scissors where they stuck out of the flesh."[15] The doctor and Tamson changed Howard's bandages and dressed his wound during the next week or more. Unable to fully use his right hand, Howard had limited usefulness for his family and for the camp until it healed.

On June 8, Heber C. Kimball, ever the patriarch, called for a reformation among those in his division. "He wanted the men to keep their women and children in subjection and not suffer them to use profane language, nor to suffer their women to ramble away from camp, nor go visiting from wagon to wagon, but to stay at home and keep themselves clean and their children and wagons clean." Kimball advised brethren not to swear, use profanity, abuse cattle, murmur, or have angry feelings. He wanted them to not sit up late at night but to go to bed early, and to see that their families observed "good hours." He urged them to make certain they held family prayers. Kimball's encampment voted unanimously to follow those instructions.[16]

Three days after the shooting, Elder Kimball organized his division into subgroups. Unlike in previous years, Howard was not picked to be a captain, probably because of his injury. He was still nursing his wound when he turned thirty-three on June 15. John D. Lee, writing in his diary on June 16, noted that both Thomas Ricks and Howard Egan were "doing well."[17] President Young, after he learned about the Indian skirmish, had Elder Kimball bring his division closer to Young's First Division.[18]

Along the Platte's North Side

On June 17 the Kimball Division crossed the Loup Fork River, assisted by teams Young's Division sent to help them.[19] Two days later the Kimball train reached the Platte River and gladly camped "to give the females a chance to do their washing, etc, which was attended to with alacrity." Tamson, having a ten-month-old in diapers, appreciated the laundry stop. One woman thought that this Platte River country "was beautiful" and noted that "the women, in small companies, were often seen walking on its banks by moonlight, or bathing in its waters."[20]

Ransom liked a fun site they saw, a prairie dog colony. "The whole earth seemed to be covered with little mounds," he said, on which they saw "dozens of the dogs at a time all sitting upright and watching our train, and if a person started towards them there would be a general barking chorus and instantly every dog would disappear and not appear again till the intruder had left to a safe distance." Children were told that if someone shot a prairie dog and the body fell into the hole, they should not reach into the hole for it because rattlesnakes lived there too.[21] During the next month, the Kimball and Young divisions traveled close together and often camped nearby. Each fifty in Kimball's company took turns in the lead. Slowly the caravans moved along the north side of the Platte, often traveling "double file" and sometimes on four tracks or roads.[22] During rare stops of a half-day or more, women "were busily engaged washing & baking."[23] By July 1, in the high plains country, the Second Division was seeing great herds of buffalo.[24] One day a stampede endangered Tamson and the boys. According to Ransom:

> I was playing near the end of the wagon tongue. Our wagon was the first on that wing of the corral. Mother caught her boys, and before I knew anything more we landed in the wagon, and she followed, and just in time, for a stampeded herd of buffalos was coming straight for the camp. They divided just a little way from the camp, some passing the back, some the front of the corral. Some of them passed over the end of our wagon tongue, doing no damage, but the part that passed the back end struck and broke a hind wheel of the last wagon in our wing. We staid there to repair damages till next day.[25]

On another travel day, Howard suddenly shouted, "Mother, quick, my gun." By the time Tamson passed it to him, it was too late. Howard had seen an antelope running between the wagon train and the river, five or six rods away. He wanted meat for dinner. Tamson, however, said it'd be a shame to kill such a pretty animal as that.[26] While the wagons moved close to buffalo herds early in July, each fifty assigned several men to be hunters. By then Tamson was learning to cook using buffalo chips. Ransom helped her gather them: "When we camped where there was plenty of them we could collect a couple sacks full and carry them to the next camp, for sometimes they would be very scarce."[27]

During their tedious travel days, Saints in the Young and Kimball divisions eagerly awaited news from the Salt Lake Valley about the crops. It was critical that farmers there produce a good harvest in 1848, enough to feed themselves and the three divisions heading their way. In mid-July the divisions received this June 9 letter, telling about the now legendary seagull-cricket encounter:

> There has been a large amount of spring crops put in, and they were doing well till within a few days. The crickets have done considerable damage to both the wheat and corn, which had discouraged some, but there is plenty left if we can save it for a few days. The sea gulls have come in large flocks from the lake and sweep the crickets as they go; it seems the hand of the Lord in our favor.[28]

Perhaps mid-July is when eight-year-old Ransom, on foot, failed to keep up with the wagons:

> One day our wagon was the last in the train and Mother who was driving the team, let me get out and walk behind the wagon. I took my time and gradually fell back till I could hardly see the wagon, when I noticed this it scared me so

I ran at my fastest speed, but soon was out of wind and went very slow again to gain my breath, and took another run, but I was getting farther behind all the time. As the train was nearing a rolling country, where I couldn't be seen, Mother got George Redding to come back and get me.

Redding threw Ransom over his back "and tried to rattle my teeth out by running at a dog trot." Ransom confessed that he'd learned a lesson, "for I never got very far from the wagon again."[29]

Wagons on Trail, *National Park Service Photo Gallery*

Camp Captain for Mississippi Saints

On July 16, a Sunday, the Kimball and Young divisions were camped close together and within sight of Chimney Rock. They held a Sabbath meeting midway between the two encampments. There, President Young requested that both trains travel in smaller companies "so that our cattle can have more time to feed." In response, each restructured itself. President Kimball's four camp leaders continued to be the captains of fifty: Titus Billings, Isaac Higbee, John Pack, and President Kimball himself assisted by Henry Herriman. However, Saints from Mississippi traveling in the Kimball Division asked to have their own fifty, and with President Kimball's approval, adopted Howard

Egan to be their captain. Apparently his wrist had healed well enough for him to handle daily tasks. Tamson and the children were now surrounded by Southern accents.

In Howard's company were fifty-six white persons, thirty-four blacks, and twenty-eight wagons pulled by oxen, horses, and mules, which had come from Mississippi and other southern states. About half of them had joined the Kimball Division the same day that Mary Fielding Smith's group did, but the others had started later in the Willard Richards's Third Division and then caught up with the Kimball division.

The southerners, well-equipped, brought along fourteen milk cows. John H. Bankhead and Nancy Crosby had three children with them as well as John's brother George. Before leaving home, the Bankheads had given their slaves a choice of freedom in Tennessee or going west with them. Eleven chose to go west. The Bankhead slaves in Howard's company included Nathan and wife Susan, Dan (a blacksmith), George, Alex, Sam, Lewis, Ike, John Priestly, and Nancy, and possibly Rose, the mother of Ike and John. The Bankheads had joined the Kimball train on May 29. John and Margaret Towery Lockhart, Mississippians, brought along five children. Francis McKown had ten whites and two blacks in his group.[30] Because these Mississippians had not lived in Nauvoo, they enjoyed conversations with the Egans about Joseph Smith, the temple, and the exodus.[31]

Crossing to the Oregon Trail

The Kimball Division decided to leave the Mormon Trail, cross the Platte, and travel on the Oregon Trail. On July 17, sometimes triple-teaming, the 180 wagons forded the river six miles west of Chimney Rock. All forded safely, the company clerk noted, "except one wagon of Brother Howard Egan tipt partialy over on the side; nothing injured, a few things wet." They now funneled onto the Oregon Trail. "The road is much the best," clerk Thompson wrote two days later.[32] A dry season made feed scarce, causing scouts to look hard to find good enough campsites. Camping spots became close together, as Thompson reported on July 20:

> Brother Howard Egan's camp moved off at 9 this morning, President Kimballs, Billings, Higbee & Herrimans at noon as Brother H. C. Kimballs camp come up to this place Brother Egan's camp had formed their carell [corral]. Brother K. carelld close by, Brother Billings camp carrelld a little distance from Brother Kimballs & Egans camps on the west. Brother Herymans [Harriman] & Higbee camped about 4 miles east of us.

That day, a Thursday, Brigham Young's big First Division also crossed the Platte. Hearing of this, Elder Kimball and Howard rode ahead to find the Young camps, but eight miles later turned back without making contact—two miles too soon. At a good camping place on the Platte bottom, with plenty of feed, wood, and water, the Kimball Company declared Friday a day to rest the cattle "and give our wives a chance to wash." That evening Porter Rockwell arrived from the Valley. He said people there were well and the wheat crop looked fine. He delivered a letter from the Valley presidency dated June 21, who reported that frost and crickets had seriously damaged wheat, beans, and peas, but the corn looked first rate.[33]

During the next several travel days, the separate fifties bunched and leap-frogged. On July 22, one day before reaching the vicinity of Fort Laramie, camp clerk Thompson filed this busy traffic report, which shows how complicated wagon train travel sometimes became:

> Camps started at 8, Brother Kimball and Pack's companies taking the lead, Brother Egan's, Higbee's & Billings followed. We left Brother Henry Herriman's camp in corall not coming on to-day. Stopt at noon to watter & feed, the feed being so poor. President Kimball & Packs companies moved on, followed by Brother Egan's, camp over the Bluffs; camped on the Platt Bottom near Laramie Creek. Brother George Billings went on from Father Billings camp & got back; stated that Brother Kimball, Pack & Egan was camped three miles ahead & they wanted us to come forward. We hitched up our teams & put ahead; got into camp about 6 p.m. after coming about 10 or 12 miles to-day. Plenty wood & water; tolerable feed. H.C.K. called the brethren of the different camps together after sundown to know their minds about traveling on the morrow [Sunday]. The brethren concluded that it was better to go on as the feed was poor here.

Drought, Feed Shortages, and Dust

On Sunday afternoon, July 23, thunder, lightning, and rain showers struck, halting the travel. Although they were close to Fort Laramie, company records don't show any contacts with it.[34] Monday, July 24, 1848, was the one-year anniversary of Brigham Young and Howard entering the Great Salt Lake Valley. Travel that day let Howard's fifty camp eleven miles past Fort Laramie. Because cattle had "scarcely any feed," the Kimball train moved out early on Tuesday but was slowed by the big Young Company ahead of it. The next day "Howard Egan went some 10 miles on the river road to ascertain about feed. Come back and reported that there was no feed as far as he went."[35]

During the night on July 27–28, campers experienced "a most tremendous shower of rain and hail with very heavy thunder and lightning."[36] That reminds us that during days and nights crossing the plains, the Egans' ears heard a rich mix of sounds. Thunder explodes and rumbles. Rain fump-fump-fumps on wagon covers and tent canvas. Wagon wheels squeak and crunch. Infants and small children, including Horace Egan, cried, sometimes in the middle of the night. Bake kettle lids clanked. Trumpet blasts

Mormon Party in a Thunderstorm,
artist William Henry Jackson, courtesy Scotts Bluff National Monument

awakened campers and announced yoke-up and departure times. Squirts of warm milk from cows' teats clanged the tin buckets' bottoms. Axe blades cracked wood. Mothers' voices yelled for children to come to supper, and sang soft lullabies to hush little ones to sleep. Blacksmiths' hammers rang on wheel rims or red-hot steel. Hunters' rifles popped. Voices high and low sang hymns. Playing children shrieked and laughed. Oxen bellowed, dogs barked, horses snorted, sheep baa-aad, pigs grunted, and roosters crowed. Campers' ears heard coughing, snoring, a profanity or two almost out of earshot of women or wagon captains, screeching fiddles and stomping feet during evening dances, and men's animated voices swapping tall tales around crackling campfires. Possibly Howard's voice was one, telling high seas adventures or about his Elkhorn shootout. Farther up the trail the Egans would hear "wolves very noisy through the night."

The wagons rolled northwesterly along the North Platte, feed continued to be scarce, and livestock suffered. On July 28, Thompson recorded that, in one of the tens, "several cattle" gave out, "staggered and fell," and "several cattle [gave] out in the different camps today." That same day "a white mule in Brother H. Egan's camp undertook to get out. The guard turned him back; he run through among the cattle & scared them." The cattle knocked over the blacksmith's wagon, breaking an axle and all the spokes but one in a wheel, and upset a wagon with a family in it, breaking one axle.[37]

The next day near Horseshoe Creek "the cattle belonging to Brother H. Egan's camp got scared through the night again although they had a number of them yoked up, & chained to the waggons. They had to let them go to save the wagons from being broke. When they started there was 11 yoke of their cattle that they had not got." More cattle problems plagued Howard's camp the next night, making three nights in a row. "Through the night 41 of cattle belonging to Brother Howard Egan's camp got scattered, supposed to be by the Indians; they were found through the day near Laramie peak, 10 or 12 miles distant, about sundown."[38]

Second Division wagons reached the Upper Ferry site on August 7 and halted to do blacksmithing and wagon repairs, shoe horses and oxen, and hunt buffalo. Howard probably related to Tamson and the boys how a year earlier he had almost drowned there trying to ferry wagons across. This year the river was so low that the wagons forded it on August 12.

Cattle Death Zone

For three days Howard led his fifty up and over the difficult divide between the Platte and the Sweetwater. They passed sagebrush growing eight or ten feet high, with limbs six inches in diameter, "the largest I saw on the road," Hosea Stout said.[39] At the saleratus lakes, Tamson was one of many who stocked up on the white soda to use for baking. According to Ransom, "One day we camped a little ways from a dry Salaratus Lake. Mother took me along with her to get some. It was very hard and smooth and we had only table knives to dig it out, but ... we got as much as Mother could carry to the wagon. It lasted for a number of years after we arrived in the valley."[40]

Reaching the Sweetwater River, travelers rejoiced to find "the only good feed for the last 200 miles."[41] Near Independence Rock, Howard and Tamson's littlest boy, Horace Adelbert, turned one year old on August 17. While the Egan fifty traveled beside the "very crooked" Sweetwater, Ransom recalled, "Mother was driving when the next wagon ahead of ours turned over into a creek or bog hole." Two children were inside. The driver called for help and men came running. "The children had not been severely hurt."[42]

West of Devil's Gate on August 18, a rider from the Valley shared good news. Some three hundred yoke of cattle and one hundred wagons from the Valley were on their way to help them. Such help was needed. Captains and teamsters felt growing concern about cattle deaths during the two weeks after they left the Platte, caused by alkali poisoning, heat, overwork, and wolves. John D. Lee recorded that "the roads are almost lined with dead cattle."[43] John Pack's camp lost nineteen by August 25. During one stretch, Thompson saw some ten to fifteen dead cattle by the wayside.

Camp at End of Day, *artist W.N. Wilson, Trails West, Utah State Historical Society*

Henry Herriman's fifty lost so many cattle they had to move some wagons aside, unhitch them, and use their oxen to help pull the other wagons. Companies sent any oxen they could spare back to help companies needing them. For those camped near the dead oxen, "the stench was awful, and the wolves as thick as sheep."[44]

Two letters from the Valley brought mixed crop news. One, from Parley P. Pratt dated August 8, reported that "many had lost their crops" to the crickets and because of poor cultivation, but the wheat crop "has exceeded all expectations," and oats and vegetables had done well. They expected a surplus of ten- to twenty-thousand bushels of corn.[45] In an August 9 letter, Valley leaders said the pioneers had plowed, planted, and sowed three thousand acres. Despite the crickets' damage, the wheat harvest exceeded expectations, and "green peas have been so plentyful for a long time that we are becoming tired of them, cucumbers, squashes, beets, carrots, parsnips, and greens are upon our tables."[46]

On August 24 Elder Kimball, while camped a mile west of the seventh and final crossing of the Sweetwater, wrote to President Brigham Young and explained why his wagons were so far behind. Howard delivered the message the next day.[47] By August

26 the Kimball Company's fifties were stretched out for at least twenty-four miles, causing Kimball to order ox teams back to assist the slow travelers.[48]

Word came on August 28 that thirty cattle recently had died in the Young Company. Presidents Young and Kimball, writing that day to Saints back near the Missouri River, said that the extensive cattle losses were due to "the very dry season, the scarcity of grass, the heavy dragging, dusty roads and inhaling so much of the alkali by breathing, eating and drinking." They admitted that some families in their divisions now lacked wagons, cattle, and even tents. If necessary, they would take those people only to the Green River and there build them huts to live in until teams from the Valley could come for them. The letter also mentioned a future assignment for Howard: "When we are all arrived in the Valley, we shall make arrangements to send to Winter Quarters, another mail by Captain Egan, Captain Roundy and others, when we shall be able, to send letters to individual persons, in addition to another General Epistle."[49]

The next day, Elder Kimball asked Howard, William Kimball, and Thomas Bullock to "take an account of his teams." This they did from 4:00 p.m. until sunset.[50] Two days later Kimball ordered a stop. Then he, Howard, Brothers Davis and Jackman, and William Kimball walked "to a bunch of willows & all knelt down," Elder Kimball prayed, "and we all felt well."[51] That night the company camped near a branch of the Sweetwater. Next morning William, Howard, and Davis "went and found our horses" and started again. One of the Mississippi Saints in Howard's company, Jane McKown, age thirteen, died on August 31 of mountain fever and diarrhea.[52]

The Kimball division started September by catching up with Brigham Young's large company. Then, when they were just east of South Pass, to their great joy and relief, about 130 yoke of cattle and wagons arrived from the Valley to help them. When Kimball polled his captains of ten, they said they needed forty-three yoke. A day was spent assigning newly arrived oxen to teams needing them. On September 4 the Egan camp and other reinforced companies crossed South Pass.[53]

Completing the Journey

Kimball's Second Division crossed the Little Sandy, Big Sandy, and on September 8 reached and forded the Green, its waters reaching only up to the axles. The next day they crossed the Black Fork and camped on Ham's Fork, with "Brother Egans, Billings, Pack & Kimball forming one large corell [corrall]."[54] On September 12, some companies in the Second Division reached Fort Bridger and camped near it. Howard had last been there at the post thirteen months before, eastbound. Undoubtedly the Egan family liked this campsite, because it had "Water pure & clear; feed first rate & wood sufficient for camping purposes."[55]

"Harmonica" pistol, possible type used by Howard Egan

Traders visited the Mormon camps trying to market buckskins and antelope hides. Son Ransom described Fort Bridger as "low dirt covered houses near the bank of the river. Indians and white men all dressed in buckskin clothes, and more dogs, half-bred wolf, than you could shake a stick at." Inside the post, Howard had an amazing experience. He "traded for the same pistol he had held in his hand, and dropped, when shot, in the fight at the Horn River. It had passed from Indian to Indian and arrived at Bridger long before we did."[56]

On September 16, when the Egans and the others awoke, they found ice a half inch thick in their water pails.[57] Two days later, the Kimball division's wagons were jostling down rocky, willow-infested Echo Canyon. Ransom liked the echoes: "we could hear the men calling and dogs barking from one cliff to another, although the ones starting the sound was far ahead of us, it went bounding from cliff to cliff, repeating the sound perfectly."

Their canyon descent produced three family stories.[58] Ransom said that Howard had to help repair a Kimball wagon, which meant Tamson had to drive the Egan wagon until he could catch up. She had two yoke of cattle and a yoke of cows, which she drove down the canyon. She missed more stumps and rocks than any other driver, or so they say, while crossing the stream twenty-seven times. Sometimes she walked ahead of the team, sometimes between the cattle and wagon. A second story is that Erastus had to ride in the wagon because he had been run over when he slipped and fell under the tongue. He would have escaped any harm, but a pig was tied under the back of the wagon, and while trying to get out of the way of the pig, Erastus' foot went under the wheel. The third story is that when Tamson was driving and her team was in the lead, those of the family who could walk were up ahead. "Those ahead would holler out. 'Here is another creek,' and Mother would say, 'D--n the creeks!'"[59]

Four days after exiting Echo Canyon the Kimball companies made the arduous ascent up Big Mountain, which Ransom did not like. "Father said we had to climb a mountain for seven miles, and I thought before we did get to the top we had come seven hundred miles, for he had us walk up every step of it." At the summit Tamson and the children looked down and saw far in the distance the southern part of Great Salt Lake Valley.[60] The wagons then descended Big Mountain's west slope on a new, "pretty good" road, locking both wheels of the wagon to slow it down. Ransom said he had to walk "down the other side, where it was awful steep, and," being humorous, "everything loose in the wagon was liable to attempt to pass the team."

Navigating carefully down Emigration Canyon on September 23, the travelers, most of them walking, "got very cold" during a rainstorm. A muddy trail forced teamsters to put from four to seven yoke of cattle to a wagon. When they finally drove out from the canyon's mouth, Ransom said, Howard "took us to one side of the road and pointed out the place where we would live" in the valley.[61] The next day, September 24, a Sunday, in pleasant weather, the Kimball fifties "almost all together" clattered and squeaked into Great Salt Lake City.[62] Daniel Davis recorded that "as We drew near the Saints came out to meet us with cheers," and proudly shared with them beef, beets, squash, carrots, corn, cucumbers, pickles, bread, biscuits, butter, and pies "that they had raised here."[63]

Upon entering the one-year-old fledgling city, Ransom said, "Father drove the team and landed the wagon near to the door of a house, near the middle of the south side of the north fort."[64] During Howard's absence, a "north fort" and "south fort" had been added to the original "Old Fort." New England-bred Tamson's reaction to her new mountain-desert home is not recorded. One in the Young Division, Zebulon Jacobs, felt disappointed: "When we arrived there the face of the land looked like a famine, it was dry and parched."[65] Disappointed or not, the five new Egan residents, by giving up covered wagon life and nighttimes of camping, felt great relief to be there. This now was home, and would be for years to come. ◆

~ 14 ~

Kanesville Mail, Nancy, and Utah Freight

When Howard halted his trail-worn wagon at the Old Fort, he hardly had time to shake dust from his clothes, hair, eyes, and teeth before heading back on the trail. Apparently he decided before leaving Winter Quarters that he'd first bring Tamson and the boys west and then go back and bring Nancy and Helen to Utah the next year. When Presidents Young and Kimball understood Howard's intent, they saw opportunity. With full trust and confidence in Howard, they asked him to take mail back to Kanesville that fall and then in spring lead a freight wagon train to Utah hauling materials needed at Church headquarters.

Three Weeks in Great Salt Lake City

Fortunately, for the three big divisions' emigrants, the Valley's food supply seemed surprisingly bounteous. Despite the cricket invasion three months back in the spring, Valley crops had proved good enough for the settlers to hold a joyous thanksgiving festival six weeks before the Egans arrived.[1] The wheat harvest was turning out "tolerably well," pioneer Leonard Harrington said, "though the Crickets injured it considerable as also our corn, beans, vines, etc., we have enough to subsist on till another harvest, and some corn to spare."[2]

The Egans moved "into a room of the Old Fort that had been provided for them," Ransom recalled. The primitive cabin, he said, had a "shed roof, covered with inch lumber, plastered with clay on the outside." The roof sagged and had "quite a depression in the center." With autumn yellows and reds lightly tinting the Wasatch Mountains, Howard and Tamson spent three weeks together arranging the cabin and rounding up food and winter necessities before Howard's departure.

Howard would leave Tamson, Ransom, Erastus, and Horace living in an undesirable cabin. After Howard left, Heber C. Kimball visited Tamson one rainy day. He saw the roof leaking and heard it settle with a "loud crack." He bolted outside and told

Tamson to get out before the roof caved in. She refused. She placed a tub under the drip and "stood up in a chair and ran a table knife up between the boards, so letting the water come down." With weight off, the roof sprang back. Kimball sent a man to erect a pole under the sagging roof, but Tamson refused to see "a post set up in the middle of her parlor." While Howard was gone, Ransom observed, "Mother would never ask for help if she could avoid it…I have heard her say that she would work her finger ends off before she would ask for assistance."[3] Tamson would move them out of the fort by the next spring.

Following the October general conference, President Young addressed an epistle for Howard to take to Elders Orson Hyde, George A. Smith, and Ezra T. Benson and Saints scattered in southwestern Iowa.[4] It told about progress with farm and city lot assignments, then detailed some of the needs the Valley's residents faced. Rather than haul surplus food for use in Utah, President Young instructed, Saints coming from Iowa should use wagon space for dry goods, vegetable seeds, bees, fowl such as ducks, doves, geese, and turkeys, and flowering and shade tree saplings. "It is our desire to build a beautiful city to the Lord," he said. Bring the best glass, steel of all kinds, saws, files, plenty of scythes and sickles, and paper and ink.

Orson Hyde, Frederick Piercy, Route From Liverpool to The Great Salt Lake Valley

That same letter instructed leaders in Kanesville about a freighting project they'd assigned to Howard, for which he'd need their help. "We wish you to send by Elder Howard Egan, the carding machine and fixtures, so that it may be placed in a suitable building, and at as early a time as possible for the convenience of the brethren. We wish him to start as early as he can, that he may arrive here by the time of sheep shearing." It advised that "we send the mail in charge of Elder Egan, from which you can obtain intelligence in regard to many items that may have been overlooked in this epistle."

Fast Mail Carrier to Council Bluffs

For this one trip, Howard's assignment was to carry mail, a new role for him. Years later, as a supervisor, rider, and driver for the Pony Express and stagecoaches, mail would become his decade-long career. On October 13, Howard bid Tamson and the boys goodbye, loaded up the eastbound mail, and left for Kanesville. This time his absence would last ten months. He went with a small party of three or four, whose names we lack.[5] The next day, while they approached the mouth of Echo Canyon, they met Willard Richard's big Third Division of the year's emigrants. They handed Howard mail they had brought. This caused him to turn around and hurry back to the city, knowing that some of that mail would require an answer he needed to carry east.[6]

When he finished that task, he and his party resumed their rush eastward. This would be Howard's fourth time traveling the thousand mile trail. What kind of transportation they used isn't known, but facing late October and all of November on the trail, they traveled as fast and mobile as possible to beat winter conditions. They covered the thousand-plus miles in fifty-six days, or half the time it took the 1847 westbound pioneers.[7] To travel at that pace indicates that they used a light wagon or carriage pulled by mules. They averaged about twenty miles a day. They suffered. They lost animals. But they reached Kanesville safely on December 7 with a lot of mail.

Grumblings greeted Howard at the post office. Back then the receivers of the mail, not the senders, paid the postage costs. Mail that Howard delivered was not U.S. mail, so postage costs were to be paid to him and his team. Some of those receiving mail he brought felt it "extortionate" to pay forty cents for a letter from the Valley, and argued for a lower price. Howard "brought many letters for poor people, widows and soldiers wives," so Kanesville leaders "advised Mr. Egan to give these out free of charge," which he did. Then they came to his defense. Because he had such a hard time "coming through with the mail, lost many of his animals on the way &c.," they "thought it more than right that he should have forty cents a letter from such as could pay it." They reasoned that "no man, or set of men, can carry a mail there or bring one back without sinking a good deal of money. One man cannot go through alone; he must have a strong guard." It was not right "to crush or oppress three or four men that endure the hardship of transporting the mail across the Plains in severely cold weather." Complainers should pay up or carry the mail themselves.[8]

Wintering in the Kanesville Area

Elders Orson Hyde, George A. Smith, and Ezra T. Benson presided over Kanesville and the dozens of surrounding settlements of Mormons. Most were not villages or hamlets but simply pockets of settlers living by a grove or stream. Many of these clusters had a school, and some set up small water- or horse-powered gristmills. Iowa then contained more Saints than Utah did. Howard reunited with his wife Nancy and fifteen-month-old daughter Helen Jeanette. Records don't show where Nancy and Helen had been living or where they and Howard lived after he joined them, but apparently it was among the Reddens. Her parents lived in the area and didn't

Major Howard Egan, Early Mormonism, and the Pioneering of the American West ~ 203

Kanesville, 1849–1851, artist George Simons, courtesy Council Bluffs Library

Ramage Printing Press,
Wendell J. Ashton,
Voice in the West

come west until 1852.[9] Howard, because of his many buying and trading trips, knew southwestern Iowa well. He knew how to provide for Nancy and Helen through the winter. That winter lasted long and the snows fell deep.

In Kanesville, a scrubby town, most houses were log cabins. The business district boasted three general stores, and advertisers included Hiram Clark's Union Hotel, Dustin Amy's tinsmith shop, a blacksmith, a tailor, and doctors and lawyers.[10] Howard found a stake operating there, replete with quorums, a high council, and nearly forty branches, many with a bishop in charge. High councilmen, circuit riders, and other authorities regularly visited the branches.

Two months after Howard arrived, Elder Hyde started publishing a four-page biweekly LDS newspaper, the *Frontier Guardian*. Its first issue is dated February 7, 1849.[11] Salt Lake City didn't have a newspaper yet, and part of Howard's mission was to haul a printing press west to end that deficit.

Outfitting the Egan Freight Company

Per President Young's October 9 letter, Elders Hyde, Smith, and Benson had to help outfit and round up freight for Howard. During the April 7–9 stake conference, inside and out, exciting news buzzed about gold discoveries in California and the gold fever sweeping the nation. Conference speakers cautioned Saints against temptations to flee west for supposedly quick riches. But one matter of conference business was to "devise means to send the public property to the Valley" with Howard. Attenders heard this appeal:

> Well now, to get the carding machine and other property to the Valley there is about five tons; it will take two wagons and five or six yoke of cattle to carry the carding machine and printing press, which we want to go with brother Egan who starts about the 15th of this month. Now we want the man that has money, oxen or wagons that can go, to come forward and let us know his name.

Several responded. Isaac Matthews provided one pair of oxen, Isaac Houston and Alexander S. Stanley one wagon each. Elder Benson appealed for more oxen, and proposed during one meeting that they "take up a collection to assist in carrying the church property to the Valley." He received $18.75 in donations. He then called for flour for the teamsters and other provisions. In response, ten men and one woman donated 490 pounds of flour, 6 hams, and 2.5 bushels of beans.[12]

With streams running high, some bridges washed out, and roads muddy, Howard spent most of April rounding up freight, recruiting wagons and teamsters, and helping Nancy and Helen prepare for the trip. He needed people to join his company to make it large enough to travel safely in Indian country. Several families enlisted, either voluntarily or by assignment from the resident apostles.

Howard recruited seven teamsters for "his" wagons. One of the best teamsters was a thirty-year-old Dane named Peter Olsen Hansen, who had previous trail experience. Born in Copenhagen, Denmark, Hansen was a sailor by trade, so he and Howard had sailing in common. Hansen joined the Church in Boston in 1844, then moved to Nauvoo where he worked on the temple and helped translate the Book of Mormon into Danish. In 1847 he had gone to Utah in the Smoot-Wallace wagon train just after Howard had been there and left. Hansen returned from Utah to the Kanesville area in 1848.[13] In Egan's 1849 company Hansen kept a diary, and, years later, he wrote several recollections about the Egan trip, from which the following account is taken.[14]

On April 18, teamsters Hansen, William Meeks, George Redden (Nancy's brother), and Franklin Edwards, acting for Howard, left "Father Redden's house" with three wagons and fourteen yoke of oxen. Nancy's father was George Redden Sr. They passed through Kanesville, where Solen McFarlin replaced George Redden, who went home. These four teamsters then drove way down to St. Joseph, Missouri, "after some goods to take with us to the Valley." They found St. Joseph swarming with men "raging with the gold fever." They loaded up goods and headed back. The heavy wagons sometimes sank in mud up to the wheel hubs. On April 27 they arrived at the Winchester family's home opposite Old Fort Kearney (Kearny misspelled), about halfway between Kanesville and St. Joseph.[15] "Here we tarried a fortnight fitting out," Hansen said.[16]

Meanwhile, Howard sent freight to the Winchester outfitting place. He needed and waited for materials being shipped up from St. Louis aboard the steamboat *Dahcota*. But, on April 25, a Wednesday, that paddle-wheeler suffered "a total wreck with great loss of property and one child" seventy miles downriver from Kanesville and about eighteen miles below Old Fort Kearney. A distraught *Dahcota* passenger dispatched an urgent appeal to Kanesville: "please send us some teams, we are on the river bank without provisions or means of transportation." Kanesville hesitated, then sent aid.[17] "The saints lost all their luggage...A number of letters and packages ... were also lost on this steamer."[18] While the boat was sinking, Orson Whitney, in charge of Howard's shipment, rushed to the Winchesters' and recruited help. They salvaged the greater part of Howard's goods. This Winchester family would join Howard's wagon company and Whitney became one of Howard's teamsters.[19] (He was *not* the Orson F. Whitney who later became an apostle.)

On May 3, Hansen said, Howard arrived with his family at the Winchesters', "after which we went to work loading up our wagons."[20] By then Nancy was about three months pregnant. On May 7, Elders Hyde, Smith, and Benson outfitted three ox-wagons with six yoke each and one yoke extra for Howard's use. Helping hands loaded Church property into the wagons, including a carding machine, printing press, printing press type, a box of cases, glue, stationery, printers ink, 872 bundles of paper, a clock, German books, and mail for the Valley.[21] Where they obtained the printing press isn't known. This press, after Howard hauled it to Utah, became the press that printed the first issues of the *Deseret News* in 1850.[22]

Howard's small wagon train had no choice but to drive into heavy traffic, gold-fever-driven trail traffic, as described by the *St. Joseph Gazette*:

> ...a large number have crossed the upper part of the State, intending to cross the river at the Bluffs [Kanesville]—say four thousand persons. We do not think it an extravagant assertion to say that at least eighteen thousand persons will leave the frontier between this place and the Bluffs; ...We have no means of knowing what number will leave Independence, but should suppose that six or eight thousand will depart from that point. This will make some 25,000 persons on the plains in a few weeks.[23]

Boulware's Ferry

Howard decided not to cross the Missouri River at Kanesville or to follow the established route along the north side of the Platte River. Instead, he outfitted his wagons forty-five miles farther south, near the Winchesters, in order to use John Boulware's ferry that crossed the Mississippi River to Old Fort Kearney. That departure point was closer to the freight that was sent up to him from St. Joseph, and, from the ferry landing across the river, a trail led northwesterly to the Oregon Trail and the south side of the Platte River.

On May 9 Howard's teamsters drove four wagons down to the ferry, but for some reason, perhaps backed-up traffic, his array of wagons didn't cross until May 15. Then, while camped on the Nebraska side on Cable Creek, Howard organized the covered wagon train. By common consent, as if there were any question, Howard was elected company captain. Elijah Elmer became captain of the guard and herdsmen, James Graham a captain of ten, and Reuben Hildreth captain of the second ten. G. H. Hoit was chosen camp clerk, although teamster Hansen's diary became the company's journal.[24]

Following the "Old Fort Kearney Trail"

Hansen said that Howard "studied the shortest route in order to make the trip as quick as possible, and we did make it in eleven weeks." Hansen's diary and one letter Howard wrote on June 1 tell how the small wagon company started out. They followed an existing Oregon Trail "feeder" called the "Old Fort Kearney Road," which soon became known as the "Ox-Bow Trail." From Old Fort Kearney, the trail traced a big bow that curved northwesterly to the south bank of the Platte, then curved southwesterly along the Platte to New Fort Kearny, for a total of 210 miles. Just east of that new fort, the trail merged onto the well-established Oregon Trail that came in from Independence, Missouri.[25]

On their first travel day, May 17, they moved fourteen miles. Ten miles the next day brought them to the Weeping Water River and a campsite where wood was scarce. On May 19 they camped on Snake Creek, where three families named Jones with three wagons joined them. Lucky for the Egan Company, Frederick Jones was a blacksmith. That day Howard started jotting down daily trip notes, which, ten days later, he sent to Elder Hyde.[26] His first entry reads, "This morning Br. Nathaniel Jones came up with us accompanied by two of his brothers with their families, with three wagons, and two young men, late from Baltimore, John Stewart and Charles Snow."

Next day, a Sunday, the little company stayed camped. Travels on Monday moved them to a landmark named Salt Creek, or Saline Creek. "The bank of this stream being high and steep, we had to let the wagons down by ropes," Hansen recorded. Before lowering the wagons, Howard undoubtedly checked the ropes and loadings to be sure the contents were tied down, especially the printing press and the carding machine. "This is the largest stream we have crossed," Hansen continued. "The water here is a little salty, owing to the existence of salt banks above, but there was plenty of cottonwood and good grass at the bottom. Most of the cattle wouldn't drink the water."[27]

California-bound people and gold-rush dropouts constantly passed and repassed Howard's party. He noted on May 21, "a few miles east of Salt Creek, met three wagons on their way back to Nodaway county, Missouri, reported that a number of their company had the measles." Then, about two miles west of Salt Creek, they "past a company, most of them from Gentry county, Missouri, had five cases of cholera, a Mr. George Thompson, of Atchison county, Mo., died on the 22, the other four are said to be recovering."[28]

Crowds of forty-niners—first crammed together on sailing ships, riverboats, and stage coaches, and then in taverns and campgrounds—caused a deadly cholera epidemic in 1849. Cholera devastated St. Louis. It caused between two hundred and four hundred trail deaths that year.[29] Reports about cholera and measles

Peter Olsen Hansen, the company's diarist, 1874, Portrait Collection, LDS Church History Library

gave Nancy and Howard cause for concern for themselves and little Helen, and the baby forming inside Nancy.

"Br. Winchester and family came up with us about 90 miles from the Missouri river," Howard wrote on May 23, "with four wagons, accompanied by two young men John Thackham and James Dimond." That evening the enlarged train overtook a company that had, Hansen said, "four cases of cholera among them." Howard noted that "We are traveling at the rate of about 15 miles a day, feed is good, the weather very cool and our cattle are doing well." Their road passed across prairie landscapes.[30]

After the Winchesters arrived, Hansen's inventory showed the company had 57 people, 23 wagons, 91 oxen, 6 horses, 5 mules, 3 young stock, 21 fowls, 6 dogs, and 1 cat. At least two yoke, apparently meaning oxen, pulled each wagon. Howard had personal responsibility for seven wagons, or one-third of the total. Traveling with him were Nancy and Helen and six teamsters. Hansen referred to Howard's wagons as "Kimball wagons," which means Heber C. Kimball had covered costs for much of the cargo they carried.[31]

Howard drove the leading wagon, pulled by mules. The men, women, children, wagons, and animals in his company relied on him for their route, feed, water, campsites, and overall well-being.[32] On May 25, rains ruined the morning travel, and then rising creek waters forced them to move camp a mile up onto higher ground. They traveled eighteen miles on May 26 to a point "above the Pawnee Village." Howard's May 27 entry, written "ten miles west of the Pawnee village," mentioned a "Pittsburgh company." It had crossed the Missouri at St. Joseph and "quarreled amongst themselves." One man had been killed and they "were heaving out sugar, coffee, and tools of all kinds, and breaking up in small companies." When Howard wrote that, his train still had fifty or sixty miles to go to reach New Fort Kearny.[33] On May 29 they met a lieutenant from Fort Kearny at Grand Island, who reported "that a great many belonging to the companies from Independence has had the cholera: he said that sixty had died between Independence and Grand Island."

Joining the Oregon Trail and Constant Traffic

On May 31, the Egan Company's long, bowed route merged into the Oregon Trail. They added to its heavy traffic, as Howard noted:

> Eight miles east of the head of Grand Island; to-day we have passed where the St. Joseph and Independence road intersect this road; there is one continual string of wagons as far as the eye can extend, both before and behind us; all seem to be moving on peaceably and quiet. They reported a great deal of sickness in the different companies for the first two or three weeks; but now mostly are

enjoying good health, and our cattle are gaining. If the Platte river is low enough I think I shall cross over to the North side when I get above the head of Grand Island, in order to get out of the crowd, that I may have more sea room. This evening there is twenty-nine camps in sight, numbering from fifteen to forty wagons in a company.

His phrase "more sea room" is further evidence he once was a sailor. On June 1 they stopped at New Fort Kearny "to feed," Hansen said. Here they learned how big, and desperate, the stampede for gold really was. Forty-niners, frustrated by slow travel, littered the landscape with discarded wagons, baggage, and food. That day Howard finished writing his ten-day trip summary and mailed it at New Fort Kearny to Elder Hyde in Kanesville. Its final entry reads:

June 1st. We arrived at Fort Kearney about noon to-day; I ascertained that there had 4131 wagons passed here up to the last of May, and there is probably about two thousand behind us. It is reported that there is 2000 wagons at the crossing of the South Fork of the Platte [up ahead], awaiting as the river is so high that they cannot cross. There is some of the companies selling their wagons and packing from this place; wagons which cost $125 dollars in the States have sold for $10 and $20 dollars, bacon has been sold for one cent per pound, flour from one to two dollars per hundred, and other articles in proportion.

Old Fort Kearny, *artist William Henry Jackson, courtesy Perry Special Collections, Lee Library, BYU*

Along the Platte, Then Fording the South Platte

This was Howard's sixth trip "crossing the plains," doing three in each direction within a three year period. After leaving the fort, the Oregon Trail hugged the south side of the Platte River for about 110 miles westward to where the South and North Platte rivers converge. During that stretch, or soon after leaving it, Howard mistakenly blamed teamster Hansen for a problem some of the younger teamsters caused. As Hansen explained it:

> The seven first teams in the company were Br. Kimballs. Capt. Egan drove the first which was a mule team. I drove an ox team, and the other five teamsters were mere boys. In one of the wagons was a barrel of whiskey, and one day 3 of the boys had bored the barrel and let out some whiskey and drank, and the Captain noticed their been acting a little silly and found that the barrel had been bored, and thinking that I must know of the doings and have shared in the fun, he kept from speaking to me a whole week.

Finally, Hansen asked Howard for an explanation. Howard said he had assumed Hansen had been "guilty with the boys." Hansen convinced Howard he played no part in the whiskey drinking. Nevertheless, Howard felt that a mature teamster like Hansen had some responsibility for guiding the young teamsters' conduct.[34]

On June 7 the Egan party's nearly two dozen wagons reached and rolled past where the North and South Platte flowed together. That day they saw their first buffalo. Two days later they forded the South Platte, but not easily. They had to double team each wagon to pull it across. From there they continued on a road westward between the two Plattes. On the tenth they saw many buffalo and killed one. Perhaps here Nancy, for her first time, tasted buffalo meat. Three days later they braked down to Ash Hollow, a favorite camping place on the Oregon Trail on the North Platte's south shore. The Egan Company, Hansen said, "descended the hills which were very steep and came down into Ash Hollow

Crossing the South Platte, *artist Irene D. Paden,* The Wake of the Prairie Schooner

which we followed down to its mouth, near the north fork of the Platte, and encamped for the night about one mile above the mouth of Ash Hollow. It rained in the evening and we found that the grass here had been eaten off by other cattle." Hansen and other teamsters "went back to the hollow" and picked currants and choke cherries.[35] Travelers liked Ash Hollow because of its sweet spring water and large, shady trees, the first they'd seen for nearly a hundred miles.[36]

Rumbling day by day along the south side of the North Platte, the Egans experienced mosquito swarms, a night of heavy rain, some good and some bad roads, and several creek crossings. On June 18 they passed sand-colored Chimney Rock, the high plains landmark.[37]

Hansen recorded that on June 20 "a regiment of dragoons [cavalry], with a great number of baggage wagons, encamped with us that night." From New Fort Kearny onward, Hansen recalled, "we saw more or less of Soldiers & gold hunters most every day, and we learned that nearly 2000 soldiers were on the road to Oregon and California, and that more than half of them deserted by the way." In one place the Egan train "found some military baggage waggons in the mud, and by the request of the officer we hitched some of our big oxen to the waggons and pulled them out." They looked at "many waggons, chests, piles of bacon and of iron left by the gold hunters when their teams gave out."[38]

To the Upper North Platte Crossing

Hot, dusty days accompanied them to Fort Laramie, which Howard had seen four times before. They made no stop at the crowded, jammed post, but continued on the well worn but rough Oregon Trail. Teamster Hansen recalled a dangerous situation that perhaps happened during this stretch of travel. He was taking Nancy Egan somewhere "when the road took us onto a very narrow ridge and as we found that we were going in a wrong direction and I had to go right off & go down the hill side, which went well as the cattle were well broke."[39]

On July 2, windy and dusty, they traveled a twenty-one mile stretch that ended at the North Platte ferry. They found good feed on the bench and bottoms. "It was with great joy," Hansen said, "that we met some of our brethren who were ferrying at this place." For more than a week the Egan procession "laid by" near the ferry, waiting for the water to subside. Howard felt fording was safer for the heavy equipment he was hauling than ferrying would be. Men used the down time to repair the wagons and rest the teams.[40]

On the Fourth of July Howard invited the Mormons operating the ferry to come for supper.[41] That day, sadly, Frederick Jones accidentally shot himself, fatally. According to Hansen:

> Our blacksmith Frederick Jones had been doing a good deal of work, mostly setting tires, and when done & we still had to wait for the water to come down, he took his rifle barrel, believing that he must have put the cartridge the wrong end in, as he could not get the gun to go off, and stuck the bud [butt] end in the fire for to melt the bullet, holding the musle [muzzle] in one hand & blowing the bellows with the other. When the iron got red hot, the powder within ignited & sent the bullet into his stomach with the conviction that it had not been put wrong end in.

As Jones's condition worsened, he expressed deathbed repentance:

> I think the poor man lingered four days before he expired. He was a brother to Nathaniel V. Jones who was with us at the time. He ... had not obeyed the gospel, which neglect he now regretted, saing that he had believed mormonism to be true, but had had a disposition to eavil & gainsay, & now he desired to be baptized for the remission of his sins & that he might die a member of the church. He was carried to the water by four of the brethren & after being baptized he was ordained ... and he felt thankful and asked his wifes forgiveness for keeping them out of the church, and exhorted her to never leave it.[42]

Brother Jones died on July 8 and was buried "not far off." After his burial, Howard forded his company across North Platte. They then drove up along the river "a little ways" and camped. There, "Jones's widow [Samantha] was baptized before going any farther."[43]

Avoiding a Robbery Near South Pass

They spent July 10 "until sundown setting tires," and then Howard led them on a twenty-four hour drive across the waterless, forty-plus miles long divide between the Platte and the Sweetwater. They traveled all night by moonlight. At the Sweetwater they found "first rate grass," Hansen said. They now moved through the deadly zone that proved fatal for cattle because of mineral water and alkali. Near Independence Rock on July 12 they spotted large numbers of dead cattle along the road. For the next five days they traveled beside, and repeatedly crossed, the twisting Sweetwater. On July 17, Sister Hannah Klingonsmith gave birth to a daughter. Three oxen and a heifer died two days later. To lose even one ox put a wagon in jeopardy.[44] On July 20 the company drove up and over South Pass and camped a few miles beyond Pacific Springs. That evening, danger lurked up ahead posed by army deserters. Said Hansen:

> Coming over by the Pacific Spring we overtook & passed by Pomeroy's merchant train. This gentleman had learned from one of his hunters that some seventy deserted Dragoons with 1–2 horses to a man, were encamped a few miles north in the direction of the Wind river mountains where we sure enough saw a

smoke, and that they were awaiting Pomeroys and the Mormon train to come, that they might plunder them for provisions.[45]

The Pomeroy brothers, Ebenezer and Thaddeus, had left Lexington, Missouri, early in May with forty heavy freight wagons and 130 yoke of oxen. The wagons carried thirty tons of provisions valued at fifty thousand dollars. The Pomeroys planned to sell their cargo in the California gold fields, but also to emigrants along the trail.[46] One of the worried brothers proposed to Captain Egan "for both camps to break up at 12 oclock in the night when the moon would rise, and thus get out of the way of the danger." Howard agreed. So "when the moon got up we were going along at a good piece," Hansen recalled, "and it is well known that cattle will travel faster by night than in the day time. The road we had before us was very good." They avoided being robbed.[47]

Needing Help from the Valley

On July 23 the Egan wagon train reached the Green River "and drove our stock over on the other side, on to most excellent feed." The wagons ferried the river the next day. That's where teamster Hansen decided he might like to marry Samantha Jones, the twenty-five-year-old widow:

> After passing down into the Green river country I proposed marrying the widow for I understood she was a good woman. But before revealing my thoughts to the lady, I spoke to Brother Nathaniel [Jones] about it to know whether he had any thoughts of marrying his brothers widow and he said he had not had any such thoughts & He had no objection to my marrying her, but then he told me that it was her wish to be married to her husbands brother otherwise she would had no objection ... and this ended my courtship.[48]

When yet another ox died on July 25, Howard's train was in trouble. So that day he went ahead in the morning with the mail for Salt Lake City, his main purpose being to bring back wagons and teams to help his company.[49] After he left, who drove the Egan wagon with Nancy and Helen isn't known. About a week later he reached the Valley. No doubt he paid a quick visit to Tamson and the boys, and then he rounded up wagons, teams, and supplies, and headed back.

Arriving Home to a New Home

On August 3, while the Egan Company jostled down Echo Canyon's lower end, Howard and his reinforcements met them with "some wagons and ox teams" to help them in. The reinforced caravan ascended and passed over Big Mountain on August

6. President Heber C. Kimball, apparently anxious to examine the machinery and cargoes Howard hauled, visited the wagon train while it carefully descended through Emigration Canyon.[50] On August 7, the Egan Company entered the Valley. Their journey from the Missouri River ferry had taken them eleven weeks.

Howard reunited with his first family. Hopefully they extended a cordial welcome to Nancy, who was in her last two months of pregnancy, and little Helen. Tamson and the boys no longer lived in the fort. The forts had been broken up "by the removal of the houses on to the city lots; and the city is already assuming the appearance of years, for any ordinary country; such is the industry and perseverance of the Saints."[51] Back in April, Ransom said, Tamson and the boys had "moved out of the Fort to our new home, on the second lot south of the corner of First North [today's Second North] and Main Street. We had a house built of adobes with a shingle roof." Ransom said, "we lived across the street from Heber C. Kimball." According to what Tamson told her son William Egan later, she lived one block north of the Salt Lake Temple block, opposite Heber C. Kimball's house, "in a little adobe house." Kimball owned the entire city block northeast of the temple block, and erected his main home there. So, the Egans lived right across the street, on the west side of Main Street close to mid-block between today's North Temple and Second North.[52] In that adobe house "Mother had a little better time of it," Ransom said, "than while living in the fort." The house had but one large room that was plastered sides and ceiling, and a lumber floor "that Mother used to mop every day. She took quite a pride in her white floor." By the house they kept a pig, some poultry, and a cow, "which helped along nicely."[53]

The Family During Howard's Absence

During Howard's first few days home Tamson updated him, telling him how the city's Saints fared during his absence. She probably related some of the same things the First Presidency had summarized about the difficult, previous winter, which had produced excessive, below-freezing cold, and frequent snow storms:

> The snow on the surrounding mountains has been much deeper, which has made the wood very difficult of access; while the cattle have become so poor, through fasting and scanty fare, that it has been difficult to draw the necessary fuel and many have had to suffer, more or less, from the want thereof. The winter … found many of the brethren without houses or fuel, and although there has been considerable suffering, there has been no death by the frost. Three attempts have been made by the brethren with pack animals or snow shoes to visit Fort Bridger, since the snow fell, but have failed. [54]

Conditions had become so dangerous by early February that the bishops took an inventory of breadstuff in the Valley and found "a little more than three-fourths of a pound per day, for each soul, until the 9th of July; and considerable was known to exist which was not reported. As a natural consequence some were nearly destitute while others had an abundance." A small outpost for agricultural and fishing purposes had been set-up sixty miles south in Utah Valley. Fish, it was hoped, could lessen calls for beef that was "rather scarce." At times Tamson and the children must have been hard-pressed and short of resources. It's likely that President Kimball kept a watchful eye on them, even though Tamson didn't like to accept help.

The Presidency's April report had lamented the short supply of cows, sheep, oxen, livestock of all kinds, geese, ducks, turkeys, guinea hens, domestics, dry goods, groceries, window glass, nails, cotton yarn, dye, paints, turpentine, paper, books, saws, files, screws, sheet tin, hardware, cutlery, iron, farm utensils, steel, copper and brass sheeting, crockery, glasses, looking glasses, shoe leather, harnesses, harness trimming, mill saws, mechanics' tools, wire, door locks and padlocks. Saints needed and hoped that the incoming 1849 Mormon emigration would bring much of what they needed, "for any of these articles here are better than gold." Howard's freight wagon train apparently brought some of the badly needed items.

And, back in June, Howard learned, crickets had invaded the crops, like they had done the year before, but with less devastation. Ransom witnessed the 1849 insect onslaught:

> Crickets.—Oh! yes, I must not forget them! Well they hatched out all along on top of the bench land, and as they grew kept working down hill, leaving nothing green behind except sage brush. The road north of our place ran along the lower level of the bench, the grain and hay fields being still farther down and a fence between the road and fields. When the crickets got near the road, war was declared and the fight was on; men, women and children walking back and forth swinging brooms made of willows or bunches of grass, trying to drive the enemy back, but with very little success.

In fact, Ransom said, this kind of warfare only made the crickets more aggressive and hopping ever-nearer to the grain,

> ...till at last, was put in operation, our biggest gun, which consisted of all the sheep, cows and horses that could be collected, These were crowded together and driven back and forth the length of the field slaying the enemy by the legions. Thus it only required about a week to save part of the crop, but a little was better than none those days.[55]

Probably the best news Tamson shared with Howard concerned the gold rush miracle then blessing the city. While Saints were facing serious shortages, the California gold rush suddenly brought them wonderful windfalls. Starting on June 16, forty-niners poured into Great Salt Lake City. An estimated five thousand to ten thousand gold rushers passed through the Valley that season.[56] Dismayed by slowness to reach California, most stayed for about a week and then pushed on. And, needing food and livestock, they paid high prices that Mormons had to charge because of shortages. In return for fresh vegetables, fruit, livestock, meals, and temporary lodgings, the forty-niners gave the Saints clothes, tools, equipment, and wagons, and almost every article, except sugar and coffee, at half the price at least for which the goods could have been purchased in the States. It was a "bargain basement atmosphere."[57]

The anxious gold rushers traded heavy wagons, worn out cattle, and merchandise for horse or mule outfits. LDS blacksmiths, wheelwrights, teamsters, laundresses, and millers were paid to service and re-outfit the overlanders. Through such transactions, Saints obtained necessities and even some luxuries. Perhaps enterprising Tamson figured out ways to benefit from the visiting forty-niners. Also a blessing was the arrival, two days after Howard's freight company, of the Pomeroy brothers' freight wagons. Their new merchandise found eager buyers.[58]

A New Baby and an Additional Wife

Howard moved into the little adobe house with Tamson and the boys. Where Nancy and Helen lived isn't recorded. It didn't take long for Howard's family to increase by two–a wife and a baby. Between August and November (the date isn't certain) Howard married Mary Ann Tuttle. She had crossed the plains with him, Tamson, and the boys the year before. She was born June 5, 1830 in Boston to Edward Tuttle and Catherine Vanever Geyer. Her father had died in August 1847 at Winter Quarters, and her mother came west in the Kimball Division in 1848.[59] Then, as the second addition, on October 13, 1849, Nancy gave birth to Vilate Louise. She was Howard's second and last daughter.

Howard now had five children. Ransom was nine, Erastus seven, Horace two, Helen Jeanette two, and Vilate newborn. Howard was thirty-four, Tamson twenty-five, Nancy twenty-four, and new bride Mary Ann nineteen. The Egan family numbered nine. Howard was able to spend four months with them and handle family obligations. Then, apparently by Church assignment, he had to leave once again, this time going to the California gold fields to operate a trading post. ◆

~ 15 ~

By a New Southern Route to the Gold Fields

Gold attracts dreamers of a better life like magnets grab steel shavings. Legends are legion about gold rings, gold medals, King Midas's Golden Touch, Jason and the Golden Fleece, and Seven Cities of Gold. "Every civilization of recorded history had its gold lust and sent its explorers to the edges of the earth to sate it."[1] Few events have had more impact on the American West than the fabulous discovery of gold in California in 1848 and the gold rush it launched. For Howard, the gold rush became another big history event he participated in, and another one that he documented in a diary that now is an invaluable historical document.[2]

Howard went to California to establish a trading company for prospectors, Mormon or otherwise. To do that he first had to survive grueling travel on a barely findable new southern route to California. Then, he opened, stocked, and operated a trading post in the Sierra Nevada foothills. He endured primitive living conditions, worked with Mormon apostles in the area, traveled frequently through the mining camps, survived cholera, and saw others undermine his business. His success in the gold regions is questionable, but his absence from home for nearly two years cost his family relationships dearly.

News About Gold in California

California, until 1848 when America seized it from Mexico, held little interest for Americans. It seemed a far away, balmy curiosity occupied by Native Americans, dotted with Catholic missions, and a source for hide and tallow coveted by Yankee merchants. Few whites had settled there. But, after Swiss settler John Sutter's hired hands, including ex-Mormon Battalion men, discovered gold in January 1848, California became front page news. The next year the rush to the gold fields was on, causing some fifty thousand "forty-niners" to push fast and hard by land and sea to California, where they scoured Sierra Nevada foothills for glittering flakes and shiny nuggets. Almost overnight California became a boisterous, single-male populated American territory, disdainful of Catholics, Mexicans, Indians, and the Mexican land-grant ranches.[3]

Mormons and the Gold Rush

Mormons helped discover the gold.[4] Late in 1847 James Marshall began constructing a grist mill and saw mill for John Sutter. Marshall's work force included former Mormon Battalion soldiers. On January 24, 1848, at the sawmill project on the South Fork of the American River, ex-Battalion private Henry Bigler recorded in his diary: "Monday, January 24. This day some kind of mettle (metal) that looks like gold was found in the tail race." Battalion member Azariah Smith recorded on January 30 that "Mr. Marshall found some precious (as we all suppose) Gold … some been found that would weigh five dollars."[5]

Excited Mormon prospectors soon found gold at sites they named Mormon Island, Mormon Bar, Mormon Gulch, and Mormon Diggings. A pack train arrived in Salt Lake City on September 28, 1848, heavily laden with bags of "Mormon gold."[6] Howard was still in the Valley when that happened. Gold news excited the community. President Young, fearing wholesale desertions to the gold fields, preached hard against it: "If we were to go to San Francisco and dig up chunks of gold or find it here in the valley it would ruin us," he warned; "to talk of going away from this valley for anything is like vinegar to my eyes. They that love the world have not their affections placed upon the Lord."[7]

Then, during his winter and spring in the Kanesville area, 1848–1849, Howard witnessed gold hysteria driving excited men to rush to California. He led his freight wagon train in 1849 amidst thousands of forty-niners streaming across the plains. Perhaps gold talk enticed Howard, at least slightly, by the time he unloaded his freight in Salt Lake City that August. On September 29, 1849, a "gold train" of eight wagons and fourteen men arrived from California, sent by Apostle Amasa Lyman. It carried $25,000 to $30,000, some of it gold that miners had paid as tithing. Utah needed hard currency, so the Church's mint turned some of the newly arrived gold dust into "2.5, 5, 10, and 20 dollar pieces," and by the end of October those coins were "quite plentiful" in the city. Possibly Howard handled a few. Every Mormon gold coin, stamped with "Holiness to the Lord," whispered a message that "there is gold to be had in California."[8]

Mormon Gold Coins, 1849

The Need for a Southern Wagon Route

California-bound Argonauts entered Salt Lake City in June 1849, and their numbers increased during the next months. Those arriving late in the season, haunted by horrific stories about the Donner Party's winter entrapment three seasons earlier, feared to push on to California. But, hating to lose time wintering in Utah, they eagerly listened to talk about a pack trail route from Great Salt Lake City to southern California.[9] Back in 1846, mountaineer Miles Goodyear had taken a mule pack train from the Great Salt Lake Valley southbound on trails he found. Then, late in 1847, Asahel Lathrop, one of Howard's fellow 1847 pioneers, led a party of nineteen Mormon riders with twenty pack animals to southern California. During Lathrop's return trip early in 1848 his group brought not only pack animals and loose livestock, but also one wagon most of the way—the first wagon ever to try that route.[10]

Frustrated forty-niners didn't want to winter in Utah and LDS leaders didn't want them staying because they would drain valuable resources,[11] so President Young encouraged the southern trail possibilities. He favored having a few Mormon frontiersmen lead the forty-niners on that route, both to get them out of town, as well as to possibly open a travelable wagon road to southern California.[12] As one guide, forty-niners recruited Jefferson Hunt, an ex-Mormon Battalion captain, who had twice traveled the route.[13] They met with Hunt on August 20, where he forthrightly described for them the trail's difficult terrain, bad roads, lack of water and feed, and Indian dangers.[14] That said, he offered to captain a large company for ten dollars per wagon. He'd lead the way but, he warned, those going with him would have to "work" the trail. To avoid heat in the desert stretches, and to let the forty-niners' already trail-weary cattle rest up, he'd not start the company until October. Hunt estimated they could cover the 825 miles to Los Angeles in sixty to seventy days.[15]

Jefferson Hunt, Miscellaneous Portrait Collection, LDS Church History Library

Gold Mining Missionaries

To blunt gold fever, Church leaders pointedly preached that people who stayed, developed farms, and raised livestock would be better off financially than nearly every gold seeker. The Lord would bless them for staying. "The saints can be better employed in raising grain and building houses in this vicinity," President Young admonished, "than in digging gold in Sacramento, unless they are counseled to do so."[16] Most accepted that counsel, but a select few received specific counsel to go. Seeing opportunity to help the Church's finances, Young let a few high authorities select and sponsor men to take missions via the southern route to find gold and bring it back. Sponsors would receive a share of what their representatives brought home.[17] Twenty to thirty men became "gold mining missionaries."[18]

The 1849 Southern Trail Companies

Talk about the southern route's possibilities raised high hopes and attracted recruits. Four or five pack groups and five wagon companies, one led by Howard, tried it in September, October, and November.[19] South of Salt Lake City, near Utah Lake, the companies organized. Many of those anxious to start first were unwilling or unable to pay Jefferson Hunt's fee. The first company, the Independent Pioneer Company or Hoover-Gruwell-Derr Company, chose not to employ him. They started on September 29 with forty-five wagons. They rarely traveled together. Theirs became a "mistake-fraught" trip because of an incompetent guide, bickering, and poor decisions.[20]

In early October the Hunt-Baxter wagon train left next, with Hunt as their guide. Henry Baxter of Michigan captained more than one hundred wagons and five hundred people. Next, a pack train led by Captain James M. Flake, a Mormon, left on October 14. They caught up with the Hunt-Baxter Company. Flake's group included young George Q. Cannon, one of the gold missionaries, and new LDS apostle Charles C. Rich, being sent to California to assist Elder Amasa Lyman in the gold fields. The large Hunt-Baxter train made slow progress. Frustrated by their pace, all but seven wagons quit near present-day Beaver, Utah and headed west to find a shortcut to Walker Pass in the Sierras. Orson Kirk Smith, who had captained a pack train of twenty men that had caught up with Hunt-Baxter, took charge of this mutinous operation. They failed to find a route that wagons could follow, so most gave up and returned to the southern trail and Hunt's leadership. Some of those who kept wandering ended up dying in the Death Valley region, giving it that name.[21]

On November 3 the Pomeroy brothers, Thaddeus and Ebenezer, started their freight wagons on the southern route. Howard had traveled with this Pomeroy train that summer on the Oregon Trail (see Chapter 14). After selling lots of commodities in Salt Lake City, they purchased livestock, and planned to drive their remaining cargo and cattle herd to southern California to sell.[22] A group of non-Mormons joined them. The company started with eighty-five men, forty-one wagons, and 480 livestock. This trip turned out to be disastrous for them; they lost almost all their cattle and more than half of their wagons. [23]

The next group was the Simpson D. Huffaker Company, composed mainly of gold mining missionaries, perhaps thirty-one in number.[24] A wagon train pulled by oxen, they left Salt Lake City between November 10 and 13.[25]

Howard's small Salt Lake Trading Company party, the final company of the season, pulled out on November 18. It consisted of fourteen men and boys, three wagons, and fifteen head of livestock. Using horses and mules to pull the wagons, instead of oxen, and being so small, the company traveled faster than the other wagon companies.[26]

Why Did Howard Go?

That Howard, home for such a short time, would leave his three wives and five children, who needed him to be provider, husband, and father, seems wrong. Why would he do that? There's no indication he went because he'd developed gold fever. And there's no hint that wanderlust drove him. And, being devoted to "the Brethren," he would have obeyed their counsel against going to the gold fields. Thus, something beyond himself must have compelled him to go. It's most likely that Church leadership sent him to California. Like gold missionaries quietly sent on their secret missions, Howard evidently received a Church assignment to develop in the mining camps a business called the Salt Lake Trading Company. No records for that company have been found, so some mystery swirls around the why and how of his California operations.[27]

It's not far-fetched to believe that Church leaders, already well aware of the amounts of gold some Mormons had been finding, felt that if those miners, and others, bought goods from Mormon traders, not "gentiles," that income could benefit the Church. It could be used to obtain food, livestock, and commodities needed in Utah, which Howard could either send or bring back. Church leaders well knew Howard's abilities as a trader, demonstrated during the Camp of Israel's Iowa crossing, his seven trade trips from Winter Quarters to Missouri, and his just-completed freight hauling mission from Kanesville.

The Route

The southern route ran roughly eight hundred and fifty miles. More than half of it "traversed some of the most forbidding desert terrain ever encountered by American pioneer companies."[28] These risk-taking 1849 wagon companies endured stretches of sandy, rocky, steep, and muddy trails, combined with days of terrible thirst and meager food, stiff winds, and stirred-up dust. They frequently lost oxen, mules, horses, and wagons. Indians stole cattle and posed life threats. Animal feed often was scarce, as were watering holes. For most who ventured on that trail, it was, as a later song says, "hard travelin'."

Because the southern course was so new, Howard kept a diary that identified sites and distances. Perhaps he had in mind generating a detailed traveler's guide, one like friend William Clayton had compiled for the Mormon Trail.[29] Howard's diary is a small bound book with pre-printed, but undated, days of the week, two per page. He wrote something for every day between November 18, 1849 and February 23, 1850. Because of its value as a historical record, his diary is accurately transcribed and published in LeRoy and Ann Hafen's *Journals of 49ers Salt Lake to Los Angeles*, as well as in *Pioneering the West*. All quotes by Howard in this chapter are from his original diary and are not separately documented.[30]

In today's Utah, the southern route basically ran where I-15 now connects Provo with Nephi and Fillmore. Just below Fillmore, where I-70 joins I-15, the wagon companies then followed what was the Old Spanish Trail. The Old Spanish Trail was a pack-trail from Santa Fe to Los Angeles since the 1830s and was not suitable for wagons. Near where Cedar City now is, the trail dog-legged west and then south to reach the lush Mountain Meadows, soon after which it dropped over the southern rim of the Great Basin. It then passed through desert regions between today's Mesquite and Las Vegas. After skirting Death Valley and wending through desert landscape to the Mojave River, it crossed Cajon Pass and dropped down into verdant southern California.

Winter Travel the Length of Utah

Howard started from Fort Utah, where Provo developed, on November 18, 1849. He carried with him a letter to deliver to Apostle Amasa Lyman in California.[31] "Our company numbered 14 men & boys," Howard penned in his diary. Despite snow, they reached the Sevier River, and on November 24 camped "with a company of ox teams & hors teams," apparently the rear section of the Pomeroy freight train.[32] On November 27, he finished organizing his little company. The next day they rolled through white

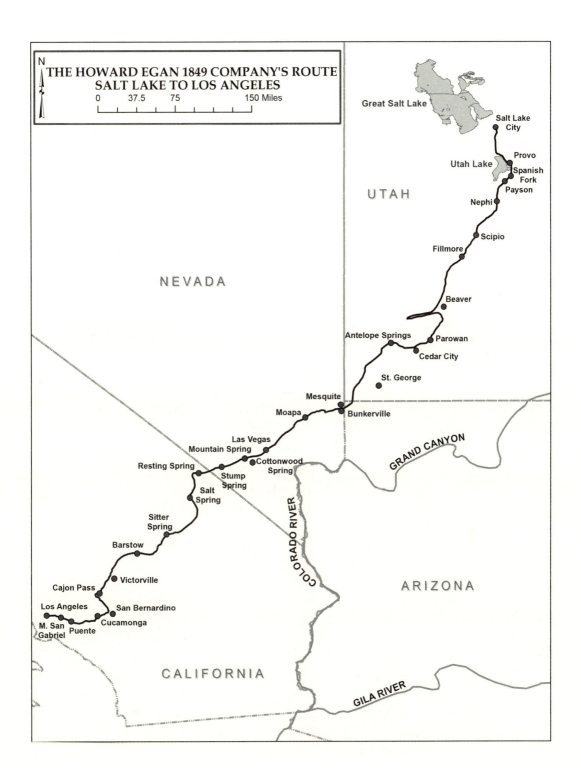

blankets of snow. They ended November in sight of Little Salt Lake, about seven miles long and a mile wide, a few miles northwest of today's Parowan.[33] On December 1 they caught up with the lumbering Pomeroy Company. One of the Pomeroys "laid up to burn coal & do some blacksmith work. He kindly oferd to have our wagon tier [tire] welded & anny other work done that we wanted." Joseph Hamblin, in the Pomeroy train, recorded that Egan had charge of "a party of Mormons & buckeyes…They have mules & horses."[34]

The next day, about where Cedar City is now, four men from Captain Kirk Smith's breakaway company that had lost their way joined the Egan Company, increasing it to at least eighteen men. Because of a threatened mutiny in the Pomeroy ranks, "Pomeroy solicited and obtained protection from Howard Egan's small Mormon company."[35] Howard stayed close to the Pomeroy company from November 29 to about December 7.

On December 4 and 5, Howard's party kept going through severe, cold, stormy weather. They rolled through Mountain Meadows.[36] On December 8, temperatures fell to twelve degrees below zero. Diaries don't say it, but the men depended for survival on their heavy coats, gloves, blankets, and campfires. They feared for the lives of their exposed mules. On December 11 they traveled through snow a foot deep. After that, having crossed the south rim of the Great Basin, they descended a thousand feet within thirty miles and reached the Virgin River at a point southwest of present-day St. George. They now enjoyed warmer climes in what's defined today as Utah's "Dixie," part of the Mojave Desert Region.[37]

Across Southern Nevada Deserts

Following the Virgin River for three days, they passed through some of "the most barren dessolate country I have ever seen," Howard said. They entered present-day southeastern Nevada about where Mesquite now is, and then traveled on "a heavy sandy road." On December 13, amid "warm and pleasant weather," they had to cross the Virgin River ten times.

During the next week, pleasant weather alternated with rain. John Bill's team gave out on December 15, so he junked his wagon and put his load into others' wagons. Discarded wagons often became firewood for later travelers. That day, according to Howard, they came to what is now known as Mormon Mesa near today's Bunkerville. To ascend and cross it "we took out part of loads & doubled teams, with a rope 250 feet long at the top of the mountain with a team and the assistance of 20 men we got up safe." After navigating the "California Crossing" of the Muddy River, travelers faced fifty "tortuous" desert miles to reach the Las Vegas springs. On ground alternating

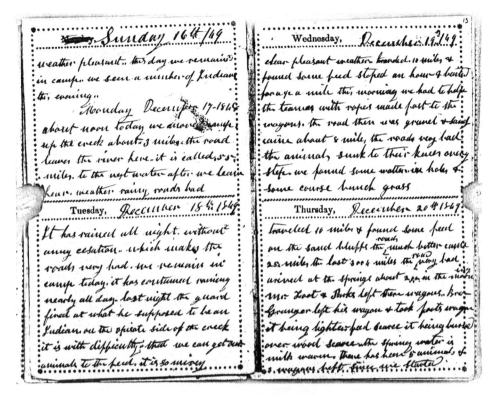

Howard Egan diary, December 1849, Beinecke Library, Yale University

between rock and sand, and lacking adequate feed and water, this was one of the most difficult segments of the trail.[38] Puddles of rain water helped quench thirst, but mud made travel difficult. It rained nearly all day on December 18. Next day, for the first half mile, Howard noted, "we had to help the teames with ropes made fast to the wagons...The roads very bad, the animals sunk to their knees every step. We found some watter in holes & some coarse bunch grass." At last they reached the welcome Las Vegas springs and meadows on December 20. Howard wrote:

> The last 3 or 4 miles of the road very bad, arived at the springs at 2 oc. In the morning. Mr. Foot & Parks left their wagons. Brother Granger left his wagon & took foots wagon it being lighter. feed scarce it being burned over. wood scarce. The spring water is milk warm. there has been 5 animals & 3 wagons left since we started.[39]

They remained camped for the day, then moved three miles to the main Vegas artesian springs. These produced clear, pure water, a treat for thirsty travelers and livestock. One of the largest springs had warm water boiling up "with such force as to buoy the swimmer like a cork."[40] After this Vegas oasis, Howard's men faced a seventy mile trek west-southwest on rough trails. On December 23 they camped by Cottonwood Springs. "2 of our company were run by some Indians who were behind." Next morning about 2:00 a.m. they heard the crack of rifle fire. Indians shot at their livestock, causing four to run off. Two men pursued and captured three of the animals.

To Cajon Pass and California Ranches

On Christmas Day, after traveling twenty-three miles "over a ruff road," they camped at Hernandez Springs (later called Resting Springs), approximately forty miles north of today's city of Baker and within twenty miles of Death Valley's edge. On December 27 the Egan party found a stray ox with an arrow stuck in his side, and saw fresh Indian tracks.[41] A guard spotted an Indian in the brush just before daylight and fired at him. That afternoon they crossed the Amargosa River several times. More wagon breakage occurred there than anywhere else on the southern trail.[42]

On December 29 they camped at Bitter Springs, which is now part of the Fort Irwin Military Reservation. Water was drinkable but cattle feed scarce. Nearby, they "found 3 wagons with nearly all there loading in, left by some of the company ahead." They ended December and the year 1849 with a flourish, covering an amazing forty miles by traveling all night. They arrived at the Mojave River at 8:00 a.m. on New Year's Day, and camped by good water and plenty of wood. "Most of our company are short of provisions," Howard noted; "we divided with them all we had to spare." The next night they camped at a site where they found crackling fires left by campers the night before. On January 3 Howard's party rested. He then started out ahead of them "for the settlements" with a "Mr. Foot."[43] Two days later the duo moved up Cajon Pass, "the watter rushing through the pass about 3 feet deep," and in places "the water would roll our horses over." The pass, elevation 4,300 feet, is in the rugged San Bernardino Mountains. Both Howard's route and today's I-15 cross the summit in the same place. Across the pass, Howard entered the mild southern California climate where grass grew abundantly and cattle ranches could provide them food and water.

In the evening on January 5, after traveling all day in the rain, Howard and Foote reached Rancho Cucamonga, the first habitation Howard had seen since leaving northern Utah.[44] A day later they arrived at Isaac Williams's Rancho del Chino, where the city of Chino is now, which Howard calculated was 769 miles from Utah Lake. "Here I found Bro Rich & Hunt & some 18 or 20 of the brethren. All well," Howard wrote.[45] "This is a beautifull valley…The hills look as green as they would be in [Salt Lake] valley at May." On the Williams Ranch, ten miles wide and thirty long, thirty thousand cattle roamed. He had never seen so many cattle before. Williams also had an orchard and a large vineyard.[46]

On January 9, Sheldon Stoddard arrived "and reported the [Egan] company ten miles from here." Captain Howard recorded that "our company arrived about noon, all well." He and they had bragging rights. Still behind them on the trail were the Pomeroy and Huffaker companies, which didn't come until February. Comparing travel times, Howard's group made the trek faster than the other wagon companies. From Fort Utah, his wagons needed forty-nine days, Flake's company fifty-eight, Hunt's eighty-one, Huffaker's eighty-seven, and Pomeroy's about 114.[47] Howard's company averaged 110 miles per week or roughly sixteen miles per day.

These five wagon companies had traveled the entire length of the crude southern trail. Their repeated hardships, sufferings, and courage, and their mule, horse, and ox teams and wagon wheels, had worn and carved a crude but passable new wagon road. They opened a new epoch in overland trail history. After that, the road became well-used. Many more miners heading for the California gold fields followed it. Mormon missionaries and the colonizers of San Bernardino and other communities traveled that way, as did an array of mail carriers, soldiers, world travelers, emigrants, and freight-wagon operators. Howard himself would be on that road again while doing California business a few years later.

Heading for the Sierra Nevada's Gold Regions

When Howard arrived at the Williams Ranch, now Chino, he found many other Mormons there who had traveled the southern trail ahead of him. The Jefferson Hunt, James Flake, Apostle Charles C. Rich, and Egan groups now needed to coordinate how best to reach the gold fields that were 450 to 500 miles northward. But, compared to what they'd just endured, their next months of travel on the Pacific Coast—among California's Mexican missions, amid verdant hills and tropical orchards and vineyards—would be scenic and pleasant. For their northward venture the men, anxious to start, accepted the leadership of Apostle Charles C. Rich.

From southern California, gold seekers chose one of two ways to reach the gold fields. Some went to Pueblo de Los Angeles and the port of San Pedro and booked passage on an infrequent ship sailing north to San Francisco. From there, riverboats conveyed them upriver to Sacramento City, where they outfitted and headed for gold regions east and north. Others, including the Mormon company Howard was in, traveled by land, using existing roads, primarily El Camino Real, or the Royal Highway.

When Howard first reached the Williams Ranch on January 7, he wrote that "the brethren are all preparing to start." The next day he penned that "Bro Rich is procuring wheat & corn & getting it ground for our company." Men spent January 10 "getting our grinding done." It took some work to organize teams and livestock. "Through the kindness of Brother Rich and Captain Hunt," George Q. Cannon noted, "ox teams were bought on credit, with which a number of us, under the leadership of Major Howard Egan, proceeded up the coast."[48] On January 11, Howard wrote that "[we] commenced our journey again," and when "Brothers Rich & Hunt came up this evening[,] we organized." The men selected Jefferson Hunt to captain their small company.

According to diarist Addison Pratt, the party was encamped along the San Gabriel River on January 13.[49] While stopped to feed on January 14, at the Mission San Gabriel, "we found plenty of oranges on the trees," Howard wrote. "The Mission has been partially deserted since the [Mexican] warr." Its location is nine miles east of today's downtown Los Angeles.

San Gabriel Mission, Henry Miller
California Mission Sketches, 1856, courtesy Bancroft Library

Continuing almost due west the next day, the company camped about a mile from "Pueble delos angles" on the San Pedro River, now called "Los Angeles River."[50] On January 16 the Mormons remained in camp "and lay in our grociers" they bought in town. Here once again Howard put his buying and trading expertise to work. In a "bill of provisions laid in by Howard Egan," he lists "200 lbs of flour $14.00, 92 lbs of Meal $8.60, grinding $1.50, 80 lbs of beef $1.60, 24 lbs sugar $4.80, 28 lbs of coffee $3.78," and salt and pepper.[51]

California introduced Howard to a fourth type of culture, Mexican, in addition to the Irish, French-Canadian, and American societies he had lived in.

A Pack Train and Egan's Wagon Company

A major travel change came the next day, after brief travel. The company split. It formed into a wagon group and a pack-animals group. "Bro Rich, Hunt & some others are preparing to pack and go a head of the wagons," Howard wrote. "The brethren were called together who were to remain with the wagons and Howard Egan elected captain by a unanimous vote of the company." On January 19, a beautiful day, Apostle Rich and Captain Hunt gave Howard fifty-three dollars for the use of his company.

Traveling Up El Camino Real

Both companies chose El Camino Real, a very old road, to be their line of march. Between 1769 and 1823, Spanish Catholics of the Franciscan Order, to spread Christianity among native peoples, established four forts or presidios and twenty-one missions along the California coast. To facilitate land travel, mission settlements were positioned approximately thirty miles apart, meaning one long day's ride on horseback, with connecting roads. The connective routes, one after the other, formed a consecutive road called El Camino Real, or King's Highway. Today's Highway 101 generally follows that route.

At and around the missions, the Franciscans introduced European fruit, vegetables, cattle, horses, and ranching. Mexico, which gained independence from Spain in 1821, secularized the California missions in 1833–1834, then gave them in land grants to settlers.[52] During their northern trek on El Camino Real, Howard's company passed nine missions in various stages of disrepair. His diary names eight: San Gabriel, San Buenaventura, Santa Barbara, Santa Ines, San Luis Obispo, San Miguel, Soledad, and San Juan Baptista.

"The pack company left us today & went ahead," Howard wrote on January 20. Apostle Rich recorded that "having organized the company with Howard Egan as captain to remain with the wagons, Capt. Hunt and myself, together with Brother Addison Pratt and ten or twelve others left the wagons and started ahead, with packs."[53] James S. Brown, who, like Pratt, was on his way to Tahiti on a mission, stayed with Howard's group. Brown was one of the original gold discoverers at Coloma two years earlier.[54] That day Egan's group traveled fourteen miles and camped in one of California's impressive oak groves. The next day, while progressing twenty-one miles, they crossed the Santa Monica Mountains using Cahuenga Pass and "came down one of the steepest mountains today that I ever saw a wagon road run over," Howard said. They sighted four or five ranches.

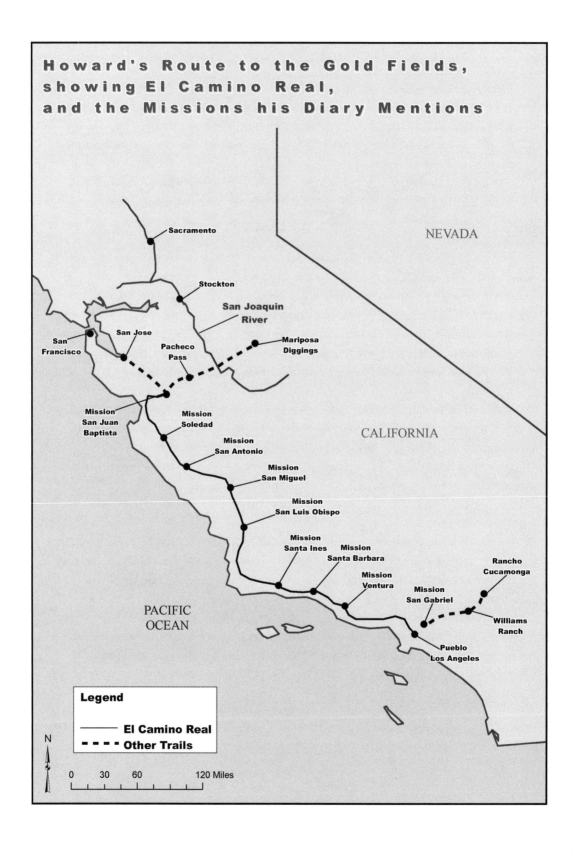

Mission San Buenaventura and Beach Travel

Their travel on January 22 brought them to Mission San Buenaventura (today's city of Ventura) "near a stream within a quarter mile of the sea shore." Howard noted his company then consisted of thirty-five men, one woman, five wagons, twenty horses and mules, and twenty oxen. These numbers indicate that each wagon had four oxen pulling it. Some horses and mules carried riders.

The little company undertook a new experience on January 23 when they traveled about sixteen miles "most of the way along the beach" on rough roads. On the beach they saw ocean waves break, heard crashing surf, saw green and brown seaweed clumps in sand, and watched screeching white seagulls circle in the sky. Howard, familiar with the Atlantic Ocean, here had a good look at the awe-inspiring Pacific. While living in Salem he must have heard stories about Yankee ships trading for California hides and tallow, such as Richard Henry Dana, Jr. memorialized in his popular novel, *Two Years Before the Mast*, published in 1840.[55] Southern California must have fascinated Howard, with its ocean and beaches, vast cattle ranches, orange and lemon groves, pomegranate and fig trees, towering palms, white stuccoed Catholic missions, enormous oak tree canopies, and Mexican music and customs.

Rain halted progress for almost two days. Then, on January 26, traveling on a "very hard road," they passed what Howard called "St. Abantres," or Mission Santa Barbara,

Santa Barbara Mission, Henry Miller
California Mission Sketches, 1856, courtesy Bancroft Library

"and traded 1 yoke of our cattle, 1 of them being broke down." In fine weather the next day, they rode and drove on a "very bad" road. That evening's campground was "a beautifull place on the seashore, the best place we have had since we started, & a beautifull grove to camp in." The next day they traveled eleven miles and camped within a quarter mile of the seashore. That evening they killed a beef.

From Mission St. Ines to Mission San Juan Baptista

On January 30, after a rainy night, they discovered five head of cattle were missing. Men hunted all day and finally learned the cattle were about four miles from the Mission St. Ines (not spelled Ynez) up ahead. This mission, constructed in 1812, three years before Howard was born, was the last one built. It sits high on a hill near the Santa Ynez River. Egan's party began February by moving down the fifty-yard-wide Santa Ynez River. They passed the Mission St. Ines, several streams and ranches, and crossed a "very steep mountain," an eighteen mile day.

San Juan Bautista Mission, Henry Miller
California Mission Sketches, 1856, courtesy Bancroft Library

On February 2 they gained eighteen miles, then fifteen the next day, both days blessed by "pleasant weather." "It was a dandy morning," Howard said of February 4. "All of the company were well except brother John Bills, who is very sick." His days, it turns out, were numbered. On the fifth, pulling two miles up a canyon and crossing a mountain, they came to "the old mission," probably San Luis Obispo de Tolosa, and then crossed the fifty-rods-wide San Miguel River. At a ranch and store, they bought two beeves for twenty-five dollars. Howard penned a rare description of California's impressive landscape when he wrote on February 6: "Last night we camped under a white oak tree that measured 21 feet in circumference and the boughs would shade 405 feet in circumference." Would that he were an artist!

That day they came to the San Miguel Mission, "which is deserted." By nightfall they had progressed thirteen miles, reached a river "about 100 yards wide," crossed it, and camped. This was the Salinas River, sometimes called the Monterrey River. They had moved through El Pase de Robles (today's city of Paso Robles), which in translation is "The Pass of the Oaks," located on the Salinas River north of San Luis Obispo.[56]

During the next day they skirted and then forded the same river, covered twenty-three miles total through "very poor country," and camped at a ranch Howard called "Las Hoetis." They killed two deer. They next reached the San Antonio Mission, which Howard failed to mention, but James Brown did.[57] That mission sits within the "Valley of the Oaks" in the valley of the San Antonio River along the Santa Lucia Mountains. On February 8, while covering nineteen miles "on first-rate roads," they crossed a mountain, descended into a beautiful valley, reached a deserted ranch, and camped by the "river Monterey." The next day, during twenty miles, they passed the Mission Nuestro Senora de la Soledad, and later crossed the "River Monterey." "By raising our wagon boxes we got over without any difficulty," Howard noted. On February 10, a Sunday, Howard's little caravan moved some twenty miles.

The next day they camped a mile beyond the San Juan Baptista Mission, near present-day Hollister. James Brown recalled that "the mission was old and dilapidated, and at that date was occupied by a very rough class of men." Addison Pratt, in the pack train group, noted that he saw Americans "merchandizing there."[58] In San Juan, the town, Howard received a letter Apostle Rich had left for him. After reading it, Howard assembled the company at 7:00 p.m. His company being out of provisions, he put Brown in charge of the ox teams so he could make an urgent ride ahead to find Apostle Rich.[59] "Brothers Staden, [Franklin] Edwards and myself started about 10 o'clock at night," Howard wrote.[60]

Supplies and Instructions at San Jose

The trio must have ridden past Gilroy's Ranch, taken a northwest fork in the road, crossed a divide, and ridden down to the vicinity of the Pueblo de San Jose. After forty-five nighttime miles they arrived about 8:00 a.m. and "found Brother Rich and company one mile from San Jose." According to Pratt's February 13 entry:

> Early this morning as we were making preparations to go to town again, Br. Egan and two or three more of the brethren came up to us and said the waggons

were at the Mission of St. Wan [San Juan], when they left them and they had hurried to overtake us, as they were out of provisions. It was the intention of Brs. Rich and Hunt to get supplies for the whole company, as they had the agency of the whole of them.[61]

Howard tallied that by then he had traveled 438 miles from the Williams Ranch to San Jose.[62] He needed provisions for his company and for the trading post he planned to open in the Sierras. "The fact that Apostle Rich was so intimately involved in Egan's operations," historians Davies and Hansen note, "seems to indicate that the latter [Egan] was operating under church direction rather than on his own."[63] The Mormons raised money for Captain Egan and his company, including a loan Apostle Rich obtained from Donner Party survivor William H. Eddy. Egan then "made arrangements to get provisions."[64] Pratt wrote that "Br. Egan told us his party were well except Br. Bills, and he was failing verry fast. Thought he would not live long."[65]

On February 13, according to Howard, "we sent Franklin Edwards back to meet the company & stop the ox teams and send the hors teams up after the provisions. Bros Rich, Hunt, Pratt, [Henry] Rollins started for San Francisco." Brown said that in the morning, while he was with the ox teams at San Juan Baptista, he received a message from Howard "ordering us to stop....The horse teams arrived" about noon, loaded up provisions, and "started out a mile and camped." Pratt noted that any of those with Elder Rich who had not gone to San Francisco "turned back for the gold mines" with Howard.[66]

The Northern and Southern Gold Regions

California's gold fields once extended 200 miles north-south along western Sierra Nevada slopes, ranged up to sixty miles wide, and reached from seven hundred to twenty-five hundred feet in altitude. A smaller core area called the Mother Lode or *Veta Madre*, 120 miles by two miles, ranged from the canyons of the American River south to the Merced River near where Howard soon set up his trading post.[67] Today's California Highway 49 in the Sierras, named in honor of the forty-niners, zigs and zags, climbs and dips, while it traces a route from one gold rush site to another.

One estimate says that between 900 and 1,000 adult Mormons may have been involved in the gold fields (northern and southern) between 1848 and 1857.[68] Where did men in Mormon-related companies choose to prospect? Most went to the northern region. In 1850, the northern miners worked east and north of Sacramento City, their main supply city, and swarmed most earnestly along branches of the American River. Most of the gold mining missionaries chose to work there. In that region are such gold rush locations as Auburn, Coloma (where gold was first discovered) and Placerville, once known as "Hangtown." At Coloma today is the Marshall Gold Discovery State Historical Park, which features a replicated Sutter's sawmill.

The southern region, where Howard ended up, saw prospectors work along the Stanislaus, Mokelumne, and Merced rivers, and their tributaries. Those miners put on the gold rush map such places as Angel's Camp (made famous by Mark Twain's and Bret Harte's stories), Sonora, Columbia, Mariposa, and Mormon Bar. Stockton, in the San Joaquin Valley west of this southern region, served as the miners' main supply center and Howard's resupply place for his trading post.[69]

Elder Rich's reason for coming to California was to assist Elder Lyman until Lyman returned to Salt Lake. At San Jose, Elder Rich instructed Howard to stop the oxen company from continuing north and send it east to the southern gold zone.[70] Howard's account gives no indication that he had any say in selecting their destination.

Howard recorded that on February 14 "about noon the hors teams arived loaded up & started out a mile & camped." The next day Howard and the horse teams traveled seventeen miles and met up with his wagons. "The brethren killed a beef and the hunters killed several deer." Howard told James Brown, who had been assigned a mission in the Pacific region, that Elder Rich thought Brown should continue with the Egan Company to the mines, which Brown did.[71]

Across Pacheco Pass and the San Joaquin River

On February 16 the reunited Egan party rode and drove to the Gilroy Ranch (about where the city of Gilroy is today), turned off of El Camino Real, and headed generally eastward toward the San Joaquin River valley and "Marapars [Mariposa] diggins," Howard said. Two concerns pressed the group: finding their way east to the river and trying to keep Brother Bills alive.[72] A trail of sorts ran from the Gilroy Ranch eastward toward and up across Pacheco Pass and then down into the San Joaquin Valley, but the trail was hard to follow. While Howard was gone from the company and negotiating in San Jose, Henry Bigler and some of the company had gone four miles eastward on a wrong road. They returned and met Captain Brown who had obtained oil at the mission to anoint Brother Bills. They started again, but Bigler and others with two wagons took a wrong road for nine miles, crossed a lake, and camped. They were lost. Captain Brown and George Q. Cannon hunted for them and found them in the dark, after wading through a creek. The rescuers "were somewhat out of humor and some sharp words past between us," Bigler confessed.[73]

On February 18 the reunited company moved ahead to "the foot of the mountain," Howard said. In order to cross Pacheco Pass they double teamed for about two miles. According to Brown they met a Frenchman who directed them across the mountains.[74] They then descended into the San Joaquin Valley. "The roads have been very hilly and hard to travel," Howard wrote, "there is plenty of feed and wood." That night, light rain fell. "This morning Brother John Bills was much worse," Howard wrote on February 19. "The company remained in camp," where "about 10 o'clock PM Bro Bills died. This evening moved camp about 5 miles."

Captain Egan appointed six men to go ahead and mark out a road because, James Brown noted, "we were again entering into a wilderness with no roads except Indian and wild animals' trails."[75] Brown, one of the six, said that at one point they were halted by a three-hour stampede of wild mustang horses, some seven or eight thousand horses running a mile in width. To Brown it sounded like "distant, heavy thunder, only it was a long, continuous roar or rumbling sound" and presented a "magnificent picture." They resumed travel, but four hours later they halted again to wait for about five hundred horses to thunder by. Arriving at the San Joaquin River, the six tried to find some way to follow it, and encountered, in Brown's words, a "grand aggregation of waterfowl" that swarmed above them. "For a time, we could not understand each other's talk, because of the clatter."[76] Another surprise they faced was a herd of about five hundred elk. Brown's scouts finally found an ill-defined wagon path to the river's edge, so they sent two men back to guide Captain Egan and the wagons to it.[77]

James S. Brown, Portrait Collection, LDS Church History Library

According to Howard's diary, his group traveled twenty-one miles on February 20 and reached the San Joaquin River. They found a man named Woods there with a boat, who was willing to sell provisions at high prices. The company "took our wagons apart & crossed them in a whale boat," Howard said, "for which we had to pay 87½ dollars," an enormous fee. They dared not disassemble Brown's wagon because it was heavily loaded and fitted with an odometer that counted road mileage, which must not be disconnected. Using a cable rope attached to Brown's wagon, men tried to pull it across. The cable broke midstream, so men jumped in and salvaged the wagon and cargo.[78]

The next day the men swam their livestock across, reassembled the wagons, and moved about eighteen miles up the south side of the in-flowing Merced River. The river originates in what is now Yosemite National Park and flows nearly 150 miles before emptying into the San Joaquin River more than one hundred miles south of Sacramento. Today's city of Merced is a half-dozen miles south of the Merced River. After all were across, Howard sent James Brown and five others ahead "to see what we could learn that would be of benefit to the company."[79] •

~ 16 ~

Running a Trading Post and Assisting Apostles

After Howard's prospectors-to-be crossed the San Joaquin River on February 20–21, 1850, their six guides found them a trail up along the Merced River. The small company's destination was the Mariposa Diggings. Who decided that, and when, isn't known, but Howard's diary shows that by February 16 he knew where he was going. "We traveled about eighteen miles up the Mercelda [Merced] river," Howard wrote on February 21, "camped in a bend of the river." The next morning the six scouts went ahead while Howard's group moved twenty miles up the river. On February 23 the company traveled about ten miles then stopped so that their livestock could feed. Howard sent out four more men to look around, after which "we traveled about four miles and camped near a spring branch." With that entry, Howard's diary stops abruptly and doesn't resume.

Searching Where to Prospect

James S. Brown, one of the six searchers, was a good man to look for gold sites because he had been a gold discoverer near Sutter's Mill in January 1848. After three days, meaning on February 24, Howard's scouting party reached a small mining camp called Burns' Diggings on the south side of the Merced River.[1] "We struck a very good prospect, and stopped until the main company came up," Brown said. Some at the site were taking twelve to fifteen dollars worth of gold per man per day. Howard's group stopped there briefly, then encamped a few miles away. They then were fifty-five miles up the Merced River. This camp ended Howard's five-hundred-mile, six-week trip from the Williams Ranch.[2]

Miners had worked the upper Merced River since 1848. Some had created a village of tents, then cabins, called "Logtown," which became the gold rush town of Mariposa. Howard's camp was not far away. Mariposa now is an entry point for Yosemite National Park. An 1851 guide to gold rush sites says the store was nine miles from "Water's Ferry" on the Merced River and six miles from Burns' Diggings near Hornitos.[3] At two thousand feet above sea level, the Egan camp's climate was mild in winter, although hot in summer.

Mormon Bar, Mariposa, courtesy Bancroft Library

Setting up a Trading Post and Prospecting

Wasting no time, Howard's party began prospecting. Because of the richness of the river gravels in the early gold rush days, searchers preferred to pan for the gold flakes. But, because panning was inefficient and backbreaking labor, it gave way to cradles, rockers, and long-toms. Using this equipment, hardworking miners could process several cubic yards of gravel a day. "Digging was the constant and endless task that faced every miner," one historian observed. "Digging on a river bar in sand, gravel and rocks, between massive boulders…digging in a dusty-dry gulch…Always

Gold Mining in California, *courtesy Bancroft Library*

digging down and down through eons of accumulation of rock and gravel that dulled pickaxes and bent shovels," seeking pay-dirt.[4] Working a creek or riverbed offered the best chance to find gold.[5]

That first day in the Egan camp, Brown said, some of the over-excited men put on "quite a laughable performance":

> Those who had been the very worst drones in camp were now the first with the pick and wash pan. They pitched into the creek as if they expected to scoop up the gold by shovelfuls, leaving their teams hitched to their wagons; while those…taking a more methodical view of things, first formed the camp, got their dinner, and then went quietly prospecting up and down the creek. By this time our drones decided that there was no gold there, and that they would go where there was some.[6]

The next day, Brown said, some men panned gold worth fifteen, twenty-five, or fifty dollars per day, some as high as a hundred. Howard joined them, but then, the next day, "Captain Egan and five others of our number were elected to go further up into the mountains and prospect for the company, while the others dug gold." Those who stayed were to give an equal share of their findings to those who went seeking better sites.[7]

Howard, Brown, and the others rode off on horseback with pack mules. In the mountains they encountered rain, then snow that became so deep the men had to walk

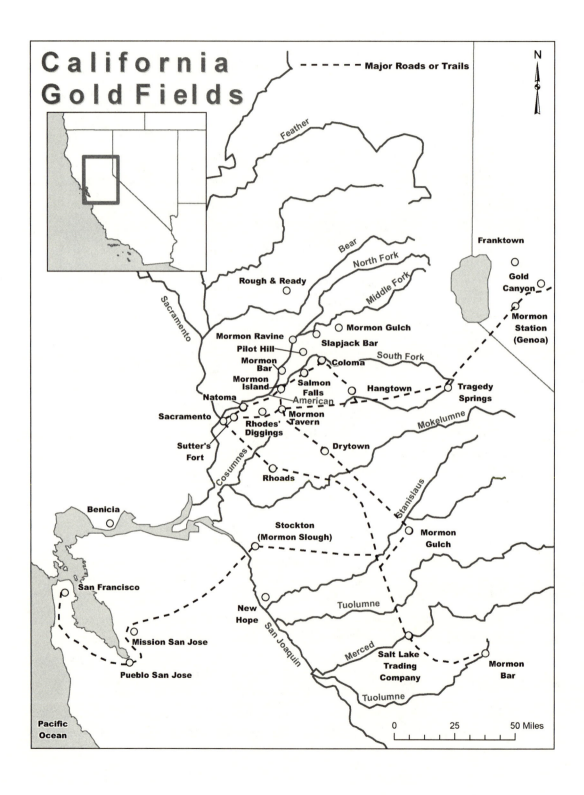

ahead of the horses to break a road. "We were soaked to the skin," Brown said, "and our bedclothes were all wet." After spending ten miserable days, and running out of provisions, they returned to camp, sometimes moving through snow two to three feet deep.[8] Earlier, Howard had returned to camp and tried to start his trading post business. Probably he opened it in a tent or a covered wagon. His initial inventory of food and merchandise supplied his own men.

Elder Rich, Captain Jefferson Hunt, and other Mormon officials came looking for the Egan group. They reached Burns' Diggings on March 7. Rich learned that some Mormon miners had gone up to Mormon Bar, some thirty miles up the slope to the east. (Bar means sand-bar, not a liquor bar.) Mormon Bar, not the same as the Mormon Bar in the northern gold region, was a mile below present-day Mariposa and along Mariposa Creek.[9] Former Mormon Battalion men had mined there in 1848, and a few still worked that area.

When Brown rode back from his snowy venture, he "found that Apostle Rich had been there, and the men had sent every dollar's worth of gold they had dug in our absence to Stockton for supplies of provisions, clothing, tools, etc. so that there was none left to pay us our proportion." Howard had gone with Elder Rich to Stockton. The apostle had left word for Brown to go to San Francisco to resume his journey to his Pacific mission.[10] Brown packed up and sold his oxen to Captain Jefferson Hunt. He prepared to bid "adieu" to the camp, but felt they owed him a hundred dollars as his share of their gold findings. He never received it. He waited in camp, perhaps hoping for some payment.[11]

Elder Rich and Egan returned, bringing supplies. Then, according to Elder Rich's diary, he, Captain Egan, and Brown rode out of the hills on March 26 and headed once more for Stockton. They followed a road that crossed the Merced, Tuolumne, and Stanislaus Rivers. At the Stanislaus River, their north-south trail intersected with one heading due west for Stockton, onto which they turned.[12] On March 30 they stopped briefly at "French Camp," five miles from Stockton. There they found nine men from the Pomeroy Train who had just arrived in the mining region and were destitute. Elder Rich advised them to go to the Mariposa mines near where the Egan men were.[13] Led by George Hickerson, they did, and spent six unsuccessful weeks in the Mariposa vicinity before heading north to find better diggings.[14]

During the rest of 1850 and part of 1851 Howard lived in the Sierra Nevada foothills. Primarily he did Salt Lake Trading Company business, either at his store or traveling back and forth to Stockton for supplies. When the 1850 census taker found him, Howard was residing briefly in a boarding house in Stockton.[15] His store business proved to be difficult to start, a challenge to keep re-supplied, and, later on, a victim of associates who betrayed his trust. When needed, he interrupted his trading post work and prospecting, to help LDS apostles Amasa Lyman and Charles C. Rich minister to and accept tithes from widely scattered Mormon prospectors.

Buying Trips to Stockton

A merchant had potential to earn more than miners did. That's what the Salt Lake Trading Company hoped to do. Miners needed pants, shirts, boots, hats, gloves, shovels, knives, guns, axes, pots and pans, matches, flour, sugar, bacon, beans, coffee, and many other items, for which they could buy or trade. The Salt Lake Trading Company's success depended on two things: miners finding gold they could spend and Howard keeping the store stocked. That meant he had to visit Stockton regularly to buy provisions.

Stockton, a San Joaquin River port city, boomed because of its proximity to the mining regions. James Brown described rip-roaring Stockton as he, Howard, and Apostle Rich found it:

> The place was at that time a point of debarkation where freight was landed for the many mining camps. There were a few trading establishments and warehouses, and three or four large gambling houses in and around which were gathered freighters, packers, and one of the most motley gangs it has ever been my lot to see. Bands of music were in the gambling halls. At one of these I noted twelve tables, four men at each, armed with bowie knives and revolvers; and to me it looked as if there were more gold and silver exposed on those twelve tables than six mules could draw.[16]

It was a time, Brown reflected, "when the strong, with revolver and bowie knife, were law, when gamblers and blacklegs ran many of the towns in California."[17]

A current tourist brochure capsulizes the unruly side of the Gold Rush this way:

> Wherever the gold seekers went, saloon keepers, dance hall girls and avaricious merchants followed. Few miners actually became rich; instead, it was those who supplied their needs who grew wealthy. Prices were high, living conditions were primitive and unhealthful, but the chance of instant wealth inspired those who endured. The yellow ore seemed to be everywhere during the early years of the Gold rush, and a man working with just a pan could sometimes glean $10 to $50 per day. More exciting were the infrequent nuggets weighing up to 100 pounds or more.[18]

Gold in 1850 was worth $20.67 per ounce.

Several steamboats ran constantly between Stockton and San Francisco "which always return heavily laden with goods and provisions for the mines."[19] Trade and business conducted in Stockton nearly equaled that in Sacramento. Howard recognized

California's business potential, particularly its demand for cattle. During that summer and fall "large speculations were made trading [live]stock," one assessment said. A good horse or mule garnered $125 to $200, compared to sixty dollars for one that had just crossed the plains. A fat cow with a young calf was worth two hundred dollars, while one just off the overland trail might fetch sixty. During upcoming years Howard would capitalize on that market by driving cattle from Utah and selling them in California (see Chapter 19).[20]

Assisting the Apostles

Elder Amasa Lyman had been in California since May 1849. On February 20, 1850, he and three associates sailed from San Francisco down to San Pedro to meet some of the southern trail arrivals and to look for a Mormon settlement site in southern California.[21] He returned to San Francisco on March 16. Soon after that, he and Elder Rich met up with each other and began visiting Mormons in the gold fields. Elder Rich's diary mentions that on April 27 he and Apostle Lyman went up the Merced River to Salt Lake Trading Company's "trading post." Howard, who was away on another trip to Stockton, returned the next day. The three had a good visit.[22]

Then, on April 29, Howard accompanied Elders Lyman and Rich to Mariposa and Mormon Bar, visiting Mormon gold miners for two days. They fellowshipped, encouraged, gave gospel advice, and collected nearly three hundred dollars in tithing.

Amasa Lyman, Frederick Piercy, Route from Liverpool to Great Salt Lake Valley

Charles C. Rich, Frederick Piercy, Route from Liverpool to Great Salt Lake Valley

Of the twenty-one miners, seven had come to California in the Flake Company, two in the Pomeroy train, two from the Mormon Battalion, and the other ten's origins aren't known. The apostles' May 1 list of tithe-payers at Mariposa doesn't include Howard, so either his post hadn't yet generated profits, was a Church venture not for his profit, or he simply paid tithes at another time. Among the tithe-payers were Henry Bigler of Howard's group, and George Hickerson, whom Howard, Elder Rich, and James Brown had advised on March 30 to go to Mariposa.[23]

Obviously, somebody else manned the trading post while Howard traveled. On May 2, Howard and Elders Lyman and Rich returned to the Salt Lake Trading Company post where they found Jefferson Hunt. The next day Rich, Captain Hunt, Howard, Henry Rollins, and William Bills left the camp, apparently on another tithing errand for Elder Rich. They crossed the Tuolumne River on May 4, and two days later reached Mormon Gulch, a few miles west of Sonora, where they found several Mormon prospectors. Elder Rich wrote down their names and gave them to Captains Hunt and Egan. Then Hunt and Howard rode to Stockton on business.[24]

On May 21, Elders Lyman and Rich, doing ecclesiastical work, visited Slap Jack Bar near present-day Auburn.[25] This was a Mormon gathering place where young George Q. Cannon operated a store. Cannon was one of the gold mining missionaries, sponsored by his uncle, Apostle John Taylor. Perhaps Cannon's store had some business

Gold Washing in Mariposa, *courtesy Bancroft Library*

connection to the Salt Lake Trading Company.[26] During that visit, Lyman and Rich advised any Mormon miners in the area who had not done well to head back to Utah in a company the two apostles were organizing. They counseled "all to go home that had not good claims or found a chance to make a lot of money in a few days." Those who packed up were ones tired of poor returns for their toil, broken in health, or homesick.

They had dug holes, hauled gravel and sand and rocks, and washed dirt using but simple tools. They had waded in icy water sometimes up to their waists, been sunburned, wind blown, covered with mud, and caked with dust. They had fought mosquitoes, eaten poorly, searched constantly for firewood, cared for mules and horses, lived outdoors, and slept on the hard ground. Broke most of the time, they still had to pay high prices for supplies. Their boots had rotted from being in water and their clothes had worn out. They had blistered hands and some had crushed fingers. But worst of all, they were heading home with little gold to show for all that labor and sacrifice.[27]

Lathrop's Tavern, or Mormon Tavern, was a gathering spot for Mormon miners in the northern gold region east of Sacramento. Asahel Lathrop operated the place, which was an inn and hotel. Lathrop's was one of perhaps two dozen Mormon-managed inns and taverns in the gold regions. Howard's friend Porter Rockwell maintained three in 1849–1850.[28] Like Howard and Rockwell, Lathrop had been one of the 1847 Pioneers.

Lathrop's Mormon Tavern, Mormon Gold

Apostles Rich and Lyman used Lathrop's inn as their home base.[29] Located on the Placerville-Sacramento Road, it was not far from such gold mining sites as Mormon Ravine and Mormon Island. On June 20, Howard attended a business meeting at Lathrop's with Elders Rich and Lyman, Jefferson Hunt, and former Mormon Battalion Captain Jesse D. Hunter, basically "all of the top Mormon leaders in California."[30]

In a July 23 letter to Brigham Young, Mormon Hiram Clark penned a compliment about Howard. Clark first told about arriving safely in California and that most of the Saints he met "were in the mines, but not doing much and a very poor prospect of doing better." He added that "many of the boys here would give their old shoes to be back" with the Saints in Utah, and that many would be better off to go back "to learn Mormonism from its beginning again." By contrast, he said, "there were many as good Saints here as we found anywhere, most of whom belong to the class who came out with Brothers Rich, Egan, Huffaker and Mr. Pomeroy's trains."[31]

Elder Amasa Lyman's recruits for the long trip to Utah met at Lathrop's Tavern, conveniently located on the road heading east to Carson Pass and over the high Sierras. They left on August 16. Lyman had them travel in small groups, then reassemble near today's Carson City, Nevada. They totaled about forty people.[32] They reached Salt Lake City on September 29, 1850. At Church headquarters, Elder Lyman reported unfavorably about the gold region, including an outbreak of cholera. That Howard didn't come with Lyman probably disappointed Tamson, Ransom, Erastus, Nancy, and Mary Ann. Mary Ann had given birth to a son, Hyrum William Egan, on July 24. Perhaps the Lyman group brought them a letter or two from Howard. Elder Lyman predicted that Elder Rich would be leaving California about October 1 to return to Utah. The Salt Lake City Egans might have hoped Howard would come in that next group.

Health and Business Troubles

Meanwhile, Howard stayed in California and continued the store business. On October 20, fellow storekeeper George Q. Cannon and others stopped at Lathrop's Tavern and found Howard there, very ill. He probably had cholera. That fall a devastating cholera epidemic struck the Mormon Tavern area, killing about half the population.[33] Cannon had a long talk with Howard about Cannon's store at Slap Jack Bar and about Howard's trading post, which was experiencing hard times. Historian J. Kenneth Davies sees this discussion as evidence the two stores might have been connected in some way.[34] Howard told Cannon that during "his sickness every thing had gone to wreck." Howard believed that "Phin[eas] Kimball had acted the scoundrel with him" and that "[Fayette] Granger was 'bad'." He blamed Granger for much of the trouble the store had experienced.[35]

Evidence of that wrong-doing is found in a notice published eighteen months later in Salt Lake City in the *Deseret News*. It appeared as a "To Whom It May Concern" item on April 17, 1852. It said anyone indebted to Hunt, Egan & Co. of Mariposa Store, and Marcede Ranch, or Egan, Cain & Co. of Woods Diggings and Middle Fork stores in California, "are cautioned against paying any person except either of the undersigned," meaning Howard or Joseph Cain. "And, all persons having payed Lafayette Granger or any other person any money on account of the above firm, since October 1850" should communicate with the two undersigned men because "said Granger has in his possession the promissory notes, books, and other papers of the concern." The notice was signed by Howard Egan, Sacramento City, and Joseph Cain, Salt Lake City.[36]

This notice reveals bits and pieces about Howard's California businesses. One is that Jefferson Hunt had a shared interest in the Salt Lake Trading Post. Another indicates Howard had ranch operations. A third says that Howard had partnered with Joseph Cain in stores operating in Woods Diggings and on the Middle Fork of the American River. Woods Dry Diggings was the early name for what became the city of Auburn.[37] No further information about these involvements has been found.

On September 24, 1850, Apostle Rich called Cannon to go on a mission to the Sandwich Islands (today's Hawaii). In October, Cannon and two others wanted to send some money to Utah, but, having doubts about a company then "going home," they left their money with Howard to "send if a company should go." If not, Howard was to use at least Cannon's money as he saw fit. What he did with the funds isn't known. On October 30, the day after California celebrated becoming the nation's thirty-first state, Cannon again met with Howard and found him "looking better." Howard "had purchased a load of flour to take to Stockton," Cannon said, which indicates that Howard's trading business continued.[38]

Historians Davies and Hansen found it "interesting to note that the Bigler, Cannon, Farrer, Keeler, and Egan accounts of the Flake Company Gold Mission and of the Salt Lake Trading Company are completely silent on Mormon religious activity in the southern mines." The two historians felt that such omissions were not coincidental. Possibly, they wondered, were those men instructed not to record those kinds of experiences in the gold fields, in case their diaries and records got lost or stolen?[39] For whatever reasons, "information on the operations of the Salt Lake trading company have been elusive."[40]

A host of unanswered questions swirl around Howard's trading company. Did a high Church authority assign Howard to set up a trade business in California? And if so, why? What did Howard's trading post/store look like? Did Howard live in the post, or somewhere else? What did its account books show? What inventory did the post carry? How was credit handled? How much gold did the store take in? Was the store's business brisk, fair, or poor? What connection did the Salt Lake Trading Company have, if any, with Cannon's and others' trading posts? Upon returning home, to whom if anyone did Howard report about the Salt Lake Trading Company? Perhaps in the future, records will surface that provide some answers.

In the front of his diary, Howard jotted a note too cryptic for us to make sense of. He first lists sub-totals, then a total: "Gold Dust 18800, Silver 4490. Gold Coin 7340." Perhaps this tally was for gold dust, silver, and gold coins his trading post business handled at some point.[41]

Leaving California via Carson Pass

By the time Howard headed for home in late June or early July 1851, he either had closed his trading business or turned some or all of it over to someone else to operate.[42] For the long and dangerous return to Utah, he probably rode a horse or mule rather than drive a wagon. Safety from robbers, who plagued the trails outbound from the gold fields, dictated that he not travel alone. He left California by way of Carson Pass. Back in 1848, forty-five discharged members of the Mormon Battalion in the Holmes-Thompson wagon company dug and hacked open a new wagon road from an old horse trail, providing an exit from California south of Lake Tahoe. They took the first wagons, seventeen, across the pass, thereby opening what became the Carson Pass Road.[43] The 1849 gold seekers favored that new route rather than the Donner-cursed Truckee Pass trail because the new Carson road brought them nearer to the gold fields than did the Truckee course. Carson Pass likewise gave eastbound travelers like Howard an easier exit from the gold camps.

Howard rode eighty miles from Lathrop's Tavern to Carson Pass. At 8,700 feet, it still had snow patches in summer. Once across, Howard descended into the Carson River Valley in today's Nevada, a location he would revisit in upcoming years. Following the Carson River, he reached "Ragtown," which was not a town but a welcome oasis on the banks of the Carson River. Before Ragtown, which is near present-day Fallon, Nevada, the Carson Trail merged into the California Trail.[44] Ragtown gained its name for the constant laundry that travelers spread out to dry on nearly every bush.[45]

The well-traveled but desolate California Trail now became a tutorial for Howard. This was the first of several travels that acquainted him with it. Beyond Ragtown he crossed the deadly "Forty Mile Desert," a waterless alkali wasteland filled with broken wagons and bleached bones. This desert was "the most dreaded section of the California Trail." A modern historical marker states that a survey in 1850 of the death toll in that area showed 1,061 dead mules, almost 5,000 horses, and 3,750 cattle, and

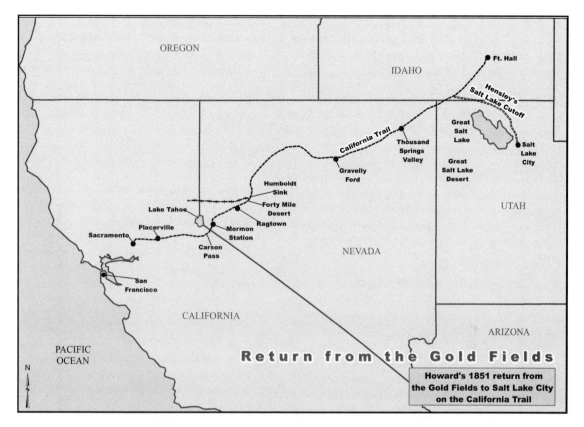

Howard's 1851 return from the Gold Fields to Salt Lake City on the California Trail

953 human graves.⁴⁶ That year, too, Joseph Cain, one of Howard's business partners, counted 1,400 head of dead livestock by the roadside and hundreds more scattered over the plain.⁴⁷ Another traveler counted 100 abandoned wagons in less than a mile, many in good order, others split into pieces and partially burned, and saw discarded clothing, tents, harnesses, tools, and even water casks.⁴⁸

The California Trail along the Humboldt River

Howard rode past the Humboldt Sink, where the 300-mile long Humboldt River, which flows from present-day Nevada's northeast corner, "expired in a vast slough surrounded by a desert." The sink is approximately twenty miles southwest of present-day Lovelock, Nevada.⁴⁹ California-bound traveler E. S. Ingalls, in 1850, said the sink was "a basin about 80 rods wide and half a mile long. It is usually the last water found [westbound] on the Humboldt, or where it loses itself in the sand, hence its name…There is no grass here whatever, nothing but desert."⁵⁰ During future years Howard came to know this awful stretch so well that he vowed to find a new route to avoid it. And he did.

The Humboldt River, once termed "nothing but horse broth seasoned with alkali and salt," and called the "Humbug River," was the California Trail's lifeline across present-day Nevada.[51] Its "water and grass sustained men and animals through three hundred miles of arid, hostile wasteland." The trail ran about where much of Interstate 80 now does: northeast from the Humboldt Sink to Winnemucca, then snaking eastward to Battle Mountain and Elko, and on to Wells, Nevada. Wells is named for the Humboldt Wells springs, near where the Humboldt River begins.

Taking the Salt Lake Cutoff

Howard and those with him passed the "Gravelly Ford" on the Humboldt, a well-known landmark, located between where Battle Mountain and Carlin are now. The trail then headed up towards the Humboldt's headwaters. From there, travelers rode northeast. At Thousand Springs, or Hot Springs Valley, Howard saw "where clusters of boiling springs watered marshy turf and sent up plumes of steam."[52] He then reached the Goose Creek Valley in present-day Nevada's extreme northeastern tip. Goose Creek flows northward to the Snake River. Howard followed down Goose Creek, and then faced "dangerously steep" Granite Pass, a rise of two thousand feet on today's Utah-Idaho border. From there, a day's travel could have taken him northward to the "City of Rocks" on the California Trail and to Ft. Hall. But, instead, he and most Mormon returnees traveled eastward onto the Salt Lake City Cutoff, also known as the Hensley Cutoff. At that point Howard was only about 190 miles from Great Salt Lake City.[53]

Riding into northern Utah, and crossing Deep Creek near today's Snowville, he found plenty of water and grass. He forded the Malad River, then the Bear River.[54] A southward course took him between the Wasatch Mountains on the east and the Great Salt Lake to his west, and past Mormon settlers and settlements. He came to Ogden. A few hours after he and his party crossed the Ogden and Weber Rivers, their excitement grew as they approached Salt Lake City.[55]

By horseback or mule, Howard would have made the dusty, dislikeable, monotonous, nine hundred mile trip from Lathrop's Tavern to Salt Lake City in five or six weeks. But, if he in fact drove a wagon, like Elder Rich's group did the previous fall, he would have needed nine weeks.[56] When entering Salt Lake City, he now had a beginning familiarity with the main route connecting Salt Lake City with Sacramento. He would travel it several more times before he could locate, through trial and error, a better and more direct way south of the Great Salt Lake.

Troubled Homecoming

During Howard's sojourn in the Sierra Nevada gold fields, President Millard Fillmore signed into law the "Compromise of 1850," which granted California statehood and gave Utah a territorial status. This changed the Egans from being residents of the Mormon state of Deseret into citizens of the Utah Territory.

According to Daniel Davis, Howard's friend who was also one of President Heber C. Kimball's adopted sons, Howard arrived home on September 10, 1851.[57] He had been away from Salt Lake City for almost twenty-two months. Normally, a man in Howard's situation would rejoice to be back home again and anticipate home-cooked meals, a real bed, a bath, clean clothes, and hugs from wives and children. And, ever the storyteller, he had a host of gold rush and trail tales to share with his family and friends.

However, this reunion became very upsetting. When he reached the Egan home, Tamson gave him a bitter pill to swallow. She introduced him to her son that was not his. ♦

~ 17 ~

The "Mountain Justice" Killing of James Monroe

When Howard approached his small adobe home in Salt Lake City on September 10, 1851, he had not seen his family for almost two years. He knew Ransom now was eleven, not nine; Ras nine, not seven; and Horace four, not two. Second wife Nancy's two girls had grown, too, so that Helen was four and Vilate almost two. Wife Mary Ann had one-year-old Hyrum William Egan to show Howard, who was born while Howard was in California. The 1850 census, taken early in 1851, shows that Nancy, Helen, and Vilate lived with John and Euphemia Banks, a couple in their early fifties.[1] Where Mary Ann and Hyrum lived isn't known.

A Homecoming Heartbreak

Tamson greeted Howard with a three-month-old son who was hers by another man. She explained as best she could. She said that tiny William M. Egan was born on June 13, 1851.[2] She admitted that the father was James M. Monroe, whom the Egans had known in Nauvoo. Howard learned then or soon afterwards that her affair with Monroe had been consensual, not forced. While digesting this betrayal, Howard felt that family honor required him to confront Monroe for defiling his family.

Perhaps Nancy and Mary Ann gave Howard a better welcome home. But, given Tamson's illegitimate infant, no Egan could feel "thank goodness Howard's back and at last we can get on with normal living." That could not happen.

During his California work, his three wives, not Howard, had the hardest rows to hoe. Credit is due them for enduring so many months as "gold rush widows." The story of how they managed isn't recorded, but without Howard's help they had put food on the table for nine mouths, clothed the family, paid bills, and kept the family going. Had Howard brought them bags filled with California gold dust, which he didn't, his absence could have provided the long-suffering families at least some small solace for his long absence.

Paramour James Monroe

Howard and Tamson had known James Madison Monroe in Nauvoo (see Chapter 4). Born January 9, 1822, in Erie, Pennsylvania, he was almost two years older than Tamson and seven years younger than Howard. His parents were William and Rebecca Reese Monroe. His father died in 1840.[3] On October 3, 1841, Monroe and his mother converted to Mormonism in Utica, New York, following in the footsteps of his two sisters and aunts and uncles.[4] According to Monroe's diary, written in an excellent hand, Utica Branch president James Blakeley ordained him to the Aaronic Priesthood. The two of them did missionary work in the surrounding area. Monroe preached often. His diary records his joy in engaging in the Lord's work, and recounts his preaching and baptizing up to April 1842. "Oh! How my heart swells with gratitude," he penned.[5]

He relocated to Nauvoo. His diary notes that on August 22, 1842, he commenced teaching "common school" there, which was about the same time when the Egans arrived from Salem. During the next months Monroe's diary names dozens of students. On April 10, 1843, he received a mission call to New York, went there, and made some converts.[6] In 1843 he was chosen secretary of the newly formed Nauvoo Young Men and Ladies Society, and in 1844 the stockholders in the Seventy's Library and Institute Association chose him as one of their seven trustees. In a Seventies meeting on January 26, 1845, he offered to teach the rudiments of English grammar to quorum members.[7] He was appointed a regent of the University of Nauvoo.[8] In April 1845 he taught school to widow Emma Smith's children in her home, and also had Apostle John Taylor's children among his students. "I feel very much interested in these children and am determined to do my best to study their characters and dispositions and thereby be enabled to pursue the best course to give them a good education." His motivation was "to give a good education to Br. Joseph's children," hoping that such effort would earn him "a reward in eternity."

On April 27, 1845 he wrote "I rode today, for the first time, 'Old Charley,' Joseph's celebrated black horse, a beautiful animal." Two days later Monroe began teaching school at Brigham Young's residence. On May 1 he "commenced the study of Botany, which I like very much…it will exercise my perceptives wonderfully."[9] Phrenology, a national fad that entailed the reading of the human head's contours to discover personality and character traits, fascinated him.

His diary contains some very private and introspective entries. These explain in part his behavior towards Tamson. "I am determined to leave off drinking tea and coffee

James Monroe Diary, May 10, 1845, LDS Church History Library

as I think they only stimulate my animal passions which are certainly large enough already," he wrote on May 10, 1845. He vowed to not commit indiscretions and to not put himself "in the way of temptation," and "may God assist me to do it, in him I put my trust."

Monroe's name is not on Nauvoo lists of those who performed baptisms for the dead or who received temple endowments. It's not known what he did between 1846 and 1850. His name is not among those on a January 1848 petition for a post office in Kanesville, Iowa.[10] No rosters of those who came west in Church-directed wagon companies include his name.[11]

Work for Uncles John and Enoch Reese, Merchants

Howard's relationship to Monroe involved several of Monroe's uncles and aunts named Reese. John Reese and Susannah Owens, emigrants from Wales, lived for a time in New York City. They had eleven children. Daughter Rebecca married William

Monroe and was the mother of James Madison Monroe. Daughter Catherine married Zephaniah Clawson and later, as a widow in Nauvoo, became Howard's plural wife. (see Chapter 6). She was Monroe's aunt. Daughter Ruth Amelia Rose, another of Monroe's aunts, became one of Heber C. Kimball's plural wives. Two sons, John and Enoch Reese, Monroe's uncles, were practicing Mormons, and they engaged Monroe to do freighting work for them to and in Salt Lake City.

The gold rush brought merchants to Great Salt Lake City in 1849, including John Reese "of New York," and Livingston & Kinkead of St. Louis. Their assortments of goods found a ready market and proved profitable. John Reese was a partner with his brother Enoch in the J. & E. Reese Mercantile firm at Salt Lake City. The store capitalized on the forty-niners passing through. During the 1850s they continued as merchants in the city and had business operations in Carson City, which was then part of Utah.[12] It seems likely that Monroe came to Utah as an employee of his uncles, probably in a Reese freight wagon train.

Tamson and her children are listed in the Utah 1850 federal census. Monroe's name isn't listed, no doubt because much of that census was taken in 1851, and by then Monroe had gone east.[13] A story surfaces now and then, folklore with no evidence, claiming that Monroe was a lodger in the Egan home. Probably he boarded there, meaning he ate there and paid Tamson for the meals. The home then was a tiny adobe house on Main Street into which the Egans had moved in April 1849. Tamson's home had no room for lodgers. The Egans didn't move to the larger home three blocks west and one block north until after Howard returned from the gold fields.

Tamson became pregnant by Monroe in mid-September 1850. Monroe was then twenty-eight years old and Tamson twenty-six. On December 1, when Tamson was about two-and-a-half months pregnant, Monroe left Salt Lake City to do "express business" in the States for "the J & E Reese and Company."[14] He covered a thousand miles "in the most perilous period of the year" and reached Kanesville on December 16 in the incredibly short time of seventeen days, if that's to be believed.[15] Because of this fast trip, the Kanesville newspaper termed him "an adventurer" and remarkably brave. "He brought no letters or papers with him, because it was feared that he perhaps would not reach the States this winter."[16]

His fast travel raises the possibility that he left Utah because he knew Tamson was pregnant and, when people found out, he'd be the prime paternity suspect. However, if he had skipped town to avoid accusations, it's unlikely he would have returned to Utah the next year. A more likely scenario is that he did not know she was pregnant and simply rushed off because of urgent Reese Company business. As their agent, his errand was to bring back wagonloads of merchandise during the next trail season, which he did.

If he did know about Tamson's pregnancy, only two reasons explain his return to Utah: his business obligation to the Reese Company or a conscience telling him to face the consequence of paternity.[17] When he hurriedly left Utah for Kanesville, and then when he started back to Utah six months later, he had no way to know when, or even if, Howard would return from California.

Monroe spent from December 1850 through June 1851 in various cities in "the States," lining up freight to haul west. On February 9 he was in Cincinnati. That day he wrote to a Mr. Carter, who had a merchandise store in Salt Lake City, where Monroe previously had witnessed "your goods were going off very rapidly." Monroe's letter reminded Carter of Carter's wish "last year" to transport goods from Bethlehem, the Missouri River town south of Kanesville, to Utah the next spring. He informed Carter: "I am about getting up a train for our Store in the Valley and am willing to take the contract of carrying your Mdze. for ten dollars per hundred" from the wharf at Bethlehem "as soon as landed and delivered in the Valley in good order and in as short a time as it is possible for us to make it."[18]

This $10.00 was a bargain price because Orson Hyde was taking contracts for $10.50 per hundred pounds, and others were asking $11.50. "I have made you the lowest offer," Monroe said. To seal the deal, Carter needed to pay by March 15. Carter needed to reply to him, Monroe instructed, not in Cincinnati or Kanesville, but in St. Louis, care of R. H. Stone, 57 Front Street.

The Reese merchandise train, with company agent Monroe, pulled out of Kanesville on June 17. At Bethlehem they stopped and loaded up more freight. Captained by William Horner, the caravan started west on July 1, consisting of thirty to forty wagons accompanied by a score of passengers. The teamsters were Dutch, Americans, and English, and about half were Mormons, including eighteen-year-old William Woodward. Monroe was responsible for the Reese merchandise.[19] During the first 150 miles, twenty axletrees broke in the poorly constructed wagons, forcing Monroe to ride ahead to Ft. Kearny and procure replacement wagons.[20]

Decision to Seek Justice

On September 12, two days after Howard came home, he dined with William Kimball, his fellow Heber C. Kimball associate. The two of them and William's wife were "poisoned by eating oysters."[21] A few days later Howard learned that the Reese train with Monroe in it was nearing the Mormon settlements. He decided to ride out and confront the wrong-doer. It's uncertain if he consulted with any law enforcement people or Church leaders about how best to deal with Monroe. Possibly he had discussed the situation with friend William Kimball while dining on the tainted oysters.

Perhaps he talked over the matter with his adopted father, President Kimball.

In pre-Civil War American society, violence was common. History makes that crystal clear. At times citizens took justice into their own hands, unwilling to trust legal channels. Newspapers reported hundreds of incidents of duels, lynchings, and mob violence. When a community or group of people faced a situation deemed dangerous or harmful, local sentiment often determined what was allowed or not allowed, no matter what some law code said. Mormons in Nauvoo had become victims of that attitude.

When Latter-day Saints first arrived in Utah, it was Mexican territory governed by nobody. They had the freedom and the obligation to govern themselves. Church leaders and Church rules and regulations became the government. That culture had no tolerance for acts like Monroe had committed. A year before Howard faced the crisis, government surveyor Major Howard Stansbury pointed this out. Stansbury, after exploring the Great Salt Lake region, returned to Fort Leavenworth on November 6, 1850. In his published account of his expedition, he included this observation about Mormon morality:

William H. Kimball,
Utah State Historical Society

> Purity of life, in all the domestic relations, is strenuously inculcated; and they do not hesitate to declare, that when they shall obtain the uncontrolled power of making their own civil laws, (which will be when they are admitted as one of the States of the Union,) they will punish the departure from chastity in the severest manner, even by death.[22]

Early settlers in Utah sometimes turned to violence. In some cases it was condoned by the Church. In some situations, fanatical individuals imposed it unjustly. The Mormon-created State of Deseret (1849–1851) was a theocracy that set some standards of behavior based on the Old Testament, New Testament, and revelations to Joseph Smith. Among the early settlers, violent punishments for stealing, immorality, and other wrongdoing were preached and at times practiced. Blood atonement, as sometimes preached during the 1850s, said that some sins a person committed were so bad that the sinner could atone for them only by the shedding of his or her own blood.[23]

Tamson's giving birth to a baby not Howard's was no secret among Egan friends and neighbors and some of the public. People from as far away as Iron County knew

about James Monroe's deed and felt that "there has to be another execution."[24] Had Howard discussed with associates how to deal with Monroe, someone could have told him about a similar case of seduction just months before.[25] Early in 1851 in Manti, Utah, Madison D. Hambleton deliberately shot Dr. John M. Vaughn for "seducing" his wife. Vaughn apparently had been having an adulterous affair with Mrs. Hambleton while her husband was out of town, and the relationship continued secretly after he returned. Thus,

> One Sunday afternoon after attending church meetings, Hambleton shot and killed Vaughn. Hambleton immediately surrendered himself to his bishop and was escorted to Salt Lake City where a court of inquiry was convened to investigate his act. Brigham Young, who had only recently been sworn in as governor, represented Hambleton. Hosea Stout acted as attorney for the prosecution. The supreme court of the territory heard the case and acquitted Hambleton. Those in attendance enthusiastically voiced their approval of the court decision.[26]

Stout wrote that Vaughn's "seduction and illicit conversation with Mrs. Hambleton was sufficiently proven insomuch that I was well satisfied of his justification as well as all who were present and plead to the case to that effect." Hambleton was acquitted. However, Mrs. Hambleton was "excommunicated for adultery by the local congregation."[27]

Whatever type of justice Howard had weighed and considered, he rode back along the Mormon Trail to confront Monroe.

Monroe's Appeal to Brigham Young

Monroe heard somehow that, when he arrived in the Valley, Howard probably would shoot him. Hoping to prevent that, when the Reese freight train reached Fort Bridger, he penned a six-page letter, dated September 16, to President Brigham Young (he had taught Brigham Young's children in Nauvoo).[28] "I am in a great difficulty: and without a favorable consideration of my case on your part, I am afraid it will prove a very serious one for me," his letter begins. "I have done very wrong and I am in your hands." For two pages he tells about his friendship with the Egans in Nauvoo and his beyond-friendship attraction to Tamson. He first became acquainted with Tamson, he says, "about ten years since," or about 1842. "From the first sight," he says regarding Tamson, "I have always admired her."

After about a year in Nauvoo, Monroe explains, a young lady with whom Monroe had been keeping company moved in with the Egans.[29] Thus, Monroe became well acquainted with the Egans and "on terms of the greatest friendship both with Br. Egan and his wife." Then for three pages Monroe says that Tamson made repeated advances. He claims he was a novice, a victim of her enticements, and that he resisted. He left to go east, returned to Nauvoo, and he and Tamson "lived as distant neighbors only."

Monroe's letter continues that he next saw Tamson in the Valley and that she was glad to see him. He took "familiarities" with her. Monroe fails to mention to the Church president that this friendship "renewal" happened while Howard was far away in the California gold fields. "I freely acknowledge that I have…sinned against the Lord and against the Church," Monroe wrote. "I throw myself entirely on your mercy. Do with me as you think fit." Monroe says nothing about his illegitimate son, Tamson's eternal soul, or how he might make restitution. His big concern is to stay alive:

> I have been informed that Mr. Egan will be advised to shoot me, and that if I come into the valley I will never leave it alive. I am aware that he will never do it, unless he thinks you will sanction it. If you think it advisable for him to pursue that course, I hope you will have sufficient charity and regard for me to tell me so, for under such circumstance I would not of course come into the valley and I do not believe you want to see a man murdered in cold blood. If, on the contrary, you take a more favorable view of my case, and think it safe for me to come into the valley, you will confer a great favor upon me and upon my friends if you will let me know it, and I trust that my future conduct will show that I have repented and am not ungrateful.

Monroe's letter is in President Young's correspondence files, but when he received it isn't certain. No answer to Monroe's letter has been found in Young's files, and it's unknown if Young tried to either dissuade or encourage Howard.

Howard Confronts and Kills Monroe

On September 20, Howard met the Reese merchandise company on the Mormon Trail near Cache Cave, close to the head of Echo Canyon. William Woodward, in the wagon train, recorded what he saw witnessed:

> As we were "rolling out" of camp a person rode in and conversed with Mr. Monroe. The man was a stranger to me. This was in the vicinity of Yellow Creek & about 70 miles from the Valley. The next I saw of him, he came riding by saying "gentlemen I have killed the seducer of my wife." He put his hand to his breast and said "vengeance is sweet to me." Our captain [Horner] rode past and gave orders to stop. I went back to see what was the matter & James Monroe lie dead, he was shot by Howard Egan, for seducing his wife.[30]

One day after the killing, Hosea Stout, once a fellow policeman with Howard in Nauvoo, and the prosecutor in the recent Hambleton-Vaughn case, noted the Monroe killing in his diary:

> Sunday, Sept. 21, 1851. I learned to day that Howard Egan, who has returned from the gold mines lately, and upon learning that his wife had been seduced or in other words had a child willingly by James M. Monroe during his absence. Said Monroe had also gone to the States for goods for Reese and was now on his return here, whereupon Egan went and met him near Cache Cave and after talking the matter over sometime Egan drew a pistol and shot him dead which makes the second man who has been deliberately shot dead for the same offence in less than one year in the Territory.[31]

Cache Cave, Utah State Historical Society

According to Juanita Brooks, the editor of Stout's diaries, the killing was mentioned by other diarists, not just Stout.[32] One was Alexander Neibaur, who on September 21 wrote: "Howard Egan returned to Great Salt Lake City from canyon whither he had gone to meet Monroe whom he shot for seducing his wife."[33] Three days after Howard killed Monroe, Elder Orson Hyde, whom Howard knew well, left Salt Lake City for Kanesville. Upon arriving there he immediately published the news of the killing in his *Frontier Guardian* newspaper:

> Mr. James Monroe, Agent for Reese & Co., was shot by Howard Egan, near Bear River in September last, while on his way to Salt Lake with a train of Goods. The cause of the difficulty was this:—While Egan was at the mines in California, Monroe took unwarrantable liberties with his (Egan's) wife, by which Egan received an unwelcome accession to his family. After the deed was executed, Egan returned to the City, told what he had done and gave himself up to be dealt with by the officers of the law.[34]

When Salt Lake City's mayor Jedediah M. Grant published a version back east of the Monroe murder seven months later, he provided details not found elsewhere.[35] He either learned these from Howard or heard them circulating. When Howard returned from the Gold Country, Grant said, "he found his wife had been unfaithful. ...Every one knew the paramour, James Monroe, merchant ... He was Egan's friend too, therefore a Traitor." Then,

> Egan did not remain long to be pointed at. He learned that Monroe was on his road out from the States, with a train carrying merchandise. He set out alone, nor did any know whither he had gone when he went forth to meet them. He came upon the party in the night time. It has been said that he had with him his old house dog, as knowing its nose would scent out the frequent lifter of his door latch. This is not true; he found his way, by himself, to the wagon in which his betrayer was, and rising upon the tongue ward looked in upon him as he lay sleeping.

Howard decided to wait until morning to deal with Monroe, so he left the camp. Then, Grant said,

> The men were getting breakfast ready round the fire, when he again appeared among them. Tapping Monroe on the shoulder; James, he said aloud, you must die! Then beckoning him apart sat down with him a few rods off to one side. Thirty minutes he assigned him to live, during which he exhorted him to contrition and preparation for his change. At the twenty-five minute, he showed by his watch that but five minutes remained of the time in which, if the criminal were so minded, he could assail his executioner. At the expiration of the thirtieth, as he did not move, Egan rose and despatched him, putting a bullet through his brain. Then, sorrowing, returned home.

At Egan's trial a month after the killing, this summary of Howard's very open dealings with Monroe was presented:

> Egan met him...and calmly saluting each other both appearantly friendly went some 100 yards from the corrall and appeared to talk peaceably some time when Egan drew a pistol and shot him in the face on the right side of the nose just below the eye. Monroe fell dead on the spot, when Egan mounted his horse, rode to the company, told his name, made a short speech, said what he did he done in the name of the Lord. That Monroe had seduced his wife, ruined his family, and destroyed his peace on earth for ever and that they would find him in this place and then blessed them and hoped that they would have a safe journey to the city and rode off informing those he overtook on the road what he had done.[36]

Back Home

The Reese wagon company didn't arrive in the city until September 29, nine days after the killing. John Reese, Monroe's uncle, probably took responsibility for Monroe's body and his personal effects. A headstone marks Monroe's grave in the Salt Lake City Cemetery.[37] Monroe's Nauvoo diary, cited above, survived, and at some point was given to Tamson and Monroe's son, William Egan.

The public quickly heard that Howard had killed Monroe. Church officials knew about it, and so did law enforcement people. There had to be a trial. The case needed to be presented to a grand jury. Ex-policeman Howard expected it. He cooperated fully and waited for it. Prosecution and defense alignments formed and prepared their arguments. Witnesses in the Reese wagon train were asked to testify. So was Tamson. ◆

James Madison Monroe grave, Salt Lake City Cemetery

~ 18 ~

A Jury Trial and Acquittal

During the days following James Monroe's killing, Utahns talked about whether or not Howard had the right to shoot him to defend the Egan family's honor. Members of the Salt Lake City seventies quorums met to "try" Howard, meaning to keep him in or drop him from quorum membership. After hearing him, they dismissed the case.[1] A criminal court case was delayed because of a judge shortage. One week after the shooting, the territory's federal judge and Supreme Court appointee, Lemuel H. Brandebury, and associate justice Perry E. Brocchus, deserted their posts and returned to "the States."[2] In essence, "the Supreme Court left the Territory without trying Howard Egan for the murder of James M. Monroe."[3] Regarding the Monroe murder, they expressed outrage "that the perpetrator of the crime was walking the streets of Salt Lake a free man."[4]

A month after the murder, Howard went on trial. Held on October 17–18, 1851, *United States vs. Howard Egan* is now a famous court case in Utah's legal history, in part because of the unusual defense arguments and partly because Utah's legal system right then was a quagmire. It was unclear what laws were in effect and what courts could or could not handle Howard's case.[5] Newly formed Utah Territory, established in mid-1850 to replace the provisional State of Deseret, had not had time for its first legislature to create and pass a code of laws before Howard's trial took place.

Grand Jury Investigation and Findings

The one remaining federal district court judge in the territory, Zerubbabel Snow, from Ohio, a Mormon, convened Utah Territory's very first federal court session on October 6, 1851. One day later, U.S. District Attorney Seth M. Blair petitioned for a grand jury to investigate the Monroe murder. As directed by Judge Snow, U.S. Marshal Joseph L. Heywood, who lived close to the Egans, formed a grand jury panel with Daniel Spencer as foreman. As its first business, it ordered Marshal Heywood to issue subpoenas to several witnesses: George Moore, William Horner, James Wade, George C. Robbins, and Dominicus Carter.[6] On October 13 the witnesses were sworn and presented to the grand jury. Based on their testimonies a warrant was issued for Howard's arrest to answer an indictment for murder.[7] Also indicted was an alleged accomplice, Thurston Larson, but why is not clear.[8]

An autopsy was performed on Monroe's body. Prosecutor Blair's indictment, much too convoluted and with too much "legalese" to include in total here, contains the following case against Howard, and mentions the autopsy findings:

Seth M. Blair, LDS Church History Library

> The Grand jurors…present that Howard Egan of the County of Great Salt Lake not having the fear of God before his eyes on the twentieth day of September in the year (1851) in the Territory & County affore said in and upon one James Monroe in the peace of God then and their being feloniously willfully & of his Own malice afore thought did make & assault with a Certain Pistol…being charged with gun powder and a Leaden bullet…Howard Egan in his right hand then & there had & held against at & upon him the said James Monroe then & …did discharge & shot off …at him the said James Monroe in & upon the right side of the nose a little under the right Eye …one mortal wound of the breath of one inch & depth of Seven inches of which said mortal wound the said James Monroe did then & there die and so the jurors …do say that the said Howard Egan did Kill & murder the said James Monroe…feloniously willfully & of his malice affore thought & against the Laws, peace & dignity of the United States.[9]

Based on this indictment, Judge Snow ordered Marshal Heywood "to arrest the said Howard Egan if he is to be found in said Territory and him safely keep in watchful custody, and have his body before this Court forthwith to answer to an Indictment found against him by the United States Grand Jury for said Territory, and hereof fail not."[10] Howard was fully compliant. Marshal Heywood arrested him without trouble.

Joseph L. Heywood, Utah State Historical Society

When arraigned on October 14 he pleaded not guilty. That day Marshal Heywood received court orders to summon thirty-six "good and lawful men" to be a jury pool. He proposed thirty-six names, then added three more, of whom twelve would become the trial's jurors.[11] That same day, William Wines Phelps and George A. Smith appeared in court as Howard's defense counsel. Both had barely received certificates to practice law and neither had argued a case in court before.[12]

Tamson, a witness crucial for the defense, needed to testify, but the court spared her from appearing in person. Instead, on defense attorney Phelps's motion, the court appointed Justice of the Peace William Snow to present an interrogatory to her, because of her "being unable on account of indisposition to attend court and wishing her testimony to be taken in the case."[13] Snow's official interrogatory report, handwritten and dated October 16, 1851, is on file in the Utah State Archives. It reads as follows, with our punctuation added for clarity:[14]

> This day at the residence of Mrs. Tamson Egan in GSL City, She the Said Tamson Egan being Duly Sworn by me, Wm Snow, Justice of the Peace, the following questions were asked:
>
> Question: Was you seduced in the year A.D. 1850?
>
> Answer: Yes
>
> Question: Under what circumstances?
>
> No answer given
>
> Question: what month & day of the month?
>
> Answer: About the middle of Sept.
>
> Question: Did you by reason of such seduction have a child by the Said James Monroe?
>
> Answer: Yes
>
> Question: How long after Such Seduction?
>
> Answer: About nine months
>
> I certify the above questions & answers to be correct as asked & answered.
>
> Wm Snow J.P.

On October 17, Judge Zerubbabel Snow convened the trial. He was the brother of Erastus Snow, who had converted the Egans in Salem. The Egan case was newly-formed Utah Territory's first jury trial. Jury selection occupied most of the morning. The names of the jurors and the city ward number each lived in were: Daniel H. Wells, 18, Truman O. Angel, 13, George D. Grant, 13, A. H. Raleigh, 19, James Mulliner, 14, Jacob F. Hutchinson, 12, Joseph Buzby, 13, Richard Petite, 8, Morgan Phelps, 13, Rodney Badger, 15, and A. C. Brower and A. J. Stout. The last two were not among the 36 names in the original jury pool, so their residencies are not indicated. Juror Raleigh was in the Egans' Nineteenth Ward bishopric, and four years later would marry Howard's then ex-wife Nancy.

Prosecutor Seth Blair read the indictment to the jury, and then presented his case against Howard. One report said that "the prosecution was very spirited."[15] Blair examined William E. Horner, captain of the Reese wagon train in which Monroe had been traveling. George C. Robbins, James Wade, and George Moore testified for the prosecution. Who they were and why they testified isn't known. William Kimball testified for the defense. Regrettably, no public record remains of what these witnesses said.[16] However, lawyer Hosea Stout attended and wrote a summary of the prosecution's case. "From the Evidence it appears that while Egan was gone to the mines, Monroe seduced his wife by whom she had a bastard child." The witnesses established that Monroe had gone to the East for goods, and during his return Egan rode out, the two saluted each other, and talked calmly about a hundred yards from the livestock. Howard then shot him with a pistol just below his right eye, killing him instantly. Egan told the wagon train and others he met along the trail what he'd done, because Monroe had "ruined his family, and destroyed his peace on earth for ever." This, Stout said, "is in short the evidence of the case, after which Blair made his first plea" against Howard. Blair was followed by defense attorney Phelps "who used Bible History, Homer, Virgil besides a large pile of law books & precedents to show that Egan was justified in his act, when the court adjourned till tomorrow at ten a.m."[17]

George A. Smith's "Mountain Common Law" Defense

Earlier events back in Missouri and Illinois had convinced Brigham Young and most Church leaders that the national legal system was corrupt, such that they should maintain their own institutions of law and government. Mormons disliked courts using "common law," which then was in favor nationally. Common law referred to that portion of *unwritten* English legal doctrine, which had been received and modified in the United States before the American Revolution. From the Mormon perspective, much common law entrenched unwise tradition and "ignorance." Legal historian Michael Homer has pointed out that "Many nineteenth-century Americans believed that the common-law power of judges needed to be checked through legislatures' codifying the laws." To cite one example, President Young criticized jurists and legislatures back east who made it almost death for a man to have two wives but refused to institute laws to do away with "whoredoms." Mormons did not want judges applying such unacceptable standards in Utah. In Egan's case, rotund defense attorney Smith argued that Egan's action was justified under "mountain common law" and that common law's usual light penalty elsewhere for adultery could not be accepted in Utah.[18]

According to Stout, during the second day of the trial George A. Smith based his defense arguments not on legal books and briefs but on Utah attitudes about right and wrong. "He justified Egan for what he had done, said it was the duty of the nearest kin to a female who was seduced to take the life of the seducer. He made an able plea & was followed by the prosecuting attorney."[19] Smith's defense is recorded in detail. It appeared first in the *Deseret News* in mid-November 1851, then in pamphlet form, and even in the Church's *Journal of Discourses*.[20] Smith, a first cousin of Joseph Smith, said the case "is of no small moment" because it involved the life of a human being. He hoped the jury was looking for justice "instead of some dark, sly or technical course by which to bias their judgment." For them he would argue in "common mountain English" based on simple, not technical, reasoning.

He stated that the prosecution admitted that Monroe "came into this place in the absence of her husband, had seduced his family, in consequence of which an illegitimate child had been brought into the world; and the disgrace which must arise from such a transaction in his family, had fallen on the head of the defendant." Thus, he argued, "in this territory, it is a principle of common mountain law, that no man can seduce the wife of another, without endangering his own life." Despite thousands of law books and court cases, "natural justice" for Utah Mormons, the justice "that beats and throbs thru the heart of the inhabitants of this Territory," was simple: "The man who seduces his neighbor's wife must die, and her nearest relative must kill him."[21]

George A. Smith, LDS Church History Library

Elder Smith reminded them that wagon captain Horner's testimony showed that he knew the "common law" of the territory, "knew that his [Monroe's] life was forfeited." Horner therefore had advised Monroe that for God's sake he should leave the train, for Horner did not wish to see him killed there. "Do leave the train," Horner told Monroe, "I would not have you travel in it for a thousand dollars." To the jury, Smith asserted that the killing accorded with "the established principles of justice known in these mountains." In fact, people would consider Howard an accessory to the crimes, Smith emphasized, had he not killed Monroe. "Don't hang a man for doing justice, for the neglect of which he'd be damned in the eyes of the whole community."[22]

Smith cited the *New Jersey vs Mercer* court case wherein a man publicly killed the seducer of his wife, and after repeated sittings the jury judged him not guilty of murder. "We will allow this to be set down as a precedent, and, if you will, call it American common law." He cited a Louisiana case where a man killed the seducer of his sister. "This is a common practice," Smith argued, "that the man who kills the seducer of his relative is set free." He told about a similar case he personally witnessed in Kentucky. He cited and criticized states like Ohio, where the penalty for such crimes was merely a civil suit for damages. "The spirit there is to prostitute female virtue and character," he accused. With invective, he termed Howard's act "the justified killing of a hyena, that entered his sheets, seduced his wife, and introduced a monster into his family."

Next, Smith hammered home an important legal technicality for acquitting Howard. Judge Snow's federal district court lacked jurisdiction. Because the killing took place within Utah Territory, territorial law and not federal law applied. This U.S. court conducting the trial, a federal court, had no legal right to hang Egan.[23]

Let's provide here a larger legal perspective for this trial. According to laws in effect in Utah from 1847 to 1849, called "Ordinances of the High Council," the punishment for someone convicted of adultery or fornication was up to thirty-nine lashes and fines up to one thousand dollars. Then, by statutes passed on January 16, 1851, the provisional State of Deseret established that the punishment for a man convicted of having sexual relations with a female not his wife, or who seduced any female, was up to five years in prison, private damages, and fines up to five thousand dollars. At the time Utah began operating as a territory in mid-1851, no territorial laws yet were on the books. The territory's first legislature first met two days after Howard killed Monroe and needed months to create and pass a new law code.

When finally enacted, the territorial laws stipulated that for adultery a person could be imprisoned for up to twenty years and not less than three, and be fined up to one thousand dollars, but not less than three hundred dollars, or be both imprisoned and fined. When such crime was committed between two parties, and one of them was married, both were guilty of adultery and should be punished accordingly. "No prosecution for adultery can be commenced but on the complaint of the husband or wife."[24] However, no doubt with the Egan case in mind, one law did establish that a homicide carried out by a male relative with respect to an actual or would-be rape was "justifiable homicide."[25]

No report contains prosecutor Blair's summation and closing arguments. Legal scholar Kenneth L. Cannon II noted that Blair admitted that Monroe had fathered a child by Tamson Egan, but that this did not warrant Egan's killing him. Cannon also speculated that Blair argued for jurisdictional reasons that the shooting took place outside the boundaries of Utah Territory, hence the federal court had jurisdiction.[26]

Judge Zerubbabel Snow's Charge to the Jury

In instructing the jury, Judge Snow gave a careful analysis of what the case involved and what needed to be proved.[27] He explained their options. He said they could decide that by law the killing was justifiable homicide, or else that Egan had no right to take the law into his hands. And, even if the law punished a seducer by death, they might determine that the injured party had no right to execute that law. By that standard, "if the deceased did seduce the defendants wife, and begat a child with her, and if for this the defendant killed him, the killing was unlawful," meaning murder.

Judge Snow then differentiated between *types* of murders and homicides. First there is murder. "Murder may be defined to be, the unlawful killing of a human being in the peace of the republic, with malice of prepence, or of forethought, by another human being who is of sound mind and discretion." Regarding Howard, he said, there was no question he was of sound mind and discretion. So, the jury must find whether or not Monroe was dead. If dead, they must inquire by what means his death came. That is, if dead by violence, then they must be satisfied Howard gave him the mortal blow. If Howard delivered the mortal wound, the jury must inquire if the killing was lawful or unlawful.

Judge Snow then explained *justifiable homicide*. Every killing of one human being by another is unlawful except as the law excuses or justifies. An accidental killing, for example, "is excusable homicide." If a person kills another during a sudden attack in defense of himself, or in defense of his wife, child, parent or servant, it is excusable homicide. Also, if an officer of the law executes the sentence of law on another, by taking his life pursuant to a judgment of a court legally rendered, that, too, is justifiable homicide. And, if an officer of the law in pursuit of a legal duty is forcibly resisted or prevented, and, with malice, kills the one who resists, that, too, is justifiable homicide. If a homicide be committed to prevent the forcible commission of an atrocious crime, such as murder, robbery, or rape, it is justified, but not if done to punish the offender after the crime has been committed. "If you find any of these in favor of the defendant," the judge pointed out, "then your verdict must be not guilty."

Zerubbabel Snow, Utah State Historical Society

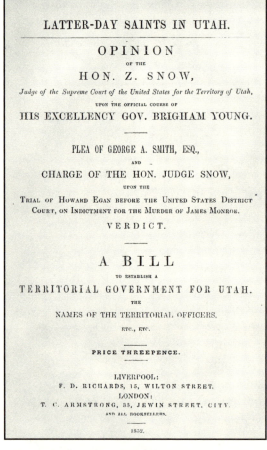

However, if none of these justifiable situations existed in the Monroe murder, then the killing, if it had taken place, was unlawful. In that event, the jury must proceed to inquire, in regard to the malice, prepence, or malice aforethought before the killing occurred, no matter if it be meditation of a few moments only or of long standing. Such malice and premeditation might be owing to an injury, real or imaginary, received by the accused from the deceased.

Judge Snow stressed that justifiable homicide does not cover a person who takes the redress of grievances into his own hands. "Though the deceased may have seduced the defendant's wife, as he now alleges, still he had no right to take the remedy into his own hands." If for a seduction the law inflicted the punishment of death, that would not justify nor excuse the injured party from guilt if he inflicted death without a judgment of the law to that effect, nor even with such a judgment, unless he be the officer of the law appointed for that purpose. Even "if as it is contended by the defendant's attorney, he killed Monroe in the name of the Lord, it does not change the law in this case." A man may violate the law of the land and be guilty even if he believes he did the act in the name of the Lord.

After that review of what constitutes murder and justifiable homicide, Judge Snow applied it to Egan's case. If, as contended by the district attorney, the defendant before he left the city formed the design of killing Monroe, or if he so formed the design after he left, and before he met him; or if he formed it while in conversation with him, "it was malice prepence or aforethought. If the deceased did seduce the defendant's wife, and begat a child with her, and if for this the defendant killed him, in law, the killing was unlawful."

Then Judge Snow elaborated about the point of law most bothersome in Egan's case, the location of the killing. That is, if the jury feels the defendant is guilty, "then the place in which the act was committed becomes material" because a crime must be committed within the jurisdiction of the court trying the accused. The jurisdiction of United States courts is separate and distinct from the jurisdiction of state courts, but in U S. territories the same judges preside in federal courts and in the territorial courts. Therefore, if the court sits as a U.S. court, like in the Egan case, it must try the accused by federal law, not territorial law. Only in an area where U.S. law applied "solely and exclusively" could a federal court like this one decide a case. Thus, if the Monroe murder took place in Utah Territory, federal law didn't apply, in which case Howard was entitled to a not guilty verdict. "This to me has been the most difficult part of the case," Judge Snow admitted to the jury. Because Utah Territory lacked any legislature-approved law code that defined crimes and set penalties, Howard could not be tried by territorial law.

"Gentlemen," the judge instructed the twelve men, "the case, for the present, is committed to your consideration."

"Not Guilty"

Jury foreman Daniel H. Wells returned the jury's verdict of "Not Guilty."[28] Said Stout, "the jury retired and was absent about 15 minutes when they returned with a virdict of not guilty as found in the Indictment whereupon the court discharged Egan." Alexander Neibaur's journal entries for October 17 and 18 say the jury acquitted Howard "on account of deficiency in the indictment," which refers to the court lacking jurisdiction.[29] It's a moot question whether or not the "in territory" issue produced the "not guilty" verdict, because even if the court did have jurisdiction, it seems unlikely that the jury would have returned anything other than an acquittal, given community animosity for seducers.

Support for Defending Family Honor

A day after the trial, Brigham Young, in a letter to Apostle Franklin D. Richards in England, said matter-of-factly that "Howard Egan was tried last week before the U.S. Circuit Court in this city for the murder of James M. Monroe, and found not guilty."[30] In the *Deseret News* account of the trial, not published until November 15, editor Willard Richards editorialized that the verdict should "prove a sufficient warning to all unchaste reprobates, that they are not wanted in our community…It may be the means of saving some from a similar fate."[31]

Showing approval for what Howard did, the Church published Apostle George A. Smith's defense of Howard's justice-taking in the *Deseret News*, in a pamphlet in England, and then in the *Journal of Discourses*. Similarly, Salt Lake's mayor, Jedediah

> 13
>
> *(From the "Deseret News" of Nov. 15th, 1851.)*
>
> INDICTMENT FOR MURDER.
>
> *October Term, 1851.*
>
> Before the Hon. Z. Snow, Judge of the First Judicial District Court of the United States for the Territory of Utah.
>
> UNITED STATES *versus* Howard Egan.
>
> SETH M. BLAIR, Esq., U. S. Prosecuting Attorney.
>
> GEORGE A. SMITH, Esq., } Counsel for Prisoner.
> W. W. PHELPS, Esq., }
>
> This case was brought before said Court by Presentment, &c.
>
> The Prosecution was very spirited, and no duty left unperformed by Mr. Blair.
>
> PLEA OF GEORGE A. SMITH, ESQ.
>
> PLEASE THE COURT, AND GENTLEMEN OF THE JURY: With the blessing of the Almighty, although not in a proper state of health, I feel disposed to offer a few reasons, and to present a few arguments, and perhaps a few authorities, upon the point in question. In the first place, I will say, gentlemen of the Jury, you will have to bear with me in my manner of communication, being but a new member of the bar, and unaccustomed to addressing a Jury. The case upon which I am called to address you is one of no small moment. It is one which presents before you, and to investigate which, involves the life of a fellow-citizen.
>
> I am not prepared to refer to authorities on legal points, as I would have been had not the trial been so hasty; but as it is, I shall present my arguments upon a plain, simple principle of reasoning. Not being acquainted with the dead languages, I shall simply talk the common mountain English, without reference to anything that may be technical. All I want is simple truth and justice. This defendant asks not his life, if he deserves to die; but if he has done nothing but an act of justice, he wishes that justice awarded to him.
>
> It is highly probable that the manner in which I may present my arguments, may be exceptionable to the learned, or to the technical policy of modern times; be that as it may, the plain simple truth is what I am aiming at.
>
> I am happy to behold an intelligent Jury, who are looking for justice instead of some dark, sly, or technical course by which to bias their judgment. I shall refer in the first instance to an item of law, which was quoted by the learned prosecutor yesterday, in which he stated to this jury, that the person killed should be, or must be, a *reasonable creature*. Now what dark meaning, what unknown interpretation the learned and deep-read men of law may give by which to interpret this language, it is impossible for me to say; as I said before, it is the plain mountain English I profess to talk. It was admitted on the part of the prosecution, that James Monroe, who is alleged in this indictment to have been killed by Howard Egan, had seduced Egan's wife; that he had come into this place in the absence of her husband, and had seduced his family, in consequence of which, an illegitimate child has been brought into the world; and the disgrace which must arise from such a transaction in his family, had fallen on

M. Grant, while in the East the next spring, published three letters in the *New York Herald* countering propaganda that the runaway judges circulated. Grant's three letters were republished together as a pamphlet that circulated in the East. In the third letter, dated April 25, 1852, Grant discusses the Monroe murder case and defends Howard's right to uphold his family's honor. "I have seen a Duellist protect Virtue and restore Honor–I never heard of the Law doing it yet," Grant said. "I say, the Murder was right," and "I hope it will not be long before an Act of our Territorial Legislature making Death the punishment of Adultery, will be up before Congress for its approval or recission. We will stand there upon the broad question of State Rights."[32]

A few years later, on May 13, 1857, beloved LDS apostle Parley P. Pratt was murdered in Arkansas, the victim of an "honor killing." He had married Eleanor Jane McComb McLean, who had separated from her abusive husband and taken custody of her children. In a trial the judge acquitted both Eleanor and Pratt of charges Hector McLean had brought. Angry, Hector tracked Pratt down and stabbed him to death. For this deed, Hector gained widespread acclaim as a hero. Historians of Pratt's murder point out that "the Southern code of honor, especially that of the antebellum south, was a man's paramount personal code…When a man's honor was impugned, it was imperative that he confront the transgressor in order to save face …In Particularly severe cases, only violence against the offending party could restore lost honor."[33]

As soon as lawyer Stout heard Egan's not guilty verdict, he saw trouble ahead. "This is like to be a precident for any one who has his wife, sister, or daughter seduced to take the law into his own hands and slay the seducer & I expect it will go still farther."[34] According to legal scholar Cannon, the Egan case gave precedent to a progeny of justifiable homicides. In 1868, for example, William Hughes was acquitted for the shooting of his daughter's abductor. The *Deseret Evening News* editorialized that "Public opinion in these mountains declares that a man who seduces a woman ought to pay the penalty with his life; and her nearest of kindred should bring him to account."[35] Cannon documented similar incidents in and outside Utah that took place even past the turn of the century.[36]

Family Repercussions

The trial showed that legally Howard committed a murder. Although not explicitly stated, the trial also found James Monroe guilty of seduction and adultery. And, the trial found that Tamson gave in to Monroe's advances and was complicit. She faced no Church hearing for her wrongdoing, no doubt because Howard chose not to prefer charges. And, apparently, Howard received no disciplinary action from the Church, other than the seventies' quorum hearing noted above.

In our day, some postings about Monroe's killing that appear on the Internet posit that Tamson's relationship with Howard cooled because he favored second wife Nancy, hence Tamson had lost affection for Howard. Therefore, her responses to Monroe's advances were justifiable. That's pure speculation. However, her "vulnerability" seems more explainable by Howard's constant absences on Church assignments, assignments that didn't carry the same kind of honor as did proselytizing missions. Between March 1846, when he and Tamson began their trek west, and September 1851, when he returned from the gold fields, their total time together adds up to just two years out of five-and-a-half years.

Loss of the Plural Wives

The marriage betrayal, the Monroe-Tamson baby, the killing, and the trial had a big impact on the five Egan adults and probably the older boys. Howard lived the rest of his life knowing he'd intentionally killed Monroe. A third-hand account in the family says that Howard told his son Ransom that he had killed in self-defense before, such as Indians, but had never tracked anyone down. Howard supposedly said that after the Monroe murder he felt as if his heart was taken out of him.[37]

Tamson and wives Nancy and Mary Ann each had to deal with the tragedy in her own way. Tamson, who was almost twenty-seven when William was born, did not have another child by Howard for ten years. It's possible the baby gap existed because of alienated feelings. Howard and Nancy had no more children after Vilate, born in 1849, which suggests that affection between Nancy and Howard suffered after his return from California. Nor did Mary Ann have any more children by Howard.

As of 1855 Howard had no plural wives. In the case of Catherine Reese Clawson, as explained earlier, it's not certain she really was his wife other than perhaps in Nauvoo. She came west under the Clawson name in 1848 in Brigham Young's Company. If she were still married to Howard in 1851, after he shot her nephew James Monroe, she had good reason to dislike him. She married Brigham Young in 1855.[38] Mary Ann Tuttle and Howard also divorced. She married Titus Billings on January 20, 1854 in Salt Lake City as his second wife.

Nancy Redden and Howard divorced in the early 1850s. She married their Nineteenth Ward's bishop, Alonzo H. Raleigh, on May 6, 1856. In 1859 Brigham Young wrote to Howard, at Nancy's request, asking Howard to provide suitable clothing to Helen and Vilate, also fuel and wood sufficient for them until spring. She requested twelve yards of linsey, twenty yards of cotton cloth, twelve of calico and two pair of shoes. Young added to the list five hundred pounds of flour and four cords of wood. "Your earliest attention to this matter will naturally benefit your own offspring."[39] This was child support, even though Nancy was married to Bishop Raleigh. Why these marriages terminated isn't known, but Howard's killing of James Monroe likely contributed. No doubt Nancy and Mary Ann felt uncomfortable being married to someone considered a murderer. It's possible, too, that Nancy and Mary Ann did not want to be linked to Tamson and her badly tarnished reputation. It's not known how well the wives got along with each other before Howard shot Monroe, or after. Even if there'd been no Monroe affair, Howard's absences could have led the two plural wives to divorce him. He followed up his recent absences with more of them. In 1852 he began making annual cattle drives to California. These drives provided him and his family with a good income, so a lack of finances wasn't a big factor in the divorces.

It is very possible that Howard took on the cattle drives as his way of getting away from home and escaping from negative treatments he was receiving from family, neighbors, and associates.

Monroe's Son William

Tamson's son William, sired by James Monroe, became part of the Egan household. "Willie" grew up with Howard as his father. At some point Willie learned that Monroe was his biological father and that Howard had killed him. One descendant, Mary Jane Egan Johnson, said she understood that the M in William's middle name stood for Monroe, his biological father's surname, even though family formal genealogical records and church records list the middle name as Moburn.[40] It needs noting here that William Moburn Egan is the "Compiler and Editor" of *Pioneering the West*, and without him that book would not exist. He was a stepson and a half-brother, but as later chapters will show, Willie was treated like a son and brother by Howard, Tamson, Erastus, and Ransom.

An interesting footnote to Monroe's death relates to his personal effects. At the time he was killed, Monroe had belongings and luggage in the Reese wagon train. No doubt wagon captain Horner brought those into Salt Lake City, where the Reese merchandise company decided what to do with the clothes, comb, watch, trail equipment, money, merchandise accounts, and whatever else had belonged to Monroe. However, because Monroe intended his previous year's fast and light trip east to be a round trip, he might have left some personal belongings in Salt Lake City at the Reeses' store. Included in the property he left were his Nauvoo journals. Those ended up in the Egan household. They rightly belonged to William, Monroe's son.[41]

In his later years William worked with half-brother Ransom to collect, organize, and make typescripts of Howard Egan's diaries and papers. They published selections from the diaries and papers in 1917 as *Pioneering the West*. William played a major role in making the book happen (see Chapter 29). To his and Ransom's credit, that book did as much as anything to give Howard Egan's name and contributions a prominent place in the annals of the American West. ◆

~ 19 ~

City, Family, and Cattle Drives

Reunited with his families, Howard needed to find work so he could provide for them. He'd been a rope-maker. He'd run a trading post business. His leading of wagon trains gave him expertise with horses, mules, and oxen. He knew trails entering Utah from the east, south, and west, and his circle of friends included influential Church and business people. His killing of James Monroe gained him respect among some, dislike from others. Facing an unsure future, he first engaged in a local business in his neighborhood and then, knowing good money could be made in California, signed up with the Livingston & Kinkead merchandising firm to drive cattle from Utah to California to sell them.

From then on for nearly two decades, although the family home was in Salt Lake, Howard's heart fixated on the wide-open western regions and how to best move cattle, people, mail, and freight across to California. Those unexplored spaces seemed to work on him, the ex-sailor, somewhat like uncharted seas attract mariners to probe the unknown.

Residents in Great Salt Lake City

About the time of his trial for killing James Monroe, Howard moved Tamson and their children into a better residence. With the household size increased by baby William and by Howard himself, the family needed more space. Stepson William later learned that when he was born on June 13, 1851, Tamson lived in the "little adobie house" opposite the Heber C. Kimball home, but that they then moved "to a Livery stable and house that father bought from Charles Snow. This was on the north and west of Main Street."[1] This purchase indicates that Howard brought some gold or money back from California. A map of Salt Lake City lot owners, based on early 1850s land records, shows Howard owning lot four in block 114. The house was on the northeast corner of where today's Third West and Third South streets intersect, catty-corner to

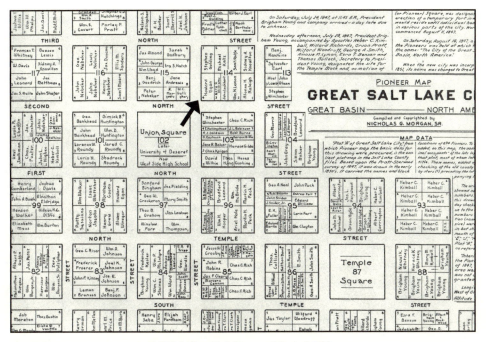

Nicholas G. Morgan Map, 1855

Union Square, where West High School now stands. That same map indicates that at some point Howard also owned lot 8 in block 98, on the corner southwest of Union Square.[2]

"When Father returned from one of his trips," Ransom said, "he got acquainted with a Mr. Moore and Mr. W. E. Horner." Together the three men bought the lot on which stood a very large barn intended for a livery stable. "The man Horner was some[thing] of a horse doctor, and Father and Moore gave him the reins to do as he thought best" in the stable business. Horner had captained the Reese wagon train in which James Monroe had been traveling when Howard killed him (see Chapter 17).

The city was divided into blocks of ten acres each, and each block contained housing lots of 1.25 acres, lots longer than wide. The Egans' corner lot ran the long way north and south. Ransom, in *Pioneering the West*, described the property.[3] He said that in the lot's middle section the big barn extended "crossways of the lot," meaning from today's Third West eastward for about half the lot. Barn access was from the west. North of the barn "the lot was fenced with a strong fence, making a secure corral to turn animals in, to feed." About sixteen feet south of the barn's southeast corner stood an adobe house. A shed at that corner of the barn was replaced by a room the same size as the adobe house and connected to its north side. A window in the adobe house faced west, and the south side contained the door, which means the house faced south toward today's Third North. The room-addition had a door and window on the west side, a window on the north, and a door on the east side. Its south wall was the north wall of the adobe house. The Egans lived in the addition and apparently rented out the adobe house section. The lot's space south of the barn and west of the house and addition "was all open ground, sometimes used by emigrants for camping."[4]

Mr. Moore didn't stay long in the partnership, and Horner went east to bring his wife across the plains, so, for a time, not much happened with the stable. When Horner came back he built a house on the lot north of the barn. After that, the stable business flourished briefly, "at least in the summer time," Ransom said. But, "taken all together, Father, when they tried to settle up, was not satisfied and bought Horner out." Howard planned "to make a dairy barn of it as soon as he could make the proper arrangements." For boys Ransom, Erastus, and Horace, the barn offered adventure. Because it had spaces underneath it, Ransom said, "us boys, and many of the neighboring boys, used to spend many an hour under there crawling from one place to another."[5]

Living right across the intersection from Union Square, the Egans witnessed the arrival of trail-worn emigrant wagon trains each August through October, and other travelers at all times of the year. During the 1850s, the "crossing the plains" wagon trains and handcart companies completed their journeys in that square.[6] Ann Lewis Clegg, who reached the Valley in 1854, recalled coming through Emigration Canyon and "through the valley and on to the public square, where we camped with hundreds of others for a few weeks until we could get located."[7]

For the Egans, that bustling campground produced dust, street traffic, garbage, manure, campfire smoke, oxen and cow bellowings, dogs barking, babies crying, and voices speaking and yelling in Danish, German, Welsh, and other languages. These emigrants gave the Egans opportunities to be helpful and charitable, and to buy from them and sell to them, and to make the livery stable business profitable.

A Tannery Business

Within days of Howard's return from the gold fields, the First Presidency issued its "Sixth General Epistle," on September 22, 1851. In it the Presidency explained that:

> Experiments at tanning hides, and making leather, have, as yet, been very limited in the Valley. Much leather is needed in this country, and many thousands of the best hides have rotted or been wasted, for want of sufficient help to erect tanneries, and convert those hides into leather…some attempts are now making at this business but more help is wanted…the laborers are few."[8]

Seeing that need, Howard, Richard Margetts, and Robert Golding started a tannery just west across the street from the Egan home. Perhaps the leather business integrated with the livestock Howard kept in and around the livery stable. How long Howard had a share of that business isn't known. "When and how he got out of it I do not know," Ransom said, "but I do know that the venture never made him a millionaire." To start the tannery business, "I think Father put in a piece of Main street property and finally took it out [years later] in boots and shoes for his Deep Creek store," which would mean 1859 or later.[9]

Nineteenth Ward Members

Officially the city's name until 1868 was "Great Salt Lake City." Early in 1849 the city had been organized into nineteen wards, each with a bishop. Howard and Tamson and the boys lived in the Nineteenth Ward in the city's northwest section. Where wives Nancy and Mary Ann lived hasn't been verified. The Egans' ward contained nine blocks, bounded on the north by Fifth (now Sixth) North, on the south by Second (now Third) North, on the east by the "brow of the hill," and on the west by the Jordan River.[10] Its primary geographic features were the high, sloped hillside to the east, and the natural warm springs to the north.[11]

In 1852 Bishop James Hendricks presided in the Nineteenth Ward. It had 303 adults and one hundred children under age eight. The ward met in the Warm Springs Bath House until they erected a school by 1850 on the northeast corner of Fourth (now Fifth) North and Second (now Third) West.[12] In 1866 the ward constructed a large and commodious building on the school site. In 1856, Alonzo Raleigh succeeded Hendricks as bishop.[13]

Willie's Boyhood

William, born in 1851, said he spent his boyhood years in Salt Lake City up to age twelve, then moved out to work on the Egans' Deep Creek ranch (see Chapter 27). As a youngster he was called "Willie." "I had good clothes when a child and they kept in good order by my mother," he said; "she had a seamstress to make them for the whole family." He often wore buckskin pants "and had some nice ones at different times with fringe all down each side. They wore well and lasted better than cloth."[14]

Children like water. William said that "our bathing and swimming places were the Jordan River and the warm springs. The latter being nearest was used the most. The Great Salt Lake was too far away and therefore seldom used. The Jordan was shallow in summer and not very cold so the boys had quite a time bathing and swimming there." At "flood time" each spring the river became quite dangerous. "Fishing was good at this season and chubs, mullets, and sucker were numerous in the stream." One of Willie's favorite winter sports was ice skating on a lake below the hot springs about four miles north. He played baseball and "town ball" on vacant lots. For hiking "we had Ensign Peak, the cave, City Creek canyon, the big bench, green bushes and many other resort places." He and Orson Pratt Jr. spent much time playing together and "walking fence poles."

While making a fire in the parlor one morning, Willie sat on a chair. Getting up to fix the fire, he brushed a ten dollar bill off the cushion. "I did not report it to my folks as I ought to have done, but appreciated it to my own use." With it he bought some candy and gave his boy friends a treat, and then, after it was mostly spent,

> I got a bottle of whiskey and before I knew it, was drunk and vomiting. I felt allright the next morning but did not know how I got home, until mother wanted to know where I got my whiskey. I found out later that some man and mother had carried me home. I never wanted whiskey after that and never was drunk again.

Utah and Church Developments

Between Howard's return home in September 1851 and his California cattle marketing trips up through 1855, several events impacted Utah and the Church. Howard and his families were aware of these and probably participated in some. In the temple block, just four blocks from Howard and Tamson's home, workmen erected a large, rectangular, adobe, peaked-roof tabernacle. It was dedicated on April 6, 1852. It proved to be too small for general conferences and large public gatherings, so a new tabernacle would replace it in 1867. During the Old Tabernacle's lifetime it seems likely Tamson, some of the children, and Howard, when he was in town, attended gatherings there.

During a conference meeting on August 29, 1852, the Church officially announced publicly for the first time that plural marriage was one of its doctrines. Not news to Howard and his wives, this was a bombshell for many recent converts from Europe, and to the world. Elder Orson Pratt made the announcement and delivered a lengthy discourse about "a plurality of wives," giving "some of the causes why the Almighty has revealed such a doctrine, and why it is considered a part and portion of our faith."[15] National and international press made the announcement big news, so sooner or later Tamson's relatives in New Hampshire and Howard's in Canada probably heard about it. If so, it no doubt darkened their opinions about the faith Howard and Tamson had embraced.

Old Tabernacle and Bowery, Lee Library, BYU

The Egan boys paid particular attention to another construction project on Temple Square. "I witnessed the first breaking of ground for the foundation of the Temple," son Ransom said. Starting on February 14, 1853, with an "immense concourse of people" watching, and, introduced by celebrations, workmen broke ground and began digging trenches up to sixteen feet deep for a foundation for the Salt Lake Temple. Then, seven weeks later, on April 6, Ransom was part of the crowds witnessing a solemn cornerstone laying ceremony. This ceremony marked the beginnings of the fulfillment of biblical prophecies that foretold the building one day of a House of the Lord in the "tops of the mountains."[16] He recalled that near the southwest corner was "an immense mound of earth" dug from foundation trenches. At the ceremony "this mound as well as the whole surrounding space was covered by a very large number of very happy people." He stood near the top of the mound "and had a good view of the southeast corner, where the stone was laid."[17]

The Egans also heard about a troubling conflict with local Native Americans, the Walker War, which took place south of Salt Lake City in 1853 and 1854. Howard, although an officer in Utah's militia, the Nauvoo Legion, played no role in that conflict due to his absences on business.

Costly Fire

On March 23, 1853, a "fine but cold day," winds blew from the south. Dust sailed like clouds "during which the large frame barn, in Ward 19, belonging to Horner and Egan, was burned."[18] A woman living in the south room had borrowed a shovel full of coals from Tamson to start a fire in her fireplace, but wind blew live coals from her shovel that set the barn on fire. Ransom described the fire:

> One day us boys took our little cart and went up on the hillside to get some oak brush for firewood. We were about to start for home when we chanced to see a small blaze at the east end of the barn. Watching this for a very few moments we saw the flame spread all over that end. We were about a half mile away. We dropped everything and ran as fast as we could for home.[19]

By the time they arrived, the fire had destroyed the Egans' barn, leaving nothing but "a huge pile of coals." Three horses in stalls got out, but two ran back through the flames and were killed. Ransom found Tamson sitting in the yard "surrounded by her household goods that had been quickly removed to a safe distance," but which "had not been handled very carefully." Tamson bemoaned that "they might as well have been left to burn as to have been smashed to pieces as some of the things were." The house, somewhat damaged, was saved. "We lost all of our chickens, and our pig had lost all of his bristles, while his pen was burning so he could escape," Ransom noted. "There was about thirty tons of hay in the barn, and the grain room was full of oats and barley. There were four sets of harness and some saddles in the harness room. All went up in smoke, besides a good many carpenter tools, the flames had spread so rapidly that it was impossible to save much that was in the barn."

Ransom's account doesn't mention Howard because he wasn't there. He was recruiting cattle up north.

Selling Cattle in California for Livingston & Kinkead

The Egans lived close to Salt Lake City's "down town" district, where Howard, an experienced trading store operator, became aware of merchants freighting in goods from Missouri River cities to sell in Utah and in California. Between 1849 and 1851, four merchant groups freighted in merchandise. One was the John and Enoch Reese firm, for which their nephew James Monroe had gone to Kanesville and returned only to face Howard's justice. Likewise, Ben Holladay and a business partner had great success selling merchandise to Mormons. John Henry Kinkead, born in Pennsylvania in 1826, went into the dry goods business in 1844 in Ohio, and in 1849 moved to Salt Lake City. There, he and I. M. Livingston founded the dry goods firm of Livingston & Kinkead. They opened their store in the John Pack home on the southwest corner of West Temple and First North.[20] Howard discussed business with them, and they employed him for a cattle project he perhaps suggested.

By 1852 Salt Lake City had "five large stores well supplied," making good profits by selling desperately wanted goods to the locals at high prices. On one occasion when freight wagons from the east resupplied those stores, an observer noted that "there is a big crowd outside the doors and upon the sidewalk, all fearful the goods will be gone before they can get in."[21] Livingston & Kinkead did well. The Church's record of Mormon Trail wagon companies shows that Livingston and Kinkead freighted store goods to Utah in 1850, 1851, and 1855.[22] Among the earliest construction projects in Salt Lake City was a store for Livingston and Kinkead, "the first mercantile building in the territory."[23]

If Howard wasn't the first, he was among the first who promoted lucrative cattle drives to California. He knew firsthand that California needed cattle and that Utah was experiencing a surplus. He knew the California Trail, and he knew where in California he could sell cattle. So, with Livingston & Kinkead, he either convinced them, or they recruited him, to drive cattle to California for market. Son Ransom explained that "Father was employed by some Salt Lake merchants to travel through the settlements both north and south in the winter time, buying up all the extra animals, cows and steers, that the people would sell." Then Howard and his crew found various places to "keep these animals till spring brought the grass up." He'd then round them up and start for California.[24]

In Utah, cattle then were currency. Church members paid their tithing, one-tenth of their increase, not in cash but in kind, so that much tithing came in as livestock. Livestock became the Church's main medium of exchange for paying obligations to merchants. News about Livingston & Kinkead's first cattle drove in 1852 influenced the Church to get involved. On April 18, 1852, the First Presidency appealed for cattle tithing. They said they had a handsome surplus of commodity tithing to pay obligations,

> but it could not be immediately converted into cash: and as the merchants were wishing stock to drive to California, it was proposed that those having extra oxen, horses, or mules, should bring them to the tithing office, to help liquidate the cash debts of the Trustee. The proposition met with a warm response from the Conference, and many cattle have already been received, and if others do as some have done, which we doubt not, old debts will be cancelled, and a handsome sum will remain in the hands of the trustee, to prosecute the public works this season.[25]

Records show that particularly large stock drives to California took place at least in the summers of 1852, 1853, and 1857. Drives were announced in Church meetings, inviting individuals to send animals in the drive, either as pay for Church obligations or for their personal income. "The 1853 drive is said to have consisted of some 2,300 work steers, which were trailed to California and sold for $100 to $125 each." Cattle and horses were Utah Territory's best exports during the 1850s.[26]

William, then a youngster, later recorded bits of information he heard from Howard or from Tamson or his brothers about Howard's cattle business. "During the time of my childhood my father was traveling most of the time to California and he was quite successful and made money in selling cattle for Mr. Livingston & Kinkaid," he said. "We had plenty and some to give."[27] He said that "Father bought cattle in the winter time and got them together and fattened them and he drove them along to California for beef."[28]

Cattle drive, University of North Texas Libraries

Howard made his first cattle drive in 1852. That's indicated by the "To Whom It May Concern" notice he and Joseph Cain posted in Salt Lake City on April 17, 1852 (see Chapter 17). It's signed by Cain of Salt Lake City and "Howard Egan, Sacramento City," which means that Howard just then was on his way there.[29] During his 1853 trip, one in the party said Howard had been from Salt Lake to California with cattle at least once before, which means 1852.[30] That he was in California in 1852 is certain, too, because on December 9, 1852, he arrived back in Salt Lake City from southern California "accompanied by the mail." Mail contractor Major George Chorpenning had just ordered that the California-Salt Lake winter mails would be transported on the southern Mormon Trail.[31] Howard had been on that same southern trail three years earlier.

Howard's Near-Death Freezing and Crippling

Howard was home for three months. Then, again, in 1853, working for Livingston & Kinkead, he headed another large herd of cattle to California. The company employed him to get the cattle there in a timely manner in order to beat the competition. In addition, he had to guide the wagons of "paying passengers anxious to leave Utah." Passenger Cornelia Ferris's journal provides a good record of the company's travels to California.[32] She was the wife of Benjamin G. Ferris, Utah Territory's recently resigned Secretary. She said that cattle broker Mr. Livingston, early in April, sent "his wagon master, Capt. Egan" and a clerk, Edgar Blodgett, to Fort Bridger "to procure a quantity of cattle for his drove." When Howard and Blodgett failed to report back on time, Livingston went looking for them. He found them, lucky to be alive, at Fort Bridger. In a sudden snowstorm they'd lost their way, exhausted their provisions, faced starvation, and crawled for miles on their hands and knees. They reached Fort Bridger with feet badly frozen. Howard was unable to walk a step without crutches, Mrs. Ferris said.[33]

In *Pioneering the West* Ransom told about that near-tragedy, but he mistakenly dated it to 1857, not 1853:

> Father went east after some cattle that he had heard were for sale. His business was buying cattle in winter to drive to California for Beef, in summer. He had a man with him and when in the mountains this heavy storm caught them and they got lost. While endeavoring to save his companion from freezing by rubbing his feet, his own froze. He lost one of his little toes entirely, and I have cut the calloused parts from his heels and toes many a time afterward. They were three days with but a pinch of cracker crumbs and after that ten days without anything to eat. His companion often said he would lie down and die, but Father would coax him and say I will try and save my life, and would go ahead and set down in a hollow and his companion would finally come along.
>
> When they got in sight of Fort Bridger the snow was crusted and their clothing and shoes were cut to pieces breaking the crust and they would leave blood in their tracks, but they tore up their blankets and wrapped their feet and legs as best they could. They finally arrived at Fort Bridger and were used up for many days. The skin of the calf of their legs could be wrapped around the bone.[34]

After Howard recovered somewhat, and being behind schedule, he, but mostly others, moved a large cattle herd to the rendezvous point for the expedition south of the Weber River near Ogden. There they joined the wagon passengers from Salt Lake City who had arrived the week before. The wagons and cattle started on May 5. Howard impressed Mrs. Ferris, even though she despised Mormons after spending a winter with them in Salt Lake City. She noted:

Capt. Egan, the conductor of our train, may fairly be termed a mountaineer. He has been back and forth from Missouri to Salt Lake, and from the latter to California, with the mail and with cattle, sundry times; and is reputed to be among the most experienced and safe for such an enterprise. The crippled condition of his feet compels him to ride in a wagon–a few times he has mounted a horse, but complains of great pain. He is a Mormon; but we have a hint that his Mormonism sits sufficiently light upon him to see that we poor Gentiles are properly cared for. So far he has been exceedingly attentive to our slightest wants.[35]

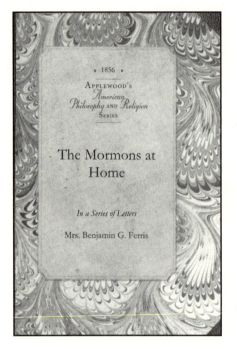

Mr. Livingston must have sent a report to Salt Lake City about Howard and Blodgett's troubles at Bridger, because Tamson traveled up to help Howard temporarily. Mrs. Ferris noted that "his wife accompanied us a few stages" and assisted to dress Howard's feet.[36] The company took the Salt Lake Cutoff and crossed the Bear and the Malad rivers. Howard and the herdsmen drove the cattle into the Bear River and swam them across. Mr. Livingston joined them there, carrying mail for California.[37]

Mrs. Ferris recorded an incident that "in a remarkable degree" illustrated Howard's "tact in managing the rough and turbulent spirits placed under his control." In a camp at the north end of the Great Salt Lake,

...while Dr. Coward was dressing his frost-bitten feet, a man near by, vexed by the contumacy of his mule, was swearing at a round rate. Egan turned to us, and, in a loud voice, said: 'I s-pose you know the regulations of the camp; no man is allowed to swear but that man; he does it so easy, that he is appointed to do all the swearing for the train.' This came out with a comical twinkle of the eye; we all laughed; the man ceased his profanity, and slunk away.[38]

Difficulties on the California Trail

They passed Steeple Rocks, or City of Rocks, and in a valley by the Goose Creek Mountains waited for a week for some cattle to arrive that Livingston had purchased at Fort Bridger. They then moved onto the California Trail. Mrs. Ferris wrote that she and her party tried to keep track of their whereabouts by using a copy of Fremont's map "but are compelled to rely much more upon Capt. Egan, who pronounces the map inaccurate." She described the landscape thus far as "a labyrinth of mountains, irregular highlands, frightful gorges," which she found "dreadfully wearisome to the traveler." She noted that "the large cattle train of Halliday & Warner, rival merchants at the city," sometimes were in advance, sometimes behind.[39]

Her observations show what kind of hard work Howard and his drovers did in order to control such herds. "It is a grand sight," Mrs. Ferris said, "the gathering of this great herd for guarding during the night–almost equal to a band of buffalo—lowing, bellowing, and rushing madly about, with any number of mock fights and playful tiltings with each other." Occasionally "some hundreds rush wildly on together in a kind of stampede, shaking the very ground beneath their feet. Sometimes our carriage is completely hemmed in by huge oxen…and we are compelled to make a grand flourish of whips to prevent mischief." One night, lightning and thunder caused a stampede: "the poor cattle turned their backs to the tempest and rushed, in a body, to the opposite highlands; and the men had to turn out and chase them for miles."[40]

On May 20 the Holladay & Warner wagons and herds caught up with them. The next day a train with perhaps four thousand sheep camped near them. On May 23 some six hundred cattle, mostly cows, joined the Livingston herd. On May 27 the Livingston-Egan company crossed a summit and reached the Thousand Springs. Then Howard, exploring ahead, led them along mountains on the south side of the Mary's (Humboldt) River.[41]

Failed Shortcut

Terrible California Trail conditions forced Howard to try a shortcut, which turned out to be a mistake. Early in June they saw the Holladay & Warner company struggling with river crossings due to high water and mud. So, "under these circumstances, Captain Egan concluded to keep on the south of the river," Mrs. Ferris wrote. She noted a time when "the Captain and four men have gone forward to explore." On June 4 "our commander returned after exploring fifty miles of the route, and reports it entirely practicable, with plenty of grass and water." The company spent that day preparing "and tomorrow we commence a route destined to be called 'Egan's Cut Off.'" The wagons and ox-teams became the vanguard "to break through the everlasting sage bushes and grease wood."[42]

Howard attempted to develop a trail variation through or around the Ruby Mountains, somewhat close to segments of the Hastings Cutoff route. Mrs. Ferris said they crossed many streams, and that some crossings upset the wagons. They had to build two bridges. One day, she said, "Capt. Egan's countenance and speech have the usual non-committalism of the leaders; but I detected in his looks, that we had a difficult task before us." Another time, scouts returned, worried about a band of Indians ahead.

Humboldt River, courtesy Trails West Inc.

"You may ask if I have any fear," Mrs. Ferris jotted. "Not the least—not even as much as I have sometimes felt around the fireside at home. Egan uses great caution."[43] They made a difficult crossing of the South Fork of the Humboldt. But Howard's route became too taxing. The men, "tired of making roads through impassable places, are almost in a state of mutiny." The detour failed. "Unfortunately for Egan, the route was not good," Egan descendant-historian Marie Irvine concluded, "in fact, it was quite bad." They took a hundred-and-fifty mile course off the normal Humboldt River trail, which exploration became a "trail not followed" again.[44]

They rejoined the normal California Trail at Gravelly Ford. But, surprisingly, by then they were ahead of their competition, the Holladay and Warner cattle herd. Being again on the normal trail that followed the Mary's (Humboldt) River, Mrs. Ferris noted that "in our journey down the river, the history of one day's ride is that of another." Howard's company passed the Humboldt Sink late in June. When ready to cross the forty-mile desert, Mrs. Ferris stated that "out of fifty teamsters, not more than five or six remained sober." They crossed the desert at night, with wagons and cattle getting stuck and mired down.[45]

While they were in the Carson Valley and near the end of their journey, the Ferrises and a handful of others decided on July 19 to leave the cattle company and cross the Sierras and enter California more quickly. So they bid adieu to the others while passing by them. Mrs. Ferris said that "when we came to Egan, he said laughing, 'You are not done with me yet,'" and he then galloped ahead and disappeared. Soon, in an "incipient village we found Egan, and a good dinner ready for us, ordered by him as a kind of complimentary farewell. This man, with all his faults, has many excellent qualities; we surely have reason to be grateful to him for numerous kind offices."[46]

In late July Howard got the Livingston cattle to the destination, apparently

Sacramento. They made it to market before the Holladay and Warner herd did. Howard's venture succeeded, but his attempted short-cut route "was anything but a success."[47]

Howard's "Fearful Fall"

"In the early days, when Father was at home for a brief time," Ransom recalled, "they used to have a sociable evening at home with friends, at one home or another." Because Howard spent so much of his time going to or coming from California, the socializers, especially the women, urged Howard "to tell them some of his thrilling experiences." One evening, after much persuasion, he related a tale about a "fearful fall" he took while selling cattle in California.

> I was selling beef to the placer miners and had to do a great deal of horseback riding to visit the different camps to get their orders for beef. On going to one camp I found the trail so steep that I thought I would walk the balance of the way, about one-fourth of a mile. So I tied my horse close to the trail and footed it on up to the camp. On the way up I noticed a good many prospect holes that had been abandoned. Some of them with large dumps and some with their windlasses still over them. I remember of thinking how dangerous it was to leave such places uncovered, as men or animals that might fall in one of them, if not killed, could not be heard by anyone, and so die of starvation or thirst.[48]

He arrived in the camp early in the afternoon. He felt "much pleased" because he had "made contracts for a good amount of beef for each week for a couple of months, which meant ten or twelve head of beef sold." His deal was with "a jolly crew" of successful miners. "By the time I had made the round of the camp and finished up my business it was dark, some of the miners wanted me to stay with them all night, but I would not, for I had left my horse tied so he could not feed, and I also thought I could find my way back down the gulch, although it had grown extremely dark." He made good time descending a well-beaten trail "when all at once I felt that I was falling. Throwing out my hands I struck what I supposed was a windlass frame, and clung to it for dear life." But the wood was rotten and it broke "almost in two, and the least move I made it would crack, and was already pinching my hands."

Horrible thoughts "ran riot through my head. How I should lie mangled at the bottom, or if dead, how long before I would be found. What would my wife and friends say as to the cause of my disappearance. Great beads of sweat came out all over me. All my life's doing, good, bad and indifferent, rushed through my mind at lightning speed, and the terror and agony of it all!" His strength finally failed, he commended his soul to God, closed his eyes, and let himself drop. At that point his listeners exclaimed "Oh, my! Dreadful! Horrible!" Then, he sheepishly admitted that he only fell "about six inches!" Finding his horse, he rode to his lodgings.

An 1854 Cattle Drive

In 1854 Howard drove cattle again, for which no account has been found. His 1855 daybook starts with January notations that show that he was then in California. His business partner John Kinkead had moved to California in 1854, and it's possible Howard left Utah with him. When Howard and Tamson's son Ras was baptized on March 17, 1854, and confirmed the next day, the Nineteenth Ward record listed father Howard as a "trader" who was in California at the time.[49]

"Tecumsee"

Ransom told a delightful story about an Indian named Tecumsee, which is illustrative of how Howard found cattle in Utah and drove them to California.[50] He didn't identify in which cattle drive year the following story about Howard took place:

> He had been very successful in buying, and when he had gone as far north as Malad River, where he camped for a few days, he had a bunch of about fifteen hundred head and a train of fifteen wagons, a hundred horses and mules, and thirty-five men, all to be looked after and taken care of till they arrived in California.

Howard's plan was to get the cattle moving in the morning, and when they were well strung out "he would select a good position and count the whole bunch, and if there were any missing he would send men out to hunt them up and bring them in." Only in cases where a lot of livestock were missing was it worth a layover to hunt for them. One day "they had traveled beyond Promontory Point and camped near Sage, or Indian Creek about sundown." Howard climbed a steep ridge and, while watching the spread-out livestock feeding, he spotted an Indian creeping close enough to stick an arrow in a cow, "an old Indian trick to get the carcass after the train moved on." Just as the Indian seemed ready to shoot the nearest steer, Howard gave a "hugh!" The Indian turned and faced Howard's six-shooter, dropped his arrows, and said "Hugh! Hugh!" Howard holstered his gun, led the Indian down to the camp, sat him by the campfire with a guard, fed him a good supper, and gave him blankets to sleep on. Next morning Howard fed the Indian all he could eat, gave him flour and bacon for his family, and told him to go.

About noon, while Howard was counting livestock passing by him, he saw the same Indian and two others watching him. When he finished the count, he turned to the Indians and held up six fingers, pointed to the cattle, and "motioned his hands over the country." The Indians understood, and went searching for six missing animals. About sundown the Indians brought in fifteen, not six. Some had the company brands, but others must have been lost by other parties. Howard then let the Indians be the cattle guards until the herd reached the Humboldt River. His final tally in California showed three cattle killed for beef, one of those for the Indians; two or three poisoned; and two or three drowned. Nevertheless, they had one more cow than when they left Malad Valley.

The next year, Howard made a similar trip. Near the same place, the same Indians came again and helped. They left, except for one, the same one at whom Howard had pointed his pistol the year before. Howard named him "Tecumsee." He "kept as close to Father as he could day and night," Ransom said. In California, when Howard stayed in a hotel, "it was always understood that Tecumsee slept on the floor by his bedroom door." One night Howard saw Tecumsee get up and search through Howard's pockets. He took a few dimes, leaving the larger money alone. Howard said nothing about it. He'd leave a few dimes in his pockets the next nights, which Tecumsee also took. Howard wondered why the Indian took the money and never spent it. One day in a store Howard let Tecumsee understand he was buying him a hat and shirt. After the fittings, Howard pretended he didn't have enough money to pay. Tecumsee took out a rag in which were tied up two or three dollars in dimes, which he slid along the counter to Howard to take what he needed.

Howard wanted Tecumsee to wear shoes while in Sacramento, so they found ones that fit, and then both paid for them. But out on the street Tecumsee took the shoes off. He could not bear to wear them. "As a general thing he tried to imitate Father's walk and actions, which caused many a smile among spectators and many a hearty laugh from Father's acquaintances." Although the old fellow once had been a war chief of a band of Shoshoni, "he came with Father to Salt Lake and never went back to his tribe." As time went on, Ransom saw him "sometimes at Mother's" and other times at different mail stations when Howard later superintended Pony Express and stagecoach mail. William Egan said Tecumsee used to sleep in Tamson's back kitchen and do chores.

"Cautious Kindness"

The Tecumsee story says a lot about Howard's tolerant attitude toward Native Americans. He had encountered them before, during the Iowa crossing, while living at Winter Quarters, during the Mormon Battalion paychecks trip, while crossing the plains four times (and being shot by them), during his gold trip to southern California, and then on the California Trail. In the case of Tecumsee, and as would happen often in years to come, Howard exhibited "cautious kindness" when he interacted with Native Americans. ◆

~ 20 ~

The "Ten Days Bet" and the New Egan Trail

Howard's 1855 daybook has spaces for every day of that year. On most of the days, but not every one, he made brief notations. At times his pencil jottings are too faint to read. During the first five months he documents where in northern California he sold cattle and at what prices. Then, in the middle part of the daybook, he jots notes about his trip back to Utah during which he explored for a shorter route, after which he documents his historic "ten day" ride back across an unproven central route he felt might become a new trail. After that fast trip to Sacramento, his daybook again records details about his cattle business in California until the end of the year.[1]

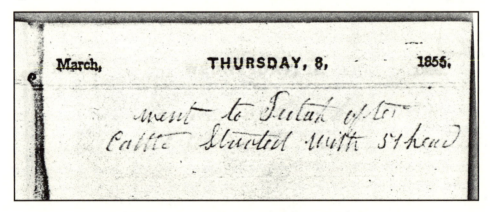

Howard Egan Diary, 1855, Beinecke Library, Yale University

Apparently, Howard drove cattle to California in 1854, because when 1855 opened he was still there, managing and selling those cattle. He continued doing selling and delivery work during much of 1855. That year he did not herd any Utah cattle to California.

About 20 miles east of Sacramento, the two-story Sloughhouse Inn was built in 1850 as a stagecoach and lodging for prospectors. It burned down in 1890 and was rebuilt that year. Sloughhouse is a registered historic landmark.

Operating out of "Sloughhouse" and Putah

When Howard's daybook entries begin on January 1, 1855, he was in California at a ranch by the San Joaquin River. His notations from January through June track his travels between Stockton, Sacramento, Auburn, Stringtown, Putah, Washington, Volcano, Jackson, Grass Valley, Georgetown, Placerville, and other places in the gold mining region. On days when he made sales, he wrote down the number of cattle, cows, or steers involved. To do his business, mostly he rode a horse. A few times he traveled on a steamboat on the combined American/San Joaquin rivers between Benicia and Sacramento and elsewhere. A time or two he traveled by stagecoach.

Paying nine dollars per week rent, Howard's primary "home" was the Commercial Building in Sloughhouse, a rest-stop settlement seventeen miles southeast of Sacramento. Sloughhouse was a favorite stopping place for travelers because it sat by a highway and stagecoach route leading to the busy mining town of Jackson.[2] Howard made use of pastures or a corral near Sloughhouse for cattle he would deliver to buyers.

Livingston & Kinkead kept its main cattle herd in a ranch area west of Sacramento called Putah. Gold Rush era records show that Putah Creek ran through the extensive 35,000 acre Rancho Las Putas, also known as the Berryessa Ranch. Most of that acreage today lies below Lake Berryessa in Napa County.[3] After negotiating a sale, Howard would arrange for the firm's cattle to be delivered or picked up from that ranch. Sometimes he herded cattle to Sloughhouse, but at other times he delivered them directly from Putah to the buyers. His daybook indicates that he had men working for him, tending or moving cattle, but doesn't say how many or who they were.

Howard's few January weather notations indicate "cloudy weather" one day, "cold foggy weather" another, and a day of "warm pleasant weather." Mr. Kinkead visited him at Sloughhouse on January 28 and stayed overnight. On February 4, Mr. Kinkead's partner, Mr. Livingston, visited Howard. During the month of February, traveling salesman Howard sold five cattle to a man named Sudbury, twelve to "C. Stebbins," fifteen head to Bill Williams in the mining town near Placerville called Diamond Springs, seven to a Mr. Spencer, and twelve to some other party on February 22. On the twenty-fourth he went to Putah for fifty-one head of cattle, which he herded to the Cosumnes River lowlands by Sloughhouse, where he and they arrived the next day. These were cattle he'd deliver to buyers who had already paid for them.

Carson Pass, courtesy Trails West, Inc.

During March Howard had sold enough cattle that he sent two thousand dollars to Livingston and Kinkead. In April he had a hundred cows brought to him from Putah and the San Joaquin River. He worked quite a bit in Jackson and northeast of there, in a mining town named Volcano. During May he did the same kind of work. He sold 115 cattle that month. In June he worked in Georgetown, Placerville, Auburn, a mining town called Nevada, and made trips to Sloughhouse, Sacramento, Putah, and San Francisco. When June ended, so did Howard's selling and delivering business. His July 1 notation says that he "started the Boys for Salt Lake."

He paid a last visit to Sacramento and Putah Creek, wrapping up business affairs, and on July 4 he boarded a stagecoach for Placerville "on the way to Salt Lake." He crossed the Sierras over the Carson Pass. On July 6 he came to Ragtown, traveling the same route he'd taken in 1851 and at other times. But he decided he'd not go back on the tedious California Trail but, instead, he'd search for a shorter and more direct way back to Salt Lake City. At some point he got off the stagecoach and bought some mules.

Prior Attempts to Find a Central Route to California

Back in 1841, the Bartleson-Bidwell party tried to take wagons from the Missouri River to California, and, after ditching their wagons, found a route along the Humboldt River. Others followed it. But "there had been no California trail until 1844," overland trail expert John Unruh emphasized, until "the Stevens-Murphy party succeeded in taking emigrant wagons across the Sierra Nevada into California" using the Truckee Pass. From then on, the Humboldt River route became the "California Trail."[4] Meanwhile, adventurous souls probed the vast unexplored reaches of the Great Basin for better ways across it. Their two biggest obstacles were the rib cage of mountain ranges running north-south and a dearth of water in the region.

In 1846 Lansford Hastings found the "Hastings Cutoff" when he led a party around the south end of Great Salt Lake, across eighty miles of salt flats, then south around the Ruby Mountains, and to the Humboldt River and the California Trail at a point about two miles west of today's Elko, Nevada. By 1850 Howard Stansbury, of the Army's Corps of Topographical Engineers, made a short probe by exploring sixty-four miles west from the Great Salt Lake.[5]

Newspaper reports in 1853 mention searches for a central way that passed south of the Great Salt Lake. Howard's friend and brother-in-law Jackson Redden/Redding learned from Indians about a stream northeast of what came to be called the Deep Creek Valley. "As far as I have traveled," Redden said, "I have found it a first rate road." His location gained the name Redding Springs.[6] In March 1853, Congress passed the Pacific Railroad Survey Act, which called for explorations to find all practical routes for a railroad to connect the East to the Pacific Ocean. In response, Lieutenant John W. Gunnison surveyed into central Utah from Kansas before Indians killed him and seven others in his party. In 1854, Lieutenant Edward G. Beckwith, one of Gunnison's subordinates, received government permission to continue the surveying to the Pacific.[7] Beckwith's party traveled a portion of the Hastings Road, then tracked southwesterly to the Ruby Mountains some distance south of the Hastings Road. His course rejoined Hastings's at the western side of Ruby Valley. Beckwith's route then turned to reach the Humboldt River about twenty-seven miles southwest of today's Winnemucca.[8]

The next probe came late in 1854, when Colonel Edward Steptoe's party, on orders to go to the Pacific coast, stopped in Salt Lake City. Wanting to find a more direct route to the coast, Steptoe sent out two exploring groups. One, led by Mormon Oliver B. Huntington, and aided by Carson Valley resident John Reese (of the Reese merchandise firm), left Salt Lake City on September 18, 1854, and followed the "Beckwith Trail" for about two hundred miles. They tried various cutoffs, but had to turn northwest to the old route along the Humboldt River, then pushed on to Carson Valley by mid-October. They returned, boasting that "from the Beckwith route we have cut off over 150 miles." They claimed that their route would produce "the best route known by white men."[9] Steptoe, distrusting Huntington's character, sent a second search group headed by Porter Rockwell and George Washington Bean. They explored some eighty miles to the west edge of the Great Salt Desert until bad weather stopped them. They returned and told Col. Steptoe that the country was not fit for wagon travel. Steptoe gave up on the central route search.[10]

Scouting the 1855 Egan Trail

After his stop at Ragtown on July 6 and 7, Howard crossed the forty-mile desert. He had other people with him, but he didn't record their names, except Tecumsee's. Undoubtedly they rode mules. On July 8 they reached the Humboldt Sink. From there, Howard's jottings somewhat track what route they tried, but who can decipher his notations? They do make clear that this was a grueling trip.

From the Sink they rode thirty-five miles and had supper, then restarted and traveled all night. About 4:00 a.m. the next morning they stopped to feed and rest. The next day they started again at 8:00 a.m. and reached an unnamed trading post about 11:00 a.m. "Left Indian Tecumsee at this point," Howard wrote. Pushing on, they camped at 9:00 p.m. On July 10 they started at 4:00 a.m. and searched all day for the Beckwith Trail. That evening three of their mules ran off, so they spent the night looking for them. By daybreak they had found the mules and got moving again. On the twelfth, they "had the pleasure of having some Indians to breakfast with us." Next, they traveled from 9:30 a.m. to about 5:00 p.m., camped and rested, restarted at 3:00 a.m. and stopped to breakfast at 5:30 a.m. They camped at 4:00 p.m. Not wanting to waste time, Howard hunted for a pass through the Humboldt Mountains "and got lost."

Howard's next jottings give descriptions of unnamed places they passed. On July 15 they traveled all day and then, like reaching an oasis in the wilderness, they "stopped at Peter Haw's and took dinner." Haws, like Howard, had spent youth years in Montreal. He'd served in the Mormon Battalion. He had lived for more than a year with his wife and daughter in a narrow valley, where they had a long cabin, garden, a corn field, mowed meadows, and a cattle herd. Haws traded with the Shoshone for furs. Of this visit, Haws said that Howard, with three mules, was eight days from Sacramento, and then went on to Salt Lake in four. Twelve days total. (Howard probably said eight days from Ragtown, not Sacramento.) "He had never made more than two hours' halt, and had never troubled himself to follow in the steps of those who had gone before him."[11] Marie Irvine determined that Howard "left the established trail eastbound near Haws's place or Gravelly Ford."[12]

They then "started a south course through a pass in the Humboldt mountains," Howard said, "traveled through a beautiful valley and stopped at 3 p.m." and then traveled ten more miles and camped. On July 17, after early morning travel on a south course for three hours, they "intersected Hastings trail, bearing east." The west end of the Hasting Cutoff Trail, now memorialized by an historic marker beside I-80, is just west of present-day Elko. Howard, enduring desert-like desolation in July heat, stopped to feed at 11:00 a.m. at Sulphur Springs. John R. Adams, "traveling in company with horses," camped with them that night. "No water," Howard noted.

On July 18 they started at 3:30 a.m. and, after bearing north, traveled about five miles and came to a large slough. They stopped to feed, then traveled for eight hours and stopped "where there is a host of Springs feed good." They resumed travel at 7:00 p.m., then stopped "on the desert" about midnight with "no grass nor water." The next day Howard started about 3:00 a.m. and traveled across "ruff barren country." They stopped at a spring on the right of "the road" about 3:00 p.m., and traveled again between 6:00 and 11:00 p.m. The next day they rode from 4:00 a.m. until 11:00 a.m., then stopped to feed. Howard's diary ends there. He finished his exploring trip by avoiding low areas near the Great Salt Lake and going south of the earlier routes.[13] In the back of his diary-daybook Howard wrote a memorandum of a route for a trail:

> Commencement of trail was ninety miles to the right of the sink of the Humboldt. Across a valley twelve miles–little water in canyon over a mountain five miles; little water to the right in the creek across a valley one miles from the road at foot of mountain, good grass and water. Thirty miles to summit of mountain. Ten miles to left, one mile over small mountain creek. Fifteen miles to Ruby Valley. Twenty miles down to valley; forty miles in same valley, creek fifteen

miles [perhaps Shell Creek, Ransom noted] on the side of a small mountain is a large spring. Twenty miles over mountain five or six springs [Spring Valley, Ransom said]. Twelve miles to summit of a little mountain; twenty-five miles to Deep Creek; thirty miles to desert; twenty miles over summit of mountain; forty-five miles to Salt Spring. To creek sixteen miles.

Howard also drew a map, but, Ransom said, "as it is only a rude drawing, with no names of places, no one but him could make much out of it."[14] Howard wrote a list of figures, perhaps distances, which likewise are not understandable.

He arrived home on July 21. He brought with him a large file of newspapers. While delivering those to the *Deseret News* office he gave the newsmen a report about his explorations. Their published version of his report reads: "Mr. Egan deviated very much from all the previously traveled routes, with the view of reconnoitering for a way that would avoid the Goose Creek Mts of one route and the miry places, in wet seasons, of the Beckwith trail."[15]

Howard's Historic Ten (Eleven) Day Trip to Sacramento

Howard, back once more in Salt Lake City, resolved to explore the Great Basin's rib cage of mountain ranges and dry valleys and find a central route. Convinced the new course he'd just probed through could be improved enough to become the long sought-after central route, he decided to prove it when summer cooled down. He spent six weeks at home. Utah then was suffering a severe drought and a devastating grasshopper invasion. Both disasters ruined farm fields and orchards (see Chapter 21). In September Howard packed up to do his exploring venture. He made a bet that he could go from Salt Lake City to Sacramento on this new route in just ten days, using mules. He arranged to haul packages for the Pacific Express Company, for whom Livingston & Kinkead were the Salt Lake City agents.[16] The *Deseret News* reported on his plan on September 19, the day he was leaving:

> Capt. Howard Egan starts on the 19th inst., for Sacramento with the Pacific Express Company's packages. He will go by way of Tooele valley and the nearest practicable route, and will doubtless make the quickest trip that has ever been made from here to Sacramento. We shall be anxious to learn the time occupied, and regret that the notice of departure was not a week earlier. It would then have afforded our citizens a better opportunity to avail themselves of the celerity, safety and certainty of the transmission and delivery of important letters and packages, and a better chance to encourage that energetic, prompt, and courteous channel for communication, the Pacific Express Co.[17]

Howard wrote daybook entries during this historic trip. On September 19, he noted that "we started from Salt Lake City to go to Sacramento." This was a Wednesday. He traveled with one other man, whose name we don't know. They stopped in Tooele for breakfast, then pushed on until 1:00 p.m., took a two-hour break, then resumed, then stopped for two hours for supper, then kept going until 2:00 a.m. They started again at 5:00 a.m., and maintained a similar grueling schedule that day. At their breakfast stop at "the Granite mountain" they found fine springs and good feed, enough for a small company. Between 11:00 a.m. and 7:00 p.m. they crossed "the desert" to Willow Springs, where the town of Callao now is. That evening they encountered Peter Haws guiding French traveler Jules Remy and traveling companion Julius Brenchley eastbound to Great Salt Lake City. These travelers were camped eight miles west from the springs. Remy described the chance meeting with Howard:

Jules Remy

> We were surprised by the arrival of two travelers, accompanied by two pack-mules. It was Mr. Egan, who stated that he had quited Salt Lake the morning of the previous day, and who hoped to be in Sacramento in ten days. This man's mode of traveling was surprising. He never followed any track but when he knew it was direct. He made but three halts in twenty-four hours, of only two hours each; he and his servant kept watch by turns. They were mounted on fine large mules, which always kept at a trot, and which could manage to work on a pound of biscuit when they could get no grass.[18]

Howard started again and traveled until 4:00 a.m. After a one hour rest, they pushed ahead until their breakfast stop at 9:00 a.m. After a five-hour ride, they took a two-hour break, then continued on until rains commenced about dark. They had seen a large Indian camp in the valley, so, for safety, they "went up a canyon" and camped for the night.

Howard's ten-day plan allowed no time for serious sleeping. "On Father's quick trip to California, straight across the great American desert, his rule was to stop but four hours out of every twenty-four," Ransom wrote, "which soon made men and mules suffer for the want of sleep as well as rest."[19] On Monday, September 24, they started at 6:00 a.m. They met some Indians "coming up the canyon on our trail." At 2:00 p.m. they stopped in the Humboldt Valley to let the animals feed for an hour, then traveled eleven straight hours, from 3:00 p.m. to 4:00 a.m. "without water." Starting again at 6:00 a.m., they found a spring of water four hours later "on the top of a mountain," so they stopped "to feed" for two hours. They traveled for one hour, stopped for an hour, then traveled all afternoon and all evening.

Ransom said that after Howard and his companion crossed about thirty miles of desert, they came to the bench or foothills of the next range of mountains, which appeared to be very dry. "Father told his partner to ride a little ways off in that direction and he would go the opposite, and if either found any water to shoot his pistol off, that the other might come to him, and if neither of them found any water they must return and climb the mountain and search the other side." Howard went as far as he thought advisable, then backtrailed. Not meeting his partner, he followed tracks, and a half mile later saw the man and mule both standing up. "The man had his hands on the horn of the saddle as if about to mount. The mule's head was down close to the bunch grass." Both man and beast were fast asleep! But the man had found water. When Howard approached, the mule awoke and raised its head a little. "The man slept till Father had dismounted and gave him a shaking up, and asked him why he had not fired the shot to let him know that he had found water. He said he was going to ride back to the top of the little ridge and do so, as the shot could be heard farther," but had fallen asleep when about to mount up. With plenty of water there, men and beasts rested "for four full hours," Ransom said.[20]

Howard believed "that man can go longer without sleep than the animals he rode, but he felt sure that the animals often slept while traveling slow." During this period, Howard hallucinated for want of sleep:

> Father said, at one time on his fast trip across the country, as he was traveling through a narrow, steep side canyon, it appeared to him that he was going through the street of a very large city. The buildings on each side appeared to be of many shapes, and some of many stories high, and occasionally a bridge would span the street, and so low down that he would duck his head to ride under them. Some of the houses seemed to be lighted up. He could see the lights in many windows, but there was no sound. Then he knew that he was suffering for the want of sleep. That made the transformation. He had often when on the desert seen the mirage take the form of buildings, bridges, forests and lakes... but he knew this was not a mirage, but lack of sleep.[21]

At another time the two men, suffering from thirst, came to a small stream of clear water. Howard's partner "jumped off his mule and threw himself flat down with his lips to the water, sucking in huge mouthfuls," Ransom said. "Father grabbed him by the legs and pushed him heels over head into the creek. Of course, when he scrambled out, he was ready to fight, but then Father said, 'Now you can drink without killing yourself, and I hope you have learned a good lesson about drinking when thirsty.'"[22]

On September 26 they stopped at 2:00 a.m., resumed the trek at 6:30 a.m., and "arrived at the Humboldt river, ninety miles from the sink." Next day they reached a trading post at the Sink at about 11:00 p.m., rested, then started again at 2:00 a.m., crossed the "Big Desert" (meaning the Forty Mile Desert), and arrived at Ragtown at

Trail Fork, Carson Trail Left, California Trail Right, courtesy Trails West, Inc.

11:30 p.m. Again, with little rest, they started at 2:30 a.m., took a two-and-a-half hour midday break, arrived at "Jack's Valley" at 7:00 p.m., changed mules, and started at 9:00 p.m. "and went on." On Saturday, September 29, having traveled all night, they stopped for breakfast at "Slippery Ford," changed mules at Silver Creek, and traveled that day and all through the next night. Having crossed the Sierras, they arrived in Placerville at 5:00 a.m., and finally reached Sacramento at 6:00 p.m., "making the trip in ten days," Howard wrote.

Howard's record-setting travel time caused quite a stir. On October 1, Mr. Kinkead sent a dispatch from San Francisco to Salt Lake City to announce he'd received word from Sacramento about Egan's arrival there "in eleven days" from Salt Lake City. "This is the fastest time on record," the *Deseret News* trumpeted, while publishing Kinkead's report.[23] Kinkead said eleven days. Howard said ten days. His diary shows it took him eleven days.

J. Raman Drake, in his 1956 thesis about Howard, pointed out that the Harold's Club Casino in Reno, Nevada, displayed a series of full color paintings depicting western subjects, and the one entitled "Muleback Champion" depicted Howard's quick trip. Next to the depiction was a generous retelling of Howard's historic venture. We've been unable to locate that painting or a photograph of it.[24]

Howard, after this debilitating regimen of four hours or less of sleep a day, reached Sacramento filthy dirty and totally exhausted. He needed a bath and sleep:

When Father arrived in Sacramento, at the end of his ten-day mule trip, his first duty was to take a bath and then a good sleep, both of which he stood very much in need of. So, after engaging his room at the hotel, he turned the water on and did not wait for the tub to fill, but got in and sat down and leaned back and — Well, the first he knew the bellboy was in the room trying to wake him up, and the water still running at full force. The first thing the bellboy knew was a battery of boots directed at him, which caused his hasty retreat. But he had broken the first real comfortable sleep Father had enjoyed for over ten days.[25]

Howard's eleven-day trip had followed somewhat the Beckwith Trail to the Humboldt River. But he refined the Beckwith Trail's course, particularly south of the Great Salt Lake and in today's eastern Nevada. Of most importance, reports of his speedy crossing gave that route's potential great public interest.

Three Months of Cattle Business in California

Howard now was back in California. Notes in his 1855 printed daybook show that from September 30 to the end of the year he traveled between San Francisco, Sacramento, Putah, and the San Jose Valley doing cattle business. For some reason the Livingston & Kinkead herd, or part of it, had to be moved from the Putah ranch lands, so Howard spent November 13 and 14 hunting for a new range. He located one in the Napa Valley, about twenty miles south of the Putah location, perhaps the San Pablo Ranch. He then went to Putah Creek "and moved the cattle." He met with James Kinkead, undoubtedly a relative of John Kinkead. One day he went with John to Putah and back to Sacramento.

On October 25 he went to San Francisco and stayed two days, then visited the San Jose Valley October 28 with one of the Kinkeads, and returned to San Francisco. He then went to Sacramento and stayed for three days. His October jottings say nothing about cattle sales. His work related to the Putah pasturage. He started on a circuit into the Sierra foothills and gold country, visiting Sloughhouse, Jackson, Sonora, and Columbia. He reached Sacramento on December 23 and spent the next week there. His 1855 daybook then concludes. How much longer he stayed in California isn't known.

By then he was paying ever closer attention to emerging national efforts to get packages and U. S. Mail delivered with some reliability and regularity to and from "the States" and California. ◆

~ 21 ~

Famine, Handcarts, Reformation, and Fort Limhi

Like ocean breakers crashing one after another, crises pounded Utah in the mid- to late-1850s, which the Egans experienced firsthand. First, they lived through a severe drought in 1855. Then drought's hot days and dryness fostered grasshopper invasions that decimated struggling gardens and crops. Following that came a terrible winter that killed half of Utah's cattle. Crop and cattle losses produced famine conditions and food rationing during the Famine of 1856. Fearing that these disasters signaled God was displeased with his people, Church leaders in 1856–1857 instituted a stern reformation. Utah's fields did produce decent harvests in 1856, but that fall's handcart disasters forced rescuers to haul off tons of the needed harvest to help the victims. Howard's family lived through these crises, but he was absent from home, as usual, during much of the time.

Drought and Grasshoppers

Far from stores in Missouri River towns or California, Utah people counted on spring plantings, rains, summer irrigation, and fall harvests for food. But during the winter of 1854–1855, the snow and rain didn't come, and then a hot and super-dry spring and summer wilted fields, orchards, and gardens. Drought set in. It spawned an invasion of hungry grasshoppers. Technically the hoppers were Rocky Mountain locusts, a voracious species whose worst outbreaks came later in the 1870s, from Colorado to Minnesota. That locust specie is now extinct.[1] The brown-gray insects averaged 1 to 1.5 inches in length. Infant locusts could only hop, but when grown and winged they flew in swarms that darkened the sky like clouds. During May through July 1855, they gorged on Utah crops north and south.[2]

This infestation was Utah's "worst grasshopper infestation" of that century.[3] According to Elder Heber C. Kimball's report late in May, "from this place south as far as we went, the grasshoppers have cut down the grain, and there is not fifty acres now standing of any kind of grain in Salt Lake Valley, and what is now standing, they are cutting it down as fast as possible."[4] Other counties suffered on the same scale. Kimball described "a great many of the gardens in the city entirely ruined."[5]

Drought and locusts must have done damage to the Egans' garden. The *Deseret News* reported one massive appearance in which "the grasshoppers filled the sky for three miles deep, or as far as they could be seen without the aid of Telescopes, and somewhat resembling a snow storm."[6] Ransom witnessed the amazing sight:

> I remember that during the heat of the day they were so thick in the sky that at times you could not see the sun, and where they would light for the night, or when the wind was too strong from the direction they wanted to travel, they destroyed everything green. All of this mighty army of hoppers were traveling in a southeasterly direction and in two or three days had finished their work here and passed on.[7]

Summer heat and strong winds are what ended the hoppers' assault. Winds blew clouds of the insects into the Great Salt Lake, creating thick rows of smelly hopper carcasses that ringed the lake's shores. Ransom described the carnage:

> There along the shore could be seen great windrows of their bodies that had been washed ashore by the north winds. Near Black Rock there were three such rows, so wide and high that a man could have filled a wagon bed with them as quick as he could have shoveled that much sand, and the whole shore line facing the north was just the same. Millions of bushels of preserved or pickled grasshoppers, that would do no more harm.[8]

That's about when Howard arrived back from California and his eastbound search for a central route. He stayed home from about August 1 until September 19. He then made his eleven-day fast trip to California (see Chapter 20).

After the infestation, a July 30, 1855 report from Salt Lake City assessed that the drought and hoppers had ruined approximately 70 percent of Utah's cereals, vegetables, and fruits.[9] Hope held for the corn and potatoes, "but the potatoes are not getting sufficient water, and will consequently be light." Grass dried up on the benches "so the cattle have to be driven high upon the mountains, or to new and distant locations for grass."[10] Desperate farmers replanted and managed to grow some late wheat and hay. The First Presidency assessed that 1855 saw "the almost total loss of crops."[11] Fortunately, communities bordering Utah Lake had a food resource others lacked: fish. The lake's fish population of trout, chub, suckers, and mullet thrived. Indians used traps and bows and arrows. Mormons set out lines and hooks and employed big nets and seines.[12]

A Cattle-Killing Winter

That fall, about the time Howard again reached California, fires broke out in Utah's tinder-dry canyons and consumed valuable timber and feed for livestock.[13] Then came winter, which proved to be "the worst weather experienced by the pioneers since the arrival." Loss of grazing grounds, caused by locusts and drought, forced herdsmen to move cattle to higher locations. Wranglers drove the Church herd and those of large cattle owners up into Cache Valley in northern Utah, a spot not favored earlier because of its cold winters. A Church ranch there soon contained about two thousand Church cattle and a thousand private ones. Then came a killer winter. Deep snows. Bitter cold. Sensing disaster, herders tried to drive the cattle back from Cache Valley towards Salt Lake Valley, but deep snow blocked them. Only 420 of the church herd survived. The others froze to death or starved. Heber C. Kimball estimated Utah lost about half of its cattle, perhaps as many as 4,000.[14]

William Egan, then four years old, recalled that "snow fell in our peach orchard nearly four feet. A crust formed on top which was strong enough to hold me up and I remember that I played on top of it. The cattle on the range over Jordan river died of starvation. My brother and others went with sleds and skinned them."[15] In *Pioneering the West* Ransom included a story, "Deep Snow, Cattle Starving," which described his experience collecting hides near the Jordan River. He dates this experience to 1857, but most likely it happened during this deadly 1855–1856 winter:

> One morning in 1857 [1856] I awoke to find a heavy snowstorm had set in, and it continued all day, all night, and all next day, and until some time in the night. The next morning when I was able to go out I found that the snow was up to my waist or about two and a half feet deep on a level. Some places eight feet deep in the valley. It was some days before the roads were broke open so travel could be resumed.[16]

Ransom and other boys heard that many cattle, on the range west of the Jordan River, were dead or dying "and that boys could make something by going over there and getting the hides off the dead ones." So he and two others "got our sleds and ropes ready and when the snow had settled and crusted so it would bear our weight we started on our exploring trip. About five miles northwest of the river bridge, "we found a bunch of ten or twelve cattle, every one dead, and laying close together. By helping each other we were able to start for home about 3 or 4 o'clock p.m., each with a hide on his sled." They repeated the gathering the next day. The boys sold the hides for three dollars apiece, "which we considered millionaire wages." Cattle losses proved catastrophic. Cattle provided milk and meat, and most farmers could not plow without them. The crisis created a good local market for any cattle being sold. Cattle dealers like Howard faced hard times.

The Famine of 1856

The positive side to such snow and freezing was that winter coated the mountains with a deep snowpack that promised good stream flows come spring, a good irrigation season, good crops, and badly needed food. But until the fall 1856 harvests, Utahns faced famine. By March, "folks had but little grain on hand, not near enough to do them till the next harvest," one bishop said, "but they began to ration out to themselves first a pound of flour per day, and then half a pound, and so on to make it last till harvest." Wheat prices shot so high "you could not get it hardly."[17] Howard's adopted father Heber Kimball put his big family on rations and assisted about a hundred others, possibly the Egans.[18] Bishops reported "unnerving destitution." Some people ate yampa roots, sego bulbs, thistle roots, and wild plants. Others begged on the streets.[19] "A great portion of the people are digging roots," President Kimball noted on April 13, "and hundreds and thousands, their teams being dead, are under the necessity of spading their ground to put in their grain."[20]

From March through July, more fishermen swarmed Utah Lake than happened in 1855. Salt Lake City wards sent fishing teams to the lake. On May 30 Wilford Woodruff said the shores of Utah Lake "are crowded like a fair with wagons, there are so many catching and drying fish."[21] Fish harvests that year were "intense."[22] Despite severe food shortages, no one died of starvation.[23] No records tell how the Egans fared during the famine.

During planting season, farmers enjoyed an abundance of irrigation water. On May 29 Wilford Woodruff felt pleased that "the potatoes, corn, squash, peas and other vegetables look well." He added that "we expect to reap a bountiful harvest."[24] But summer sun and winds scorched almost as hot and dry as the year before, and "much destitution was experienced by the masses of the people through the want of provisions."[25] The food crisis lessened, but continued.

Near year's end the First Presidency reported that "the wheat crop of this season was good, but corn was rather light and potatoes were almost an entire failure."[26] As of December 31, 1855, Howard was in California, but he probably returned home by spring 1856. He knew, because he'd been home the previous summer, about grasshopper and drought conditions, so it's likely he brought supplies and some food from California for his family. Also, he made money in California, so when he arrived home he could buy for the family, even at the high prices caused by the famine.

A Gap in Howard's Record

Documents and family traditions are silent about Howard's doings during 1856. What's known is that as of December 31, 1855, he was in California. He either returned home by spring 1856 and then returned to California by year's end, or else stayed in California all during 1856. It's known that he returned from California to Salt Lake City in March 1857. There is some indication that Howard's work in California early in 1856 might have been related to mail and express matters (see below).[27]

Helping Handcart Emigrants

Every August, if not sooner, Mormon emigrant wagon trains started rolling into Great Salt Lake Valley. For the year 1856, the Church instituted low-cost handcart companies in which emigrants pulled and pushed handcarts. Five handcart companies outfitted in Iowa City. During September and October about 800 travelers in the Ellsworth, McArthur, and Bunker handcart brigades pulled into Great Salt Lake Valley after a taxing but successful crossing of the plains. Wagon trains also arrived. As in years past, these 1856 companies terminated their journey at Union Square, catty-corner to the Egans' home.

But early in October 1856, troubling word came that 1,200 people in the Willie and Martin handcart companies and the Hunt and Hodgett wagon trains were far behind schedule and in trouble. Immediately, rescue teams loaded up food, clothing, bedding, and supplies, and headed out to the blizzard-trapped companies. Rescuers brought survivors by the scores into Salt Lake Valley. Those in need of nursing were sent to various communities.[28] It's not known what, if anything, the Egans donated to this rescue effort or if they took in any of the survivors, but in that year or at other times, the Egans did aid some handcart and wagon emigrants who reached Union Square. According to Ransom:

> When the immigrants came in with trains each season and also with the hand cart companies there was much suffering for want of the necessaries of life which they were entirely deficient of, during the early years after first ones began to arrive. This would have been much greater but for the benevolence of those that were here who were able to help them. Father was doing well during this period with his beef trade in California and Mother had means to use and being naturally very benevolent she helped them a great deal. We were situated close to the Union Square on which they could get some better quarters. I remember Mother saying that she kept an account one season and found that she had purchased $1500 worth of provisions which she had given emigrants of the hand cart companies and others that were in need. She told Father about it and the only comment he made was, "That is right Mother and you shall be blessed for your good heart."[29]

The "Mormon Reformation"

Drought, pestilence, harsh winter, and famine seemed to be signs that "modern Israel's problems were rooted in disobedience and unrighteousness." Why else did God allow the Saints "to be on the receiving end of nature's fiery darts"? By March of 1856, President Young felt that the people needed "sermons like peals of thunder" to wake them up. The annual influx of emigrants consisted primarily of converts, new to the faith. Homeless and destitute, they felt more concern for food, shelter, and surviving than religion. So, at conferences held in Kaysville on September 13–16, a spirited crusade now termed the "Mormon Reformation" started.[30] It aimed to inculcate deeper spirituality, firmer commitments to Church teachings and requirements, remorse and repentance for past wrongs, better behavior, and, ultimately, a society worthy to merit God's blessing and protection. People were asked to repent, get their lives in order, and be worthy to renew their original baptismal covenants by being rebaptized.[31]

During general conference in October 1856 at least 12,000 people gathered in and around the bowery. They heard handcart reports and appeals for rescuers; they also listened to stern calls for reform. President Woodruff said that the First Presidency had preached such messages to the people for the last month, and the last year:

> I have thought that it was a good deal like throwing a ball against a rock. It did not penetrate but bounced back...They have told us that we were asleep as a people...we have had more stealing, more lying, more swearing in one year than there should have been in a thousand...What is the use of our saying that we have been righteous, that we have been holy when we have actually been in a sound sleep...the time for sifting and purifying the Saints has come.[32]

The reform crusade spread even to mission areas overseas.[33] Meetings and sermons called for repentance and rebaptisms. President Brigham Young and general authorities were rebaptized. The crusade's rhetoric urged adults to enter into plural marriage relationships.[34] By early November bishops and ward teachers visited members in their homes to review a Church-produced catechism of nearly thirty questions dealing with murder, betrayal, adultery, misuse of others' property, lying, swearing, intoxication, debt payment, branding someone else's animal, use of someone else's horses or animals without permission, misappropriation of irrigation water, Sabbath church attendance, payment of tithes, speaking against Church doctrines or the First Presidency, keeping the body washed and clean, family and private prayer, and earning pay.[35]

Very likely the Nineteenth Ward's bishop or block teachers visited the Egan family and read through the catechism with them. What Tamson and Howard felt during this repentance crusade and catechizing isn't known, but probably by then they had worked things out between themselves and the Lord. Ras said he was baptized on March 5, 1857, when he was fifteen, which must have been a rebaptism as part of the Reformation.[36] *Pioneering the West* doesn't mention the Reformation.

Some Reformation rhetoric became too harsh and judgmental, causing fanatical members to justify threatening, harming, and in a few cases killing, those whose behavior they judged improper.[37] The crusade lasted into the first half of 1857. And, although strong teachings let some feel license to do despicable acts, overall the push to improve behaviors produced a "significant improvement" spiritually and physically throughout the Church. Meeting attendance rose, tithes and offerings increased, community morale improved, and, as a mixed-bonus for the believers, many backsliders and apostates left the territory—some of whom felt forced out.[38]

With President Young's Caravan to Fort Limhi

On March 28, 1857, Howard arrived in Salt Lake City from California. Four others were with him, including Orson K. Whitney, returning from his mission to the Sandwich Islands (Hawaii). Howard made that trip, which was mail-related, in near-record time. He left San Francisco on March 5, reached San Bernardino on March 10, left there two days later, and "passed the incoming mail which started on March 8th, at the Mountain Springs, 50 miles beyond Los Vegas." He traveled from San Bernardino to Salt Lake City in ten days. He brought with him a March 5 edition of the *San Francisco Bulletin* and the February 5 issue of the *New York Herald*. Howard had lobbied with the postmaster in San Francisco to expedite mail from that city to San Bernardino in a way that would allow mail for Utah to leave at the end of the month instead of in the next month's mail.[39]

During April conference back in 1855, President Young sent men to establish a farming settlement among Native Americans far north near today's Montana-Idaho border. For thirty days and 380 miles from Salt Lake City, Thomas S. Smith led a first company north past Fort Hall (near present-day Pocatello) and into the Salmon Mountains. This region was part of the Oregon Territory. They settled in a narrow mountain valley by a stream flowing into the Salmon River. There, 5,000 feet above sea level, the men built Fort Limhi, named after a Book of Mormon king. The name later became misspelled Lemhi. They named a nearby stream, which was a favorite fishing center for Bannock, Shoshoni, and Nez Perce Indians, the Limhi River.[40]

The tribes permitted the Mormons to occupy the land, and to fish, hunt, and cut timber, but not for profit. The men constructed a fort having a palisade of logs nine feet high that surrounded the log cabins within. They built a corral and fences, and planted several acres of land. The settlement developed for three years. Dozens of Indians were taught the gospel by the few missionaries who knew some of the Indian languages, and a number received baptism. In 1856, when grasshoppers ruined the Limhi crops, the fort's residents lived on cow's milk and salmon. The fort population by 1857 was 116 men, women, and children.

Late in April 1857, President Young decided to visit Fort Limhi and see firsthand how the mission fared and to scout the region for future settlement. To protect the president's caravan, some of the Church's best military men went along, including Howard. He had been home less than a month. He was part of a large, well-staffed company of 115 men, twenty-two women, and five boys, who started out from Brigham City on April 26. Most of the following account of Young's trip, unless otherwise documented, is from the official company journal.[41] Nauvoo Legion colonel Robert T. Burton served as the company commander. He chose five captains of tens. Howard was not one of the captains but traveled in the second ten.[42] The caravan included twenty-eight carriages, twenty-three wagons, 104 horses and sixty-four mules.

On May 1 they reached the Snake River, six miles above Fort Hall. Using strapped-together canoes and small boats, the captains ferried people and vehicles across the swift Snake, and swam the animals across the next day. The ferry site was 193 miles from Salt Lake City. After storing and camouflaging the canoes and boats, they traveled up along the Snake. This probably was territory Howard had never seen before. Some areas lacked roads. The procession faced wind and dust. Sagebrush covered the country, which deep ravines indented.

On Sunday afternoon, May 3, Howard's eyes lit up when the company passed Frederick Burr, who oversaw a considerable herd of cattle and horses. These animals had wintered in the Flat Head country (now western Montana). Howard talked cattle business with Burr. According to historian David Bigler:

> Frederick Burr, the cattle trader from Bitterroot Valley, was driving a small herd, which he intended to sell before going on to California. Burr recorded

the meeting that day: "Two Mormons passed on an express to Salmon River; they reported Gov. Brigham with 118 men coming on behind." On 3 May, when he met Governor Young's main company ..."Howard Egan made me an offer for my cattle."[43]

Burr sold his herd to Egan, for later delivery, then went to Salt Lake City. Howard might have been acting in behalf of Livingston & Kinkead or some other dealer. It's doubtful he could afford to buy the cattle with his own money.

On May 8 the Mormon company reached Fort Limhi, finishing a twelve-day journey. Howard's experience there broadened his understanding of Native Americans. Soon, Chief Snag moved his Shoshoni band and sixteen lodges near the fort. He and others came to the fort, sat by the fire, smoked, and talked with Chief Kanosh of the Utes who had accompanied the Young party. On May 11 some expedition men repaired wagons, while others visited Indians at their lodges. Howard found Indians and whites regularly pulled two- to five-pound salmon from the nearby river.

With business finished on May 13, the Young Company headed home. On May 18 they came again to the Snake River, and on May 20, by reusing their stored canoes and boats, they ferried across. On May 21 Howard paid close attention as they passed a camp of mountaineers with livestock. Two days later he left the Young party and

Fort Lemhi in 1918, Utah State Historical Society

hurried ahead to the Bear River crossing near Brigham City. There, Frederick Burr turned his herd over to Howard.[44] Howard must have arranged to graze the cattle there, because the next day he was in Salt Lake City, bringing news that Young's party soon would arrive.[45] It's not known what became of the cattle Howard bought. Previous patterns suggest they became part of a cattle drive to California that Howard may have led that summer or fall. ◆

~ 22 ~

Difficult Assignments During the "Utah War"

A pleasant spring, 1857, brought Utahns optimism, which summer news from the plains killed. A substantial United States Army force was heading toward Utah Territory to suppress a purported Mormon "rebellion" against the federal government. The news came while snowmelt watered irrigated fields, crops flourished, cattle herds replenished, and business thrived. The shocking news of the army on the march made Church leaders agonize and ponder how to respond. Brigham Young still was the territorial governor. The territory's militia, the Nauvoo Legion, although rusty, could be mobilized, but it needed arms, ammunition, and powder. Thank goodness that farmers would have time to gather a good harvest before any army regiments could reach Utah. Scouts were sent to explore nooks and crannies to find retreat places if civilians became endangered. War fear permeated the Mormon settlements.

The army's actions, coupled with Utah's resistance, produced a conflict popularly called the "Utah War."[1] Historians Bigler and Bagley argue a good case that the Utah War could and should be called "The Mormon Rebellion, America's First Civil War." Howard, as a Nauvoo Legion officer and California trader, became directly involved in it, and his family endured months of uncertainty, worries about him, and displacement from their home.

A Federal Territory or a Theocracy?

Brigham Young's term as territorial governor expired in 1854. But when Col. Edward Steptoe declined appointment to be Young's successor, and his troops flaunted behavior offensive to the Saints, President Fillmore appointed Governor Young to a second term. In that same year, the federal government sent appointees to fill several territorial positions. These "outsiders" became frustrated by Mormon interferences and hostile talk. Clashes came. Differences and disrespect reached a volcanic state during 1855. Utah's federal appointees and the national establishment felt obligated to bear down hard on Utah's theocracy-in-progress.[2]

New Associate Justices George P. Stiles and W. W. Drummond stirred up eastern sentiment against the Mormons by claiming, incorrectly, that United States court records in Salt Lake City had been burned. In 1856, mail contractor William M. F. McGraw, upset because he'd lost a mail contract to Mormon bidders, purported that "no vestige of law and order, no protection for life or property," existed in Utah. Indian agent on the Upper Platte, Thomas S. Twiss, and the Surveyor General in Utah, David Burr, complained about Mormon misuse of land. Such reports, read by a nation already enraged by Mormon polygamy, raised cries for federal action. Senator Stephen A. Douglas termed Utah "an ulcer on the body politic" that should be cut out.[3]

In 1856, the new Republican Party, which replaced the old Whig party, nominated John C. Fremont to be their presidential candidate, a man who felt contempt for Mormons. The Republican platform pledged to take action against the "twin relics of barbarism," polygamy and slavery. Fremont lost the election to Democrat James Buchanan.

The United States Army's "Utah Expedition"

"A contentious struggle between an American republic and a homegrown frontier theocracy" simmered.[4] Church control of Utah Territory clashed with the federal government's role in territorial matters. To deal with a public upset about the "Mormon problem," President Buchanan decided to install a new governor in Utah with the aid of army troops. He presumed Utahns would not oppose the army, that the army could find provisions and forage in Utah, and that unhappy Mormons would welcome a chance to free themselves from church domination.[5] All three presumptions proved wrong.

President James Buchanan, Utah State Historical Society

The army, to form a "Utah Expedition," began assembling up to 2500 soldiers to escort the new governor, Alfred Cumming, as well as three new judges and new superintendent of Indian Affairs Jacob Forney. Cumming was a former mayor of Atlanta and superintendent of Indian Affairs in St. Louis. On July 18, advance army detachments left

Fort Leavenworth, led temporarily by Col. Edmund Alexander until Col. Albert Sidney Johnston replaced him in late August.[6] The army hired teamsters, bought horses and wagons, and purchased tons of food to be hauled to Utah by the Russell, Majors, and Waddell freighting firm. Advance army units reached Fort Laramie on September 3. By September's end the army units, with supply trains in the lead, "stretched all the way across the Great Plains."[7]

Harper's Weekly, April 24, 1858, Utah State Historical Society

Nauvoo Legion Readiness

Months before news about the Utah Expedition reached Utah, the territorial legislature had reorganized the Nauvoo Legion. In April 1857, General Daniel H. Wells, as the hands-on commander, issued General Order Number One, which decreed that all able-bodied white males between ages eighteen and forty-five were subject to military duty. Howard already was a major in the Legion, dating from Nauvoo days, and often was referred to as "Major Egan." General Wells's order divided the Legion into platoons, companies, battalions, regiments, brigades, divisions, and departments, and carved Utah into thirteen military districts. Howard's participation became limited by his absences from home.[8]

Legion men had to supply their own arms, equipment, uniforms, and mounts. The authorized uniform consisted of long, dark blue trousers, which men in the mounted service tucked into their boots. A dark blue blouse with long tails, double- or single-breasted, bore gold buttons and gold shoulder tabs displaying the rank of the officers. Soldiers wore a straight "choke" collar of medium height and a black flat-crowned and flat-rimmed hat, turned up on the right side, with a black ostrich feather attached. Sometimes the officers wore shoulder sashes, the color representing their branch of service.[9] When doing officer duties, Howard wore such a uniform, but no photographs exist showing him in military dress. One of his descendants today possesses his Legion sword.[10]

Nauvoo Legion, Utah State Historical Society

Because Governor Young received no *official* notification of his replacement, or of the sending of the Utah Expedition, he considered the approaching army an invading mob. As governor he pledged to protect Utah citizens from such a menace.[11] Utah prepared to resist. The Legion sent out observation corps to monitor the trail approaches into Utah. One order warned that "the time may come when we shall have to lay everything waste and go into the mountains, therefore let us be preparing for such an event." Grain must be secured and conserved, and garden produce used economically. Residents should be "storing up clothing of a substantial kind. Fix up and keep in repair our wagons and take care of our property and not let anything go to waste." Also, they should "find a safe retreat in the mountains for [live]stock."[12] Some reassignments of Legion officers placed Ephraim Hanks in charge of West Jordan, Willow Creek, Cottonwood, and Millcreek, and Major Egan in charge of Sugarhouse. However, Howard was probably in, or headed for, California.[13]

In September, Mormon patrols in present-day Wyoming spotted infantry moving rapidly towards Fort Bridger. Spies reported that soldiers were boasting they would drive and plunder the Utah pioneers and "scalp old Brigham."[14] By September 21 the military expedition had four thousand horses and mules transporting men and supplies.[15] Near South Pass on September 24, Legion Colonel Robert Burton's cavalry stampeded army cattle. Meanwhile, Captain James S. Brown and a small unit from the Weber military district circled Bear Lake looking for army intrusions that might bypass the Echo Canyon road.[16]

Captain Steward Van Vliet, of the army's Quartermaster Corps, rode ahead to Salt Lake City to arrange for the army's arrival there and to obtain provisions. He consulted with LDS leaders, advising them that the army had peaceful intent. Doubting that, leaders told him they would resist the expedition and that the Mormons would destroy their own communities if the army tried to come in.[17] Utahns expected that the army "would certainly shatter the peace of the Valley and might even destroy the Church."[18] Capt. Van Vliet rode back to Col. Alexander, west of South Pass, and reported the Mormon response. Given the lateness of the season, Captain Van Vliet recommended the Utah Expedition not push all the way to the Great Salt Lake Valley that year, but that it should winter near Fort Bridger.[19]

Defensive Actions to Protect the Territory

After Captain Van Vliet left, Governor Young proclaimed martial law in Utah Territory. "We are invaded by a hostile force," his order reads, "who are evidently assailing us to accomplish our overthrow and destruction." It forbade all armed forces from entering the territory.[20] Under martial law no one could pass into or through Utah without a permit from territorial officials.[21] Military commanders were advised to be ready for "a big fight next year." In case the army could not be stopped, the plan called for Saints to desolate the territory, hide families and livestock in the safety of the mountains, attack the army from ambush, stampede the soldiers' livestock, capture supply trains, and "lay waste everything that will burn."[22]

By September 25, 1857, horrible news from southern Utah said that a large company of non-Mormon emigrants had been massacred near Cedar City at Mountain Meadows on September 11. First reports said Indians did the killing, but rumors claimed correctly that Mormons had perpetrated it. This horrific act committed by overzealous Saints, infused with the war hysteria and fear the Church leaders had whipped up, still taints Mormons and Utah to this day.

The Church, which had recently purchased Fort Bridger and nearby Fort Supply, authorized Nauvoo Legion patrols to burn the enclosures on October 3 so that the army could not use them. Col. Alexander's advance troops approached today's Utah-Wyoming border and planned, when reinforcements caught up, to head into Great Salt Lake Valley through Echo Canyon, the usual Mormon Trail route. He set up a temporary Camp Winfield for his disorganized troops and then, afraid the Echo Canyon route might be a death trap, he headed his Tenth Infantry northward to try a Bear River Road entry point.[23]

Meanwhile, Major Lot Smith's Mormon patrol of forty-three men rode from Bridger's ashes, met unguarded supply trains, and torched three of them. Smith's men then joined Porter Rockwell and burned grass ahead of the army at Ham's Fork. Their "most significant accomplishment," though, was taking possession of fourteen hundred of the army's two thousand head of cattle, while startled guards watched. Rockwell took the livestock into Salt Lake Valley for safe keeping, later to be returned, while Lot Smith continued to patrol the countryside.[24]

Expecting a protracted conflict, President Young ordered that distant Mormon outposts at Elk Mountain in southeastern Utah, Carson Valley, and San Bernardino be abandoned and the colonists "come home to Zion." The Church recalled several hundred missionaries from around the world, and it stopped publishing its two principal non-Utah newspapers, the *Western Standard* in San Francisco and *The Mormon* in New York City.[25] Howard was then in California, having probably driven the cattle he'd obtained on his Fort Limhi expedition.

Camp Scott and "Johnston's Army"

General Albert S. Johnston, Utah State Historical Society

Snow caught Col. Alexander's infantrymen thirty-five miles from Camp Winfield. On November 2, Colonel Albert Sidney Johnston finally caught up and assumed command of the Utah Expedition. He realized its wisest alternative was to encamp for winter near Fort Bridger's ruins.[26] On November 6 a mountain blizzard hit. Axle grease froze. Horses, mules, and oxen died by the hundreds. Meanwhile, back at South Pass, Lt. Colonel Philip St. George Cooke, the former commander of the Mormon Battalion, led his cavalry "through temperatures that dropped to 44 degrees below zero at night." Col. Johnston's advance units reached the ruins of Fort Bridger on November 17. Cooke's dragoons and the civilian officers arrived two days later, having lost 130 of their original 144 horses to the cold and to feed shortages.[27]

Finally, most of the army units combined together and, near the Bridger site, General Johnston created Camp Scott, a campsite that stretched out for several miles.[28] Governor Cumming stayed in a nearby civilian camp called "Eckelsville."[29] By now Mormons used the nickname "Johnston's Army" for the Utah Expedition.

Mormons' Echo Canyon Defenses

From his frigid headquarters, Governor Cumming on November 21 issued a proclamation to Utahns. It announced his appointment, warned that their behavior was treason, and ordered all Utah militia units to disband. He promised a just administration and freedom of conscience. He criticized former Governor Young for "violent and treasonable acts." When Mormons heard his insulting proclamation, red-blooded militiamen by the hundreds itched for battle. General Johnston, himself eager to attack Mormon forces, felt Cumming's message was too lenient.[30]

During September and October, Mormon infantry and cavalry entered East and Echo canyons and erected fortifications and stone walls on upper slopes of the narrow ravines. They excavated trenches in sides of the canyon where snipers could hide. They positioned boulders to push down the slopes. Muscles and shovels dug deep water ditches in Echo Canyon's floor and constructed dams which, if opened, would send water through the conduits into the army's path. On October 14 the Legion's commissary general reported it had eleven-hundred militia in the mountains, seven hundred more were awaiting orders in Salt Lake City, and three thousand troops could be thrown into the canyon on fifteen hours notice.[31] Had Howard not been away on business, as a Legion officer he would have been helping erect the canyon's defenses. Within three months, though, he'd be on duty there.

Winter Lull and Spring War Preparations

On November 11 a mountain snowstorm set in, and winter soon put the "Utah War" on hold.[32] The army's entire command of men and officers then numbered two thousand. Col. Johnston's troops endured storms and bitter cold in Camp Scott's thin tents, while the Legion men went home to comfortable firesides.[33] Army troops suffered shortages of everything—clothing, medicine, rations, salt, mounts for the cavalry, and animals to draw wagons and artillery. Some three thousand cattle died that winter from starvation and freezing.[34] Desperate for draft animals, General Johnston sent a small contingent under Captain Randolph Marcy to far-off Fort Union in New Mexico Territory to bring back more, which they did by early spring.

Benjamin F. Ficklin, authorized by both Johnston and Cumming, led ten civilians north from Camp Scott on December 9 to contract with mountaineers located near the headwaters of the Columbia and Missouri rivers for five hundred head of cattle to be delivered to Camp Scott by spring. Only Fort Limhi had the number of cattle Ficklin needed. His urgings "lit the fuse" that made Bannock and Shoshoni attack Fort Limhi and steal more than thirty horses and three hundred cattle. Six weeks later Ficklin and his men arrived with animals for the army.[35] After those raids, President Young ordered the Fort Limhi mission closed down.

Howard Brings Ammunition from California

In California, meanwhile, mail and travelers brought information about the pending invasion of Utah. Word reached Howard that Mormon troops desperately needed arms and ammunition. Militia soldiers outnumbered guns available in Utah. Half of the Legion was unarmed. A gun shop on Temple Square began producing about twenty revolvers per week. Gunpowder mills were established at Cedar City, Provo, and Salt Lake City. President Young sent instructions to returning brethren in the eastern states "to provide yourselves with good Rifles, and Pistols, and bring with you all the powder and lead which you are able to purchase and freight through."[36] Young sent a small command of experienced LDS frontiersmen to northern California, led by Legion colonel Peter Conover and Oliver B. Huntington, to, among other tasks, "secure a cargo of guns and ammunition in San Francisco for delivery to Utah." Saints in San Bernardino shipped five hundred revolvers, those in Carson Valley forwarded 2,700 pounds of ammunition and a large amount of arms, and from San Francisco came eight hundred dollars worth of war munitions.[37]

As Howard's first involvement in the Utah War, he scoured California for all the gunpowder he could transport. His was a dangerous mission: "Egan had to deal with the cumulative uproar created in California by Conover's slightly earlier activities, the sensational Mormon evacuations of Carson Valley and San Bernardino, and the widespread anti-Mormon animosity created by travelers' accounts of the carnage at Mountain Meadows." He rounded up gunpowder and packed it up for Utah. "The resourceful Egan operated not only clandestinely but largely alone."[38] In a letter to George Q. Cannon, Howard said that he'd left Stockton, California on November 23 with all the gunpowder he could carry.[39]

He then made his way south in order to travel the southern route back to Utah, the road he'd helped blaze (see Chapter 15). He sent word to Church headquarters about his cargo and asked for assistance. While approaching Cedar City he must have passed by the unburied bodies of victims at the massacre site at Mountain Meadows. On January 6, 1858, the General Tithing Office in Salt Lake City sent him a letter, which he received in southern Utah. It said they had learned he was returning to the city with ammunition and that he needed assistance. "This will be readily afforded you by the Bishops and brethren South upon showing them this letter." They were to furnish Howard any supplies and horse feed he asked for. "We send you four of your mules in the charge of John Larson to relieve your team." With regards to disposing of any of the powder in the southern Utah settlements, a concern he had raised, the letter advised that "they are making powder in Iron county and we trust will be able to supply themselves, you had therefore better bring it all through." The letter certified that Howard had paid tithing full "to date," not just an annual tithe, amounting to $753.12.[40]

Traveling through winter conditions, Howard arrived in Salt Lake City on January 19, 1858.[41] He delivered to the Nauvoo Legion's ordinance depot more than eight hundred pounds of ammunition, which a receipt lists as:[42]

27 Kegs (FFFG) Rifle Powder 25 lb each
30 M Percussion Caps
100 lbs Lead

Preparations for a Spring Invasion

Back home again, Howard found the Nauvoo Legion, and a unit called the Standing Army, getting ready for a spring face-off with the vast army. President Young knew that when he was replaced as governor, which soon could happen, the Nauvoo Legion would be under the direction of the new governor and not Church leaders. So, back in October 1857, he turned wheels to create an independent, paramilitary body he called the Standing Army. He wanted a thousand-man cavalry unit, a Church entity, with well equipped troops available for indefinite, not short-term, service. This mounted unit, one plan said, would spearhead the Nauvoo Legion's spring attack of Fort Bridger and Fort Laramie.[43]

By early February the Standing Army had been organized as a brigade commanded by Brig. Gen. William H. Kimball, then a colonel in the Nauvoo Legion. Subordinate units were regiments, battalions, and companies. Howard became one of the battalion heads, as did Thomas Callister, Lot Smith, M. D. Hambleston, Warren Snow, Henson Walker, Brigham Young Jr., Chauncey West, and others.[44] Men selected for the Standing Army, Elder George A. Smith observed, were "well mounted, expert riders, and dead shots–armed with Rifles and Revolvers."[45] Some winter socializing took place among the top militia officers. One, Col. Robert T. Burton, enjoyed many dinners with officers, and military parties in the social hall. He particularly enjoyed the company of Lot Smith, Nathaniel V. Jones, William Kimball, and Howard.[46]

The surprise arrival of Thomas L. Kane from Philadelphia in late February put a new player into the mix.[47] Organizational tangles and situation changes became such that by late March "the Standing Army was a dead issue." Historian MacKinnon said it's doubtful that this force every campaigned offensively.[48] Howard, however, continued to carry out Nauvoo Legion assignments.

Thomas L. Kane's Peace Mission

Unknown to anyone in Utah, Kane, the Church's Philadelphia friend, volunteered to be a private peace envoy for President Buchanan.[49] "Feisty, combative, and quixotically brave almost to the point of foolhardiness," he was somewhat well connected in the nation's capital.[50] President Buchanan reluctantly authorized him to clandestinely head to Utah and negotiate with General Johnston, Governor Cumming, and Brigham Young. Posing as a Philadelphia botanist named Dr. Osborn, Kane sailed to Panama, crossed the isthmus by train, and then went by boat to San Francisco and then San Pedro. He left San Bernardino on February 6 and arrived in Salt Lake City on February 25, where he stayed until March 8 talking with Church leaders.[51]

Thomas L. Kane,
Utah State Historical Society

On March 8 he left for Camp Scott to talk with Gov. Cumming and army commander Johnston. He "traveled under protection of a few frontiersmen hand-picked by Brigham Young from among his reliable 'b'hoys': Brig. Gen. Lewis Robinson, Major Howard Egan, Capt. Orrin Porter Rockwell, and others." These special guards delivered Kane, exhausted, at the army camp on March 12.[52] Howard knew Kane. Eleven years earlier, back in 1846 when Howard's family, as Nauvoo exiles, crossed the Missouri River about July 8, they heard about Kane's appearance to help recruit Mormons for Mexican War duty (see Chapter 7). Kane had visited Heber C. Kimball's encampment, which included Howard and Tamson and the boys, where he spoke to the people.

Kane spent March 12 to April 5 at Camp Scott. Howard was part of a cluster of men who remained close by, whom Kane could communicate with when needed. Kane was unwilling to discuss his thinking with them. He waited for William Kimball, whom he trusted more.[53] Howard and others encamped at a command post at Quaking Asp Hill (near today's Evanston, Wyoming).[54] Kane tried to negotiate with General Johnston and Governor Cumming, two men who didn't get along with each other.[55]

At one point Kane and Johnston's arguments escalated such that Kane challenged Johnston to a duel.[56]

Kane did convince Cumming to go to Salt Lake City and talk with Mormon leaders. On April 5, Kane and Gov. Cumming, with two black servants as drivers, left the camp, made slow progress, and ended the day with their wagon stuck fast in a snowdrift. The next morning they encountered a mounted party of some thirty select Mormon militia in uniforms, including William Kimball, Porter Rockwell, and Howard. These riders became the new governor's protective guard and escort.[57]

After difficult travel in a snowstorm, the party found an excellent dinner awaiting them that night, fixed by a chef President Young had sent. During the following night, the escort took Cumming and Kane past fortifications, bonfires, and troop parades in Echo Canyon. Soldiers formed two lines and presented arms as Kane and Cumming passed by. Because snow blocked the Mormon Trail over Big and Little Mountains, the party followed down the Weber River toward Ogden, then came into Salt Lake City from the north. They found the northern settlements vacated because of the "Move South" (see below). President Young arranged an elaborate reception for them at Warm Springs, very close to the Egans' home.[58] When Cumming arrived in the city, he saw roads lined with Mormon families evacuating southward.[59] He and Kane took up rooms in William Staines's residence (also known as the Devereaux House).[60]

Kane's Peace Negotiations

On April 12, Brigham Young called on Gov. Cumming at the Staines home. Kane introduced the new governor to the ex-governor. Knowing that officers at Camp Scott had warned Governor Cumming that Mormons would poison him, "it was contrived by Elder Staines that Howard Egan should eat at the same table with him and partake of the same food." That way Cumming felt assured that "death was not in the pot." Howard survived just fine.[61]

On April 21, Howard, along with William H. Kimball and government Surveyor General Jesse W. Fox, left for Rush Valley, about twenty miles southwest of Tooele, to scout out a possible military reserve for Johnston's Army.[62] Few knew that region better than Howard. Then, for a time, Howard was in charge of guards posted at Governor Cumming's temporary residence in the Staines mansion. People with grievances against

Governor Alfred Cumming,
LDS Church History Library

Church control in Utah tried to talk with Cumming, but guards turned them away unless they had obtained Brigham Young's permission.[63] Guards protected as well as isolated Cumming from Mormon society. When Cumming visited Provo in early May, his guard consisted of Howard, John Kay, Fayette Worthen, David Candland, William Kimball, and Col. Kane.[64]

Kane spent several weeks mediating between Cumming and Young, and collecting evidence that rebutted the allegations the disgruntled federal officials had filed. Cumming and Young reached agreement for an "unofficial truce."[65]

Escorting Colonel Kane Across the Plains

Gov. Cumming needed to head back to Camp Scott to consult with Col. Johnston, now advanced in rank to general, and then to formally reenter Utah with the army and take office. Kane went with him. Howard was assigned to guide them to Camp Scott safely. Then Kane, his negotiating work finished, returned to the city, apparently guarded by Howard, to wrap up his business and prepare for a long overland journey back to Philadelphia. President Young assigned Howard to accompany and guard Kane. "In May, 1858, Father was sent with a company to escort Colonel Kane to Florence [Nebraska]," son Ransom wrote. *Pioneering the West* contains a transcript of Governor Cumming's recommendation to the army commander at Fort Laramie to give the Kane-Egan party safe passage:

Executive office
Great Salt Lake City U.T. May 12, 1858
Commanding at Ft. Laramie

I beg to recommend to your favorable attention Majors Egan, Murdock, West, Knowlton, Van Eltan [Ettan], Worthing, & Mather. The company escorting my friend Col. Kane to Florence- on their way to the States and upon their return. Any assistance which you may furnish in providing forage; (or animals if they stand in need of them). will oblige

Yours truly

A. Cumming, Governor of Utah Territory [66]

Howard headed Kane's escort party, which included John R. Murdock, John Q. Knowlton, Elisha W. Van Ettan, Lafayette Shaw Worthen (a non-Mormon), and men surnamed West and Mather.[67] Governor Cumming gave Kane a similar message to the army commander at Fort Kearny in Nebraska, "recommending assistance for the company escorting Thomas L. Kane to Florence." It noted that Kane had been in Utah as a mediator during the Utah War.[68] Howard also carried a May 12 letter from Salt

Lake City businessman Nicholas Groesbeck asking John Richard at the Platte Bridge to "Please let Mr. Howard Egan, or Bearer, have animals and goods as he may require."[69]

On May 13 the Kane-Egan group left Salt Lake City. Given the speed at which they traveled to the Missouri River, it appears that Howard drove Kane in a wagon or carriage pulled by mule teams, and the other men rode on horseback. They arrived at Camp Scott on the sixteenth. There they found the still-encamped army nearly destitute of food, having ten days of short-rations in store, and learned that soldiers felt very dissatisfied. Many were deserting. General Johnston seemed in bad humor towards Governor Cumming and toward mankind generally, because of peace terms being reached. He had come to fight.[70] He was slow to accept Cumming's assurances that the war was over. The military and the civilian authorities still needed to de-fang the conflict, but Kane, no longer needed, headed out on the trail, trusting in Howard's trail savvy, driving skills, and protection. Kane felt anxious to report to Washington, D.C.

This was Howard's sixth time "crossing the plains." In 1847 he went west and east over it, in 1848 west and east, and west in 1849. Quite a pair, Howard and Kane. A genuine western frontiersman traveling long days with a refined, prominent eastern gentleman. No doubt Howard, ever the story-teller, shared stories with Kane about such experiences as his Battalion pay errand, the 1847 pioneers, getting shot at the Elkhorn, wagon train mishaps, river fordings, the gold rush, and California's prosperity. During this 1858 trip, some westbound Saints encountered the Egan-Kane company. One was Thomas Bullock near Chimney Rock on May 27, who gave them a letter to carry east.[71] Likewise, Howard gave Bullock's group a letter of instruction and counsel from President Young, and told them "many items of interest."[72] On June 6, Oscar Stoddard, in the westbound Horace S. Eldredge wagon train, noted that "Near noon met Col. Kane with an escort of Mountain boys who brought correct news from the Valley...we all nooned together."[73]

On June 8, Howard's party pulled into Florence, Nebraska Territory, the Mormon outfitting location for the few wagon trains going west that year. "In drove Col. Thomas L. Kane and suite," one emigrant wrote, "whom the brethren hailed."[74] They had reached Florence in twenty-three days, averaging forty miles per day. Florence, which sprouted as a brand new town in 1855, stood where Winter Quarters once was and where Howard and Tamson had once lived.

When he arrived, Kane was "in delicate health and somewhat worn and indisposed." Nevertheless, he gave his fellow travelers a supper "with kind expressions of gratitude for their attentions and watchfulness over him on so long and toilsome a journey."[75] Just across the Missouri River and twelve miles south stood Council Bluffs, Iowa, which originally had been Kanesville, named after Kane. Howard had last been in that formerly Mormon region in 1849.

From Florence to Philadelphia

At Florence, Kane's escort men were dismissed but told to wait there for Howard. He alone would accompany Kane the rest of the way to Philadelphia.[76] Kane's wife Elizabeth's diary indicates that Kane and Egan went to St. Louis by riverboat.[77] From there they took the "St. Louis train" to Cincinnati and then continued east. The two-week trip from Florence seemed to improve Kane's health. During the trip, he "spoke often with reporters, leaving a trail of newspaper articles" that credited Cumming for making the peace happen.[78]

A Philadelphia newspaper reported that Kane arrived at his home on June 18 "in buoyant spirits and hearty good health, after one of the most romantic, dangerous and successful expeditions on record." It didn't mention Howard, who was with him. Kane then proceeded to Washington on June 19 with dispatches from Gov. Cumming "to the Government" saying that the Mormons had received him peacefully.[79] The administration refused to trust these reports, so cabinet members quizzed Kane closely and then debated the matter for two weeks. Finally, they accepted that the hostilities were over.[80]

With Thomas and Elizabeth Kane in Philadelphia

Elizabeth Kane recorded on June 24 that Thomas returned that day to their Philadelphia home from Washington, D.C. Her diary documents that Howard was in the Philadelphia area for at least three weeks, from June 27 to July 19. He waited for a report from Washington D.C., to Kane, which Howard needed to courier back to Brigham Young.[81]

Howard impressed Elizabeth. He was then age forty-three, she twenty-two, and her husband Thomas thirty-six. On June 27 she wrote in her diary: "There were two Mormons here, one an exceedingly striking, distinguished-looking fellow, named Howard Egan, the other a vulgar-looking reporter." The reporter was T. B. H. Stenhouse.[82] It's certain that Howard had cleaned up and bought new clothes after the weeks on the trail. Indeed, on the riverboats and in Philadelphia he needed to be appropriate in appearance while traveling with the illustrious Col. Kane. On July 18, a Sunday, Elizabeth noted:

> Messrs Stenhouse and Egan, Mormons both, dined with us. Egan is an exceedingly noble looking fellow, who has been devoted to Tom. He was speaking of his detention in Phila (where he is waiting for a despatch from Tom to B. Young) and Tom said "You haven't regretted it, have you?" He answered "Well, I had my doubts for a while—when I thought something might have

happened—it did seem hard to be shut up here, losing my privileges. After a fellow's been trotting in the snow all winter, it is rather hard he shouldn't be allowed to lay a finger on them." Tom said "when the true history of the Peace came to be written, B. Young would receive due credit as the peace-maker." After listening patiently till he ended, knitting his brows & folding his hands E[gan] said–"I have a strong faith in Bro. Brigham as any one, but I can't allow Mrs K. and Mr S., who don't know the truth as I do, to believe that Gov. Cumming would ever have felt to enter the city without Johnston to back him, or been allowed to enter if he did, without another man" referring to the critical role played by Thomas Kane].

"Egan said Grace for us, as simply and Christianly as it could have been done," Elizabeth noted. She, a photographer, "attempted to take his likeness, and Mr Stenhouse formerly a practical photographer made a similar attempt. His was worse than mine I am glad to say." On July 19 she wrote: "Monday Mr. Egan came to take leave. I took a good portrait of him." Thus far, searches through her photographs and personal papers have turned up no Howard Egan likeness.[83]

Thomas Kane's health problems resumed. He was recovering from illness, again, when Howard left Philadelphia for home.[84] To return to Florence, Howard most likely traveled by train to Chicago and Iowa City, and then by stagecoach to Florence. There he rejoined his traveling companions. They then crossed the plains, the seventh time for Howard. He arrived home on August 20, only a month after he left Philadelphia. His important Church/military errand to guard Kane between May 13 to August 20 meant Howard was away from Tamson and his children for three months and a week. He brought two letters to Brigham Young, one from Utah's spokesman in Washington, D.C., John M. Bernhisel, and one from Kane, along with a Kane letter to Gov. Cumming.[85]

Elizabeth Kane, courtesy Perry Special Collections, HBL, BYU

For Kane's friendship toward Utah and Mormons, Utah Territory in 1860 named Kane County after him. A statue honoring him stands in the Utah Capitol building and the Church maintained the Kane Memorial Chapel in Pennsylvania from 1970 until donating it to the Kane Historic Preservation Society in 2014.

Egans Join the "Move South"

Back on March 21, 1858, President Young announced in the Tabernacle a "desert your homes" strategy, a retreat instead of warfare. He said that fighting would be futile and that desert regions somewhere in the Great Basin could provide safe havens for the Saints if they needed to escape the soldiers. Copying Russia's destruction and evacuation of Sevastopol in 1855 during the Crimean War (a flight that created worldwide sympathy for its refugees), in 1858 President Young ordered that everyone living north of Utah County move southward. A few men were to stay behind to burn buildings and lay waste to farms and orchards if army depredations made that necessary. Families were to take food, clothing, and personal possessions, including furniture. More than just a few Saints disliked this plan, complained loudly, and resisted it.[86] The Egans and others had labored for ten years to build their homes, gardens, fences, stock pens, and farms, which they now had to desert.

On April 25, 1858, John Pulsipher said, perhaps tongue-in-cheek, "the Saints are leaving their homes, beautiful habitations, farms & gardens, shade & fruit trees & go joyfully to the toils and hardships of camp life."[87] During April and May, the main roads southbound saw heavy traffic of people on foot, wagons, horses, cows, sheep, pigs, dogs, and other animals, as well as clouds of dust and noise. As much as possible ward members traveled together. Wards north of Utah Valley were assigned destinations in Utah, Juab, Millard, or Iron counties. When such families halted, they lived in their wagons, tents, or huts they built of logs, boards, or willow branches. By early May the traffic jam extended for one hundred miles, from Box Elder County to Provo.[88] During the first two weeks of May, an average of six hundred wagons passed daily through Salt Lake City.[89] The exodus involved perhaps thirty thousand people, twice the size of the Mormon exodus from Illinois twelve years earlier.

Pioneering the West records that the Egans, except Ransom and Howard, joined the mass evacuation. "While Father was east escorting Colonel Kane, the family moved south with the rest of the Saints," Ransom said. He stayed behind to guard the house and to set it on fire if army activity made that necessary. The family went first to Provo. "I ran along behind the wagons while moving," recalled William Egan, "and well remember the big crickets that filled the track of the wagon as it proceeded. I also remember well going down the dug way to cross the Provo River where men were catching fish in large quantities." At some point the family "returned as far as Mulliner's Mill, where the Lehi Sugar Factory now stands," Ransom said, "and lived in a dugout." While the Egans were there, William said, "the mill dam broke away three times and was repaired each time. It made a large pond of water and a good bathing place for us youngsters."[90]

The Move South had a devastating economic and family impact on Mormon communities. When settlers should have been engaged in spring planting, they were uprooted. It took Utah years to recover from the disruptions and dislocations.[91]

Peace Settlement and a Presidential Pardon

Two men, Lazarus W. Powell and Ben McCulloch, carried a pardon signed by the president. He offered "a free pardon for the seditions and treasons heretofore by them committed" to all who would obey the laws.[92] Powell and McCulloch left Washington, D.C. on April 12. Their party crossed the plains westbound while the Egan-Kane group pushed eastward. The peace commissioners reached Camp Scott on May 29, two weeks after Howard and Kane had left there. They consulted with Governor Cumming and General Johnston, then went to Salt Lake City, which, on June 7, they found deserted. They held meetings with Mormon leaders. Brigham Young was not allowed to negotiate. Powell and McCulloch controlled the discussions in unyielding fashion. They extended the President's pardon on a federally dictated take-it-or-leave-it basis.[93] On June 12 Church leaders accepted the President's terms, and the pardon. They pledged that the Mormons would not oppose the army marching through Salt Lake City and camping away from Mormon settlements. Mr. Powell announced that day that all difficulties had been settled, and invited General Johnston to bring the army into the valley. Two days later, Governor Cumming made a formal announcement of the peace settlement. The so-called "Utah War" was over.[94]

With peace in place, the Utah Expedition broke camp on June 13. A week later it slowly filed through Echo Canyon.[95] All day on June 26, long columns of soldiers marched through a virtually deserted Salt Lake City. The army encamped, temporarily, on the west side of the Jordan River while scouts searched for a location for a military base.[96] General Johnston decided to establish his camp four dozen miles southwesterly in Cedar Valley, twenty miles west of Utah Lake.[97] As such, the post, named Camp Floyd, was equidistant from Salt Lake City and Provo, somewhat convenient for the army to march to those major Mormon centers in case of trouble.

On July 2 the "Move South" ended. Saints began returning to their homes, although some chose new places to live. "After the Federal Army had passed on to Fort Crittenden [Camp Floyd] in Cedar Valley," Ransom wrote, "we returned to our home in Salt Lake City."[98] By the time Howard got back to his Nineteenth Ward home from the Kane assignment, Camp Floyd was halfway through its four-month construction period.

Camp Floyd Army Post

The presence of a large army and military base in the territory altered dramatically how the Mormon leadership dealt with matters of civic governance. Tensions became commonplace between Mormons and a growing population of "gentiles." Saints had reasons to chafe at some attitudes and practices of non-Mormon newcomers, and the influence they were gaining. To ease tensions, the Church announced a policy change in mid-summer. An edict, recognizing that "an enthusiastic Mormon is more dangerous than an apostate," cancelled all Church public meetings. In towns and villages, private prayer meetings took place, but not Sunday worship meetings. Spanish Fork held no more general worship meetings that year. The lack of church meetings hurt the members spiritually.[99] This period of cancelled meetings underscored that Mormon life in Utah would never be the same as long as the army stayed in the territory.

Camp Floyd sprang up in Cedar Valley twenty-five miles southwest of Lehi, at a site on Howard's newly developing central trail.[100] Pioneers' sawmills supplied lumber. Mormon workmen molded thousands of adobe bricks. By year's end, workmen and federal funds created a military camp of almost four hundred adobe huts, each housing six or eight soldiers, and extensive warehouses, headquarters buildings, mess halls, blacksmith shops, and stables.[101] On November 9, by which date Howard had resumed mail work for George Chorpenning (see Chapter 24), the army formally dedicated Camp Floyd with a grand review of the troops and the raising of a forty-foot United States flag atop a 100-foot flagpole. Camp Floyd's sprawl extended for five miles. Such

Camp Floyd Stagecoach Inn, Utah State Historical Society

a pool of soldiers generated markets for pioneers' fruit and vegetables, and it supported jobs for local blacksmiths and craftsmen.[102] Mail business would put Howard in frequent contact with Camp Floyd.

The negotiated peace became "an armed truce, for it left two hostile factions wrestling with each other for control of the Territory." General Johnston felt "loathing for Mormon customs and disdain for Governor Cumming."[103] But to his credit the commander provided "rigid protection of Mormon life and property." Camp Floyd soldiers published a four-page newspaper called the *Valley Tan*, which openly ridiculed Mormons.[104] In 1858 and 1859, at least 2,400 soldiers were in Utah Territory. Across a creek from the base, "camp followers developed a Gentile suburb called Frogtown, or Dobietown, where soldiers could find women, gambling, and drinking saloons." In Fairfield, six miles away, shootings and murders became common. One soldier said Fairfield included "Saints, Gentiles, Mountaineers, Greasers, Loafers, Thieves, Black Legs [swindlers], Rum sellers, Lager Beer Brewers and the Lord know what else; every house is [a] grog shop—or a Beer-shanty."[105]

For supplies, the big army base needed a direct route to California. So they sent Captain James H. Simpson, a topographical engineer, to explore a central route close to one Howard had opened (see Chapter 24). When Secretary of War John B. Floyd, for whom the camp was named, sided with the secessionists in 1860, the Army renamed the base Fort Crittenden. In subsequent months Civil War demands for Union soldiers closed it down. Soldiers headed east. The post was vacated and disassembled. But, before its demise, it served as a Pony Express station, and after that a stagecoach station and inn, which is now a registered historic building.

Historian MacKinnon's Assessment of Howard's Utah War Service

Our finest Utah War scholar, Bill MacKinnon, found that, contrary to what well-entrenched Mormon folklore portrays, the Utah War had no winners, only losers.[106] The list of losses and costs and bad conduct by both sides requires a long set of parallel columns. But, "if any individuals emerged as heroes from the Utah War," MacKinnon concluded, "my candidates are Capt. Randolph B. Marcy of the Fifth U.S. Infantry and Maj. Howard Egan of the Nauvoo Legion." On the surface, MacKinnon said, "Howard Egan might seem an unlikely hero. He was, after all, the defendant in one of Utah's first murder trials in 1851 and a prominent member of Brigham Young's inner circle of rough operatives dubbed the 'b'hoys.'"

But in Howard's case, still waters ran deep, and he served the Mormon side of the war in important, hazardous assignments ranging from acquiring gunpowder in California to escorting Thomas L. Kane first to Fort Bridger and then to Philadelphia.

That Egan did so dependably and without the flamboyance of homicidal peers like Porter Rockwell and Bill Hickman may have been what prompted Brigham Young to select him repeatedly for such independent assignments. During the Utah War, no Nauvoo Legion officer traveled as extensively and alone across unfriendly territory as did Egan . . . Egan's postwar role in operating the Pony Express west of Salt Lake City is well known; historians need to understand as thoroughly his remarkable exploits during 1856–1857.[107] ◆

~ 23 ~

Howard and the Chorpenning Western Mail

California, lacking decent cross-country mail service after it gained statehood in 1850, began to demand improved mail services. That posed prickly problems for the United States Postal Department. Missouri River states, from whence wagon and pack trains and private merchants began their treks west, pushed for mail routes across the well-established Oregon-California Trail. But opponents always played the trump card: snow. Rocky Mountain and Sierra snows made any regular mail service on the Oregon-California trail route unpredictable every winter. Southern politicians lobbied for a southern overland service to California while steamship owners fought hard for the California mail to go by ocean vessels, utilizing short land crossings in Panama or Nicaragua.

Congressional sword-fights broke out about the California mail problem. Every time Congress tried to pass post office appropriations, vociferous sectional and business interests competed for their pet projects and favorite routes.[1] Lucrative government mail contracts were at stake. One enterpriser, George Chorpenning Jr., pursued those contracts with some success, and he enlisted Howard's expertise and services for a non-southern, overland mail system.

A Bird with Poorly Flapping Wings

A postal service of sorts developed for isolated Utah Territory. It was like a bird flapping two wings, which did not flap equally well. The bird's body was Salt Lake City. One wing was mail to and from the east, the other wing was mail to and from the Pacific Coast. For the city's first decade, "pitiful" best described its mail service on both wings. In 1850 the postal department granted a mail contract to Samuel Woodson of Independence, Missouri, allowing him thirty days to deliver mail each way between Independence and Salt Lake City. This put an "east wing" in place. He established no mail stations along the way, and during the early 1850s this mail was irregular and unreliable. Woodson's mail zone extended only to the intermountain region, not to California, and his service "at all seasons was poor at best, but it was practically suspended during the winter."[2]

George Chorpenning and the "West Wing" Mail

George Chorpenning

The "west wing" mail operated separately from the east operations. In April 1851, George Chorpenning Jr., and Absalom Woodward, through Woodward & Company, won a contract to deliver monthly mail between Salt Lake City and Sacramento.[3] Their pack mule teams, called the "jackass mail," left the first of each month from both cities and delivered at each end within thirty days. Their teams traveled the Salt Lake Cutoff around the north end of the Great Salt Lake, joined the California Trail in Idaho, and followed that standard trail to the Sierras and on to Sacramento.

An Egan family source says that when Howard returned from his lengthy Salt Lake Trading Company efforts in the gold fields in 1851, he accompanied a Woodward & Company's Utah-bound mail party.[4] Chorpenning-Woodward faced two primary start-up challenges: snows in the Goose Creek Mountains on today's Utah-Nevada border and in the Sierras, and the Indian "menaces" north of the Great Salt Lake. One Indian attack killed partner Woodward. Struggling to keep the company profitable, Chorpenning decided his mail pack trains needed to also convey freight and passengers.[5] After interruptions and irregularities cost him his contract, he went east and lobbied personally with the Postmaster General. He received back the contract. Howard, busy driving cattle to California, using the same route, crossed paths with the Chorpenning mule trains.

By the time Chorpenning's first contract ended in 1854, he had given up on the troublesome northern route and shifted his pack train operations south, to travel the southern Mormon Trail between Los Angeles and Salt Lake City.[6] Meanwhile, ocean steamers carried most of the California mail.

After Chorpenning's contract renewed, his firm's mail deliveries became more regular than before. For a time the rival Adams Express Company operated, and when it went defunct in 1855 the Pacific Express Company succeeded it. Livingston & Kinkead, the firm for whom Howard drove cattle to California, was the Pacific Express

Company agent in Salt Lake City. That explains why Howard, during his famous "ten day trip" to Sacramento in 1855 (see Chapter 20), carried Pacific Express Company packages. On November 12, 1855, John Y. Greene arrived from Sacramento, bringing express matter to the Salt Lake City office of Pacific Express, located in the Livingston & Kinkead store. Every month that express, not the U.S. mail, brought a package or two to the *Deseret News* offices containing copies of newspapers from around the world.[7]

From newspapers they received, the *News* selected items they wanted to republish. One that was printed in its November 14, 1855 edition involved Howard's famous ride, without mentioning his name. The "News from Sacramento" notice said the Pacific Express Company's "messenger" left Salt Lake on September 20 and arrived in Sacramento on October 1. The story focused on the fact that the U.S. mail had left Salt Lake City on September 1 and did not arrive in San Francisco until October 11. Therefore, it took thirty-one days longer than the private express. The article spoke decidedly "against Uncle Sam's old fogy postal facilities and for the express companies. And the difference is by no means altogether in time, for the expressed letters and packages are with certainty as well as dispatch, which cannot be said of mail matter." The postal department, the write-up concluded, needed to take steps to "remove those glaring and gross deficiencies," for, if not, "the Expresses will take the lead in that business."

Family News from Canada

It's likely that Howard received news from his relatives in Canada that his brother Richard Egan, age thirty-eight, died on October 5, 1858. That left Howard the only male still alive of his parents' four sons. Two of his sisters also were dead. By age forty-three he had lost seven of his nine siblings to death. His sister Catherine Egan Ransom, fifty, was then still living, and perhaps Margaret was, too.

Rivalries on the "East Wing"

For the overland mail on the "east wing" of the central route, William F. McGraw won the contract in 1854 for two years to carry monthly mail, using four-horse coaches. Then, in 1856, the Church submitted a low bid through Hiram Kimball and replaced McGraw as the contractor. The Church wanted to build up a great express line from the Missouri River to the Pacific coast, covering both "wings." By early spring 1857, the Church sent companies of men to form settlements along the "east wing" stagecoach line, and provide relays of horses and mules. But, by midsummer, when U.S. President James Buchanan ordered army units to Utah to suppress the purported

Mormon rebellion, the government cancelled Kimball's mail contract. As a result the "east wing" saw no government mail service that fall and winter. In 1858, when deliveries were resumed, S. B. Miles became the new "east wing" contractor. He was to carry the mail on pack mules in winter and use coaches in summer.[8]

Butterfield Overland Mail Competition on a Southern Route

In 1857 a new competitor for the overland mail contracts emerged. That March, Congress authorized the Postmaster General to contract for six years for all letter mail to be conveyed overland from a point on the Mississippi River to San Francisco,

utilizing four-horse coaches or spring wagons suitable for passengers. Each trip should take twenty-five days. Among nine bids submitted, Postmaster Aaron Brown, a Tennessean, selected a proposal from John Butterfield and associates to create a new southern route. It ran from St. Louis down to Memphis, across to Little Rock, through Texas and above El Paso, across New Mexico and Arizona to Ft. Yuma, Arizona, to Los Angeles, then up the central valley to Pacheco Pass and on to San Francisco. This snow-free semi-circular "ox-bow" route totaled some 2,800 miles. Thus was born the Butterfield Overland Mail, which operated with 139 relay stations, 1,800 head of stock, and 250 Concord stagecoaches.[9] The Butterfield line gained such favor that by 1860 it carried more letter mail between the Mississippi and California than did the ocean steamers.[10]

Chorpenning Shifts to the Egan Route

Places along the central route still needed mail service. While contractors on the "east wing," the Missouri-to-Utah half of the central overland mail route, came and went (there were six between 1850 and 1861), "the service west from Utah was held by one man, Major George Chorpenning."[11] Interest in his west wing perked up beginning in 1858, after half of the nation's regular army stationed itself in Utah Territory. When Chorpenning's contract expired in 1858, he signed a new and lucrative $130,000 agreement to carry mail weekly in twenty days between Placerville and Salt Lake City, for the period from July 1, 1858 to June 30, 1862. He chose to transport the mail using the standard but risky old route via the Salt Lake Cutoff and the California Trail. This mail service started out semi-weekly, using twenty days each way, but later became weekly. Contract in hand, Chorpenning assembled men and equipment. "Gone were the days when Chorpenning himself led a few pack mules over the line."[12] He ordered twenty new Concord stagecoaches. He appointed his brother Frank Chorpenning to be the company's general agent in California. Jared Crandall became Chorpenning's overall supervisor of the mail operations. By July 1858 the firm had set up primitive mail camps along the Humboldt route, interspersed among existing summer trading posts. Stations were twenty-five miles apart.[13]

With bare-bone, haphazard arrangements, Chorpenning's men transported the first mail without incident. On July 19, 1858, the first weekly mail from Utah reached Placerville in fourteen days. Once the mail traffic became routine, the "west wing" stagecoach line was grouped into two divisions. Jared Crandall managed the operations west of Gravelly Ford, midway up the Humboldt, and Jefferson Hunt moved up from the southern Mormon Trail operations to oversee the eastern segment between Gravelly Ford and Salt Lake City.[14] However, Indians started making the Salt Lake Cutoff too dangerous. Chorpenning's coaches needed a less hazardous route. Besides, Indian troubles or not, he wanted a shorter route. Several more direct ways to cross the Great Basin had been explored, including the 1855 Egan Trail, but the question yet to answer was, could any of those desert trails be suitable for "wheeled traffic" like stagecoaches and wagons?

The Egan Trail, the route Howard had located in 1855, ran from Salt Lake City southwesterly, skirting the southern edge of the Great Salt Lake Desert, then headed westerly to today's Utah-Nevada border. From there it passed through a "rib-cage" of mountain ranges that most earlier explorers had avoided, but where Howard had located passes and water springs. These lined up enough to make an almost direct pathway across western Utah and in today's eastern Nevada parallel to and just north of today's U.S. Highway 50. Then, at Ruby Valley, directly south of today's Elko, Howard's route angled northwest to the Humboldt River near Gravelly Ford, west of today's Carlin, Nevada, and joined the regular California Trail. This south-of-Great Salt Lake course shaved about 280 miles off the normal route, and cut travel time from thirty-nine days to thirty. After 1855, for the next three or four years, this new Egan route served some emigrants, riders on horseback, mule pack trains, and cattle drives. But the wagon test awaited.

Needing a stagecoach route, Chorpenning left Salt Lake City on October 30, 1858, to turn the Egan Trail into a wagon trail, no doubt with Howard's help. On November 21 Chorpenning dispatched fifty wagons and three hundred animals southwest from Salt Lake City and headed them to Ruby Valley and on to the Humboldt.[15] By December his mail started using that route. Never again would mail move over the "north around the Great Salt Lake" road.

To promote his business and the shorter route, Chorpenning concocted for the nation a historic delivery race in December 1858.[16] To prove the year-round superiority of a central route, Chorpenning challenged both the Butterfield line and a new steamship line to a competition. At issue was who could deliver a copy of President James Buchanan's December 1858 annual message to Congress the fastest. Copies of the message were to be handed simultaneously to the three firms' representatives in St. Louis. For the central route, Chorpenning for the west wing and John M. Hockaday for the east wing spent eight thousand dollars setting up a pony relay system. Chorpenning engaged Jared Crandall to stock and superintend the west part of the western wing with Howard responsible for the three-hundred mile segment from Ruby Valley to Salt Lake City.[17]

Chorpenning's competitors sabotaged him. On race day, December 6, in St. Louis, a courier delivered two packets containing the President's message, but not a third one for the central route team. Not until December 14, eight days later, did the central route team see the Buchanan message thanks to a St. Louis newspaper publishing it. Finally, behind schedule, the couriers raced off. Weather hammered the riders along the trail to Salt Lake City. Then, Lot Huntington, the rider out of Salt Lake City, ran into deeply drifted snow. In San Francisco, meanwhile, Butterfield's firm delivered the message on December 16, and the steamship firm did the same on December 18. Chorpenning's rider didn't arrive until New Year's Day. Therefore, the central route lost because skulduggery had denied them the message for eight days. Impressive, nonetheless, they had made the delivery in seventeen travel days and twelve hours, which was two days faster than the Butterfield Mail and four days faster than the steamship company. "Their riders had proved the unquestionable superiority of the Central Route over any other."[18] The contest also demonstrated the viability of a fast pony express system on the central route. Pony Express operations would start there within two years.[19]

The Postmaster General's annual report for 1858 said the route from St. Joseph to Salt Lake City and from Salt Lake City to Placerville (not yet using the Egan route) had been so improved that trips "are performed once a week in thirty-eight days each way. For some months past this service has been performed with remarkable regularity." That service received "warmest applause" and enthusiastic public demonstrations from California citizens.[20] This central route now proved to be competitive with the Butterfield stagecoach mail.[21]

But then came the 1858–1859 winter. Could the "east wing" and "west wing" contractors make good? As weeks went by, mail suffered some delays in the Sierras but was "rather regular." A correspondent in Salt Lake City wrote in February 1859 that "Major Chorpenning is always ahead of time." When his teams were unable to get coaches through, his men put mail on the backs of horses. Chorpenning utilized snow plows, sleighs, and sometimes ski couriers to carry the mail across the mountains during the winter of 1858–1859.[22] John Albert "Snowshoe" Thompson did heroic work. Chorpenning hired Thompson to keep mail crossing the Genoa-to-Placerville passes. Locals called Thompson's ten-foot skis "snow shoes." Using a single, sturdy pole generally held in both hands at once, his version of cross-country skiing helped deliver the mail.[23]

Indian Doctor Cures Howard's Snow Blindness

While Howard was out on the mail line one hot spring-like day before the snow had melted, the snow's brightness burned his eyes so badly he was completely blind. He couldn't stand the least bit of light. He bandaged his eyes with tea leaves but they did not seem to get any better. After a couple of days of misery, two Indians came to the station. "Egan sick?" one asked. Station men said Howard had snow blindness. "Me see Egan," the Indian said. He came up close to Howard. "Eyes big sick," Howard said, "you fix them?" The Indian jumped and caught Howard's head in both hands, pushed the bandages off, placed his mouth over one eye, "and set to sucking with all his strength." Howard thought his eye would be sucked out, if not his brains, too. Before Howard could push him off, the Indian stepped back a little and spit up a tablespoon or more of blood.

After a little rest he said, "Fix more?" Howard agreed. He gave the other eye the same treatment, with the same result. After about an hour the Indian asked "a little more fix eye?" He gave Howard another treatment and then said, "Big Chief see all right two days." That proved true. In two days there was no pain. Howard joined the pack train and went to Salt Lake, his eyes perfectly cured of snow blindness. He said he'd sooner stand the Indian treatment than suffer any length of time without it.[24]

Creating a Stagecoach Route on the Egan Trail

At the end of 1858, United States Attorney General Jeremiah S. Black informed George Chorpenning that Dr. Jacob Forney, Utah's superintendent of Indian affairs, needed to be replaced and would be if the department could find a man in Utah who could do the job better. Chorpenning wrote to Mr. Black "and recommended Howard Egan as a suitable person for the office of superintendent."[25] Forney, however, kept his job until 1860.

Because Congress in 1858 failed to pass an appropriations bill, the government withheld Chorpenning's quarterly payments, which he counted on. Instead, the

Postmaster General issued obligation notes. Unable to pay creditors with such notes, Chorpenning faced bankruptcy. In financial straits and fearful of rumored competition, in January 1859, right after hiring Howard as a manager, he went to Washington, D.C. while his "creditors and unpaid staff clamored for payment of bills due since summer." A payment did reach his brother Frank in California in late January 1859.[26] Other firms, including Ben Holladay and Russell, Majors, and Waddell, waited like vultures to see if Chorpenning's company would collapse.[27]

Despite the payments shortage, Chorpenning ordered his men to reroute the mail line. He wanted the weekly mail coaches to travel the Egan route to the Ruby Valley. The firm spent the 1858–1859 holiday season transferring stock and equipment there from the upper Humboldt stations. Now, Egan's crude trail needed to be a stagecoach road. Early in 1859, starting in harsh winter conditions, Howard worked to get that route ready. He searched for and selected station locations, set up stations and corrals, staffed them, and supplied them with necessities and extra horses.

Henry J. Faust, Utah State Historical Society

One of his best employees was Henry J. "Doc" Faust. Faust had been driving Chorpenning mail coaches on the regular Salt Lake City-to-Carson route, but in November 1858 he was told to move his stock and station material to the new route. Years later, Faust recalled that in 1859 he, Howard, and Lot Huntington discovered Pleasant Valley (southwest of Fish Springs in Juab County, next to today's Nevada border) while exploring the country for a mail route to California. "We had been out in a storm for about a week in February, cold, snowing, and unpleasant." On the divide on a mountain, "Mr. Egan turned to me and said, Henry, what will you call this place? I said 'Pleasant Valley.' We went down to the valley and found a beautiful spring, fine grass and a good camping place."[28]

The three explorers needed to find more locations. They spotted and tracked down an Indian. Huntington was a good interpreter. They gave the Indian something to eat. "He proved a valuable guide." In going through the passes west of Pleasant Valley, the Indian would say "the Whoa Haw could go through, but the [expletive] could not." He had heard the emigrants say "Whoa, Haw, [expletive]," and "came to the conclusion that the Whoa, Haw, was the team and the [expletive] was the wagon." They named him "Egan Jack." Along the track they were staking out, they had Egan Jack gather Indians together, and the trio of Mormons made treaties with them. "The treaties lasted long enough for us to establish stations, but the Indians soon after broke out."[29]

A Cutoff Avoiding the Forty Mile Desert

Howard, ever the explorer, tried to find a more direct route westerly from Ruby Valley, one that could avoid veering up to the Humboldt route. "It is not known whether Chorpenning had ordered the change prior to his trip east, or whether it was Egan's own decision. The western division also took part in the search in early February."[30] Finally on March 9, 1859, the *Sacramento Union* reported that Howard had found a cutoff that bypassed the "much dreaded" Forty Mile Desert. He put men to work grading the new route via the Reese River and Sand Springs Pass to Carson Valley, so the *Union* predicted that by "next summer passengers will find this as comfortable and pleasant a road to travel as almost any other land route of the same distance not navigated by railroads."[31] In March 1859, Frank Chorpenning dispatched crews east from Carson Lake to Howard's new route, building stations and improving mountain passes.

Distracting an Annoying Indian

While Howard was trying to put a line of mail coaches across the desert to California, Ransom drove for him a little spring wagon or ambulance. The route at that time ran through Pleasant Valley. About ten miles west of there, an Indian began trotting along beside the front wheel. He kept dodging sagebrush to keep up. Annoyed, and fearing for the Indian's safety, Howard had Ransom dump some loose gunpowder from his powder flask into his hand. The Indian, knowing it was for him, grinned. In pouring the powder, Howard let it fall and scatter in the dust and sage leaves. "The Indian dropped like he had been shot, to his knees, and as far as we could see him, was working to pick up the powder."

Arriving at a camp eight miles farther on, they had their grub ready to eat when the Indian walked up to their fire. Ransom asked the Indian how much powder he saved. "The Indian showed us that he had tied it up in one corner of his shirt tail, which was all the clothing he had on." Howard asked to see it and the Indian showed it. "To our surprise we could not detect a particle of dirt. It was as clean as that in my flask." What he'd done was take off his shirt, scoop the powder onto it, then blow away dust and pick out gravel and dirt. "Well, he earned his supper, and got it."[32]

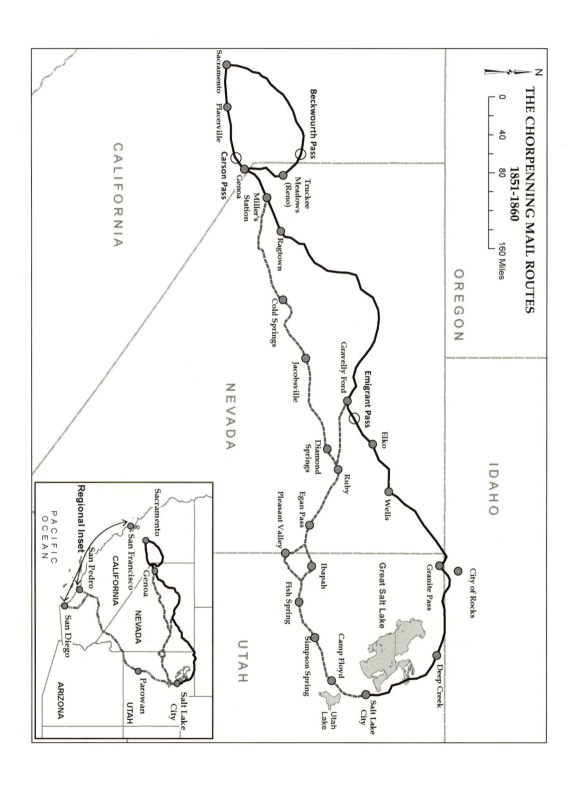

Capt. Simpson's Refinements of Egan's Route

Because of the Utah War (see Chapter 22), the United States Army in 1858 established Camp Floyd southwest of Salt Lake City in Cedar Valley. Its hundreds of troops needed supplies from California. To the camp's commander, General Albert Sidney Johnston, the Egan Trail seemed like a possible route for such transportings. So, late that year, he had Captain James H. Simpson of the Army Corps of Topographical Engineers lead an expedition to survey the Egan Trail for use as a military road.[33] Capt. Simpson explored about eighty miles of the existing trail to Dugway Mountain, then returned.

Captain James Simpson, Library of Congress Prints and Photographs Division

The next spring, while Howard and Chorpenning's men were busy transforming the trail into a wagon road and setting up stagecoach stations and relay stations, Captain Simpson started again. He led a military expedition of sixty-four men and fourteen wagons back to Dugway Mountain and then beyond. He basically followed the Egan Trail to Ruby Valley. Useful for our account, Simpson's official journal made note of Chorpenning's stagecoach stations, road builders, and mule teams carrying the mail.

On May 3 the Simpson expedition reached and camped by Meadow Creek, now Faust Creek. There they saw the Chorpenning company's makeshift mail station, "at present consisting of a Sibley tent, and a cedar-picket corral for stock is being made." Of conical design, the tent stood about twelve feet, was eighteen feet in diameter, and could house a dozen men. At the soldiers' next camp, at Simpson Springs, the mail station was "a Sibley tent set upon a circular stone wall." From Simpson Springs they reached a pass through which "Chorpenning & Company, the mail-contractors, have made a road, but it is so crooked and steep as to scarcely permit our wagons to get up it." At the foot of Dugway Pass the soldiers found a couple of mail company men who were living in a tent while improving the road through the pass and digging for water. At Fish Springs on May 6 the army unit found a mail station that was but a "thatched shed." That day, Captain Simpson said his intent was "to follow Chorpenning's extension of my route to Hasting's Pass,"

U.S. Pack Mule, Utah State Historical Society

which was west of Ruby Valley in the Humboldt Mountains, some 166 miles ahead. On May 8, in the surveyors' camp and in the dark, two six-mule teams from Ruby Valley stopped, watered, and hustled eastward on to Fish Springs. The "Jack Ass Mail" drivers told Simpson's people that road work was done to Ruby Valley, and that the next westbound mail would run on stage coaches not just to Simpson Springs but all the way to Ruby Valley. From there the mail would be carried on pack mules.[34]

At Pleasant Valley, Simpson's party talked with station agent Faust. He reported that Gosiutes (spelled in Simpson's report "Go-shoot" and "Go-sha-utes") had stolen twelve head of cattle and as many mules. Faust said that twenty-five miles west and north from his station the government, under Indian agent Robert Jarvis, had opened a farm for Gosiutes at Deep Creek. He noted that Deep Creek Valley was quite large and fertile and had fine timber nearby. The next day, May 10, after leaving Pleasant Valley, the soldiers found a road hardly ready for wheeled vehicles. "The mail company have done on this portion of the route some little work, but not enough to make the road what it should be."[35]

On May 12 the expedition reached the Steptoe Valley on a "good wagon road." They met up with Lot Huntington, who said he was in charge of the mail company's operations from Pleasant Valley to the Humboldt River. At a primitive mail station on the valley's east side, with only a shed and a tent, Simpson learned that "the mail company's road-party, consisting of eight men, have worked the road no farther than this camp. From this point onward we will have to open the road ourselves."

Simpson also learned that "Mr. Egan, the principal agent of the Chorpenning & Company, tried twice to get south from Ruby Valley, toward Genoa, in Carson Valley, but was defeated by snow, and once business in Salt Lake City diverted him." This report contradicts the February news reports, noted above, that Howard had found just such a route. That was where Simpson planned to do important exploring and to try to get his wagons through to Genoa. "The mail from Camp Floyd passed this afternoon, on mule-back, to California," Simpson recorded, "and the carrier reported two stages at Pleasant Valley Station, just through from Salt Lake City."[36] Chorpenning's mail stagecoaches were now using the new route.

On May 14 the Simpson expedition reached Egan Canyon, "down which a fine, rapid stream runs, and on which we encamp." Simpson had heard that the canyon required considerable work to enable wagons to pass through, but found instead that very little needed to be done. That day one of the mail men from Steptoe Valley "joined us at my request and by direction of Mr. Egan." Egan Canyon passed through a mountain range that, Simpson learned, "is the boundary between the Go-shoot and Sho-sho-nee tribes of Indians; the latter ranging to the west of the line." He found the road across Butte Valley "generally good."[37]

Egan Canyon, author's photo

At that point in his official diary, Simpson took time to record what he'd learned about the mail company operations:

The mail company has three traveling agents between Salt Lake City and the Humboldt River–Howard Egan, superintending agent; Ball [Bolivar] Roberts, district agent between Salt Lake City and Pleasant Valley; and Lott Huntingdon, the agent for the district between Pleasant Valley and the Humboldt. Then they have an agent called station agent, and from three to seven persons at each station, one being the mail-carrier. The number of mules varies at these stations from 8 to 15. The mail during this winter was carried on pack-mule, which was sometimes led and sometimes driven. The required rate of travel (which was accomplished) was 60 miles in every twenty-four hours, changing every 20 to 30 miles. The superintending agent [meaning Howard Egan] is said to get from $200 to $250 per month, the district agent $100, the station agent from $50 to $75, and the hands from $25 to $50, according to worth.[38]

Simpson's men camped on the east slope of Ruby Valley on May 17, where, one of the mail party said, as many as fifteen hundred Shoshoni had stayed the previous winter. "One of the mail company informs me that along the route from this station to the Humboldt they had last winter to subsist themselves on mule and coyote (wolf) meat," Simpson said.[39] The Ruby Valley mail station was a "mere shed," but "Pine-log houses are at present being put up."[40]

At Ruby Valley, Simpson reached the point where his men needed to explore to find a cutoff that eliminated trips northward to the Humboldt. His men turned southwest into lightly explored territory, where Howard already had found a route. "On May 18 the men moved through Hastings Pass in the Humboldt Range and then headed southwest "over an unknown country, toward the most northern end of the Walker's River." They were "guided by the country entirely as it unfolds itself," their heavy wagons breaking a trail passable for anyone to follow. On May 19 they moved up a steep pass where they did some hill cutting. Simpson felt that a road of good grade could be made up that pass, and, when he returned from this expedition, he learned that the mail company made a road there. While blazing the needed cutoff, Simpson met Shoshoni chief Cho-kup, a "respectful, intelligent, well behaved Indian," who "seems to have gained the approbation of the California Mail Company."[41] Howard had a good relationship with Cho-kup.

Simpson pushed his expedition on to California. Then, during its return trip to Camp Floyd, they scouted for better route possibilities. In total, Capt. Simpson mapped and reported both an "outbound" route and a "return" route. His "outbound" travels to Genoa, which included much of the Egan Trail, became known by many as the "Simpson Trail." In 1859 and 1860 the Army improved the trail and some springs along it for use by wagons and stagecoaches. It then served as the Central Overland Trail.[42] However, at the end of the Egan Trail in Ruby Valley, travelers and trail hands the next year favored Howard's cutoff to Carson City over Simpson's. "The *employees* of the route prefer Egan's line," stagecoach traveler Richard Burton learned, "declaring that on Simpson's there is little grass, that the springs are mere fiumaras of melted snow, and that the wells are waterless."[43]

The Egan-Simpson Road

Money triggered the personal disputes that broke out between the two divisions of Chorpenning's "west wing." The west segment under Jared Crandall grew uneasy about irregular paydays and competitors' threats. But the east segment, which Mormon station keepers and riders manned, "functioned effectively under Howard Egan." The "authority of the church" kept Egan's line "loyal and operational."[44] Permanent structures replaced shanties. Each station located near arable land received plows and farm implements to cultivate for food and forage. In the spring, Chorpenning's agents arranged for improvements: more stock, more coaches, more stations, and road upgrades. When this was done, "considerable passenger traffic was now carried by this line." However, "shortages of capital and lack of credit delayed Chorpenning from using the new bypass from Ruby Valley to Carson until November 1859."[45]

Faust said that after the stagecoach road was established, he was sent to Pleasant Valley to build a station. He and two others did the work and guarded the stock. Mail came once a week each way. They built a log house, chinked it, and used wagon floorboards for a door. Simpson Springs was one hundred miles away. Faust's Pleasant Valley station was one of three sleeping stations on the route to California. Passengers from Salt Lake City slept here on their second day out. When spring arrived, Faust added on a room for his wife, using a wagon cover for a floor covering and a washed out flour sack to cover the window cut out of one log. The Fausts entertained "many notable passengers," including newspaper editor Horace Greeley (see Chapter 26). "The drivers would make good time from Salt Lake to here so as to have a long rest." At some point he sent his men north to Deep Creek "to build another station, as we wanted to move the line further north."[46]

While hostile Gosiute Indians were threatening to kill Faust, his wife, and an ill man left behind by the stagecoach, a group of Shoshone Indians rode in from Ruby Valley. Their chief, Cho-kup, told the Gosiutes that if they harmed even a hair of the head of the three whites, he would come and kill every last one of their tribe. "I will kill you for I made a treaty with the mail company and will protect them."[47] Given Howard's relationship with Cho-kup, it's most likely he had negotiated that treaty.

On June 17, 1859, Utah Territory's Indian agent Jacob Forney wrote a note to "Howard Egan, Esq., General Mail Agent." He asked Howard to "inform me, as soon as convenient, of Indian depredations committed on the United States mail property under your charge," information Howard had shared with him verbally earlier that day.[48] Howard had perhaps one of the best sets of eyes and ears for that mid-Great Basin section.

Howard's Road Improvements

Early in July 1859, while Howard was the superintendent for the Chorpenning mail between Salt Lake City and Gravelly Ford, he helped guide an enormous cattle herd over his Egan Trail. In a letter written at the Humboldt River on July 22, a correspondent with the initial "H" sent this report to the *Deseret News*:

> One of the finest herds of cattle that has ever passed through this country has just arrived here by the Salt Lake and California mail route. The drove numbered over one thousand head, besides some mules. It belonged to Mr. B. Holladay, of your city, in charge of Capt. D. M. Yates. Howard Egan, superintendent of the mail line from here to the city, has piloted them through. They arrived at Gravelly Ford in the remarkably short time of seventeen days from Camp Floyd, including two days they laid by to rest, without losing a single head. The cattle appear and feel remarkably well, presenting a marked contrast to most of the stock that has come the northern route. This has demonstrated the practicability of the mail route, as a road for large cattle droves as well as for emigrants generally. Mr. Egan returns with this mail, to pilot out some mules for the same party.

The correspondent added that "there is a very strong probability that the mail route will soon avoid the Humboldt altogether." He reported, too, that Mr. George F. Jones, agent for the western division of the California and Salt Lake Mail Line, as Chorpenning's system now was called, had learned that their service would not be reduced to bi-weekly but would continue weekly. He praised Major Chorpenning's "energetic perseverance" and concluded with a toast: "Prosperity to the mail route; and may the railroad soon follow."[49] Howard returned to Salt Lake City, then headed back out.

On September 18, 1859, Howard returned "from another of his exploring trips, this one to seek a way to avoid a portion of the Salt Desert." Ever since the previous November he had been "almost constantly exploring" in order to make the Central Route better. On this trip he had found a more direct route for the Egan Trail between Fish Springs and Shell Creek that avoided Pleasant Valley by passing farther to the north through Deep Creek. "By this means, the second half of the Great Desert is greatly reduced, or almost avoided, leaving only one long stretch–from Simpson to Fish Springs–on this end of the route." He announced that "this is the last change he designs making between Camp Floyd and Ruby Valley, and he considers the road will be as straight and perfect as it can be made to that point."[50] He rerouted the Chorpenning traffic to Deep Creek in September 1859.[51]

Gosiutes, Deep Creek, and the Indian Farm

The Gosiutes (today usually spelled Goshutes), a Shoshonean people, ranged as far west as Ruby Valley. But they concentrated in the Deep Creek Valley (which they called Ibapah), the Simpson Springs area, and Skull and Tooele valleys.[52] The word *Gosiute* derives from a word meaning "desert people." On May 9, 1859, Captain Simpson wrote an unflattering description of the first "Go-shoot Indians" he and his exploring party encountered:

> They are the most wretched-looking creatures I have ever seen…Both men and women wear a cape made of strips of rabbit-skins, twisted and dried, and then tied together with strings, and drawn around the neck by a cord. This cape extends to just below the hip, and is but a scant protection to the body. They seldom wear leggings or moccasins, and the women appear not to be conscious of any impropriety in exposing their persons down to the waist. Children at the breast are perfectly naked, and this at a time when overcoats were required by us. The men wear their hair cut square in front, just above the eyes, and it is allowed to extend in streamers at the temples. The women let their hair grow at random. They live on rats, lizards, snakes, insects, grass-seed, and roots, and their largest game is the rabbit…They use generally the bow and arrow, there being only one gun to about 25 men.[53]

Early in 1859 Jacob Forney, the Superintendent of Indian Affairs for Utah Territory, became interested in establishing permanent farms among the Gosiutes. He instructed Indian agent Robert Jarvis to proceed to Deep Creek and Ruby Valley and open farms at those places. On March 25 Jarvis met with about one hundred Gosiutes from several bands and convinced them to try farming and stop raiding and stealing from whites. He tried to induce the "miserably starving fragments of the Gosha-Utes" to try farming at Deep Creek. The Indians left for Deep Creek on April 3. Wilford Hudson and other Mormons from Grantsville started a settlement, and Harrison Severe acted as the government agent for the Indian farm, "the place being a government reservation."

Jacob Forney, Utah State Historical Society

Later, a hostile group arrived at Jarvis's camp, but with Howard and George Chorpenning's help, Jarvis convinced them to join those who had agreed to farm. A third group also joined who were as anxious to obtain farm implements as to be instructed. In September 1859, agent Forney wrote that the Gosiute band was broken and subdivided into small groups, but that some sixty had a "quiet and well-disposed chief to control them" and were at that time "permanently located on the Deep Creek Indian farm." Most of the Indians, however, found it hard to adapt to such a radically new way of life.⁵⁴

In September 1859, because Howard had just brought in "a bunch of wheat" from Ibapah, a friend praised what Mr. Severe, the supervisor there, had accomplished in a short time. Ibapah had gardens and two hundred acres of wheat, and thousands of adobe bricks being used to build houses for the few men and families there with Mr. Severe. The friend, in his report to *Deseret News* readers, pointed out that not long ago the regions west of Great Salt Lake were barren, uncultivated desert inhabited only by Indians, but now there were gardens and farms scattered in that region, "little oases in the desert." Those improvements, he said, were due primarily "to the mail route and its gentlemanly and energetic managers, and the names Chorpenning, Schell, and Egan will be had in remembrance by the children of the pioneer settlers of these valleys."⁵⁵

> **From our Western Correspondent.**
>
> C. & S. L. M. Route, Sept. 18, 1859.
>
> Editor News:—Dear Sir—
>
> I was forcibly reminded of the prediction that the "desert shall blossom as the rose," upon seeing a bunch of wheat which Capt. Howard Egan brought with him from the settlement at Iba-pah or Deep creek.

After Howard set up the mail station at Deep Creek, he developed a ranch there to support it. Deep Creek soon became the largest station west of Camp Floyd that was within Utah's present borders.

Chorpenning's Express Company Failure

Back in February 1859, Chorpenning reached Washington, D.C., and worked out payment difficulties. Verbally, Postmaster General Aaron Brown assured Chorpenning his annual fee would increase from $130,000 to $190,000, which would cover most of the company's outstanding debt. But, bad luck for Chorpenning, Brown died in March. At that time the postal service had six lines operating on various routes and schedules. New postmaster Joseph Holt, facing big deficits, rejected his predecessor's view that the mail service existed to help develop the nation. To cut costs he cancelled some route segments and reduced mail frequency.

Chorpenning's payments were cut and his delivery times reduced from weekly to semi-monthly. Then, Congress failed to pass the usual postal appropriation, leaving contractors high and dry. When Chorpenning could not pay his obligations, his company's stock and some properties were attached. On October 6, 1859, Lewis Brady, owner of the Pioneer Stage Line, bought virtually all of the confiscated property and blocked Chorpenning men from picking up mail at the California end, even though Chorpenning's contract was still in force. Brady's underhanded efforts to deliver mail to Utah turned into a disaster:

By the time he met Egan at Ruby Valley, his wagon was in shambles. Egan offered to carry the mail the rest of the way, but Brady refused. He did, however, accept the loan of fresh stock and finally reached Salt Lake City far behind schedule. Although the Salt Lake city postmaster refused to turn over mails to him, Brady apparently made at least three deliveries of mail from Placerville to Zion.[56]

When the Placerville newspaper published "false assertions and unjust insinuations" about Howard, one of his company associates defended "our able superintendent." His defense, penned on August 5 and published in the *Deseret News*, challenged the Placerville account.[57] He charged that the paper's editor, "in slightly disguised terms," attacked Egan and called him unfit for the position while praising Major Jared Crandall, "the sub-agent on that end," to the skies. The Placerville newspaper also urged Major Chorpenning to replace Howard with Crandall. Howard's defender countered that they should leave it to the traveling public to decide which of the two divisions had the best "arrangements" but as to speed "we are prepared to make better time than any they ever have done on that end *when there exists any necessity for it.*"

He alleged that Crandall's plans to increase speed would risk ruining the coaches while wearing out and endangering the passengers. "Last winter when it was necessary to make as quick time as possible, they were nearly always behind time on that end of the route and our mail carriers had to make it up." Chorpenning's team, he said, "are prepared to institute a comparison, or to compete with that end of the route in any way, shape or manner they may please." Then he asserted: "I do not believe Major C. could find a more suitable man for superintendent than Mr. Egan."

Early in November 1859 Howard left Salt Lake City to establish some stations. A November 8 report said that "certain parties" had placed an attachment upon the property of the "western division" of the line "by virtue of which they took all the stock from that end of the road." This crippled Chorpenning's company. As soon as Howard learned of it, "with his usual energy and promptitude" he hurriedly made his own arrangements to transport the mail the whole distance from Salt Lake City to Placerville, "which he has now completed, and is prepared to carry the mail each way with the regularity and dispatch for which this line has been noted."

That report contained an historical announcement: "the mail is now carried on the new route, which avoids the Humboldt altogether." Even more historic, it added that "Mr. E. has just taken out the first coach upon it." Howard's stagecoach went as far as the last station on his half of the line, Ruby Valley, which took him only five days. From there "he has sent an agent to Placerville, who will call for the mail there regularly, and if it is not delivered to Salt Lake City as punctually as heretofore, it will be owing to the non-deliverance to Geo. Chorpenning's authorized agent, or to the malicious and unlawful interference of certain parties at that end of the route."[58]

But the Placerville postmaster continued to deal only with usurper Lewis Brady.

Brady connived to undermine the Chorpenning contract. He recruited Chorpenning's employees. He had local newspapers try to convince the public that a change in contractors was needed. Then winter conditions and Indian hostilities taught Mr. Brady a lesson, and by late December he decided that commandeering Chorpenning's service was a lost cause. He withdrew from the contest. Nevertheless, the Placerville postmaster refused to give mail to Howard's crews until the Postmaster General in March 1860 directed him to ditch his bogus contract with Brady. Thus, from March until May of 1860, Howard's teams carried the semi-monthly mail on the entire "west wing" without dispute.[59] At that point, the line operated ten stagecoaches.[60]

When news about the attachment of Chorpenning's property reached Washington, D.C., it damaged his reputation. So, in November 1859, the Postmaster General annulled Chorpenning's contract on grounds of bad management and failure to provide means to fulfill their agreement. Chorpenning later insisted payments to him had been deliberately withheld to force his company into bankruptcy. His claim lacks proof. The best study of Chorpenning's mail career observes that the failure perhaps was a "classic case of undercapitalization."[61] Years later, he presented a claim to Congress for his losses incurred carrying the mail from 1851 to 1860. The claim was allowed and he received a Treasury warrant for $443,010.60. However, payment on it was stopped. He didn't receive even one dollar due to him. He died a poor man in 1894.[62]

To Mr. Chorpenning's credit, and due to Howard's assistance and fortitude, he did establish the first scheduled mail service over what later became the preferred route for the Pony Express, transcontinental telegraph, and the Overland Mail. He instituted, and for nine years had maintained, fairly regular mail delivery between California and Salt Lake City. He introduced wheeled transportation to the western wing's central route. And "he reoriented the Utah-California route to a shorter, safer, and more dependable trace." It's unfortunate that his ambitions exceeded his resources.

Frustrations About Not Being Paid

In *Pioneering the West*, Ransom gives a brief summary of how Chorpenning's financial troubles forced Howard to come up with pay for men in his district:

> Father was George Chorpenning's agent or partner, when he had the contract to carry the mail from Salt Lake to California...As the time came that money failed to come to pay off the men or other expenses, Father was forced to dig up and use every resource to keep the Mail going, expecting every day to receive the money that he had been told by letter from the boss had been sent by a trusty agent by way of California...Chorpenning had written that he would soon have another payment from the government and for Father to keep the mails running as long as possible, but after a few months there came a change of contractors.[63]

The firm of Jones, Russell, and Company, acting for Russell, Majors, and Waddell, replaced Chorpenning's operation by seizing and using Chorpenning's stations, stock, and equipment. A geyser percolates and bubbles, then erupts. Chorpenning's "jackass mail" and then the stagecoach mail percolated and bubbled, and then suddenly erupted into historic importance when mail contracts produced the Pony Express. In April 1860, Russell's team launched the Pony Express, and from May to termination of the Pony Express in October 1861, Russell's company and the U.S. mail followed the route and utilized the stations established by the Chorpenning mail.[64]

Chorpenning's employees, including Howard, resented how Chorpenning's successors used them and their stations and equipment without paying compensation. Howard's associate, William H. Shearman, vented the men's anger in an April 16, 1861 letter, written from the "C. & S. L. M, Line" station at Ruby Valley, which the *Deseret News* published.[65] In it he said the mail station people were tired of being fed promises by Jones, Russell, and Company. "When Geo. Chorpenning failed, there was plenty of his property on this end of the line to have paid off his employees." But his successors used the stock and stations without paying anything to the owners for it. The station owners lost mule after mule while carrying the company's express and mail, but received no compensation from Russell-Jones. Shearman continued:

> Chorpenning was a badly abused man. The contract was taken from him without any just reason. But I cannot conceive by what right another company avails itself of the proceeds of the labor of his employees without paying them. We have been promised time after time that they would pay us–but it seems to me they put it off to get all they can out of us and then leave us to help ourselves…If justice were done the contract would be given to those who have made the road, carried the mail thro' snow and storm, and lived, or starved, on mule meat and dogs' to do it. But we don't ask this. All we ask is, that they should take the road stations, and property and pay us for our labor.

By the time Shearman wrote this letter, the Russell people had been operating the Pony Express for a year, thanks to the Chorpenning property and men. They recognized how essential Howard was to their venture, so they hired him to supervise the Pony Express and stagecoach mail within his usual district from Salt Lake City to Ruby Valley and a bit beyond it to Roberts Creek. That gave Howard a new and central role in a brief but exciting and now legendary Pony Express chapter in the history of the American West. ◆

~ 24 ~

A "Ramrod" for the Pony Express

The Pony Express lasted only nineteen months, from April 1860 to November 1861, but its story is legendary and its exploits exciting. Young, lean riders. Fast horses. Super-quick changes of mounts and mail pouches. "The mail must go through" determination. Heroic endurance. Daring riders racing night and day through deserts, heat, wind, and snow. Narrow escapes from Indians. Mail stations burned and remounts stolen.[1]

Among names prominently associated with making the Pony Express work, Howard's is near the very top of the list. He, Ransom, and Ras Egan are well-known Pony Express participants. All three were riders, but the sons rode the most. Howard managed a Pony Express division, its stations, riders, remounts, supplies, and safety for 323 miles in western Utah and eastern Nevada desert regions. Some of the Egans' Pony Express experiences became good campfire stories back then and, thanks to *Pioneering the West*, are still good reads.

With Howard's help, stagecoach mail had been running for a year on the Central Route when the Pony Express partnered with it and recruited his management skills. Pony Express riders and stagecoaches regularly passed each other in both directions.

A "web of fantasy" wraps around the Pony Express. By now, the facts, fiction, truth, half-truth, and hyperbole are "so thoroughly blended that, after nearly a century," one historian said, "legend has largely replaced and superseded a clear and unclouded record, if indeed such a chronicle ever existed."[2] Concentrating on the basic facts and setting the record straight is a challenge we take on here.

Why the Pony Express?

Before the Pony Express, a letter took six to eight weeks to travel coast to coast. People joked that the "East" would forget events before the "West" ever heard of them.[3] Faster communication was needed. For promotional purposes, and without a

Pony Express mail stolen by Indians in 1860, later recovered in 1862.

direct government contract, William Russell's Central Overland California and Pike's Peak Express Company (COC&PPX Co.) created the Pony Express. They knew it would lose big money but they hoped its successful deliveries would demonstrate that daily mail could travel over the Central Route all seasons long and on time. Once they proved that, they could seek a lucrative near-daily stagecoach overland mail contract. By setting up the Pony Express they voted to lose money in the short term in order to win big money in the long term.[4]

On January 27, 1860, William Russell proposed that his COC&PPX Co. establish a pony express to start from Sacramento on April 3 to take mail to St. Joseph, Missouri, in ten days. He induced reluctant partners Alexander Majors and William B. Waddell to go along with the plan. The company then pushed the venture "with vigor." The firm already had many stations in the "east wing" but the "west wing" from Salt Lake City to California needed enhancement. (This is where Chorpenning's coaches operated.) Russell took managerial charge of the east wing. For the west wing, Benjamin F. Ficklin managed in Salt Lake City and W. W. Finney in San Francisco. The new operation was named "the Central Overland Pony Express Company."[5]

While the Pony Express was being set up, Major Chorpenning still held the "west wing" mail contract, being paid $75,000 a year for semi-monthly stagecoach mail service with a sixteen-day delivery time. But on May 11, 1860, just five weeks after the Pony Express went into operation, the Postmaster General annulled Chorpenning's contract due to alleged failures (see Chapter 23).[6] That same day the post office contracted with Russell's COC&PPX Co. to operate that semi-monthly stagecoach mail service.⁷ Russell's company, by gaining Chorpenning's "west wing," now controlled the entire route, both wings. "From May 1860 to July 1861, William Russell and the COC&PPX and its Pony Express held a monopoly over federal mail service between Missouri and the Pacific."⁸ Among the COC&PPX Co. directors were Russell, Majors, and Waddell, with Russell as president. The COC&PPX Company technically organized the Pony Express, but the Russell, Majors & Waddell freighting firm financed it.⁹

Ramrod Howard: One of Five District Superintendents

The COC&PPX Co. representatives visited Chorpenning's stations west of Salt Lake City in February and March of 1860, while his contract was still valid and his coaches running. They claimed "they represented new mail contractors," and then "paid a trifle of their past-due wages, and took over lock, stock, and barrel." The company created five Pony Express divisions, each with a superintendent. They picked Howard to be one. These five key managers, along with general superintendent Ficklin and western superintendent Finney, "were the ramrods of the Pony Express. All problems on the trail fell upon their strong shoulders."¹⁰ The five superintendents took orders directly from Mr. Ficklin in Salt Lake City, and each was paid ninety dollars a month.¹¹

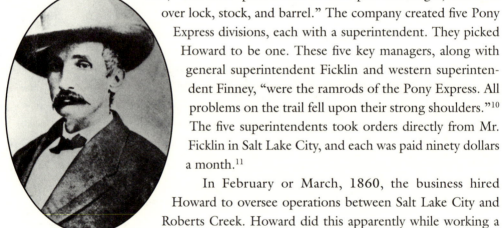

Benjamin Ficklin, VMI Archives Digital Collections

In February or March, 1860, the business hired Howard to oversee operations between Salt Lake City and Roberts Creek. Howard did this apparently while working a few final weeks for Chorpenning. For the district west of Roberts Creek to Sacramento, the Pony Express hired Bolivar (Bolly) Roberts, stationed in Carson City.¹² Howard's and Roberts's districts met at Roberts Creek, named for Bolivar Roberts. That location is twenty miles northwest of today's Eureka, Nevada. Two noted historians of the Pony Express said of Howard that "his knowledge of the West was inferior to none." Chorpenning had eight or ten stage stations in Howard's district, which the new company took over. For the pony relay to work, Howard needed to double the number of stations. Bill Roberts, a former wagon boss for the Russell, Majors and Waddell freighting firm, assisted him.³ The most difficult and dangerous section on the entire Pony Express line from St. Joseph to San Francisco was Howard's district.

The Mail Relay System

The pony relay mail needed to cover 250 miles per day. Initially the system used about four hundred horses, 119 stations (increased to between 150 and 200), and eighty experienced riders.[14] The horses trotted or jogged at about ten miles per hour, and at times they galloped at up to twenty-five miles per hour.[15] The Pony Express route basically followed the Oregon and California Trails to Fort Bridger in Wyoming and then the Mormon Trail into Salt Lake City. From there it went along the central Nevada route to Carson City before passing over the Sierras into Sacramento.

Along that 1,996 mile-long course the company created two kinds of stations: "swing," or relay stations, and "home" stations. At swing stations the rider changed his trail-weary mount for a new, fresh one. At first these relay stations were placed about twenty-five miles apart, but by fall of 1860 they were on average ten to twenty miles apart. On one ride, the rider changed horses six to eight times. Each relay station had a station keeper, perhaps a stock tender, a corral, stable, haystack, water, and at least two fresh horses.[16] The "home stations" were seventy-five to one hundred miles apart.

The Changing of Horses, *artist William Henry Jackson,*
courtesy Utah State Historical Society

That's where the rider ended his ride, handed the mail to the next rider, stayed a few days waiting for the mail coming from the other direction, then carried it back the way he had come. Mail ran both directions twice weekly. Staffing each home station were an agent plus two or three stock tenders and two riders. Home stations had better living accommodations than the primitive relay stations.[17]

To get the system started and then keep it operational, Howard selected a number of new station locations. One example is a Point Lookout station about twenty-five miles west of Camp Floyd. Howard built a station there in April of 1860. It was a small two-room log house. By September, however, Indians reduced it to ruins.[18] Howard recruited stock tenders and bought relay horses that he placed in stations along the line. He helped hire the best riders obtainable. Sons Ransom and Ras were two of them. By the spring of 1860 Ransom was twenty and Ras eighteen. One of Howard's first hires was William F. (Billy) Fisher, who rode a section between Ruby Valley and Schell Creek. Fisher later transferred to the Salt Lake City-to-Rush Valley ride.[19] Other Mormon riders in Howard's division, at one time or another, included Henry J. Faust, George Washington Perkins, Lot Huntington, and perhaps Porter Rockwell. Thomas Dobson rode for Howard between Deep Creek and Ruby Valley.[20]

Historic First Pony Express Ride

Amid fanfare in San Francisco and in St. Joseph, the first Pony Express riders galloped off in directions toward each other on April 3, 1860. In the Sierra Nevadas, pack trains of mules and horses kept the route open through snow sometimes thirty feet deep. Both the east and the west runs succeeded. The San Francisco *Bulletin* recorded, "The arrangements were so well planned and executed that the express was carried through in excellent time, as per schedule. The receptions of the ponies along the route and at the opposite ends of the line were very enthusiastic."[21]

On April 13, crowds in St. Joseph celebrated the historic first rider from the west with a parade, cannon fire, bonfires, fireworks, church bells, and "three cheers" over and over. For the westbound mail, riders used 175 ponies and reached San Francisco from St. Joseph in ten-and-a-half days.[22] In Sacramento on April 13, when the first rider arrived, a hundred people lined the road, flags flew, merchants had appropriate displays in their windows, church and fire house bells clanged, a cannon boomed forty times, and crowds roared cheer after cheer. The heralded rider rode between "a double line of almost a hundred wildly cheering horsemen." He then continued on by boat to San Francisco for another glorious reception.[23] In the midst of the California excitement, writer Bret Harte, soon to be revered for his California gold rush stories, penned a poem titled "The Pony Express." One verse conveys the rhythm of the rider and horse:

Trip lightly, trip lightly, just out of the town,
Then canter and canter, o'er upland and down,
Then trot, pony, trot, over upland and hill,
Then gallop, boy, gallop, and galloping still,
Till the ring of each horse-hoof, as forward ye press,
Is lost in the track of the Pony Express.[24]

Newspapers across the nation praised the Pony Express. In Washington, D.C., congressional cloakrooms "buzzed with talk of it."[25]

Howard Carries the First Pony Express Mail to Salt Lake City

Howard was one of the riders in that historic first Pony Express run. Being in Salt Lake City, he feared that the rider coming from the west might reach Rush Valley, seventy-five miles from Salt Lake City, faster than expected, which meant the relay rider, who would come from the east, would not be there to receive the mail and bring it to the city. So, Howard rode to Rush Valley. The eastbound mail did come early. The rider transferred the mail to Howard, and on a stormy afternoon Howard headed for Salt Lake City. Ransom described his father's fast, nighttime ride:

> The pony on this run was a very swift, fiery and fractious animal. The night was so dark that it was impossible to see the road, and there was a strong wind blowing from the north, carrying a sleet that cut the face while trying to look ahead. But as long as he could hear the pony's feet pounding the road, he sent him ahead at full speed. All went well, but when he got to Mill Creek [on Salt Lake City's southern edge], that was covered by a plank bridge, he heard the pony's feet strike the bridge and the next instant pony and rider landed in the creek, which wet Father above the knees, but the next instant, with one spring, the little brute was out and pounding the road again...And here let me say, it was a very long time before the regular riders came up to the time made on this first trip, if they ever did.

Howard reached the Salt Lake City headquarters station just before midnight on April 7, a Saturday, during the Church's general conference weekend. At that late and stormy hour, the city gave no celebration of welcome. The Pony Express rider from the east did not show up until two days later, on April 9.[26] When he came, Ras Egan took the westbound mail pouches from him and carried them to Rush Valley in four and a half hours.[27]

Howard's First Ride, *artist Bob Child*, Pony Express Adventures

Riders and Horses

Riders were a special breed. They could ride long hours in all weather across rough and sometimes unfriendly land. They were young men "selected for their nerve, light weight, and general fitness." Their average weight was 125 pounds. They committed to the Pony Express motto that "the mail must go through." Most riders were older than eighteen, but Howard ranks as the oldest Pony Express rider.[28] Being a rider "was not a fit position for a tender-foot or a coward" because "if a rider galloped into a station and found that his relief had been killed or disabled, then he must go double service."[29] Riders were armed, but depended on pony speed for safety from Indian attacks. Weapons were limited, for weight purposes, to a knife and a revolver. At first, riders carried a horn to blow to announce their approach to a station, but those became discarded as nuisances.[30]

As a rule, riders were screened for "high moral quality." Pony Express backer

Pony Express Monument, This Is The Place Heritage Park, Catherine Blake photo

Alexander Majors, a religious man, insisted that new hires sign "the Majors' oath," which was:

> I, (name), do hereby swear before the great living God that during my engagement and while I am an employee of Russell, Majors, and Waddell, I will under no circumstances use profane language, that I will not quarrel or fight with any other employee of the firm, and that in every respect, I will conduct myself honestly, be faithful to my duties, and so direct all my acts as to win the confidence of my employers, so help me God.[31]

Mr. Majors provided each rider with an 1858 Bible, on the cover of which was imprinted, in gold letters, "presented by Russell, Majors & Waddell-1858."[32] He wanted riders to read the Bible during down time when not riding. No such Bible has been found among Howard Egan's descendants.

Though the company never had more than eighty riders at any one time, nearly two hundred men are known to have ridden for the Pony Express. Perhaps twenty lasted the entire nineteen months. But the service never lacked riders. Pay was good, at least fifty dollars a month plus board and room. "To ride for the Pony was one of the greatest honors a young man could achieve. The riders had status and respect wherever they went." One primary attraction for becoming a rider was to experience "the real sense of adventure."[33] The oft published ad in Pony Express histories that says "Orphans Preferred" probably isn't authentic. No such 1860 or 1861 ads have been found. Apparently the orphan bit was created later to capture what was popularly believed.[34]

For clothing, riders typically wore a buckskin hunting shirt, cloth trousers tucked into high boots, and a jockey cap or slouch hat. In stormy weather they donned "a complete buckskin suit with the hair on the outside" to shed rain or snow.[35] Horses were the best obtainable. A large percentage was half-breed California mustangs "famous for speed, endurance, and dependability." They were fed and housed with the greatest of care, for they needed to measure up to the severest tests. Each had to cover ten, fifteen, or twenty-five miles "with scarcely a breathing-spell."[36]

Mail and Postage

The Pony Express carried two kinds of mail: letters in stamped envelopes and telegraph dispatches. Telegraph lines extended east from the California coast to Carson City, Nevada, so telegraph messages could be sent east to Carson City just before the east-bound rider arrived to pick up the telegrams. The same telegraph facilities developed at the eastern end. Normal delivery time was to be ten days for letters, and eight days for mailed telegrams. During winter months the letter time extended to between twelve and sixteen days.[37] For its day, this was considered fast communication.

Common people couldn't afford Pony Express mail prices. At first a half ounce of mail or fraction thereof cost the sender five dollars, or about $147 today.[38] Later, in August 1860, one-fourth-ounce letters were accepted at $2.50 each, and then for two dollars in April 1861. As of July 1, 1861, the half-ounce rate reduced to a dollar. In addition, each letter had to pay the government's normal ten cents postage.[39] Letters were written on the thinnest tissue paper available, but they had to be in envelopes. Before being placed in the mail pouches, letters were wrapped in oiled silk to preserve them from moisture. Large newspapers in New York and California readily patronized the Pony Express, so "the issues of their papers were printed on tissue manufactured purposely for this novel way of transmitting the news."[40] The maximum weight for any rider's mail was twenty pounds. Apparently this limit was "rarely reached."[41]

The mail was carried in four small leather bags called *cantinas*, about six-by-twelve inches in size, sewed to a square *mochila* that fit over the saddle such that one letter bag was in front and one behind each leg of the rider. Three *cantinas* contained "through mail" and were locked and not opened from start

Russell, Majors and Waddell Memorial Plaque, Salt Lake City, Utah

to finish. One *cantina* carried "way mail" to be delivered along the way. Riders, when changing mounts, transferred the *mochila* from pony to pony.

The Stations Howard Supervised

As a superintendent, Howard had responsibility for both the Pony Express and the stagecoach mail between Salt Lake City and Roberts Creek, a distance of 323 miles. Keeping each station supplied required regular freight shipments. In Salt Lake City, Chorpenning's office had previously given its employee Frederick W. Hurst a job at Ruby Valley. According to Hurst's April 8, 1860 diary entry, "I saw Mr. Egan. He told me he wanted me to start with the first team which would start on the 13th of April." This was a supply team being sent just days after Howard brought the first Pony Express mail into the city. "He also said he would give me 34 dollars per month to start on," in return for "making a garden." On April 13 Hurst started out, riding in one of several large freight wagons, each pulled by six mules. "I understood Mr. Egan that I was to ride out to Ruby, but after we started we were given to understand that the wagon was too heavily loaded, consequently we had to walk."[42]

At Camp Floyd on April 15 they loaded in bacon, sugar and "lumber for well curbs," filling the wagon "to the top of the box." There, "Mr. Egan also hired ten or a dozen of the worst black guards and black legs, loafers that could be scared up." Ten miles from Camp Floyd, Hurst's wagon broke down. On April 17 some nine hundred head of cattle passed by, "also three rough looking fellows, stating they had been hired by Mr. Egan, which statement afterward proved false." Hurst said the stations at Dugway and at Willow Springs both were "nothing but a small tent." They arrived at Deep Creek Station on the twenty-first. On April 29 they reached the Ruby Valley Station, which was a log building with six rooms and a blacksmith shop. Main station agent William H. Shearman was absent, but two other employees were there, as was a Pony Express rider.

That day Hurst "received a nice letter from Howard Egan" by Pony Express, "telling me to take charge of the station and all of the mail property belonging to the same ... and proceed with all the necessary improvements as fast as possible." Hurst learned that Indians had killed three men farther west and set fire to one station, that stations from Diamond Springs (twenty-five miles to the west) to Carson had been deserted, and that Indians had killed sixty men near Carson (see "Paiute War" below). Hurst "sat down and wrote to H. Egan explaining the particulars and sent it off by express."[43] Riders and stagecoach drivers gave Howard regular reports about situations that developed along the line.

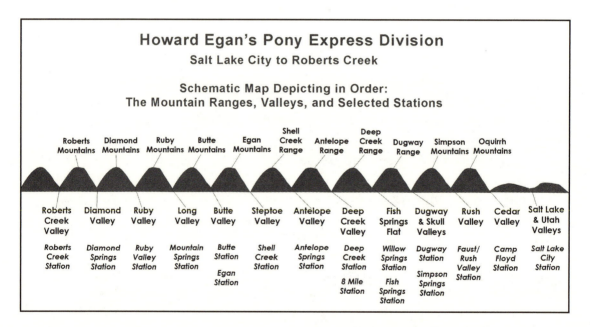

Howard and the line's other four superintendents shifted some station locations to make the relay system work at top speed. One trail expert noted that "the Pony Express enterprise was in an almost constant state of flux. Stations were often being added, some as replacements, some as new ones. Stations were destroyed and some abandoned...A temporary station might be replaced by another structure in the same area."[44] Because the route changed slightly from time to time, an etched-in-stone list of stations in place at the same time isn't possible. A list drawn up in March 1861—one week before Congress created the Territory of Nevada out of the western half of Utah and ten months after the Pony Express started—shows forty-eight stations on the entire "west wing," the first twenty-two of which, to Roberts Creek, were in Howard's district:

> Traders' Rest, Rockwell, Dug Out, Camp Floyd, Rush Valley, Point Lookout, Simpson's Springs, Dugway, Fish Springs, Willow Springs, Deep Creek, Antelope Springs, Schell Creek, Egan Canyon, Bates', Mountain Springs, Ruby Valley, Jacob's Wells, Diamond Springs, Sulphur Springs, Roberts Creek, Camp Station, Dry Creek, Simpson's Park, Reese, Dry Wells, Smith's Creek, Edwards' Creek, Cold Springs, Middle Gate, Sand Springs, Sand Hill, Carson Sink, Desert Station, Fort Churchill, Clugage's, Nevada, Carson City, Genoa, Friday's, Yank's, Strawberry, Webster's, Moss, Sportsman's Hall, Placerville, Duroc, and Folsom (by rail) to Sacramento.[45]

The most important stations in Howard's zone, and their approximate distances apart, along with the total distance from Salt Lake City, were as follows (home stations are capitalized):[46]

SALT LAKE CITY	00		Butte Station	18	254
Camp Floyd	39	39	FISH SPRINGS	23	126
Antelope Springs (Nevada)	26	199	RUBY STATION	20	274
RUSH VALLEY	20	59	Willow Springs	20	146
SCHELL CREEK	25	224	Diamonds	24	298
Simpson Springs	26	85	DEEP CREEK	27	173
Egan Canyon	12	236	ROBERTS CREEK	25	323
Dugway	18	103			

Practically the entire trail landscape was desert-like, barren, dry, and desolate, so the company placed relay and stage stations near the rare water sources and scarce patches of vegetation. On today's maps most of Howard's district's route in Nevada runs roughly parallel to and north of U. S. Highway 50, considered "the loneliest highway in America." The landscape in Howard's district resembled eleven fingers on a table: valley, mountain range, valley, mountain range, one after another. One traveler described the region as a "vast basin desert through which north and south run subsidiary ranges of mountains, averaging at least one to every fifty miles."[47] The travel route worked because Howard and others had found canyon passes through the mountain ranges or else ways over or around them. Egan Canyon, which cuts through the Egan Mountains from Steptoe Valley to Butte Valley, is a prime example.

A decade after Congress created Nevada Territory in March 1861, Nevada's eastern border became what it is today, a north-south line just west of the Deep Creek Station, or Ibapah.[48]

Top: Simpson Springs Obelisk. Above: Simpson Springs Station, author's photos.

"Paiute War" and Costly Damage to Howard's Line

Only during one period did the Pony Express mail not go through. Right after completing eight once-a-week trips in both directions, the service suspended operations because of the Paiute or Pyramid Lake Indian War in May 1860.[49] Some six thousand Paiutes in northwestern Nevada had suffered a winter of fierce blizzards. The federal Indian agency failed to provide food and clothing the Indians had been led to expect.[50] Fed up with white encroachments on their lands and resources, and angry with belligerent miners, that spring the tribes spoiled for war. Unfortunately, during the winter of 1859–1860, the War Department ordered a severe reduction in troops stationed at Camp Floyd, despite Utah Territory's chronic troubles with the Shoshone and Bannock along its northern border. On February 29, 1860, Colonel Charles Ferguson Smith replaced the reassigned General Albert Sidney Johnston in command of Camp Floyd. Smith inherited an undermanned department.[51]

As a Nauvoo Legion officer, Howard had opposed the United States army coming against Mormon settlements. Therefore, he initially disliked the unfriendly-to-Mormons Camp Floyd post. But, as a U.S. mail carrier, he represented government interests as did the army. He superintended mail that included army mail. The army, needing to patrol in the Great Basin and among desert tribes, recognized Howard's expertise and called on it. He helped Captain Simpson's explorations westward. Details are lacking, but in 1859 Howard acted as a guide to General Johnston for an extended surveying tour through the north.[52]

When reassignments drained troops from the post, the Mormon side of Howard might have felt "good riddance," but his mail and coach side didn't. When Indians attacked mail stations and carriers, Howard and the mail company called on Camp Floyd's troops for help.

In the disastrous "Battle of Pyramid Lake" on May 12, 1860, forty miles northeast of Reno, Paiutes killed most of the 105 white volunteers fighting them. Indian attacks spread across the Great Basin. Gosiutes raided mail stations, including some in Howard's district. Emboldened by each success, "howling like wolves, a band of a hundred or more would swoop down on a lonely post, killing keeper, hostler, and guards; pillaging, burning buildings and haystacks, and driving away relay horses." By late May, all mail stations between Carson Valley and Ruby Valley became deserted.[53]

Howard needed Army protection for his stations and men. Right then, the regular dragoons (cavalry) had been sent up to protect the Oregon-California Trail. As a result, artillery men at Camp Floyd, whom commander Smith assigned to mount up and serve as light dragoons, "accompanied Major Egan to protect the express line between here and Carson Valley."[54] Col. Smith sent one mounted patrol out under

Uncle Sam Guarding the Mail, *artist William Henry Jackson,
courtesy Perry Special Collections, HBL, BYU*

Lt. Delavan Duane Perkins and another under Lt. Stephen H. Weed. Before Weed's patrol got underway, Howard joined it and served as its guide and interpreter. The mission was to protect mail stations and pacify Indians. Lt. Weed's instructions were to escort and protect Major Egan in the distribution of goods to Indians in order to reward friendly ones and bring in those not deeply engaged in the hostilities.[55]

The first day out, a friendly Indian reported that a war party had burned the Deep Creek mail station, wounded several keepers, and driven off a score of horses and mules.[56] The soldiers and Howard reached Deep Creek on May 28. They captured a "bad" Indian and threatened to kill him, causing nearby Indians to flee to the mountains. The Weed patrol took the Indian with them as they rode west. The government Indian agent at Deep Creek, Harrison Severe, reported that as soon as the military left, Indians returned, attacked the station, shot an express employee, and stole considerable stock. They attacked the next station west, whose employees fled to Deep Creek for safety.[57]

Weed commanded twenty troops compared to Lt. Perkins's forty; between them, they probably could have kept the route open from Camp Floyd to Ruby Valley and safeguarded the mail. However, they had no assignment for the 'war zone' between Ruby Valley and Carson. By early June, citizens in Utah wondered if stage drivers would take the western mail beyond Ruby Valley or Diamond Springs.[58] Wilford Hudson and other settlers at Deep Creek abandoned the place and brought their belongings back to the Tooele area. Hudson reported that Indians who had previously been friendly had become as hostile as others, shooting at whites whenever they saw them.[59]

Howard, accompanied by Lt. Weed and his twenty troops, arrived in Ruby Valley on June 2. Weed's orders were to stay there until Lt. Perkins arrived, but, being several days ahead of Perkins and anxious to help keep the mail route open, he consented to go fifty miles farther to Roberts Creek. The Weed contingent reached Roberts Creek on June 4 and found it " a mass of smouldering ruins," burned two days earlier. They stayed the night, but sent out a small scouting party to find "some of the savages." The night being stormy and foggy, they found no Indians. On June 6 they rode back to Ruby Valley. The Indian whom they had taken prisoner at Deep Creek tried to escape and was killed.[60]

Pony Express Rider, *artist William Henry Jackson, courtesy Utah State Historical Society*

That morning the Pony Express mail from the east arrived, brought by Peter Niece from the Schell Creek station. He reported that on June 8 thirty or more Indians came to his station and demanded he surrender all provisions in his charge. The station had four thousand pounds of bacon, two thousand pounds of flour, and other supplies delivered there a few days prior, purchased from Russell, Majors, and Waddell. Niece told the Indians no. They said they'd kill him and the two men with him. A resulting gunfight killed several Indians. Niece and his men captured bows and four rifles, sending them to Deep Creek. They then gathered up all the stock, and the two men drove it towards Deep Creek because they knew the natives would soon return to Schell Creek with a larger force.[61]

Niece met westbound mail riders, and with them he headed back to his Schell Creek Station. They found it in ashes and three natives dead. Niece's earlier coolness and courage had saved his life and those of his men and livestock. He and two others rode east to Antelope Springs, which they found deserted. The two riders carried mail that included a letter from Mr. Faust at Rush Valley, stating that Indians had commenced shooting at station men there, too. At Ruby Valley, Lt. Perkins arrived on June 10. On that day Howard's operations faced "trouble in front and rear."[62] On June 19, a Pony Express rider brought news to Salt Lake City that "The Indians are still troublesome, annoying the stations," despite the army patrols. Some of the troops were stationed at School Creek, others at Ruby Valley, while the balance went west to escort the mail "in company with Major Egan."[63]

At Roberts Creek on June 16, supervisor Bolivar Roberts and thirteen men met "Major Egan and party" carrying mail from Salt Lake City that had left on June 6. Lt. Perkins and part of his command were Howard's escort. A large company of emigrants, mostly from Davis County in Utah, were traveling with the Egan-Perkins group or camping there. The soldiers intended to continue westward to protect the mail and the emigrants. The Indians were following in the rear of the troops, destroying the rebuilt stations or whatever was left behind, even before the soldiers were out of view.[64]

Howard turned around and headed back toward Salt Lake City. He passed through Ruby Valley and kept going. Within an hour after he left Butte Station, twenty-three miles east of Ruby Valley, Indians attacked and burned it.[65] On June 27 the *Deseret News* published that "Major Egan, accompanied by Mr. Shearman, arrived here at early dawn yesterday." Howard proposed that he return to the road in a few days with reinforcements "of his own selection" to protect the stations between the city and Roberts Creek.[66]

On July 2, 1860, while Indians were still a threat, rider Billy Fisher, brother to Minnie Fisher whom Ras would marry, carried mail east from Roberts Creek. Because of burned stations, stolen animals, and missing riders, Fisher rode the entire distance to Salt Lake City, arriving on July 4. He covered "300 miles in 30 hours," he said, "using 8 horses and mules."[67] This was one of the longest and most amazing rides by any Pony Express rider.

On July 11 the *Deseret News* reported that two men recently had been wounded at Deep Creek, and that the route beyond Ruby Valley was not open. There was no prospect of communication by mail or Pony Express between the valley and California. However, all was quiet at Ruby Valley.[68] The Pony Express brought word from Deep Creek that government herdsmen in Rush Valley might be supplying Indians with food and clothing, as well as ammunition. Because Indians had stolen three or four dozen head of stock at Deep Creek, the report said, Howard had been out with a party of men to find and chastise the Indians involved. He couldn't find them, but rumor said some of them had gone to Rush Valley to receive "aid and comfort" from the herdsmen.[69]

Range Boys

To deal with Indians who had stolen horses from the Deep Creek range, Howard, hard-pressed for manpower, recruited some "range boys" from saloons in Salt Lake City, including Jesse Earl. Howard and Earl rode in a covered spring wagon pulled by two mules while the other men rode on horses. Near Schell Creek Station a man named Bill rode up to the wagon and shot Earl in the back, killing him instantly. This was on July 20, 1860. Hearing the shot, the other riders caught up with the wagon, and "were for killing Bill on the spot." Howard asked Bill if he'd mistakenly killed the wrong man. "No," Bill said, but claimed that while checking his pistol his thumb slipped off the hammer, and the shooting was accidental. They gave Bill the benefit of the doubt, but intended to turn him over to the officers when back in the city. During their unsuccessful hunt for the missing horses, one of the men accidentally shot one of his own arms off because he dragged his gun through the brush. "This satisfied Father," Ras Egan said, "of the value of a 'City Rough' in an Indian country, for, said he, he would not give a half dozen of his mail boys for a hundred saloon bred 'Roughs.'" During the return trip, Bill disappeared in the night near Simpson Springs and fled. A posse near Fort Bridger killed Bill, who was wanted for horse stealing and murder.[70]

Danger characterized Howard's 300-mile district. It was a fact of life that men working out there lived in a dangerous zone where nature, Native Americans, and men evading the law could cause them harm. They lived a precarious distance from others who could help them. Theirs was risky work. Tamson had reason to worry about Howard and her sons who worked with him. But she, like the men who hired him and the men who worked for him, must have felt confident in his proven skills, wisdom, and toughness. ◆

~ 25 ~

Pony Express, Egan Adventures, and the Telegraph

Richard Burton, who had been a British soldier, explorer in Arabia and Africa, and observer of world cultures, came to the United States and traveled by stagecoach to Salt Lake City to assess the Mormons. In September and October, 1860, he continued on to California, riding in an ambulance wagon. The next year he published an account of his adventures, *The City of the Saints and Across the Rocky Mountains to California*. For twenty-one pages he described his wagon journey along the west wing of the Central Route, and he noted Pony Express activity and stations, including damage done by Indians. What he experienced was a fairly well-operating pony mail system, despite the recent Indian depredations. One of Burton's observations would have pleased Howard: "The central route is called Egan's by the Mormons, Simpson's by the Gentiles."[1] Perhaps the world adventurer and explorer saw in Howard something of a kindred spirit:

Richard Burton, Utah State Historical Society

> Mr. or Major Howard Egan is a Saint and well-known guide, an indefatigable mountaineer, who for some time drove stock to California in the employ of Messrs. Livingston, and who afterwards became mail agent under Messrs. Chorpenning and Russell …he claims to have explored the present post-office route between 1850 and 1857–58.[2]

Soldiers Help Quell the Violence

On July 20, 1860, two months before Burton traveled the mail route, the Army, because of the Indian issues, began constructing adobe Fort Churchill on the Carson River about thirty miles from Carson City. Soldiers assigned there helped guard the Pony Express and stagecoach mail routes.[3] The Carson area disbanded its volunteer defenders.[4] Troop escorts slowed the swift Pony Express to a mere forty miles a day. These delays continued throughout the month of July 1860. It appeared that hostile Indians had disappeared, not because of the soldiers but to obtain more horses and prepare for future operations. "Hostilities measurably terminated," a July 17 report said.[5]

Violence renewed in August. Unlike in the May attacks, the station employees were prepared. In late July, the acting Adjutant General in Utah had issued one hundred revolvers and eight hundred cartridges to the Pony Express office in Salt Lake City, which were distributed to the riders in order to defend themselves against Indian attack.[6] This time the trouble broke out at Egan Canyon Station, and affected the Schell Creek and Dry Creek Stations as well. On August 14 Howard, in Salt Lake City, showed the *Deseret News* letters he had just received by Pony Express from Deep Creek and other points along the line. One letter said that, on August 11, between 150 and 200 Indians went to the Egan Canyon station and demanded powder and lead. Denied those, they wanted provisions. The station men gave them two sacks of flour, sugar, and coffee. Then, Lt. Weed with twenty-five soldiers attacked, driving off the Indians and saving the stock.[7]

A fuller account soon arrived. It said that in early August mail riders from Ruby Valley to Deep Creek were shot at in Antelope Canyon, without injury. Indians then attacked an emigrant company in Antelope Canyon, killing a rider's horse. When the emigrants reached Ruby Valley, they informed Lt. Perkins of the attack. On August 11, Lt. Weed led twenty-six soldiers to "chastize" the Indians in Antelope Canyon. When they were within eight miles of Egan Canyon, an express rider from the west overtook them and rode ahead of them. In view of the Egan Canyon Station near the west entry to the canyon, he discovered it surrounded by Indians and its doors closed. He galloped back to inform Lt. Weed.

The officer immediately took eighteen mounted men to relieve the station. Lt. Weed's command came just in time. In the station were two men manning it and four emigrants headed for California. "The Indians had already got all the provisions of the station house" and no doubt would have killed the men and destroyed the station had not Weed arrived. Weed's soldiers tried in vain to surround the Indians. The Indians "poured a volley of balls" at them. Of the 150 or more Indians, half were armed with good rifles. The detachment charged, forcing Indians to flee to "get behind rocks, or on top of them ...and whoop and yell like fiends, daring the troops to follow them." Soldiers "found it anything but fun to fight well-armed Indians, when concealed behind rocks and trees." A station man, armed with a Sharp's rifle, shot one at an "incredible distance." During the skirmish, one soldier was killed and two badly wounded, but the soldiers estimated the Indians lost fourteen and had fourteen wounded. Apparently some Bannock Indians took part in that fight.[8]

Another report Howard received said that on August 12 a half dozen Indians ordered men mowing hay near Deep Creek to leave. They didn't. The next morning the Indians came back, but six hidden soldiers fired at them, wounded two, and the others fled. That same day, after Indians had attacked the Egan Canyon Station, two Indian parties attacked the Schell Creek station. They fired into the house, then drove off stock. An hour later, Lt. Weed and his men rode in from Ruby Valley. They found and attacked the Indians, killed seventeen, wounded others, and relieved the station from peril. That same day three soldiers who came in to the Schell Creek Station with the Pony Express killed four Indians.[9]

After those battles, the main violence ended. But by then nearly half of the twenty mail stations within the Great Basin had been razed, sixteen employees killed, and 150 horses stolen.[10] During the rest of 1860 and into 1861, small skirmishes took place, but army patrols stunned the hostiles and saved the Pony Express. Howard's firm, the C.O.C. & P.P. Express Company, placed at each station along this portion of the route five additional men, who rebuilt and guarded the corrals and stations. They used stone and adobe materials, where available, to fortify the facilities.[11]

By the end of 1860, Camp Floyd barely had three hundred soldiers. Because the man for whom the camp was named, Secretary of War John B. Floyd, sided with southerners seceding from the Union, the Army renamed the post Ft. Crittenden that December.[12]

Traveler Burton's Descriptions of Howard's Operations

After leaving Great Salt Lake City for California in September 1860, traveler Burton found two types of stations: mail stagecoach stations with five or six "boys" and Pony Express stations with a station master and rider. For station hands, he said, "the work is severe" and "the diet is sometimes reduced to wolf-mutton, or a little boiled wheat and rye, and drink brackish water." At Fish Springs, Burton found two men in charge of ten horses and mules. Heading for Willow Creek Station (today's Callao), they met Lt. Weed, two officers, and ninety dragoons returning from missions against the Gosiutes. At the station after Willow Creek, Burton saw a Pony Express rider who was "a handsome young Mormon," and an Irish station keeper, but noted that "nothing could be fouler than the log hut; the flies soon drove us out of doors." He'd heard that a "little war" had been waged near Willow Springs back in June when a small band of Gosiutes shot and scalped three whites.[13]

From near a summit in the Deep Creek range, Burton's group looked down on Deep Creek Valley, "the first patch of cultivation" he'd seen since leaving Salt Lake City. He said the area's Gosiute name, Ibapah, was spelled Ayba-pa and meant "clay colored water." He noted that "an Indian model farm had been established here," but recent warfare had prevented cultivation. Indians had burned down the house "and several of them had been killed by the soldiers." The Deep Creek Station, he said, was "two huts and a station-house, a large and respectable-looking building of unburnt brick, surrounded by fenced fields, water-courses, and stacks of good adobe." The passengers met the Mormon station master, Harrison Severe, and others. They were "mostly farm-laborers," Burton said, "who spend the summer here and supply the road with provisions; in the winter they return to Grantsville, where their families are settled." He found that "the Mormons were not wanting in kindness":

> They supplied us with excellent potatoes, and told us to make their house our home. We preferred, however, living and cooking afield. The station was dirty to the last degree; the flies suggested the Egyptian plague; they could be brushed from the walls in thousands; but, though sage makes good brooms, no one cares to sweep clean. This, I repeat, is not Mormon, but Western: the people, like the Spaniards, apparently disdain any occupation save that of herding cattle; and will do so till the land is settled.[14]

The next day Burton's party traveled on a road "dusty to the hub" with the west wind howling. That night their only fuel was sagebrush, "which crackled merrily, like

Desert Scene, author's photo

thorns, under the pot, but tainted the contents with its medicinal odor." On October 4 they found the Antelope Springs station had been burned in June and never rebuilt. A corral still stood. Burton's little company next reached the Schell Creek Station. At Spring Valley the log hut station showed bullet marks of a recent Indian attack. Its station master was a Frenchman, and the Pony Express riders there were "three roughs, one was a Mormon."[15]

On October 5 Burton's party crossed a barren plain, Steptoe Valley, by way of "a heavy road" that rabbits and prairie hens seemed to like. They then entered Egan Canyon. The canyon road "was vile, now winding along, then crossing the stream—hedged in with thicket and dotted with boulders." They found that Egan Station, at the canyon's east end, had been reduced to a chimney-stack and a few charred posts. Gosiutes had burned it two or three days before, as revenge for Lt. Weed's troops killing seventeen of their men. At Butte Station a Mr. Thomas, "a Cambrian Mormon," was the station master. Tables were roughly dressed planks two feet by two feet. Utensils included a tin coffee pot and mess tins, rough knives, "pitchforks," pewter spoons, a tin skillet, and a dipper. Wall pegs supported spurs, pistols, whips, gloves, and leggings. Soap was a handful of gravel; evaporation served as the towel. Rifles, pistols, and guns lay and hung all about the house.[16]

Burton considered the Ruby Valley Station the "halfway house," three hundred miles from both Salt Lake City and the Carson Valley. On October 10 his group reached "Roberts Spring Valley." From this point, Burton recorded, "'Simpson's Road' strikes off to the S.E. and as Mr. Howard Egan's rule here terminates, it is considered the latter end [terminus] of Mormondom."[17]

Civil War Shifts Butterfield to the Central Route

Despite the first month's success of the Pony Express, the Postmaster General's hostility toward and distrust of the overland central route continued. During 1860 he supported the ocean service instead of investing in improvements for the overland operations. His stance meant that "there was but little alteration in the Overland Mail service during 1860."[18]

After Indian raids ended, to draw heightened public attention to the Pony Express service, the company staged a super-sprint crossing that set a speed record. Riders carried news of Abraham Lincoln's election to the presidency in November 1860, covering the distance between the telegraph terminals at Fort Kearny, Nebraska and Fort Churchill in western Nevada in six days.[19] This was one of the most praised accomplishments of the Pony Express.

Winter brought the Pony Express's biggest test, which the *San Francisco Bulletin* underscored in December 1860: "A few weeks are to perhaps settle the fact whether the first Daily Overland Mail, telegraph, and railroad shall enter California by the shortest and most central route, or be compelled by the inclemency of winters on that route to seek a passage-way by making a long circuit through a milder climate."[20] During the winter, runs extended to eleven days between the telegraph end points, and to fifteen days between St. Joseph and San Francisco.

Fortunate for the Central Route, the Civil War shattered the Butterfield southern mail connection to California. By February 1861 five southern states, including Texas, had seceded from the Union. The Confederacy began. The southern U.S. mail line was "cut up by the roots" in southern Missouri and Texas by Confederates. But the Postmaster General could not simply cancel the contract with the Butterfield operation, now termed the Overland Mail Company. So, to keep the mail moving to and from California, Congress authorized the Overland Mail Company to relocate its southern equipment and operations to the Central Route. A scandal had ruined the reputation of Russell, Majors, and Waddell, and their freighting firm soon collapsed into bankruptcy. Though they failed, their Central Overland California and Pikes Peak Express Company was a separate entity and it continued to operate the

"east wing." Neither company could afford to run the entire line alone in its present state, so the two negotiated a working agreement with postal officials. According to the agreement, the government would subsidize the Pony Express to keep it working until the overland telegraph opened. Also, the two companies decided that the C.O.C. & P.P. Express Co. would subcontract to run the mail from St. Joseph to Salt Lake City, and the Overland Mail would run it from Salt Lake City to California using C.O.C. & P.P. Express Co.'s facilities.[21] The Overland Mail Company (formerly Butterfield), however, was firmly in the driver's seat for both wings.[22]

Contracts authorized the stagecoach mail to run on the Central Route six days a week, and the Pony Express semi-weekly at a scheduled time of ten days for eight regular months and twelve days during winter months. For the government, the Pony Express must carry, free of charge, five pounds of mail matter, but the charge to transport letters for the public should not exceed one dollar per half ounce. For both the stagecoach and Pony Express mail, Congress authorized one million dollars per year, a lucrative mail contract.[23] Civil War conditions made it necessary to substitute Atchison, Kansas for St. Joseph as the eastern terminal.[24] The Wells Fargo banking and express

Howard Ransom Egan, Egan Family Archives

firm, then prominent in California, had deep interests in the "financial fabric" of the Overland Mail Company.[25] Pony Express letters mailed in California needed a Wells Fargo Pony Express postage stamp, in addition to U.S. postage.[26]

On April 16, 1861, Howard's man at Ruby Valley, William Shearman, reported Indian talk of "cleaning out" all the stations. He complained that all stations along the line from Simpson Springs to Ruby Valley had needed to furnish Indians out of their own provisions because Indian Agent Benjamin Davis failed to keep his promises to provide provisions, clothing, and presents. Indians constantly asked "When is Davis coming?" Shearman asked if the mail's own contractors want a "double dose of last summer's losses in stock, extra hands, etc.," or do they "wish communication with the west cut off?" He appealed again for Russell's COC&PPX Company to pay Chorpenning and his men seven months pay, which had been promised "again and again," and to reimburse them for the livestock and stations they had commandeered.[27] Agent Charles L. Hawley at Diamond Springs told Howard that "Davis ought to be hung for making promises to the natives and not fulfilling them," thereby "signing the death warrant of the boys on the mail line."[28]

Richard Erastus Egan, Egan Family Archives

By the middle of July 1861, two things concerning the Pony Express were clear: "it was operating with clock-like regularity; and it was not paying, and never would pay, even the expense of operation."[29] Nevertheless, people and businesses in Salt Lake City, San Francisco, Atchison, and points in between counted on the Pony Express mail until October. Newspapers continued to grab up fresh news the riders brought and publish it in special columns called "Pony Express News" or "News from the West" or "News from the East."

Egan Family Pony Express Stories

Howard, Ransom, and Ras Egan played vital roles in the Pony Express saga. Appropriately, the Daughters of Utah Pioneers Museum in Salt Lake City displays several Egan Pony Express items, including leather boots tailored to fit rider Ransom's crippled foot, two pair of eye glasses belonging to Howard, and Howard's Pony Express lantern. *Pioneering the West* is highly valued for its exciting Pony Express stories and reminiscences, selections of which follow here. As happens often with family stories, these lack dates and sometimes places.

The author at the Civil Conservation Corps's 1935 Faust Station Memorial, 2014

Near-Ambush in Egan Canyon

When an express rider at Schell Creek once was too sick to ride, Ransom volunteered to take his place. His ride was from the creek to Butte Station, "there being no station at Egan Canyon at that time." Because they needed to go fourteen miles to Egan Canyon and then eighteen to Butte, Ransom tried not to overtax the pony. In the middle of Egan Canyon, an ideal ambush setting, he saw Indians ahead on both sides of the trail. He decided not to turn back and detour six or eight miles around the canyon, but chose to rush through.

> Taking my pistol in hand, I rode on as close as I dared, then striking in the spurs and giving an awful yell, a few jumps of the pony brought me to about the middle of the camp, when my gun began to talk, though pointed up in the air, and my yells accompanied each shot. I got a glimpse of several Indians who were doing their best to make themselves scarce, not knowing but there might be a large party of whites after them.

Ransom reached the little valley at the head of the canyon safely and raced on to the next station. Later, he learned from friendly Indians that he'd dodged a trap set to catch an express rider "for the purpose of seeing what he carried to make him travel so fast." Had Ransom turned back and tried another canyon "probably there would have been one 'Express' lost."[30]

Reprimand for Taking a Shortcut

Ransom was at the Rush Valley Station south of Tooele where Henry J. Faust became a station keeper and part-time rider in 1860. That's the station where the first Pony Express ride from Salt Lake City ended. The next ride went from there west to Willow Springs. When the rider came in from Salt Lake City, the next rider didn't feel well and said he couldn't stand the ride. So Ransom volunteered to ride in his place. He rode to Simpson Springs "at the edge of the desert," then galloped "to the Dugway" and over a mountain to where the road "ran nearly west across the worst part of the desert" where "nothing but mud grows" and horse hoofs sank and had trouble getting out. The route then made a big "U." It went north past Fish Springs, around a mountain point, then back to where Boyd Station later was set up, just across from Fish Springs. Then it headed on a straight line westerly to the Willow Springs Station. Three miles after leaving Simpson Springs Ransom chose not to make the "U" but "took a straight line for Willow Springs." He made good time, but the desert became softer. He rode into flat land covered by an inch of water "as far as I could see in any direction" and his pony's hooves sank in the mud, making it "slow traveling." After five miles he reached a little higher ground. He made it to Willow Springs and "saved a good many hours of time."

He expected to receive "considerable praise." But, the next time he saw Howard, "he asked me what kind of traveling I found it to be across the way I took with that express." After hearing the shortcut story, Howard said, "Well, don't ever do anything

Willow Springs Station, Utah State Historical Society

like that again without orders," and "that was all, and plenty. I never did, for that was a cold bath for me."[31]

Circle Ride in a Snowstorm

For about sixteen months Ras rode the Pony Express stretch between Salt Lake City and the Rush Valley Station. On his first trip he rode "Miss Lightning," the "famous and beautiful sorrel mare." They reached the first station, twenty-two miles away, in one hour and five minutes. The scheduled time for his full run was five and a half hours. "At first the ride seemed long and a tiresome one but after becoming accustomed in that kind of riding it seemed only play."[32]

One time Ras rode the fifty miles to the Fort Crittenden (Camp Floyd) stop, then started at sundown for Rush Valley in a very heavy snowstorm. Snow stood knee-deep to his horse. When darkness set in he couldn't see the road. "I had to depend entirely on the wind" that was striking his right cheek. He kept the wind there, but it changed and led him off course. Instead of going westward he rode southward all night "on a high trot." He then discovered that he now was at the same place he'd left the evening before, "with both myself and horse very tired." He jumped on the horse he'd ridden the evening before and took the mail the twenty-five miles he'd failed to cover while

Pony Express Rider Fording a River, *artist William Henry Jackson, courtesy Utah State Historical Society*

riding in a circle. Then, "instead of having a night's rest at my home station, I was riding all night, in consequence of which I met the 'Pony' from Sacramento and was compelled to start immediately on my eastward trip to Salt Lake City. This made my continuous ride 150 miles besides all night in deep snow."[33]

Continuous Ride of 330 Miles

Ras and his future brother-in-law, probably Billy Fisher, concocted a plan so the latter could see his sweetheart in Salt Lake City.[34] The man had the route after Ras, so Ras was supposed to pass on to him the westbound mail at Rush Valley. Instead, they planned to supposedly pass in the night, such that Ras kept going west after Rush Valley, and the man kept going east to Salt Lake City. That way he could spend a day there before covering Ras's route back to Rush Valley. But after Ras did his own run and the man's run, a double route of 165 miles, he met the "Pony" from the west and had to ride the double route again. So, he rode continuously for 330 miles, a remarkable feat for any Pony Express rider. The longest ride is credited to Jack Keetley, 340 miles in thirty-one hours.[35]

Riding Out an Attack

About the time when Indians attacked a stagecoach, killed the driver and passenger, rifled the mail, and took four horses, Ras did his express run near the site where it happened. As he rode along a lone Indian, armed with a rifle and a bow and arrows, started chasing him. Ras, thinking he had the best horse, played along, staying just out of easy gun shot from the Indian. Then, "I thought I would play a bluff on him." Ras turned and he raced at the Indian full speed "swinging my pistol and yelling at the top of my voice." The Indian immediately left the road "kicking and whipping his pony and kept it up as far as I could see him."[36]

Fatal Horse Fall

Ras noted that his agent (probably in the Salt Lake City office) encouraged the "boys" to make good time by saying, "Boys if you kill a horse by riding fast we will buy a better one."[37] Ras admitted that he once killed a horse. "One trip I was riding a lovely rangey bay, $300.00 horse at a 20 mile an hour clip, when the poor animal missed his footing and fell, breaking his neck and almost sent me to St. Joseph. When I gathered myself up and found my horse dead, I had to walk about five miles and carry my saddle and express matter."[38]

Saving Nick Wilson's Life

One of Howard's riders was Elijah Nicholas (Nick) Wilson, later known as the "White Indian Boy," who had lived for a time among the Shoshone. Nick was shot in the head by an arrow. Men pulled out the shaft, but not the arrowhead. They rolled him under a tree, thinking he would die. When they came back to bury him, he was still alive. They carried him to the Cedar Wells station and sent word to Ruby Valley for a doctor. For six days the boy waited. Then Howard came along. He sent for a doctor and this time one came. "If Mr. Egan had not happened along when he did, I think I should not be here now telling about it," Wilson wrote in *White Indian Boy*.[39]

Ras's Wedding in Between Rides

On New Year's Day 1861, Ras, almost nineteen, married Mary Ann (Minnie) Fisher, sixteen, in the Endowment House in Salt Lake City. Ras took a furlough from his assigned ride, which caused problems for his substitute:

> I was married January 1st, 1861, and of course, wanted a short furlough, but was only permitted to substitute a rider for one trip, and the poor fellow thought that was plenty. I had warned him about the horse he would start with from "Rush" on his return trip, telling him that he would either buck or fall over backwards when he got on him. 'Oh,' said he, 'I am used to that kind of business.' 'But,' said I, 'Bucking Bally is a whole team and a horse to let, and a little dog under the wagon, so be careful.' So as a precaution, after he had tightened the saddle, he led him out about a quarter of a mile from the station and got on; when the horse true to his habit, got busy, and the next thing the rider knew he was hanging by the back of his overcoat on a high stake with his feet from the ground.[40]

He could not reach behind to unhitch himself. He could not unbutton his coat so as to crawl out of it, but "he could get his hands in his pocket for his knife to cut the buttons off and release himself; after which a search was made for the horse in the darkness of the night. He finally found him and made the trip, getting a black eye for loss of time. He said to the boys, 'No more Bucking Bally for me.'"

On Ras and Minnie's wedding day, Howard presented them with a Melodian, an organ-like instrument that was a luxury in those days. It was the only instrument of its kind in the community, and people in the town would come by to practice on it. For about two years the couple made their home in Salt Lake City while Ras continued to ride for the Pony Express and then helped with the stagecoach mail.[41]

Soon after his marriage, Ras, the westbound rider for the first leg from Salt Lake

City, waited at the downtown office for the Pony Express to come from St. Joseph. Deep snow in the Rockies made him presume the rider would be long delayed. The hostler (handler of the horses) through sympathy told him, "You go home to your new wife and if the express comes I will jump on a horse and come after you." Of course Ras accepted. "Oh! what luck," he said. "About midnight here comes the pesky fellow and I had to jump out of a snug warm bed and start off in a howling blizzard to ride seventy five miles."[42]

Telegraph Terminates the Pony Express

Late in 1861, Pony Express riders on the west wing galloped past workmen planting tall poles and stringing wire for a transcontinental telegraph system. Samuel Morse patented his telegraph invention in 1830, and in 1844 the government funded him to build a telegraph line from Baltimore to Washington, D.C. California put up telegraph lines from San Francisco to Sacramento and interior cities in 1853. Lines then headed for a Sierra crossing. In 1860 Congress passed the Pacific Telegraph Act, offering funding to any company connecting Missouri to San Francisco. The Overland Telegraph Company and the Pacific Telegraph Company (Western Union) were formed. The

The Transcontinental Telegraph, *artist William Henry Jackson, courtesy Utah State Historical Society*

latter started erecting poles and lines from Omaha to Salt Lake City, and the former worked eastward from California. The route selected on the "east wing" went by way of Omaha, up the South Platte, via old Fort Kearny and Fort Laramie, up the Sweetwater and through the South Pass to Salt Lake City. On the "west wing," installers basically followed the Pony Express route east from Virginia City, Nevada. Both projects faced labor and supply shortages caused by the Civil War.

James Gamble, who oversaw construction of the Nevada and Utah lines, described how the lines were erected and how the Pony Express and stagecoaches interacted with the project.[43] Loggers cut trees in the mountains in California, Nevada, and Utah, which were trimmed into telegraph poles. Wire, connectors, and telegraph keys came by ships to California. Wagons hauled poles by the hundreds and the wire and equipment to where the pole installers were.

> The line was first measured and staked off; the hole-diggers followed; then came the pole-setters, and next the wire party. The line was strung up at the rate of from three to eight miles a day. An advance telegraph station was kept up with the head of the line, and the progress of the work reported each day. At this advance station the news was received on the arrival of the Pony Express, and telegraphed to San Francisco and other points. Commercial dispatches were also sent and received daily, as the Pony Express arrived at or departed from our camp. In this way the newspapers in San Francisco were supplied with telegraphic news, and were daily gaining on time as the lines advanced east and west across the continent toward their meeting point.

Deserts had to be crossed, which taxed the efforts and strength of the expedition to its very utmost. In one instance, sixteen miles of line were built in one day in order to reach a point where water could be obtained. Because the weather was extremely hot, teams with barrels of water had to be kept with the different parties when crossing these deserts. When the line from California approached central Nevada, pole suppliers could not keep up with the installers. Said Gamble:

> It began to be apparent that the pole contractors were going to fail on that section. Mountaineers and Indians were at once secured to scour the mountains, and procure, if possible, a sufficient number of poles to complete the remaining portion of the line. As the season was growing late, and cold weather coming on, I began to have serious fears that it would be impossible to complete it before winter. The men were also getting frightened, and many of them wanted to return home, as they feared we would be over taken by the snow.

Gamble learned that poles could be had on the top of a high mountain about fifteen miles from Egan Canyon, "but that the only way to procure them was with our own men and teams. This I directed done, and with as little delay as possible." By stagecoach, he rode to Egan Canyon and spent two days supervising the men. They secured twenty wagon-loads of poles and began putting them in place.[44]

On October 18, 1861, the western telegraph lines reached Salt Lake City, meeting the line from Omaha on October 24. That day President Lincoln received a telegraph message from California saying "the telegraph to California this day has been completed." Super-fast electronic dot-dot-dash messages flashing along transcontinental telegraph wires killed the Pony Express. Telegrams took but a few hours or less to pass between the east and west coasts. "The pony was fast, but he could not compete with the lightning."[45] In early November the last eastbound Pony Express mail was delivered in Atchison, and on November 18 the last westbound run ended in Sacramento and San Francisco. The Pony Express was no more.[46]

The company then was sold at auction to Ben Holladay in March of 1862. Many of the Pony Express stations, employees, and animals stayed put and concentrated on the cross-country stagecoach business.

Pony Express Legacies

The Pony Express was a "successful failure." Its organizers hoped not to profit but to prove the viability of the Central Route, which they did. With exaggeration, Alexander Majors said that "the business transacted over this line was not sufficient to pay one-tenth of capital invested." Riders made a total of 308 runs each direction, covering a total of 616,000 miles, and carried 23,356 pieces of mail going east and 11,397 pieces going west, a total of 34,753 pieces. That averaged about 113 pieces per run. Californians used the Pony service more than people in the East, so more Pony Express mail items went east than west. Totals receipted for the eighteen months were $90,141, only a little more than the initial cost of horses alone.[47] The promoters' hopes that the venture would land them good government mail contracts failed. The pony relay experiment drove the financially precarious Russell, Majors, and Waddell firm deeper into debt, contributing to, but not causing, its financial collapse.[48]

But the Pony Express did prove the suitability of the central route, which became an ever-busier thoroughfare. It stayed very much alive with stagecoaches and their stations, telegraph stations, emigrants bound for California, soldier patrols, cattle drives, and freight wagon trains. A "thriving wagon trade" developed between California and Utah Territory when mining booms struck Virginia City, Austin, and other Nevada sites.[49] A half-century later, the nation's first transcontinental highway for automobiles, the Lincoln Highway, followed parts of the Pony Express and stagecoach routes that Howard once located and supervised.

The Pony Express helped save the Union when the Civil War broke out. Historian

LeRoy Hafen pointed out that the speed of the Pony mail "helped to unite the Pacific Coast and the Rocky Mountain region to the Union during that first ominous year of Civil War."[50] "That long, slender line of communication, which a handful of hostile Indians might easily break any day, was their sole reliance for keeping abreast of swiftly moving [Civil War] events."[51] With the nation stumbling into a lengthy war, the Pony Express conveyed big news items when timing greatly mattered, such as Lincoln's election, President Buchanan's last message to Congress, and details of Lincoln's inauguration. David Rhodes, one of Howard's descendants, penned a poem, "We Are the Riders," that doesn't exaggerate:

> What we carry runs the nation
> And we execute our duty well.
> We're the Pony Express riders,
> The boys who carry the mail.[52]

Today, the National Park Service oversees the nearly two-thousand-mile-long Pony Express National Historic Trail across eight states. It's a ghost trail. Most of it has been erased by wind, rain, snow, floods, sagebrush, livestock, farms, ranches, roads, houses, military installations, and off-road vehicles. But, where once it was well etched into the landscape, at least now it is fairly well-mapped and identified in guidebooks. Much of it is off road, and some segments are on private property and inaccessible. All along the historic route are markers, panels, monuments, and a few station ruins.

Egan descendants perhaps more than anyone else have honored their Pony Express heritage by driving, riding horses or bicycles, flying over, or walking on portions of the original Pony Express Trail.[53] Poet Rhodes, while riding the trail by himself one night and imagining what Howard might have been thinking, wrote "Take Me Back to Tullamore." The poem captures what could have been Ireland-born Howard's thoughts, and his sense of humor, while he rode alone one night on that quiet trail far from everywhere. One verse reads thus:

> I start to dream of our Irish home,
> And hear the songs mother sings.
> Lord, take me back to Tullamore,
> Or, at least, get me to Antelope Springs.[54] ◆

~ 26 ~

Overland Stagecoach Supervisor

When the telegraph killed the Pony Express, the overland stagecoach transportation business expanded, with Howard's supervisory help. On scales of importance, stagecoaches far outweigh the Pony Express. One Pony Express *mochila* carrying twenty pounds or less of mail overland cannot compare to the packages, passengers, and mail bags a single stagecoach carried that same distance. The epic era of overland stagecoach operations between the Missouri and the Pacific started in 1859 and lasted almost a decade. The business thrived because demand rose for transporting packages, freight, mail, and passengers. Travelers, needing to cross the western half of the country as fast as possible, realistically had no choice but the stagecoach. Their other options were to walk, ride a horse or mule, or join a wagon train.

During the 1860s the stagecoach system was "rightly judged one of the wonders of the age; an American phenomenon unequaled for sheer magnitude anywhere in the world."[1] Howard, from company offices in Salt Lake City and his headquarters in remote Deep Creek, but mostly out on the road, supervised and promoted nearly six hundred miles of stagecoach operations for almost a decade. For his contributions, Howard's name in overland stagecoach history needs to be written large in bold letters.

Ex-Sailor on the Desert Sea

Howard supervised coach operations in the most desolate division of the 1,900 mile overland stagecoach route. His zone reached from Salt Lake City to Ruby Valley, at first, but soon extended to Carson City. This mostly arid landscape was hardly fit for human habitation. Native Americans barely survived there. Ex-sailor Howard was the high desert's equivalent of a seaman. At sea his world primarily was water, sometimes horizon to horizon. By stark contrast, this west central desert gave him sometimes endless dry landscapes. Mark Twain termed one stretch of that desert "a vast, waveless ocean stricken dead." Howard's stagecoaches were the desert's version of ships on the sea. World traveler Richard Burton saw covered wagons and coaches in that region as "ships of the great American Sahara" carrying people "between the eastern and the western shores of a waste, which is everywhere like a sea."[2] Covered wagons often were called "prairie schooners," a schooner being a sailing ship.

"American Sahara," along the Pony Express trail, author's photo

For ships, weather mattered, and so it did for stagecoaches that faced summer heat, spring and fall rain and mud, winter snows, and bitter cold. If wind and currents propelled sailing ships, mighty teams of horses or mules powered the coaches. Instead of unpredictable ocean waves, coaches navigated ruts and gullies, rocks and hills, corduroy ripples, sand, hub-deep dust, and tight curves. As with a fleet at sea, Howard's desert vehicles needed captains and crews, harbors (stations) for safety and sustenance, regular maintenance, and sometimes daring rescues.

Stagecoach Mail Starts on the West Wing

Howard's serious stagecoach experiences began when Chorpenning's mail operations shifted from pack trains to stagecoaches in 1858 for some parts of the journey (see Chapter 23). His coaches followed the Humboldt route, and then, in 1859, began trying the Egan central route. Howard superintended the segment between Salt Lake and Gravelly Ford. Then, eventually, the stagecoaches favored the more direct route via Ruby Valley, Reese River, and Carson Valley.

In July 1859, *New York Tribune* editor Horace Greeley, in a mail coach, traveled along the Egan Trail route to Ruby Valley and then northwest to the Humboldt River. He published his observations in 1860 in *An Overland Journey from New York to San Francisco*.³ His is the earliest account found of stagecoach travel on that new central road. He said that the vegetation along it "was the same eternal sage-bush and grease-wood." He found that "from the Jordan to the Humboldt is about three hundred and fifty miles by the route I traveled, and in all that distance the brooks and rills I crossed or saw, could they be collected into one channel, would barely form a decent mill-stream." Greeley complained about the passengers' "usual rations of pork, bread and coffee." He didn't describe his stagecoach, or mention Howard, or tell about the mail stations other than his coach's mule changes there.

Horace Greeley, LDS Church History Library

Howard continued to supervise his district when company ownership changed from Chorpenning to the Overland Mail Company, then to stagecoach king Ben Holladay, and finally to Wells Fargo. He became a stagecoach expert. He learned how coaches were built and how to repair them, what kind of loads they could and couldn't carry, the best types of horses or mules to use, how to pick and handle drivers and conductors, and what the "swing" and "home" relay stations needed. His working days engaged him with hired hands, horses, mules, cows, hay, saddles, mail bags, stagecoaches, drivers, telegraph lines, bandits ("road agents"), and Native Americans. From the Wasatch Mountains and across the Great Basin to the Sierras, Howard made many trips riding in a stagecoach, checking on coaches, and sometimes driving one.

The Concord Stagecoach

Prim, uniquely shaped, colorful stagecoaches are one of the Old West's best-known icons, like the Winchester rifle and saloon swinging doors.⁴ They were unique vehicles, impressive then and fascinating today in museums and as replicas.⁵ Express firms bought Concord coaches manufactured by the Abbott-Downing Company in Concord, New Hampshire. They measured 8.5 feet long and tall, and five feet wide. Empty, they weighed about 2,500 pounds. Their rear wheels' diameter was five-feet-one-inch and the front wheels, which had to be able to turn under the carriage's front, were three-feet-ten-inches in diameter. The oval shaped body was suspended on two 3-inch thick leather thorough-braces running the length of the coach. Like a swing, the coach body rocked slightly forward and back. "Our coach," Mark Twain wrote, was "an imposing

Concord Stagecoach, Wagons, Mules and Men, *Nick Eggenhoffer*

cradle on wheels."[6] The carefully painted coach's color was sometimes green, more often red.

The coaches' insides measured a bit over four feet wide, and about 4.5 feet high. The interior was upholstered in padded leather and damask cloth. Seats had leather-covered pads, sometimes harder than the wood beneath them. Overland trail stagecoaches seated six or nine passengers inside. One or more might ride topside. If nine passengers, they sat three to a seat. Back and middle rows both faced forward, and a forward row faced rearward. Those in the forward and middle rows had their knees almost dovetailing those of the facing passengers. Center seat passengers, to support their backs, had a leather strap running the coach's width. Each person was allowed twenty-five pounds of luggage, two blankets, and a canteen. Small windows and roll up leather curtains let in air and kept out some rain and snow. A few coaches had glass windows. At night a dim oil lamp glimmered inside.[7]

Topside, the driver's seat and boot could hold two passengers, besides the driver and mail bags. The driver had a locked box under his cushion. To apply brakes "his right foot is planted upon an iron bar which presses by a leverage upon the rear wheels."[8] When short on passengers or mail, "we loaded up with grain or other provisions to be distributed along at the various stations," one driver recalled, "so we were nearly always well loaded. Often we carried more than a ton of mail in the 'boot' and strapped on the back platform."[9]

Depending on the road and distance, four or six horses pulled a coach. Mule teams sometimes handled the sandy stretches. By the end of 1863, Wells Fargo & Company had replaced all mules on Howard's division with horses.[10] In hot weather a bucket for watering the animals hung over one of the coach lamps. Stagecoaches, by traveling day and night and changing their teams regularly, could get freight, passengers, and mail to and from Missouri River towns and California in about twenty-five to twenty-eight days. A coach's speed "on average is five miles an hour; six is good; between seven and eight is the maximum."[11] Most drivers "trotted at gate awhile, then dropped to a walk to let the team get its wind, then brought them back to trot."[12] Every twelve to fifteen miles, meaning every two to three hours, the stagecoach line had "swing stations," and about every forty-five miles was a "home station." During quick stops at the swing stations, fresh teams replaced the tired ones. At home stations, the driver got off the coach to drive the next coach heading back the direction from which he'd come and a new driver took over his coach. Also at home stations, wagon wheels had to be greased, or "doped," and passengers sometimes could get a meal. In 1863 passengers paid $225 (more than $3000 in 2015 dollars) for a ticket to travel from Atchison, Kansas to Placerville, California.[13]

Supervisors, Conductors, Drivers, and Station Hands

In the summer of 1861, Samuel Clemens (Mark Twain) traveled the overland stage to the new territory of Nevada, carved that year from Utah Territory. In his 1872 book, *Roughing It*, Twain penned descriptions of his long trip.[14] Awed by the stagecoach system, he termed it a "vast machinery–these hundreds of men and coaches, and thousands of mules and horses."[15] He ranked the district agent, Howard's position, "of top importance," followed by the conductor, then the driver, and then the station hands. The district agent held great authority within his 250-mile district: "He purchased horses, mules' harnesses, and food for men and beasts, and distributed these things among his stage stations, from time to time…He erected station buildings and dug wells. He paid the station keepers, hostlers, drivers, and blacksmiths, and discharged them whenever he chose." An agent "was like a king" in his division. Not necessarily

Farrell R. Collett drawing from The Stagecoach in Utah History, *Dixon Paper Company of Salt Lake City, 1962*

a gentleman, the agent nevertheless "was always a general in administrative ability, and a bulldog in courage and determination."[16]

Next in rank, Twain said, came the conductor, who rode the length of the division. He sat with the driver and had absolute charge of the mails, express matter, passengers, and stagecoach, until he delivered them to the next conductor. Third in importance was the driver, left hand holding reins and right hand a whip, determining the fate of the coach and the passengers. As a rule the passengers "idolized most drivers."[17] Every driver was armed.[18] Least respected were the station keepers and hostlers (animal handlers) whom Twain described as "low, rough characters," a considerable sprinkling of whom might be outlaws. He didn't mention blacksmiths, who, at the home stations, were indispensable.[19]

Butterfield Overland Mail Moves to the Central Route

As shown in Chapter Twenty-five, Congress approved an act on February 27, 1861, for the establishment of post routes that conducted stagecoach mail service on the Central Route six days a week.[20] But when secession by southern states interfered with the Butterfield Overland Mail operations on the southern route, arbitrators assigned the Overland Mail people to manage the "west wing" from Placerville to Salt Lake City. Only eighteen Butterfield coaches moved to the central route. Bela M. Hughes was acting president. This takeover made Howard an Overland Mail employee. He continued to oversee stagecoaching for most of the west wing.[21] On June 5, 1861, the Overland Mail agreed to purchase some 600 horses for the route between Salt Lake City and Carson City, along with twenty-five stagecoaches, twenty-five drivers and twelve conductors, plus station keepers and stock tenders, for a total of nearly 150 men. On July 1, 1861, Wells Fargo acquired the Butterfield line but let it retain the Overland Mail Company name. Louis McLane, an "efficient general agent," handled the line between Folsom, California (a railroad ran from Sacramento to Folsom) and Carson City. Company president A. H. Barney represented the company between Carson City and Salt Lake City, so Howard's division worked under him.[22]

Overland Mail Operations, 1861–1862

In 1861 the western wing, which included Howard's division, contained fifty-three stage stations. Each station kept eight horses for stages and two for the Pony Express. The total number of horses was more than five hundred. About fifty wagons and stagecoaches were put on the line. Drivers' routes averaged fifty miles. Their wages were seventy-five dollars per month and board. The official schedule between Sacramento and Salt Lake City required seven days and about six hours.[23] In October 1861 the overland telegraph opened and the Pony Express stopped. On the whole, the stagecoach service during 1861 was good, but when winter set in, stagecoaches came through irregularly.

Financial troubles on the east wing let stagecoach mogul Ben Holladay, a "black bearded dynamo," buy that contract in March 1862 and assume "sole charge and management."[24] He named the new east wing company the "Overland Stage Line."[25] Congress passed the Pacific Railroad Bill in July 1862, which authorized construction of a transcontinental railroad but also called for a major shortening of the "east wing" mail route. No more would coaches take the long loop from Fort Laramie up and across South Pass. To service Denver with a branch line, the new stagecoach route ran from the South Platte to Julesburg in Colorado's extreme northeast corner, then to Bridger's Pass, down to Bitter Creek, and to the Green River. This shortcut saved 150 miles. The new route ran approximately where the Union Pacific railroad soon would lay track, and where Interstate 80 now is.

Mormon leaders felt "badly disposed," even "hostile," towards the east wing mail system, which they wanted Mormons to operate, but the Overland Mail's managing of the west wing "commands their undivided confidence, friendship and affection." So said treasurer Hiram Rumfield in 1862. That good opinion came in part because the Overland spent thousands of dollars in Utah for their supplies, and because Howard's management of his west wing district helped shape it.[26]

Appointed Overland Stagecoach Superintendent

Howard's appointment as an Overland Mail Company superintendent, dated July 1, 1862, is addressed to "agents and employees" of the company, and reads: "Major Egan this day becomes Superintendent of the Overland Mail Line from Salt Lake City to Carson in place of Rowe resigned. You will please regard his directions accordingly." It is signed by Frank Cook, assistant treasurer, Salt Lake City.[27] Each of the company's three divisions—Atchison to Denver, Denver to Salt Lake City, and Salt Lake to Placerville—had a superintendent for roughly six hundred miles. Howard's spanned 563 miles. Below the superintendent level, a division agent had responsibility for two hundred miles. Howard supervised three such division agents, although he might have done double-duty and served as one division agent himself.[28]

When not out on the line, Howard worked from his Deep Creek Ranch or in the company office in Salt Lake City. That office, housed in the Salt Lake House at about 150 South Main Street, was the Overland Mail's "most important administrative center on the line."[29] A granite monument with bronze plaques marks the location today.

Pony Express Station in downtown Salt Lake City, Utah, Egan Family Archives

For Howard's division, the company supplied its service shops in Salt Lake City with parts sent from the Concord coach manufacturer, and it sent out traveling horseshoe men, harness repairers, and blacksmiths who, as needed, "kept the horses shod, and the stages in repair."[30]

Deep Creek, a home station, was Howard's road headquarters. It had a coach and repair shop, a blacksmith, and a harness shop. It and Ruby Valley, and perhaps other home stations, set up ranches and grew hay in order to provision the swing stations. Wagons regularly hauled and distributed provisions, forage, and other necessary supplies to the stations. Howard's sons often drove those wagons.[31]

With Camp Crittenden, formerly Camp Floyd, deserted by mid-1861, travelers soon preferred a new bypass that headed west from Salt Lake City to Tooele and turned south past Stockton and through Rush Valley to reach the main stagecoach road just east of Faust Station.[32] In 1866 Howard shifted the Overland's stagecoaches to that route.[33]

An 1864 Denver advertisement for Ben Holladay's Overland Stage Line reads: "Carrying the Great Through Mail Between the Atlantic and Pacific States." The company, it said, "is now running its Daily Coaches to and from Atchison, Kansas, and Placerville, California, through the City of Denver." The ad promised "Quick time, and every convenience afforded to passengers." The trip from Denver to Salt Lake City took five days, and from Salt Lake City to Placerville took thirteen.[34] By 1866 passengers paid three hundred dollars to go from Fort Kearny to Salt Lake City or five hundred dollars all the way to California. Fares included twenty-five pounds of baggage. Meals cost extra, so passengers at home stations paid fifty cents to two dollars to eat there.[35]

Passengers and "Hard Traveling"

TV westerns and such classic movies as "Stagecoach" give some sense of what stagecoach travel was like for the passengers. For income reasons, the company gave passengers preference over mail sacks. The stagecoaches that Howard and his sons assisted, guarded, and rode in and on transported hundreds if not thousands of passengers, "characters of every kind."[36] One traveler noted that "passengers often sang hymns, recounted their own experiences, or bored their fellow travelers with recitals of their misfortunes," and then toward evening "nerves became frazzled, tempers flared, children cried, and the everlasting dust and jolting seemed intolerable. There was no such thing as a night's sleep." In winter, "wind-blown snow seeped in around the curtains to cover the floor, the seats, and the passengers ... Passengers wrapped themselves in buffalo robes and huddled tightly together."[37] "One can hardly imagine worse punishment," one study concluded, "than riding day and night continuously for twenty days in a crowded coach."[38]

Passenger Samuel Bowles complained about "jolts of the rocks" and the "chuck holes" in the road, "to which the drivers in their rapid progress could give no heed, kept us in a somewhat perpetual and not altogether graceful motion." The alkali dust, "dry with a season's sun, fine with the grinding of the season's stages and freight trains, was thick and constant and penetrating beyond experience and comparison. It filled the air—it was the air; it covered our bodies—it penetrated them." It begrimed clean clothes packed in the traveler's bags and trunks.[39]

In *Roughing It*, Mark Twain penned descriptions of his 1861 trip and of some stations in Howard's division. He made no mention of Howard or the boys.[40] Leaving Salt Lake City, Twain's group provided themselves with "enough bread, boiled ham, and hard-boiled eggs to last double the six hundred miles of staging we had still to do."[41] He described the west Utah desert region as a "solemn waste tufted with ash-dusted sagebushes" amid "the lifeless silence and solitude that belong to such a place." Of one wilderness stretch he used such phrases as "it was so hot…so tiresome and dull …the tedious hours did lag and drag and limp along," and "the alkali dust cut through our lips… our eyes." That desert trip was "a thirsty, sweltering, longing, hateful reality!" He said the coach's mules, "under violent swearing, coaxing, and whip-cracking, would make at stated intervals a 'spurt,' and drag the coach a hundred or maybe two hundred yards, stirring up a billowy cloud of dust that rolled back, enveloping the vehicle in the wheel tops or higher, and making it seem afloat in a fog." A rest followed, then another "spurt," and another rest. "All day long we kept this up."[42] At Reese River Station, his stagecoach encountered eastward-bound telegraph construction workers, then the coach crossed the forty-mile desert and reached their destination, Carson City.

Mark Twain, 1867, Library of Congress Prints and Photographs Division

Ransom's Three Days Without Food

Sometime between 1862 and 1865, Ben Holladay, owner of the east wing's Overland Stage Line, decided to make a super-fast trip across the continent, starting from California. Times were set for Holladay's starts and arrivals. For that speedy run,

Howard made all the necessary preparations in his division. He positioned extra relay teams between stations, which gave each driver a fresh team at halfway points between stations and enabled greater speed. He told Ransom to send a relay back to a particular point at a certain time "and wait for me till I come." Ransom and Mr. Ball, called "Boley," took four mules to Egan Canyon.

Two hands from the Shell Creek station showed up, "hungry as wolves," so the four men ate all the food the station had. The stage didn't come that night, as expected, nor did it come the next day. At first daylight on the third day, Howard and Ben Holladay's coach roared in, received a fresh team, gave Ransom and Boley some dry, hard bread, and sped off. Ransom and Boley walked the tired team of horses to the next station and relished a meal there.

Holladay made the trip from San Francisco to Atchison, Kansas in twelve days, but it cost him an estimated $12,000 in damage to horses and equipment.[43]

Stagecoach king Ben Holladay, Beaverton, Oregon Historical Photo Gallery

Desert Pirates

In stagecoach days, the desert's equivalent to ship pirates were "road agents." Robbers targeted stagecoaches. Nick Wilson said that "Some drivers, when these outlaws came upon them, would put the whip to their horses and try to dash by them to safety. At times the boys managed to give the robbers the slip, but oftener the driver would be shot down in the attempt to escape." Minus a driver, "the horses, mad with fright, if no passenger was aboard to grab the lines, would run away, upset the coach, perhaps, and string things along the trail in great shape."[44] When Nick was at Canyon Station, Howard drove up in a coach whose driver was dead in the boot, and a wounded passenger rode inside. "They had been shot by stage robbers, or 'road agents,' as we called them," Wilson said. The stagecoach was shot full of holes. Howard needed a replacement driver. The station keepers said they couldn't drive four horses, so Howard told Wilson to do it. "I hadn't had any experience handling a stage, but I tried it." Howard promised to send someone to relieve Wilson, but didn't, "so I kept on driving."[45]

Ransom dodged being robbed of cattle.[46] In the fall of 1862 while he was in Salt Lake City "on a furlough," Howard telegraphed a message from Ruby Valley that changed his plans. Howard needed fifty or sixty head of beef cattle herded from Salt

Lake City to Ruby Valley, 274 miles. "I want you to take these animals out to Ruby, and you must start tomorrow, for they need them there now. Everything is ready, a wagon loaded with about a ton of supplies, three yoke of broken oxen, two ponies for the two Indian night herders, and an ox driver or teamster." Ransom's own outfit was simply his riding pony. "I was told to make as good time as I could, but get the beef through in the best shape possible, and keep a good watch on the animals, as there was a good deal of stealing going on about that time."

On his second day out from Salt Lake City he and his men stopped to eat lunch. Lot Huntington rode into their camp and ate with them. Huntington was going west and said he might join them later and travel with them to Rush Valley. "This was the last I ever saw of Lot," Ransom said. The next night, camped in Rush Valley, he heard a stagecoach pass by westbound. That didn't seem right because it was not a mail day. The next morning another stagecoach approached from the west and stopped. Porter Rockwell sang out "Hello kids, all right?" Rockwell was either a sheriff or a deputy. "Yes, all right so far," Ransom answered. "Good!" said Rockwell, "Your Father told me to tell you," and then he stopped speaking. "What did Father say?" "He said for you to be very careful and keep a good watch on the cattle and guard them well." Because the men on the stagecoach were heavily armed, Ransom thought that maybe they were on a rabbit hunt, a common fall activity. The stage rolled on.

When Ransom reached Faust Station, he learned that Rockwell and the armed men had been on a man hunt, not a rabbit hunt, and that the hunted men were inside that stagecoach with Rockwell. One was Lot Huntington, dead. Later, Ransom learned that a certain gang had planned to steal his herd before he got them to Ruby, then sell them in California.

Col. Connor Establishes Camp Douglas

Camp Crittenden closed in the summer of 1861, after which the Army had no post in Utah or nearby for a full year.[47] Early in 1862, when winter ended, Indians troubled the overland trails northeast of Salt Lake City. They burned mail stations between Fort Bridger and the North Platte, destroyed mail and coaches, drove off stock, and killed several men. Ben Holladay, the east wing's stagecoach company owner at the time, wanted soldiers positioned every hundred miles along his mail line.[48] President Young and Utah Territory federal officials desired that "a regiment of mounted men be raised" to protect the mail, emigration, and telegraph routes. On April 28, 1862, by "express direction of the President of the United States," President Young sent out a company of cavalry for several weeks under Captain Lot Smith to protect the telegraph and overland mail near Independence Rock.[49]

Army leaders, seeking a better solution than the Mormon patrol, sent a unit of California volunteers under Col. Patrick Connor to Salt Lake City. In August 1862, Connor assumed command of the military's District of Utah, which included the Utah and Nevada Territories. Five infantry and two cavalry companies composed his command. On his way to Salt Lake City, Col. Connor left a few men to build a fort in Ruby Valley, about two miles from Howard's Overland Mail station. By stagecoach Col. Connor reached Salt Lake City on September 4. He quickly judged the Mormons to be a "community of traitors, murderers, fanatics and whores." Wanting a camp location better than the old Camp Floyd site, he created Camp Douglas on bench lands overlooking Salt Lake City, where the University of Utah now stands.

Colonel Patrick Connor, LDS Church History Library

Col. Connor then went back and marched his men toward Salt Lake City. At Deep Creek they obtained thirty barrels of water and noticed rich bunch grass available for their animals.[50] After the troops entered Salt Lake City, the Overland Mail Company, the Post-Office Department, and the Department of the Interior all urged Connor's superiors to move Connor's soldiers to Fort Bridger "as a check upon the Indians." Connor sent one or two detachments from Camp Douglas to occupy Fort Bridger.[51]

Bear River Massacre

Shoshone attacks on mining parties and murders of miners and express men near Cache Valley prompted Col. Connor to lead a punitive expedition against Shoshone chief Bear Hunter's winter camp on Bear River in Cache Valley and deliver a "vigorous chastisement of the murderers." In the "Battle of Bear River" on January 29, 1863, Connor's men killed approximately two hundred Shoshone, then pillaged the village, killed women and children, raped women, and savagely killed wounded warriors. Cache Valley Mormons praised his victory. Because of Connor's "splendid victory," the Army promoted him to brigadier-general. For a century, western history accorded Connor hero status for the victory. Today, the event is judged a horrible massacre. Of the top five massacres in western history, including the Sand Creek Massacre and the Wounded Knee fight, each had less Native Americans killed than the Bear River Massacre. Approximately 250 Shoshone were killed, including ninety women and children. The massacre site, which is now well-marked with illustrated wayside panels, is north of present-day Preston, Idaho.[52]

The Gosiute Indian War in 1863

In the summer of 1862, Overland Mail treasurer Hiram Rumfield, stationed in Salt Lake City, reported that a mile above the Egans' Deep Creek house was a large Indian encampment. Because the mail service had put its route right through their lands, game had left the valley, leaving the Indians with no means of subsistence. To help out, Overland Mail was feeding them "liberally." During a previous quarter, the company "paid Mr. Egan 1792 dollars for beef furnished [to] these Indians[,] and his bill for the present quarter will scarcely be less." The company spent $12,000 on provisions. Rumfield said the company on the west wing agreed that "it is cheaper to feed than to fight them."[53]

The Bear River Massacre, when added to the ongoing white encroachments onto Indian lands and the failure of government promises of supplies, produced the "Gosiute War" in 1863. Indians attacked soldiers and stagecoach stations, employees, and coaches for six months, and the army's counter-efforts led to deaths and destruction on both sides. In a series of massacres, soldiers from Fort Ruby killed fifty-three Gosiutes. The stagecoach company lost a total of seventeen stations, 150 horses, and sixteen men in this short but intense conflict.[54]

Downing-the-nigh-Leader, *Frederic Remington*,
courtesy Utah State Historical Society

Near-Killing of Ransom at Deep Creek

In 1863 Howard engaged John Fisher to ride horseback to Deep Creek and from there to drive cattle to Fort Ruby to fill a government beef contract. At Deep Creek Ransom helped Fisher gather up cattle, aided by three white men from the farm and "three of the best Indians."[55] Ransom had heard that some Shoshone Indians, now nearby, talked of revenge for the Bear River Massacre. On March 22, when his Indian herders didn't show up, he sensed trouble, ordered all the windows covered in the Deep Creek buildings, and had men load their rifles. The next morning Ransom rode to the Indian's camp. Friendly Egan Jack, a local Gosiute, refused to tell him where the herders were, then wanted him to ride back home ducked to the side of his horse. Ransom did, and later learned that the Pah Van Ute with Egan Jack had planned to shoot Ransom when he rode off.[56]

Stagecoach Driver Killed Near Eight Mile Station

During that same troubled morning, some Deep Creek hands saw Indians riding over a bluff toward Eight Mile Station, eight miles westbound from the Egans' Deep Creek ranch.[57] Fearful, Ransom told his men to round up cattle before Indians stole them all. Then, seeing smoke from the direction of Eight Mile Station, he, John Fisher, and others rode home to Deep Creek Station. There they found the eastbound stage had arrived after it had been attacked, and Hank Harper, the coach driver, was dead, stretched out in the dooryard. On the floor in the sitting room, John Liverton, a passenger from California, was bleeding from a head wound, his two young sons crying next to him.[58]

Near the Eight Mile Station, Indians had attacked Harper's coach. Badly wounded, Harper called to passenger Gordon Mott, Nevada's candidate for Congress, to come up and drive the team. While horses raced at full speed, Mott did as Harper asked. He should have stopped at Eight Mile Station for a change of horses but bypassed it and reached Deep Creek Station. The wounded father recovered enough in two weeks to resume his journey east on a bed in a stagecoach.[59] When a telegraph message from Deep Creek shared news of the stagecoach killing, company officers urged Col. Connor to send help. A stagecoach immediately started from the city, conveying a doctor and five soldiers. Conner notified Fort Ruby, which sent soldiers by stagecoach to the Eight Mile Station.[60]

Eight Mile Station, built of adobe, had two rooms, about sixteen feet apart. Next morning Ransom and others rode to check on it. What they found turned their stomachs:[61]

The cook was lying just outside of the space between the rooms, stripped, scalped and cut all over his body. They had even cut his tongue out before, or after, death, I don't know which, but I think it was before, because they had dobbed his face with blood and then covered that over with flour to make him a white man again.

Ransom's party found the haystacker, Mr. Wood, dead about seventy-five yards north of the house in the rabbit brush. "They had taken off every stitch of clothing and left him as naked as he was when born." They left three or four broken arrows near his body, which they had pulled out of him to get his clothes off. Ransom and his men left, then returned that evening and buried the men. Back at Deep Creek they buried the driver about a half of a mile from the station. Despite the bloodshed, the mail was not interrupted.[62]

This attack at Eight Mile Station started the Gosiute War. "This is the first Indian difficulty we have had upon our road since the line was started," Overland treasurer Rumfield emphasized, admitting that until then "passengers and employees were seldom armed when upon the road."[63] General Connor dispatched a full company of cavalry under Captain Sam Smith and a separate detachment under Lt. Quinn toward Ruby Valley on March 25.[64]

A telegraph report published on March 22 said raiders ran off with "about forty horses belonging to Major Howard Egan, from Deep Creek ranch." For about a week Ransom, Fisher, and others hunted for missing livestock. Out of twelve milk cows and calves once in their corral they found but two or three cows with young calves.[65]

Howard Drives a Stagecoach After the Driver Is Killed

Depredations continued, and "for a time the Indians were so troublesome that a soldier was sent with every stage."[66] In late March Indians attacked at Willow Springs (now Callao) and Boyd's Station, and then in April at Faust Station. On May 19, Indians targeted an eastbound stagecoach on which Howard was riding next to the driver, W. R. Simpson. The passengers were soldiers. Indians shot and killed Simpson, so Howard "pulled him into the boot, got the reins, stopped the coach, and ordered out the soldiers to return the fire." Because the Indians hid in the rocks, the soldiers' shots were ineffective.[67]

Two California newspapers published such far-fetched lies about this episode that Howard felt compelled to correct them. A woman claimed that she and her small child were the only passengers on that coach, saying that when the driver was killed she leaped out and took the reins, cut a horse loose that the Indians had killed, and drove two miles to safety. "I have been not a little amused in reading the romantic story of the 'brave woman,' clipped from the San Francisco Alta," Howard wrote to that newspaper.[68] He also corrected a newspaper account given by a soldier who likewise had not been there, John C. Allen, which, seeking to ridicule Mormons, incorrectly claimed that Howard sped the coach off so as to "not give the soldiers a chance to have a shot at the Indians" and let the Indians get away. Howard sent a factual account, a corrective, to the *Sacramento Daily Union*:

> I stopped the coach within a rod after the driver was shot, and the soldiers jumped out and opened fire upon the Indians, and they supposed that one of the redskins was hit. We were in pistol range, and a little incident of the time will show how far I whipped the horses out of the way to give the Indians a chance. One of the soldiers was a son of Ireland, with a rich brogue of the mother country. A ball struck at his feet, scattering the dust around him. "J—!" says Pat, "Did you see that?" After they had opened upon the Indians, I ordered them into the coach, not to be exposed to the enemy, hid behind rocks, while they loaded; and I took the reins and drove further for our advantage, but the soldiers had no hindrance from me for "a chance to have a show at the Indians." I seldom make such statements, but it is only common justice to one's self, and a set-off to [Allen's] slur upon "Major Egan of Mormondom," to say that I have done more to preserve the Overland Mail Line from Indian depredations than any person in or out of Mormondom.[69]

Killings and Arson at Canyon Station

A small squad of soldiers patrolling the mail line found an Indian camp about fifteen or twenty miles from Simpson Springs and killed all that were in camp, men, women, and children, leaving none to tell the tale.[70] The camp's men, who had been out hunting, returned and found their families murdered. Until then, this band had been friendly to the whites. Getting reinforcements, the angry Indians sought revenge. They chose Canyon Station, fourteen miles by trail east from Deep Creek, for a surprise attack on July 8.

Two Indians spied on the station, then reported that five or six men there slept in a barn but went into the dugout for meals, without their guns. The next morning Indians waited until the men were called to breakfast, then shot arrows that set the barn's canvas roof on fire. When the men at breakfast rushed out of the dug-out to fetch their firearms, nearly all were killed. Indians killed two hostlers and five of Connor's soldiers, and looted and burned the station. They threw one man on a woodpile and set it on fire. They killed a man who was bald and had a beard, scalping him in both places. The Indians took four head of horses, as much of the harness as suited them, all the guns and ammunition that were there, all the provisions and cooking utensils they thought worth carrying away, and then burned everything else. They took the clothes off of every man and left the bodies just where they fell. All this had been done without the victims firing a shot. "A most complete surprise and massacre," Ransom termed it.[71] The water hauler and three soldiers coming from Deep Creek witnessed the finish of the massacre. Ransom's brother Ras and half-brother Willie, hauling grain from Salt Lake City to the mail stations, arrived at the scene a day later.[72]

The 1863 Gosiute Peace Treaty

On October 13, 1863, a "Treaty of Peace and Friendship" was signed in Tooele Valley between the United States and the Shoshone-Gosiute tribe. The treaty was not one of land cession, nor did the Gosiutes give up their sovereignty. They did, however, agree to end all hostile actions against the whites and to allow several routes of travel to pass through their country. They agreed to the construction of military posts and station houses wherever necessary. Stage lines, telegraph lines, and railways could be built. Mines, mills, and ranches would be permitted. Timber could be cut. In return, the federal government agreed to compensate the Gosiutes $1,000 per year for twenty years in payment for the destruction of their game. Signing for the Gosiutes were Tabby, Adaseim, Tintsa-pa-gin, and Harry-nup, while James Duane Doty, Indian Commissioner, and Brigadier-General Connor signed for the United States. The treaty was ratified in 1864 and announced by President Lincoln on January 17, 1865.[73] The Gosiutes refused to relocate to designated places, including in the Uintah Valley, Fort Hall in Idaho, or the Indian Territory (Oklahoma). During the 1870s they still farmed in the Deep Creek area.[74]

Wells Fargo's "Grand Consolidation"

Despite Indian attacks during 1863, the stagecoach mail that year went through well enough. Then, as usual, winter cold and snow disrupted schedules. In the spring of 1864, high water hampered runs, which meant that the coach mail didn't become regular until June. That month the Overland Mail contract expired. Ben Holladay won the new four-year contract for the east wing, from the Missouri River to Salt Lake City. Nationally he was considered the "stagecoach king." But the west wing contract, from Salt Lake City to Folsom, California, once again went to the Overland Mail Company controlled by Wells Fargo. Howard continued to serve as division manager for the next four years, from October 1, 1864 to September 30, 1868. The new contract called for stagecoaches to move the letter mail between the Missouri River and California in sixteen days for the eight "good" months of the year and twenty days during the other four months. Heavier mail would be shipped by sea. What kept the stagecoach business profitable were the passenger and express handling.[75]

The overland mail "achieved its greatest success" during the mid-1860s.[76] In 1865 the service on the west wing performed with "reasonable regularity," but not so the east wing. That year the superintendent of Wells Fargo and Company made a record run on the west wing on an express that went from San Francisco to Salt Lake City in three days and seventeen hours. That year, too, Speaker of the U.S. House of Representatives Schuyler Colfax and his party traveled from Salt Lake City to Virginia City, Nevada (575 miles) in a fast seventy-two hours.[77]

A passenger with Colfax, Samuel Bowles, reported that the Overland Mail stations "are ten to fifteen miles apart; at every station fresh horses, already harnessed, took the place of the old, with a delay of from two to four minutes only; every fifty miles a new driver took his place on the box; whatever meals were to be eaten, they were ready to serve on arrival." Horses were "ever fresh and fat," and drivers were "gentlemanly, intelligent and better dressed than their passengers." Division superintendents traveled with the contingent "for each two hundred miles," although Bowles mentioned no

Farrell R. Collett drawing from The Stagecoach in Utah History, *Dixon Paper Company of Salt Lake City, 1962*

names. "The speed rarely fell below eight miles an hour, and often ran up to twelve."[78]

After the Civil War ended, traffic picked up considerably, and two or more stages were required in nearly every run of passengers and mail.[79] During the severe winter of 1865–66 the system carried the mail with "fair speed and regularity," although December and January saw slowdowns. A letter from Ruby Valley dated December 29, 1865 said the snow was fifteen inches deep on the level and three to fifteen feet deep where the road crossed summits, but

> ...notwithstanding these difficulties the Overland Mail Company's stages arrive and depart with their usual regularity, making the trip from Salt Lake City to Virginia [City] in 120 hours; distance six hundred miles. This company never was in finer condition for winter service, having an abundance of grain for their horses, as well as hay; plenty of provisions for their men, and sleighs and light coaches distributed so well along the route that it is impossible for snow or anything else almost to stop them.[80]

It seemed to be like a well-oiled machine. But then, because of track-laying railroad crews, the overland stagecoaches' days were numbered. The overland route shrank with every new mile of rails laid. Stagecoach terminals constantly moved to where the tracks had extended. In 1866 Ben Holladay had a far-flung and highly successful transportation network, even extending from Salt Lake City into Oregon and Montana. He renamed his main overland route, the "Overland Stage Line," in 1866, calling it the "Holladay Overland Mail & Express Company." But then, seeing the fading overland stagecoach future, he bailed out.

Wells Fargo and Co. Overland Stage

On November 1, 1866, the "grand consolidation" occurred. The Holladay interests, the Overland Mail Company, Wells Fargo & Co., and other stage companies combined into one giant enterprise controlling all transportation and mail facilities west of the Missouri River.[81] By this purchase, Wells Fargo "became owners of all stage lines of any consequence between the Missouri River and California." They reduced passenger fares sharply, replaced worn-out equipment, and stocked the entire line with horses as fine as any. "Under Wells Fargo ownership, coaching in the West reached its ultimate peak of glory, efficiency, and service to the public," anticipating a bright future through connector lines to the railroad towns and by gaining contracts to ship utilizing the railroads.[82]

In 1867, Theodore F. Tracy, the former general agent of Wells Fargo's California subsidiary, the Pioneer Stage Company, became the general agent for Wells, Fargo & Company in Salt Lake City to supervise both banking and express operations. Howard had a new boss. A photo taken about 1868 shows Wells Fargo stables, repair shops, and storage sheds on Second East between South Temple and First South.[83]

The "Golden Spike" Forces Stagecoach Relocations

In the Pacific Railway Act of July 1, 1862, Congress authorized the Union Pacific and Central Pacific railroads to "lay out, locate, construct, furnish, maintain and enjoy a continuous railroad and telegraph" from the Missouri River to the Pacific Ocean. The Central Pacific would build east from Sacramento while the Union Pacific would build west from Omaha. The two sets of tracks would connect in or near Utah.[84] Funds for the ambitious project came from government bonds and from extensive grants to the railroads of salable government land. The Central Pacific drove its first spike on October 26, 1863, in Sacramento. The Union Pacific didn't start construction until the Civil War ended and freed up manpower and equipment, which meant they laid their first track in Omaha, Nebraska on July 10, 1865. As the two companies' track crews advanced towards each other, trains traveled as far as the new tracks allowed.

The Central Pacific Railroad's progress held great interest for Howard's stagecoach division. The Sierras required tunnels and bridges, so tracks did not reach Reno, Nevada until May 4, 1868. On June 18 the first passenger train crossed the Sierras and puffed into Reno. That August Howard failed to convince Central Pacific officials that their best and shortest track course was the central trail route rather than up and along the Humboldt River.[85] Two months later, with stagecoach overland mail contracts scheduled to expire, the government authorized the contract holders to stay in business until the railroad opened. In November 1868 the stage route westbound ran only as far as Austin, Nevada, some fifty miles west of Roberts Creek, and then the coaches cut directly north on a new route to Argenta (twelve miles east of today's

Battle Mountain) to connect with the Central Pacific railroad.[86] With two sets of tracks nearing each other, the overland stagecoach people lost enthusiasm, such that "the overland mail service during the winter of 1868–1869 was very unsatisfactory." On April 10, 1869, when the approaching railroads were but 110 miles apart, the stages began running directly between the termini. Stagecoach operations between Salt Lake City and Austin were abandoned and their thirty-six stations "stripped of valuables."[87] Before the railroad tracks met, Howard, under contract to Wells Fargo, located a new stage route from Humboldt Wells to Bear River by way of Promontory City. Wells Fargo then placed stagecoaches on this route.[88]

On May 10, 1869, at Promontory Summit, Utah Territory, the famous "driving of the golden spike" connected the Central Pacific and Union Pacific tracks. The transcontinental railroad opened, replacing forever the overland stagecoach business.[89] The railroad line meant a partial victory to proponents, including Howard, who had lobbied long and hard since the mid-1850s, and proved by pony and stagecoach that the main transportation route to and from California should be along or near a central route, not a southern one.

The golden spike didn't end stagecoaching. Rather, the railroad's stopping places all along its line became opportunities for needed feeder stagecoach lines. At the silver-rush town of Austin, Nevada, for example, a stagecoach route opened north-south connecting with the Central Pacific at Argenta.[90] Wells Fargo and Company's surplus equipment in Utah, including $70,000 worth of excellent Concord coaches, found new homes, particularly in the mining regions of the Dakotas and Montana and in the Northwest.[91] Until near the close of the nineteenth century, these feeder stagecoach lines remained "the chief means of travel throughout the mountainous and sparsely inhabited regions of the west."[92]

Of Howard's sixty-two years of life, he spent more years in the stagecoach business (ten) than in any other type of employment.[93] Any monument to Howard or painting depicting him should include in it a stagecoach, but not with him as a driver, for that would misrepresent his role. He did hands-on management and supervisory work during those years. He shouldered responsibilities for hundreds of employees, hundreds of expensive vehicles, thousands of livestock, tons of U.S. mail and freight, hundreds if not thousands of passengers, dozens of home and relay stations, and scores of Native Americans. Because of his responsibilities, he personally interacted with and had the trust and respect of top business leaders, LDS officials, military officers, and government agents. To do his job well and right, Howard spent most of his time out on dirt roads and byways monitoring, inspecting, and finding solutions to problems. ♦

~ 27 ~

The 1860s, Deep Creek Ranch, and the Family

At Deep Creek, Howard developed a well-supplied and staffed "home" station for the Pony Express and stagecoach operations, as well as a telegraph station, sizeable ranch with flocks and herds, sawmill, and store. The Egan spread was a prime oasis on the traffic-filled road west. Deep Creek became his home-away-from-home. It produced income for him and the family, as did the store he set up a hundred miles west at the Ruby Valley Station in Nevada. Because Howard needed his sons' help, he gave them responsibilities from young ages. They became valuable contributors to his work. Deep Creek had other settlers, so the Egan properties had neighbors. A traveler in 1868 found "quite a little town" there.[1]

Family Changes

When the 1860s opened, Howard was forty-four and Tamson thirty-five. They entered the stage of life when children start to reach adulthood, marry, leave home, find livelihoods, produce grandchildren, and perhaps serve Church missions. That decade brought the family several big changes. As noted earlier, on January 1, 1861, Ras was the first of the Egan children to marry.[2] A month later, on February 5, Tamson gave birth to her and Howard's final child, Ira Ernest. Then, a year after that, Tamson and Howard lost their son Horace Adelbert. He died on March 24, 1862, at age fourteen. He was the child born at Winter Quarters while Howard was away with Brigham Young's 1847 pioneer company. Horace is buried in Salt Lake City.[3]

Another family event happened on March 2, 1863, when Howard and Tamson became grandparents for the first time, with the birth of Ras and Minnie's daughter

Tamson Minnie, in Salt Lake City. After her birth, Ras moved his little family out to Ruby Valley, Nevada. On October 10, 1863, Ransom married Amanda Andrus in Salt Lake City. He was twenty-three, she fifteen.[4] Howard's daughter by Nancy Redding, Helen Jeanette, was married in 1866 to John K. Irvine.[5] They had a son, John K. Irvine, born on February 7, 1867, giving Howard another grandchild. Then, in 1868–1869, Ras was the first of the Egan children to serve an LDS proselytizing mission. His wife Minnie gave birth to another child while Ras was in England. By the time the 1860s ended, Howard and Tamson had two sons married and through them seven grandchildren—Ras's four and Ransom's three. In addition, Howard had a married daughter who had a son, giving Howard eight grandchildren.

Mary Ann Fisher Egan with baby Tamson, Egan Family Archives

Deep Creek Valley

The Egan story during the 1860s centers in Deep Creek, an isolated valley roughly 170 miles southwest of Salt Lake City.[6] Tamson continued to live in the family home in Salt Lake City, a place much safer, cleaner, and liveable for her and little Ira than the distant, dirty, fly-infested, far-from-everything Deep Creek stagecoach station and ranch house, where she rarely visited. The Deep Creek Valley is about four miles wide and thirty-five miles long, bordered on the east by the Deep Creek Mountains and on the west by rolling hills of the Antelope Range. The Great Salt Desert borders Deep Creek Valley on the north. Namesake Deep Creek runs through the valley, fed by three small streams known as East, Middle, and West Forks. These flow together in the north part of the valley, just north of the Egan station and property.[7]

Deep Creek Valley, author's photo

Today the small, unincorporated community of Ibapah, originally called Deep Creek, is the valley's only settlement. It is in southwestern Tooele County about seventy miles south of Wendover, Nevada and reachable by one paved highway accessible from Highway 93A.[8] Next to Ibapah are the headquarters for the Confederated Tribes of the Goshute (current spelling) Reservation, an area which consists of scattered farm and ranch lands and a trading post. While living at Deep Creek, the Egans constantly interacted with Gosiutes.

Egan Station and the Ranch

When the short-lived Pony Express ended late in 1861, Howard continued to manage the ongoing mail and passenger stagecoach operations. Deep Creek served as a home station. Howard's ranch supported livestock essential to his business. The Egans recorded the brands they'd put on their livestock. Howard, listing the Salt Lake City Nineteenth Ward as his residence, registered his "HE" brand on April 1, 1861. On April 1, 1862, Ransom, with residences in Salt Lake City and Ruby Valley, registered an "HRE" brand, and Ras, of Salt Lake City and Deep Creek, filed an "REE" brand.[9] In 1860, Howard opened a store close to the Deep Creek Station.[10] The station served as Howard's on-the-trail headquarters. Constantly busy superintending the mail and stage, he initially turned ranch operations over to Harrison Severe. Then in June 1862 he put son Ransom in charge, and Severe returned to Grantsville.[11]

Deep Creek Station, LDS Church History Library

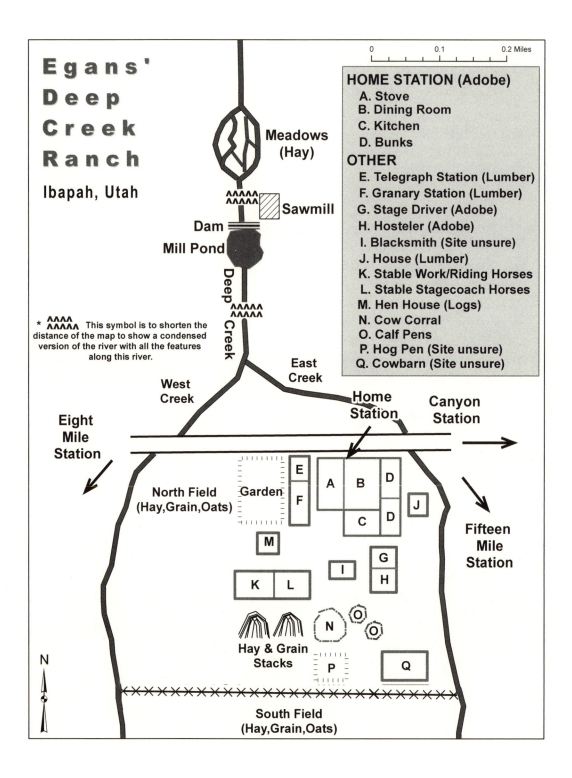

John Fisher, who was Ras's wife's brother, described the Egan holdings as they were in 1863 when he visited Deep Creek:

> Major Egan owned an extensive ranch, raising a large amount of grain and keeping a large number of cattle, also some horses which were used for both saddle and harness. Besides this he kept the hotel, and boarding house, at which the overland mail employees boarded. It was called a "home" station, that is where the drivers change; it was a regular meal station for passengers to take their meals, which taken together and including the ranchmen made it quite a busy little place to be so far from any settlement...Major Egan kept a general store, also the Western Union Telegraph company kept a regular office there.[12]

Ransom said Deep Creek was "our [the Egan sons'] principal home." There, "Father and his sons were quite successful in raising hay and grain for the mail stations and in ranching." They supplied "stations along the road" with beef and mutton. They kept about twenty cows for milking, which chore "fell to the lot" of Ransom and Hyrum, Howard's son by Mary Ann Tuttle. Egan sons, too, had "the cowboy job of riding the range for beef cattle, hunting horses and herding sheep," as well as helping on the farm, plowing, planting, irrigating, and hauling hay.[13]

Both Ransom and half-brother William wrote fairly good descriptions of the Deep Creek Station and ranch.[14] It spread out for several miles. Ransom positioned the main adobe station house and its auxiliary operations in a prime location a half-mile south (upstream) from where Deep Creek's three branches came together. The East Creek was east of them and the West Creek a short distance to the west. Downstream, two miles north of the station house, workers built a dam and erected a sawmill. Even farther downstream (north) the combined waters in Deep Creek fanned out into a meadow. From the meadow, workers put up hay each season for the mail station.

Ransom said the home station was a one-story adobe building, apparently facing north. Two rooms on its east were rest or bunk rooms. In the middle were a big dining room and a kitchen. At the west end was a store. William's account says a lumber addition on the west housed the telegraph office in the north part and a granary in the south. Howard's people operated the telegraph until 1868 when Jim Ferguson moved there and took it over.[15] In line with the east end of the main building but a bit south, William said, the stage driver and the hostler had rooms built of adobe. Across a yard about forty feet west from the kitchen stood a large chicken house made of logs. On the south side of that yard and a few rods from the house were stables, those on the east for stagecoach horses and those on the west for riding and work horses. South of the stables were hay stacks and grain stacks when in season. East of the stack yard were the cow corral and calf pens. Somewhere the complex had a blacksmith shop. Nearby too, but not too near, was a hog pen. The complex must have had a barn for the milk cows.

Some sixteen feet west of the telegraph office was the northeast corner of a field, and in that field's corner was a garden, fenced off along the road and from the corner up to the hen house. That field was the complex's north field, which ran west of the station through to the West Creek. An upper or south field was about a half mile from the station. It was fenced with a "stake and rider"-type fence.[16] In the north and south fields the ranch hands raised some hay but mostly grain and oats for the stagecoach horses.

Egan Stories About Deep Creek

Pioneering the West contains several stories, mostly told by Ransom, about happenings at or near the Deep Creek home and ranch, and about Howard. One humorous episode Ransom titled "Irrigation":

> When Father and his partner (Mr. Severe) had got some land cleared, plowed and seeded to wheat on their new location at Deep Creek, Mr. Severe running the place while Father tended to his mail business, Father, in passing that way, stopped over long enough to ride over the place with the boss to see what had been done and lay plans for the future. In going along a small field of grain Father said, "This looks fine, but don't it need irrigating?" "Yes," said the boss, "I sent a couple of hands early this morning with their dinners to turn the creek and water it. I wonder where they are." This was about the middle of the afternoon. In going around a clump of willows they found the two men lying on their backs, on the west side of the willows, both sound asleep, paying no heed to the sting of flies or mosquitos. After they had been awakened Father said, "Boys, if you had wanted to take a little rest why didn't you get in the shade?" "Why," said one, "it was shady here when we laid down." They must have been very tired, for they had lain there at least six or eight hours.[17]

Another story, "Coyote in Chicken House," delightfully shows Howard's fun sense of humor:

> It was just at dusk as father came out of the stable, he saw a coyote enter the hen house, the door of which had not yet been closed for the night. He ran as fast as he could and pulled the door shut; he then ran to the telegraph office for the shotgun that most always could be found there. "Ed (the operator's name), hand me the shotgun, quick!" "What is it?" "Oh, only a coyote in the hen house." In place of handing out the gun he came out with it, and excited, ran for the hen house, but seeing the door shut, he said, "Where is the coyote?" "Inside," said Father, "give me the gun and I will get him." "No, let me shoot him. Open the door." The door was opened, but it was so dark inside that they could not see very plain. But finally Ed said, "I see him" and he fired. There was a terrible commotion in that hen house, for there were about one hundred

chickens and a coyote very badly scared. The coyote was trying to escape by way of the roosts, knocking the chickens to the floor, but it was not chicken he wanted just then. Father said, "No use to shoot again till we get a lantern so we can see the thief. Stay in the door till I get a light." "Alright, hurry up."[18]

When Howard brought the light, they could see the coyote squatted in one corner watching for a chance to spring out the door, "chickens fairly climbing all over him." Ed fired again "causing another outburst of squawks and cacklings." When the smoke cleared, Howard dragged the coyote outside and then picked up five or six large chickens that Ed had shot. He said, jesting, "See here, young man, what you have done, and on purpose, too, I believe."

The next morning Father was up early. He took the coyote that had frozen stiff during the night and set it up about thirty yards from the house in the garden and propped it up with some sticks to appear as if alive. Then going to the office, he called Ed to hand out the gun. "What for?" "A coyote in the garden—the gun quick before he goes." The gun comes and Ed with it. "Where is he?" and turning around the corner of the house, said, "I see him; that's my hide," and he fired. The coyote seemed to squat a little. Father said, "You missed him." Ed fired again. This time the coyote fell down. "I got him this time," he said, and stood the gun up against the house while he climbed over the fence to get the coyote to place beside the one he killed last night.

He found it frozen stiff. He then knew he'd been tricked. He turned around to accuse Howard, but Howard "was in the mess-room telling the boys how Ed had killed a dead coyote, and when breakfast was called, every one Ed met had a grin on his face."

But the fun wasn't done. At dinner when all were seated around the table, the cook placed cooked chickens on the table, looked at Ed, and nodded. Ed said, "Is this the chickens the coyote killed?" "I guess so," came the answer, "for they were plumb full of shot." The diners burst out laughing.

Another coyote story tells about one of the men who went outside and left the bunkhouse door open. The blacksmith, whose bunk faced the door, saw a coyote come into the room. He kept still until the man came back, then he said, "Close the door quick! There is a coyote in here." One man was frightened and feared the coyote would bite his bare legs, so he attempted to leave. But the blacksmith said, "Stand still a minute while I light the candle. Then we can get him." The man obeyed, and when the light was made, there in one corner and under the bunks crouched the coyote. It was "soon made ready for skinning."[19]

One dark evening a coyote had the misfortune to look for dinner in the hog pen. A ranch hand passed by and heard the old sow making a terrible fuss. He went to the side of the pen and swung his lantern over. "He could see the old sow backed up in a corner with her six or eight young pigs behind her, her bristles sticking straight up and her mouth open. In the opposite corner crouched a large coyote. Ransom left the rest of the story to our imagination by simply noting, "Well, his hide was worth one dollar."[20]

A large dog named Pompy, which had black curly hair, became the subject of several Deep Creek stories. William called it a Newfoundland dog.[21] Pompy had been taught to carry things in his mouth, such as a full bucket of water. Once he carried a large dinner basket for four workmen fixing the sawmill. One day Ransom rode two miles to pick up a plastering trowel he'd loaned a man. Pompy put his paws high up on the saddle and signaled he wanted to carry the trowel. "So I placed the handle of it in his mouth." Pompy laid down with the trowel between his paws. When Ransom started for home Pompy picked up the trowel and followed close behind the horse. When almost home, Ransom saw Pompy had dropped the trowel. The dog, knowing he was in trouble, indicated he wanted to go back down the trail. Ransom followed him to a bend in the creek, where Pompy waded in, stood still, and stuck his nose in the water. He'd dropped the trowel earlier while drinking from the creek, but now couldn't find it. Ransom located it four feet down stream, eighteen inches deep, and coaxed Pompy there. The dog lunged and came up with the handle in his mouth, and carried it home.

Treasurer Rumfield's Visit

Overland Mail treasurer Hiram Rumfield stopped at Deep Creek Station in June 1862 on his way by stagecoach to Carson City. From Rush Valley, he said, "our road lay through one of the most dreary regions to be found on the American continent. It is … the 100 mile desert in the great basin. It is nothing, in fact, but a succession of brazen looking, barren mountains, and alkalie flats." But of Deep Creek, he said, "this valley is a beautiful one…the only settlement is close to this station. Some half dozen Mormon families reside here." He noted that "a young married man named Egan," meaning Ransom, owned and kept the station. This Egan was the "son of Major Egan, a man who occupies a prominent place in the history of the Mormons."

Rumfield found Mrs. Egan, Minnie, to be young, beautiful, and accomplished. "While I write this," he said in a letter, "this generous and simple hearted woman is engaged in singing an accompaniment to the tones of the Melodean. How home-like the associations, and how chastening to the soul of the weary way-faring stranger, are the gentle tones of the female voice." He felt impressed by "many of the comforts and some of the refinements of eastern life" he found in that home.[22]

William Egan's Recollections

William Egan, Tamson's son by James Monroe, had a lot to say about his experiences at the Deep Creek ranch. When he was about eleven, around 1862, Howard took him and his mother for a stagecoach ride from their city home to the Army's new Camp Douglas, where the University of Utah is now, and then a long way to Rush Valley, almost to Tooele. Willie, as he was called, liked the sites but especially liked their lunch, which had pineapple they'd brought from Camp Douglas, the first he'd ever tasted.[23]

His biggest and best memory was of a long trip he made in 1863 at age twelve to Carson City and back to Deep Creek.[24] This trip introduced the lad to what his often-absent stepfather Howard spent so much time doing. City-boy Willie went as a night herder of two teams of six mules, with his older brother Ras in charge. These were father Howard's teams, and one of Ras's main jobs was stocking mail stations from Salt Lake City to Placerville with grain for the stagecoach horses. The assembly camp for Ras's wagons and animals was "over Jordan." Willie visited the camp with other boys and Ras. Eri Butler, nearly Willie's age, was a night herder going with Willie. Willie's half-brother Hyrum William, Howard's son by Mary Ann Tuttle, also went, and likewise entered into father Howard's real world. Young Hyrum's mother had remarried Titus Billings and had three children with him. It's likely her hard circumstances in Manti caused her to let Hyrum go live and work with the Egans.[25]

In addition to mules, the boys' travel party took wagons pulled by oxen. "The mule teams being faster took the lead." They followed the usual stagecoach trail. One night, soon after passing Simpson Springs, both night-herd boys fell asleep "and the mules were nowhere to be seen the next morning." Ras searched and found them near Dugway, the next station. Before reaching Fish Springs the party crossed an alkali flat that was "a sea of white sticky mud" where wheels went down to the hub and ox teams had "a bad time." The gnats and mosquitoes were awful. Then they came upon a grisly scene at Canyon Station right after Indians had burned it and killed two station men, four soldiers, and a wagon man, according to William. They reached Deep Creek, but while there the Eight Mile station was burned up and the station men killed (see "The Gosiute Indian War" in Chapter Twenty-six).

Willie's group rested a few days at Deep Creek, "it being our own ranch and home headquarters. The ox teams staid longer than we did." Hyrum remained at Deep

Creek and, after Willie returned from Carson, the two boys became ranch hands. In his trip account, William names every stagecoach station along the way, a listing that underscores how many stations Howard supervised and how rough and desolate the road was. After Deep Creek, William noted, came the Schell Creek Mountains, Steptoe Valley, and narrow, rock-bound Egan Canyon, through what he termed the Ruby Valley Bluffs. "We had no trouble herding the mules through these places where the road and water was good." From the bluffs' summit they moved down into Ruby Valley. The store there, he said, "was kept, owned by Father and W. H. Shearman and there was a camp of soldiers a short distance away that had been called out to protect the Overland Mail." They crossed the "Ruby Valley mountains," came to Jacob's Well, "and had rough roads and high summits to cross over to Diamond Springs." From then on they found "not so much mountain country." After Sulphur Springs they proceeded to Roberts Creek, Camp Station, Dry Creek, Cape Horn, and Simpson Park.

"At Reese River they sent me out from camp to get a bucket of water from the River," William wrote. West of camp he found a stream so small he assumed it was a branch of the river. He filled the bucket there, returned, and learned that the little stream was in fact the Reese River. From the Reese River Station to the Mount Airey Station was twelve miles, but "the roads were rough." At Castle Rock, Edwards Creek, Cold Springs, and Middle Gate "we had no trouble with the night herding." Fairview, he said, "was quite a nice looking place we camped early that afternoon and I went under the wagon and slept until the sun was about one hour high above the level prairie and I felt sure it was morning but found out it was just near sunset." Mountain Wells's water came from hand-dug wells. Next they came to Still Water in "a sandy desert country." At Sand Springs the wheels of the wagons sank halfway to the hubs. The drifting sands formed mounds as big as a haystack at places where some bush gathered the drifting sands. After crossing the long stretch of sand "we came to alkali flats for some distance." They reached Bisbys Station then "passed Rag Town a place composed of canvass tents. Here we saw some Hurdy Girls dancing with the miners. The town was nearly abandoned." Their next stations were Nevada Station, Desert Wells, and Dayton. "At Dayton the stamp mills were crushing the ore from Gold Hill and other mines near." At last they reached their destination, Carson City, Nevada's capital. They had traveled 390 miles from Deep Creek, quite a trip for twelve-year-old Willie.

In Carson City, William said, they bought goods for the store at Ruby and the one at Deep Creek. They ate meals in a restaurant, "which was a change from our normal fare on the road of bacon and flap jacks and gravey with very few other changes." Loading up quickly, they "made tracks back to Ruby Valley as fast as it was possible." They unloaded part of their cargo into the store at Ruby Valley and sent the rest on to the Deep Creek store. Willie stayed at Ruby Valley for a time and assisted on the ranch

Howard had set up there. After helping put up hay, he "went on back to Deep Creek with the mule teams, but my brother Erastus staid on the Ruby Valley Ranch where he later on moved his wife and family from Salt Lake and lived there for several years." After returning to Deep Creek, Willie stayed there for the next six years.

Young Ranch Hands

At the Deep Creek ranch, Willie and Hyrum, ages twelve and thirteen, had to milk the cows, about twenty head.[26] "We allowed the calves to do nearly one-half of the milking," William wrote. The two boys slept together in the granary most of the time "and Father would call us in the morning to get and milk the cows and used to say we should answer by our feet striking floor as the sailors did. He had been an old sailor." The two boys had to ride the range, mostly at the upper end of the valley, "and hunt for beef cattle and new milk cows from the stock that were turned out on the range." When hunting stock, "we always carried six shooter revolvers and a shot gun or rifle." He and Hyrum "were pretty good chums" during the six years William stayed there. Deep Creek became Hyrum's home well into adulthood. He homesteaded, married, and had two children there.[27]

The ranch needed lumber. A millwright named Thompson came from Salt Lake City. Near the dam site two miles north of the station, he directed men to construct a sash sawmill. Ranch hands, including Gosiutes, felled trees and hauled logs from Eight Mile Canyon and Fifteen Mile Creek. "The mill worked all right but being an upright sashsaw done slow work," William said, but "from lumber cut from the logs which I helped to haul from 15 Mile Creek a house was built a short distance east of the regular original ranch house." A bonus for Willie and Hyrum was that the mill pond "made us a good place to swim in and we took advantage of it often."[28]

Howard bought about a thousand sheep. He assigned Willie to tend the sheep during the day and drive them into the willow-and-slats sheep-pen at night. Nearly every evening five or more sheep were killed to supply mutton to other mail stations. "This reduced the flock until they were all gone," William said.

The Egan spread used whatever hired hands they could recruit. These included stranded prospectors, visitors, and Indians. Willie thought the Gosiutes were

> …pretty good workers at some things as pitching hay, and they would work at it all day for the food we gave them. The old men were very awkward at it, but the young men such as father had made use of for many years could do as much work as any of us. We most often had to furnish the loaders as they could not do it.

The Indians "could not milk cows." At the lower end of Deep Creek Valley, the ranch had "many acres of wild hay land," so the ranch "employed these natives every year to help us" pitch the hay. "They were a great help to us," William said. Some work the Indians could not be taught to do, "so father hired men going to California gold hunting," some of whom stayed with him from year to year. "These men with the Indians and ourselves done the harvesting and other work connected with the Ranch Farm."[29]

Willie and Hyrum also had to irrigate during the summer. "There was always something to keep us busy," he said. "Father never punished us and never spoke a cross word but once to me." That happened, Will explained, "when we were taking grain to Eight Mile Station. I was driving two yoke of cattle with a loaded wagon and in crossing some cordoroy bridge...I missed the bridge and we had to unload, which made him a little angry." Then, crossing a bridge over the West Creek, the wagon's hind wheels pulled off a plank, so they had to unload again.

> After I delivered the load and was returning home Father rode up behind me and said for me to take his horse and come on in to milk the cow and he would bring the team. He said I must not notice him when he spoke a little angry at me in the lane as he was a little excited. The idea of his apologizing to me hurt me much more than a good licking would do.[30]

Deep Creek, author's photo

Will said that the stack yard in the fall became a threshing floor. A circle of bundles of oats or other grain was stood up, and several yoke of cattle were driven around on the grain until it was pretty well tramped out. Then it was run through a "fanning mill and cleaned." In time they brought a threshing machine from Carson City to do the work.

On January 1, 1865, Willie, then thirteen, started for Skull Valley for beef cattle. He went alone with a good horse, saddle, bedding, pistol, and dog. On day three he reached Grantsville and met, by previous arrangement, a Mr. Lynch. They rounded up about twenty beef cattle and started them west. They had to push the cattle through snow and across alkaline flats and icy sloughs, and once they had to track down cattle that wandered off during the night. They drove the cattle to Deep Creek ranch, where, over time, they were slaughtered to furnish beef for stations along the stage line.[31]

Ruby Valley Store and Farm

Howard operated a store in Ruby Valley, which was halfway between Salt Lake City and Carson City. On today's maps it is forty miles south of Elko. Ruby Valley is one of the most beautiful areas of Nevada. In 1859 Colonel "Uncle Billy" Rogers opened a trading post there. Likewise, George Chorpenning's mail, the Pony Express, and the Overland Mail operated stations there. In September 1862 Col. Patrick Connor established Fort Ruby in the area.

That year, Ransom was helping at Willow Springs (today's Callao), and, not wanting to work there as a hostler, rode back to Ruby Valley where Howard and his partner,

Ruby Valley Pony Express and Stagecoach Station, 1944 photograph.
The restored station is displayed in Elko, Nevada.

W. H. Shearman, "had a good-sized supply store." Howard and Shearman owned the station and were doing a good store business, especially when emigrants traveled through. An 1862 emigrant found "camping ground good with a good spring close by."[32] Ransom had not been paid for a long time, so his father offered to give him an outfit and furnish the necessary supplies and said, "if I would go down the valley and pick out a good place and start a farm, and he would wait till I raised the grain to pay him back. That sounded good to me."[33]

Ransom went out some twenty miles and set up the first farm in Ruby Valley. "It was a fine location," he said; "a mountain stream coming out of a heavy timbered canyon ran through the land down to the lake in the valley below, with an immense strip of meadow land all around it." He built a log house, then plowed to get land ready for fall planting. But then, his father sent him orders to pull up stakes and head for Deep Creek right away. Howard had learned from Dimick Huntington that Indians were going to make raids in that area. "I did not believe it, but then, Father must be obeyed," Ransom said. Using ox teams, he plodded one hundred miles to Deep Creek.

He thought the agreement stipulated he'd be a partner with his father and his brother Ras at Ruby Valley, but something bothered Howard such that he had Ras move there in 1863 and take charge of the business. Ras became the partner instead of Ransom, and farmed the place Ransom had started. Ransom didn't say out loud in *Pioneering the West* that he got treated unfairly, but he implied it.[34] Ras lived at Ruby Valley, except for the period of his Church mission, until 1877.

"Ruby Valley was one of the most important places on the Central Overland Trail," historian Jesse Peterson noted, because "there was plenty of water and grass, and some other provisions soon became available for purchase or trade."[35] In 1864, traveler Mary Warner saw a stagecoach station and half a dozen houses at Ruby Valley. Her emigrant company obtained milk there.[36] In 1865, the Overland employed an estimated fifty men at Ruby. Around 1866, the Overland pushed agriculture development in the valley to support its way stations. It added a twenty-five acre garden, a thousand acre farm, and imported a thresher and three reapers just to handle the hay crop. In 1867 Ruby Valley set up eastern Nevada's first flour mill.[37] Howard, Ransom, and Ras deserve credit for being pioneer developers of that valley. After the overland stagecoach business closed in 1869, ranching took over in Ruby Valley and continues to the present day.

Military Officer in the Short "Morrisite War"

In June 1862 the "Morrisite War" near Ogden pulled Howard from stagecoach work into military duty for a week. He helped enforce a District Court order issued against a zealous religious group led by Joseph Morris who were holding prisoners.[38] "Major Egan" proved to be a key participant.

Morris, an English LDS convert, arrived in Utah in 1853. He became dissatisfied with his income prospects and with the Church, especially its polygamy practices. He claimed to receive revelations commissioning him to be a prophet. He became evangelical, telling people about his visions and gift of prophecy. He gained converts, particularly from the South Weber area. In February 1861, the Church excommunicated him and seventeen followers. He organized his own church, then gathered followers to the abandoned Fort Kingston at the mouth of Weber Canyon. By the spring of 1862 the Morrisites numbered 507 members.[39]

Morris announced dates for Christ's second coming. The dates came and went, so he lost followers, some of whom he forbid to claim property they had turned over to his church. About May 8 or 10, 1862, more than two dozen armed Morrisites captured three dissidents, whom Morris kept imprisoned in a log cabin in the fort. Friends asked the courts for help. When Morrisite leaders burned Utah Supreme Court Chief Justice John F. Kinney's writ of habeas corpus, he ordered their arrest for contempt of court. Acting Utah Governor Frank Fuller ordered deputy U.S. marshal Col. Robert T. Burton to make the arrests. Burton insisted he must have "a strong, overwhelming posse" to awe the Morrisites into compliance and avoid bloodshed.[40] Howard, in Salt Lake City at the time, was recruited into a five-hundred-man posse of horsemen, infantry and artillery. It positioned itself on June 13 on heights above the Kingston fort, which consisted of log cabins, tents, a schoolhouse, a bowery, and a corral.[41]

Col. Burton "deputed Major Howard Egan and another to proceed towards the fort with a white flag, anticipating to be met half way by a like deputation from the fort; but as no notice was taken of the circumstances, the party returned."[42] Morris told his concerned followers that revelation told him God would deliver the group.[43] Col. Burton's men sent a Morrisite herdboy to the fort with a message. It demanded that Morrisite leaders surrender and release their prisoners within a half hour. If they chose to resist they should send their women and children to safety. Soon thereafter, the posse's artillery fired twice, and one cannon ball killed two women and a young girl in the fort. How soon Morrisites returned fire is in dispute. Col. Burton, seventeen years later, said that when small arms fire came from the fort,

Robert Taylor Burton, courtesy Janet Seegmiller

> I interpreted this as an indication that they did not intend to surrender. I then directed Major Howard Egan, with considerable force, to form a line around the east side of the fort, and Major Cunningham was sent to the west side and both received heavy fire before they got into position…firing was done on both sides, and my orders were…to avoid the shedding of blood as far as possible.[44]

"Pretty heavy fire" from the fort killed one posse member.[45] Cannon and small arms fire continued through the day. At dusk the posse withdrew, except for a guard to prevent escapes. On Saturday, rains halted the fighting. By the day's end, Acting Governor Fuller ordered Burton's force to make the arrests or request more force if needed. Sunday morning Col. Burton ordered his men to storm the fort. "Soon the entire fort was surrounded by skirmishing parties under the command of Col. Ross on the north, on the south and east sides under the command of Major Howard Egan and Col. Merrill [of Ogden] together with Capt. Jack's Enfield Rifles.[46]

After meeting considerable resistance, by evening Col. Burton and more than a score of men rushed the fort and ordered the Morrisites to stack their arms. In an escape rush, four Morrisites were killed. Col. Burton regretted the deaths but felt "it could not be helped."[47] Years later Burton was tried for murder, but acquitted. Morrisite War historian LeRoy Anderson concluded that Morris's last actions precipitated the killing of the four.[48]

On Monday evening, June 17, the posse arrived back in Salt Lake City. The next day ninety prisoners appeared before Judge Kinney and were jailed or placed under bond. Ultimately seven Morrisites were convicted of second degree murder and sentenced, but new Utah governor Stephen S. Harding, antagonistic to Mormon dominance in the territory, pardoned them.[49] Howard, meanwhile, returned to his stagecoach responsibilities.

Third District Court Deputy Clerk

In 1862 Howard became a court clerk. "Reposing special trust and confidence in the capacity and integrity of Howard Egan," his certificate of appointment reads, Patrick Lynch, the clerk of the Third Judicial District in the Territory of Utah, appoints Howard "to be my deputy clerk and empower him to fulfill the duties of that office… during my pleasure." Lynch signed the document on April 21, 1862. Apparently Howard's stagecoach work in Salt Lake City made him available to help the court. It's possible his clerk responsibilities had something to do with legal issues out on the stagecoach route.[50]

Old Indian Left to Die

Howard felt compassion for his Indian neighbors, and in one case he showed too much. He learned from a stage driver that Indians had left an old Indian to die not far from the road a mile north of Fish Spring Station, within a semi-circle of gathered sagebrush protecting him from the wind. He was totally blind, almost skeletal, and clothed only with a strip of rabbit skin robe hung around his neck. So, the first time Howard passed that way he tried to help. He told the driver to turn off the road and go to the old man's camp. They found him beside a spring, pulling tiny fish out and eating them. Howard "raised him from the spring and tried to make him understand that he would give him something to eat and a blanket to keep him warm. But he soon found that the old man was very deaf and did not seem to understand a word." Howard helped him back to the sagebrush circle, gave him food and a gallon can of water to last several days, and placed a good blanket around him. He left the old man eating sparingly, as if to make the food last as long as possible.

Howard continued west, but told the stage driver to take food for the man every time he passed that way. On his return trip, Howard asked about the old man. The driver said the man was alive and "seemed some stronger when we left him," but the blanket was gone. Howard rounded up another blanket, more food, and a water can and visited the old man. He found him asleep, woke him, put bread in one hand, a can of water in the other and left him to himself. Howard planned to move the old man near to the station to be supplied and cared for, but on his next trip the man was gone and the sagebrush circle burned. Howard then learned that the old man's relatives, or the band he belonged to, did not want anyone prolonging the man's life. They felt it was time for him to die, which he would do if Howard let him alone.[51]

Wagon Train Ruins and Skeletons

A man named James Pearce, writing in 1902, said that in 1866 he met Howard in Salt Lake City. Pearce told him about his trip in 1849 across the desert west of Skull Valley. Pearce's company of thirty-five men had fourteen wagons drawn by horses, mules, and oxen. They filled their water barrels in present-day Grantsville, but two days into the desert many of their livestock perished. Desperate, the group took four light wagons and the strongest animals and dashed ahead for water, leaving most of their equipage and ten wagons on the desert. They managed to reach California.

Hearing Pearce's account, Howard told Pearce that he himself had been out to those abandoned wagons. He had burned some of them "for the purpose of securing iron," a scarce item. Because of the number of wagons and the animal skeletons,

Howard had presumed the entire train had perished. Pearce put two and two together and said Egan's conclusion probably "is how the record of our death was started," which was untrue.[52]

Tamson's Family Letters

"Mother came to Deep Creek," William noted. Her letters say she was there in January and February 1868. He said she took charge of the kitchen. She "made cheese from the large amount of milk that we had." A few of her letters written during the 1860s survive. On November 24, 1867, she wrote from Salt Lake City to her brother Richard Parshley, probably in New Hampshire.[53] She requested him to send likenesses of several relatives she named. She said she weighed 148 pounds, down from 176. She sent him postcards that depicted Salt Lake City. "I have none of my family [at] home only Ira since July," she said, and "have not seen Mr Egan since then, he is pretty well but busy and I have not seen Howard [Ransom] nor Willie for a year." Willie would be home soon, she said, and son Ransom "is one hundred miles south of here with the threshing machine and Erastus' wife has another fine son, now she has three sons and one daughter, so you see that I have six Grandchildren, that makes one seem old." Ira would be seven in February, and "he says tell his cousins that he will come and see them sometime when the railroad gets here and it is within four days travel now by stage."[54]

On February 9, 1868, Tamson, while visiting Deep Creek, wrote again to her brother Richard. She told him to be sure to address letters for her to *her* and not to husband Howard in Salt Lake City. Otherwise the post office would forward the letters to Howard at Deep Creek. "I left home for this place on the 10th of January," she said, "was thirty four hours coming to this place by stage two hundred miles had a pleasant trip found all well. It has been very cold weather ever since I came here." Given Howard's position with the company, Tamson no doubt rode the stagecoach for free. Big news in that day was the transcontinental railroad construction, so she again told her brother that the tracks then were "within four days stage travel of Salt Lake City." She and little Ira were counting the days for their train trip. "Ira says Mother can we go pretty soon to see them, the fifth of this month was his birthday seven years old." Tamson and Ira later did go to East Barnstead to visit her family.[55]

At Deep Creek, she said, Ira played with an Indian boy who brought water and wood in for the family. The Indian killed six birds with his bow and arrow, which became dinner. Tamson found her son Willie there, now age seventeen, and "he is lots of company for his father, he is always on the move and asking questions." Willie had a quiver filled with arrows and was something of a sportsman. Tamson said her son Ras was "a good boy," then jested that "they say he is like his Ma." She complained to Richard that her brother Charles didn't write to her. She said she had sent Richard two newspapers, the *Deseret News* and the *Salt Lake Telegraph*. "Mr. Egan," she added, "was glad to get hold of an eastern paper. I wish you could send him some." She signed her letter "Your affectionate sister, Tamson P. Egan."[56]

Ras's Mission to England, 1868–1869

After Ras and Minnie Egan's first baby was born in March 1863, the three of them moved to Ruby Valley, where Ras did ranching in connection with the stagecoach station there. Minnie made butter, sending it packed in forty-gallon barrels to Eureka, a mining town that sprang up in 1864 some fifty miles south-southwest. Then, in 1868–1869, Ras served a Church proselytizing mission in England. Before leaving he moved his family to Bountiful to his wife's family home, the Thomas Frederick Fisher home. Minnie and the children stayed there until her father built a home for them in Bountiful, where they lived until Ras returned.

One of Ras's assignments in England was to preside over the Birmingham District. He reported to Tamson in a letter home that "he has lots of uncles and cousins" and they treated him "first rate." Who these relatives were isn't clear. Tamson learned that Ras was "traveling from one town to another all the time preaching or trying to."[57] Just before his release, Ras wrote from Birmingham to his uncle Richard Parshley in New Hampshire, Tamson's younger brother, and said he'd try to visit the Parshley relatives on the way home: "I look forward and with pleasure to the time when I will have the privelege of visiting those whom I have known so long through hearing my Dear Mother speak of them." Ras added that he'd "not heard from Father or Mother for a long time but I hear of them," probably from his wife Minnie, and "they are well as are also my family."[58]

He returned to America by steamship, arriving on August 9, 1869. From Staten Island he wrote again to his uncle, thanked him for directions, and said he'd soon visit.[59] He did. After Ras's visit, and with the transcontinental railroad now running, uncle Richard hoped to go west and visit Tamson and the family. But he died eighteen months after Ras's visit, on April 25, 1871.[60] After his New Hampshire stop, Ras headed home, riding the new transcontinental railroad part of the way:

> I was about ten days coming from N. Y. home. It was longer than I expected to be, but we had to lay over more than I thought we should. Besides there were places where we had to drive very slow. One place, I think it was in Iowa there had been such a flood that there was about a foot of water on the track for miles. But we came through it all right by being cautious. Then after we left Omaha one of the baggage cars caught on fire and raised quite an excitement for a few minutes, but there was no harm done.[61]

Salt Lake City had no rail connection yet, so Ras deboarded from the Union Pacific train in Ogden. His son and father-in-law met him and took him to Bountiful. He found his wife and children "comfortably situated in a new house." In a September 23 letter to his uncle Richard, Ras said he thought he'd go out to Ruby Valley for two weeks and settle some business before returning to Bountiful for the winter. "I have seen Mother she is pretty well and is building a new house. Father left the City the same day I arrived in Ogden so I did not get to see him."[62] He closed by sending his love to "My Dear Old Grandmother."[63] Howard would not see his returned-missionary son for another seven months.

After his mission, Ras and Minnie rented out their Bountiful home and moved back to Ruby Valley. Ras sent his uncle Richard a letter from Ruby Valley, dated April 29, 1870. In it Ras says he's "an honest farmer again" and "very crowded lately with work" and has got "about 75 acres of ground planted and most of it sowed. I hope to plow 40 or 50 acres more yet. I am putting in several acres of Potatos but the most of my crop is barley." He saw "fine prospects" for good crops and a good market for their produce. He advised his uncle that Tamson wouldn't be going east to see the relatives until the next spring.

He also described a difficult herding he'd just survived, during which he managed to see his father for the first time since his mission. He said that on April 22 he and some helpers left Salt Lake City, driving livestock to Ruby Valley. Eighty miles out, in a severe blizzard, they "lost all our stock and came near freezing ourselves." They hunted for six days, sleeping on the ground every night, and found all the cattle but none of the horses. So they continued on foot. A wagon came along and took them to within twenty-seven miles of Deep Creek "where Father and Howard [Ransom] live." They got another ride but had to leave the cattle. "I found the folks all well at Deep Creek, it was the first time I had seen Father and Howard since my return home. I stayed with them about a week and then borrowed a horse and struck out again for Ruby, 100 miles yet to ride, a good two days trip."[64] Ras and his family continued ranching in Ruby Valley until 1877 when they moved to Bountiful for the children's schooling.

Stagecoach Supervisor Out of a Job

Technology twice changed Howard's work situation. First, the transcontinental telegraph ended his Pony Express supervisory job in 1861. Then, in May 1869, transcontinental steam locomotives and coast-to-coast steel rails killed his stagecoach employment and ranch businesses. After the driving of the famous golden spike, the relay and home stations east and west stood deserted. The Egans' markets and employment dried up.

At fifty-three years old, how would resourceful Howard next earn a living? And where? He saw prospectors swarming the mountains and valleys all along the Central Route, some making worthwhile strikes. But he also knew Salt Lake City well, and many prominent people there were his friends. The family home was in the city, where Tamson and Ira lived; daughter Helen lived there also and Willie was moving to Salt Lake. Howard had good reasons to move to the city. But he chose not to. ◆

Promontory Point, Utah State Historical Society

~ 28 ~

Miner, Missionary, City Life, and Final Days

The termination of Howard's stagecoach employment, final as it was, didn't catch him by surprise. He had prepared for it. Pick and shovel projects in nearby hills beckoned. So, after shutting the stagecoach door, he pushed open, with a pick and shovel, a mining door he'd been developing for nearly a decade. Between 1869 and 1874 he staked almost a dozen claims. Only when that work fizzled out did he finally move into Salt Lake City, where he spent his final years.

Prospector

It's no surprise that Howard prospected. Forty-niner impulses flowed in his blood. He knew from the California gold rush and from miners near Deep Creek that lucky prospectors could find wealth. Some nearby bleak hills and rugged vales contained silver and gold and other precious minerals. At nearby Dutch Mountain, an 1874 mining report says, "the first mineral was discovered there in 1860, by Major Howard Egan and other employees of the Overland Mail Co., but the hostility of the Utes, Piutes, and other marauding bands of Indians retarded the development of its mineral resources."[1]

Historical sources generally credit Col. Patrick Connor and his troops for opening Utah and eastern Nevada to mining. Following the 1863 peace treaty ending the "Gosiute War," several soldiers discovered gold veins in Egan Canyon, sixty-three miles west of Deep Creek.[2] This Egan Canyon Mining District soon had mines, a hundred miners, stamp mills, blacksmith shops, and a small town named Egan with stores, a school, residences, and a post office.[3] The mines there died in 1893 when the federal government demonetized silver. Today, ruins of wooden cabins and mines mark the ghost town's site.[4]

The *Egan Ledge* Claim

By 1866 a Clifton Mining District formed ten miles beyond Howard's Deep Creek ranch. District records show that on June 20, 1869, six weeks after the transcontinental railroad started running, Howard and Ransom and ten others, acting as the "Clifton Mining Company," filed an *Egan Ledge* claim for 2,400 feet of "rock and ore," including "all Dips, Spurs, angles & various offshoots and outcrops of the same."[5] It contained silver. The *Egan Ledge* was on Dutch Mountain, ten miles north of the mining town of Clifton and about fifteen direct miles northeast of Deep Creek. A Salt Lake City newspaper headline on September 9, 1869 reads "Precious Metals in Deep Creek," followed by this report related to the *Egan Ledge* claim:

> Major Egan and Mr. Barbee have just come in from Deep Creek for 1,500 fire bricks to start a furnace 15 miles from Deep Creek, to reduce the silver ore found in that neighborhood, and have engaged a man from Swansea, Wales, who for twenty years has been engaged in the business, to take charge of the works. The Major has located a road to Toano [Nevada], the nearest station on the Central Pacific Railroad, distant about seventy miles from Deep Creek, which will be the traveled road for four or five districts south of that place.[6]

Twice Howard and his partner-claimants forfeited the *Egan Ledge* because of "non-compliance to the by-laws" of the district. But Howard and two of the partners reclaimed fifteen hundred feet of the "Egan Lode or Mineral Vein" on January 4, 1874. It had silver.[7]

1871 silver coins

Helping Direct the Clifton Mining District

Filing claims. Scouting a route to the railroad. Constructing a smelter. Clearly Howard felt fully committed to mining. In 1869 he helped reorganize the Clifton Mining District after a fire had damaged its records.[8] The District's minute book documents his participation for the next five years.[9] The district was compact, measuring six miles by twelve. On October 18, 1869, after Howard and Ransom and six other miners called for a meeting of the miners of the district, they met and enacted a "code of laws" for the district.[10] A half dozen by-laws spelled out that the district's claim holders would meet the first of June each year to elect a president and a recorder and conduct business. The code detailed steps that prospectors must take in order to make and keep a claim. The recorder wrote down all notices, kept meeting minutes, went to the sites to see that proper monuments and notices were placed thereon, and made a list each quarter of forfeited mining claims and posted those in a conspicuous place near his office. When miners extended any ledge, they requested the recorder to measure the original location to determine the beginning point of the extension. He also monitored unworked claims that became forfeitures.

To mark a claim, miners needed to erect a stone monument on it at least two feet high, and place on it a notice listing the date and location, number of feet claimed on the whole, number of feet claimed on each side of the monument, and name or names of the owner of the location. Owners could claim one hundred feet on each side of their ledge or deposit, as long as that space didn't conflict with anyone's adjoining rights. They filed their claim with the recorder.

On December 23, 1869, the miners called a meeting. With Howard presiding, they elected a Mr. Barbee to be their recorder. At the first annual meeting, held on June 1, 1870, Howard again presided. Voters elected him president of the Clifton Mining District for the next year. At the next annual meeting, which Howard didn't attend, miners elected H. C. Longmore president and John Woodruff recorder. Bickering about the by-laws broke out and the meeting became "boisterous." The members changed the by-laws to spell out how long tunnels needed to be to comply with the first year's requirements to work the mine.

At the third annual meeting, on June 1, 1872, George W. Brown became the recorder with Howard and W. R. Sheldon conducting the balloting. The miners once again elected Howard president. The attendees heard and accepted the mining laws just passed by Congress entitled "An Act to Promote the Development of Mining Resources in the United States." Members agreed to extend the number of days for filing a claim from ten to twenty. Howard's name doesn't appear in the 1873 annual meeting's minutes, but in 1874 he conducted the annual meeting where G. F. Hendry was elected president. That was the last District meeting where Howard's name is mentioned in the minutes. By late 1874, at least forty-one miners worked in the district. Howard retired from mining prior to the 1875 annual meeting.

Howard's Mining Claims

Between 1869 and 1874, counting the *Egan Ledge*, Howard alone or with others recorded at least eleven claims. Names of the mines, claimants, filing dates, and length of claims are as follows:

Date	Mine	Claimant	Length
July 29, 1870	*Major Lode*	Major Egan Quayl Co.	1000 linear feet.
Sep. 16, 1870	*Montrelona Lode*	Egan Co.	1400
Sep. 16, 1870	*Hibernia Lode*	Egan Co.	1800
July 24, 1873	*Keystone*	Egan & Co.	1200
Dec. 31, 1873	*Egan Claim*	Egan & Co.	1500
Dec. 31, 1873	*New York No. 2*	Egan & Co.	1500
Jan. 04, 1874	*Waterloo*	Egan & Co.	1500
June 05, 1874	*Mountain Boy*	Egan & Co.	1500
June 05, 1874	*Highs Lode*	Egan & Co.	1500[11]

Howard Egan & Company's claim for the *Keystone*'s "mineral bearing rock" is signed by Howard and T. A. Cunningham. The *New York No. 2* claim was located in Dutch Mountain ten miles from Clifton, and its claimants were Howard, J. Berry, and G. Brown, the same three still claiming the *Egan Ledge*. The *Waterloo* claim was in the same area, ten miles from Clifton, and its claimants were Howard, J. Despain, and G. Brown. The *Mountain Boy*, which Howard claimed by himself, ran three hundred feet easterly and twelve hundred feet westerly from his monument and was "situated 4 miles northwest of the Gold Hill Mining on the west end of Dutch Mountain." The *Highs Lode*, also claimed by Howard himself, was "situated on Dutch Mountain & a parallel ledge to the *Spring America* Ledge."[12]

An 1872 mining study noted that the ledges in Clifton District showed thicknesses ranging from four to ten feet and depths from ten to fifty feet.[13] It said two travel routes connected the Clifton District and Salt Lake City. One ran west from the city and through Grantsville, Hooper's Ranch, and Redding Springs for 150 miles total. The other went via the Utah Central Railroad from Salt Lake City north to Ogden, then on the Central Pacific westerly to Toano, Nevada, or 216 miles by rail, and then by livery seventy-five miles to Deep Creek and ten miles to the mines. This route totaled 301 miles. The 1872 study pointed out that gold had been discovered at Deep Creek "but not in paying quantities."[14]

In 1872, mining interests built a furnace near Clifton that smelted about 1,500 tons of lead. In 1874 the furnace moved a few miles northwest to the new town of Gold Hill, and a stack furnace was set up with three blacksmith bellows.[15] That year the entirety of Tooele County had four stamp mills and seven smelters. One smelter was at Deep Creek, so perhaps Howard had invested in it. By then the county's "lively mining camps" were at Stockton, Ophir, Jacobs City, and Lewiston.[16]

An 1874 directory for Tooele County's mining districts noted a failing, one that probably irked ex-mail transporter Howard: "The citizens of that [Clifton] district have been deprived of all mail facilities since the withdrawal of the stage line through the building of the railroad." The directory also said that the "most promising mines" in the Clifton District then were the *Gilberson, Black Jack, Stonewall, Mayflower, Young America*, and the *Douglas Mine* owned by "Egan & Co." Howard's *Douglas Mine*, an eleventh claim for him, was located on Dutch Mountain. In 1874 this mine was producing milling ore essaying at $169 to $223 per ton in silver, 25 percent lead, with traces of gold, and "there are seven ledges adjacent of equal character and value," the directory said. The Clifton District then numbered about one hundred mines. Along with precious metals, the district contained copper, sandstone, fire-clay, and other substances suitable for the erection of furnaces and mills.[17]

"Living is Very Hard"

Either Howard camped while mining his claims or he built a basic shack or cabin. Ransom, prospecting with a Mr. Shell, a well-educated New Yorker, located a claim "and built a small log cabin." Howard probably cracked into his "ledges" using picks and shovels, and blasting. Ransom and Mr. Shell sank a mining shaft by drilling holes for blasting. They had several drills.[18] Miners had access to blasting powder, and dynamite became available about 1868. For deep probes, tunnels had to be dug and shored up using timber. Partners assisted on some claims. District minutes show that Ransom sometimes worked with Howard. When needing more help, Howard might have recruited Deep Creek associates or Gosiutes. Among miners swarming the Clifton District, Howard no doubt interacted with some dredges of society, men who were ignorant, crude, profane, mean, heavy drinkers, and dishonest. It's safe to assume that some miners expressed contempt for Mormons and received such themselves.

Howard's site work involved digging and picking, shoveling out the dislodged rock, loading the ore into a wagon, hauling it to a stamp mill at Clifton about ten miles away, and having the ore assayed. To haul mined ore required a sturdy wagon and more than one horse or mule to pull it. The ant-hill of mines on Dutch Mountain must have forced miners to carve out a few primitive roads. Aside from mining, the men regularly had to bring water, food, and firewood to their sites. Clothes were rarely laundered. As a miner, Howard did physically hard outdoor or underground work—dirty, boring, dangerous, lonely work. On occasion he spent time back at the Deep Creek Ranch. In April 1870, for example, Ras spent a week at the ranch with Howard and Ransom. This was about when Ransom packed up and left Deep Creek.[19]

Howard sometimes wrote to Tamson and sent her money. One of his letters survives. Dated July 14, 1874, a Tuesday, it's written in pencil on letterhead titled "Deep Creek Consolidated Co., Mining, Smelting and Merchandising, Gold Hill, Utah."[20] "My dear wife," it starts, "I write you early in the week as I must start tomorrow to go a 40 mile trip to see if there is watter [sic] at the sink of Deep Creek. If I should find water I will have to pilot a train of wagons the next day over that rout [sic] and would not [be] back time enough for Friday's mail." The trip he mentioned indicates that someone who knew his exploring reputation called on him for help.

Howard told Tamson he distrusted the mail service between Gold Hill and Salt Lake City. "I have sent money in the letters that I wrote but was uneasy and I don't [know] whether you received them or not." In this letter he enclosed fifty-seven dollars for her. He had received but two newspapers recently. One was the July 1, 1874, *Deseret News*. "There is not a pen nor ink in camp have to use pencil and am writing on a piece of board for a table on my knee and it is just beginning to rain." Apparently he'd been ill recently, for he told Tamson,

> My health has improved, but I am on the move about all the time I don't have time to get rested and living is very hard and have to stay out in the sage brush that is here. Our store house is [not] up yet but there has been a lot of lumber arrive and today will be comfortable. We have showers every day. It is hard to keep bedding dry.

He said he'd heard good reports about Indian conversions nearby that pleased him: "There has been about 425 Indians baptized since the first of June at Deep Creek how is that." He closed the letter with "I remain your effectionat [sic] Husband & God bless you all, Howard Egan."

Exit from Ranching and Mining

In *Pioneering the West*, son William's summary of Howard's mining efforts says they didn't pay off:

> After the completion of the railroad from the east to the west across the continent, the route having been chosen north of the Salt Lake, there was no more use for the Mail Line and there was not much left at Deep Creek for activity

except in connection with the mines that had been discovered during the many years that the ranch had been in operation, so Father turned his attention to them. He seemed to be quite successful in developing some good properties in partnership with two other men and could have sold out for $50,000 which Father wanted to do, but his partners wanted more and they got nothing, as all the railroad projects failed to reach there, and as the ore was low grade it would not pay to ship. The mines failed to reimburse him for the means he had expended in them, which was the substance of the entire Deep Creek Ranch farm land.[21]

Howard's judgment about wealth in the Dutch Mountain area was sound. In the early 1890s several thousand dollars in gold was shipped out of the Clifton Mining District. In 1918, Western Utah Copper shipped tons of copper daily, plus lead and silver. From 1917 to 1925 up to 1,500 people resided in nearby Gold Hill, when the Deep Creek Railroad hauled out hundreds of tons of tungsten.[22]

Disposing of the Ranch

After his lack of success at mining, Howard returned to the ranch for a short time "with most of his resources used up."[23] In the late 1860s and during the 1870s, several settlers moved to the Deep Creek Valley. They each claimed land and water. These included John Devine, Edward Ferguson, Sheldon Bates, William Lee, Charles Felt, James Worthington and his sons, and the Larkin family. Ronald R. Bateman's *Deep Creek Reflections* provides a fine history of the community from its beginnings.[24] About 1874–1875 Howard sold his Deep Creek properties. James Martin's biography of Howard asserts that Howard owed a debt to W. C. Rydalch, who hired a man named John Gillespie to collect it. Arriving at Deep Creek, Gillespie learned that Howard had sold the property, but not the cattle, to John Binley (who'd been one of Howard's mining partners). So, Gillespie gathered up cattle in the area, some that didn't belong to Howard, and then encountered Howard.

According to Gillespie's diary, "We separated Egan's cattle from the rest, and then turned the others out. Mssrs. Egan and Binley were very excited and wanted to know what I intended doing." Gillespie claimed the cattle, based on the writ of attachment he carried. "They talked of burning the corral and letting the cattle out. I told them the corral was mine and to leave it alone and I guarded it all night." The next morning Gillespie "attached a set of blacksmith's tools and some other property" and started herding the cattle to Grantsville. "I levied on about Three thousand Dollars worth of property," he said.[25]

Amazing Spiritual Outpouring Among Native Americans

Gosiutes, despite government efforts to move them to the Uintah Basin or a reservation near Fort Hall, Idaho, liked and stayed at their Ibapah "homeland" south of the Deep Creek ranch.[26] By about 1873, a strange spirit began stirring among Native Americans, which extended from Ibapah to northwestern and southwestern Nevada and into Utah and Idaho. It resulted in several thousand Indians being baptized by Mormon officiators. At Deep Creek the stirring caught "Indian Farm" missionaries by surprise. In a story dated June 2, 1874, at Deep Creek, the *Deseret News* reported that "One hundred Indians were submerged and confirmed into the 'Mormon' faith here yesterday."

On November 7, 1874, the Church's *Juvenile Instructor* published an explanation for why the Indians near Deep Creek wanted to be baptized. The movement, it said, resulted from a dream Torbuka, a leading chief of the Gosiutes, experienced, and from visits he received from heaven-sent strangers.[27] Reporter John Nicholson's source for the story was his interview with Torbuka. Nicholson said that during the previous spring Torbuka and the greater portion of his band had encamped some distance west of Deep Creek. One night Torbuka had "a singular and very pleasant dream, in which he thought he saw a beautiful meadow, through which flowed a fine stream of clear water." He thought he saw Elder William Lee, the Mormon interpreter and missionary, who told him that he and his people must wash in that stream. Torbuka awoke in the morning and had very pleasant feelings. He told his people they must go and wash themselves in the creek nearby, which they and he did.

> Subsequently Torbuka was sitting alone in his tent, when a man entered, whom he later described as having a white or rather a grey beard, and a very handsome countenance. As may be imagined, he had peculiar feelings on seeing this stranger so suddenly. He gazed at this personage for a few moments, when he the stranger addressed Torbuka, the substance of his words being that the time had come for the Indians to be buried in water, baptized; that the "Mormons" were their friends; that they had a book which told about their fathers, that Brigham held communion with God, and they must hear him. He also told Torbuka that the enemies of the Indians had driven, robbed, plundered, and abused them, but the time when their enemies could do that was nearly past, that the time had almost arrived when those who had wronged them would be like the "dry wood upon the mountains that would be consumed, and they, the Indians, would walk over the ashes."

The stranger left. Torbuka walked toward the corner of the bluff around which the person had turned, to see which direction he was going, but could not see where he'd gone. Soon, two more personages visited Torbuka in the same manner and repeated what the first visitor had told him word for word. Then Torbuka had a third visit, this time by one of those two personages, who repeated the same exact utterances. Torbuka related these events in a Grantsville LDS meetinghouse in the presence of several individuals. These visitations prompted Torbuka to gather his people and travel to Ibapah where he sent for "Interpreter William Lee."

The *Juvenile Instructor* article then details the baptisms that resulted from Torbuka's vision and visitors. With Bishop John Rowberry's approval, interpreter Lee and William H. Lee (not related) preached the gospel in a simple manner to the Gosiutes and invited them to be baptized in a stream a half mile away. One elder did the baptizing and others stood on the bank with a chair where those who had been baptized sat and received confirmations through the laying on of hands. Gosiutes under age eight received blessings from the elders. The baptisms took place within sixty minutes in the midst of a downpour of rain. Seven Gosiute men were ordained elders, and they were instructed about their duties.

These were among the 425 Indian baptisms Howard mentioned in his July 14, 1874 letter to Tamson. That December Elder Lafayette Ball of Deep Creek brought to Salt Lake City a book containing a record of the Indian baptisms performed since June in Ibapah. "It included the names of eight hundred." The Indians had come from "quite long distances" and were "wearied with travel," Ball said. A Deep Creek Branch membership roster of October 1, 1874 shows Indians from White Pine, Ruby Valley, Diamond Springs, Humboldt River, and southwest Nevada, plus Box Elder, Utah. Many of these were listed as being baptized at the "Indian Ranch" at Ibapah. Elder Ball said he expected more baptisms the next spring because the Indians claimed the heavenly messengers wanted more Indians to come. They would gather at Ibapah to be baptized, then commence farming. However, no records tell us about such a subsequent gathering.[28]

Similar mass baptisms took place elsewhere. In March 1875 about two hundred Shebit Indians "came and demanded baptism, the result of some supernatural influence through their prophets and 'medicine men.'" In June 1875 Bishop Culbert King baptized eighty-five Indians at Kanosh Settlement in Millard County, Utah. In August George W. Hill baptized more than three hundred Indians in the Malad River in Box Elder County. Historian B. H. Roberts found that "Indian conversions and baptisms continued through a number of years."[29]

Howard's Gosiute Mission

Church leaders felt astonished by the outpouring of spiritual manifestations among Native Americans. Apostle Orson Pratt explained in Salt Lake City's Twentieth Ward on February 7, 1875 that it seemed the Lord was working among the remnants of Joseph "scattered all around us," and that "messengers are visiting these wild tribes in the basin, and in the regions round about hundreds of miles apart. These messengers come to them, and they speak in their own languages in great plainness, and tell them what to do." Pratt said, "the messengers are the three disciples told about in the Book of Mormon." He reported that Church leaders had heard of at least 1,400 Indians who had been baptized. "Here is a work for us to do."[30]

Gosiute Indians, Detroit Publishing Company

Lamanite conversions became a major topic at the Church's April 1875 General Conference. In Apostle Orson Hyde's sermon he admitted that "we have labored in our weakness among the Indians, trying to convert them from the error of their ways" and "we have not been able to accomplish much." But,

...for some time past, the Indians have been telling us very strange stories. They say that certain strange men have visited them and spoken to them, and have taught them what to do in order to be saved in the kingdom of God. Strange men have come to and talked with them perhaps an hour at a time, and while the Indians are looking at them they vanish out of sight, and they know not where they go.[31]

Elder John Taylor affirmed what Elder Hyde said.[32] Elder Pratt pointed out that the Indians in that spiritual movement "are in these western deserts, in the northwest hundreds of miles, in the west and in the southwest," and "some of them have come hundreds of miles to be baptized, and they are now desirous of laying aside their savage disposition, their roaming habits, and they want to learn to cultivate the earth."[33]

During the conference, the Church called Howard and three other Deep Creek men to teach the gospel to the Gosiutes: James Worthington, Edwin Tadlock, and Lafayette Ball.[34]

But Howard, by then newly returned to Salt Lake City, didn't go until October, according to the Nineteenth Ward Historical Record.[35] How long he served or what he accomplished isn't known. *Pioneering the West* merely says that Howard "aided much" in teaching Gosiutes and "imparting to them a knowledge of the Gospel."[36]

Howard's last effort to help the Gosiutes came in 1877. He proposed that the Deep Creek land intended to be a reservation be sold to raise funds to supply the Gosiutes with farming equipment.[37] That never happened. Decades passed with no permanent reservation being set up. Finally, on March 23, 1914, the federal government allotted them more than 34,000 acres at the south end of Deep Creek Valley and extending into White Pine County, Nevada.[38] Today, the Confederated Tribes of the Goshute Reservation consists of 122,085 acres in White Pine County, Nevada, and Juab and Tooele counties in Utah, on which live (in 2014) approximately two hundred tribal members. Headquarters are adjacent to Ibapah, Utah.[39]

At Home in Salt Lake City

The Salt Lake City directory for 1874 lists Howard, occupation miner, living at the northeast corner of 2nd North (now 3rd North) and 2nd West (now 3rd West).[40] William Egan explained that "having exhausted all his resources at Deep Creek Father came to Salt Lake about 1875 and lived at the old home with his family (what were left at home)."[41] Tamson was there, and so was fourteen-year-old Ira, Howard's youngest child. Howard now was situated to get well acquainted with Ira. About 1875 William moved back home, too, and attended Beck's School, making four persons in the Egan household. Howard found living at home with Tamson was cleaner, healthier, more comfortable, and more convenient, and probably that meals were the best he'd regularly eaten in years.

By then the Nineteenth Ward's meetings were held in a "large and commodious" building erected in 1866 on the southwest corner of Fifth North and Third West. The bishop still was Alonzo Raleigh, who had married Howard's ex-wife Nancy two decades earlier. In 1876 Richard V. Morris replaced him as bishop. Perhaps Howard resumed some kind of activity in the Seventeenth Quorum of Seventies, in which he had been one of the seven presidents a quarter-century earlier.

Howard by then had seen several changes in the city, such as a growing gentile population, often anti-Mormon; the newer Tabernacle (1867); Zion's Cooperative Mercantile Institution, or ZCMI (1868); street lamps (1868); and a streetcar system, using horses and mules (1872). His good friend and adopted father Heber C. Kimball had passed away in 1868. Convert-emigrants continued to arrive, but now at the Utah Northern Railroad depot (starting in 1870) instead of Union Square by the Egan home. And, newcomers came in every season of the year. The city now had an anti-Mormon newspaper, the *Salt Lake Tribune* (1870). Municipal elections pitted two new political parties against each other: the Mormon-backed People's Party and the anti-Mormon Liberal Party.

Nineteenth Ward United Order Soap Factory

Utah suffered from an economic depression that hammered the nation in 1873. Church leaders, reacting to the economic disruptions and wanting more unity and cooperation among the Saints, instituted a United Order movement. They established one of four types of United Orders in nearly every Mormon community in the intermountain west.

President Young established the first United Order in St. George.[42] It became a prototype that other small communities adopted. In it, members assigned productive economic property, such as land, livestock, and tools, to the community cooperative. Then, elected managers directed the labor of all. Each member shared in what their united efforts produced, according to what they contributed and how they labored.[43] A second type was the "Order of Enoch," a rigid communal system developed most fully in Orderville. They became organized like a "well-regulated family" wherein communal cooking, dining, laundry, sewing, and field work replaced individual duplications of work each household normally did. The "Brigham City Order," a third type, was but a coordinating of various cooperatives already thriving in Brigham City. It required no consecrating of property. A fourth approach was the "large city type" adopted in Salt Lake City, a lesser version of the Brigham City model wherein city wards each developed one particular industry as parts of a whole. During 1874 and 1875 some two hundred community and ward United Orders were created, at least on paper, in Utah, Idaho, Arizona, Nevada, and Wyoming. Almost all failed within one or two years.[44]

In the Salt Lake Stake, all but one of the twenty-seven wards formed Order organizations. The norm was for members to join the ward Order by donating capital to launch a single enterprise. Its products then would be marketed through the Zion's Cooperative Mercantile Institution (ZCMI) central store, which wholesaled to cooperative retail stores in most Utah communities. That way, the city's Orders collectively accomplished what a single Order could do in smaller communities. The Eighth Ward operated a hat factory, the Eleventh Ward a tailor's shop, the Twentieth Ward a boot and shoe shop. But in practice only a few of the city's ward Orders did more than elect officers.

On May 23, 1874, the Egans' Nineteenth Ward organized a United Order enterprise, with Bishop Raleigh as its president. About four hundred and thirty members committed to join the Order.[45] The Order manufactured soap.[46] An advertisement for their ward's "Utah Soap Manufacturing Company" says it offered several brands of first class soaps to territory merchants, brands such as "Pale Savon," Castile, Walnut Oil Shaving, and Variegated Toilets, "including the celebrated Thomas Patent Soap." They also produced "Scouring or Fuller's Soap" and "Miners' Candles." To make soap they needed grease, and it's likely that Tamson contributed some grease. The soap products were sold at the factory and at a Scandinavian store near the corner of Second South and First East streets.[47] When Howard moved home in 1875, the soap factory was operating, so he might have helped support it financially. It stayed in business for "many years."[48]

Policeman, Deputy Sheriff, and Guard Work

William said Howard became "one of the Salt Lake Police and also Deputy Sheriff." Will's papers include Howard's appointment as deputy sheriff, although Will did not include it in *Pioneering the West*:

> To all whom it may concern, Know ye that Howard Egan of Salt Lake City, Salt Lake County, Utah Territory, has been duly appointed a Deputy Sheriff in and for the said County. Given under my hand this ninth day of January A.D. 1876. (signed) Theodore McKune, Deputy Sheriff.[49]

What Howard's police and sheriff work entailed isn't known. According to Will, Howard also "became a special guard for Pres. Brigham Young at the Lion House and Church offices."[50] The guard assignment demonstrates the trust and confidence

President Young placed in Howard. Their friendship and relationship went way back, at least to 1845 in Nauvoo. Based on their long association, President Young asked Howard to help guard him and be stationed at the Lion House and Church Offices. This was not a token appointment. Howard, then about age fifty-nine, was not an old man and probably wasn't given a watchman-type job out of sympathy. Young needed toughness and dependability. Perhaps the guard job was part of Howard's duties as a deputy sheriff or policeman.

Lion House, Utah State Historical Society

Several situations between 1875 and Young's death in August 1877 involved protection and safety, some of which probably engaged Howard: general conferences, visits by President Ulysses S. Grant and Civil War hero General William T. Sherman, Brigham Young's arrest for contempt of court, a bank burning, an escape by seven prisoners from the penitentiary, a massive explosion of gunpowder on Arsenal Hill, a visit by a band of Navajo people, and tensions related to John D. Lee's trial and execution for his role in the Mountain Meadows massacre.

Nursing Fatally Ill Brigham Young

Brigham Young fell ill on August 23, 1877 and died six days later. William Egan said that, "at the time of Pres. Brigham Young's last illness," Howard "acted as special nurse, in which capacity he had many times acted before in various cases, and was often called a doctor. Brigham Young would tell him to get him a pitcher of cold water and

Brigham Young,
LDS Church History Library

pump it full forty times. Many other attentions he would render for him."⁵¹

Although Young's six-day illness is well-documented, it's difficult to pinpoint when Howard did this water errand. On Thursday afternoon, August 23, Young fell ill and was "inclined to vomit," but he participated in that evening's bishops' meeting in the Council House. That night he was attacked by "cholera morbus" and suffered through the night from vomiting and purging.⁵² He had intense pain and muscle cramping. On Saturday his bowels became inflamed. His condition worsened. Small doses of opium helped him sleep quietly. Sunday and Monday he received a milk and brandy medicine, and "various brethren" administered to him, as happened most days. That evening he became semi-comatose and hard to arouse, but he was able to swallow the milk mixture and a teaspoonful of ice water now and then.⁵³ By 4:00 a.m. he sank down in bed "apparently lifeless." Artificial respiration for nine consecutive hours kept his lungs inflated and hot poultices stimulated his heart. He spent that night semi-comatose. During Tuesday night and into Wednesday, doctors F. D. Benedict and W. F. Anderson attended him, frequently checking pulse and temperature. On Wednesday about two hours before his demise, when several brethren administered to him, he voiced a clear and distinct "amen."⁵⁴

The traditional cause of death ascribed to Brigham Young is peritonitis following the rupture of his appendix.⁵⁵ An alternate view, that Young died of arsenic poisoning, isn't given much credence.⁵⁶ The most recent assessment by a Young biographer is that Young might have died from food poisoning.⁵⁷

Brigham Young's death impacted Utah and beyond. He had led the Church for thirty-three years and had directed the founding and pioneering of Utah. His followers in Utah numbered nearly 105,000.⁵⁸ He'd become a national figure, sometimes admired but mostly vilified. Throughout Utah Territory, flags were lowered to half-mast.⁵⁹ His death dissolved the First Presidency. Presidency duties reverted to the

Quorum of the Twelve, presided over by senior apostle Elder John Taylor. He did not become Church president until three years later, in October 1880.

Guard Duty at Brigham Young's Grave

Saturday morning, September 1, President Young's body was taken to the Tabernacle. It rested in state all day. An estimated 25,000 people came to the public viewing to pay respects, some to grieve. Almost certainly Howard and Tamson attended. Perhaps Howard did police duty there. Then, for the funeral at noon on Sunday, the Tabernacle was filled, including aisles, doorways, and every available standing place. Howard and Tamson would have been there if at all possible. Organ and choir performances preceded eulogies by Elders Daniel H. Wells, Wilford Woodruff, Erastus Snow, John Taylor, and George Q. Cannon.[60]

Brigham Young's will specified that his body be taken to the "little burying ground, which I have reserved on my lot east of the White House on the hill, and in the southeast corner of this lot, have a vault built of mason work large enough to receive my coffin." So, following the funeral, about four thousand people marched in a specified order and ranking, eight abreast, to the grave site. Young was buried in a wooden casket placed in a stone vault. Elder Woodruff dedicated the ground, vault, and the body to

Brigham Young grave, courtesy Perry Special Collections, HBL, BYU

the Lord. The grave site today is within The Mormon Pioneer Memorial Monument, also known as the Brigham Young Cemetery, located on First Avenue between State Street and A Street.[61]

"After the death of Pres. Young Father was the special guard at his grave," William Egan said. The grave needed to be protected from vandalism and from any disgruntled Mormon or Gentile who might try to dig up the body and desecrate or steal it. Guards took turns, each doing a shift. For Howard, William said, "a building was erected so that he could look out on the grave any time of night, without getting out of bed, by the light that was kept burning."[62]

Along with Howard, Egan family friend William L. Ball, age forty-four, served as a guard at the grave. Ball had worked at Deep Creek before and had known the Egans there. He was related to Lafayette Ball, who was called with Howard and others to be a missionary to the Gosiutes. William Ball's journal shows that he was at the Young grave nearly every day from January 1 through March 19, 1878.[63] He often stayed there overnight. On January 1 he spent part of the day at the grave but took breakfast and dinner at "Bro. Egans." On January 6 he and Howard attended morning and afternoon meetings of the stake conference, held in the Fourteenth Ward. He noted on January 10 that a "stone cutter is dressing a big rock to put over the grave." On January 24 Ball and Ras went to a lecture, and the next day both of them did guard duty at the grave.

On February 3, Ball recorded that "Bro. Egan and me done some visiting before meeting time." On February 8, "Sis Egan gave me a Bottle of Wine for the Cold." A week later he noted that "Bro Worthington wants me to go with him to Deep Creek. Says he is in charge of Indian affairs out there." On February 20, Ball "help[ed] to make some fence for Bro Egan on his place," and two days later he "worked for Bro Egan helping William make some gates for his yard." On the twenty-third he noted: "work some for Bro Egan," and two days later, "some work for Bro Egan at his fence. Bro Egan got me a pass to American Fork & back from Bro. Sharp, superintendent [railroad]." On February 26 Ball worked "a little" for Egan. He then took a trip out of town to American Fork. That Ball's diary never mentions Howard doing guard duty at the grave indicates that Howard and Ball did different watchman shifts.

Howard's Death on March 16, 1878

"In March 1878 Father got his feet wet one dark night and took sick," William Egan said, "which resulted in inflammation of the bowels."[64] When Ball returned from his trip on March 5 he "found Bro Egan very sick, with his request layed hands on him & asked God to heal him. Went to grave to stay the night."[65] The next day he went to Brother Egan's: "he is very sick, got a bottle of oil, took it to the office, had it blessed, gave him some, prayed for him. Brother Cushion [Cushing] and me anointed and layed hands on Bro Egan." The next morning, Howard was "a little better." That afternoon he had the hiccoughs "very bad." Ball and Cushion anointed him again. On March 8 "Egan seems a little better. They anointed him again and I asked God to heal him." Ball spent part of the next day with Howard. Ball's diary entries for the next week document Howard's decline and death:

10 He is very weak…I pray all the time for Bro Egan hoping he will get well.
11 found bro Egan very weak this morning when I went down to his house … he is better this evening.
12 Bro Egan is very sick, yet stayed with him most of the day.
13 he very sick this morn, seemed better this evening.
14 seemed a little better this morn. Dr. Bendick called on him today.
15 seems worse this morning. Dr. Bendick said they can't do anything for him, he will live till tomorrow … I am staying with him all of the time. I anointed, Bro Egan layed hands on him, Erastus. Went with him tonight.

While Will Egan guarded Brigham Young's grave that night, Howard died.[66] Ball's journal noted his passing: "16 Bro Howard Egan died. 10 minutes past 12 this morning. I feel like I have lost a good friend. Brother James Jack gave me orders to pay funeral expenses which I feel thankful for." James Jack had been Brigham Young's chief secretary, so he probably now served the same duty for John Taylor. As a grave guard, Howard had been a Church employee, so the Church paid for his funeral expenses. Howard died six months after Brigham Young did. His cause of death was inflammation of the bowels after a two-week sickness.[67] He was sixty-two years old, almost sixty-three. He died three decades after he first entered Great Salt Lake Valley with Brigham Young as one of the original 1847 pioneers.

Nineteenth Ward Funeral

One day after Howard died, his funeral took place in the Nineteenth Ward meetinghouse. So many attended that "numbers could not get in." Apostle Orson Pratt spoke and gave "a highly instructive discourse." After the funeral, Howard's remains "were followed to the grave by a large cortege of mourners." His grave is in the Salt Lake City Cemetery, where daughter Vilate and son Horace are buried.[68] "We buried

Orson Pratt,
LDS Church History Library

Bro Egan today," Ball wrote, "and it has been a sorrowful day to me for I loved him. Bro. Orsen Pratt preach Bro James A Cushing done all he could to help. But I miss a true friend…I payed him goodby for a short time."[69]

One obituary for Howard, titled "An Old Citizen Gone," referred to him as an "old and respected citizen of this Territory," then summarized that "he resided principally in Salt Lake City, but during the last few years, and until recently, he labored as a missionary among the Indians in the vicinity of Deep Creek, seeking to impart to them a knowledge of the gospel and train them to the habits of honesty and industry." The notice lauded him for his mail and stagecoach work and for being "a promoter of progress on the borders." Another obituary praised that "his career was characterized by numerous acts of heroism and many were his hair-breath escapes. His reputation for being friendly to everyone was good, and his enemies in the territory were very few."[70]

Two days after Howard's funeral, Ball turned in his guard house keys to a Church headquarters secretary George Reynolds and then "Stayed the night at sister Egans." At the end of March, he went out to Deep Creek. There he "stayed with Hiram Egan," Howard's son. Ball worked with teams of men at the Indian Ranch. On April 1 he penned, "I miss Bro Egan." On the sixth he wrote a few lines, a letter, to William Egan.

Funerals.

The funeral obsequies of Major Howard Egan were largely attended on Sunday, at the 19th ward meeting house. Elder Orson Pratt addressed the assemblage and imparted words of comfort and instruction to all. A long cortege followed the remains to the cemetery.

On April 13 he went to Hyrum's. Ball worked there through the summer, but then died on September 19.

For decades a reddish headstone standing four feet tall and two feet wide marked Howard's grave. Then, apparently when it was falling apart and needed replacement, it was removed and disappeared. In 1990 a man discovered it while gardening in the yard behind the State Capitol and donated it to the Daughters of Utah Pioneers Museum in Salt Lake City. Its inscription reads: "In memory of Howard Egan, son of

Howard and Ann Egan," and gives his birth and death dates.[71] Today a more recent, flat headstone marks the grave. ◆

~ 29 ~

Tamson, the Family, and Publishing *Pioneering the West*

Howard ranks among fortunate ones whom history and family have not forgotten. His death in 1878 at the not-so-old-age of sixty-two meant Tamson would be a widow for more than a quarter century. After his passing, his children developed useful lives, and memories of him began to fade. But a series of happenings about a quarter century after his death triggered new interest in his life and his records, particularly by his sons Ransom and William. Through their efforts, Howard's diaries and many of his life contributions became published in 1917 in the book *Pioneering the West*, which a century later continues to stay in print.

Widow Tamson

During the late 1840s and throughout the 1850s, Howard and Tamson's marriage endured constant separations caused by his work and Church calls to duty. During the 1860s, Howard spent much time at the Deep Creek Ranch while Tamson stayed at the family home. Howard had employment responsibilities that required him to be out in the west desert. It was work too valuable to quit. It provided well for his family. She visited Deep Creek a couple of times that we know of, and he spent time at home with her while in the city doing work at the stagecoach headquarters. The question arises, why did she not join him at Deep Creek? Could not a better arrangement have been set up?

Their separate living arrangement was not principally due to estrangements of feelings. Rather, several understandable reasons are evident for why he and Tamson decided she should stay in the city. (1) The uncertainty of the mail contracts, which bounced from one owner to another, and the struggles of the Pony Express and then the stagecoach owners, raised doubts about how long the Deep Creek operation would last. (2) Tamson's pregnancy from June 1860, just after the Pony Express started, until February 1, 1861, when Ira was born, was not a good time for her to be out there. (3) Primitive housing and cleanliness issues, coupled with distance from doctors and stores, made Deep Creek undesirable for Ira while he was a newborn or toddler. (4) Living at isolated Deep Creek was dangerous, as shown by Indian attacks in 1860 and 1863 and intermittent stagecoach robberies. (5) Fairly often Howard was in Salt Lake City doing business with company headquarters. (6) Regular mail service and then the telegraph after October 1861 kept Deep Creek and Salt Lake City in communication. (7) By about 1866 Ira needed to attend school, and Deep Creek had no school.

Tamson Parshley Egan, Egan Family Archives

With Howard away so much, Tamson felt some sense of independence and freedom. By personality she was resourceful, as her letters below show. Living alone, like it or not, prepared her somewhat for the twenty-seven years of widowhood she faced after Howard died. Not a lot is known about her during that last, long period of her life. A sampling of city directories shows that by the early 1880s she had moved and was living a block to the north. She is listed in 1885 through 1905 as a widow living at 312 North 200 West (which today would be 412 North and 300 West). Apparently son William lived with her for several years. He's listed as living at her address in the city's 1884 and 1885 directories. In 1886 he married and moved to Provo. Ira lived with her between 1885 and 1890.[1]

A letter Tamson wrote to William on February 27, 1893 gives some insights about her and the family.[2] She said Ira was her only child then living in Salt Lake City, and that Ira's baby, a "little mite of a thing," had something like pneumonia, and Ira's wife Emma was not very well. "They have no help, so I go back and forth and assist all I can. Iras health is very poor, very thin, children have bad coughs, myself I have been very sick, but able get round now but long ways from well." The rest of the Egans were "pretty well." Erastus's wife Mary Beatrice Noble Egan "was here yesterday an hour or two she said they all well." Tamson said that she heard from Ransom's family "once in a while they are all well."

Her yard, she said, had three inches of snow. She promised to send Will some tree tomato seeds. On March 2 Tamson added a postscript to the letter. "Iras baby died on the 21, buried on 22 rest getting better." The baby had been blessed and named Jeanne Tamson Egan. "Erastus wife caught cold," she reported. "Some of my chickens have

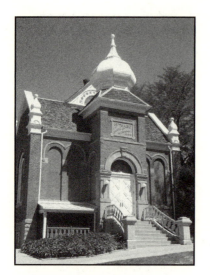

Nineteenth Ward Chapel, constructed 1890, 168 West 500 North, Salt Lake City, where Tamson attended church.

laid all winter." She had brown roosters. "Now how is your stock of chicks ducks and turkey?" She offered to send Will some red pepper seeds. She signed the letter, "kind love to you and yours and as ever I remain your affectionate mother, Tamson P. Egan," then added "Ta Ta write soon."

Somewhere in her house Tamson stored Howard's records, which were extensive. "If we had all of Father's papers that were kept during Mother's lifetime," Will observed, "we would need several volumes to contain them." The papers stayed there until she died, but after that, Will lamented, "many of them were destroyed." Ransom saved some, which became texts in *Pioneering the West* in 1917.

Tamson died in Salt Lake City on March 31, 1905 of pernicious anemia at age eighty.[3] She is buried beside Howard at the Egan plot in the Salt Lake City Cemetery.[4]

Postscripts About Howard's Former Wives

As told about earlier, Howard's plural wives did not stay married to him for very long. By 1855 he was a monogamist again.

On June 10, 1855, Catherine Reese Clawson became one of Brigham Young's wives, indicating she had divorced Howard by then. Her grandson Rudger J. Clawson became an apostle of the Church.[5] She died on November 7, 1860.[6]

Nancy Ann Redden's marriage to Howard did not last long after the Monroe killing. Less than three years later she became a plural wife of Alonzo Hazeltine Raleigh on April 27, 1854, the bishop in the Egans' Nineteenth Ward. The 1860 census lists Nancy Redding as age thirty-three, living in Salt Lake City.[7] By then her married name was Raleigh, but not on the census. Howard and Nancy's daughter Helen Jeanette married in 1866 to John K. Irvine. They were sealed together in the Endowment House on September 30, 1872. By the time Howard died, Helen and John Irvine had given Howard and Nancy five grandchildren.[8] Nancy died in 1892.

Howard and Mary Ann Tuttle Egan's marriage was dissolved by Brigham Young because of unidentified "disagreeable conditions" between Howard and her.[9] She married Titus Billings, on January 20, 1854, and spent the rest of her life in Sevier and Sanpete counties. Her marriage to Billings didn't work out. She married again, this time to Walter Elias Gardner on November 28, 1866. Howard kept in contact with their son Hyrum, and in time Hyrum worked at the Deep Creek ranch with him. Mary Ann had three children by Titus Billings, and one by Walter Gardner. She died on December 10, 1910, in Thurber, Wayne County, Utah.

The Egan Sons

Howard valued his boys; he employed them and they stayed loyal to him. He knew what it was like to grow up without a father. Even stepson William had such regard for Howard that he worked dedicatedly with Ransom to get *Pioneering the West* published, to honor Howard.

Howard Ransom Egan. Thus far this history has referred to Howard Ransom as Ransom, for clarity's sake. From here on, after father Howard's demise, the narrative calls him Howard R., the name he preferred. When the transcontinental railroad opened, killing the overland stagecoach business, Howard R. and Amanda moved to Richmond, Utah. There he bought a sawmill in High Creek Canyon northeast of Richmond and managed it for many years. He was also involved with a sawmill in Logan Canyon. He homesteaded eighty acres. Reportedly he was elected the first president of the Utah Cattlemen's Association when it first organized in 1870. His livelihood came from farming and threshing. He also had a mining company which, when it produced, sent ore to a smelter in the Salt Lake Valley.[10] From at least 1910 until 1916 he wrote remembrances and recruited funds for *Pioneering the West,* also steering forward the book's publication.

Four sons of Howard Egan, Egan Family Archives

He and Amanda had twelve children.[11] On March 17, 1916, he died at home of pneumonia.[12] At his funeral, held in the Richmond meetinghouse on March 22, his son-in-law Walter Hill spoke, praising Howard R. for his interest in genealogical work and Egan family history.[13] Howard R. was survived by his wife, three brothers (Erastus, William, and Ira), six sons, two daughters, forty-seven grandchildren, and ten great-grandchildren.[14] He is buried in the Richmond Cemetery.

Howard Ransom Egan, Egan Family Archives

Richard Erastus Egan. After his LDS mission to England, Erastus and Minnie moved back to Ruby Valley, where Ras resumed farming and stock raising. They went back to Bountiful in 1877 for the children's schooling. Ras engaged in fruit farming and sheep raising and was involved with the Bountiful Livestock Company. In 1885 he became a Justice of the Peace and served two terms. On December 26, 1887, his wife Minnie died in childbirth at age forty-three. Erastus then married Mary Beatrice Noble, who was much younger, in the Logan Temple on July 10, 1889. They had seven children of their own in addition to Minnie's fifteen.[15]

Richard Erastus Egan, Egan Family Archives

In politics Ras identified with the Democratic Party. He was Davis County assessor and tax collector from 1889 to 1899, and filled two terms on the Bountiful City Council. On January 8, 1893, he was sustained as bishop of the South Bountiful Ward. In 1896 he served in Utah's first state legislature—Utah had been a territory until then.

Between 1885 and 1900 about 178 genealogy missionaries traveled, most of them from Utah, to their ancestral homes to search out their family history.[16] Although most were self-appointed missions, they received missionary status and were set apart by General Authorities and sent out. Erastus was one. "When he was set apart, he was promised that he would find his people and be received with open arms, which is what occurred."[17] He went to the old home in Tullamore, King's County, Ireland (pictured in *Pioneering the West*), which was built by Howard Egan's grandfather Bernard Egan and where Howard and his father were born. He obtained the genealogy of relatives there, and visited with a kinsman, the poet Edward Egan. He then went to Montreal, Canada, where he found a considerable number of the family and obtained more genealogical information. He also visited Massachusetts and New Hampshire and copied down considerable genealogy of Tamson's Parshley and Caverly relatives. At home, Ras did the temple work that would be done for them.[18]

Because of Erastus's visit with the Canadian Egans, Richard Egan in Montreal wrote to the officials in Tullamore seeking a history of the Egan lands there. His letter was forwarded to poet Edward Egan, a bachelor, prompting Edward to reply to Richard on February 19, 1900, saying "I am the only surviving member of the Egan family in this country," and therefore "I am delighted to hear from you as we have lost all traces of our relations in Canada."[19]

In 1905 Erastus resigned as bishop after twelve years and accepted a mission call to help colonize the Little Big Horn territory in Wyoming. He, his second wife Mary Beatrice Noble, two of his married sons, one unmarried son, and five other children by Mary left Bountiful in April 1905. They homesteaded eighty acres between Byron and Lovell and obtained forty acres in Byron. They cleared sagebrush, leveled sand knolls, and plowed and planted hay, wheat, corn, and a main cash crop, asparagus. Ras opened a small general merchandise store in Byron. He was elected a school trustee for two years. In 1910, because of failing health, he sold the store business. He devoted the next few years to farming, and started a dairy.[20] His son Byron Egan said Erastus was "God-fearing," kindhearted, generous, fair-minded, and had a "keen sense of humor."[21] Erastus was ordained a patriarch in 1914.

His health began to fail late in 1916. A cancerous growth in his stomach caused intense suffering. While he lay on his death bed—he had been paralyzed and unable to sit up for days—he sat up suddenly, looked ahead, and said, "Oh Minnie, you have come for me," then fell back, dead. This was in the farmhouse in Byron on April 20, 1918.[22] His wife Mary lived as a widow for forty years, passing away of pneumonia on March 3, 1959 at age ninety-four. She is buried next to Ras in Bountiful.

William Moburn Egan. Although he was the son of Tamson by James Monroe, Howard treated him like he was his own son. Willy called Howard "Father."[23] In 1863, Howard, busily engaged in stagecoach supervising, had "Willy" come out to the Deep Creek Ranch and help, after which he lived at Deep Creek for five or six years before moving back to Salt Lake City. Tamson and little brother Ira were away, so Willy boarded with neighbors and went to work at a smelter.

He grew up basically unchurched, but began pondering "the object of life." After reading Parley P. Pratt's *Voice of Warning* he started attending church meetings, "was converted to the Gospel as they taught it," and on June 3, 1869 was baptized by Henry Grow and confirmed by Luther Twitchell in the Egans' Nineteenth Ward. He taught a Sunday School class, was ordained an elder in 1871, and received temple ordinances in the Endowment House "before I was 20 years old." He participated in the new Young Men's Mutual Improvement Association.[24]

William Moburn Egan, Egan Family Archives

As an adult Willy stood five feet, seven inches tall and weighed 150 pounds, had brown hair and blue eyes, was near-sighted, and had a rheumatic condition. When older brother Howard R. came in from Deep Creek and moved his family to Richmond in Cache Valley he induced Will to go with him. Will lived with them "mostly" for five years. A Salt Lake City directory for 1874 lists Will as a clerk and living with Tamson.[25] He went to Beck's school in the Seventeenth Ward and then to Morgan's College, where he studied bookkeeping and business training. He started bookkeeping, then took up bee-keeping and the honey business. With honey profits he bought a printing press and equipment, and for three years he published a monthly journal called *Our Deseret Home*. An 1885 directory lists him as a printer and publisher, living at Tamson's address. In time he felt unable to do both the editorial work and manage the business, so he quit.

In 1886, at the age of thirty-four, he married Ruth Nicholls, a native of Chatham, Kent, England. She was eleven years older than William. They had no children. They moved to Provo where Will and a partner, D. P. Felt, obtained another press and published the *Provo Utah Industrialist Monthly*. After three years, Will sold his share.[26] He had used Tamson's money to buy the printing plant, but its sale involved promissory notes that didn't get paid. Tamson sued the buyer, got judgment, but received nothing when the buyer declared bankruptcy.

Willy was ordained a seventy (comparable to a stake officer then) on March 28, 1890. He served a mission in the Eastern States while in his fifties. He returned home on April 11, 1905, just over a week after Tamson died. According to the 1906 Salt Lake City directory, he was a bookkeeper for People's Building and Savings Company.[27] He became especially interested in genealogy, science, and theology. He compiled a genealogical record book containing New England ancestry of his father, James Monroe, and another with extensive genealogical records for the Egan family.[28] He helped Howard R. compile and publish *Pioneering the West* in 1917.

Hyrum William Egan, Egan Family Archives

Ruth died on April 20, 1921 in the city at age eighty-one.[29] On June 15, 1921, William married for a second time to Lula Mazonna Winnie. They made their home at 3 Girard Avenue in the Capitol Hill neighborhood of Salt Lake City. William died on April 17, 1929. He is buried in the Salt Lake City Cemetery next to Tamson.[30] Lulu remarried, then died July 10, 1947, also in Salt Lake City.

Hyrum William Egan. He was Howard's son by Mary Ann Tuttle. He went to Deep Creek as a boy and worked there for six years. Father Howard stayed at Deep Creek until the mid-1870s, and Hyrum made the area his home. He homesteaded a ranch of 120 acres about three miles southeast of his father's place. He built a home, farmed, and had livestock. About 1877 Richard Preator, his wife Mary, and their family moved to Deep Creek. Hyrum then was twenty-six years old and so was the Preators' daughter, Mary Salome. The two fell in love and married at Deep Creek. They had two children born there, Hyrum Lorenzo in 1872 and Emily Theresa in 1874.[31]

The Hyrum Egans moved to Goose Creek, Idaho in 1880. They had two children born there, Mary in 1883 and Vida in 1885. Hyrum died in Albion, Idaho on March 4, 1888, at age thirty-seven. As of 1917, when *Pioneering the West* was published, his wife and family were living in Burley, Idaho and they had "quite a posterity."[32] Widow Mary died in 1930. She and Hyrum both are buried in Oakley, Idaho.[33]

Ira Ernest Egan. On February 5, 1861, Tamson gave birth to her and Howard's last child, Ira Ernest Egan. He lived in Salt Lake City through his early life, received schooling there, and at some point was a messenger boy for a telegraph company.[34] He married Emma Moss (1860–1925) on August 24, 1881. They had five children, born between 1883 and 1893.[35] The 1885 city directory says Ira was living a block south of Tamson and his occupation was "brewer." An 1889 directory terms him a "laborer," living at Tamson's address. The 1890 listing shows him still residing there and working as a "barkeep" for the P. T. Nystrom Commercial Saloon at 40 East and First South. In 1917, when *Pioneering the West* came off the press, Ira was living near Smithfield, Cache County. He died on December 13, 1933 at age 72 in Maywood, Los Angeles County, California.

*Ira Ernest Egan,
Egan Family Archives*

Howard Egan's Hundredth Birthday Reunion

By the turn of the century, 1900, four developments produced renewed family interest in Howard Egan. The first was the wave of genealogy concerns, which the Church was actively promoting, that washed over Richard Erastus, Howard R., and William. William collected genealogy data from family members. He created the William M. Egan Temple Record Book. Ras filled a genealogy mission to Ireland, Canada, and New Hampshire, then compiled what's catalogued in the LDS Church Family

History Library as the Richard Erastus Egan Book of Genealogy. Howard R. became the one who arranged for temple work to be done for the relatives. In March 1913 Ras told William that "it'd be a good thing to have the family organized into a society so as to have this work attended to systematically."[36]

A second stirring of interest in Howard undoubtedly was the big 1897 celebration marking the 50th anniversary of the 1847 pioneers. A four-day "Utah Pioneer Jubilee" took place in July 1897.[37] Recognition and accolades for the original pioneers permeated Utah on a grand scale that year. Howard, of course, featured prominently in the original group of pioneers.

A third development was Howard R.'s rescue of father Howard's papers after Tamson died in March 1905. The loose and random papers were going to be destroyed when her house was torn down. Howard R., in town for Tamson's funeral, gathered up some of the most valuable. To make those records available to family members, he arranged for them to be transcribed. He and William decided to publish a book about Howard. Linked to the book idea, the two of them hoped to erect a monument to honor Howard.

As a fourth motivator, the brothers realized that their generation soon would be gone, removing the glue that held the family together. To somehow pass a leadership torch along, they felt the need for an Egan family organization. To make that happen, they held a reunion of Howard's descendants on the centennial of Howard's birth, June 15, 1915.

On that occasion, 185 of Howard's descendants gathered in Salt Lake City's Nineteenth Ward chapel. "After the preliminary exercises and during the address of welcome, various members of the family were introduced to each other and the roll was called." Each branch of the family was represented on a large-size family tree graph that Howard R. had prepared with the help of son-in-law Walter Hill. In attendance were sixty-one from Howard R.'s family, sixty-three from Richard Erastus's family, and others who were not identified by family branch. Relatives far away in Idaho and Wyoming were "not represented well."[38] After readings and a poem, those present voted to make the Egan organization perpetual. However, there's no record that any future meetings of the Egan organization happened. President Howard R.'s death in March 1916 appears to be why the organization fizzled.[39]

But Howard R.'s death didn't terminate the book idea. William took charge of it and pushed the problem-plagued project through, getting *Pioneering the West* published in 1917. Even though the perpetual Egan organization failed, as did the plans for a monument, that book fulfilled Howard's children's goal early in the twentieth century to ensure that he not be forgotten.

Plans to Publish Howard's Diaries

While Howard was alive he "had a private desk packed full of papers," Will said, "but that any of them had any thing of value more than private correspondence none of the family knew. Even at the time of his death no attempt was made to examine his papers and see if there was anything worthy of preservation until Mother died." Will knew that Howard's life story, if written, would make a "remarkably interesting book," but "neither himself [Howard] or family were of a literary turn of mind, and hence much that would be of great interest was never committed to paper. During his life time no thought was ever given to anything of a literary nature."[40]

When Tamson died, Will was a missionary in the eastern United States and unable to return for the funeral. By then "the old home had been ransacked ready to be pulled down." Just in time, Howard R. rummaged through his father's desk and records and gathered up writings that he wanted to read when back home in Richmond, Utah. He saw more of his father's papers scattered over the floor. Right after that, the house was pulled down, and out went many of Howard's "voluminous papers."[41] One winter when Howard R. was unable to work, he hand-copied Howard's entire hard-to-read diary of the 1847 Pioneers' trip, in order to make the account more readable. He also found diaries his father wrote during other trips.[42]

He had Howard's diaries on his mind when, in 1910, the Skelton Publishing Company of Salt Lake City published a little book called *Among the Shoshones*.[43] Written by Elijah Nicholas "Uncle Nick" Wilson, it told about his life as a "white Indian boy" and experiences with the Pony Express and stagecoaching, including some with Major Egan. It's extremely likely that Wilson's accounts inspired Howard R. and Will to want a similar book about Howard, or at least it reinforced such an idea that they already had. Within a year they asked publisher Robert Skelton to take on their project. Will, of a "literary mind," had engaged in publishing, printing, and writing before, having edited and published *Our Desert Home* and *The Utah Industrialist*, as well as operating a printing business Tamson had helped fund.[44]

Book Contract with Skelton Publishing Company

Will and Howard R.'s correspondence about the project is in a file called "Publishing Pioneering the West" in the Beinecke Library at Yale University.[45] According to Howard R.'s March 26, 1911 letter to Will, the diary project then was well underway. Willy, as Howard R. called him, had a typist transcribing father Howard's journals. Howard R. had shopped the book idea and received estimates of costs. That summer, 1911, Howard R. signed an agreement with Skelton Publishing Company, located at

45 Richards Street in Salt Lake City, to publish one thousand books, similar to *Among the Shoshones*.[46]

The initial plan proved impossible for the writers and their finances. Howard R., the book's financier, suffered income reversals. His health interfered, too. "I have had a very bad time with my Eyes & Head, but am getting better now," he wrote early in 1913.[47] The book project didn't generate much family support. Late in 1914, Howard expressed frustration: "Let me say that if the Egan family doesn't show more interest than at present I am afraid we can not raise the money to publish the book."[48] By then, Howard R., Will, and Mr. Skelton knew that the book would not be published anytime soon. On April 13, 1915, Howard R. still was struggling financially.

Howard R.'s Additions of "Thrilling Experiences"

Also causing delays, Howard R. and Will kept adding materials to include in the book. Because he was "unable to walk or work much," Howard R. wrote down some of his recollections of "thrilling" Egan experiences and sent those to Will to possibly add to the manuscript. Howard R. continually sent Will story after story. He also sent Will original documents "that might be of interest." [49]

When the family gathered on June 15, 1915 to honor father Howard's 100th birthday, the book manuscript was far from finished. On July 13 Howard R. faced a problem. His typist's typewriter became unusable and he needed to buy "an Underwood machine" as soon as he was able.[50] On August 29 Howard R. thanked "dear brother" Will for "the great interest you are taking in the work we are trying to accomplish," and discussed finances for the book and the monument.[51] Skelton called on Howard R. on November 15 and they "closed the bargain for 2 thousand books," or double the number originally projected.[52] On December 7 Howard R. believed the book was nearing completion, so he was studying "different ways and means to make a quick sell out." They felt they should give complimentary copies to each leading newspaper in Salt Lake City, so they might "give us good commentary." He wondered about running an ad for good reliable agents in each town. "Brother Skelton told me he would bind in leather twelve or fifteen copies complimentary," so Howard R. thought Church President Joseph F. Smith should get one.[53]

Selling books and paying print costs became challenges. Howard R. praised the promotional handbills Will had produced "so cheap and good."[54] Will, probably to Mr. Skelton's consternation, still was working on the manuscript. "You may stop the number of pages any where you please after the 300 pages," Howard R. told Will; "of course the more pages put in the more money for printing and less for us at the same price." He told Will not to sell books until they were printed. Delays hurt, because

Howard R. had to pay interest on money he borrowed to advance to Skelton, and because they were losing "the best selling season," meaning the holidays.[55]

Printing and Delays

Skelton started printing some signatures of the book. Howard R. rejoiced on February 6, 1916 that the manuscript was "again on the press with the prospect of being completed immediately." Expecting his own death, he urged Will to finish the job at once. "Push the Printer and give him to understand that the sooner he finishes the job the better it will be for him as well as us."[56] Howard R. had paid $338 cash down out of a total cost of $997.00. Books if sold at $1.50 apiece would generate $3,000, which would mean profits of $2,003.[57] Howard R. became irate that Skelton had used the Egan project's paper, bought at one price, on another project, which meant the price of paper went up and Skelton had no means to buy paper for *Pioneering the West*.[58] On February 18, news that the project was on course kept him from "acting harshly." Since Christmas, his feeling had reduced to "just smouldering."[59]

With Howard R.'s patience running out and his health failing, his son Horace warned Will that "something has got to be done, father is worrying his self to death about it and we have got to get it threw some way and that rite away."[60] Howard R. died the next day, March 17, 1916. Will now carried the sole family responsibility to get the book published. He struggled to feed final pages to the printer.[61] Meanwhile, Skelton battled financial problems.[62] For the rest of 1916 and into 1917 the project staggered along.

Pioneering the West is Born

On July 27, 1917, Skelton sent great news to Howard R. and Amanda's son James Alva Egan in Central Idaho. Skelton wrote that by the time James received his letter "we will have *Pioneering the West* finished." He proposed that "you remit with your various orders half the retail price of the books" and that the Egans keep the other half to pay their expenses. He asked for some indication of what number he should bind "for immediate requirements."[63] On August 10 Skelton's concern was "paying money we borrowed at different times to make the book in consequence of your family failure to do so." Books must be sold, he urged: "We made you a very liberal offer of half the retail price. You should be able to reduce your loan in the same proportion." Skelton needed to know "who are the lawful successors to your Father, and who will assume and carry out his part of this matter?" Skelton wrote with "no feeling of ill will" but "we must have money soon to pay what we have borrowed to finish the book."[64]

On November 3, 1917, the *Deseret Evening News* announced the publication.[65] On November 29 Alva wrote to Will that he received copies of the book "a few days ago." Like music to Will's ears, Alva added, "I sure like the books."[66]

The formal title is *Pioneering the West, 1846 to 1847: Major Howard Egan's Diary. Also Thrilling Experiences of Pre-Frontier Life Among Indians; Their Traits, Civil and Savage, and Part of Autobiography, Inter-Related to His Father's by Howard R. Egan.* The book contains 302 pages and its hardcover has green or gray or brown cloth-covered boards, with the title stamped in black on the front board and the spine strip. On some is a horseman illustration in black on the front board.[67] The title page credits Wm. M. Egan, who "Edited, Compiled, and Connected In Nearly chronological Order" the contents. The book's publisher and copyright holder is the Howard R. Egan Estate, Richmond, Utah, 1917. Books sold for $1.50 and $1.75.[68]

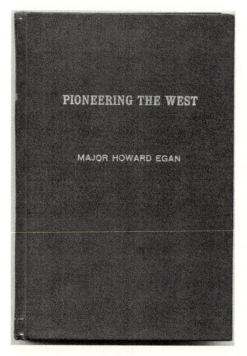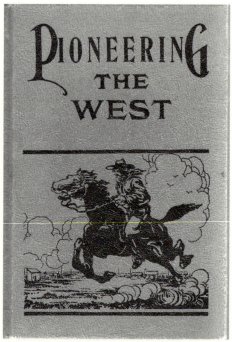

The preface tells readers that the book "contains no fiction, but is the actual experiences and personal views of the writers." It stresses that "the book is not written from a religious nor scientific standpoint; nor is it written in poise of a hero, ostentation or self praise, but is simple in style and diction." In 1915 Howard R. had told Will that the book must "take a non-Mormon view," an outside-of-family view.[69] *Pioneering the West* is divided into four parts: (1) Pioneering: Nauvoo to Salt Lake, (2) Salt Lake: Incidents of Early Settlement, (3) Pioneering: Salt Lake To California, and (4) Thrilling Experiences of Pre-Frontier Life. A concluding section finishes Howard's life story and brings Egan history down to Howard R. and William's time. An Appendix contains genealogy and family organization information.

It's not known how many books Skelton finally printed or how well the books sold during the first few years. After the book's copyright expired in 1942, no evidence indicates that the book was re-copyrighted. It now is in the public domain, and early in this current century several firms reprinted it. It is widely available, though first edition copies are hard to find and as of 2015 rare book sites sold them for prices near or above $200.

The Egan Papers at Yale University

When Skelton finished with the typed manuscript, he returned it, the documents, and the photos to Will. What happened next to the Egan original journals and other papers isn't known. That Will last possessed them is a good bet, because when a wealthy collector of Western Americana bought the Egan collection containing the diaries, Will's own materials were part of the collection.

Mr. William Robertson Coe (1869–1955) was an insurance, railroad, and business executive, a generous philanthropist for the academic discipline of American Studies, and an avid collector of books and documents related to the Old West. For forty-five years, starting about 1914, he built up a fine collection of pioneer-era original diaries, manuscripts, letters, photographs, newspapers, and publications that depicted life in the western United States. One part of Coe's collection focused on early Utah and on Mormonism.[70] Edward Eberstadt, a New York dealer in rare books and documents, served as Mr. Coe's agent to locate and purchase what became known as the Coe Collection.[71]

Eberstadt went to Salt Lake City, hoping to buy Mormon pioneer William Clayton's original 1847 journal from the Clayton family. He had lunch with John A. Widtsoe, secretary to Church president Heber J. Grant. Dr. Widtsoe shocked the collector while mentioning an Egan journal: "Eberstadt, you got Egan's journal out of the state, but you are just one day too late on the Clayton records," which the Church had just obtained.[72] Apparently Eberstadt helped Coe obtain the Egan items, including Howard's journals for 1847, 1849–1850, and 1855, James M. Monroe's diary for 1841–1845, and William M. Egan's 1863 diary and personal papers. By 1948 Coe had donated his collections to Yale University in New Haven, Connecticut. The Coe Collection opened to the public in September 1952. Currently it is catalogued as "Western Americana Collection, Beinecke Rare Book and Manuscript Library, Yale University." The Egan Papers are a treasured component of that collection.[73] Microfilms of the Egan materials are available in several research libraries in the West. ◆

~ 30 ~

Major Howard Egan: The Man And His Legacy

A simple summary of Howard's life shows that, during his six decades and two years, he lived in Ireland, Canada, on a man-of-war ship, in Salem, Nauvoo, Winter Quarters, Salt Lake City, California, and Deep Creek. He became an orphan at age thirteen. Religiously, he came from an Irish-Protestant family background, and in his mid-twenties joined The Church of Jesus Christ of Latter-day Saints. His adult endeavors include being a sailor, rope maker, policeman, money collector, pioneer, freighter, trading post operator, cattle drover and merchant, explorer, mail carrier, Nauvoo Legion major, manager of Pony Express and stagecoach operations, store operator, assister of Native Americans, silver miner, and security guard. He had four wives, three of whom divorced him. He fathered six sons, two daughters, and parented one stepson.

Previous chapters tell *what he did*, but scattered in them are mosaic pieces, which, positioned together, show *who he was* as a person. They produce a reasonably good portrait of his personality and character, which follows here.

Impressive Presence

Only one photograph of Howard exists, and it misleads. Salt Lake City photographer Edward Martin's studio view of Howard taken circa 1865 shows a rather unattractive man with a dark, heavy beard. Photographs taken in that time period typically made the subjects look serious and dour. In contrast to that unflattering picture, Elizabeth Kane described Howard as "an exceedingly noble looking fellow." Her diary gives evidence that Howard conveyed a good impression physically and personally. He had some kind of appeal that convinced four women to marry him. People of standing regarded Howard well and trusted him. His obituary praised his good reputation for "being friendly to everyone" and that he had very few enemies.[1]

Major Howard Egan, 1865, Egan Family Archives

Howard was a well-regarded "somebody." Church presidents Joseph Smith and Brigham Young both took Howard into their confidences. LDS apostle Heber C. Kimball adopted Howard as a son, in terms of priesthood operations. In social circles people recognized his military rank and addressed him as "Major Egan." A leading Church apostle, George A. Smith, served as Howard's defense attorney in the Monroe murder trial. The big merchandising firm of Livingston and Kinkead relied on him to drive cattle to California, sell them, and handle large sums of money. Philadelphia lawyer Thomas Kane entrusted his life to him. Mail contractor George Chorpenning hired him to handle government-contracted mail shipments. The Pony Express and stagecoach executives gave him superintendency responsibilities. Miners elected him their district president. Government Indian agents respected his insights. Gosiute Indians befriended him. LDS Apostle Orson Pratt spoke at his funeral.

Perhaps more revealing of the regard held for him, Howard made a positive impression on his children. They felt proud of him. Son Richard Erastus's first son's middle name is Howard. Daughter Helen named her second son Howard. Tamson and the children erected a four-foot-tall headstone marking his grave. Nearly forty years after Howard's death, his aging son Howard R. and stepson William labored and, with scarce money, created, and published *Pioneering the West* to honor Howard's life and contributions. They also tried to erect a fine monument honoring him, but the effort fell short.

Storyteller with a Sense of Humor

One of Howard's traits that people liked was that he was an entertaining conversationalist and had a good sense of humor. Helen Mar Kimball and other Nauvoo young people liked when Howard guarded Brigham Young's home because they enjoyed Howard's "interesting yarns and anecdotes." While a large party of riders, returning to Nauvoo, stopped to rest, Brigham Young requested Howard to tell them an entertaining story. Son Richard Erastus reported in *Pioneering the West* that "when Father was at home for a brief time, they used to have a sociable evening at home with friends, at one home or another. As Father put in most all his time in going or coming, or in California, the good folks, especially the women folks, were always urging him to tell them some of his thrilling experiences."[2]

His humor shines through in the "Coyote in Chicken House" story, when he stood up a frozen dead coyote so that it looked like it was alive, prompting a ranch hand to shoot it. Another example is when he tricked an 1847 pioneer about the hornet tree.[3] Similarly, Mrs. Ferris told how Howard used humor when dealing with a man in camp who "swore at a round rate." In a loud voice Howard announced to the camp, with "a comical twinkle of the eye," that camp regulations disallowed swearing except by that man, because "he does it so easy, that he is appointed to do all the swearing for the train."[4]

Dependable Toughness

In unusual proportions, Howard possessed a toughness that blended courage, fearlessness, confidence, survival skills, and physical strength. In his youth he developed independence after losing first his mother and then his father, and then by being a sailor on a naval vessel. Waves, storms, winds, rocks, leaks, tangled ropes, and slippery decks steeled sailors to hardships and danger. So did living and working with sailors, a breed of men for whom good manners and politeness often didn't matter. In his thirties, his tenacity drew recognition. Hancock County deputy sheriff H. G. Ferris praised Howard as "a man who attends to his duty strictly and will never be taken or caught by surprise nor will never be seen running from danger." Later, Howard's military associate John R. Young named him as one of the Church's few "strong, fearless men." John D. Lee's biographer Juanita Brooks said Howard "was a stranger to fear." Utah War scholar Bill MacKinnon labeled Howard as "one of Brigham Young's most trusted agents," adding that "no Nauvoo Legion officer traveled as extensively and alone across unfriendly territory as did Egan."[5] A list of Howard's difficult and dangerous assignments during his adult years is long and impressive:

> Nauvoo police work, especially at night
> Protecting and guarding Joseph Smith in Nauvoo
> Protecting Brigham Young in Nauvoo and Utah
> Patrolling on horseback to monitor and control anti-Mormon vigilantes near Nauvoo
> Constant trading trips into isolated Missouri locations and back during 1846–1847
> Fulfilling a secret and danger-filled mission conveying Mormon Battalion money
> Being a captain in the 1847 Pioneer Company's trek into barely explored regions
> Leading an 1849 company on an undeveloped, dangerous southern route to California
> Operating a trading post in California's basically lawless southern gold region
> Dealing with James Monroe's crime against his family
> Droving a number of big herds of cattle nine hundred miles to California
> Exploring desolate sections of Nevada and Utah to find a central trail route
> Hauling ammunition secretly from California during the "Utah War"
> Escorting and guarding presidential emissary Thomas Kane from Utah to Philadelphia
> Establishing, supervising, riding with, and protecting Pony Express operations
> Establishing, supervising, driving for, and protecting stagecoach operations
> Dealing with Native American depredations on his mail stations and stagecoaches
> Directing posse members under fire during the "Morrisite War"
> Dealing fairly and taking risks with Gosiutes who surrounded his Deep Creek operations
> Establishing unprotected, isolated Deep Creek Station, ranch, sawmill, farm, and store

Porter Rockwell
Church History Library

Hosea Stout
Church History Library

Lot Smith
Church History Library

Robert T. Burton
Church History Library

Jacob Hamblin
Utah State Hist. Society

William Henry Kimball
Utah State Hist. Society

Ephraim Hanks
Utah State Hist. Society

Discussions about sturdy, seasoned Mormon and Utah frontiersmen usually start with Porter Rockwell, but Howard ranks near the top with Rockwell. The book *Rugged Men of the West*, published by the Daughters of Utah Pioneers (1995), focuses on Rockwell, Ephraim Hanks, Lot Smith, Jacob Hamblin, and Major Howard Egan, among others. In *Brigham's Boys* (1999), author Marlene Bateman Sullivan gives short biographies of sixteen men on whom Brigham Young relied to help "tame the West" and build up the Great Basin. Young often referred to these trusted can-do friends as his reliable "b'hoys." Howard is one of them.[6]

What Kind of Mormon?

After his conversion in 1842, Howard committed himself to The Church of Jesus Christ of Latter-day Saints and its well-being. Because converts needed to "gather to Zion," he sacrificed his rope-making job and home in Salem and moved Tamson and the boys to Nauvoo. There, he participated fully in Mormonism. He worked on the Nauvoo Temple construction project, paid tithing, and filled a mission to New England in 1844 to campaign for Joseph Smith for President and to proselytize. He accepted the new teaching about baptisms for the dead and had that ordinance performed for some of his kin. He made an extremely difficult faith commitment by entering into plural marriage. He and Tamson and plural wife Nancy received the newly introduced ordinances of the temple endowment and sealing. In Nauvoo, Howard was ordained a seventy and served in the seven-man presidency of the Seventeenth Quorum.

After Joseph Smith's murder, Howard accepted the Twelve Apostles as Smith's successors, and he gave lifetime support to Brigham Young's leadership of the Church. He embraced Elder Heber C. Kimball, Young's counselor, as a substitute father. Howard carried out numerous special, difficult assignments that Elders Young and Kimball gave him.

Howard didn't fit well today's description of an "active Mormon." In fact, neither did most people in the pioneer generation.[7] Given his constant travels and isolation, he couldn't be a go-to-meeting Saint. He didn't hold ward or stake positions. His name is absent from his seventies quorum's minutes, no doubt because he spent little time in the city. His principle church service was the special and difficult assignments that leaders gave him. In California's gold fields he helped Apostles Amasa Lyman and Charles C. Rich minister to LDS miners and collect tithes. He paid tithing. He donated to the Perpetual Emigrating Fund. Howard showed great charity toward Native Americans, and three years before he died he did missionary work among his Deep Creek Gosiute friends.

His 1855 diary shows that when he was far from church meetings he didn't do much to keep the Sabbath Day holy. In the early days of Mormonism, including the pioneer period, leaders urged Saints to keep the "Word of Wisdom," but didn't require it. Howard drank alcohol and used coffee, as did many "good Mormons" back then. With no temple in Utah until 1877, Howard, like most ex-Nauvooers, never entered a temple other than the one in Nauvoo. Although his three plural marriages ended in divorce, he did keep his temple marriage vows to Tamson, despite the Monroe betrayal.

In his personal writings Howard expressed his faith many times. Not effusive statements, they usually offered thanks to God. In his 1847 Pioneer Company journal, for example, on April 17 he wrote that "I thank the Lord for the privilege of being one of the number and enjoying the society of father Heber [Kimball]." One Sunday he termed the day as "set apart by Almighty God for His people to rest," so "we do not intend to travel." On April 19 word arrived from Winter Quarters "that my family was all well, which I thank the Lord for." In his April 21 letter to Tamson he urged her to be humble and prayerful, and to pray for her husband. A few days later he wrote in his diary, "thank the Lord the morrow is a day of rest." May 4: "Thank the Lord we are now in buffalo country." May 6: "Last night the Lord sent a light shower." Early in May he wrote to Tamson and asked her to "pray for me for I do not forget you night or morning." On May 13 he felt improved health "and I thank the Lord for it." On May 16 Howard said of Elder Kimball's talk to the camp that "the Spirit of the Lord rested upon him and he spoke with power, which cheered my soul." Regarding the Pioneer Company's progress as of May 31, Howard recorded, "The Lord has blessed and prospered us on our journey." On July 14, a wait-in-camp day, Howard and others

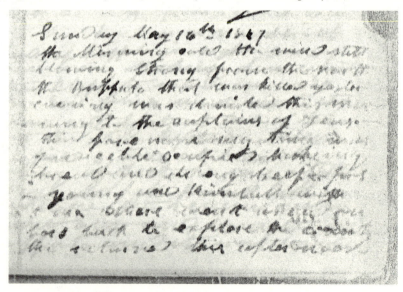

Howard Egan Diary, 1847, Beinecke Library, Yale University. Partial decipherment: "The morning cold[.] The wind still blowing strong from the north[.]"

retreated to the tops of "the Needles" where they "offered our prayers to the Almighty God in behalf of the sick and for our dear families." Upon reaching their Great Salt Lake Valley destination, Howard penned that "the saints have reason to rejoice and thank the Lord for this goodly land unpopulated by the Gentiles."

While he was a guest in the non-Mormon home of Thomas and Elizabeth Kane in Philadelphia, Elizabeth noted that "Egan said Grace for us, as simply and Christianly as it could have been done."

Howard's boys embraced the faith, although during their youth years the Church didn't yet have Sunday School, Primary, or Mutual. Erastus spent two years in England as a missionary. Stepson William wasn't baptized until he was eighteen. After he was married, he filled a mission. Erastus served as a bishop for twelve years, and long after Howard's death he went on a genealogy mission and visited Egan relatives in Ireland and Canada, promoted Egan family genealogy work, and saw that temple work was done for Egan kin. Howard R. likewise stayed committed to Mormonism.

A striking measure of father Howard's commitment to Mormonism is that he did not become a Californian. Howard knew California well, north and south. His constant trips there showed him how much better California was than Utah in terms of land, climate, and opportunities. Had Howard wanted the economic betterments or seasonal mildness that California offered him and his family, or had he wanted to distance himself from Mormon leadership or Mormon practices, he would have left Utah. Many dissatisfied Saints did, but he chose to stay within his church's Great Basin Kingdom.

Pioneering the Untamed West

A favorite Latter-day Saint hymn praises the "Blessed, honored Pioneer!"[8] A common image of Mormon pioneers is men and women colonizing untamed parts of the Great Basin, establishing villages, plowing, planting fields and orchards and gardens, irrigating, fencing, and building roads and bridges. They were community builders. Their men responded to mission calls, while their families learned to get along without them. The pioneer designation comfortably fits Howard and his family, both in the Salt Lake Valley and the western edge of Utah and parts of Nevada.

As an original pioneer in 1847, Howard helped to start turning the barren Great Salt Lake Valley into a city by plowing, planting, and building houses and fences. In 1848 and afterwards, he and Tamson planted orchards and gardens. He developed a fledgling leather industry. In a similar manner, although without a specific colonizing call, he pioneered and helped settle Deep Creek. He established a mail transfer station and ranch at isolated Ibapah, and developed roads, a farm, irrigation, pastures, sawmill, store, a cattle herd, and sheep flock. His exploring, and then setting up relay stations, led to the development of a few western communities. One traveler in 1859 observed that,

> I was forcibly reminded of the prediction that "the desert shall blossom as the rose," upon seeing a bunch of wheat which Capt. Howard Egan brought with him from the settlement at Iba-pah, or Deep Creek...Only a short time since, nothing was to be found west of the Great Salt Lake, but barren deserts and uncultivated and, except for the red man, uninhabited valleys and water courses...Now there are gardens and farms scattered throughout these western mountains, beautiful little oases in the desert...No one acquainted with the facts, will question for a moment that you are indebted for these improvements in the western portion of your Territory, primarily, to the mail route and its gentlemanly and energetic managers, and the names of Chorpenning, Schell, and Egan will be had in remembrance by the children of the pioneer settlers of these valleys.[9]

Businessman

Howard was a businessman. He engaged in at least eight businesses, and he succeeded in all but one or two. He manufactured and sold ropes. He ran a trading post in Gold Rush California. He partnered in a Salt Lake City leather manufactory. As an agent for the Livingston & Kinkead company, he bought, beefed up, and drove cattle to California and sold them. He superintended and supervised Pony Express operations and stagecoach operations, and in both positions he was responsible for land, buildings, livestock, coaches, equipment, and dozens of employees. He operated the Deep Creek ranch and store and "a good-sized supply store" in Ruby Valley. After stagecoaching closed down, Howard worked mining claims as "Egan & Company" in partnership with other miners, which venture failed.

For each of these businesses, Howard had to learn its distinctive tools and techniques. He had to understand contracts, financing, purchasing, payrolls, paying bills, bookkeeping, salesmanship, hiring, firing, motivating, government rules and regulations, and land titles.

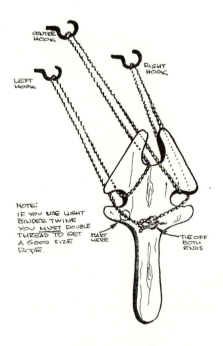

Ropemaking tool

Livestock Skills

In Howard's day, few worked with livestock more, or knew them better, than he did. He captained and drove in four covered wagon companies pulled by oxen, mules, and horses. He had charge of several pack-mule trains between Utah and California. He bought and sold livestock. He drove several big cattle herds from Utah to California. He bought and rode mustangs for the Pony Express. He bought mule and horse teams for and drove them ahead of stagecoaches. He knew how to feed, care for, round up, brand, hitch, shoe, drive, buy and sell, and nurse oxen, mules, and horses. On the Deep Creek Ranch he grazed sheep as well as cattle. His hands knew well the feel of cowhide, fleece, horseflesh, ropes, reins, harnesses, whips, saddles, bridles, and stirrups. His back and arm muscles tossed tons of hay. His feet and nose endured manure. Head-to-foot, Howard was a livestock man.

Literate

Howard penned and pencilled three diaries that we know of. He wrote letters to Tamson, Church officials, federal Indian agents, transportation agents, and newspapers. In Ireland, Canada, on board ship, or somewhere else, Howard learned to write. He wrote with a good hand, sometimes, and for his day he had good spelling, fairly good punctuation, and he expressed himself well. He probably became a diarist through the example of colleagues Hosea Stout, John D. Lee, and William Clayton.

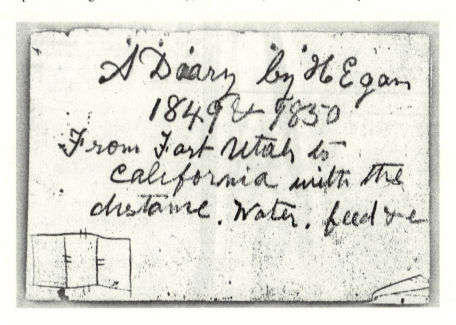

His diary documenting his 1847 Pioneer Company journey is considered one of the best accounts written during that historic trek. Then in 1849, while his wagon company struggled to help open up the southern route to California, his diary listed and numbered campsites and distances and described early California. That diary merited publication in the Hafens's *Journals of the Forty-niners Salt Lake to Los Angeles.* In 1855 Howard made diary entries during a trip to California, then while exploring on the way back, and then while selling cattle in the Sierras. It documents his finding of what became the central route's "Egan Trail."

Comfortable Being Away

By obligation and choice, Howard was not a homebody. That he had the emotional ability to be gone for long periods of time probably resulted from patterning. That is, he lost his mother while young, and his father soon after that. He grew up with no model of married life or family life to learn from. He became a sailor, which probably took him away from his siblings in Canada for extended periods. After the Saints left Nauvoo, Howard spent long periods away from home. Except for three years in Nauvoo and perhaps four in Salt Lake City when he had a home life, his was mostly an isolated existence on western trails, ranches, and mining claims.

His gold rush separation, cattle droving, and then mail trips across the Great Basin in both directions, accustomed him to being away from home. Between 1858 and 1873 he resided mostly in the remote Deep Creek region, and worked within a stretch of five hundred inhospitable miles between Salt Lake City and Carson City. The Deep Creek Station and ranch required him to live there while going out on location, supervising the Pony Express and stagecoach operations. He did visit Tamson during business stops in the city, but in the Egan home in the Nineteenth Ward he was more visitor than resident. Howard managed to handle being far from home and constantly traveling. Son Ransom estimated that Howard had made more than fifty trips across the central routes during his mail explorations and cattle drives.[10]

Sense of Fairness and Generosity

To our generation, Howard's killing of James Monroe seems unreasonable and excessive. Yet the trial evidence shows that he carried out the avenging calmly and deliberately, not viciously or in anger. Monroe committed an extremely serious crime against the Egan family, so Howard felt justified in defending his family's honor. His "Rocky Mountain justice," severe by modern society's morally casual standards, had its place among many citizens back then. Howard's sense of fairness caused him to raise stepson William, the result of Monroe and Tamson's affair, as his own son. William, lifelong, referred to Howard as "Father."

William documented Howard's kind nature toward the Egan boys. "Father never punished us," he said, and "never spoke a cross word but once to me." In that one case, Howard apologized, which hurt Will "more than a good licking."[11] Howard did expect his boys to follow his orders, as Ransom learned when he took an unauthorized shortcut (see Chap. 25) and Howard instructed him never to do anything like that again without orders. "I never did," Ransom said, "for that was a cold bath for me." Will said that Tamson told him that one year she had purchased fifteen hundred dollars worth of provisions, an enormous expenditure, which she gave to handcart companies and others in need. When she told Howard about it, he didn't criticize her. Instead, his only comment was, "that is right Mother and you shall be blessed for your good heart."[12]

Howard donated generously to assist poor English converts to emigrate to Utah and didn't begrudge it. He gave a hundred dollar gold coin, more than two thousand dollars in our day, to his associate William H. Shearman, who was leaving for a mission to England, to use to help as many converts to emigrate as possible. Shearman made loans, and each recipient signed a note for the amount received, and promised to pay Howard back after reaching Utah. About four years from the date of the last note, Howard figured out how much the thirty notes totaled in American money. He had hoped to use the paybacks to finance another round of emigrant loans, in the spirit of the Church's Perpetual Emigrating Fund. He briefly thought he "might be able to collect the most of it by calling on each person owing him," but then decided not to press the matter because, "probably they needed the money." So he had his son Ransom burn the notes.[13]

Mrs. Ferris, at the end of her 1853 journey with Howard's cattle drive, said that while they were in the Carson Valley, he rode ahead. Soon, they found Egan had a good dinner waiting for them. "This man, with all his faults, has many excellent qualities; we surely have reason to be grateful to him for numerous kind offices."[14]

Cautious Compassion for Native Americans

Howard's years of travel, trading, Church assignments, and transportation work gave him familiarity with Native Americans. During a skirmish on the Elkhorn River in June 1848, an Otoe or Omaha Indian shot Howard through the wrist. During his trip on the southern trail to California during the gold rush, Indians seemed a constant menace to his party's men and livestock. He encountered Indians regularly during long cattle trips to and from California and during his Pony Express and stagecoach work.

In 1857, with the Brigham Young traveling party, he had visited Indians as far north as Fort Limhi. He used Indians to help him explore and locate mail stations. He hired Indian workers for his Deep Creek operations.

Howard became one of but a score of Mormon frontiersmen known for understanding how Indians thought and why they acted the way they did, and for being able to work with them. Constant interactions gave him the ability to gauge whom among Indians to trust, when to be cautious, and how to settle differences. As noted, late in 1858, the federal government asked George Chorpenning to recommend someone to be Utah's superintendent of Indian affairs. Chorpenning recommended Howard as suitable for that daunting task.[15]

Howard recognized that encroachments by Mormons and other whites had deprived Gosiutes of prime hunting and gathering lands. That's why, in February 1859, in a letter to Superintendent of Indian Affairs Jacob Forney, Howard argued: "Years of experience has led me to believe that the depredations committed by the Indians on the Deep Creek and at Ruby Valley is simply owing to the fact that no provision of any kind is made to meet the ever recurring want of the Indian viz, food and raiment. Now Sir, a life of predatory warfare on persons and property is the result."[16] When Howard heard that soldiers might be sent and a post established, he argued that such was no solution because "the same evils [raids] would still persist." Instead, an Indian farm would reduce Indian hostilities. Superintendent Forney appreciated Howard's insight and worked to implement it.

While involved with the Pony Express, stagecoaching, and the Deep Creek ranch, both Howard and his son Ransom made many friends among the Gosiutes by kind treatment, "and were counted as big chiefs by them." They were protected "many times" by these Indians.[17] *Pioneering the West* documents that Howard had friends among the Gosiutes, and describes many situations in which he showed compassion and concern for ones in dire conditions.

His treatment of his Indian friend Tecumsee on cattle drives, in Sacramento, and in the Egan home is a good example. Another is the "Old Man left to Die" story, when Howard provided food and clothing to a dying Indian whom tribesmen intended should die.[18] Stepson William observed that

> ...while Father was working the mining property he was also engaged in missionary work among the Indians, who were induced through his influence to settle down to civilized life, and have since became quite successful in farming, for they had been used as farm and hay hands many years on the Deep Creek property and now they were shown how to work for themselves. He also aided much in teaching them and also imparting to them a knowledge of the Gospel, as well as in good habits of honesty and industry.

Published histories dealing with Anglo and Native American interactions in the American West spotlight hostilities. It's refreshing, therefore, to find how Howard got along with his Indian neighbors near and beyond today's Utah-Nevada border.

His Place in the History of the American West

History celebrates best those people who were the firsts, the most influential, the most colorful, or the most notorious. Likewise, stage plays have leading actors and key supporting actors. A *Deseret Evening News* assessment of Howard, published in 1917, called him "one of the best known characters of his day throughout the western country," a person "prominent in all the early activities of the community."[19] Those comments show that, even two decades after his death, he was recognized for his supporting and starring roles in history. In 1950, in the wake of 1947 celebrations of the Mormon Pioneers centennial, the *Deseret News* asked "Who is Utah's outstanding outdoorsman of the 1850–1950 century?" It then answered, "His name, Major Howard Egan," and summarized his ventures with the 1847 Pioneers, Pony Express, Indians, game, and trails.[20]

According to Will Bagley, a leading historian of the American West, "Egan was a Western frontiersman of the first order," and his involvement with the Pony Express "would secure his place in the annals of the West." Pony Express scholar Joseph J. Di Certo said "Howard Egan...stands out as one of the great names in pioneer history."[21] It is disconcerting to find, therefore, that Howard's name rarely appears in general histories of, and reference books about, the American West. *The Oxford History of the American West* (1994) doesn't mention him, and gives the Pony Express less than a page of discussion. The *Encyclopedia of the American West* (1997) has no entry for Howard, nor does the *New*

Encyclopedia of the American West (1998).[22] Even the fine regional reference volume, *Utah History Encyclopedia*, has no entry for Howard, although it does mention him in its "Pony Express in Utah" entry, and cites *Pioneering the West* as a best source to read.[23]

Howard served lead roles, starring roles, in four western history developments. The first was his being a lead drover of herds of cattle to help California during its early years. Unfortunately, the importance of that livestock flow for California's development and for Utah's economy is under-recognized by historians. Howard, as much as anyone, made that economic movement happen.

He deserves star billing, too, for locating and making usable a vital central trail route from Salt Lake City to California that ran south of the Great Salt Lake. While a great national debate argued about how best to service California by trail, Howard was one of several who probed for a better, more direct way than along the Humboldt River. By difficult searches he discovered such a better trail. Captain James Simpson receives accolades for supposedly finding that route, but Howard's "Egan Trail" made Simpson's work possible. That trail, then road, became *the* major western wing route for the Pony Express and the overland stagecoach relays. Pioneering that route is Howard's most impactful contribution to history.

His other two "starring roles" were management ones. He set up and supervised most of the "west wing" of the Pony Express. He was the district agent for much of the "west wing" of the overland stagecoach mail for nearly a decade. He is the one man who primarily made the west wing operational for both of those enterprises. The Pony Express and the stagecoaches changed the West, and manager Howard made the riders and coaches keep going as much or more than anyone else on the ground.

History generally considers George Chorpenning and government explorer Captain James Simpson the lead actors in the central trail story. And in the Pony Express saga, Russell, Majors, and Waddell usually take center stage. Then, in the overland stagecoach's west-wing studies, Wells Fargo receives top billing. However, Howard deserves to share the center-stage spotlight and applause with those "stars."

Howard does receive deserved attention in some regional and specialized histories, such as books and articles about the 1847 Mormon Pioneers, gold rush, Pony Express, development of western trails, the U.S. mail, Utah legal history, Mormon Trail emigrating companies, Native Americans, Tooele County, Deep Creek, and eastern Nevada. When these separate examinations of Howard's involvements are looked at all together as a whole, they show how very widespread his contributions were to developing the trans-West's commerce, transportation, communication, and settlement.

His Place in Mormon History

In the sub-field of Mormon history, Howard played no starring roles but was a key supporting actor in many events. During the Camp of Israel's crossing of Iowa and then through the Saints' first winter at Winter Quarters, he performed extraordinary service as a buyer and trader, getting needed supplies for the Mormon refugees from farms and businesses in various Missouri locations. His secret errand with John D. Lee to Santa Fe to bring back badly needed Mormon Battalion pay to Winter Quarters was crucial for the Church. His work as a captain of ten in the 1847 Pioneer Company, and then as one of those who started the first buildings and farms in the Great Salt Lake Valley,

Utah State Historical Society

are notable contributions. The story of Mormons in the gold rush features his work with the Salt Lake Trading Company and his helping two apostles minister to LDS prospectors. In the legal history of Mormonism and discussions of pioneer violence, Howard's trial for the Egan murder receives major attention. Histories of the Utah War, Fort Limhi, and the Morrisite affair include Howard's involvements.[24] Howard receives attention, too, in biographies of Brigham Young, Heber C. Kimball, Hosea Stout, William Clayton, John D. Lee, Thomas L. Kane, Robert T. Burton, and others.

However, historians have yet to appreciate two of Howard's vital roles that affected Mormon history, not just western history. One is the cattle business he helped develop between Utah and California, and its benefits to Mormon stock raisers and to the LDS Church's finances. The other is how his mail delivery and stagecoach transportation between Salt Lake City and California contributed to the well-being of Mormonism during the 1850s and 1860s. When those two gaps in Mormon history are filled, Howard's contributions in Mormon history will be enhanced, perhaps giving him star billings.

Monuments, Markers, Namings, and Events

A "Brigham Young Monument," also called the "Pioneer Monument," with Young's statue atop it, dominates the plaza between Temple Square and the LDS office block in downtown Salt Lake City. As the statue and the sculpts and plaques around it demonstrate, one with Howard's name on it, society uses monuments and markers to recognize and publicly honor important historical events and people. Back in 1917, the Egan family organization made plans for a monument to honor him, which would be seven feet across, supporting a "not high" monument.[25] It was never finished.

Kanesville Tabernacle Interior (2015), courtesy Kenneth Mays

Howard's name is also on a plaque at This Is the Place State Park. It is inscribed on several Pony Express monuments. A plaque in downtown Salt Lake City, at the site where the Pony Express division headquarters once stood, in part reads: "Here Ben Ficklin, General Superintendent and Major Howard Egan and James C. Bromley, division superintendents, had their headquarters." Then it lists fifteen "honoured Utah Riders," including Howard, Richard E., and Howard R. Egan.[26] At Ibapah, Utah, Howard's Deep Creek efforts are praised on a large monument. On a more modest scale, his importance is memorialized by objects on display at the Daughters of Utah Pioneers Museum.

His name endures today on geographic features in the west desert landscape, where he spent so much time and energy. Most apparent is Egan Canyon and its Egan

Creek. At the canyon's west mouth, the Pony Express and then the Overland Mail operated Egan Station, and because prospectors discovered gold there, for a few years a mining town named Egan stood there. It's now a ghost town.[27] The "Egan Range" of mountains extends from Egan Creek, near the historic community of Cherry Creek, southward for approximately a hundred miles. North of Egan Canyon, in what is now the Cherry Creek Range, is Egan Peak, 7,440 feet high. On government topographical maps, Egan Peak is in the "Egan Quad." Also, northwest of Egan Canyon's west side is a region the United States Geological Survey quad maps called "Egan Basin," and marked within it is an "Egan Basin Well." Near Ely, Nevada is a recently designated "South Egan Range Wilderness."

Left and below: Brigham Young Monument, Main Street, Salt Lake City, Utah (with names of the 1847 Pioneers). Above: Ibapah Monument.

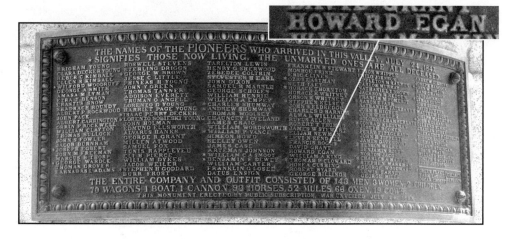

Celebrations and commemorations likewise honor and recognize important historical events and persons. For that reason, a Major Howard Egan jubilee took place June 11–13, 2015, honoring his two-hundredth birthday. Sponsored by the Egan family, Brigham Young University's Charles Redd Center for Western Studies, and the Sons of the Utah Pioneers, it drew more than six hundred attendees. At an evening symposium, four scholars presented papers evaluating Howard's life and contributions, and a temporary museum displayed rare Egan-related items including his Nauvoo Legion sword, and a Joseph Smith note ordering that Howard be paid for police service. To appreciate Howard's Pony Express work, more than forty vehicles traveled much of the Utah section of the Pony Express Trail. About sixty-five people hiked the 4.5 mile long, unpaved mountain trail east of Salt Lake City's Emigration Canyon, which is part of the original 1847 pioneers' route that Howard had traveled about ten times. Also, many visited Egan sites in Salt Lake City, including Howard's grave. The finale was an Egan family day at This Is the Place Heritage Park that featured Egan history-linked events and period activities.

Many in Howard's posterity meaningfully feel related to him and his life story, particularly his work as an 1847 pioneer and Pony Express rider. They own and cherish rare and costly original editions of *Pioneering the West* or recent paperback reprints. That jam-packed, small book still serves as the primary memorial to Howard's life. To the book's lasting credit, its crisp title distills succinctly and well what Major Howard Egan's life, in large measure, was all about—pioneering in the great American West.

With devotion to duty,
Courage, strength, and foresight,
He pioneered in so many ways,
The pre-railroad American West
And its vital institutions,
And made it and them better. ◆

Egan family reunion, 2015

Notes

Chapter 1

1. Brian de Breffny, *Irish Family Names*; Grenham, *Irish Family Names*; Conor Mac Hale, "The Mac Egan Inheritance."

2. It was known as Kings County until it was informally changed to Offaly when the Irish Free State was established in 1922.

3. Dsomhnaill, "The Townlands of Offaly." "Meeleghans is more like a townland or an address or a farm," Irish genealogist James Hennessy to Janet Sloan, June 10, 1992, copy in author's files.

4. Eamonn O. Dsomhnaill, "The Townslands of Offaly," in *Ireland's Own* (Summer Asnual, 1988), photocopy in author's possession. Edward Egan to Richard Egan, Feb. 19, 1900. An Edward letter to Richard Erastus Egan dated March 24, 1900 states that "William was the oldest brother and as such inherited the whole place until he afterwards admitted his brother Howard to partnership."

5. The cottage picture is in Egan, *Pioneering the West*, 10. The cottage's exact latitude and longitude are: 53 degrees 15' and 24.83" longitude, and 7 degrees, 25' and 53.12" West. See Google Earth. Re Lord Digby's land ownership see Elayne Stanton Allebest, "Howard Egan's Irish Heritage," 10.

6. Killeigh Parish of the Church of Ireland was in the Diocese of Kildare as of 1808–1835.

7. James Hennessy to Robert and Janet Sloan, June 6, 1991. He notes baptisms from 1713 to 1799 in Geashill and Killeigh.

8. Hegarty, *The Story of Ireland*.

9. *Traveller's New Guide Through Ireland*, 125.

10. Byrne, *A Walk Through Tullamore*, 1.

11. Ibid., 2.

12. Ibid., 3.

13. Lewis, *Topographical Dictionary of Ireland*, 2nd ed., 605.

14. Table of prices for 1811 for Kings County, *Farming in Offaly Down the Years*.

15. Lewis, *Topographical Dictionary*, 183, 185, 187.

16. Otuathaigh, *Ireland Before the Famine*, 135–136.

17. Stommel and Stommel, *Volcano Weather: 1816*, 44.

18. *Traveller's New Guide*, 128–129.

19. Ibid., 228, 128.
20. Byrne, *Sources for Offaly History*, 100.
21. Kearney, *The Long Ridge*, 117–126.
22. Stewart, *The Shape of Irish History*, 3–4.
23. Quoted in Hagerty, *The Story of Ireland*, 190.
24. "Year without a Summer," *Wikipedia*.
25. "Parochial Schools Returns for 1824."
26. "Protestant Schools," in *The Long Ridge*, 76–77.
27. Parish Records of Killeigh, Diocese of Kildare, King's County (Offaly), Ireland, Baptisms 1808–1823, Marriages 1808–1932, Deaths 1808–1835. FHL film 990092. Her death record gives, "Anne Eagan, female, birth 1778 of Meelahans, County Offaly, Ireland, spouse Howard Eagan, death Feb. 15 Feb, 1823 at Killeigh, County Offaly, Ireland."
28. Edward Egan to Richard Erastus Egan, Feb. 19, 1900.
29. For the 1825 position see Knudson, "A Brief History of the Family of Howard Egan and Anne Meath." She suggests the Egans took advantage of Peter Robinson's crusade. On Robinson-related ship passenger lists, which are few, Howard Egan and his family are not listed. See: http://www.geni.com/projects/Irish-Peter-Robinson-Settlers-Canada/2553.
30. Peter Robinson's emigration program is well celebrated in Irish and Canadian history and on genealogy sites. See "Peter Robinson Settlers in Canada" and "Details of Peter Robinson's Transport of Emigrants to Canada."
31. "St. Lawrence Steamboat Co. Passenger Records, Part II," http://www.theshipslist.com/ships/passengerlists/1819_36stlawrence.shtml.
32. Peter Robinson Report, May 4, 1827, reproduced at www.theshipslist.com/ships/passengers/
33. www.theshipslist.com.
34. Egan, *Pioneering the West*, 9.
35. A report by James Hennessy, accredited genealogist, to Robert and Janet Sloan, June 6, 1991, notes that in the Offaly area the Egan surname was also spoken in dialect as "Ayghen." The *Chambly* passengers continued on from Montreal, as the emigration plan called for, but then on to Upper Canada and to Peterborough where land, cabins, and tools awaited them. Those favoring the 1825 dating say the Egans, being part of the Robinson program (which is speculation), dropped out at Montreal because of sick children.
36. www.theshipslist.com.
37. "Details of Peter Robinson's Transport of Emigrants to Canada."
38. Vaughan, *A New History of Ireland, Vol. 5*, 606.

39. Leacock, *Montreal: Seaport and City*, 148.
40. Cooper, *Montreal: A Brief History*, 18–19.
41. www.theshipslist.com.
42. Houston and Smyth, *Irish Emigration*, 109.
43. Ibid.
44. Nora Corley, "The St. Lawrence Ship Channell, 1805–1865," 280.
45. Knudson, "Brief History of the Family of Howard Egan and Anne Meath."
46. Jenkins, *Montreal, Island City of the St. Lawrence*, 252, 274. An 1822 Irish immigrant group transferred at Quebec to a steamer heading to Montreal, see Davin, *The Irishman In Canada*, 341.
47. Corley, "The St. Lawrence Ship Channell," 278–279. The first steamer to go all the way up the St. Lawrence from its mouth to Montreal unaided was the tow boat *Hercules* in 1823.
48. Davin, *The Irishman in Canada*, 260.
49. Cooper, *Montreal: A Brief History*, 11–13.
50. A fine pictorial history of Tullamore in the twentieth century is Byrne, *Tullamore Tour Album*. Among prominent Tullamorites it showcases (its pages are unnumbered) are political and economic leader Henry Egan (1847–1919), his son Henry James Egan (died 1907), and Patrick Egan (died 1897). A good guidebook for visitors to Tullamore today is Byrne's *A Walk Through Tullamore*.
51. Edward Egan to Richard Egan, Feb. 19, 1900, photocopy in Janet Sloan's files.
52. Howard Sr.'s brother Edward (1783–1848) married Margaret Coffey in 1811. They had a son William (1815–1865), who married Maria Murphy in 1857. The poet Edward was their son. Poet Edward was buried at the Killeigh Parish's (Church of Ireland) cemetery in an unmarked grave.
53. Byrne, "Some Members of the Egan Family of the Meelaghans, Tullamore Pioneers and Poets."

Chapter 2

1. Jenkins, *Montreal, Island City of the St. Lawrence*, 253.
2. Corley, "The St. Lawrence Ship Channell, 1805–1865," 277.
3. Jenkins, *Montreal, Island City*, 253–254.
4. Davin, *The Irishman in Canada*. A comprehensive list of books, articles, and theses dealing with the Irish in Canada is in Metress and Baker, "A Bibliography of the History of the Irish in Canada," and in Driscoll and Reynolds, *The Untold Story: The Irish in Canada* Vol. 2, ed., 977–1001.

5. An Act of Union in 1841 brought better government to the two provinces and renamed them Canada East and Canada West. Then, in 1867, these two provinces along with Nova Scotia and New Brunswick formed the Canadian Federation, which in time enlarged to become the modern nation of Canada.

6. Drake, *Howard Egan: Frontiersman, Pioneer, and Pony Express Rider*, 6. Drake interview with Fred H. Egan (a great-grandson), January 6, 1956. My research in the Canadian National Archives in Ottawa found no place name in Quebec province resembling the name Callander. Researcher Barbara Ann Aye found a Callander far up in Ontario Province but censuses there didn't show our Egans. In the 1820s several Irish settlements developed at St. Columbe, a somewhat similar name, which today is an hour's drive northwest of downtown Montreal; see Davin, *The Irishman in Canada*, 245.

7. Doige, *An Alphabetical List of the Merchants, Traders, and Housekeepers Residing in Montreal*, 8.

8. Jenkins, *Montreal, Island City*, 253–258.

9. Ibid; Doige, *Alphabetical List*, 12, 25.

10. Jenkins, *Montreal, Island City*, 262.

11. Elliott, *Irish Migrants in the Canadas*, iv.

12. Corley, "The St. Lawrence Ship Channell," 279.

13. Charles Stotsburry from Cove of Cork, in Davin, *The Irishman in Canada*, 259.

14. Death of Howard Hagan of Montreal, Laborer, August 5, 1828, in Montreal Anglican Christ Church Cathedral, Actes (Proceedings), in Drouin, *Quebec Vital and Church Records, 1621–1967*.

15. Leacock, *Montreal: Seaport and City*, 149.

16. Creighton, *The Commercial Empire of the St. Lawrence, 1760–1850*, 24.

17. Jenkins, *Montreal, Island City*, 258–259; Doige, *Alphabetical List*, 22–23.

18. Bosworth, *Hochelaga Depicta: The Early History and Present State of the City and Island of Montreal*, 179.

19. *Quebec Vital and Church Records*.

20. Doige, *An Alphabetical List*, 10–11; Corley, "The St. Lawrence Ship Channell," 280.

21. Doige, *Alphabetical List*, 20–21, 41.

22. Ibid., 10–11; Bosworth, *The Early History…Montreal*, 220.

23. Death of Evelina, daughter of Howard Hagan and Ann Maid, June 30, 1825; death of Ann, daughter of Howard Hagan and Ann Maid, July 20, 1825;

death of Barnard, son of Howard Hagan and Ann Maid, July 27, 1825; death of Howard Hagan of Montreal, August 5, 1828, in Montreal Anglican Christ Church Cathedral, Actes (Proceedings), in *Quebec Vital and Church Records*. Research hasn't identified where the deceased three children and the father are buried.

24. "Lines composed by Edward Egan, Meelaghans, while viewing Killeigh and surrounding scenery," *King's County Chronicle*, June 5, 1879, copy in author's file.

25. *Quebec Vital and Church Records*.

26. Ibid.

27. Ibid.

28. Mary, "of Montreal," died on June 6, 1857. See ibid.

29. Ibid.

30. Immigrants on a vessel from Dublin brought the disease to Montreal. Cholera deaths began on June 8, 1832 and lasted into September. Of 4,420 reported cases of cholera, 1,904 people died. See Sandham, *Ville-Marie, or, Sketches of Montreal, Past & Present*, 110.

31. *Quebec Vital and Church Records*.

32. Egan, *Pioneering the West*, 9.

33. Brooks, ed., "[John D. Lee] Diary of the Mormon Battalion Mission," 198–199.

34. "W.M. Egan: Trip from Carson City in 1863."

35. John Egan to the author, email, Dec. 6, 2015.

36. "Man of War," *Wikipedia*.

37. Wilson, comp., *This Was Montreal in 1814, 1815, 1816, and 1817*, 183. Hopeful pursers were told by the advertisement to report to the Deputy Naval Storekeepers Office or to purser on board the *Champlain* docked at the Isle aux Noir. See also *The St. Lawrence Survey Journals of Captain Henry Wolsey Bayfield, 1829–1853*, xv and xvii.

38. http://someinterestingfacts.net/man-of-war-ship/. British Vice-Admiral Lord Nelson's flagship at the Battle of Trafalgar, the *HMS Victory*, today is the only surviving "ship of the line," and is in drydock at Portsmouth, England.

39. http://www.thedearsurprise.com/a-brief-history-of-royal-navy-uniforms/.

40. Sager, *Seafaring Labour: The Merchant Marine of Atlantic Canada, 1820–1914*, 5.

41. Ibid., 242.

42. *The St. Lawrence Survey Journals of Captain Henry Wolsey Bayfield, 1829–1853*, xlii.

43. Sager, *Seafaring Labour*, 49.
44. Ibid., 3, 55–56, 136–137, 162.
45. Sager, *Seafaring Labour*, cites Froude, *On the High Seas: The Diary of Capt. Jon W. Froude* (St John's: Jesperson Press, 1983), 162, 183.
46. Tiger, *Men in Groups*, 231.
47. The surviving children were Francis Howard, William John, Richard, Eliza, Henry Adam, and Maria. A variant list shows no Francis Howard but a Robert. Younger brother Richard Egan and wife Maria had six children. On October 5, 1858, Richard died in Montreal at the young age of thirty-nine. Maria died in Quebec on January 9, 1896. Howard's oldest sister Eliza and husband Henry Benallack continued to live in Montreal, where their eight children were born, two of whom died very young. Eliza died in Montreal at age forty-one, on January 2, 1848. Husband Henry lived until September 1, 1877. Howard's sister Catherine, married to John Ransom, apparently continued to live in Montreal until her death there on August 16, 1869. They had eight children, all born in Montreal. He died May 25, 1877. Howard's sister Mary and husband Adam Higgins had eight children, all born in Montreal. She died in Montreal on June 6, 1857. He died November 16, 1875. With respect to John Ransom, see www.ancestry.com-mcclintock/ransomjohn.htm and www.ancestry.com-mcclintock/higginsadam.htm.
48. Sager, *Seafaring Labour*, 138.

Chapter 3

1. "Brief History of the Family of [handwritten in the provided space: Howard Egan]," followed by a handwritten life sketch, in Richard E. Egan, "Genealogical Record of the Ancestors, Descendants and Relatives of [handwritten in the provided blank: Richard E. Egan of Bountiful, Utah: Father's side]", copy in author's "Egans in Ireland" folder.
2. "Salem, Massachusetts," from various sites posted on the Internet and from tourist literature in the author's files.
3. *The Salem Directory and City Register, 1837*.
4. *The Salem Directory and City Register, 1842*.
5. *The Salem Directory and City Register, 1837*.
6. Barber, *Historical Collections. . . Relating to the History and Antiquities of Every Town in Massachusetts, with Geographical Descriptions*, 28–29, 224.
7. Ibid., and *Vital Records of Salem, Massachusetts to the End of the Year 1849*, 3:328.
8. Tamson's death certificate says she died on March 31, 1905 at age 80

years, 8 months, and 3 days. Doing the math, her birthday would be August 28, 1824, which it wasn't.

9. Some records say she was born in 1825. But her tombstone and death certificate list her birth year as 1824, and she celebrated her twenty-first birthday in Nauvoo in 1845 (see Chap 5). However, *Pioneering the West* (pp. 9 and 289), Ancestry.com, the LDS Family History Library, and some family sources say 1825. The month and day were July 27, as noted in Egan, *Pioneering the West*, (p. 9) and in her patriarchal blessing record on Sept. 24, 1843.

10. *The Salem Directory and City Register* and *Vital Records of Salem, Massachusetts to the End of the Year 1849*. Vol 3: Marriages (Salem: The Essex Institute, 1924), mentions the following: there were children born to Charles and Adelaine Parshley in 1843–1846; Mary E., who was a daughter of Nathaniel and Nancy Parshley; Sylvester Parshley, who died of cholera in 1849; a daughter of Charles Parshley in 1839; and a daughter of Calvin H. and Martha Jane Parshley in 1846.

11. Egan genealogist Sandra Day shows their marriage taking place Dec. 1, 1839, using marriage records in Salem Massachusetts Vital Records. Janet Sloan Conversation with Maryan Egan-Baker, May 14, 1994, communicated to the author.

12. *Salem Observer*, December 7, 1839.

13. Reverend Marta Morris Flanagan, Minister, First Universalist Church, 211 Bridge Street, Salem, MA, to Robert and Janet Sloan, Oct. 10, 1995, in Janet Sloan files. Rev. Flanagan said the First Universalist Church was established in Salem in 1805 and its building was erected in 1808.

14. Demos and Demos, "Adolescence in Historical Perspective," 632–638; Kett, *Rite of Passage: Adolescence in America, 1790 to the Present*, 1–45.

15. J. Raman Drake interview with Mrs. John Simmons, cited in Drake, "Howard Egan: Frontiersman, Pioneer and Pony Express Rider," 7, n7.

16. Janet Sloan conversation with Maryan Egan-Baker, May 14, 1994. Maryan's mother, Irma Egan Baker, used to tell this story when Maryan was a child. Maryan couldn't say the story was true but felt it had at least a kernel of truth in it.

17. Mary Jane Egan Johnson, Personal History. Mary Jane was the aunt of Janet's husband, Robert C. Sloan, Jr., and daughter of David Egan. Howard Egan was her great-grandfather.

18. Howard N. Egan (grandson), Remarks, Aug. 2, 1972, at Pioneer Village unveiling of oil painting of Howard done by great-grandson William Egan Sylvester. Photocopy in Janet Sloan files.

19. Prince, "The Great 'Riot Year': Jacksonian Democracy and Patterns

of Violence in 1834" and "The Year Was 1834" in a "24–7 Family History Circle." Post on: http://blogs.ancestry.com/circle/.

20. Egan, *Pioneering the West*, 9.

21. *The Annals of the Caverlys*, 18–19, 53.

22. Charles and Molly Danielson Caverly Family Group Chart comp. by Sandra R. Day, on file in author's "Tamson Parshley" file.

23. Jewett and Caverly, *History of Barnstead from the First Settlement in 1727 to 1872*. A township is an official subdivision of a county, and townships might or might not contain any villages or cities.

24. Hayward's *New England Gazetteer of 1839*, link posted to "Barnstead" entry on *Wikipedia* (Nov. 23, 2012). Barnstead became part of Belknap County, which was organized in 1840.

25. Revolutionary War Rolls, State Papers of New Hampshire, Vol. 1. New Hampshire Revolutionary War Rolls, Vol. 5, p. 10 and Vol. 11, p. 747.

26. Hammond, *Vital Records of Barrington, New Hampshire, 1720–1851*.

27. The children and their birthdates are Joseph Hill (1812), Ira (1814), Sarah (1817), Mary Ann (1820), Meribah Jane (1822), Tamson (1824), Richard J. (1833), and Charles (1833).

28. "Howard Ransom Egan," in Bateman, *Deep Creek Reflections*, 86. The Daughters of Utah Pioneers Memorial Museum in Salt Lake City has Ransom's specially made leather boot from when he was a Pony Express rider.

29. "Brief History of the Family of [handwritten in the provided space: Howard Egan]," followed by a handwritten life sketch, in Egan, "Genealogical Record of the Ancestors, Descendants and Relatives of Richard E. Egan of Bountiful, Utah.

30. *The Salem Directory and City Register, 1842*.

31. Ibid. An 1851 Salem directory lists a Joseph Chisholm at 18 South Street who was a "line and twine manufacturer." Adams, *The Salem Directory... For 1851*.

32. "The Story of Rope Making," on website http://www.the-rope-walk.co.uk/ks2th2.pdf.

33. Salem Maritime National Historic Site https://www.nps.gov/sama/index.htm

34. "The Story of Rope Making."

35. http://www.lowtechmagazine.com/2010/06/lost-knowledge-ropes-and-knots.html.

36. Journal History, Aug. 10, 1841.

37. Ibid., Aug. 16, 1841.

38. Doctrine and Covenants 111:2, 4, 10; Larson, *Erastus Snow*, 67.
39. Larson, *Erastus Snow*, 68.
40. Journal History, Sept. 18, 1841; Larson, *Erastus Snow*, 68–69.
41. Larson, *Erastus Snow*, 69.
42. Journal History, Oct. 10, 1841; also *Times and Seasons* 3:602.
43. Larson, *Erastus Snow*, 69–70.
44. Ibid., 71.
45. Ibid., 70.
46. Journal History, Feb. 4, 1842.
47. Larson, *Erastus Snow*, 70–71; Godfrey, "More Treasures Than One," 199.
48. Badger, "A Sketch of the Life of Susan Hammond Ashby Noble."
49. Ibid.
50. Larson, *Erastus Snow*, 90.

Chapter 4

1. General information presented here about Nauvoo is from Roberts, *History of The Church of Jesus Christ of Latter-day Saints*, Vols. 4–6; Roberts, *Comprehensive History of The Church of Jesus Christ of Latter-day Saints,* Vol. 2; Allen and Leonard, *The Story of the Latter-day Saints* (1992), chaps. 5 and 6; and the 1841–1845 issues of the Nauvoo newspaper, *Times and Seasons*. Valuable Nauvoo studies include Leonard, *Nauvoo: A Place of Peace, A People of Promise*; Flanders, *Nauvoo, Kingdom on the Mississippi*; Givens, *In Old Nauvoo: Everyday Life in the City of Joseph*; George and Sylvia Givens, *Nauvoo Fact Book*; and Holzapfel and Cottle, *Old Mormon Nauvoo and Southeastern Iowa: Historic Photographs and Guide*.

2. Fuchsia Stringham, "History of Nathaniel Ashby," posted on www.findagrave.com, entry for Nathaniel Ashby, Sr.

3. The Egans are not listed in the 1842 Nauvoo census, so they must have arrived in the last half of the year.

4. Flanders, *Nauvoo*, 156. The Smiths moved into the Mansion House on August 31, 1843.

5. Both the riverboats *Mermaid* and the *Osprey* stopped at Nauvoo going up and going back. See *Nauvoo Neighbor* clipping included as an illustration in Cannon, *Nauvoo Panorama*, 27.

6. Holzapfel, *Women of Nauvoo*, 41.

7. Perkins and Cannon, *Sacred Places, A Comprehensive Guide to Early LDS Historical Sites, Volume Three, Ohio and Illinois*, 115 (Kimball Landing), 117

(Upper Stone Landing), 133 (Foot of Main Street Landing), and 195 (Lower Stone House Landing).

8. Letter of John Needham, *Millennial Star* 4 (Sept. and Oct. 1843).

9. Nauvoo Tax Records, 1842, 1843, Church History Library.

10. Egan, *Pioneering the West*, 11–12.

11. Joseph Smith's statement about partaking of Nauvoo's poverty is in *History of the Church* 4:178.

12. Water Street today doesn't continue east of Durphey and Lumber Street, once parallel to and south of Water Street, no longer exists except as a little cul-de-sac west of Highway 96.

13. Egan, *Pioneering the West*, 11–12. Howard Egan files, Nauvoo LDS Lands and Records Office, Nauvoo, Illinois.

14. Two men named Sanders living in Nauvoo were Ellis M. Sanders and Moses Martin Sanders.

15. Brooks, *On the Mormon Frontier: The Diary of Hosea Stout, Volume One 1844–1861*, entry for May 26, 1845. Cited hereafter as Stout Diary.

16. "Howard Egan Bill of Cordage," Feb. 3, 1846, Newel Kimball Whitney Papers.

17. Brigham Young to Wilford Woodruff, June 27, 1845, in Clark, *Messages of the First Presidency,* 1:273–74. Leonard, *Nauvoo*, 438, 479; *History of the Church* 7:430-1; and Watson, "The Nauvoo Tabernacle," 416–421.

18. Nauvoo Trustee-in-Trust Nauvoo, Illinois Tithing Day Book B, 1842–1844, pp. 58, 63, 97, 146, 148, 179, 188, 251, 259.

19. Cook, *Nauvoo Deaths and Marriages 1839–1845*, 23*; Nauvoo Neighbor*, Oct. 7, 1844.

20. Derr, Cannon, and Beecher, *Women of Covenant: The Story of the Relief Society,* 23–58; Holzapfels, *Women of Nauvoo*, 104–126.

21. *History of the Relief Society, 1842–1966*, 18.

22. Nauvoo Relief Society Minutes, Church History Library. Derr, et. al, eds., *The First Fifty Years of Relief Society*.

23. Unless otherwise cited, this chapter's summary about household matters and everyday life in Nauvoo relies on Givens, *In Old Nauvoo,* chapters 15 ("Homes and Home Life") and 16 ("Food and Drink").

24. James Palmer, Reminiscences, 72.

25. Brooks, *John Doyle Lee; Zealot, Pioneer Builder, Scapegoat*, 69–70.

26. "All buy their own stoves," Ann Pitchforth wrote in May 1845; see her letter to her parents, May 1845, in Madsen, *In Their Own Words: Women and the Story of Nauvoo*, 152.

27. Givens, *In Old Nauvoo*, 182–193.
28. Perkins and Cannon, *Sacred Places, Ohio and Illinois*, 140.
29. Givens and Givens, *Nauvoo Fact Book*, 79.
30. The store was called "Red Brick" because the inside of the first floor merchandise room was painted a rich red color. Givens and Givens, *Nauvoo Fact Book*, 144.
31. Givens, *In Old Nauvoo*, chapter 7 "The Merchants" and chapter 8 "Crafts and Craftsmen."
32. Givens and Givens, *Nauvoo Fact Book*, 100.
33. *History of the Church*, 4:454.
34. Palmer Reminiscences, 69.
35. Nauvoo High Council Minutes.
36. Hartley, "Nauvoo Stake, Priesthood Quorums, and the Church's First Wards."
37. Ibid.
38. Stout Diary, entries for May 15, June 12, July 10, Aug. 14, 1845.
39. Journal History, May 15, 1845.
40. Palmer, Reminiscences, 68.
41. *Times and Seasons* 4 (Oct. 1843): 87–90.
42. Arrington, "Church Leaders in Liberty Jail," *BYU Studies* 13 (Autumn 1972), 23.
43. Porter and Backman, "Doctrine and the Temple in Nauvoo," 49, and Allen and Leonard, *Story of the Latter-day Saints*, 180–87 A general discussion of the beginnings of plural marriage is on pp. 185–186.
44. Doctrines introduced at Nauvoo are listed by Lyon in his "Historical Highlights of the Saints in Illinois," The First Annual Church Educational System Religious Educators Symposium, 19–20 August 1977.
45. *History of the Church* 6:302–317; Cannon and Dahl, "The King Follett Discourse."
46. Bennett, Black, and Cannon, *The Nauvoo Legion*, 119–121.
47. *History of the Church*, 4:300, 601.
48. Ibid., 4:356.
49. Egan, *Pioneering the West*, 9.
50. Bennett, et. al., *The Nauvoo Legion*, 125, command chart on p. 116. The most complete Legion rosters now available are found in Appendices D and E.
51. Flanders, *Kingdom on the Mississippi*, 111–13; Leonard, "Picturing the Nauvoo Legion"; *History of the Church* 4:601, 5:3, 5:283–384.
52. Hogan, *Mormonism and Freemasonry: The Illinois Episode*.

53. Nauvoo Freemason Lodge, Minutes; Hogan, "The Vital Statistics of Nauvoo Lodge."

54. Hogan, *Mormonism and Freemasonry*, 298.

55. Hogan, "Record of Nauvoo Lodge Petitions, Nov. 2, 1843 to April 8, 1846."

56. Hogan, "The Official Minutes of the Nauvoo Lodge." The typescript includes a "Complete Roster of Nauvoo Lodge from December 29, 1841 to April 8, 1846."

57. Holzapfel and Cottle, *Old Mormon Nauvoo*, 108–110.

58. Godfrey, "Freemasonry in Nauvoo."

59. Egan, *Pioneering the West*, 9; "Patriarchal Blessing of Howard Egan," as copied in Drake, "Howard Egan: Frontiersman, Pioneer, and Pony Express Rider," 161. See Ogden, "Two from Judah Ministering to Joseph." Ogden (p. 227) notes: "Later descendants of Egan used this information [being of Judah] to trace the Egan line back through the Milesian kings (of Ireland) all the way to Adam." For an example, see Egan, *Pioneering the West*, 285–287.

60. The blessing is fully quoted in Martin, *The Story of Major Howard Egan*, 88, from Patriarchal Blessing Book 3, page 183. Her birth year is listed there as 1824.

61. Hogan, "The Curious Case of James Madison Monroe," *Sunstone Magazine*.

62. Monroe to Brigham Young, Sept. 16, 1851.

63. Nauvoo City Council Minutes, May 19, 1842, Jan. 14 and 30, June 29, and Dec. 12, 1843. The minutes have been published in Dinger, ed., *Nauvoo City and High Council Minutes,* and references here to the Council's activities are cited by dates, not page numbers.

64. Certificate authorizing the Nauvoo City Council to pay Howard Egan for sixteen days of service done as a City Watch. Certificate in the Bob and Carol Campbell Collection. Our narrative in next paragraphs contains the certificate's text.

65. Nauvoo City Council Minutes, Dec. 12, 1843; Jonathan Dunham account book; Stout's diary provided the best record about the police. Also see Parkin, "Police Work on the Mormon Trail, 1846–1848," and read with caution Allaman's flawed study, "Policing in Mormon Nauvoo." The police names are in *History of the Church* 6:149–150.

66. The text of this valuable document is used here courtesy of the Bob and Carol Campbell Collection.

67. City Council Minutes, Dec. 21, 1843.

68. *History of the Church* 6:150–153. During that same meeting, John P. Greene became Nauvoo's new marshal. Unlike the police, the marshal's main duties

dealt with carrying out orders for the municipal court, such as serving subpoenas, warrants, and summonses.

69. Jonathan Dunham account book.
70. *History of the Church* 6:162–165.
71. Ibid., 6:169.
72. City Council Minutes, Jan. 13, 1844.
73. Egan, *Pioneering the West*, 9.
74. "Robbery and Lynching," *Nauvoo Neighbor*, April 3, 1844.
75. City Council Minutes, April 13, 1844.
76. Allen, "Was Joseph Smith a serious candidate for the presidency of the United States?" 21–22; Robertson, "The Campaign and the Kingdom: The Activity of the Electioneers in Joseph Smith's Presidential Campaign," 147.
77. *The Prophet Joseph Smith's Views on the Powers and Policy of the Government of the United States*.
78. *History of the Church* 6:334–335; Robertson, "The Campaign and the Kingdom," 147.
79. Robertson, "The Campaign and the Kingdom," 147–180.
80. Leonard, *Nauvoo*, 339, 392.
81. *History of the Church* 6:325.
82. Ibid., 6:340.
83. Journal History, May 21, 1844, p. 1.
84. Robertson, "The Campaign and the Kingdom," 156–160.
85. Ibid., 151–152; Leonard, *Nauvoo*, 339.
86. Robertson, "The Campaign and the Kingdom," 152–157. During his labors Franklin D. Richards baptized thirteen.
87. Ibid., 158–161.

Chapter 5

1. *History of the Church*, 6:519.
2. Robertson, "The Campaign and the Kingdom," 149, 163.
3. *Nauvoo Expositor*, June 7, 1844.
4. *History of the Church* 6:444–49. "It appears that the destruction of the press was the work of both the Legion and the police," Bennett, et. al., *The Nauvoo Legion*, 235.
5. *History of the Church* 6:492–497.
6. Ibid., 6:612–22; Leonard, *Nauvoo*, 415–17; Oaks and Hill, *Carthage Conspiracy*.
7. James Palmer, Reminiscences, 69.

8. "The Murder," *Times and Seasons* 5 (July 15, 1844), 584.

9. The East Grove location is identified in George and Sylvia Givens, *Nauvoo Fact Book*, 8.

10. England, "George Laub's Nauvoo Journal," 166, entry for May 1846.

11. Jesse C. Little to Brigham Young, Dec. 30, 1844, Church History Library.

12. William M. Egan's statement in Egan, *Pioneering the West*, 11.

13. Regarding the controversy about the actuality of the event and folklore surrounding it see Harper, "The Mantle of Joseph: Creation of a Mormon Miracle," and Jorgenson and BYU Studies Staff, "The Mantle of the Prophet Joseph Passes to Brother Brigham: A Collection of Spiritual Witness." Jorgenson includes the most extensive list yet assembled of accounts written by people who say they witnessed the "mantle" manifestation.

14. Quinn, "The Mormon Succession Crisis of 1844."

15. Young, "The Seventies: A Historical Perspective," and Baumgarten, "The Role and Function of the Seventies in L.D.S. Church History."

16. First Council of Seventy, Minutes and Genealogy Book B, p. 31.

17. *History of the Church* 6:318–19.

18. Hartley, "From Men to Boys: LDS Aaronic Priesthood Offices, 1829–1996."

19. *History of the Church* 7:305–07.

20. Seventies Record Book B, Selections, notation showing Seventeenth Quorum's founding officers and members.

21. Sally Murdock to "Respected Friends," Aug. 12, 1845, typescript copy in Holzapfel, "Women's Letters from Nauvoo," 16.

22. Seventies Record Book B, 47.

23. Dinger, *Nauvoo City and High Council Minutes*, July 13 and Aug. 10, 1844.

24. Ibid., Sept. 14, 1844.

25. Ibid., Jan. 11, 1845.

26. Dinger's observation in his City Council Minutes, 310, 313–14.

27. Leonard, *Nauvoo*, 465–67; *History of the Church* 7:370.

28. Leonard, *Nauvoo*, 467.

29. Ibid., 468.

30. Ibid., 467.

31. Ibid., 467–68.

32. *History of the Church* 7:370.

33. Stout Diary and Journal History, Feb. 8, 1845.
34. Ibid.
35. Stout Diary, Feb. 19, 1845, material inserted into his April 1, 1845 entry.
36. Stout Diary, Feb. 25 and 26, 1845; *History of the Church* 7:376–77.
37. Holzapfels, *Women of Nauvoo*, 142.
38. See Dinger's observation in *City Council Minutes*, 336.
39. Leonard, *Nauvoo*, 469.
40. From Mace's diary in BYU Special Collections, as quoted in Moody, "Nauvoo's Whistling and Whittling Brigade," 481, and from Wandle Mace's Journal, in the same repository.
41. Moody, "Whistling and Whittling Brigade," 486.
42. Stout Diary, March 14, 1845.
43. Leonard, *Nauvoo*, 471; *History of the Church* 7:388.
44. Moody, "Whistling and Whittling Brigade," 484; Journal History, April 14, 1845.
45. Stout Diary, April 5 and 6, 1845; Leonard, *Nauvoo*, 471.
46. Journal History, April 12, 1845.
47. Ibid., April 16, 1845.
48. Leonard, *Nauvoo*, 473.
49. Stout Diary, April 27, 1844.
50. Journal History, May 6, 1845.
51. If this meant "Bryant's goods" and "Egan's goods" and not goods belonging to a company named Bryant and Egan, then Egan's goods probably were an inventory of rope materials not yet sold.
52. Stout Diary. The Church's health law, the "Word of Wisdom," which is Doctrine and Covenants Section 89 today, speaks against the use of wine and strong drinks, tobacco, and other harmful substances. Introduced in 1833, it was presented as counsel and advice, not a binding commandment. As a result, compliance among many was slack until well into the 1920s. Before that, the Church had no binding policy that members needed to abide by it, and records are replete with instances where Saints, including some top leaders, used alcohol, tobacco, coffee, or tea. "Word of Wisdom" in *Encyclopedia of Mormonism* (1992), 4:1584.
53. Tamson's death record indicates she was born on July 28, but Egan, *Pioneering the West*, says July 27, and so does her patriarchal blessing, recorded on Sept. 24, 1843.
54. Stout Diary, July 29, 1845.

55. Ibid., Sept. 14, 1845.

56. Ibid., Sept. 14 and 19, 1845.

57. Journal History, Sept. 19, 1845, 3.

58. Howard Egan to Brigham Young, Sept. 20, 1845, original in L. Tom Perry Special Collections, Lee Library, Brigham Young University, Vault MSS 192.

59. Journal History, Sept. 23, 1845.

60. Ibid., Sept. 24 and 25, 1845.

61. Stout Diary, Sept. 27, 1845.

62. Ibid., and Stout Diary, Sept. 27–28, 1845.

63. Journal History, Sept. 28, 1845, 1.

64. "It is supposed that the Mormons inhabiting this city are fully 12,000 souls, and of the surrounding country, 5,000 more." *History of the Church* 7:435.

Chapter 6

1. Temple capstone ceremony description is from "Zina Diantha Huntington Jacobs' Nauvoo Diary," entry for May 24, 1845.

2. Egan, *Pioneering the West*, 11.

3. William Clayton certificate for Howard Egan, MS d 6372, Church History Library.

4. Nauvoo Baptismal Records, Original Record 1, Church History Library. Note: these baptisms are not listed in the Blacks' *Annotated Record of Baptisms for the Dead, 1840–1845, Nauvoo, Hancock County Illinois*, Vol. 2 (C-F).

5. Leonard, *Nauvoo*, 324, 326, 509–20.

6. *History of the Church*, 6:243–44.

7. "Rocky Mountain Prophecy," in *Encyclopedia of Latter-day Saint History*, 1038–39; *History of the Church*, 5:85.

8. Leonard, *Nauvoo*, 509–520.

9. Christian, "Mormon Foreknowledge of the American West"; Esplin, "'A Place Prepared': Joseph, Brigham and the Quest for Promised Refuge in the West," 88–91; Walker, "Seeking the 'Remnant': The Native American During Joseph Smith's Period."

10. Regarding the Council of Fifty, see Quinn, "The Council of Fifty and Its Members"; Ehat, "'It Seems Like Heaven Began on Earth': Joseph Smith and the Constitution of the Kingdom of God"; and Rogers, *The Council of Fifty: A Documentary History*.

11. *History of the Church,* 6:260–61, 275–77, 318–19.

12. Hartley, *My Best for the Kingdom: History and Autobiography of John Lowe Butler*. Chaps. 13, 14, and 16 deal with the Emmett Company.

13. Leonard, *Nauvoo*, 441.

14. Ibid., 514.

15. Ibid.; Howard Egan Journal, April 23, 1845, Yale University, cited in the Millers' *Nauvoo, the City of Joseph*, 192–93.

16. Leonard, *Nauvoo*, 511.

17. Roberts, *Comprehensive History*, 2:504–20.

18. Gregg, *The History of Hancock County, Illinois*, 296, cited in the Holzapfels' *Women of Nauvoo*, 38.

19. Conference proceedings are in *History of the Church* 7:456–77, and Journal History, Oct. 6–8, 1845.

20. Hartley, "'How Shall I Gather?'"

21. *History of the Church* 7:456–77, and Journal History, Oct. 6–8, 1845.

22. Irene Haskell Pomeroy to Capt. Ashbel G. Haskell, Oct. 1845, in "Letters of a Proselyte: The Haskell-Pomeroy Correspondence," 138–39.

23. Journal History, Oct. 11, 1845.

24. Black, "How Large Was the Population of Nauvoo?"

25. Roberts, *Comprehensive History* 2:539–40.

26. Ibid., and Journal History, Oct.11, 1845. The list was published in the *Nauvoo Neighbor*, Oct. 29, 1845.

27. *History of the Church* 7:532 and Journal History, Nov. 23, 1845.

28. Journal History, Nov. 30, 1854, 2.

29. "Farming Lands for Sale," *Nauvoo New Citizen,* April 10, 1846, as cited in Cannon, *Nauvoo Panorama*, 47.

30. Journal History, those dates.

31. Ibid., Dec. 31, 1845.

32. "Howard Egan Bill of Cordage," Feb. 3, 1846, in Newel Kimball Whitney Papers.

33. Anderson and Bergera, *The Nauvoo Endowment Companies, 1845–1846*, xv-xix, xxxv.

34. Ibid., xxxvi-xli.

35. Ibid., 55, 57, 58.

36. Doctrine and Covenants Section 132.

37. Danel Bachman and Ronald K. Esplin, "Plural Marriage" in *Encyclopedia of Mormonism,* Vol. 3:1091–95; Doctrine and Covenants Section 132, verses 1–4, 28–40.

38. Leonard, *Nauvoo*, 345.

39. Ibid., 343–49.

40. Ibid., 347.

41. Daynes, "Family Ties: Belief and Practice in Nauvoo," 68.

42. Journal History, Oct. 9, 1869.

43. https://archive.org/stream/AffidavitsOnCelestialMarriage/MS_3423_5-6#page/n71/mode/1up, p. 64. John D. Lee's sometimes inaccurate confessions claimed that police chief Hosea Stout one day ordered him to "watch the house of a widow woman named Clawson" because "a man went there nearly every night about ten o'clock, and left about day light." Lee was to wound or kill him. But Hyrum Smith told Lee that the man was Egan and "had been sealed to Mrs. Clawson, and that their marriage was a most holy one." Lee, *Mormonism Unveiled: Life and Confessions of John D. Lee*, 293–94.

44. Johnson, "Determining and Defining 'Wife': The Brigham Young Households," 69 n48.

45. Anderson and Bergera, *Nauvoo Endowment Companies*, 473. The name Redden appears in some sources as Redding, but records closest to the Redden family as of the Nauvoo period spell it Redden. We use that spelling throughout this history.

46. Brooks, Stout Diary, p. 91 n48 has a biographical sketch about Return Jackson Redden.

47. Anderson and Bergera, *Nauvoo Endowment Companies*, 551. Heber C. Kimball's Diary for Nauvoo up to Dec. 9, 1845, when it ends, makes no mention of Howard Egan; see Kimball, *On the Potter's Wheel: The Diaries of Heber C. Kimball*.

48. "Adoption, Law of," in Arnold K. Garr, et. al., *Encyclopedia of Latter-day Saint History*; see also Irving, "The Law of Adoption: One Phase of the Development of the Mormon Concept of Salvation, 1830–1900."

49. Kimball, *Heber C. Kimball: Mormon Patriarch and Pioneer*, 141.

50. Bennett, *Mormons at the Missouri 1846–1852*, 191–93; See adoption wording in George Laub's adoption, in Anderson and Bergera, *Nauvoo Endowment Companies*, 584.

51. Camp of Israel (Iowa) Record of Organization and List of Members, 1846 and Mormon Battalion, Roster of "A" and "B" Companies, 1846.

52. Brigham Young Manuscript History, Jan. 20 and 23, 1846; Stout Diary, Jan. 30, 1846.

53. Governor Ford's letter is in Journal History, Jan. 4, 1846.

54. Journal History, Jan. 13, 1846.

55. Ibid., Jan. 18, 1846.

56. Ibid., Jan. 20, 1846.

57. Ibid.
58. Ibid., Jan. 24, 1846.
59. Ibid., Jan. 29, 1846.
60. Ibid., Feb. 2, 1846.
61. Crockett, *Saints in Exile: A Day-by-Day Pioneer Experience, Nauvoo to Council Bluffs*, 145. Godfrey, *Charles Shumway, A Pioneer's Life*.
62. Journal History, Feb. 8, 1846.
63. *History of the Church*, 7:582.
64. Beecher, "The Iowa Journal of Lorenzo Snow."
65. Journal History, Feb. 10, 1846.
66. Lorenzo Snow Journal, 267.
67. Egan, *Pioneering the West*, 13.
68. Journal History, Feb. 15, 1846.
69. Journal History, Feb. 17, 1846; Kimball, *Heber C. Kimball*, 129.
70. On Feb. 24, 1846, a son was born to "John" Redding in the camp at Sugar Creek. See Brigham Young's Manuscript History, that date.
71. Orson Pratt Diary, Feb. 14, 1846; Patty Sessions Diary, Feb. 16, 1846; Helen Mar Whitney Autobiography.
72. Lorenzo Snow Iowa Journal, 265.
73. Brigham Young's Manuscript History, Feb. 18–25, 1846.
74. Horace K. Whitney Diary, Feb. 25, 1846, and *History of the Church* 7:598–600.
75. Brigham Young estimated 400 wagons (families) in the Camp of Israel on Feb. 28 (Brigham Young Manuscript History). Some 300 single men were serving as pioneers, guards, or artillerymen. On March 9 Horace K. Whitney (Diary) said the number in camp "somewhat exceeds 2,000." Young's History on March 31 says that when the camp reorganized at the Chariton River on March 27, six companies of fifty were formed—300 to 400 wagons (families) or 1,800 to 2,400 people. But by March 31, nearly 100 wagons had returned to Nauvoo.
76. Hartley, "The Saints' Three-stage Exodus from Nauvoo"; also, Hartley, "Spring Exodus from Nauvoo: Act Two in the 1846 Mormon Evacuation Drama."
77. Bennett, *Mormons at the Missouri*, 101.

Chapter 7

1. Regarding the Camp of Israel crossing Iowa, see Richard E. Bennett, *Mormons at the Missouri, 1846–1852* (Norman: University of Oklahoma Press,

1987); Susan Easton Black and William G. Hartley, *The Iowa Mormon Trail: Legacy of Faith and Courage* (Orem, UT: Helix Publishing, 1997); and Hartley and A. Gary Anderson, *Sacred Places: Iowa and Nebraska, a Comprehensive Guide to Early LDS Historical Sites* (Salt Lake City, UT: Deseret Book, 2006).

2. My 320 mile figure disagrees with others' tallies, but I base it on my very careful scrutiny of the diaries, pinpointing every campsite. The route across southern Iowa is now part of the 1,300-mile-long "Mormon Pioneer National Historic Trail."

3. Brigham Young Manuscript History, March 2, 1846.
4. Beecher, "The Iowa Diary of Lorenzo Snow," 264.
5. Brigham Young Manuscript History, March 5, 1846.
6. Eliza R. Snow, Diary, March 7, 1846.
7. Ibid., March 9, 1846.
8. Brigham Young Manuscript History, March 7–9, 1846.
9. Eliza R. Snow Diary, March 12–14, 1846.
10. William Clayton Journal.
11. Brigham Young Manuscript History, March 19, 1846.
12. Eliza R. Snow Diary, March 22, 1846; Brigham Young Manuscript History, March 22, 1846.
13. A historic marker now designates the area and identifies the ruts.
14. Stout Diary, March 22, 1846.
15. Eliza R. Snow Diary, March 22–25, 1846.
16. William Clayton Journal and Orson Pratt Journal, March 25, 1846.
17. Brigham Young Manuscript History, March 26, 1846.
18. Ibid., May 21, 1846.
19. Brigham Young Manuscript History, March 31, 1846.
20. Clayton Journal, March 27, 1846, says Hales was the clerk. Both Willard Richards's and Brigham Young's records for that day err and say Lorenzo Snow was the Fourth Fifty's clerk. Clayton was the Camp of Israel's official historian. Also, Lorenzo Snow's diary says he was in another fifty (Beecher, "The Iowa Diary of Lorenzo Snow").
21. Ibid.
22. Lorenzo Snow Diary, 267.
23. Brigham Young Manuscript History and Willard Richards Journal, March 29, 1846.
24. Orson Pratt Journal.
25. Brigham Young Manuscript History.
26. Eliza R. Snow Diary and Clayton Journal, April 5, 1846.

27. Eliza R. Snow Diary, April 8, 1846.
28. Clayton Journal, April 5, 1846.
29. Brigham Young Manuscript History, April 6, 1846.
30. "Pioneer and Patriarch Closes Eventful Career," obituary for Richard Erastus Egan, *Deseret Evening News*, April 23, 1918.
31. Clayton Journal and Brigham Young Manuscript History, April 6–8, 1846.
32. Stout Diary, March 26, 1846; Clayton Journal, April 8, 1846.
33. Orson Pratt Journal, April 8, 1846.
34. Clayton Journal, April 5, 1846.
35. Clayton Journal. See also Eliza R. Snow Diary, Orson Pratt Diary, and Brigham Young Manuscript History, entries for April 9, 1846.
36. Egan, *Pioneering the West*, 13.
37. Clayton Journal, April 10, 1846.
38. Ibid., April 11, 1846.
39. Brigham Young Manuscript History, March 16, 1846.
40. Ibid., and Orson Pratt Journal, April 12, 1846.
41. Eliza R. Snow Diary, April 14, 1846.
42. Today a marker designates the approximate location where Clayton's and the Egans' campsite was, three miles south of present Seymour, Iowa in front of the private Tharp Cemetery. In today's Corydon, Iowa, the Prairie Trails Museum of Wayne County features an impressive tribute to Clayton and his "Hymn Heard Round the World."
43. "'Come, Come Ye Saints' Site Marked by Plaque," *Ensign*, Sept. 1990, 30.
44. Brigham Young Manuscript History, April 18, 1846, and Huntington Diary.
45. "Zion's Camp Supply List, Pleasant Point, April 18, 1846," Church History Library, posted online at: https://eadview.lds.org/rosettaAsset/image/full/FL2189408.
46. Clayton Diary, April 24, 1846.
47. Brigham Young Manuscript History, April 24, 1846.
48. Eliza R. Snow Diary, April 26 and May 5, 1846.
49. Egan, *Pioneering the West*, 14.
50. John D. Lee Diary and Brigham Young Manuscript History, entries for April 26 and 28, 1846.
51. Clayton Journal, May 15, 1846.
52. Patty Sessions's diary, May 15, 1846. Wilford Woodruff left Nauvoo

on May 19 and reached Mt. Pisgah on June 15 (Woodruff Journal). The Newel Knight family left Nauvoo about April 24 and reached Pisgah on May 25 (Newel Knight Journal, Church History Library).

53. Brigham Young Manuscript History, April 21, 1846.

54. Patty Sessions's diary entries for March through May 1846 tell about laundry and ironing clothes.

55. Regarding women's experiences, see the diaries of Eliza R. Snow and Patty Sessions.

56. John D. Lee Diary, June 7–8, 1846.

57. Heber C. Kimball Journal, kept by Peter Hansen, June 16, 1846.

58. Daniel Davis Diaries, June 6, 1846.

59. Brigham Young Manuscript History, June 7, 1846.

60. Wilford Woodruff Diary, July 3, 1846.

61. John D. Lee Diary, June 8, 1846.

62. Ibid.; Horace K. Whitney Diary, June 8, 1846; Kimball Journal, June 9, 1846.

63. Brigham Young Manuscript History, June 17, 1846.

64. Whitney Diary, June 20, 1846.

65. Brigham Young Manuscript History, June 21, 1846.

66. Whitney Diary, June 15 to July 7, 1846.

67. "Excerpts from the Journal of John Taylor, June 5 to Aug. 5, 1846."

68. Kane, *The Mormons*, 25–26.

69. Ibid., 26, 30.

70. Bigler and Bagley, *The Army of Israel*, 31–44.

71. Golder, *Journal of Henry Standage*, 102.

72. Bennett, *Mormons at the Missouri*, 58; Journal History, July 1, 1846.

73. Brigham Young to President Samuel Bent & Council and Saints at Garden Grove, Mt. Pisgah, 7 July 1846, reproduced in Bigler and Bagley, *Army of Israel: Mormon Battalion Narratives*, 47–49.

74. Journal History, July 16, 1846.

75. W. Medill and Major Thomas H. Harvey, statement, copy reproduced in Bigler and Bagley, *Army of Israel*, 64–65.

Chapter 8

1. Heber C. Kimball Journal (kept by Peter Hansen), March 1846 to Feb. 1847, entry for June 8–9, 1846.

2. Heber C. Kimball Journal, July 9 and 10, 1846.

3. "Col. Cane [sic] manifested the spirit of a Gentleman and much interest in our welfare," Wilford Woodruff noted in his journal, July 11, 1846.

4. Grow, *"Liberty to the Downtrodden," Thomas L. Kane, Romantic Reformer*, 47–67; Kimball Journal, July 12, 1846.

5. Kimball Journal, July 14, 1846.

6. Kimball Journal, August 1846 entries.

7. For Battalion history see Yurtinus, "A Ram in the Thicket: The Mormon Battalion in the Mexican War"; Tyler, *A Concise History of the Mormon Battalion in the Mexican War, 1846–47*; Ricketts, *The Mormon Battalion: U.S. Army of the West*; Bigler and Bagley, *Army of Israel: Mormon Battalion Narratives*; and Fleek, *History May Be Searched in Vain: A Military History of the Mormon Battalion*.

8. Fleek, *History May Be Searched in Vain*, 140–41.

9. Yurtinus, "Ram in the Thicket," 1:76.

10. Fleek, *History May Be Searched in Vain*, 177–80.

11. Willard Richards Journal, Aug. 28, 1846.

12. That Pace was one of Lee's adopted sons is documented in Juanita Brooks's introduction to her edited "John D. Lee: Diary of the Mormon Battalion Mission," Part 1:173.

13. Kelly, *Journals of John D. Lee, 1846–47 and 1859*, Nov. 21, 1846.

14. Brooks, *John Doyle Lee: Zealot, Pioneer Builder, Scapegoat*, 97.

15. See Brooks's Lee biography, 97, and Bishop, *Mormonism Unveiled, or Life & Confession of John D. Lee*, 190.

16. Entry for Aug. 27, 1846, in Brooks, "Diary of the Mormon Battalion Mission: John D. Lee," 1:175.

17. Willard Richards Journal, Aug. 30, 1846, and Lee Diary, that date.

18. Brooks, "Diary of the Mormon Battalion Mission: John D. Lee," Parts 1 and 2.

19. Ibid., Aug. 30, 1846, Brooks's comment, 1:174.

20. Lee Diary; James Pace Diary.

21. Brooks's comments in Lee Diary, 1:204, based on Lt. Pace's journal.

22. Probably a fifteen-shot sliding breech, or "harmonica," rifle, like ones that gun maker Jonathan Browning sold to customers in Nauvoo ("Jonathan Browning Slide Rifle," *Wikipedia*).

23. William Coray Journal, included in Sept. 9, 1846 entry, cited in Yurtinus, "Ram in the Thicket," 143.

24. Fleek, *History May Be Searched in Vain*, 206.

25. Lee, *Confessions*, 192.

26. Yurtinus, "Ram in the Thicket," 143.

27. Jefferson Hunt and Jesse Hunter to Brigham Young, Santa Fe, Oct. 18, 1846, cited in Yurtinus, "Ram in the Thicket," 146.

28. Standage Journal, Sept. 19, 1846.

29. William Coray Journal, Sept. 19, 1846, cited in Yurtinus, "Ram in the Thicket," 147.

30. Lee Diary, Sept. 19, 1846; Yurtinus, "Ram in the Thicket," 146–147; Hunt and Hunter to Brigham Young, Oct. 18, 1846.

31. Jefferson Hunt, J. D. Hunter, D. C. Davis, George Oman, Lorenzo Clark, William W. Willis, Philemon C. Merrill, Sylvester Hulet, Cyrus C. Canfield, Ruel Barrus, and Robert Clift to Howard Egan [for Brigham Young], Santa Fe, Oct. 13, 1846, copy in Yurtinus, "Ram in the Thicket,"150–52.

32. Brooks, Lee Diary, 1:199.

33. Ibid., 2:281; Jefferson Hunt, et. al. to Egan for Brigham Young, Oct. 13, 1846.

34. Levi Ward Hancock Journal, Oct. 3, 1846.

35. Hancock Journal, Oct. 12, 1846; Standage Journal, Oct. 9, 1846.

36. Journal History, Oct. 18, 1846.

37. Jefferson Hunt, et. al., to Egan, Oct. 13, 1846.

38. Standage Journal, Oct. 15, 1846.

39. *Mormonism Unveiled*, 194. On that same page Lee claimed that he was "troubled with Egan considerably, for he was drunk every day, and I feared he would be robbed." Given uneven truthfulness in Lee's "Confession" book, this might have been an exaggeration.

40. Hancock Journal, Oct. 17, 1846.

41. Bieber, *Exploring Southwestern Trails 1846–1854 by Philip St. George Cooke, William Henry Chase Whiting, Francois Xavier Aubrey*, 67.

42. Standage Journal, Oct. 18, 1846.

43. Hancock Journal and Standage Journal, entries on Oct. 18, 1846.

44. Brooks, biography of Lee, 102. For comparative dollar values consult Samuel H. Williamson, "Seven Ways to Compute the Relative Value of a U.S. Dollar Amount, 1774 to Present," MeasuringWorth, 2016, at measuringworth.com

45. Brooks, commentary in Lee Diary, 1:204.

46. Kelly, Lee journals 1846–1847, Nov. 21, 1846; Journal History, Nov. 22, 1846.

47. Kelly, Lee journals 1846–1847, Nov. 21, 1846.

48. Ibid., Nov. 21–25, 1846 and Jan. 19, 1847.

Chapter 9

1. Regarding Winter Quarters history see Bennett, *Mormons at the Missouri, 1846–1852*; Conrey Bryson, *Winter Quarters*; Karen M. and Paul D. Larsen, *Remembering Winter Quarters/Council Bluffs*; Ward, *Winter Quarters: The 1846–1848 Life Writings of Mary Haskin Parker Richards*; Kenneth W. Godfrey, "Winter Quarters: Glimmering Glimpses into Mormon Religious and Social Life"; and Hartley and Anderson, *Sacred Places: Iowa and Nebraska, a Comprehensive Guide to Early LDS Historical Sites*, 207–16 (Winter Quarters section).
2. Bennett, *Mormons at the Missouri*, 74–77.
3. Whitney Diary, November 1846 entries.
4. Heber C. Kimball Journal (kept by Peter Hansen), March 1846 to Feb. 1847, entry for Nov. 29, 1846.
5. Whitney Diary, Nov. 30, 1846.
6. Ibid., Dec. 5, 1846.
7. Ibid., Dec. 7, 1846.
8. Ibid., Dec. 8, 1846.
9. Bennett, *Mormons at the Missouri*, 116–17.
10. Willard Richards Journal, Dec. 9, 1846; Journal History, Dec. 9, 1846.
11. Ibid., Dec. 11, 1846.
12. Heber C. Kimball Diary, Dec. 13, 1846.
13. Egan, *Pioneering the West*, 139–40; Bateman, *Deep Creek Reflections*, 62.
14. Whitney Diary, Dec. 20, 1846.
15. Whitney Diary.
16. Heber C. Kimball Journal, Jan. 1, 1847.
17. Stout Diary, Jan. 2, 1847.
18. Willard Richards Journal, Dec. 19, 1846.
19. Horace K. Whitney Diary, Dec. 20, 1846. Winter Quarters was divided into 13 wards on Oct. 4 and then on Nov. 26 into 22 wards. A map of the blocks is in Bennett, *Mormons at the Missouri*, 75.
20. Stout Diary, Nov. 17–19, 1846.
21. Stout Diary, Dec. 14, 1846.
22. "Old Sow," *Deseret News*, June 13, 1908; Glen M. Leonard, "Cannon was first 'pulpit' in salt lake valley," *Church News*, March 17, 1990.
23. Bob Mickelson, "Did 'Old Sow' go to slaughterhouse?" *The Davis Clipper*, Sept. 13, 2004.

24. Whitney Diary, Dec. 25, 1846.
25. Daniel Davis Diary.
26. Whitney Diary, Jan. 3, 1847.
27. Davis Diary.
28. Willard Richards Diary, March 9, 1847.
29. Davis Diary.
30. Heber C. Kimball Diary, Jan. 19, 1846.
31. Doctrine and Covenants Section 136.
32. Davis Diary.
33. Whitney and Davis diaries.
34. Whitney and Davis diaries. Merritt Rockwell was the brother of Porter Rockwell. Merritt had been taken into Heber C. Kimball's family.
35. Whitney Diary, Jan. 31, 1846.
36. Ibid., Feb. 15, 1846.
37. Whitney Diary.
38. Heber C. Kimball Journal, Feb. 23, 1846.
39. Whitney Diary.
40. Ibid.
41. Bennett, *Mormons at the Missouri*, Chapter 7, "Sickness and Death at Winter Quarters," 131–147.
42. Whitney Diary, March 18, 1847.
43. Beecher, "Women in Winter Quarters," 16. Tamson and Nancy both gave birth that August.
44. Egan, *Pioneering the West*, 16.
45. Ursula B. Hastings Hascall to Col. Wilson Andrews, April 1847.
46. Mary H. Richards Journal, Nov. 28, 1846 to 19 May 1847, as edited in Ward, *Life Writings of Mary Haskin Parker Richards*, 59–140.
47. Mary H. Richards Journal, Dec. 26, 1846, and Jan. 15 and May 14, 1847.
48. Beecher, "Women in Winter Quarters," 13.
49. Mary H. Richards Journal.
50. Beecher, "Women at Winter Quarters," 14.

Chapter 10

1. The best published diary accounts of the 1847 trek are those of Norton Jacob and William Clayton. See Ronald O. Barney, ed., *The Mormon Vanguard Brigade of 1847: Norton Jacob's Record* (Logan: Utah State University Press, 2005)

and William Clayton, *Journal* (Salt Lake City, Utah: Deseret News, 1921). Others in the group whose diaries have been published include Brigham Young, Heber C. Kimball, Wilford Woodruff, Howard Egan, Erastus Snow, and Thomas Bullock.

2. Howard Egan Journal, 1847, is among his papers at the Beinecke Library and Yale University. For the convenience of the reader we use, with a few exceptions, the edited version in *Pioneering the West*, 21–113. My comparisons of the *Pioneering the West* version with the original shows a few additions, a number of insignificant spelling and format changes, and no significant deletions.

3. Esplin, "'A Place Prepared': Joseph, Brigham and the Quest for Promised Refuge in the West," and Esplin, "A 'Place Prepared' in the Rockies." Young recalled saying during the trek west that "I have seen it in vision, and when my natural eyes behold it, I shall know it." Brigham Young Discourse, Sept. 14, 1873, Journal of Discourses, 16:207.

4. Wilford Woodruff Discourse, in Conference Report, Apr. 1898, 57.

5. Brigham Young Discourse, March 16, 1856, Journal of Discourses, 3:257–58. In regards to the "Rocky Mountain Prophecy," see Esplin, "Quest for Promised Refuge," 92.

6. Wilford Woodruff Journal, April 8, 1844, and Thomas Bullock Minutes, April 8, 1844.

7. John D. Lee Diary, 13 Jan. 1846.

8. Esplin, "Quest for Promised Refuge," 105.

9. Doctrine and Covenants Section 136.

10. Kimball, *Heber C. Kimball*, 150.

11. The captains were: (1) Wilford Woodruff, (2) Ezra T. Benson, (3) Phineas H. Young, (4) Luke S. Johnson, (5) Stephen H. Goddard, (6) Charles Shumway, (7) James Case, (8) Seth Taft, (9) Howard Egan, (10) Appleton Harmon, (11) John S. Higbee, (12) Norton Jacob, (13) John Brown, and (14) Joseph Matthews.

12. Stegner, *The Gathering of Zion*, 114. Narratives about the 1847 pioneers include Stegner's, *The Gathering of Zion*; Bennett's *We'll Find the Place*; and Nibley's *Exodus to Greatness*. The best published diary accounts are Barney, *The Mormon Vanguard Brigade of 1847: Norton Jacob's Record* and the *William Clayton Journal*. Also published are the diaries of Brigham Young, Heber C. Kimball, Wilford Woodruff, Erastus Snow, Orson Pratt, Horace K. Whitney, and Thomas Bullock, among others. For day-by-day accounts, see Knight and Kimball, *111 Days to Zion*; Jenson, *Day by Day with the Utah Pioneers of 1847*; and Crockett, *Saints Find the Place*.

13. Norton Jacob's diary regularly refers to Redden as "Jack Redden."

14. That became a common quip about rivers, including the Mississippi (Mark Twain) and the Colorado, as shown by an Internet search for "too thin to plow."

15. Clayton Journal, 18 April 1847.

16. The year before, about 500 Saints in three companies went this way for some 120 miles from the Missouri River ferry. Led by Bishop George Miller and a high council, this group ended up far north with Ponca Indians and wintering at "Camp Ponca." Redden and the others had accompanied them up the Platte, but then returned to Winter Quarters. See the author's *My Best for the Kingdom*, 209–30.

17. See three Mattes publications: *The Great Platte River Road;* "The Council Bluffs Road: Northern Branch of the Great Platte River Road"; and "The Northern Route of the Non-Mormons."

18. Kimball, *Heber C. Kimball*, 151.

19. Clayton, *The Latter-day Saints' Emigrants' Guide,* lists campsites, mileages, and geographic features of the trail. Modern trail site guides include Franswa, *The Mormon Trail Revisited*; Hartley and Anderson, *Sacred Places: Iowa and Nebraska*; Hill, *The Mormon Trail: Yesterday and Today*, and Kimball, *Historic Sites and Markers along the Mormon and Other Great Western Trails*.

20. An axletree is a bar, fixed crosswise under an animal-drawn vehicle, with a rounded spindle at each end upon which a wheel rotates.

21. Kimball Diary, April 19, 1847.

22. Knight and Kimball, *111 Days to Zion*, 36.

23. Nibley, *Exodus to Greatness*, 371.

24. The letter is in the Daughters of Utah Pioneers headquarters in Salt Lake City. It is published in "Three Letters" in the Daughters of Utah Pioneers' *Our Pioneer Heritage*, 14.

25. Hartley, *My Best for the Kingdom*, 210. The Pawnee village and mission location is about eight miles southwest of present-day Genoa, Nebraska.

26. *Clayton's Journal*. The real name of Ellen Sanders Kimball, Kimball's wife, is Aagaata Sondra Ystensdatter. She was eighteen years old when she entered the valley as an 1847 pioneer. See Mulder, "Scandinavian Saga," 145.

27. Clayton Journal, April 24, 1847.

28. Stegner, *Gathering of Zion*, 124.

29. In 1823 Major Stephen Long, a government surveyor, produced a map labeling the area the "Great American Desert."

30. Egan diary, April entries.

31. Piercy, *Route from Liverpool*, 116.

32. Quaife and Shaw, *Across the Plains in Forty-nine*, 37; Johnston, *Overland to California*, 58; and Internet word search for "buffalo chips."

33. Stegner, *Gathering of Zion*, 130.

34. Clayton Journal, May 1, 1847. A fifteen-shot rifle, also called a "harmonica" rifle, has a breech through which fifteen chambers slide from side to side. Howard could have obtained his from gunmaker Jonathan Browning in Nauvoo, who sold them. See "Jonathan Browning Slide Rifle," *Wikipedia*.

35. Clayton Journal.

36. Levi Jackman Journal, May 2, 1847.

37. "Three Letters."

38. Clayton Journal, May 6, 1847.

39. Egan Diary, May 31, 1847.

40. Knight and Kimball, *111 Days to Zion*, 105.

41. Clayton Journal, May 12, 1847.

42. Wright, "The Mormon Pioneer Odometers."

43. Knight and Kimball, *111 Days to Zion*, 85, 92, 97.

44. Clayton, *The Latter-day Saints' Emigrants' Guide*.

45. The "Word of Wisdom," an 1833 revelation to Joseph Smith, enjoined Saints to abstain from wine, strong drinks, tobacco, and "hot drinks." As early as 1842 Hyrum Smith asserted that hot drinks meant tea and coffee, but the interpretation remained unsettled for decades. The 1847 pioneers' use of coffee was not unusual. See Bashore, "Quitting Tea and Coffee," 73–74.

46. Knight and Kimball, *111 Days to Zion*, 101.

47. Clayton Journal, May 23, 1847.

48. Ibid., May 27, 1847.

49. Young had received a revelation the day before, on May 28, which stated that "Except you repent, and humble yourselves before the Lord, you shall not have power to accomplish your mission." Revelation received Friday, May 28, 1847, Platte River, Nebraska, Brigham Young Papers, Church History Library. Published by Fred Collier in *Unpublished Revelations of the Prophets and Presidents of the Church*, Vol. 2: 166–67 and on the Internet by Fred Collier in "The Book of the Prophet Brigham Young."

Chapter 11

1. Egan Diary, June 1, 1847. Fur traders built Fort Laramie in 1834 to be a trading post. It was first known as Fort William, then Fort John. In 1849 the government purchased it and turned it into a military post. Today, the city of

Cheyenne is about 100 miles south of the Fort Laramie National Historic Site.

    2. Nibley, *Exodus to Greatness,* 396. While all parts of pigweed plants are edible, some parts have more popular uses than others. The young plants and growing tips of older plants make nutritious vegetables that can be boiled like spinach or eaten raw as salad. The greens are rich in iron, calcium, niacin, and vitamins A and C (American Indian Health and Diet website, 2016).

    3. Egan Diary, June 3, 1847.

    4. Nibley, *Exodus to Greatness,* 397.

    5. Tourists today can walk in the parallel ruts, shoulder deep, in Guernsey State Park. See *Historic Sites and Markers,* 79–80.

    6. Clayton Journal, June 7, 1847.

    7. Levi Jackman Journal, June 14, 1847.

    8. Jackman Journal, June 17, 1847.

    9. Stegner, *Gathering of Zion,* 149.

    10. Saleratus is a leavening agent consisting of potassium or sodium bicarbonate.

    11. Clayton Journal, June 21, 1847.

    12. Woodruff Journal, June 21, 1847.

    13. Jackman Journal, June 26, 1847.

    14. Measurement at the actual pass itself by the U.S. Geological Survey; see Will Bagley, "South Pass," article at www.wyohistory.org.

    15. Clayton Journal, June 27, 1847.

    16. Woodruff Journal, July 9, 1847.

    17. Stegner, *Gathering of Zion,* 157.

    18. Baptism for health was a healing ritual common among Latter-day Saints from 1841 to 1922; see Stapley and Wright, "'They Shall Be Made Whole': A History of Baptism for Health."

    19. Nibley, *Exodus to Greatness,* 413.

    20. Woodruff Journal, July 16, 1847.

    21. Nibley, *Exodus to Greatness,* 414.

    22. Orson Pratt Journal, July 9, 1847.

    23. Nibley, *Exodus to Greatness,* 417.

    24. Ibid., 418.

    25. Horace K. Whitney said Young was pale and emaciated, see ibid., 421.

    26. Woodruff Journal, July 16, 1847.

    27. Clayton Journal, July 16, 1847.

    28. Knight and Kimball, *111 Days to Zion,* 239.

    29. Clayton Journal, July 19, 1847.

30. Willard Richards and George A. Smith to Orson Pratt, July 21, 1847, Journal History, that date.

31. Today this four-mile stretch from Mormon Flats to Big Mountain's summit is part of the original Mormon Trail preserved and maintained by the Utah State Parks Department.

32. Brigham Young Manuscript History, July 23, 1847.

33. Bennett, *We'll Find the Place*, 215–16.

34. Brigham Young Manuscript History, July 23, 1847; Wilford Woodruff sermon, July 24, 1880, cited in Nibley, *Exodus to Greatness,* 428; Roberts, *Comprehensive History 3:224.*

35. Bennett weighs the evidence in *We'll Find the Place,* 218. He favors the latter spot, identified by Woodruff. See four different versions of the account quoted in Crockett, *Saints Find the Place,* 385n43.

36. Egan Diary, July 24, 1847.

37. Nibley, *Exodus to Greatness,* 354.

Chapter 12

1. Clayton Journal, July 25, 1847.

2. Ibid.

3. Egan Diary, July 24, 1847.

4. George A. Smith Discourse, June 2, 1869, *Journal of Discourses* 13:8. See Journal of Discourses, 26 vols. (Liverpool: Latter-day Saint Book Depot, 1853–86.

5. Wilford Woodruff Diary, July 28, 1847.

6. Walker, "A Banner is Unfurled: Mormonism's Ensign Peak"; Wright and Westrup, "Ensign Peak."

7. Brigham Young Manuscript History, July 28, 1847.

8. "The Hornets," Egan, *Pioneering the West,* 163.

9. Rebaptism was first practiced in Nauvoo and was continued in the Utah Territory. Many members were rebaptized as an act of rededication. It served as a ritual of recommitment but was not viewed as essential to salvation. See H. Dean Garrett, "Rebaptism," *Encyclopedia of Mormonism* 3:1194.

10. Brigham Young Manuscript History and Journal History, Aug. 8, 1847.

11. Horace K. Whitney Journal, Aug. 9, 1847.

12. Kimball, *Heber C. Kimball,* 172.

13. Ibid., 172–173.

14. Heber C. Kimball Journal.
15. Wilford Woodruff Journal, cited in Bancroft, *History of Utah,* 266.
16. William Thompson, the Heber C. Kimball Camp Journal, Aug. 6, 1848, copied in Journal History, Sept. 24, 1848.
17. No copy of this letter has been found.
18. Bennett, *We'll Find the Place;* Chapter 9 in *"The Emigration Camp of 1847,"* 251–78.
19. Horace K. Whitney Diary.
20. Journal History, Sept. 9, 1847.
21. Ibid., Sept. 12, 1847.
22. Ibid., Sept. 16, 1847.
23. Journal History, Sept. 23, 1847. See also the account that *Pioneering the West* borrowed (p. 136) from *The Life of Heber C. Kimball.*
24. Journal History, Sept. 24, 1847.
25. "The Stampede Is Stopped," Egan, *Pioneering the West,* 164. Ransom Egan related the story "as told by Father, as near as I can remember." He said, "The place where this happened could be located by reading Father's journal giving a description of the camps and country along the Platte River. This was a few years after the Pioneers." The story doesn't fit Howard's westbound trips in 1847, 1848, or 1849, and he never went east again.
26. The riders and the two wagons had met the ox-team division on Oct. 14 at the Loup Fork River. Clayton, in his diary, said the little relief party was part of the "old police."
27. "Three Letters," 505–506.
28. Wilford Woodruff Journal, Oct. 31, 1847.
29. Ibid., Nov. 1, 1847.
30. Sally Randall to Dear Father and Mother, Oct. 3, 1847.
31. William Appleby Diary, Dec. 9 and 14, 1847.
32. Roberts, *Comprehensive History of the Church,* 3:308–14.
33. The conference is summarized in ibid., 3:315–16.
34. Ibid., 3:317–18.
35. Journal History, Jan. 16–21, 1848, and Wilford Woodruff's Journal, those dates.
36. Journal History, Jan. 18, 1848, and Wilford Woodruff Journal, same date.
37. Journal History, Jan. 20, 1848.
38. Daniel Davis Diary.

Chapter 13

1. Conference proceedings are in Journal History, April 6–8, 1848.
2. Stout Journal, May 9, 1848.
3. Egan, *Pioneering the West*, 138.
4. Cleland and Brooks, eds., *A Mormon Chronicle: The Diaries of John D. Lee, 1848–1876*, May 24, 1848. Cited hereafter as Lee 1848 Diary.
5. First 100, schedule, 1848 July, in Camp of Israel schedules and reports, 1845–1849.
6. Kimball Camp Journal, June 18, 1848.
7. Ibid., June 6, 1848.
8. Daniel Davis Diary, June 3, 1848.
9. Kimball, *Historic Resource Study: Mormon Pioneer National Historic Trail*, 25.
10. Hartley, "Howard Egan, the Elkhorn Skirmish." Details about the encounter are found in the Kimball Camp Journal, June 6, 1848; Manuscript History of Heber C. Kimball, June 6, 1848 (cited in Journal History that date); Jacob and Jacob, *The Record of Norton Jacob*; Wyler, *Thomas E. Ricks*, 13–15; "Journal of Peter Wilson Conover," *Chronicles of Courage* (1990), I:201–30; and John D. Lee 1848 Diary, June 15, 1848. Son Ransom's recollections are in *Pioneering the West*, 140.
11. Manuscript History of Heber C. Kimball, June 6, 1848, cited in Journal History, that date.
12. Camp of Israel, Division Report, schedules and returns, July 16, 1848, Church History Library, MS 14290. Summary of the skirmish by NWB, meaning Noah Wills Bartholomew.
13. Dr. Bernhisel, born June 23, 1799, graduated in medicine from the University of Pennsylvania School of Medicine in 1827. He practiced in New York City. After joining and affiliating with the Latter-day Saints, he moved to Nauvoo, Illinois, in 1843. He served as the personal physician to Joseph Smith, lived in the Smith home, and delivered one of Emma Smith's children.
14. Egan, *Pioneering the West*, 140.
15. Ibid.
16. Manuscript History of Second Division, 1848, Church Emigration Book, June 8, 1848.
17. Wyler, *Thomas E. Ricks*. Ricks later helped colonize Idaho. He laid out the town of Rexburg, where Ricks College (now Brigham Young University-Idaho) was located and named after him.

520 ~ Faithful and Fearless

18. Manuscript History of Second Division, 1848, June 16, 1848.
19. William Thompson comment in Kimball Camp Journal, June 17, 1848.
20. Manuscript History of Second Division, June 19, 1848; "Journal of Louisa Barnes Pratt," 244.
21. Egan, *Pioneering the West,* 141.
22. Kimball Camp Journal, June 18, 1848.
23. Lee Diary, June 27, 1848.
24. William Thompson to Willard Richards and Amasa Lyman, July 23, 1848, Journal History, that date.
25. Egan, *Pioneering the West,* 141.
26. Ibid., 141–42.
27. Ibid., 142.
28. John Smith, Charles C. Rich, and John Young to Brigham Young and Council of the Twelve, June 9, 1848, in Journal History, that date.
29. Egan, *Pioneering the West,* 142.
30. Daughters of Utah Pioneers, "The Negro Pioneer," 513–14, 516–19.
31. Ibid.
32. William Thompson to Willard Richards and Amasa Lyman, July 23, 1848, Journal History, that date.
33. Journal History, July 21, 1848; Kimball Camp Journal, July 21, 1848.
34. Kimball Camp Journal, July 23, 1848; Thompson to Richards and Lyman, July 23, 1848.
35. Kimball Camp Journal, July 26, 1848.
36. Thomas Bullock Journal, July 28, 1848, in Journal History, that date.
37. Ibid., and Kimball Camp Journal.
38. Ibid.
39. Stout Diary, Aug. 9, 1848.
40. Egan, *Pioneering the West,* 143.
41. Lee Diary, Aug. 9, 1848.
42. Egan, *Pioneering the West,* 143–44.
43. Lee Diary, Aug. 18, 1848.
44. Kimball Camp Journal, Aug. 25 to 28, 1848; "Journal of Rachel Emma Woolley Simmons," 162.
45. Parley P. Pratt to Brigham Young, Aug. 8, 1848, in Journal History, that date.
46. Great Salt Lake Valley Leaders to Brigham Young and Quorum, Aug. 9, 1848, in Journal History, that date.

47. Heber C. Kimball to Brigham Young, Aug. 14, 1848, Journal History that date.
48. Kimball Camp Journal, Aug. 25, 1848.
49. Brigham Young and Heber C. Kimball, Epistle to the Saints at Winter Quarters, Aug. 28, 1848, Journal History, that date.
50. Thomas Bullock Journal, Aug. 29, 1848, Journal History, that date.
51. Daniel Davis Diary, Sept. 1, 1848.
52. Thomas Bullock Journal, Aug. 31, 1848; Journal History, that date.
53. Kimball Camp Journal, Sept. 1–4, 1848.
54. Ibid., Sept. 5–9, 1848.
55. Lee Diary, Sept. 12, 1848.
56. Egan, *Pioneering the West*, 145.
57. Kimball Camp Journal, Sept. 16, 1848.
58. Egan, *Pioneering the West*, 144–45.
59. Ibid.
60. Kimball Camp Journal, Sept. 22, 1848.
61. Egan, *Pioneering the West*, 145.
62. William Burton Journal in Journal History, Sept. 24, 1848.
63. Daniel Davis Diary, Sept. 24, 1848.
64. Egan, *Pioneering the West*, 145.
65. Zebulon Jacobs, Reminiscences and Diaries.

Chapter 14

1. Esplin, "Utah's First Thanksgiving."
2. "Journal of Leonard E. Harrington," Oct. 24, 1848.
3. Egan, *Pioneering the West*, 147–48.
4. Brigham Young, "Epistle from Salt Lake City," Oct. 9, 1846, in *Frontier Guardian I* (Feb. 7, 1849).
5. "Captain" Roundy had been assigned to travel with Howard, so presumably he was in the party, per Brigham Young and Heber C. Kimball, Epistle to the Saints at Winter Quarters, Aug. 28, 1848, Journal History, that date.
6. Journal History, Oct. 14, 1848.
7. Ibid., Dec. 7, 1849.
8. "Salt Lake Postage," *Frontier Guardian*, March 7, 1849.
9. In 1852 the David Wood Wagon Train passengers included Adelia Ellen Redden, 25; Adelia Higley Redden, 60; George Grant Redden, 61; and George Grant Redden, 22. For some reason the list also includes Nancy Ann

Redden, 26, birthday Oct. 6, 1825. Possibly she returned to the Kanesville area late in 1851 in order to help her parents move west. But her daughter Helen is not mentioned.

    10.   *Frontier Guardian*, Feb. 7, 1849.

    11.   Regarding Kanesville see the author's "Council Bluffs/Kanesville, Iowa: A Hub for Mormon Settlements" and "Pushing on to Zion: Kanesville, Iowa, 1846–1853"; also, Black, *The Best of the Frontier Guardian*.

    12.   Ibid.

    13.   Hansen might have been part of Howard's mail-carrying party late in 1848. He accompanied Erastus Snow on the first Latter-day Saint mission to Denmark (1849–1855), leaving Utah soon after this Egan wagon train arrived in 1849. He became the first editor of the *Skandinaviens Stjerne*. He served additional missions in Denmark, 1873–75, and 1880–82.

    14.   Peter Olsen Hansen, Diary, 1849, Journal History, Aug. 7, 1849, 1–11, and Hansen Journal, 1876.

    15.   Old Fort Kearney (misspelled with an extra "e") was built in 1847 at Nebraska City, about half-way between Kanesville and St. Joseph. It was a log blockhouse on the hill looking down on the Missouri River. Soldiers returning across the plains from the war with Mexico wintered there. The next year its name was taken away and given to the new fort first called Fort Childs, two hundred miles west in the Platte valley, which became the Fort Kearny best known in overland trail history. The forts were named for Army officer Stephen Watts Kearny, who spelled his name with just one letter "e." Today's city of Kearney, Nebraska misspells his name.

    16.   Hansen Diary, entries those dates.

    17.   Journal History, April 25, 1849.

    18.   *Frontier Guardian*, May 16, 1849.

    19.   Hansen Journal.

    20.   Hansen Diary, May 3, 1849.

    21.   Journal History, May 7, 1849.

    22.   Regarding the *Deseret News* printing press see Ashton, *Voice in the West*, 16–24.

    23.   "California Emigrants," *Frontier Guardian*, May 16, 1849.

    24.   Hansen Journal, 75–77.

    25.   "The Ox-Bow Trail in Nebraska," Kimball, *Historic Sites and Markers*, 135–37.

    26.   Howard Egan to Orson Hyde, "From the Plains, Bro. Orson Hyde, by H. Egan," *Frontier Guardian* I (July 11 1849). The newspaper dated the letter

19 May, but Howard mailed it from Ft. Kearny on June 1.

27. Hansen Diary, these dates.
28. Egan to Hyde, May 19, 1849.
29. Stewart, *The California Trail*, 227–28.
30. Egan to Hyde, June 1, 1849; and Hansen Diary, May 23, 1849.
31. A Heber C. Kimball letter read during the April 1849 conference in Kanesville listed 12 teamsters whom Kimball recommended because they had worked for him. Howard recruited three of them: Peter O. Hansen, Orson Whitney, and Franklin Edwards. ("Conference Minutes," April 7, 1849, *Frontier Guardian 1* April 18, 1849).
32. Hansen Journal.
33. Mattes's *The Great Platte River Road* has maps in the front part of his book. One called "The Great Platte River Road [Part 2]" shows the Old Fort Kearny Road and the other trails to New Fort Kearny. A map shows a Pawnee Village 1 and a Pawnee Village 2. Hansen's mileage, about 53 miles, identifies Pawnee Village 2, which Mattes's map indicates is roughly 60 miles from Ft. Kearny. On Mattes's map, Pawnee is roughly 115 miles from Ft. Kearny.
34. Hansen Journal, 75–77.
35. Ibid.
36. "Ash Hollow" in Kimball, *Historic Sites and Markers*, 122–24.
37. Hansen Diary.
38. Ibid., those dates.
39. Hansen Journal, 75–77.
40. Hansen Diary, July 2–3, 1849.
41. Ibid.
42. Ibid.
43. Ibid.
44. Hansen Diary, those dates.
45. Hansen Journal, 75–77.
46. Owens, *Gold Rush Saints*, 275.
47. Hansen Journal, 75–77.
48. Ibid.
49. Hansen Diary, July 25, 1849.
50. Hansen Journal, 75–77.
51. First General Epistle of the First Presidency, April 1849, in Clark, *Messages* 1:353. Clark dates the message "between March 30 and April 4, 1849, quite likely the latter date" (p. 348). The epistle was published in the Frontier Guardian on May 30, 1849, three weeks after Howard left Kanesville.

52. Egan, *Pioneering the West*, 148–49; William M. Egan Journal.

53. Egan, *Pioneering the West*, 148.

54. "First General Epistle of the First Presidency," in James R. Clark, *Messages of the First Presidency, Volume 1* (Salt Lake City: Bookcraft, 1965), 350–359.

55. Egan, *Pioneering the West*, 150.

56. Dale L. Morgan estimated 5,000 to 8,000 gold seekers passed through; see his edited "Letters by Forty-niners Written from Great Salt Lake City in 1849," 98; Brigham Madsen estimated about 10,000 in *Gold Rush Sojourners*, 33.

57. "The Mail Arrived from Salt Lake City," *Frontier Guardian 1* (Sept. 5, 1849); Madsen, *Gold Rush Sojourners*, 59.

58. Owens, *Gold Rush Saints*, 276.

59. Billings, "Mary Ann Tuttle Egan/Billings/Gardner/Billings." See a sketch about her in Chapter 29 of this book.

Chapter 15

1. Walker, *Eldorado: The California Gold Rush*, 16.

2. Hafen and Hafen, *Journals of the Forty-niners Salt Lake to Los Angeles, Part VIII*, "The Howard Egan Wagon Train," includes much of Howard's diary, 307–19.

3. General gold rush histories we consulted are Walker's *El Dorado;* J. S. Holliday, *The World Rushed In;* and Holliday's *Rush for Riches: Gold Fever and the Making of California.*

4. An outstanding history of Mormons and the California gold rush is Davies and Hansen, *Mormon Gold*. A collection of narratives by participants is in Owens, *Gold Rush Saints*.

5. Both quotes about the discovery are in Davies and Hansen, *Mormon Gold*, 17.

6. Ibid., 73.

7. Brigham Young talk, Journal History, Oct. 1, 1848.

8. Journal History, Sept. 28, 1849; Davies and Hansen, *Mormon Gold*, Chapter 11, "The Rhoades Mormon Gold Train," 143–53, and Chapter 12, "Apostle Charles C. Rich and the Gold Missionaries," 155–67. The gold denominations and the "quite plentiful" quote are from William Appleby, Journal History, Oct. 27, 1849, 23.

9. Lyman's *The Overland Journey from Utah to California* is the definitive

study of the southern trail. Regarding the five LDS-related companies taking the southern route late in 1849, see Davies and Hansen, *Mormon Gold*, chapters 11–15.

10. Lyman, *The Overland Journey*, 39–41, and Hafen and Hafen, *Journals of the Forty-niners*, 24–26. Captain Jefferson Hunt usually is credited with bringing the first wagon over that route, but in fact his party abandoned the wagon before reaching Salt Lake City.

11. At October 1849 general conference, President Young said if forty-niners wintered there, this "large accession of mouths, in addition to those of our own emigration, threatened almost a famine for bread" in Utah Journal History, Oct. 8, 1849.

12. Lyman, *The Overland Journey*.

13. Pauline Smith, *Captain Jefferson Hunt*.

14. Thomas Bullock Minutes, Aug. 20, 1849, "Meeting of Emigrants at Stand at 8 a m to hear instructions from Jefferson Hunt," 15–17.

15. Bullock Minutes, Aug. 20, 1849.

16. Brigham Young Manuscript History, Sept. 28, 1849.

17. The gold mission is explained in Campbell, "Mormon Gold Mining Mission of 1849"; Arrington, *Great Basin Kingdom*, 72–76; Davies and Hansen, *Mormon Gold*, Chaps. 12 and 14; and Owens, *Gold Rush Saints*, 226–36, 267–69, 275, 309.

18. See Davies and Hansen, *Mormon Gold*, Chapter 12, "Apostle Charles C. Rich and the Gold Missionaries," 255–67. No list exists of all of those missionaries but reasonable estimates say they number at least twenty. Davies and Hansen (p. 167) list 21 men in the Flake Company but that includes Captain Flake, who wasn't a gold missionary.

19. Regarding the five wagon companies taking the southern route late in 1849 see Davies and Hansen, *Mormon Gold*, chapters 11–15.

20. Lyman, *The Overland Journey*, 46–58.

21. Lyman, *The Overland Journey*, 58–63; Davies and Hansen, *Mormon Gold*, Chapter 12.

22. Owens, *Gold Rush Saints*, 276–77.

23. Lyman, *The Overland Journey*, 71–74; Davies and Hansen, *Mormon Gold*, Chapter 13, "The Gentile Pomeroy Wagon Train," 169–77; Owens, *Gold Rush Saints*, 276–77.

24. Campbell, "Gold Mining Mission," says there were 31 men in the company, and he names 23 of them. Davies and Hansen say it's not certain that the company was largely a group of gold missionaries and suggest that a number of those whom Campbell names were probably not in the original group but met the

Huffaker company in California. See Davies and Hansen, *Mormon Gold,* 179.

25. Davies and Hansen, *Mormon Gold,* Chapter 14, *"The Huffaker Company,"* 179–87.

26. Hafen and Hafen, *Journals of the Forty-niners,* 307–319; Davies and Hansen, *Mormon Gold,* Chapter 15, "The Salt Lake Trading Company," 189–93.

27. See Davies and Hansen, *Mormon Gold,* Chap. 15, "The Salt Lake Trading Company," 189–93.

28. Lyman, *The Overland Journey,* 17.

29. Kimball, *The Latter-day Saints' Emigrants' Guide* by W. Clayton. Soon after the Egan Company departed, President Young dispatched Apostle Parley P. Pratt on a major exploring expedition into present-day southern Utah. Pratt's explorations provided information the Church used for years to plant colonizing ventures, and his reports preempted Howard's site findings by the time Howard returned to Utah in 1851. See Smart and Smart, *Over the Rim: The Parley P. Pratt Exploring Expedition.*

30. Egan, *Pioneering the West,* 169–81; Hafen and Hafen, *Journals of Forty-niners,* 307–19. The original diary, "A Diary by H Egan 1849 & 1850 From Fort Utah to California with the distance, water, feed, &c," is in the Egan Papers at Yale University.

31. Davies and Hansen, *Mormon Gold,* 189, 202.

32. Hafen and Hafen, *Journals of Forty-niners,* 309. Howard's original diary mentions the ox and horse teams, but that sentence is missing in Egan, *Pioneering the West.*

33. Landon, *The Journals of George Q. Cannon,* Volume I, 98.

34. Joseph P. Hamblin Jr., Journal, Dec. 1, 1849.

35. Lyman, *The Overland Journey,* 245 n2.

36. In these meadowlands in September 1857 occurred the terrible Mountain Meadows Massacre, which forever damaged the once-high opinion travelers held for this choice camping spot.

37. Lyman, *The Overland Journey,* 5.

38. Ibid., 109.

39. Probably George H. Foote. Mr. Parks isn't identifiable. See name index in Davies and Hansen, *Mormon Gold.*

40. Lyman, *The Overland Journey,* 8–9; Walter Van Dyke account quoted in Hafen and Hafen, *Journals of Forty-niners,* 303.

41. Egan, *Pioneering the West,* 174, mistakenly says they found a man with an arrow in his side, but the original diary says an ox, not a man.

42. Lt. Sylvester Mowry's 1855 report, cited in Lyman, *The Overland Journey,* 10.

43. Possibly George A. Foote.

44. Davies and Hansen, *Mormon Gold*, 183 n12. Today's city of Cucamonga.

45. Both Apostle Charles Rich and Captain Jefferson Hunt had been there since middle or late December. Hafen and Hafen, *Journals of the Forty-niners,* 108, 128.

46. Addison Pratt account quoted in Hafen and Hafen, *Journals of the Forty-niners,* 109.

47. Based on departure and arrival information included in the companies' chapter discussions in Davies and Hansen, *Mormon Gold*.

48. "George Q. Cannon Narrative," in Hafen and Hafen, *Journals of the Forty-niners,* 260; Landon, *Journals of George Q. Cannon: Vol. I,* 77.

49. Ellsworth, *The Journals of Addison Pratt,* 418. A life sketch of Pratt is in Davies and Hansen, *Mormon Gold,* 70.

50. Henry Bigler Diary, Jan. 15, 1850, quoted in Hafen and Hafen, *Journals of Forty-niners,* 180.

51. Egan diary, Yale copy.

52. An informative website regarding California missions is "The Spanish Missions of California" at http://www.californias-missions.org/.

53. Charles C. Rich, quoted in Davies and Hansen, *Mormon Gold,* 162; Pratt's entries in Ellsworth, *Journals of Addison Pratt.* Also see Arrington, *Charles C. Rich.*

54. Brown, *Giant of the Lord,* 77–81.

55. Richard Henry Dana, Jr.'s *Two Years Before the Mast,* very popular after being published in 1840, described his experience in the mid-1830s sailing from Boston to California and back via Cape Horn; the California hide business his ship engaged in; and villages, peoples, and customs he encountered there.

56. Website for Paso Robles, California: www.prcity.com.

57. Brown, *Giant of the Lord,* 112.

58. Ibid., 113; Addison Pratt Journal, 418.

59. Brown, *Giant of the Lord,* 113.

60. "Edwards" probably was Franklin Edwards, who came to California in Egan's company, but the identity of a man named Staden isn't known (Davies and Hansen, *California Gold,* 193 n14).

61. Addison Pratt Journal.

62. In the back of Howard's diary (the Yale copy), he listed mileages and calculated that total.

63. Davies, *Mormon Gold: The Story of California's Mormon Argonauts,*

1984. This was the predecessor study that later became Davies and Hansen, *Mormon Gold*.

64. Davies and Hansen, *Mormon Gold*, 164.
65. Addison Pratt Journal.
66. Addison Pratt Journal.
67. Walker, *Eldorado: The California Gold Rush*, 258–59.
68. Davies, "Mormons and California Gold," 83.
69. The Automobile Club of Southern California, "The Mother Lode" section of its highway, multi-folded map-type guide and maps titled "California's Mother Lode." Undated. Copy in author's possession.
70. Egan Diary, Feb. 16, 1850.
71. Brown, *Giant of the Lord*, 113.
72. During the next days, Howard's diary mentions moving past places that are mis-transcribed in *Pioneering the West* as "Gillar's Ranch" (Gilroy) and "Patgher's Pass" (Pacheco Pass).
73. Henry Bigler Diary, Book B, Feb. 12, 1850, quoted in Landon, *George Q. Cannon Journal I*, 78.
74. Brown, *Giant of the Lord*, 113.
75. Ibid.
76. Ibid., 114.
77. Brown, *Giant of the Lord*, 115.
78. Davies and Hansen, *Mormon Gold*, 191.
79. Brown, *Giant of the Lord*, 116.

Chapter 16

1. Burns' Diggings, or Burns Creek, or Burns Camp, was located southeast of and about two miles upstream from Hornitos, as explained in Landon, *The Journals of George Q. Cannon, Volume I*, 79 n17.
2. Brown, *Giant of the Lord*, 116. When Charles C. Rich went to Howard's post in early March he traveled 55 miles up the Merced River. See Davies and Hansen, *Mormon Gold*, 164. Howard, on the last page in his diary (the original copy at Yale) listed daily miles "up the Mercede river" as 18, 20, and 10, then 4 miles to the spring branch.
3. "The Salt Lake Trading Company was probably located a few miles upriver from present-day Merced Falls near where the Old Highway from Mariposa crosses the Merced River," Davies and Hansen, *Mormon Gold*, 192.
4. Holliday, *The World Rushed In*, 306.

5. Ibid., 393, 307.
6. Brown, *Giant of the Lord,* 116.
7. Ibid., 116–17.
8. Ibid., 117.
9. "Mormon Bar (North)" was located between Beals and Laceys Bars on the North Fork of the American River at the Placer and El Dorado County line near present day Auburn, according to "Inventory of California LDS Historic Sites," compiled March 1, 2001 by S. Dennis Holland, posted at www.californiapioneer.org/destinations, a site maintained by the California Pioneer Heritage Foundation. Also see Davies and Hansen, *Mormon Gold,* 109, 192, and 319.
10. Brown, *Giant of the Lord,* 117.
11. Ibid.
12. Brown, *Giant of the Lord,* 117. A map showing the gold rush trails is in the front of Davies and Hansen, *Mormon Gold,* xvi.
13. Davies and Hansen, *Mormon Gold,* 175.
14. Landon, *George Q. Cannon Journal,* 80.
15. Federal census, 1850, California, San Joaquin County, Stockton District. Howard's place of birth is listed as Massachusetts, indicating perhaps that an associate gave the census taker Howard's information, who knew he had lived in Massachusetts.
16. Brown, *Giant of the Lord,* 117.
17. Ibid., 118.
18. The Automobile Club of Southern California, "The Mother Lode."
19. Street, *California in 1850,* 46–47.
20. Ibid.
21. Elders Lyman and Rich soon became involved in land purchases that led to the founding, under their guidance, of a Mormon settlement in San Bernardino. See Lyman, *San Bernardino.*
22. Rich Diary.
23. Davies and Hansen, *Mormon Gold,* 197 and tithing list on p. 208.
24. Rich Diary.
25. Lyman, *Amasa Mason Lyman,* 183.
26. Davies and Hansen, *Mormon Gold,* 192, 211.
27. Hartley, *Another Kind of Gold: The Life of Albert King Thurber,* 79; also, Holliday, *The World Rushed In,* 395.
28. Davies, "Mormons and California Gold," 119–22; 315–27.
29. Lathrop's Tavern was located on the Placerville-Sacramento Road in El Dorado County between Shingle Springs and White Rock near the Sacramento

County line. Clarksville, located near Lathrop's, was midway between Sacramento and Placerville on Highway 50, just east of Folsom. Today's Highway 50 cuts through the hill at the actual site of the Mormon Tavern, which today would be slightly east of the south end of the El Dorado Hills Golf Course. Lathrop's was a few miles east of where Folsom, California now is. See Davies and Hansen, *Mormon Gold,* 322; also, Asahel Lathrop and Clarksville, CA entries on the Internet.

30. Davies and Hansen, *Mormon Gold,* 107.
31. Ibid., 227.
32. Ibid., 235.
33. Davies and Hansen, *Mormon Gold,* 213.
34. Ibid.
35. Cannon diary, quoted in Davies and Hansen, *Mormon Gold,* 213, citation to Cannon is in 215 n17. Lafayette Granger was 27 years old, born in New York, and had come to Utah in 1847 (*Mormon Gold,* 213, 333). Phineas Kimball also was age 27, born in Vermont, and was a disaffected Mormon who had reached Utah in 1847 and come to California in 1848 "avoiding a stay in Utah" *(Mormon Gold,* 215, 338).
36. "To Whom It May Concern," *Deseret News,* April 7, 1852.
37. Davies and Hansen, *Mormon Gold,* 284.
38. Ibid., 213, 214.
39. Ibid., 211, and Davies, *Mormon Gold* (first edition), 227.
40. Davies and Hansen, *Mormon Gold,* 192.
41. Egan 1849–1850 Diary, the original version at Yale.
42. Based on his arriving in Salt Lake Valley by September 10, as shown in this chapter's final paragraph.
43. Ricketts, *The Mormon Battalion,* 205–22. Carson Pass was named after Kit Carson, who rode through it in 1844.
44. "The Carson Pass Wagon Road was shorter and less difficult than the Truckee route…It became the most heavily used branch of the California Trail from 1849 to 1851." Owens, *Gold Rush Saints,* 160.
45. Text as posted on Nevada's "Forty Mile Desert" website.
46. Text on "Forty Mile Desert" historical marker along U.S. 50, one mile east of the junction with U.S. 50 Alternate, in western Churchill County.
47. Joseph Cain account in Journal History, Sept. 29, 1850.
48. Bryon McKinstry, quote provided on OCTA (Oregon-California Trails Association) marker at south end of the Forty Mile Desert, a picture of which is shown on www.emigranttrailswest.org.
49. Holliday, *The World Rushed In,* 247.

50. Quote posted at www.octa-trails.org.
51. Holliday, *The World Rushed In,* 225.
52. Ibid.
53. Stewart, *The California Trail,* trail map and mileages, 134.
54. James Henry Rollins, Reminiscences, 42–43.
55. Carter, "The Salt Lake Cutoff and the California Trail."
56. Rich started on Oct. 5, 1850 and reached Great Salt Lake City on Dec. 12, requiring 67 days or 9.5 weeks. Rich Diary.
57. Daniel Davis Diary. Davis said that two days after Howard returned, Howard, William Kimball, and William's wife "were poisoned by eating oysters."

Chapter 17

1. Utah Territory 1850–51 Census, MS 2672, Reel 1, Church History Library. Also in the John and Euphemia Banks household were Mary Davis, age 16, and John Lee, 12, both born in Wales, and John Killpack, age 32, from Ireland.
2. Some Egan descendants swear the M stood for Monroe, but that claim lacks evidence. Official records use the name William Moburn Egan. The Egan Family Record Book (FHL #1598329 Item 1), also known as William M Egan Temple Record Book, was compiled by William Moburn Egan. Howard probably would not have allowed William to have Monroe in his name.
3. James M. Monroe Journal, 1841–1842 and 1845, microfilm of holograph, Church History Library, MS 7061. The diary mistakenly is labeled as being Howard Egan's, not Monroe's. The library has a second version, basically a recopy of the first done by Monroe to make it more attractive, as well as a microfilm of a holography. See MS 8829, Item 5. Both of the original diaries are in the Egan Papers in the Beinecke Library at Yale University.
4. Enoch Reese Journal. Reese was born in 1811 or 1812, moved to Utica, New York, then moved to New York City, and then moved back to Utica, where he married in 1841. A note at the end of the journal says Enoch probably was baptized the same year as James M. Monroe and his mother.
5. Monroe Journal.
6. Journal History, April 10, 1843.
7. Journal History, March 28, 1843, Dec. 24, 1844, and Jan. 26, 1845.
8. Stout Diary, I:12–13 n26. See also Hogan, "The Curious Case of James Madison Monroe."
9. Monroe Journal.
10. Journal History, Jan. 20, 1848.

11. Based on name search in the LDS Church's website, "Mormon Pioneer Overland Travel."

12. The Reese brothers came to Utah in 1849 and established a mercantile firm in Salt Lake City. They established Mormon Station in 1850, which became Genoa, Nevada. Regarding the brothers see Davies, *Mormon Gold*, 254; Arrington, *Great Basin Kingdom*, 81, 86; and *Journal History Index for Enoch Reese, John Reese, and Reese & Co.* Enoch Reese's obituary is in *Deseret News*, July 26, 1876. The Enoch Reese Private Journal is cited in an earlier note. Also see "John Taylor for the Guardian," in *Frontier Guardian*, Jan. 9, 1850, and www.genoanevada.org.

13. Kearl, Pope, and Wimmer, *Index to the 1850, 1860 & 1870 Censuses of Utah*.

14. Journal History, Dec. 1, 1850.

15. "From Salt Lake," *Frontier Guardian*, Jan. 22, 1851. To cover 1000 miles in 16 days means he'd have to average 62 miles a day, which, if riding 12 hours a day he'd be traveling at just over 5 miles per hour. He must have been galloping on horseback.

16. Ibid.

17. Orson Hyde, "Shot," *Frontier Guardian*, Nov. 14, 1851.

18. Jas. M. Monroe to G. F. Carter, Feb. 9, 1851, in Wilford Woodruff Papers, Correspondence 1851, Box 6, Folder 20, Church History Library, MS 1352.

19. William Woodward, reminiscent account, posted on the LDS Church website, "Mormon Pioneer Overland Travel," for the 1851 John Reese Wagon Train.

20. William Woodward account, published in the *Juvenile Instructor*, July 15, 1896, 415.

21. Daniel Davis Diary, Sept. 12, 1851.

22. Stansbury, *An Expedition to the Valley of the Great Salt Lake*, 137.

23. Quinn, *The Mormon Hierarchy: Extensions of Power*, Chapter 7, "Post-1844 Theocracy and a Culture of Violence," 226–261; "Blood Atonement," *Encyclopedia of Mormonism*, 1:131.

24. George A. Smith statement during the defense case for Howard that he presented to the jury. See *Deseret News*, Nov. 15, 1851.

25. Unlike rape, which involves forced conduct, seduction means to entice, persuade, beguile, lure, or tempt. Seduction in the nineteenth century also included adultery, and the term had legal meaning only because of then current notions of male dominance over women. But, during the twentieth century,

seduction became and still is "almost entirely archaic as a legal concept." Kenneth L. Cannon II, "Mountain Common Law," 310 n4.

26. Cannon, "Mountain Common Law," 310.
27. Stout Diary, March 17, 1851, and Homer, "The Judiciary and the Common Law in Utah Territory, 1850–61," 100.
28. James M. Monroe to Brigham Young, Sept.16, 1851, in Brigham Young Papers. Restricted document, used by special permission.
29. By 1851 she was Delia Ann Pratt.
30. William Woodward, reminiscent account, for the 1851 John Reese Wagon Train.
31. Stout Diary, Sept. 21, 1851
32. Stout Diary, 2:406 n72.
33. Neibaur's Journal, excerpted in Journal History, Sept. 21, 1851.
34. Hyde, "Shot," *Frontier Guardian,* Nov. 14, 1851.
35. Jedediah M. Grant, *Three Letters to the New York Herald.* The Egan-Monroe discussion is in Letter 3, dated April 25, 1852, specifically on pages 42–50. The pamphlet, composed of the three letters, was Grant's rebuttal to the report of three runaway officials to the U.S. President about political conditions in Utah.
36. Stout Diary, Oct. 17, 1851.
37. The body was brought to Salt Lake City before Howard's trial. The marker for Monroe's grave is in the Salt Lake City Cemetery at Salt Lake County Plot: B2, 6, 1W.

Chapter 18

1. Journal History, Oct. 3, 1851. On July 1, 1853 Howard's 17th Quorum of Seventy did disfellowship him, but his constant absences in California could also have been the reason. (Martin, *The Story of Major Howard Egan,* 56).
2. Roberts, *Comprehensive History* 3:520–44.
3. Journal History, Sept. 28, 1851.
4. Whitney, *History of Utah,* I:480–81.
5. Cannon, "Mountain Common Law," 311 n6.
6. The trial records are in the Utah State Archives, in a file named "1851: People vs. Egan, Series 25011, Box 2, file 9." A paper shortage caused the *Deseret News* to not publish during this investigation and trial period. On Nov. 15 it provided trial information.
7. People vs. Egan, "Journal A," 7.
8. Utah vs. Egan, Journal A, #114–116. Why Larson was suspected of being an accomplice isn't recorded.

9. "United States vs. Howard Egan, Murder Case, A True Bill, Daniel Spencer, foreman, Witnesses: G C Robbins, Wm Horner, James Wade, Moore," 125–27.

10. Photocopy of the order, handwritten by clerk W. I. Appleby of the First Judicial District Court for the Territory of Utah, in author's possession. Original in the trial papers at the Utah State Archives.

11. A list of the 36 men, in clerk Appleby's handwriting, is on file in the Utah State Archives, photocopy in the author's possession.

12. "United States vs. Howard Egan, Case Murder."

13. "The United States vs. Howard Egan, On Presentment of US Grand Jury for Murder," Utah State Archives, Box A96A1, #61–3, 1533, TJ-1 03.18.

14. Tamson Egan Interrogatory, photocopy of original, in author's possession. In the trial papers at the Utah State Archives.

15. "Indictment for Murder," *Deseret News,* Nov. 15, 1851.

16. Utah vs. Egan, "Journal A," 11–12.

17. Stout Diary, Oct. 17, 1851.

18. Homer, "The Judiciary and the Common Law in Utah Territory, 1850–1861," 97–100.

19. Stout Diary, Oct. 17, 1851.

20. "Indictment for Murder" and "Judge Snow's Charge to the Jury," *Deseret News,* Nov. 15, 1851; "Mormonism! Indictment for the murder of James Monroe," referred to in the report of the returned judges from the Territory of Utah … (Liverpool, England: R. James, 1852); and "Charge of Hon. Z. Snow…to the Jury, on the Trial of Howard Egan for the Murder of James Monroe," October Term, 1851, *Journal of Discourses* I:100–103.

21. "Indictment for Murder," *Deseret News,* Nov. 15, 1851.

22. Ibid.

23. Ibid.

24. Morgan, "The State of Deseret," *Utah Historical Quarterly,* 234–35. Morgan, *The State of Deseret,* has in an appendix the "Deseret Constitution and Ordinances 1849–1851: Acts, Resolutions and Memorials Passed by the First Annual, and Special Sessions, of the Legislative Assembly, of the Territory of Utah, Begun and Held at Great Salt Lake City, on the 22nd Day of September, A.D. 1851," G.S.L. City, U. T.: Brigham S. Young, Printer, 1852.

25. Homer, "Judiciary and the Common Law in Utah Territory," 101.

26. Cannon, "Mountain Common Law," 311.

27. "Judge Snow's Charge to the Jury," *Deseret News,* Nov. 15, 1851, and "Charge of Hon. Z. Snow…to the Jury, on the Trial of Howard Egan for

the Murder of James Monroe," October Term, 1851, in *Journal of Discourses* I:100–103.

    28. Utah vs. Howard Egan, "Journal A," 13.

    29. Alexander Neibaur Journal.

    30. Brigham Young to Franklin D. Richards, Letter Draft, Oct. 19, 1851.

    31. "Indictment for Murder," *Deseret News,* Nov 15, 1851.

    32. Grant, *Three Letters to the New York Herald*. The Egan-Monroe discussion is in Letter 3, dated 25 April 1852, pp. 42–50. The quotes are on pp. 45 and 48.

    33. Pratt, "Contexts for the Murder of Parley P. Pratt," 40, based on Mason, "Honor, the Unwritten Law and Extralegal Violence: Contextualising Parley Pratt's Murder," 250.

    34. Stout Diary, Oct. 18, 1851.

    35. *Deseret Evening News,* Feb. 4, 1868, quoted in Cannon, "Mountain Common Law," 318.

    36. Cannon, "Mountain Common Law," 319–27.

    37. Janet Sloan notes, telephone conversation with Afton Green, granddaughter of Howard Ransom Egan, Oct. 7, 1993, copy in author's files.

    38. Jeffrey Ogden Johnson, "Determining and Defining 'Wife': The Brigham Young Households," 69 n48.

    39. Brigham Young to Howard Egan, Sept. 29, 1859, Brigham Young Letterbook 5.

    40. Mary Jane Egan Johnson to Janet Sloan, phone conversation, Feb. 19, 1994. Mrs. Johnson said she met William during visits with "Uncle Willy and Aunt Lulu."

    41. The Monroe journals are part of the Howard Egan and William Egan Papers at Yale. Archivists there at first mislabeled the Monroe journals as being Howard's journals.

Chapter 19

    1. William M. Egan Journal.

    2. Nicholas G. Morgan, compiler, "Pioneer Map of Great Salt Lake City."

    3. Egan, *Pioneering the West,* 151.

    4. Ibid.

    5. Ibid.

    6. Woods, "The Arrival of Nineteenth-Century Mormon Emigrants in Salt Lake City."

7. "Autobiographical Sketch of Ann Lewis Clegg," 2–3.

8. "Sixth General Epistle of the Presidency," Sept. 22, 1851, in Clark, *Messages of the First Presidency*, 2:83.

9. Egan, *Pioneering the West*, 154.

10. The city has changed the original street designations. Instead of letting the street name numberings begin after North Temple and West Temple, the city counted North Temple as First North and West Temple as First West (without changing their names); hence what had been First North now is Second North and what had been First West now is Second West, etc.

11. Union Square then was bounded by streets using the old designations: Second North and First North, and Second West and Third West.

12. The bath house was located at the equivalent of today's Eighth North and Third West and is a city park at 840 north Beck Street. It now has no hot springs access.

13. "Salt Lake City Nineteenth Ward," in Jenson, *Encyclopedic History of the Church*, 753.

14. William M. Egan, "Interesting reminiscence of the boyhood life of W. M. Egan in Salt Lake City from 1854–1863."

15. Roberts, *Comprehensive History of the Church*, 4:55–58; and *Deseret News, Extra*, Sept. 14, 1852.

16. "Ninth General Epistle of the Presidency," April 13, 1853, in Clark, *Messages of the First Presidency*, 2:114.

17. Egan, *Pioneering the West*, 149.

18. Journal History, March 23 and April 1 and 2, 1853.

19. Egan, *Pioneering the West*, 152.

20. R. Scott Lloyd, "Birthplace of the University of Utah Is Replicated," *Church News*, Nov. 17, 2001.

21. 1852 overland emigrant Addison Crane, quoted in Arrington, *Great Basin Kingdom*, 82.

22. LDS Church website "Mormon Pioneer Overland Travel" at www.lds.org/resources/churchhistory.

23. Arrington, *Great Basin Kingdom*, 111.

24. Egan, *Pioneering the West*, 182.

25. "Seventh General Epistle of the Presidency," in Clark, *Messages of the First Presidency*, 2:97.

26. Arrington, *Great Basin Kingdom*, 135–36.

27. William M. Egan Journal.

28. Ibid.

29. "To Whom It May Concern," *Deseret News,* April 17, 1852.
30. Cornelia Woodcock (Mrs. B. G.) Ferris, *The Mormons at Home: With Some Incidents of Travel from Missouri to California, 1852–1853,* 211.
31. *Deseret News,* Dec. 11, 1852.
32. Ferris, *Mormons at Home.* Her account of the company's journey spans pp. 206–92.
33. Ibid., 207.
34. Egan, *Pioneering the West,* 155.
35. Ferris, *Mormons at Home,* 211.
36. Ibid.
37. Ibid., 217–25.
38. Ibid., 291–92.
39. Ibid., 226–28, 230.
40. Ibid., 236–37.
41. Ibid., 238–39, 245.
42. Ibid., 252–53.
43. Ibid., 259, 265.
44. Marie Irvine, "The Trail Not Followed," 8–10.
45. Ferris, *Mormons at Home,* 270, 278, 283.
46. Ibid., 291.
47. Irvine, "The Trail Not Followed."
48. Egan, *Pioneering the West,* 190–91.
49. "Salt Lake City Nineteenth Ward Records," 98.
50. Egan, *Pioneering the West,* 182–86.

Chapter 20

1. "Unidentified 1855 Daybook," Howard Egan's Daybook, in Egan Yale papers. Excerpts, transcribed differently in a few particulars, are in Egan, *Pioneering the West,* 191–92.
2. www.calgoldrush.com/extra/sloughhouse.html.
3. "Rancho Las Putas," *Wikipedia.* Lake Berryessa was formed when the Monticello Dam was completed in 1957.
4. Billington, *The Far Western Frontier,* 94–106; Unruh, *The Plains Across: The Overland Emigrants and the Trans-Mississippi West, 1840–1860,* 351.
5. Lorry, "Unveiling the Black Rock: A History of Exploration in Nevada's Remote Northwest Corner," 17.
6. *Deseret Weekly News,* Dec. 1, 1853, and Bateman, *Deep Creek*

Reflections, 41. Bateman cites Cyrene Bagley of Callao, Utah, as saying that Redding Springs are on the northeast side of the Deep Creek Range.

7. Lorry, "Unveiling the Black Rock," 17.
8. Peterson, *A Route for the Overland Stage: James H. Simpson's 1859 Trail Across the Great Basin*, 53–55.
9. "O. B. and C. A. Huntington, New Route," *Deseret News*, Dec. 7, 1854.
10. Peterson, *Simpson's 1859 Trail*, 231 n2; Schindler, *Orrin Porter Rockwell*, 214–18.
11. Remy and Brenchley, *A Journey To The Great-Salt-Lake City*, 122–39, 148–49.
12. Irvine, "Howard Egan: Muleback Champion and Stagecoach Hero."
13. Ibid.
14. Egan, *Pioneering the West*, 197.
15. News item in the *Deseret News*, pasted into *Journal History*, July 21, 1855.
16. Egan, *Pioneering the West*, 197; Pacific Express Company announcement in *Deseret News*, Aug. 8, 1855, listing Livingston & Kinkead as the company's agents.
17. Deseret News, Sept. 19, 1855.
18. Remy and Brenchley, *A Journey To The Great-Salt-Lake City*, 167.
19. Egan, *Pioneering the West*, 188.
20. Ibid.
21. Ibid., 189.
22. Ibid., 188.
23. Journal History, Oct. 1, 1855, 1.
24. Drake, "Howard Egan," 110. The Harold's Club Casino closed in 1995 and the building was demolished in 1999.
25. Egan, *Pioneering the West*, 189.

Chapter 21

1. The last major swarms of Rocky Mountain locust happened between 1873 and 1877. The last recorded sighting of a live specimen was in 1902 in southern Canada. See "Rocky Mountain Locust," *Wikipedia* (2014).
2. Carter, "Fish and the Famine of 1855–56," 93–97.
3. Bitton and Wilcox, "Pestiferous Ironclads: The Grasshopper Problem in Pioneer Utah," 342–43.

4. Journal History, May 29, 1855.
5. Ibid.
6. *Deseret News*, June 25, 1855.
7. Egan, *Pioneering the West*, 150.
8. Ibid.
9. Carter, "Fish and the Famine," 98–99. Drought and grasshoppers historically have made joint appearances; see Bitton and Wilcox, "Pestiferous Ironclads," 336–55.
10. Brigham Young to Franklin D. Richards, July 30, 1855, in Journal History, that date.
11. "Fourteenth General Epistle of the Presidency," Dec. 10, 1856, in Clark, *Messages of the First Presidency* 2:202.
12. Carter, "Fish and the Famine," 97, 101–103.
13. Ibid., 100.
14. Arrington, *Great Basin Kingdom*, 150–51; Carter, "Fish and Famine," 107–8.
15. William M. Egan, "Interesting reminiscence of the boyhood life."
16. Egan, *Pioneering the West*, 155.
17. Warner, *The History of Spanish Fork*, 48; Hicks, "History of Spanish Fork," 9.
18. Arrington, *Great Basin Kingdom*, 154.
19. Minutes of Presiding Bishop's Meetings with the Bishops, March 11, 1856; Carter, "Fish and Famine," 108, 110, 113.
20. Heber C. Kimball to son William Kimball, April 13, 1856, in Journal History, that date, p. 4.
21. Carter, "Fish and Famine," 118.
22. Ibid., 101–103.
23. Arrington, *Great Basin Kingdom*, 156.
24. Wilford Woodruff to John Taylor, May 29, 1856, in Journal History that date.
25. "Fourteenth General Epistle of the Presidency," Dec. 10, 1856, in Clark, *Messages of the First Presidency* 2:203.
26. Ibid., 202.
27. Journal History, March 28, 1857, 1.
28. Hafen and Hafen, *Handcarts to Zion*, and Cornwall and Arrington, *Rescue of the 1856 Handcart Companies*, 28, 33.
29. Egan, *Pioneering the West*, 282–83.
30. Peterson, "The Mormon Reformation," dissertation, and Peterson's

article, "The Mormon Reformation of 1856–1857." For negative aspects of the Reformation from critical scholars' viewpoints see Bigler and Bagley, *The Mormon Rebellion: America's First Civil War, 1857–1858*, Chapter 5, "The Cleansing Blood of Sinners: The Reformation," 94–128.

31. Hartley, *Another Kind of Gold: The Life of Albert King Thurber*, 124–25.

32. Wilford Woodruff conference address, Oct. 6, 1856, in Journal History, that date, p. 2.

33. Peterson, "The Mormon Reformation," article, 66.

34. A responsible evaluation of nineteenth century LDS plural marriage is B. Carmon Hardy's "That 'Same Old Question of Polygamy and Polygamous Living': Some Recent Findings Regarding Nineteenth and Early Twentieth-Century Mormon Polygamy."

35. Peterson, "The Mormon Reformation," article, 70.

36. "Richard Erastus Egan," in Jensen, *Biographical Encyclopedia*, 1:816.

37. Peterson, "The Mormon Reformation," dissertation, 49–54; Bigler and Bagley, *The Mormon Rebellion*, 113.

38. Peterson, "The Mormon Reformation," article, 76–77.

39. Journal History, March 28, 1857, 1.

40. Regarding Fort Limhi see David L. Bigler, *Fort Limhi;* Jacob Miller, the "Salmon River Mission Journal"; Daughters of Utah Pioneers, "The Salmon River Mission," which includes numerous journal accounts; Hartley, *Kindred Saints*, chap. 6, "Dangerous Mission at Fort Limhi;" and Nash, "The Salmon River Mission of 1855."

41. "James A. Cummings, A journal of the travels by Pres. B Young and Company...to Fort Limhi." A slightly edited version of the journal appeared in the *Deseret News* as "Excursion to Fort Limhi," June 10, 1857.

42. The official journal lists Howard as captain of the second ten, but Bigler, *Fort Limhi*, 137, lists Col. Burton as the captain.

43. Bigler, *Fort Limhi*, 142.

44. Ibid., 242–43.

45. Journal History, May 24, 1857, 1

Chapter 22

1. Regarding the Utah War see MacKinnon, *At Sword's Point, Part One and Part Two: A Documentary History of the Utah War to 1858*; Bigler and Bagley, *The Mormon Rebellion, America's First Civil War 1857–1858*; Hafen and Hafen, *The Utah Expedition 1857–1858*; and Furniss, *The Mormon Conflict 1850–1859*.

2. MacKinnon, *At Sword's Point, Vol. One*, 52–53.
3. Ibid., 56–7, 60, 102, 116–17, and 437; Roberts, *Comprehensive History of the Church* 4:198, 202, 210, and 222.
4. Bigler and Bagley, *The Mormon Rebellion*, x.
5. Furniss, *The Mormon Conflict*, 69.
6. Roland, *Albert Sidney Johnston*, 189.
7. Isaac Sorensen Journal, excerpted on LDS Church's Mormon Pioneer Overland Travel Accounts website, 1857 Matthias Cowley Company. On August 17 in central Wyoming, Mormon travelers met two companies of about two dozen government wagons each; see Briant Stringham and S. W. Richards to Brigham Young, Deer Creek Station, 18 Aug.1857, same website, 1857 William G. Young Company.
8. Hansen, "Administrative History of the Nauvoo Legion in Utah," 10, 12–14.
9. Gardner, "Pioneer Military Leaders of Utah," 37.
10. As of 2015 the sword was privately held by the Stanley J. Pitcher family.
11. Furniss, *The Mormon Conflict*, 119.
12. Brigadier General's Office to Col. W. B. Pace, August 13, 1857, Military Records, Reel 25. Efforts to find hiding places are studied in Stott, *Search for Sanctuary*.
13. Gardner, "The Utah Territorial Militia," 368.
14. Sutton, *Utah–A Centennial History*, Vol. II, 593.
15. MacKinnon, *At Sword's Point, Vol. One*, 256.
16. Furniss, *The Mormon Conflict*, 139–140.
17. Stott, *Search for Sanctuary*, 31.
18. Furniss, *The Mormon Conflict*, 122.
19. Ibid., 105.
20. Stott, *Search for Sanctuary*, 31.
21. Proclamation, Aug. 5, 1857, Brigham Young Papers, Church History Library.
22. MacKinnon, *At Sword's Point, Vol. One*, 286–288.
23. Furniss, *The Mormon Conflict*, 37, 111–113; MacKinnon, *At Sword's Point, Vol. One*, 330, 356–57.
24. Furniss, *The Mormon Conflict*, 144; Arrington, *Brigham Young: American Moses*, 255.
25. Furniss, *The Mormon Conflict*, 123, 130; Arrington, *Brigham Young*, 261.
26. Furniss, *The Mormon Conflict*, 115.

27. Ibid.
28. Ibid., 149.
29. Roland, *Albert Sidney Johnston*, 194–96.
30. Furniss, *The Mormon Conflict*, 165.
31. Ibid., 141.
32. "Diary of John Pulsipher," in Hafen and Hafen, *The Utah Expedition*, 206–207.
33. Roland, *Albert Sidney Johnston*, 197.
34. Furniss, *Mormon Conflict*, 117–118.
35. Bigler and Bagley, *The Mormon Rebellion*, 276–279.
36. Brigham Young to William Appleby in New York and Jeter Clinton in Philadelphia, Sept. 12, 1857, quoted in MacKinnon, *At Sword's Point, Vol. One*, 275.
37. Arrington, *Brigham Young*, 261; Furniss, *The Mormon Conflict*, 135; Stott, *Search for Sanctuary*, 32; and "Secure as Much Ammunition as You Can" section in Owens, *Gold Rush Saints*, 328–41.
38. MacKinnon, *At Sword's Point, Vol One*, 268.
39. Ibid., 268–70.
40. General Tithing Office to Howard Egan, Jan. 6, 1858, Horace K. Whitney, clerk, copy in Janet Sloan Files.
41. Journal History, Jan. 19, 1858, 1.
42. *Pioneering the West*, 157, has a facsimile of the handwritten receipt, dated Feb. 3, 1858.
43. MacKinnon, *At Sword's Point, Vol. Two*, 68–69.
44. Journal History, Jan. 19 and Feb. 1 and 5, 1858. Regarding the "Standing Army" unit, see Bigler, *Forgotten Kingdom*, 183.
45. MacKinnon, *At Sword's Point, Part Two*, 248, 253. George A. Smith to John L. Smith, Feb. 5, 1858, is quoted on p. 248.
46. Seegmiller, *"Be Kind to the Poor": The Life Story of Robert Taylor Burton*, 183.
47. Ibid., 253; Furniss, *Mormon Conflict*, 147. Regarding Kane's peacemaking role in the Utah War, see Grow, *Kane*, chapters 9 and 10.
48. MacKinnon, *At Sword's Point, Part Two*, 248, 253.
49. Grow, *Kane*.
50. Bigler, *Forgotten Kingdom*, 185.
51. Grow, *Kane*, 167.
52. MacKinnon, *At Sword's Point, Vol. Two*, 276; Grow, *Kane*, 174.
53. Ibid., 315 n18.

54. Journal History, May 10, 1858.
55. Furniss, *Mormon Conflict*, 173; Grow, *Kane*, 194–95.
56. Grow, *Kane*, 177.
57. Bigler and Bagley, *The Mormon Rebellion*, 302; Grow, *Kane*, 187.
58. Bigler and Bagley, *The Mormon Rebellion*, 302.
59. Journal History, Jan. 19, Feb. 5, and April 8 and 21, 1858.
60. Grow, *Kane*, 187.
61. Gates, *The Life Story of Brigham Young*, 182.
62. Journal History, April 21, 1858, 1.
63. Bigler and Bagley, *The Mormon Rebellion*, 309.
64. MacKinnon, *At Sword's Point, Vol. Two*, 449.
65. Grow, *Kane*, 188.
66. Egan, *Pioneering the West*, 154.
67. Regarding Worthen see Grow, *Kane*, 321 n41.
68. Alfred Cumming letter, Salt Lake City, Utah, May 12, 1858, Church History Library, MS 14659.
69. Nicholas Groesbeck to John Richard, May 12, 1858, in Brigham Young Letterbook 4, file 3.
70. "Arrival of Col. Kane at Florence," *Crescent City Oracle*, in Journal History, June 8, 1858, 1; and Hafen and Hafen, *The Utah Expedition*, 289–92.
71. Thomas Bullock, Chimney Rock, Nebraska, to editor, *Millennial Star*, May 27, 1858, in Journal History, that date, p. 2.
72. Journal of Eli Pierce, in the Bullock Company, May 27, 1858, in Journal History, that date.
73. Oscar Orlando Stoddard, Journals and Record Book 1856–1860, June 6, 1858, in Horace S. Eldredge Company, 1858, posted on the LDS Mormon Pioneer Overland Travel Accounts website.
74. Joseph Orton Autobiography, in Horace Eldredge wagon train, posted on Mormon Pioneers Overland Travel Accounts website.
75. "Arrival of Col. Kane at Florence."
76. Ibid.
77. Elizabeth W. Kane Journal, June 29, 1857 to Aug. 8, 1858.
78. "Col. Kane," *Cincinnati Com*, reprinted in the *Deseret News*, Sept. 8, 1858; Grow, *Kane*, 193.
79. "Arrival of Col. Thomas L. Kane," *Germantown Telegraph*, Philadelphia, June 23, 1858, quoted in Hafen and Hafen, *The Utah Expedition*, 292.
80. Furniss, *Mormon Conflict*, 173; Grow, *Kane*, 194–95.

81. Elizabeth W. Kane Journal, June 29, 1857 to Aug. 8, 1858.

82. Thomas Brown Holmes Stenhouse, an English LDS convert and vigorous missionary, emigrated in late 1855, stopped in New York City, helped edit the LDS newspaper, *The Mormon*, and reported for the *New York Herald*. He came to Utah in 1859.

83. Kane Collection, Box 77, file 24, Elizabeth Kane's Ambrotype photographs, photographs of "unknown males" in folders 355, 358, 367, 368.

84. Journal History, Aug. 24, 1858, 1.

85. As noted in Young to Bernhisel, Sept. 8, 1858, and Young to Kane, Sept. 10, 1858, both in Young Letterbook 4, file 5; MacKinnon, *At Sword's Point, Vol. Two*, 503. The Journal History for August 24, 1858, includes a *Deseret News* clipping that says Howard and his group arrived on August 23.

86. Arrington, *Brigham Young*, 264, 266; and Furniss, *Mormon Conflict*, 188.

87. John Pulsipher Diary, April 25, 1858, in Hafen and Hafen, *The Utah Expedition*, 218.

88. Bigler and Bagley, *The Mormon Rebellion*, 295.

89. Arrington, *Brigham Young*, 266–67; Furniss, *Mormon Conflict*, 187.

90. William M. Egan, "Interesting reminiscence of the boyhood life," and "Howard Ransom Egan," in Jenson, *LDS Biographical Encyclopedia*, I:816.

91. MacKinnon, *At Sword's Point, Vol. Two*, 618.

92. Furniss, *Mormon Conflict*, 170.

93. MacKinnon, *At Sword's Point, Vol. Two*, 618.

94. Furniss, *Mormon Conflict*, 192–197.

95. Roland, *Albert Sidney Johnston*, 201, 204, 210–211.

96. Ibid., 211–216.

97. Roberts, *Comprehensive History of the Church*, 4:441.

98. Egan, *Pioneering the West*, 154.

99. Spanish Fork Ward, Record of Members, entries for July 4 and 11, 1858, and to end of 1858. The "enthusiastic Mormon" phrase appears later in Presiding Bishop's Meetings with Bishops, Minutes, Oct. 28 and Dec. 9, 1858; Alexander, *Utah, The Right Place*, 136.

100. Moorman and Sessions, *Camp Floyd and the Mormons*. Today, Camp Floyd State Park features a museum, the Carson Stagecoach Inn, and a cemetery.

101. Roland, *Albert Sidney Johnston*, 218–219; Moorman and Sessions, *Camp Floyd*, 57–58.

102. Furniss, *Mormon Conflict*, 205, 219.

103. Ibid., 205–11.

104. Ibid., 211.
105. Ibid., 219–21; Stowers and Ellis, eds., "Charles A. Scott's Diary of the Utah Expedition, 1857–1861," 175–176; Audrey M. Godfrey, "Housewives, Hussies and Heroines, or the Women of Johnston's Army," 167.
106. MacKinnon, *At Sword's Point, Part Two*, 618–19.
107. Ibid., 620.

Chapter 23

1. Hafen, *The Overland Mail 1849–1869*.
2. Ibid., 59.
3. George Chorpenning was born in Somerset, Pennsylvania in 1820. He went to California during the 1849 gold rush. After his mail freighting career he served in the Civil War in the 1st regiment of Maryland Volunteer Infantry. He died in 1894. See Biographical Supplement in Settle, *War Drums and Wagon Wheels: The Story of Russell, Majors and Waddell*, 250–251.
4. Ora Simmons, "Life Sketch of Howard Egan"; John M. Townley, "Stalking Horse for the Pony Express: The Chorpenning Mail Contracts between California and Utah, 1851–1860," 239 n25.
5. Townley, "Stalking Horse," 230–32.
6. Ibid., 234–37.
7. *Deseret News*, Nov. 14, 1855:1.
8. Hafen, *Overland Mail*, 62–67.
9. Moody, *Stagecoach West*, 97–114.
10. Hafen, *Overland Mail*, 98.
11. Townley, *The Overland Stage: A History and Guidebook*, 9.
12. Ibid.
13. Townley, "Stalking Horse," 240, and Townley, *The Overland Stage*, 9.
14. Townley, "Stalking Horse," 241, and Townley, *The Overland Stage*, 9.
15. Townley, "Stalking Horse," 244–45.
16. Moody, *Stagecoach West*, 128–32.
17. Ibid., 128.
18. Moody, *Stagecoach West*, 128–32.
19. Townley, "Stalking Horse," 245.
20. Hafen, *Overland Mail*, 113.
21. Ibid., 112–15.
22. Townley, "Stalking Horse," 246; Chorpenning report, quoted in Hafen, *Overland Mail*, 114 n247.

23. "Snowshoe Thompson," *Wikipedia*.
24. *Pioneering the West*, 216–17.
25. Journal History, Dec. 25, 1858.
26. Townley, "Stalking Horse," 246–47.
27. William Russell, Alexander Majors, and William B. Waddell. See Majors, *Seventy Years on the Frontier* (1893).
28. H. J. Faust Recollections, "Pony Express and Stage Coach: How News Was Transmitted, Mail Carried, and Passengers Transported in Early Day Utah," *Deseret Evening News*, May 29, 1897.
29. Faust Recollections.
30. Townley, "Stalking Horse," 248.
31. Ibid.
32. Egan, *Pioneering the West*, 202.
33. Townley, "Stalking Horse," 248. An outstanding trail guide and history of the Simpson explorations is Petersen, *A Route for the Overland Stage: James H. Simpson's 1859 Trail across the Great Basin*.
34. J. H. Simpson, *Report of Explorations across the Great Basin*, 1876, 46–52.
35. Ibid., 52. Spelled "Go-shoot" there. With respect to the spelling of "Go-sha-utes," see agent Garland Hurt's report that is Appendix O in the Simpson Report, 460.
36. Ibid., 53–58.
37. Ibid., 60–61.
38. Ibid., 61.
39. Ibid.
40. Ibid., 63–64.
41. Ibid., 64–67.
42. Petersen, *West from Salt Lake: Diaries from the Central Overland Trail*, 19–20. Petersen details route variations as identified in diarists' accounts on pp. 21–25.
43. Burton, *The City of the Saints*, 508.
44. Townley, "Stalking Horse," 247.
45. Ibid., 248.
46. Faust Recollections.
47. Ibid.
48. Egan, *Pioneering the West*, 215.
49. "From Our Humboldt Correspondent," Correspondent "H" to Editor News, Humboldt River, July 22, 1859, *Deseret News*, Aug. 5, 1859.

50. "From Our Western Correspondent," Letter from correspondent named simply Sirius to the *Deseret News*, clipping in Journal History, Sept. 18, 1859.

51. Bateman, *Deep Creek Reflections*, 54.

52. Bluth, "Confrontation with an Arid Land."

53. Simpson, *Explorations*, 52–53.

54. Blanthorn, *History of Tooele County*, 19–27; "Deep Creek Branch," in Jenson, *Encyclopedic History of the Church*, 177.

55. "From Our Western Correspondent," *Deseret News*, Sept. 18, 1859.

56. Townley, "Stalking Horse," 249.

57. "From Our Western Correspondent," *Deseret News*, Aug. 12, 1859.

58. "Matters relative to the Salt Lake and California Mail," C. & S. L. Mail Line, Nov. 8, 1859 to Editor, *Deseret News*, Journal History, that date.

59. Townley, "Stalking Horse," 250.

60. Settle and Settle, *War Drums and Wagon Wheels*, 115–16.

61. Townley, "Stalking Horse," 250–51.

62. Settle and Settle, *War Drums and Wagon Wheels*, 250–51.

63. Egan, *Pioneering the West*, 211–13.

64. Townley, "Stalking Horse," 251.

65. W. H. Shearman to Editor, *Deseret News*, April 16, 1861, in Journal History, that date. Shearman joined the LDS Church in California in the 1850s and came to Utah in 1857. In 1862 he went to his native England as a missionary and returned in 1865. He then became a merchant in Salt Lake City and then in Logan. He was considered a "shrewd, all around business man." See Walker, *Wayward Saints: The Godbeites and Brigham Young*, 131–34. Shearman's obituary is in *Deseret News*, Dec. 24, 1892.

Chapter 24

1. Regarding Pony Express history see Hafen, *The Overland Mail 1849–1869*; Settle and Settle, *Saddles and Spurs: The Pony Express Saga*; Settle and Settle, *War Drums and Wagon Wheels: The Story of Russell, Majors, and Waddell*; Guthrie, *The Pony Express: An Illustrated History*; Root and Connelly, *The Overland Stage to California*; Corbett, *Orphans Preferred: The Twisted Truth and Lasting Legend of the Pony Express*; Di Certo, *The Saga of the Pony Express*; Visscher, *A Thrilling and Truthful History of the Pony Express*; and the Pony Express Museum website, www.xphomestation.com.

2. William H. Floyd, *Phantom Riders of the Pony Express*, quoted by Corbett, *Orphans Preferred*, 215.

3. Jessop, "The Pony Express left lasting imprints in Tooele County," *Tooele Transcript Bulletin*, Dec. 6, 2005.

4. Hafen, *Overland Mail*, 165–66. His Chapter 8 (pp. 165–91) is titled "The Pony Express, Demonstrator of the Central Route."

5. Hafen, *Overland Mail*, 165–91.

6. Townley, *The Overland Stage: A History and Guidebook*, 10.

7. Settle and Settle, *War Drums and Wagon Wheels*, 115–16.

8. Townley, *The Overland Stage*, 10.

9. Settle and Settle, *Saddles and Spurs*, 38.

10. Di Certo, *The Saga of the Pony Express*, 59.

11. Ibid., 39–41, 44.

12. Ibid., 59, 64–67. Chorpenning employee Bolivar Roberts set up a relay station at the spot. He went to work for Russell, Majors, and Waddell when the Pony Express joined the mail route. The area became known as Roberts Spring Valley, and the creek as Roberts Creek. It is midway across Nevada, northwest of Eureka and some fifteen miles north of Highway 50.

13. Settle and Settle, *Saddles and Spurs*, 41.

14. Visscher, *The Pony Express*, 14; Settle and Settle, *Saddles and Spurs*, 42; Bensen's *The Traveler's Guide to the Pony Express Trail* (Helena, MT: Falcon Press Publishing, 1995), 5.

15. "How fast did the horses run?" Frequently asked Pony Express questions on the Pony Express Museum's website: www.xphomestation.com/faq. All horses move naturally with four basic gaits: the four-beat walk, which averages four miles per hour; the two-beat trot or jog at eight to twelve miles per hour; the cantor or lope that is a three-beat gait at twelve to fifteen miles per hour; and the gallop at 25 to 30 miles per hour (Internet site: www.speedofanimals.com/animals/horse).

16. Hafen, *Overland Mail*, 176–79.

17. Burton, *City of the Saints*, 515; Hill, *The Pony Express Trail Yesterday and Today*, 23–24.

18. Pat Hearty posting regarding Utah Pony Express stations, on the Pony Express Museum website: www.xphomestation.com/utsta.

19. Settle and Settle, *Saddles and Spurs*, 90.

20. "Utah and the Pony Express," *Our Pioneer Heritage* 3 (1960), 365–68.

21. Hafen, *Overland Mail*, 173.

22. Ibid.

23. Settle and Settle, *Saddles and Spurs*, 65, 68–72.

24. Bret Harte, "The Pony Express," *Golden Era* (newspaper), July 1, 1860, posted on Pony Express Museum website: "Bret Harte," www.xphomestation.com/facts; Settle and Settle, *Saddles and Spurs*, 65, 68.

25. Settle and Settle, *Saddles and Spurs*, 65, 68–72.

26. Egan, *Pioneering the West*, 198–200.

27. Settle and Settle, *Saddles and Spurs*, 59.

28. Bensen, *The Traveler's Guide*, 11.

29. Hafen, *Overland Mail*, 177, 178.

30. Visscher, *The Pony Express*, 17; Settle and Settle, *Saddles and Spurs*, 50. Riders carried either an 1851 model Navy Colt six-shooter or a shorter, five shot Wells Fargo model Colt; see "Weapons" at the Pony Express Museum website: www.xphomestation.com/weapons.

31. See "Oath" on Pony Express Museum website, www.xphomestation.com/facts.

32. Twelve Pony Express Bibles are known to exist. In Salt Lake City, the Sons of Utah Pioneers have one and the Daughters of Utah Pioneers have two. See "The Bible" entry on the Pony Express Museum's website: www.xphomestation.com/facts.

33. Benson, *The Traveler's Guide*, 11; Settle and Settle in *Saddles and Spurs* identify 120 riders by name (pp. 74–76).

34. See the ad in Benson, *Traveler's Guide*, x. Hill, in his *The Pony Express Trail*, considers it folklore (p. 8). That skepticism is at the heart of the fine study by Corbett, *Orphans Preferred*, especially pp. 252–55.

35. Hafen, *Overland Mail*, 179.

36. Ibid., 176, 179.

37. Hill, *Pony Express Trail*, 19.

38. A dollar in 1860 would be worth somewhere close to $29.40 in 2015. See website: http://www.measuringworth.com/calculators/uscompare/relativevalue.php

39. Hafen, *Overland Mail*, 180, 189–90.

40. Visscher, *The Pony Express*, 27.

41. Hafen, *Overland Mail*, 180.

42. "Frederick William Hurst," in Petersen, *West from Salt Lake*, 89–92.

43. Ibid.

44. Hill, *Pony Express Trail*, 23.

45. "Certified Contract with Overland Mail Company, March 12, 1861; Senate Executive Document 21, 46th Congress, 3rd Session," pp. 7–8.

46. Based on Burton's "Itinerary of the Mail Route from Great Salt

Lake City to San Francisco," in his *City of the Saints*, 574–578, and the figures that *Pioneering the West* used (197–193), which were taken from Root and Connelly, *The Overland Stage to California*, 102–103.

47. Bowles, *Across the Continent: A Summer's Journey to the Rocky Mountains, the Mormons, and the Pacific States, with Speaker Colfax*, 132.

48. Pony Express experts and the National Park Service, as well as several Internet sites, provide site and route guides. For the entire Pony Express Trail see Hill, *The Pony Express Trail Yesterday and Today*, and Bensen's *The Traveler's Guide*. For Utah see Hearty and Hatch, *The Pony Express Stations in Utah* and their pictorial guide, *The Pony Express in Utah*. For Nevada, consult Hall, *Romancing Nevada's Past: Ghost Towns and Historic Sites of Eureka, Lander, and White Pine Counties*. The website www.expeditionutah.com provides useful Pony Express site guides for Utah and Nevada. The National Park Service publishes a foldout brochure about the Pony Express National Historic Trail that includes a map. The Bureau of Land Management publishes a brochure entitled "Utah Pony Express Trail National Back Country Byway."

49. Pony Express Museum website: www.xphomestation.com/paiute war.

50. Moorman and Sessions, *Camp Floyd and the Mormons*, 221.

51. Ibid., 218–19.

52. Howard Egan Obituary in *Salt Lake Daily Herald*, March 17, 1878.

53. "Indian Difficulties in the West," *Deseret News*, May 30, 1860.

54. "Camp Floyd and Its Environs," *Deseret News*, June 6, 1860.

55. Moormon and Sessions, *Camp Floyd*, 221–23.

56. Ibid., 223.

57. "Latest from the West," *Deseret News*, June 6, 1860.

58. Ibid.

59. "Latest from the Seat of War!," *Deseret News*, June 13, 1860.

60. Ibid.

61. Ibid.

62. Ibid.

63. "News from the West," *Deseret News*, June 20, 1860.

64. "News from the West," *Deseret News*, June 27, 1860.

65. "Western Pony Express," *Deseret News*, June 27, 1860.

66. "Late from the West," *Deseret News*, June 27, 1860.

67. Di Certo, *The Saga of the Pony Express*, 183–86; William Frederick Fisher, undated letter, posted at www.xphomestation.com.

68. "The Pony Express," and "The Indian Difficulty Not Ended," *Deseret News*, July 11, 1860.

69. "Extending 'Aid and Comfort' to the Hostile Indians," *Deseret News*, July 18, 1860.

70. Egan, *Pioneering the West*, 264–65; "Latest from the West," *Deseret News*, July 25, 1860; and W. P. Appleby, "Some Pony Express Addenda," *Deseret News*, Sept. 4, 1897.

Chapter 25

1. Burton, *City of the Saints*, 508.
2. Ibid.
3. "Fort Churchill" on website: www.nv.gov/parks.
4. "Latest from the West!," *Deseret News*, July 18 and Aug. 8, 1860.
5. Ibid.; Godfrey, *Pony Express, Historic Resource Study*.
6. Ibid.
7. "More Indian Difficulties on the Central Route," *Deseret News*, Aug. 15, 1860.
8. "Latest from the West," *Deseret News*, Aug. 29, 1860; Madsen, "Shoshoni-Bannock Marauders on the Oregon Trail, 1859–1863."
9. "More Indian Difficulties on the Central Route," *Deseret News*, Aug. 15, 1860.
10. "Paiute War," on Pony Express Museum website: www.xphomestation.com/paiutewar.
11. Godfrey, *Pony Express, Historic Resource Study*.
12. Moorman and Sessions, *Camp Floyd*, 226, 274.
13. Burton, *City of the Saints*, 515–17.
14. Ibid., 518–20.
15. Ibid., 520–22.
16. Ibid., 523–26.
17. Ibid., 527, 540.
18. Hafen, *Overland Mail*, 206–7.
19. Ibid., 182.
20. Quoted in ibid., 185.
21. "Overland California and Pikes Peak Express Company," *Wikipedia*.
22. Moody, *Stagecoach West*, 202.
23. Hafen, *Overland Mail*, 189.
24. Settle and Settle, *War Drums and Wagon Wheels*, 161–62.
25. Jackson, "A New Look at Wells Fargo, Stagecoaches, and the Pony Express," 303. Wells Fargo and Company was founded in 1852 by Henry Wells,

William G. Fargo, and others and gained prominence in the express and banking businesses. On April 30, 1860, the *San Francisco Bulletin* reported that "it is understood here that the Overland Mail contract is now under the control of Wells, Fargo & Co." (Moody, *Stagecoach West*, 205).

26. Moody, *Stagecoach West*, 205.
27. "Ruby Valley," W. H. Shearman to Editor, April 16 and May 16, 1861, in Journal History on those dates.
28. Hawley letter, May 4, 1861, in *Deseret News*, May 8, 1861.
29. Settle and Settle, *War Drums and Wagon Wheels*, 114.
30. "A Little Surprise," Egan, *Pioneering the West*, 226–27.
31. "Short Line Cut Off," ibid., 220–21.
32. Egan, *Pioneering the West*, 280.
33. "A Rather Unpleasant Experience," Egan, *Pioneering the West*, 281.
34. Billy Fisher was Ras's wife's brother.
35. Egan, *Pioneering the West*, 281; Hafen, *Overland Mail*, 182; "The Longest Ride," in Guthrie, *The Pony Express*, 34.
36. Egan, *Pioneering the West*, 281.
37. Ibid.
38. Ibid.
39. Wilson, *The White Indian Boy*, 142.
40. Egan, *Pioneering the West*, 280. Richard Erastus Egan was born in Salem, Mass., on March 29, 1842. Mary (Minnie) Fisher was born on May 21, 1844, in Woolwich, England.
41. "Pony Express in My Family," http://whoweareandwhere wecamefrom.blogspot.com/, posted 08/2011.
42. "A Rather Unpleasant Experience," Egan, *Pioneering the West*, 281–82.
43. Gamble, "Wiring a Continent: The Making of the U.S. Transcontinental Telegraph Line,"1881.
44. Ibid.
45. Hafen, *Overland Mail*, 187.
46. Hill, *Pony Express Trail Yesterday and Today*, 72.
47. Settle and Settle, *War Drums and Wagon Wheels*, 113–14.
48. Hill, *Pony Express Trail Yesterday and Today*, xv.
49. Pugh, "History of Utah-California Wagon Freighting," thesis, 1949.
50. Hafen, *Overland Mail*, 190–191.
51. Godfrey, *Pony Express, Historic Resource Study*.
52. Rhodes, *Spirits in the Desert: Poetry of the Pony Express*. Used by permission of David Rhodes.

53. On June 11–13, 2015, descendants celebrated Howard Egan's 200th birthday (see Chap. 30). Some 84 people in 30–35 vehicles drove the Pony Express route from Lehi, Utah to Simpson Springs (mostly gravel road), and 20 vehicles continued from there on dirt roads to Ibapah (Deep Creek). Egan descendant Jack Rhodes, who helped lead the caravan, is one of the national Pony Express annual re-enactment horse riders.

54. Rhodes, *Spirits in the Desert: Poetry of the Pony Express*.

Chapter 26

1. Townley, *The Overland Stage*, 55.
2. Mark Twain, *Roughing It*, 113; Burton, *City of the Saints*, 26.
3. Greeley, *An Overland Journey from New York to San Francisco in the Summer of 1859*, 260–70.
4. Moody, *Stagecoach West*, 239; Eggenhofer, *Wagons, Mules and Men: How the Frontier Moved West*, 145. For mountainous trips, a "mud wagon," which was a scaled down and lighter version of a stagecoach, sometimes replaced the Concord coach.
5. The stagecoach descriptions that follow, unless documented otherwise, are a composite drawn from several sources. The most important sources are Root and Connelly, *The Overland Stage to California*; Hafen, *The Overland Mail*, Chapter 13, "In the Days of the Stage-coach"; Moody's *Stage Coach West* Chapter 2, "Yankee Ingenuity"; Eggenhofer, *Wagons, Mules and Men*, 200–01; and "stage coach" sites searched on the Internet.
6. Twain, *Roughing It*, 33.
7. Townley, *The Overland Stage*, 61.
8. Moody, *Stagecoach West*, 239.
9. Wilson, *The White Indian Boy*, 169.
10. Moody, *Stagecoach West*, 239.
11. Burton, *City of the Saints*, 18; Hafen, *Overland Mail*, 309.
12. Townley, *The Overland Stage*, 62.
13. Hafen, *Overland Mail*, 312; www.measuringworth.com/uscompare/.
14. Twain, *Roughing It*.
15. Ibid., 53.
16. Ibid.
17. Winther, *Via Western Express*, 61.
18. Root and Connelly, *The Overland Stage to California*, 269.
19. Twain, *Roughing It*, 54–55.
20. Hafen, *Overland Mail*, 189.

21. Ahnert, "Identifying Butterfield's Overland Mail Company Stages on the Southern Trail, 1858–1861," 162–63; Settle and Settle, *War Drums and Wagon Wheels*, 161–62.

22. Winther, *Via Western Express*, 139.

23. Winther, *Via Western Express*, 142.

24. Hiram S. Rumfield letter to Dear Doctor, June 8, 1862, in Hulbert, ed., *Letters of An Overland Mail Agent in Utah*, 267; Winther, *Via Western Express*, 140.

25. Hafen, *Overland Mail*, 225; Winther, *Via Western Express*, 139–40; see "Trustee Sale" document, Feb. 15, 1862, in Frederick, *Ben Holladay, the Stagecoach King*, 62, 282.

26. Rumfield to Dear Doctor, June 8, 1862.

27. Egan, *Pioneering the West*, 212.

28. We lack their names.

29. Townley, *The Overland Stage*, 215.

30. Wilson, *The White Indian Boy*, 168.

31. Hafen, *Overland Mail*, 304–06.

32. See, for example, the Albert Jefferson Young diary entries for Aug. 7–9, 1862, in Peterson, ed., *West from Salt Lake: Diaries from the Central Overland Trail*, 148, and the B. P. Lewis diary entries for June 20–22, 1863, 154.

33. Peterson, *West from Salt Lake*, 272 n2; Townley, *The Overland Stage*, 205. On today's map the new route ran about where I-80 goes west from Salt Lake City to Utah 36, then south through Tooele and Stockton to Faust's Station.

34. Frederick, *Ben Holladay*, 127.

35. Hafen, *Overland Mail*, 310–13.

36. Robert L. Hinshaw, CMSgt, USAF, Retired, poem "Stage to San Francisco," posted on website: www.poetrysoup.com, subject /long/stagecoach.

37. Moody, *Stagecoach West*, 244–45.

38. Hafen, *Overland Mail*, 310–13.

39. Bowles, *Across the Continent*, 136–37.

40. Twain, *Roughing It*.

41. Ibid., 115.

42. Ibid., 116.

43. Winther, *Via Western Express*, 141; Frederick, *Ben Holladay*, 88–91.

44. Wilson, *The White Indian Boy*, 170.

45. Ibid., 168.

46. "Trip to Ruby," Egan, *Pioneering the West*, 217–20.

47. Moorman and Sessions, *Camp Floyd*.

48. Varley, *Brigham and the Brigadier: General Patrick Connor and His California Volunteers*, 37–39.
49. Moorman and Sessions, *Camp Floyd*, 17.
50. Bateman, *Deep Creek Reflections*, 77, citing *Soldiers of the Overland*, 38.
51. Varley, *Brigham and the Brigadier*, 49; Moorman and Sessions, *Camp Floyd*, 29. In 1878 Camp Douglas was renamed Fort Douglas, and continued to be an army installation until officially terminated in 1991. It is now part of the University of Utah campus.
52. Madsen, *The Shoshone Frontier and the Bear River Massacre*; and Madsen, *Glory Hunter: A Biography of Patrick Edward Connor*, 78–87.
53. Hiram S. Rumfield to Dear Frank, June 22, 1862, in *Letters of An Overland Mail Agent in Utah*, 271; Bateman, *Deep Creek Reflections*, 77–78.
54. Allen and Warner, "Gosiute Indians in Pioneer Utah," 167; Bluth, "Confrontation with an Arid land," 80; Bancroft, *History of Nevada, Colorado and Wyoming*, 219.
55. John Fisher, "An Incident in Western Life," *Davis County Clipper*, April 29, 1892.
56. "The Indian Outbreak," Egan, *Pioneering the West*, 256.
57. Varley, *Brigham and the Brigadier*, 127.
58. Fisher, "An Incident in Western Life."
59. Ibid.
60. Rumfield to Dear Frank, March 24, 1863, in *Letters of An Overland Mail Agent in Utah*, 295–96.
61. Egan, *Pioneering the West*, 261.
62. Egan, *Pioneering the West*, 261–62. The two men were named Wood and McCarty.
63. Rumfield to Dear Frank, March 24, 1863; also, Journal History, March 23 and 25, 1863.
64. Varley, *Brigham and the Brigadier*, 127.
65. "More Indian difficulties," *Deseret News*, March 22, 1863; Egan, *Pioneering the West*, 262.
66. Wilson, *The White Indian Boy*, 169.
67. "Another Stage Driver Killed," *Deseret* News, May 27, 1863; *San Francisco Bulletin*, May 22, 1863; "Indian Raids" in Egan, *Pioneering the West*, 200.
68. "Noble Heroism of a Woman," *Daily Alta California*, May 31, 1863, and "A Brave Woman," *Sacramento Daily Union*, June 23, 1863; Howard Egan, "That Affair on the Plains," Salt Lake City, July 2, 1863, published in

Sacramento Daily Union, July 14, 1863, cited by Marie Irvine in a talk she gave to the Crossroads Chapter of the Oregon-California Trails Association, published in its newsletter *Crossroads* 20 (June 2009), 6.

  69. Egan, "That Affair on the Plains."
  70. Egan, *Pioneering the West,* 263–264.
  71. Ibid.
  72. "Burning of Canyon Station," in Egan, *Pioneering the West,* 263–64; Bateman, *Deep Creek Reflections,* 80–81. We share William Egan's account in Chapter 28.
  73. Allen and Warner, "Gosiute Indians in Pioneer Utah," 82.
  74. Bateman, *Deep Creek Reflections,* 80.
  75. Hafen, *Overland Mail,* 276.
  76. Ibid., 296.
  77. Ibid., 285–88.
  78. Bowles, *Across the Continent,* 135.
  79. Townley, *The Overland Stage,* 68.
  80. Hafen, *Overland Mail,* 288.
  81. Winther, *Via Western Express,* 140–44; Jackson, "Salt Lake City: Wells Fargo's Transportation Depot During the Stagecoach Era," 12.
  82. Hafen, *Overland Mail,* 319; Moody, *Stagecoach West,* 294; and Winther, *Via Western Express,* 140–44.
  83. Jackson, "Salt Lake City: Wells Fargo's Transportation Depot," 15, photo on p. 21; "Gould," in *Alta California,* 20 Nov. 1868, 3, cited in Bluth, "Confrontation with an Arid Land," 120.
  84. Moody, *Stagecoach West,* 239.
  85. Bateman, *Deep Creek Reflections,* 85; *Deseret News,* Aug. 18, 1868.
  86. Hafen, *Overland Mail,* 325. By 1863 Austin, in Lander County due south of today's Battle Mountain, became a silver mining boom town. It was about 50 miles west of Roberts Creek Station. The Overland Stage moved its station to Austin and closed down the Jacob's Well/Reese River Station and Simpson's Park Station. See Hall, *Romancing Nevada's Past,* "Austin," 50–52; "Jacobsville (Jacobs Well, Reese River Station)," 94–95; "Simpson Park," 108.
  87. Hafen, *Overland Mail,* 327; Townley, *The Overland Stage,* 71.
  88. Jackson, "Salt Lake City: Wells Fargo's Transportation Depot," 34; "New Stage Route," *Deseret News,* Feb. 5, 1869.
  89. Ibid., 328.
  90. Ibid., 325.
  91. Moody, *Stagecoach West,* 296.

92. Ibid., 295–96, 301.

93. How long he was a sailor isn't known. His career as a sailor is poorly documented, but as noted in Chapter 3 of this book, his sailing years probably started not before 1830 and finished by 1838.

Chapter 27

1. Bateman, *Deep Creek Reflections*; "Mary Hall Jatta," Diary entry for Aug. 8, 1868, in Petersen, *West from Salt Lake*, 305.

2. See Chapter 25. Mary Ann (Minnie) Fisher was born on May 21, 1844 in Woolwich, England. Her parents were Thomas Frederick and Jane Christton Fisher. When she was ten she crossed the plains in the Robert L. Campbell wagon train with her parents, three older brothers, and a younger sister.

3. Plot E-7-7, Salt Lake City Cemetery, 200 "N" Street, where Howard, Tamson, William M., and Vilate Egan are buried, as are other Egan relatives.

4. Amanda Andrus was born on Nov. 19, 1847, at Council Bluffs, Iowa. Her parents were Milo Andrus and Abigail Jane Daley. As an infant she came west in 1848 in the Heber C. Kimball Company.

5. He was born Jan. 3, 1844. Egan, *Pioneering the West*, 292.

6. Nevada Territory was formed in 1861, in the west half of Utah Territory. The original eastern boundary of Nevada was the 116th meridian, but the Nevada territorial delegation convinced Congress in 1862 to move the boundary east to the 115th meridian. In 1866 the border shifted east again, to the 114th meridian, in part due to the discovery of gold deposits. That borderline, which with a slight correction in 1870 is the current one, meant Nevada was but a few miles from the Deep Creek station. See *Deseret News*, Nov. 13, 1870.

7. "Deep Creek Branch," in Jenson, *Encyclopedic History of the Church*, 177.

8. The turnoff for Ibapah Road is about 27 miles south of Wendover on Highway 93A. Ibapah Road meanders southeasterly, enters Utah, and then reaches Ibapah.

9. Bateman, *Deep Creek Reflections*, 491, citing the *Record of Marks & Brands Utah Territory 1849–1874* ledger at the Utah State Archives.

10. Bateman, *Deep Creek Reflections*, 18, 19, and 54. In September 1859 Howard changed the route so the mail avoided Pleasant Valley and went through Deep Creek. He set up the ranch there to be the new station. Ransom said that after the ranch was bought "it was made a station," but gives no date; see Egan, *Pioneering the West*, 201.

11. Bateman, *Deep Creek Reflections*, 62.

12. John Fisher, "An Incident in Western Life," *Davis County Clipper*, April 29, 1892.

13. Egan, *Pioneering the West*, 201.

14. Ibid., 223, and William M. Egan's notes re Deep Creek found in "W. M. Egan: Trip from Carson City in 1863."

15. James Ferguson and his new bride Elizabeth Dunlap moved to Ibapah in 1868. Jim had charge of the telegraph there until it ceased operating in 1883. See Mrs. Wade Parrish, "The Early History of Ibapah," on website: www.feltonline.com.

16. A stake and rider fence is a rail fence assembled without the use of post holes. Two stakes are crossed, forming a crotch near their upper ends. A horizontal rail (called the rider) is supported by the crotch, then this assembly is bound together at the crotch; a series of such assemblies is required to form the fence, often with additional horizontal rails below the rider.

17. "Irrigation" in Egan, *Pioneering the West*, 222.

18. "Coyote in Chicken House" in Egan, *Pioneering the West*, 223–24.

19. Egan, *Pioneering the West*, 224.

20. Ibid., 224–25.

21. "The Dog Pompy," in Egan, *Pioneering the West*, 269–72.

22. Hiram S. Rumfield to Dear Frank, June 22, 1862, in Hulbert, ed., *Letters of An Overland Mail Agent in Utah*, 270–71.

23. W. M. Egan, 1863 Journal.

24. Ibid.

25. "Mary Ann Tuttle Egan Billings Gardner," *Pioneer Women of Faith and Fortitude*, 1059–1060. By 1863, when her son Hyrum joined the Egans, her children by Titus Billings were Emily (born Nov. 12, 1854), Theresa (born Jan. 28, 1859), and Alonzo (born Feb. 25, 1862).

26. Hyrum was born on July 24, 1850 and William was born on June 13, 1851.

27. Hyrum William Egan married Mary Salome Preator in 1871. She was born on May 18, 1851. They had four children. Egan, *Pioneering the West*, 292.

28. William Egan's 1863 account. Also "Wagon Going without a Team," in Egan, *Pioneering the West*, 268.

29. W. M. Egan, "Native Utes of Utah," typescript, 23 pp., and original handwritten. In William M. Egan Papers.

30. William Egan's 1863 account. Also "Wagon Going without a Team" in Egan, *Pioneering the West*, 268.

31. William Egan's 1863 account.

32. "Mary Kartchner," diary entry July 30, 1862, in Peterson, *West from Salt Lake*, 142.

33. Egan, *Pioneering the West*, 213–14.

34. Ibid.

35. Peterson, *West from Salt Lake*, 88 n6.

36. "Mary Warner," diary entry for June 14, 1864, in Peterson, *West from Salt Lake*, 191.

37. Townley, *The Overland Stage*, 243–44; Hall, *Romancing Nevada's Past: Ghost towns and Historic Sites*, 180–81.

38. Anderson, *Joseph Morris and the Saga of the Morrisites*.

39. Journal History, June 12, 1862, 3.

40. Seegmiller, *Robert Taylor Burton*, 217–18.

41. Journal History, June 12, 1862, 2; Seegmiller, *Burton*, 214.

42. Anderson, *Morris*, 132; Journal History, June 13–15, 1862.

43. Seegmiller, *Burton*, 219.

44. Ibid., 218–19.

45. Anderson, *Morris*, 129. Anderson cites an account by John Banks entitled "A document History of the Morrisites in Utah," 71–72.

46. Anderson, *Morris*, 135–37 and Journal History, June 13–15, 1862.

47. Anderson, *Morris*, 139, and 140–41 based on a quote from Wilford Woodruff's Journal entry for June 18, 1862.

48. Ibid., 142.

49. Bigler, *Forgotten Kingdom: The Mormon Theocracy in the American West*, 213–214; Anderson, *Morris*, 144–45, 148–49. Morris's followers scattered, and the movement gradually fizzled out with the passing of generations. A last iteration of a Morrisite-rooted church officially terminated in 1969.

50. Egan, *Pioneering the West*, 159.

51. "The Old Man Left to Die," in Egan, *Pioneering the West*, 251–52.

52. Hoshide, "Salt Desert Trails Revisited," 5. Hoshide cites Pearce's account, "A Park City Forty-Niner Discusses the Gruesome Story—the Abandoned Wagon Part All Saved," *Salt Lake Tribune*, May 11, 1902, p. 31, col. 4–7.

53. Tamson to Dear Brother Richard, from Salt Lake City, 24 Nov. 1867, in Richard E. Egan correspondence, Church History Library.

54. Tamson to Dear Brother Richard, Nov. 24, 1867.

55. William M. Egan Journal.

56. Tamson P. Egan to Dear Brother Richard [Parshley], Deep Creek, Feb. 9, 1867 [1868], in Richard E. Egan correspondence.

57. Tamson to Dear Brother Richard, Nov. 14, 1867.

58. R. E. Egan to R. J. Parshley, April 23, 1869, from 26 Tenby Street, Birmingham, England, in Richard E. Egan correspondence.

59. R. E. Egan to Dear Uncle, Aug. 12, 1869, from New York City, in Richard E. Egan correspondence.

60. Janet Sloan email to the author, Oct. 7, 2015.

61. R. E. Egan to My Dear Uncle, from Bountiful, Sept. 23, 1869, in Richard E. Egan correspondence.

62. Nothing further is known about the house Tamson was building. Her address in city directories did change by the 1880s to a location one block north (see Chapter 29).

63. R. E. Egan to My Dear Uncle, Sept. 23, 1869, in Richard E. Egan Correspondence.

64. R. E. Egan to Dear Uncle Richard, Ruby Valley NV, April 29, 1870, in Richard E. Egan correspondence.

Chapter 28

1. Sloan, *Gazeteer of Utah, and Salt Lake City Directory, 1874*, 122–23.

2. "Egan Canyon" at website: http://www.ghosttowns.com/states/nv/egancanyon.htm and http://theusgenweb.org/nv/whitepine/ponyexpress/eganstation.htm.

3. http://www.nevadadventures.com/ghost%20towns/map.html.

4. "Egan Canyon" at website: http://www.ghosttowns.com/states/nv/egancanyon.htm and http://theusgenweb.org/nv/whitepine/ponyexpress/eganstation.htm.

5. The Clifton Mining District's Recorder's Office recorded the Clifton Mining Company claim the next day, 21 June 1869. See Clifton Mining District Recorder, Location Notices 1869–1938. The ten were W. T. Barbee, John Johnston, W. R. Sheldon, W. R. Davis, F. Merrill, S. Straus, G. D. Shell, John W. Binley, John Fisher, G. W. Brown, and Howard.

6. "The Precious Metals in Deep Creek," copied into Journal History, Sept. 9, 1869, 2.

7. Notice of Egan Claim, Clifton District Recorder file Book C, p. 40, Series 24331, reel 1, 42, Utah Division of Archives & Records Service.

8. Sloan, *Gazeteer*, 1874, 122–23.

9. Clifton Mining District (Utah) Recorder, Miners' Meeting Minutes, Utah State Archives, series 24163, reel 1, microfilm of holograph notebook.

10. Clifton Mining District Minutes, Oct. 9, 1869. The six besides

Howard and Ransom were G. D. Shell, Jn Devine, W. R. Davis, W. R. Sheldon, Frank Morris, and John Johnson.

11. Clifton Mining District, Utah, Recorder File Books, Series 24333.

12. Clifton Mining District, Utah, Recorder File Book C, 197, 198, 205, 206.

13. Murphy, *The Mineral Resources of the Territory of Utah with Mining Statistics and Maps*, 1872, 7.

14. Ibid., 50.

15. Bluth, "Confrontation with an Arid land," 128.

16. Sloan, *Gazeteer*, 1874, 90, 122–23.

17. Ibid.

18. Egan, *Pioneering the West*, 272.

19. R. E. Egan to Dear Uncle Richard, Ruby Valley, Nev., April 29, 1870, in Richard E. Egan correspondence.

20. Howard Egan to My Dear Wife, July 14, 1874, Gold Hill, Utah. Copy in possession of Egan descendant Patti Timmons. The letterhead lists as Deep Creek Consolidated Co. officers: John H. Lightner, President; Chas G. Ganter, Vice President; M. J. Hartnett, Secretary-Treasurer; and J. W. Harker, Manager.

21. Egan, *Pioneering the West*, 283.

22. "History of Deep Creek Mountains, Utah," www.onlineutah.com; "Deep Creek Mine Is Bringing Out Its Lead Shoots," *Deseret Evening News*, March 25, 1918:2. Tungsten was needed in large quantities after 1910 for light bulb filaments.

23. Bateman, *Deep Creek Reflections*, 85, and Egan, *Pioneering the West*, 283.

24. Bluth, "Confrontation with an Arid land," 124; Bateman, *Deep Creek Reflections*.

25. Martin, *The Story of Major Howard Egan*, 83. Martin quotes from Gillespie's diary but provides no footnote or source location. His lack of documentation throughout his Egan biography makes it untrustworthy.

26. Bateman, *Deep Creek Reflections*, 97; Allen and Warner, "Gosiute Indians in Pioneer Utah," 175–76.

27. Nicholson, "The Lamanites," 274–75.

28. Nicholson, "The Lamanites," 274–75, 291–92, 303; Bateman, *Deep Creek Reflections*, 175–78.

29. Roberts, *A Comprehensive History of the Church*, 5:164–65.

30. Orson Pratt Discourse, Twentieth Ward, Feb. 7, 1875, in *Journal of Discourses*, 17:298–301.

31. Orson Hyde Discourse, April 6, 1875, *Journal of Discourses* 17: 354–55.

32. John Taylor Discourse, April 8, 1875, *Journal of Discourses* 18:2.

33. Orson Pratt Discourse, April 11, 1875, *Journal of Discourses* 18:19–22.

34. Journal History, April 9, 1875.

35. The 19th Ward Historical Record, LR 6092 Series 2, says in October 1875 he went on a mission to Lamanites at Deep Creek.

36. Egan, *Pioneering the West*, 283.

37. Allen and Warner, "Gosiute Indians in Pioneer Utah," 176. Their source according to their footnote 45 is: "Deposition of Howard Egan, Dec. 13, 1877, with papers of George Q. Cannon, Letters Received."

38. Bateman, *Deep Creek Reflections*, 83.

39. www.goshutetribe.com.

40. Sloan, *Gazeteer*, 1874.

41. Egan, *Pioneering the West*, 283.

42. Arrington, Fox, and May, *Building the City of God*, 177. This is the most important one-volume study to date of United Orders in Utah.

43. Fox, "Experiment in Utopia: The United Order of Richfield, 1871–1877," 355–56.

44. L. Dwight Israelsen, "United Orders," *Encyclopedia of Mormonism*, 4:1494, and Arrington, et. al., *Building the City of God*. A list of all the United Orders thus far identified is in appendices 8 and 9 in *Building the City of God*, 407–19.

45. Journal History, May 24, 1874, 5.

46. Arrington, et. al., *Building the City of God*, 221–22.

47. Arrington, et. al., *Building the City of God*, 219.

48. "Salt Lake City 19th Ward," in Jenson, *Encyclopedic History of the Church*, 753.

49. McKune note, in William Egan Papers.

50. Egan, *Pioneering the West*, 283.

51. Ibid.

52. *Cholera morbus,* a term no longer used, is defined as a gastrointestinal disturbance characterized by abdominal pain, diarrhea, and sometimes vomiting (source: various online dictionaries).

53. "Last Moments of President Brigham Young." *Deseret News*, Aug. 31, 1877.

54. Ibid.

55. Bush, "Brigham Young in Life and Death: A Medical Overview." Peritonitis is an inflammation of the membrane which lines the inside of the abdomen and all of the internal organs.

56. Samuel W. Taylor, "Who Done It?: The Nagging Mystery of Brigham Young's Last Moments," posted at www.saintsalive.com/mormonism/whodoneit.html.

57. Lloyd, "Brigham Young enigmatic, larger than life," report of Ronald W. Walker's address to the Mormon History Association," *Church News*, June 9, 2013.

58. Hartley, "The Priesthood Reorganization of 1877: Brigham Young's Last Achievement."

59. "Last Moments of President Brigham Young."

60. The history of the funeral, procession, and internment is published in the *Deseret News Weekly* of Sept. 5, 1877.

61. "Brigham Young's Last Will and Testament," web search, posted at various Internet sites.

62. Egan, *Pioneering the West*, 283.

63. William L. Ball Journal. Ball's life spanned from 1834–1878.

64. Egan, *Pioneering the West*, 283.

65. Ball Journal.

66. William Egan, in Volume: W. M. Egan 4 Items, William Egan Papers.

67. *Salt Lake Daily Herald,* March 17, 1878.

68. "Obsequies," Journal History, March 17, 1878, 1. The graves are in the Salt Lake City Cemetery in Section E, Block 7, Lot 7.

69. Ball Journal.

70. "An Old Citizen Gone," Journal History, March 16, 1878, 1; *Salt Lake Daily Herald*, March 17, 1878.

71. "Salt Laker finds marker from Express rider's grave," *Deseret News*, March, 1990, and "Pony Express rider's tombstone found in yard," unidentified source and date, photocopy of both clippings in author's file.

Chapter 29

1. Salt Lake City directories, 1869 (Sloan), 1884 (U. S. Directory Publishing), 1889 (Kelly), 1890 (Polk), 1898 (Polk), 1900 (Polk), 1906 (Polk).

2. Tamson Egan to My Dear Son Wm M. Egan, Salt Lake City, Feb. 17, 1893, handwritten, in William M. Egan Papers.

3. Pernicious anemia is an autoimmune disorder in which the body fails to

make enough healthy red blood cells. The body requires vitamin B-12 and a type of protein called intrinsic factor (IF) to make red blood cells.

4. Salt Lake County, Records of Death #026554, 1890–1914, 1895–1908, 6498 pt 2, B p. 271, #10281.

5. www.findagrave.com.

6. Clawson, "Crossing the Plains," 217–18; *Pioneer Women of Faith and Fortitude*, 606; Johnson, "Determining and Defining 'Wife': The Brigham Young Households," 69 n48; and www.findagrave.com.

7. Kearl, Pope, and Wimmer, *Index to the 1850, 1860, 1870 Censuses of Utah*.

8. Helen's children by John Irvine, born between 1867 and 1886, all in Salt Lake City, were John, Howard G., Helen N., William E., Clarence E., Maud M., Luella A., and Robert L.

9. "Mary Ann Tuttle Egan Billings Gardner," *Pioneer Women of Faith and Fortitude*, 1059–1060.

10. H. R. Egan [Richmond] to Will Egan, Feb. 27, 1913, and April 13, July 13, and Dec. 7, 1915, William M. Egan Papers.

11. Martin, *The Story of Major Howard Egan*, 95–96.

12. "Richmond Pioneer Dies," Journal History, March 17, 1916, 3, and "Funeral Services, Howard R. Egan," Journal History, March 21, 1916, 2.

13. "Howard R. Egan: Funeral Services," *Deseret News*, March 25, 1916, 8.

14. His surviving sons were Howard M., John R., Charles E., George H., Walter, and Alva. His surviving daughters were Mrs. Linnie Egan Bair and Mrs. Inez Egan Maiben.

15. Richard Erastus Egan's 16 children by Mary Ann (Minnie Fisher), born between 1862 and 1887, were Erastus Howard, Tamson Minnie, Howard, Harry Olson, Horace Fredric, John Leroy, William Fisher, Willard Richard, Joseph Ransom, Ira Irvin, a baby girl, Linne Jane, Mary Adelaide, Charles Merritt, David, and a baby boy. His children by second wife Mary Beatrice Noble, born between 1893 and 1907, were Nellie Loretta, Harold, Eugene, Ora May, Emma Alberta, Byron Noble, Howard Noble, and Richard Noble.

16. Embry, "Missionaries for the Dead: The Story of the Genealogical Missionaries of the Nineteenth Century."

17. "Richard Erastus Egan," in volume *Settlement of Northern & Central Nevada by Utah Pioneers* in *Pioneer Pathways* 19:176.

18. Egan, *Pioneering the West*, 215.

19. Edward Egan, Meelaghans Tullamore, Ireland to Richard Egan of Montreal, Feb. 19, 1900, photocopy in Janet Sloan files.

20. Byron N. Egan, Untitled sketch of his father, Richard Erastus Egan.
21. Ibid.
22. Richard Erastus Egan, Journal History, April 21, 1918.
23. William M. Egan, Life Sketch. Details about the Byron farm and Ras's death experience are from Ras's descendant John Howard Egan in email to the author, March 5, 2017.
24. 19th Ward Historical Record.
25. Sloan, *Gazeteer*, 1874.
26. Alter's *Early Utah Journalism* refers to William in its listing for "Provo Utah Industrialist Monthly, 1887–1888 Wm. M. Egan, Editor; D. P. Felt, Mgr.," 387.
27. R. L. Polk & Co., Directory, 1906.
28. Both record books are on microfilm through the LDS Family History Library. See Egan Family Record Book (FHL #1598329 Item 1) also known as William M. Egan Temple Record Book compiled by William Moburn Egan. This has information on Egan relatives in the USA and Canada and Egan ancestry in Ireland. Regarding his Monroe ancestry, see Monroe/Munro Temple Record Book (FHL #1598329 Item 4), compiled by William Moburn Egan. As a child Mary Jane Egan Johnson and her father David Egan visited David's uncle, William M. Egan, at his home on Capitol Hill. She saw papers and books stacked upon his work table. She also met his wife Lulu. After William's death, Lulu gave these record books to David Egan. Later, Mary Jane took possession of the record books and kept them under her bed for safekeeping. During the 1994 Worldwide Clan Egan Rally in Salt Lake City, the records were taken to the Family History Library, which filmed them in 1996.
29. Her official death record says her marital status was "divorced."
30. He is buried in section E-7-7. Both the sexton's record and the tombstone give the wrong birth date of 1862: "William M. Egan 1862–1929."
31. Bateman, *Deep Creek Reflections*, 87.
32. Egan, *Pioneering the West*, 282–84.
33. Bateman, *Deep Creek Reflections*, 87, and Martin, *The Story of Major Howard Egan*, 102–103.
34. Egan, *Pioneering the West*, 282–84.
35. Ira Ernest and Emma Moss Egan's five children were: Effie Irene, Emma Myrtle, Ernest LeRoy, Ira Erastus, and Jeanne Tamson.
36. Erastus Egan to Will Egan, March 26, 1913, William Egan Papers.
37. www.dupinternational.org/jubilee/main; Hunter, "The Monument to Brigham Young and the Pioneers: One Hundred Years of Controversy," 68 (Fall 2000), 332–50.

38. Clipping, "Observe Centenary of Howard Egan," no source, no date, in William M. Egan Papers.

39. Ibid.

40. Egan, *Pioneering the West*, 4.

41. Ibid., 4, 284.

42. Ibid., 4, and H. R. Egan to Will Egan, April 13, 1915, William Egan Papers.

43. Wilson, *Among the Shoshones* (1910).

44. The 1885 Salt Lake City directory lists Will as a printer and publisher. Will stamped on a letter Tamson sent him, dated Feb. 19, 1893, "W. M. Egan, Printer and Apiarian," in William Egan Papers.

45. William Egan Papers.

46. Skelton Publishing Co. and H. R. Egan of Richmond, Utah, Agreement in Duplicate, a form with information typed on it, Aug. 20, 1911, unsigned copy, in William Egan Papers; Letterhead, Robert Skelton to J. A. [Alva] Egan and Howard Egan Estate, July 27, 1917, William Egan Papers.

47. H. R. Egan to Will Egan, Feb. 27, 1913, William Egan Papers.

48. H. R. Egan to Dear Brother, Nov. 18, 1914, William Egan Papers.

49. H. R. Egan to Will Egan, April 27, 1914, William Egan Papers.

50. H. R. Egan to Will Egan, July 13, 1915, William Egan Papers.

51. H. R. Egan to Will Egan, Aug. 29, 1915, William Egan Papers.

52. H. R. Egan to Dear Brother, Nov. 16, 1915, William Egan Papers.

53. H. R. Egan to Will Egan, Dec. 7, 1915, William Egan Papers.

54. H. R. Egan to Will Egan, Dec. 30, 1915, William Egan Papers.

55. Ibid.

56. Howard R. Egan, Handwritten page, no date, evidently an add-on to his letter to Will, Feb. 6, 1916, William Egan Papers.

57. Howard R. Egan to Will Egan, Feb. 6, 1916, William Egan Papers.

58. Howard R. Egan to Will Egan, Feb. 13, 1916, William Egan Papers.

59. H. R. Egan to Robert Skelton, then changed to Will Egan, Feb. 18, 1916, William Egan Papers.

60. H. W. [Horace Walter] Egan for H. R. Egan to Will Egan, March 16, 1916, William Egan Papers.

61. H. W. Egan to Dear Uncle, March 28, 1916, and H. W. Egan to Will Egan, April 1, 1916, William Egan Papers.

62. H. W. Egan to Will Egan, April 3, 1916, William Egan Papers.

63. Robert Skelton to J. A. [Alva] Egan and Howard Egan Estate, July 27, 1917, William Egan Papers.

64. Skelton to J. A. Egan, August 10, 1917.

65. "PIONEERING THE WEST," *Deseret Evening News*, Nov. 3, 1917, clipping in Journal History, Oct. 30, 1917.

66. Mrs. George Egan to W. M. Egan, Nov. 8, 1917, and J. A. Egan to W. M. Egan, Nov. 29, 1917, William Egan Papers.

67. Two descendants of Howard Ransom Egan have shown the author 1917 books with green, brownish, and gray covers.

68. *Pioneering the West, 1846 to 1847: Major Howard Egan's Diary. Also Thrilling Experiences of Pre-Frontier Life Among Indians; Their Traits, Civil and Savage, and Part of Autobiography, Inter-Related to His Father's by Howard R. Egan* (Richmond, UT: Howard R. Egan Estate, 1917).

69. Howard R. Egan to Will Egan, Sept. 8, 1915, William Egan Papers.

70. James T. Babb, *William Robertson Coe and His Library of Western Americana*, address given July 23, 1945 to and published by the University of Wyoming Library Associates, 1954; Edward Eberstadt, *The William Robertson Coe Collection* (1952).

71. "Edward Eberstadt & Sons, Records," Catalog, Beinecke Library, Yale University. Most of the Eberstadt material document Eberstadt's business relationship with William Robertson Coe (Eberstadt was Coe's agent), and the formation of the Coe Collection of Western Americana. Records include financial records, acquisition records, and correspondence between Eberstadt and Coe and between Eberstadt and other dealers.

72. Vinson, *Edward Eberstadt & Sons*, 53–54.

73. In 1952, Mary C. Withington published a guide to the collection: *A Catalogue of Manuscripts in the Collection of Western Americana Founded By William Robertson Coe*.

Chapter 30

1. "An Old Citizen Gone," Journal History, March 16, 1878, 1; *Salt Lake Daily Herald*, March 17, 1878.

2. Egan, *Pioneering the West*, 190.

3. Ibid., 222–25.

4. Ibid., 291–92.

5. Journal History, Sept. 28, 1845, 1; Seegmiller, *Be Kind to the Poor": The Life Story of Robert Taylor Burton*, 421; Brooks, *John Doyle Lee*, 97; MacKinnon, *At Sword's Point, Part 1: A Documentary History of the Utah War to 1858*, 268.

6. Malouf, *Rugged Men of the West*, and Sullivan, *Brigham's Boys*. The

sixteen are Jacob Hamblin, Hosea Stout, Porter Rockwell, Thomas Rhoades, George Bean, Ephraim Hanks, John D. Lee, John M. Bernhisel, Jesse C. Little, Howard Egan, Isaac Morley, Lot Smith, James Brown, Tom Ricks, Edward Hunter, and Daniel W. Jones.

7. Hartley, "Common People: Church Activity during the Brigham Young Era."

8. "They, the Builders of the Nation," Hymns—The Church of Jesus Christ of Latter-day Saints, No. 36.

9. "Sirius" to Editor, *Deseret News*, Sept. 18, 1859, Journal History, that date.

10. Bateman, *Deep Creek Reflections*, 54.

11. W. M. Egan, Notebook, in his papers.

12. Egan, *Pioneering the West*, 282–84.

13. Egan, *Pioneering the West*, 157–58.

14. Ferris, *The Mormons at Home*, 291.

15. Journal History, Dec. 25, 1858.

16. Howard Egan to J. Forney, Superintendent of Indian Affairs, Feb. 19, 1859, in Jacob Forney Letterbooks, 514.

17. "Another Pioneer Crosses the River" [Howard R. Egan obituary], clipping, no date or source, in W. H. Egan Papers.

18. Egan, *Pioneering the West*, 182, 282–84.

19. "Pioneering the West," *Deseret Evening News*, Nov. 3, 1917, clipping in Journal History, Oct. 30, 1917.

20. "Howard Egan, Utah's Top Outdoorsman," *Deseret News*, undated clipping, in Janet Sloan files.

21. Will Bagley review of manuscript of Marie Irving history of Howard Egan, Jan. 9, 2004, copy in author's files; Di Certo, *The Saga of the Pony Express*, 64.

22. Utley, ed., *Encyclopedia of the American West*, and Lamar, ed., *The New Encyclopedia of the American West*.

23. "Pony Express in Utah" in Powell, *Utah History Encyclopedia*.

24. Roberts, *Comprehensive History of the Church*, mentions Howard in regard to those events.

25. H. R. Egan to Will Egan, Aug. 29, 1915, William Egan Papers.

26. The marker is at 143 South Main, Salt Lake City. It has a bas relief depiction of a rider and a Pony Express map.

27. "Egan Canyon," Internet search; Leigh, *Nevada Place Names*, 56–58; "Egan Canyon" at www.ghosttowns.com/states/nv/egancanyon and theusgenweb.org/nv/whitepine/ponyexpress/eganstation.

Bibliography

Books

Adams, George. *The Salem Directory. . . For 1851*. Salem: Henry Whipple, Publisher. 1851.

Alexander, Thomas G. *Utah, The Right Place*. Salt Lake City: Gibbs-Smith Publisher, 1995.

Allen, James B. and Glen M. Leonard. *The Story of the Latter-day Saints*. Salt Lake City, UT: Deseret Book 1992.

Alter, J. Cecil. *Early Utah Journalism*. Salt Lake City, UT: Utah State Historical Society, 1938.

Anderson, C. LeRoy. *Joseph Morris and the Saga of the Morrisites*. Logan: Utah State University Press, 1988.

Anderson, Devery S. and Gary James Bergera. *The Nauvoo Endowment Companies, 1845–1846*. Salt Lake City, UT: Signature Books, 2005.

The Annals of the Caverlys. Lowell, MA: House, Goodwin & Co., 1879.

Arrington, Leonard J. *Brigham Young, American Moses*. New York: Knopf, 1985.

_____, *Charles C. Rich: Mormon General and Western Frontiersman*. Provo, UT: Brigham Young University Press, 1974.

_____, *Great Basin Kingdom*. Lincoln: University of Nebraska Press, 1958.

Ashton, Wendell J. *Voice in the West: Biography of a Pioneer Newspaper*. New York: Duell, Sloan & Pearce, 1950.

Bancroft, Hubert Howe. *History of Nevada, Colorado and Wyoming, 1540–1880*. San Francisco: A. L. Bancroft & Company, 1890.

_____, *History of Utah 1540–1886*. San Francisco: History Company, 1889.

Barber, John Warner. *Historical Collections, Being a General Collection of Interesting facts, Traditions, Biographical Sketches, Anecdotes, &c., Relating to the History and Antiquities of Every Town in Massachusetts, with Geographical Descriptions*. Worcester: Dorr, Howland & Co., 1839.

Barney, Ronald O. *The Mormon Vanguard Brigade: Norton Jacob's Record*. Logan: Utah State University Press, 2005.

Bateman, Ronald R. *Deep Creek Reflections: 125 Years of Settlement at Ibapah, Utah 1859–1984*. Salt Lake City, UT: Ronald R. Bateman, 1991.

Bennett, Richard E. *Mormons at the Missouri 1846–1852*. Norman: Univ. of Oklahoma Press, 1987.

_____, *We'll Find the Place: The Mormon Exodus 1846–1848*. Norman: Univ. of Oklahoma Press, 2009.

Bennett, Richard E., Susan Easton Black, and Donald Q. Cannon. *The Nauvoo Legion: A History of the Mormon Militia, 1841–1846*. Norman, OK: Arthur H. Clark, 2010.

Bensen, Joe. *The Traveler's Guide to the Pony Express Trail*. Helena, MT: Falcon Press Publishing, 1995.

Bieber, Ralph P., ed. *Exploring Southwestern Trails 1846–1854 by Philip St. George Cooke, William Henry Chase Whiting, Francois Xavier Aubrey*. Glendale, CA: Arthur H. Clark Co., 1938.

Bigler, David L. *Forgotten Kingdom: The Mormon Theocracy in the American West, 1847–1896*. Logan: Utah State University Press, 1998.

_____, *Fort Limhi: The Mormon Adventure in Oregon Territory, 1855–1858*. Logan: Utah State University Press, 2004.

Bigler, David L. and Will Bagley, eds. *Army of Israel: Mormon Battalion Narratives*. Spokane, WA: Arthur H. Clark Co., 2000.

Bigler, David L. and Will Bagley. *The Mormon Rebellion: America's First Civil War, 1857–1858*. Norman: University of Oklahoma Press, 2011.

Billington, Ray Allen. *The Far Western Frontier*. New York: Harper & Row, 1956.

Bishop, William W., ed. *Mormonism Unveiled, or Life & Confession of John D. Lee*. Albuquerque, NM: Fierra Blanca Publications, 2001. Reprint of 1877 first edition.

Black, Susan Easton and Harvey Bischoff Black. *Annotated Record of Baptisms for the Dead, 1840–1845, Nauvoo, Hancock County Illinois*. Provo, UT: Brigham Young University Center for Family History and Genealogy, 2002.

Black, Susan Easton and William G. Hartley, eds. *The Iowa Mormon Trail*. Orem, UT: Helix Publishing, 1997.

Blanthorn, Ouida. *History of Tooele County*. Salt Lake City: Daughters of Utah Pioneers, 1961.

Bosworth, Newton. *Hochelaga Depicta: The Early History and Present State of the City and Island of Montreal*. Montreal: William Greig, 1839.

Bowles, Samuel. *Across the Continent: A Summer's Journey to the Rocky Mountains, the Mormons, and the Pacific States, with Speaker Colfax*. Springfield, MA: Samuel Bowles & Company, 1865.

Brooks, Juanita. *John Doyle Lee: Zealot, Pioneer Builder, Scapegoat*. Logan: Utah State University Press, 1992.

Brooks, Juanita, ed. *On the Mormon Frontier: The Diary of Hosea Stout, Volume One, 1844–1848*, and *Volume Two: 1848–1861*. Salt Lake City, UT: University of Utah Press and Utah State Historical Society, 1964.

Brown, James S. *Giant of the Lord, Life of a Pioneer: The Autobiography of James. S. Brown*. N.p.: D. A. Thompson, 2015. Reprint. Originally was published in Salt Lake City by Geo. Q. Cannon & Sons, in 1900 as *Life of a Pioneer: Being the Atobiography of James S. Brown*. Bookcraft in Salt Lake City reformatted and reprinted it in 1960 with the title *Giant of the Lord*.

Bryson, Conrey. *Winter Quarters*. Salt Lake City: Deseret Book, 1986.

Buffum, Edward. *Six Months in the Gold Mines: From a Journal of Three Years' Residence in Upper and Lower California 1847-8-9*. Philadelphia: Lea and Blanchard, 1850. Reprint by Readex Microprint Corporations, 1966.

Burton, Richard F. *The City of the Saints and Across the Rocky Mountains to California [1862]*. Fawn M. Brodie, ed. New York: Alfred A. Knopf, 1963.

Byrne, Michael. *Sources for Offaly History*. Tullamore: Offaly Research Library, 1978.

_____, *Tullamore Tour Album*. Tullamore: Esker Press, 1988.

_____, *A Walk Through Tullamore*. Tullamore: Eskar Press.

Cannon, Janeth R. *Nauvoo Panorama*. Salt Lake City, UT: Nauvoo Restoration Inc., 1991.

Clark, James R. *Messages of the First Presidency, Volume 1*. Salt Lake City: Bookcraft, 1965.

Clayton, William. *The Latter-day Saints' Emigrants' Guide. . .from Council Bluffs to the Valley of the Great Salt Lake*. St. Louis: Republican Steam Power Press–Chambers & Knapp, 1848. Reissued as Stanley B. Kimball, ed., *W. Clayton's The Latter-day Saints Emigrant Guide*. St. Louis: The Patrice Press, 1983.

Clayton Family Organization. *William Clayton's Journal*. Salt Lake City, UT: Deseret News Press, 1921.

Cleland, Robert G. and Juanita Brooks, eds. *A Mormon Chronicle: The Diaries of John D. Lee: 1848–1876, Vol. 1*. Salt Lake City: University of Utah Press, 1983.

Collier, Fred C., comp. *Unpublished Revelations of the Prophets and Presidents of The Church of Jesus Christ of Latter Day Saints*. Hanna, UT: Colliers Publishing Co., 3rd. ed., 2011.

Cook, Lyndon W., comp. *Nauvoo Deaths and Marriages 1839–1845*. Orem UT: Grandin Book Company, 1994.

Cooper, John Irwin. *Montreal: A Brief History*. Montreal: McGill-Queens University Press, 1969.

Corbett, Christopher. *Orphans Preferred: The Twisted Truth and Lasting Legend of the Pony Express*. New York: Broadway Books, 2003.

Cornwall, Rebecca and Leonard J. Arrington. *Rescue of the 1856 Handcart Companies*. Provo, UT: Charles Redd Center for Western Studies, 1982.

Creighton, D. G. *The Commercial Empire of the St. Lawrence, 1760–1850.* Toronto: Ryerson Press, 1937.

Crockett, David R. *Saints Find the Place: A Day-by-Day Pioneer Experience, Winter Quarters to the Salt Lake Valley.* Tucson, AZ: LDS-Gems Press, 1997.

_____, *Saints in Exile: A Day-by-Day Pioneer Experience, Nauvoo to Council Bluffs.* Tucson, AZ: LDS-Gems Press, 1996.

Daughters of Utah Pioneers, *Pioneer Women of Faith and Fortitude.* 4 Vols. Salt Lake City: Daughters of Utah Pioneers, 1998.

_____, *Settlement of Northern & Central Nevada by Utah Pioneers.* Vol. 19 in the *Pioneer Pathways* series. Salt Lake City: Daughters of Utah Pioneers, 2007.

Davies, J. Kenneth. *Mormon Gold: The Story of California's Mormon Argonauts.* Salt Lake City: Olympus Publishing Company, 1984.

Davies, J. Kenneth and Lorin Hansen. *Mormon Gold: The Story of California's Mormon Argonauts.* Rev. ed. North Salt Lake, UT: Granite Mountain Publishing Company, 2010.

Davin, Nicholas Flood. *The Irishman in Canada.* Shannon Ireland: Irish University Press, 1969.

De Breffny, Brian. *Irish Family Names: Arms, Origins, and Locations.* Gill and MacMillan, 1989.

Derr, Jill Mulvay, Carol Cornwall Madsen, Kate Holbrook, and Matthew J. Grow. *The First Fifty Years of the Relief Society.* Salt Lake City, UT: Church Historian's Press, 2016.

Derr, Jill Mulvay, Janeth Russell Cannon, and Maureen Ursenbach Beecher. *Women of Covenant: The Story of the Relief Society.* Salt Lake City: Deseret Book Company, 1992.

Di Certo, Joseph J. *The Saga of the Pony Express.* New York: MJF Books, 2005; posted on the Pony Express Museum website, xphomestation.com/.

Dinger, John S., ed. *The Nauvoo City and High Council Minutes.* Salt Lake City: Signature Books, 2011.

Doctrine and Covenants. Scripture published by The Church of Jesus Christ of Latter-day Saints.

Doige, Thomas. *An Alphabetical List of the Merchants, Traders, and Housekeepers Residing in Montreal.* Montreal: James Lane Printing, 1819.

Drouin, Gabriel, comp. *Quebec Vital and Church Records, 1621–1967.* Available at Ancestry.com.

Eberstadt, Edward. *The William Robertson Coe Collection of Western Americana.* New Haven: Yale University Library, 1952.

Egan, William M. Egan, ed. and comp. *Pioneering the West, 1846 to 1847: Major*

Howard Egan's Diary. Also Thrilling Experiences of Pre-Frontier Life Among Indians; Their Traits, Civil and Savage, and Part of Autobiography, Inter-Related to His Father's by Howard R. Egan. Richmond, UT: Howard R. Egan Estate, 1917.

Eggenhofer, Nick. *Wagons, Mules and Men: How the Frontier Moved West*. New York: Hastings House Publishers, 1961.

Elliott, Bruce S. *Irish Migrants in the Canadas: A New Approach*. Kingston and Montreal: McGill-Queens University Press, 1988.

Ellsworth, George S., ed. *The Journals of Addison Pratt*. Salt Lake City: University of Utah Press, 1990.

Esplin, Scott C. and Kenneth L. Alford, eds. *Salt Lake City: The Place Which God Prepared*. Provo, UT: Religious Studies Center, Brigham Young University, and Salt Lake City: Deseret Book, 2011.

Esshom, Frank. Compiler. *Pioneers and Prominent Men of Utah*. Salt Lake City: Utah Pioneer Book Publishing Company, 1913.

Farming in Offaly Down the Years: A Miscellany in Stories and Pictures. Tullamore: Offaly Historical Society, 1987.

Ferris, Cornelia Woodcock [Mrs. B. G. Ferris]. *The Mormons at Home: With Some Incidents of Travel from Missouri to California, 1852–1853*. New York: Dix & Edwards, 1856. Reprinted as *The Mormons at Home: In a Series of Letters*. Bedford, MA: Applewood Books, 2015, print on demand.

Fox, Feramorz Y., Leonard J. Arrington, and Dean L. May. *Building the City of God: Community and Cooperation Among the Mormons*. Salt Lake City: Deseret Book Company, 1976.

Firmage, Edwin B. and Richard Collin Mangrum. *Zion in the Courts: A Legal History of the Church of Jesus Christ of Latter-day Saints, 1830–1900*. Urbana and Chicago: University of Illinois Press, 1988.

Flanders, Robert B. *Nauvoo, Kingdom on the Mississippi*. Urbana: University of Illinois Press, 1985.

Fleek, Sherman L. *History May Be Searched in Vain: A Military History of the Mormon Battalion*. Spokane, WA: Arthur H. Clark Company, 2006.

Franswa, Gregory. *The Mormon Trail Revisited*. Tooele, UT: Patrice Press, 2007.

Frederick, J. V. *Ben Holladay, the Stagecoach King: A Chapter in the Development of Transcontinental Transportation*. Lincoln: University of Nebraska Press Bison Edition, 1989. The book was first published in 1940.

Furniss, Norman F. *The Mormon Conflict 1950–1959*. New Haven, CT: Yale University Press, 1960.

Gates, Susa Young. *The Life Story of Brigham Young*. New York: The Macmillan Co., 1930.

Givens, George W. *In Old Nauvoo: Everyday Life in the City of Joseph.* Salt Lake City: Deseret Book, 1990.

Givens, George and Sylvia Givens. *Nauvoo Fact Book.* Lynchburg, VA: Parley Street Publishers, 2000.

Glass, Robert and Juanita Brooks, eds. *A Mormon Chronicle: The Diaries of John D. Lee, 1848–1876.* 2 vols. San Marino California: Huntington Library, 1955.

Godfrey, Anthony. *Pony Express, Historic Resource Study.* Washington D.C.: U.S. Department of Interior, National Park Service, August 1994, online at www.nps.gov/archive/poex/hrs/hrs3b.htm.

Godfrey, Kenneth W. *Charles Shumway, A Pioneer's Life.* Provo, UT: J. Grant Stevenson, 1974.

Golder, Frank Alfred, Thomas A. Bailey, and J. Lyman Smith, eds. *The March of the Mormon Battalion From Council Bluffs to California, Taken from the Journal of Henry Standage.* New York: The Century Co., 1928.

Grant, Jedediah M. *Three Letters to the New York Herald.* New York: New York Herald, March 9, 1852. Brigham Young University Library published the pamphlet electronically in 2003–2004 and it's available online.

Greeley, Horace. *An Overland Journey from New York to San Francisco in the Summer of 1859.* Lincoln: Univ. of Nebraska Press, 1999. Originally published in 1860 by C. M. Saxton.

Gregg, Thomas. *The History of Hancock County, Illinois.* Chicago: Charles E. Chapman, 1880.

Grenham, John. *Irish Family Names.* Roberts Wholesale Books, 2000.

Grow, Matthew L. *"Liberty to the Downtrodden": Thomas L. Lane, Romantic Reformer.* New Haven, CT: Yale Univ. Press, 2009.

Hafen, LeRoy R. *The Overland Mail 1849–1869: Promoter of Settlement, Precursor of Railroads.* Norman: Univ. of Oklahoma Press, 2004. Originally published in 1926 by Arthur H. Clark Company, Cleveland, OH.

Hafen, LeRoy R. and Ann W. Hafen. *Handcarts to Zion.* Glendale, CA: Arthur H. Clark Co., 1976.

Hafen, LeRoy R. and Ann W. Hafen, eds. *The Utah Expedition 1857–1858.* Glendale, CA: Arthur H. Clark Company, 1958.

_____, *Journals of the Forty-niners Salt Lake to Los Angeles.* Lincoln and London: University of Nebraska Press, 1998 reprint of 1954 Arthur H. Clark publication.

Hall, Shawn. *Romancing Nevada's Past: Ghost Towns and Historic Sites of Eureka, Lander, and White Pine Counties.* Reno and Las Vegas: University of Nevada Press, 1994.

Hammond, Priscilla, comp. *Vital Records of Barrington, New Hampshire, 1720–1851.* Concord NH: 1934.

Hartley, William G. *Another Kind of Gold: The Life of Albert King Thurber, a Utah Pioneer, Explorer and Community Builder.* Troy, ID: C. L. Dalton Enterprises, 2011.

_____, *My Best for the Kingdom: History and Autobiography of John Lowe Butler, a Mormon Frontiersman.* Salt Lake City: Aspen Books, 1993.

Hartley, William G. and A. Gary Anderson. *Sacred Places: Iowa and Nebraska, a Comprehensive Guide to Early LDS Historical Sites.* Salt Lake City: Deseret Book, 2006.

Hearty, Patrick and Joseph Hatch. *The Pony Express in Utah.* Charleston, SC: Arcadia Publishing, 2015.

_____, *The Pony Express Stations in Utah.* Salt Lake City: The Authors, 2012.

Hegarty, Neil. *The Story of Ireland: A History of the Irish People.* New York: St. Martin's Press, 2011.

Hill, William E. *The Mormon Trail: Yesterday and Today.* Logan: Utah State Univ. Press, 1996.

History of the Relief Society, 1842–1966. Salt Lake City: Relief Society, 1966.

Hogan, Mervin B. *Mormonism and Freemasonry: The Illinois Episode.* Richmond, VA: Macey Publishing of Masonic Supply Company, 1977.

Holliday, J. S. *The World Rushed In: The California Gold Rush Experience.* New York: Simon and Schuster, Touchstone Edition, 1983.

_____, *Rush for Riches: Gold Fever and the Making of California.* Berkeley and Los Angeles: Oakland Museum of California and University of California, 1999.

Holzapfel, Richard Neitzel and T. Jeffery Cottle. *Old Mormon Nauvoo and Southeastern Iowa: Historic Photographs and Guide.* Santa Ana, CA: Fieldbrook Productions, 1991.

Houston, J. Cecil and William J. Smyth. *Irish Emigration and Canadian Settlement: Patterns, Links and Letters.* Toronto, Ontario, Canada: Univ. of Toronto Press, 1990.

Hulbert, Archer Butler, ed. *Letters of An Overland Mail Agent in Utah.* Worcester, MA: The American Antiquarian Society, 1909.

Jacob, C. Edward and Ruth S. Jacob, eds. *The Record of Norton Jacob.* Salt Lake City: Norton Jacob Family Association, 1949.

Jenkins, Kathleen. *Montreal, Island City of the St. Lawrence.* Garden City, NY: Doubleday, 1996.

Jenson, Andrew. *Church Chronology.* 2nd Ed. Salt Lake City: Deseret News, 1899.

_____, *Day by Day with the Utah Pioneers of 1847.* Salt Lake City: Deseret News, 1934.

_____, *Biographical Encyclopedia*. Salt Lake City: Deseret News Press, 1888.

_____, *Encyclopedic History of the Church of Jesus Christ of Latter-day Saints*. Salt Lake City: Deseret News Publishing Company, 1941.

Jewett, Jeremiah P. and Robert B. Caverly. *History of Barnstead from the First Settlement in 1727 to 1872*. Lowell, MA: Marden & Rowell, 1872.

Johnson, Alan P. *Aaron Johnson, Faithful Steward*. Salt Lake City: Publishers Press, 1991.

Johnston, William G. *Overland to California*. Pittsburg, PA: privately printed, 1892.

Kane, Elizabeth L. *Twelve Mormon Homes Visited in Succession on a Journey from Utah to Arizona*. Philadelphia: J. P. Lippincott, 1874. reprinted by Everett L. Cooley, editor, Salt Lake City: Tanner Trust Fund and University of Utah Press, 1974.

Kane, Elizabeth L. *A Gentile Account of Life in Utah's Dixie*. Salt Lake City: Tanner Trust Fund and University of Utah Press, 1995.

Kane, Thomas L. *The Mormons: A Discourse Delivered before the Historical Society of Pennsylvania, March 26, 1850*. Philadelphia: King and Baird, Printers, 1850.

Kearl, J. R., Clayne L. Pope, and Larry T. Wimmer. *Index to the 1850, 1860 & 1870 Censuses of Utah, Heads of Households*. Baltimore: Genealogical Publishing Co., 1981.

Kearney, John. *The Long Ridge, Towards a History of Killeigh Parish*. Tullamore, County Offaly, Ireland: Esker Press, 1992.

Kelly, Charles Kelly, ed. *Journals of John D. Lee, 1846–47 and 1859*. Salt Lake City, UT: University of Utah Press, 1984.

Kenney, Scott G., ed., *Wilford Woodruff's Journals*. 9 Vols. Midvale, UT: Signature Books, 1985.

Kett, Joseph F. *Rite of Passage: Adolescence in America, 1790 to the Present*. New York: Basic Books, 1977.

Kimball, Stanley B. *Heber C. Kimball, Mormon Patriarch and Pioneer*. Urbana: University of Illinois Press, 1981.

_____, *Historic Resource Study: Mormon Pioneer National Historic Trail*. Washington D.C.: U.S. Department of Interior, National Park Service, 1991.

_____, *Historic Sites and Markers along the Mormon and Other Great Western Trails*. Chicago: University of Illinois Press, 1988.

Kimball, Stanley B., ed. *The Latter-day Saints' Emigrants' Guide by W. Clayton*. St. Louis, MO: Patrice Press, 1983. The guide originally was published in St. Louis in 1848 by Chambers & Knapp.

_____, *On the Potter's Wheel: The Diaries of Heber C. Kimball*. Salt Lake City:

Signature Books and Smith Research Associates, 1987.

The King's County. Parsonstown: Printing House Buildings, 1890.

Knight, Hal and Stanley B. Kimball. *111 Days to Zion*. Salt Lake City: Deseret News, 1978.

Lamar, Howard R. Ed. *The New Encyclopedia of the American West*. New Haven and London: Yale University Press, 1998.

Landon, Michael N., ed. *The Journals of George Q. Cannon, Volume I, To California in '49*. Salt Lake City, UT: Deseret Book and LDS Church Historical Department, 1999.

Larsen, Karen M. and Paul D. Larsen. *Remembering Winter Quarters/Council Bluffs*. Elkhorn, NE: Paul D. Larsen, 1998.

Larson, Andrew Karl. *Erastus Snow: The Life of a Missionary and Pioneer for the Early Mormon Church*. Salt Lake City: Univ. of Utah Press, 1971.

Leacock, Stephen. *Montreal: Seaport and City*. Garden City, NY: Doubleday, Doran & Co., 1942.

Lee, John D. *Mormonism Unveiled: Life and Confessions of John D. Lee*. Albuquerque, NM: Fierra Blanca Publications 2001. Reprint of 1891 edition. Lee's narration was originally published in St. Louis in 1877 by Bryan, Brand & Co.

Leigh, Rufus Wood. *Nevada Place Names: Their Origin and Significance*. Las Vegas and Boulder City: Southern Nevada Historical Society and Lake Mead Natural History Association, 1964.

Leonard, Glen M. *Nauvoo: A Place of Peace, A People of Promise*. Salt Lake City: Deseret Book, 2002.

Lewis, Samuel. *Topographical Dictionary of Ireland . . . Vols. I and II*. 2nd ed. London: S. Lewis and Co., 1847.

Little, James A. *From Kirtland to Salt Lake City*. Salt Lake City: Juvenile Instructor, 1890.

Ludlow, Daniel H., ed. *Encyclopedia of Mormonism*. 5 Vols. New York: Macmillan Publishing Company, 1992.

Lyman, Edward Leo. *Amasa Mason Lyman, Mormon Apostle and Apostate*. Salt Lake City: Univ. of Utah Press, 2009.

_____, *The Overland Journey from Utah to California: Wagon Travel from the City of Saints to the City of Angels*. Reno and Las Vegas: Univ. of Nevada Press, 2004.

_____, *San Bernardino, The Rise and Fall of a California Community*. Salt Lake City: Signature Books, 1996.

MacKinnon, William P. *At Sword's Point, Part One and Part Two: A Documentary*

History of the Utah War to 1858. Norman, OK: The Arthur H. Clark Company, 2008, 2016..

Madsen, Brigham D. *Glory Hunter: A Biography of Patrick Edward Connor.* Salt Lake City: Univ. of Utah Press, 1990.

———, *Gold Rush Sojourners in Great Salt Lake City, 1849 and 1850.* Salt Lake City: University of Utah Press, 1983.

———, *The Shoshone Frontier and the Bear River Massacre.* Salt Lake City: University of Utah Press, 1985.

Madsen, Carol Cornwall. *In Their Own Words: Women and the Story of Nauvoo.* Salt Lake City, UT: Deseret Book, 1994.

Majors, Alexander. *Seventy Years on the Frontier, Alexander Majors Memoirs of a Lifetime on the Border.* Chicago: Rand McNally, 1893.

Malouf, Beatrice B. *Rugged Men of the West.* Salt Lake City: Daughters of Utah Pioneers, 1995.

Martin, James D. *The Story of Major Howard Egan: Rugged Pioneer and Tireless Trail Blazer.* N.p.: James D. Martin, 2000.

Mattes, Merrill J. *The Great Platte River Road.* Lincoln: Nebraska State Historical Society, 1969.

Metress, Seamus P. and William M. Baker. "A Bibliography of the History of the Irish in Canada." In *The Untold Story: The Irish in Canada* Vol. 2, ed. by Robert O. Driscoll and Lorna Reynolds. Toronto: Celtic Arts of Canada, 1988, 977–1001.

Miller, David E. and Della S. Miller. *Nauvoo, the City of Joseph.* Santa Barbara and Salt Lake City: Peregrine Smith, Inc., 1974.

Milner, Clyde A, III, Carol A. O'Connor and Martha A. Sandweiss. *The Oxford History of the American West.* New York: Oxford Univ. Press, 1994.

Moody, Ralph. *Stagecoach West.* Lincoln: Univ. of Nebraska Press, 1998. A reprint of the original 1967 edition.

Moorman, Donald R. and Gene A. Sessions. *Camp Floyd and the Mormons: The Utah War.* Salt Lake City: Univ. of Utah Press, 1992.

Morgan, Dale L. *The State of Deseret.* Logan: Utah State Univ. Press and the Utah Historical Society, 1987.

Mormonism"! Indictment for the murder of James Monroe, referred to in the report of the returned judges from the Territory of Utah . . . Liverpool, England: R. James, 1852.

Murphy, John R. *The Mineral Resources of the Territory of Utah with Mining Statistics and Maps.* Salt Lake City: James Dwyer, 1872.

Nibley, Preston. *Exodus to Greatness: The Story of the Mormon Migration.* Salt Lake City: Deseret News Press, 1947.

Oaks, Dallin H. and Marvin S. Hill. *Carthage Conspiracy*. Univ. of Illinois Press, 1979.

O'Tuathaigh, Gearoid. *Ireland Before the Famine, 1798–1848: The Gill History of Ireland*. Irish Book Center: 1972.

Owens, Kenneth N. *Gold Rush Saints: California Mormons and the Great Rush for Riches*. Spokane, WA: Arthur H. Clark Company, 2004.

Palmer, A. Kingsmill. *Notes on the Parish of Geashill and Killeigh*. Leinster Leader, Jan. 1964.

Perkins, Keith W. and Donald Q. Cannon. *Sacred Places, A Comprehensive Guide to Early LDS Historical Sites, Volume Three, Ohio and Illinois*. Salt Lake City: Deseret Book, 2002.

Peterson, Jesse G. *A Route for the Overland Stage: James H. Simpson's 1859 Trail Across the Great Basin*. Logan: Utah State Univ. Press, 2008.

_____, *West from Salt Lake: Diaries from the Central Overland Trail*. Norman, OK: The Arthur H. Clark Company, 2012.

Piercy, Frederick. *Route from Liverpool to Great Salt Lake Valley*. Fawn M. Brodie, ed. Cambridge, MA: Harvard Univ. Press, 1962.

Powell, Allan Kent, ed. *Utah History Encyclopedia*. Salt Lake City: Univ. of Utah Press, 1994.

The Prophet Joseph Smith's Views on the Powers and Policy of the Government of the United States. Reprinted in Salt Lake City, UT: Jos. Hyrum Parry & Co., 1886.

Quaife, Milo Milton and Reuben Cole Shaw. *Across the Plains in Forty-nine*. New York City: Citadel Press, 1977.

Quinn, D. Michael. *The Mormon Hierarchy: Extensions of Power*. Salt Lake City: Signature Books, 1997.

Remy, Jules, and Julius Brenchley. *A Journey to Great Salt Lake City*. Vol. I. London: W. Jeffs, 1861.

Rhodes, David. *Spirits in the Desert: Poetry of the Pony Express*. Privately published, no date.

Ricketts, Norma B. *The Mormon Battalion: U.S. Army of the West*. Logan: Utah State Univ. Press, 1996.

Roberts, Brigham H. *A Comprehensive History of The Church of Jesus Christ of Latter-day Saints*. 6 Vols. Provo, UT: Brigham Young Univ. Press, reprint, 1965. Originally published in 1930.

Roberts, B. H., ed. *History of The Church of Jesus Christ of Latter-day Saints*. 7 Vols. Salt Lake City: Deseret Book Company, 1974.

Rogers, Jedediah S. *The Council of Fifty: A Documentary History*. Salt Lake City: Signature Books, 2014.

Roland, Charles Pierce. *Albert Sidney Johnston, Soldier of Three Republics*. Austin: Univ. of Texas Press, 1964.

Root, Frank A. and William Elsey Connelly. *The Overland Stage to California*. Topeka, KS: Crane & Co., 1901.

Remy, J. and J. Brenchley. *A Journey To The Great-Salt-Lake City*. London: W Jeffs, 1861. Translated from French.

Sager, Eric W. *Seafaring Labour: The Merchant Marine of Atlantic Canada, 1820–1914*. Kingston, Montreal, and London: McGill-Queen's Univ. Press, 1989.

The Salem Directory and City Register. Salem: Henry Whipple, 1837.

The Salem Directory and City Register, 1842.

The Salt Lake City Directory and Business Guide for 1869. Salt Lake City: E. L. Sloan and Company, 1869.

Salt Lake City Directory. New York, San Francisco, and Chicago: U. S. Directory Publishing of California, 1885.

Salt Lake City Directory for 1889. Salt Lake City: Kelly & Co., 1889.

Salt Lake City Directory for 1890. Salt Lake City: R. L. Polk & Co., 1890.

Salt Lake City Directory for 1898. R. L. Polk & Co., 1898.

Salt Lake City Directory for 1900. R. L. Polk & Co., 1900.

Salt Lake City Directory for 1906. R. L. Polk & Co., 1906.

Sandham, Andrew. *Ville-Marie, or, Sketches of Montreal, Past & Present*. Montreal: George Bishop & Co., 1870.

Schindler, Harold. *Orrin Porter Rockwell, Man of God Son of Thunder*. Salt Lake City: Univ. of Utah Press, 1983.

Seegmiller, Janet Burton. *"Be Kind to the Poor": The Life Story of Robert Taylor Burton*. N.p.: Robert Taylor Burton Family Organization, 1988.

Settle, Raymond W. and Mary Lund Settle. *Saddles and Spurs: The Pony Express Saga*. Lincoln: Univ. of Nebraska Press, 1955.

———, *War Drums and Wagon Wheels: The Story of Russell, Majors and Waddell*. Lincoln: Univ. of Nebraska Press, 1966.

Simpson, Captain J. H. *Report of Explorations across the Great Basin of the Territory of Utah for a Direct Wagon-route from Camp Floyd to Genoa, in Carson Valley, in 1859*. Washington D.C: Engineer Department, U.S. Army/Government Printing Office, 1876.

Sloan, Edward L. *Gazeteer of Utah and Salt Lake City Directory*. Salt Lake City: Salt Lake Herald Publishing, 1874.

Smart, Donna Toland. *Mormon Midwife: The 1846–1888 Diaries of Patty Bartlett Sessions*. Logan: Utah State Univ. Press, 1997.

Smart, William B. Smart and Donna T. Smart, eds. *Over the Rim: The Parley P. Pratt*

Exploring Expedition to Southern Utah, 1849–1850. Logan: Utah State Univ. Press, 1999.

Smith, Pauline Udall. *Captain Jefferson Hunt of the Mormon Battalion.* Salt Lake City, UT: Nicholas G. Morgan Sr., Foundation, 1958.

Stansbury, Howard. *An Expedition to the Valley of the Great Salt Lake.* N.p.: U.S. Army Corps of Topographical Engineers, 1852. Readex Microprint Corporation, 1966.

Stegner, Wallace. *The Gathering of Zion: The Story of the Mormon Trail.* Lincoln: Univ. of Nebraska Press, 1981. Originally published in New York by McGraw Hill, 1964.

Stewart, George R. *The California Trail: An Epic with Many Heroes.* Lincoln and London: Univ. of Nebraska Press, 1962.

Stewart, Anthony Terence Quincey. *The Shape of Irish History.* Ithaca, NY: McGill-Queens Univ. Press, 2001.

Stommel, Henry and Elizabeth. *Volcano Weather: 1816 The Story of the Year without a Summer.* Newport, R.I.: Seven Seas Press, 1983.

Stott, Clifford L. *Search for Sanctuary: Brigham Young and the White Mountain Expedition.* Salt Lake City: Univ. of Utah Press, 1984.

Stout, Hosea. Diary. See entry for Juanita Brooks, editor.

Street, Franklin. *California in 1850.* Cincinnati, OH: R. E. Edwards & Co., 1851.

Sullivan, Marlene Bateman. *Brigham's Boys.* Springville, UT: Cedar Fort, 2009.

Sutton, Wain, ed.. *Utah–A Centennial History. Vol. II.* New York: Lewis Historical Publishing Company, 1949.

Tiger, Lionel and Robin Fox. *Men in Groups.* Edinburgh, Scotland: Thomas Nelson & Sons, 1969.

Townley, John W. *The Overland Stage: A History and Guidebook.* Reno, NV: Jamison Station Press and Great Basin Studies Center, 1994.

Traveller's New Guide Through Ireland . . . Dublin, Ireland: Longman, Hurst, Rees, Oreme and Brown, 1819.

Tullidge, Edward W. *History of Salt Lake.* Salt Lake City: Star Printing, 1886.

Twain, Mark. *Roughing It.* New York: Penguin Books, 1962. The book was originally published in 1872 by the American Publishing Company, Hartford, CT.

Tyler, Daniel. *A Concise History of the Mormon Battalion in the Mexican War, 1846–47.* Glorieta, New Mexico: Rio Grande Press, 1969. Originally published 1881.

Unruh, John D., Jr. *The Plains Across: The Overland Emigrants and the Trans-Mississippi West, 1840–1860.* Urbana and Chicago: Univ. of Illinois Press, 1979.

Utley, Robert M., ed. *Encyclopedia of the American West*. New York: Wings Books, 1997.

Varley, James F. *Brigham and the Brigadier: General Patrick Connor and His California Volunteers in Utah and Along the Overland Trail*. Tucson, AZ: Westernlore Press, 1989.

Vaughan, W. E., ed. *A New History of Ireland, Vol. 5, Ireland under the Union, 1801–1870*. New York: Oxford Univ. Press, 2010.

Vinson, Michael. *Edward Eberstadt & Sons: Rare Booksellers of Western Americana*. Norman, OK: Arthur H. Clark Company, 2016.

Visscher, William Lightfoot. *The Pony Express, a Thrilling and Truthful History*. Golden, CO: Outbooks, 1980, excerpts from original 1908 study by that name.

Vital Records of Salem, Massachusetts to the End of the Year 1849. Vol 3: Marriages. Salem: the Essex Institute, 1924.

Walker, Dale L. *Eldorado: The California Gold Rush*. New York: Tom Doherty Associates, 2003.

Walker, Ronald W. *Wayward Saints: The Godbeites and Brigham Young*. Urbana and Chicago: Univ. of Illinois Press, 1998.

Walker, Ronald W. and Doris Dant, eds. *Nearly Everything Imaginable: The Everyday Life of Utah's Mormon Pioneers*. Provo, Utah: Brigham Young Univ. Press, 1999.

Ward, Maurine Carr, ed. *Winter Quarters: The 1846–1848 Life Writings of Mary Haskin Parker Richards*. Logan: Utah State Univ. Press, 1996.

Warner, Elisha. *The History of Spanish Fork*. Spanish Fork, UT: Press Publishing Co., 1930.

Watson, Elden J., comp. *Manuscript History of Brigham Young*. Salt Lake City: Elden J. Watson, 1971.

Watson, Elden J., comp. *The Orson Pratt Journals*. Salt Lake City: Elden J. Watson, 1975.

Whitney, Orson F. *History of Utah, Vol. I*. Salt Lake City: Cannon & Sons, 1892.

Wilson, Elijah Nicholas. *"UNCLE NICK" Among the Shoshones*. Salt Lake City: Skelton Publishing, 1910.

Wilson, E. N. *The White Indian Boy*. Rev. and ed. by Howard Driggs. Yonkers-on-Hudson, New York: World Book Company, 1922.

Wilson, Lawrence M., comp., *This Was Montreal in 1814, 1815, 1816, and 1817*. Montreal: Chateau de Ramezay, 1960.

Winther, Oscar Osburn. *Via Western Express & Stagecoach: California's Transportation Links with the Nation, 1848–1869*. Lincoln: Univ. of Nebraska Press, Bison Book, 1969. First published in 1945.

Withington, Mary C. *A Catalogue of Manuscripts in the Collection of Western Americana Founded By William Robertson Coe, Yale University Library.* New Haven, CT: Yale University Press, 1952.

Woodruff, Wilford. Journal. See Scott G. Kenney, ed.

Wyler, Wanda Ricks. *Thomas E. Ricks, Colonizer and Founder.* 2nd ed. Sacramento, CA: The Author, 1989.

Articles/Chapters/ Brochures

Ahnert, Gerald T. "Identifying Butterfield's Overland Mail Company Stages on the Southern Trail, 1858–1861." *Overland Journal* 32 (Winter 2014–2015), 140–64.

Allaman, John Lee. "Policing in Mormon Nauvoo." *Illinois Historical Journal* 89 (Summer 1996), 85–98.

Allen, James B. "Was Joseph Smith a serious candidate for the presidency of the United States, or was he only attempting to publicize gospel views on public issues?" *Ensign* (Sept. 1973), 21–22.

Allen, James B. and Ted J. Warner. "Gosiute Indians in Pioneer Utah." *Utah Historical Quarterly* 39 (Spring 1971), 162–77.

Arrington, Leonard J. "Church Leaders in Liberty Jail." *BYU Studies* 13 (Autumn 1972), 20–26.

Bachman, Danel and Ronald K. Esplin. "Plural Marriage." *Encyclopedia of Mormonism,* Vol. 3. New York: Macmillan Publishing Company, 1992, 1091–95.

Bashore, Melvin L. "Quitting Tea and Coffee: Marketing Alternative Hot Drinks to Mormons." *Journal of Mormon History* 42 (Jan. 2016), 73–104.

Beecher, Maureen Ursenbach. "Women in Winter Quarters." *Sunstone*, 8 (July-August 1983).

Beecher, Maureen Ursenbach, ed. "All Things Move in Order in the City: The Nauvoo Diary of Zina Diantha Huntington Jacobs." *BYU Studies* (Spring 1979), 1–34.

Beecher, Maureen Ursenbach, ed. "The Iowa Diary of Lorenzo Snow." *BYU Studies* 24 (Summer 1984), 261–274.

Bitton, Davis and Linda P. Wilcox. "Pestiferous Ironclads: The Grasshopper Problem in Pioneer Utah." *Utah Historical Quarterly* 44 (Fall 1978), 336–355.

Black, Susan Easton. "How Large Was the Population of Nauvoo?" *BYU Studies* 35 (No. 2, 1995): 91–95.

Brooks, Juanita, ed. "[John D. Lee] Diary of the Mormon Battalion Mission, Part 1," *New Mexico Historical Review* 43 (July 1967), 165–209, and Part 2, (Oct. 1967), 281–333.

Bureau of Land Management, United States Government. "Utah Pony Express Trail National Back Country Byway." Brochure.

Bush, Lester E., Jr. "Brigham Young in Life and Death: A Medical Overview," *Journal of Mormon History* 3 (1978), 79–103.

Campbell, Eugene. "Mormon Gold Mining Mission of 1849." *BYU Studies* 1 (Autumn 1959), 19–31.

Cannon, Donald Q. Larry E. Dahl. "The King Follett Discourse: Joseph Smith's Greatest Sermon in Historical Perspective." *BYU Studies* 18 (Winter 1978), 179–192.

Cannon II, Kenneth L. "'Mountain Common Law': The Extralegal Punishment of Seducers in Early Utah." *Utah Historical Quarterly* 51 (Fall 1983), 308–327.

Carter, Lyndia. "The Salt Lake Cutoff and the California Trail." *History Blazer*, Dec. 1996, posted on historytogo.utah.gov website.

Carter, D. Robert. "Fish and the Famine of 1855–56." *Journal of Mormon History* 27 (Fall 2001), 93–97.

"Charge of Hon. Z. Snow. . . to the Jury, on the Trial of Howard Egan for the Murder of James Monroe." October Term, 1851. *Journal of Discourses* I:100–103.

Christian, Lewis Clark. "Mormon Foreknowledge of the American West." *BYU Studies* 21 (Fall 1981), 403–15.

Clawson, Hiram B. "Crossing the Plains." *Young Woman's Journal* (May 1907), 217–18.

Conover, Peter. "Journal of Peter Wilson Conover (1807–1892)." Daughters of the Utah Pioneers, *Chronicles of Courage* (1990), I:201–30.

Corley, Nora. "The St. Lawrence Ship Channell, 1805–1865." *Cahiers de géographie du Québec* 11, (November 23, 1967).

Daughters of Utah Pioneers. "The Negro Pioneer." *Our Pioneer Heritage* 8 (1965), 513–19.

_____, "The Prophet's Guard." *Our Pioneer Heritage* 15 (1972), 420–22.

_____, "The Salmon River Mission," *Our Pioneer Heritage* 7 (1964), 141–200.

_____, "Utah and the Pony Express," *Our Pioneer Heritage* 3 (1960), 333–420.

Daynes, Kathryn M. "Family Ties: Belief and Practice in Nauvoo." *The John Whitmer Historical Association Journal* 8 (1988), 63–75.

Davies, J. Kenneth. "Mormons and California Gold." *Journal of Mormon History* 7 (1980), 83–99.

Demos, John and Virginia. "Adolescence in Historical Perspective." *Journal of Marriage and Family* Vol. 31 (Nov. 1969), 632–638.

Ehat, Andrew F. "'It Seems Like Heaven Began on Earth': Joseph Smith and the Constitution of the Kingdom of God." *BYU Studies 20* (Spring 1980), 253–280.

Egan, Howard. "Three Letters." *Our Pioneer Heritage* 14 (1970–71): 505–06.

Embry, Jessie L. "Missionaries for the Dead: The Story of the Genealogical Missionaries of the Nineteenth Century." *BYU Studies* 17 (Spring 1977), 355–360.

England, Eugene, ed. "George Laub's Nauvoo Journal." *BYU Studies* 18 (Winter 1978), 151–178.

Esplin, Ronald K. "'A Place Prepared:' Joseph, Brigham and the Quest for Promised Refuge in the West. " *Journal of Mormon History*, 9 (1982):85–111.

_____, "A 'Place Prepared' in the Rockies." *Ensign* (July 1988), 6–13.

_____, "Utah's First Thanksgiving." *Ensign* (October 1982), 48–51.

Faust, H. J. "Pony Express and Stage Coach: How News Was Transmitted, Mail Carried, and Passengers Transported in Early Day Utah." [H. J. Faust's Recollections.] *Deseret Evening News*, May 29, 1897.

Fox, Feramorz Y. "Experiment in Utopia: The United Order of Richfield, 1871–1877." *Utah Historical Quarterly* 32 (Fall 1964), 355–356.

Gamble, James. "Wiring a Continent: The Making of the U.S. Transcontinental Telegraph Line." Published in the *Californian Magazine*, 1881, reproduced on the internet at: http://www.telegraph-history.org/transcontinental-telegraph/

Godfrey, Audrey M. "Housewives, Hussies and Heroines, or the Women of Johnston's Army." *Utah Historical Quarterly* 54 (Spring 1986), 157–78.

Godfrey, Kenneth W., "Freemasonry in Nauvoo," *The Encyclopedia of Mormonism,* 1992.

_____, "More Treasures Than One." In *Hearken O Ye People.* Sandy, UT: Randall Books, 1984.

_____, "Winter Quarters: Glimmering Glimpses into Mormon Religious and Social Life." In *A Sesquicentennial Look at Church History: Proceedings of the Sidney B. Sperry Symposium, January 26, 1980* (Provo, UT: Brigham Young University, 1980).

"Great Men of the Pony Express: Major Howard Egan." *Our Pioneer Heritage* 3 (1960), 365–368.

Hamelin, Joseph P., Jr. "The Hamelin Journal." In LeRoy R. And Ann W. Hafen, eds, *Far West and the Rockies: Supplement to the Journals of Forty-Niners*

Salt Lake to Los Angeles. Glendale, CA: Arthur H. Clark Company, 1961, 79–101.

Hardy, B. Carmon. "That 'Same Old Question of Polygamy and Polygamous Living:' Some Recent Findings Regarding Nineteenth and Early Twentieth-Century Mormon Polygamy." *Utah Historical Quarterly* 73 (Summer 2005), 212–224.

Harper, Reid L. "The Mantle of Joseph: Creation of a Mormon Miracle." *Journal of Mormon History* 22 (Fall 1996), 35–71.

Harrington. "Journal of Leonard E. Harrington." *Utah Historical Quarterly* 8 (Jan. 1940), 3–64.

Hartley, William G. "Common People: Church Activity during the Brigham Young Era." In *Nearly Everything Imaginable: The Everyday Life of Utah's Mormon Pioneers,* ed. Ronald W. Walker and Doris R. Dant. Provo, Utah: Brigham Young University Press, 1999, 249–95.

———, "Council Bluffs/Kanesville, Iowa : A Hub for Mormon Settlements, Operations, and Emigration, 1846–1852." *John Whitmer Historical Association Journal* (26: 2006), 17–47.

———, "Dangerous Mission at Fort Limhi." Chapter 6 in *Kindred Saints*. Salt Lake City: Eden Hill, 1982, 71–83.

———, "From Men to Boys: LDS Aaronic Priesthood Offices, 1829–1996." *Journal of Mormon History* 22 (Spring 1996): 80–136.

———, "'How Shall I Gather?'" *Ensign* (Oct. 1997): 5–17.

———, "Howard Egan, the Elkhorn Skirmish, and Mormon Trail Emigration in 1848." *Mormon Historical Studies* 1(Spring 2000), 37–59.

———, "Nauvoo Stake, Priesthood Quorums, and the Church's First Wards." *BYU Studies* 32 (Winter and Spring 1991), 57–80.

———, "Pushing on to Zion: Kanesville, Iowa, 1846–1853." *Ensign* (August 2002): 14–23.

———, "The Priesthood Reorganization of 1877: Brigham Young's Last Achievement." *BYU Studies* 20:1 (1979), 3–36.

———, "The Saints' Three-stage Exodus from Nauvoo," in *History of the Saints* (American Fork, UT: Covenant Books, 2012), Chap. 2.

———, "Spring Exodus from Nauvoo: Act Two in the 1846 Mormon Evacuation Drama." In Susan Easton Black and William G. Hartley, eds., *The Iowa Mormon Trail*. Orem, UT: Helix Publishing, 1997, 3–20.

Hogan, Edward. "The Curious Case of James Madison Monroe." *Sunstone* 6 (Sept. 2013), posted on Sunstone website.

Holzapfel, Richard Neitzel. "Women's Letters from Nauvoo." *The Nauvoo Journal* 7 (Spring 1995).

Homer, Michael W. "The Judiciary and the Common Law in Utah Territory, 1850–61." *Dialogue* 21 (Spring 1988), 100.

Hoshide, Robert K. "Salt Desert Trails Revisited," *Crossroads* [Utah Crossroads Chapter of OCTA newsletter]), Spring 1994, 5.

"Howard Egan--Captain Ninth Tenth," in "The First Company to Enter Salt Lake Valley," *Our Pioneer Heritage* 2 (1959), 573–574.

Hunter, J. Michael. "The Monument to Brigham Young and the Pioneers: One Hundred Years of Controversy." *Utah Historical Quarterly* 68 (Fall 2000), 332–50.

Irvine, Marie. "Howard Egan: Muleback Champion and Stagecoach Hero," talk given to the Crossroads Chapter of OCTA (the Oregon-California Trails Association), and published in its newsletter *Crossroads*, June 2009.

_____, "The Trail Not Followed." Talk to Utah's Crossroads Chapter of the Oregon-California Trails Association meeting, 11 April 2002, summarized in the chapter's newsletter *Crossroads*, Summer 2002, 8–10.

Irving, Gordon L. "The Law of Adoption: One Phase of the Development of the Mormon Concept of Salvation, 1830–1900." *BYU Studies* 14 (Spring 1974), 291–314.

Jackson, W. Turrentine. "A New Look at Wells Fargo, Stagecoaches, and the Pony Express." Reprint from the *California Historical Society Quarterly* (December 1966).

_____, "Salt Lake City: Wells Fargo's Transportation Depot during the Stagecoach Era." *Utah Historical Quarterly* 53 (Winter 1985), 5–39.

Jessop, Jaromy. "The Pony Express left lasting imprints in Tooele County," *Tooele Transcript Bulletin*, Dec. 6, 2005.

Johnson, Jeffrey Ogden. "Determining and Defining 'Wife': The Brigham Young Households," *Dialogue* 20 (Autumn 1987), 57–70.

Jorgenson, Lynne Watkins and BYU Studies Staff. "The Mantle of the Prophet Joseph Passes to Brother Brigham: A Collection of Spiritual Witness." *BYU Studies* 36 (1996–97), 125–204.

Leonard, Glen M. "Picturing the Nauvoo Legion." *BYU Studies* 35 No. 2 (1995), 95–127+.

"Letters of a Proselyte: The Hascall-Pomeroy Correspondence." *Utah Historical Quarterly* 25 (a 4-part article, January to October 1957).

Lloyd, R. Scott. "Birthplace of the University of Utah Is Replicated." *Church News*, Nov. 17, 2001.

_____, "Brigham Young enigmatic, larger than life: Report of Ronald W. Walker's address to the Mormon History Association." *Church News*, June 9, 2013.

Lorry, Jerome L. "Unveiling the Black Rock: A History of Exploration in Nevada's Remote Northwest Corner." *Nevada Historical Society Quarterly* 51 (Spring 2008), 3–24.

Lyon, T. Edgar. "Historical Highlights of the Saints in Illinois." *Church Education System Symposium, 1977, Proceedings.*

Madsen, Brigham D. "Shoshoni-Bannock Marauders on the Oregon Trail, 1859–1863." *Utah Historical Quarterly* 35 (Winter 1967), 3–30.

Mason, Patrick O. "Honor, the Unwritten Law and Extralegal Violence: Contextualising Parley Pratt's Murder." In Gregory E. Armstrong, Matthew J. Grow, and Dennis J. Stiler, eds., *Parley P. Pratt and the making of Mormonism*. Oklahoma: Arthur H. Clark, 2011.

Mattes, Merrill J. "The Council Bluffs Road: Northern Branch of the Great Platte River Road." *Nebraska History* 65 (Summer 1984), 179–84.

———, "The Northern Route of the Non-Mormons: Rediscovery of Nebraska's Forgotten Historic Trail." *Overland Journal* 8 (No. 2, 1990), 2–14.

Mickelson, Bob. "Did 'Old Sow' go to slaughterhouse?" *The Davis Clipper*, Sept. 13, 2004.

Moody, Thurmon Dean. "Nauvoo's Whistling and Whittling Brigade." *BYU Studies* 15 (Summer 1975), 480–90.

Morgan, Dale L. "Letters by Forty-niners Written from Great Salt Lake City in 1849." *Western Humanities Review* 3 (April 1949).

———, "The State of Deseret." Published in special issue of the *Utah Historical Quarterly* 8 (1940 for April, July, and October).

Mulder, William. "Scandinavian Saga," in Helen Z. Papanikolas, ed. *The Peoples of Utah*, 141–186. Salt Lake City: Utah State Historical Society, 1976.

Nash, John D. "The Salmon River Mission of 1855." *Idaho Yesterdays* 11 (Spring 1967) 22–31.

Nicholson, John. "The Lamanites," *The Juvenile Instructor* 9 (Nov. 7, 1874), 274–275, 291–292, 303.

Ogden, D. Kelly. "Two from Judah Ministering to Joseph." In H. Dean Garrett, ed., *Regional Studies in Latter-day Saint History: Illinois*. Brigham Young University: Department of Church History and Doctrine, 1995, 225–239.

"Parochial Schools Returns for 1824." In Fr. Martin Brenan, *Schools of Kildare and Leighlin*, 1935.

"Peter Robinson Settlers in Canada." In /www.geni.com/projects/Irish-Peter-Robinson- Settlers-Canada/2553.

Peterson, Paul H. "The Mormon Reformation of 1856–1857: The Rhetoric and the Reality." *Journal of Mormon History* 15 (1989), 59–88.

Porter, Larry C. and Milton V. Backman, Jr. "Doctrine and the Temple in Nauvoo." *BYU Studies* 32 (Winter/Spring 1992), 41–56.

Pratt, Louisa Barnes. "Journal of Louisa Barnes Pratt," *Heartthrobs of the West* 8 (1947), 189–244.

Pratt, Mitchell O. "Contexts for the Murder of Parley P. Pratt." *Pioneer* 62 (Number 3, 2015): 37–46.

Prince, Carl E. "The Great 'Riot Year': Jacksonian Democracy and Patterns of Violence in 1834." *Journal of the Early Republic* 5 (Spring 1985), 1–19.

Quinn, D. Michael. "The Council of Fifty and Its Members." *BYU Studies* 20 (Winter 1980), 163–197.

———, "The Mormon Succession Crisis of 1844." *BYU Studies* 16:2 (Winter 1976), 187–233.

"Richard Erastus Egan." *LDS Biographical Encyclopedia*, 1:816.

Robertson, Margaret C., "The Campaign and the Kingdom: The Activity of the Electioneers in Joseph Smith's Presidential Campaign." *Brigham Young University Studies* #3, 2000, 147–80.

Robinson, Peter. "Details of Peter Robinson's Transport of Emigrants to Canada," posted on DIPPAM's "Irish Immigration Database," DIPPAM stands for "Documenting Ireland: Parliament, People and Migration." Internet address: dippam.ac.uk/ied/records/24947.

Simmons, Rachel. "Journal of Rachel Emma Woolley Simmons." *Heartthrobs of the West* 11 (1950), 153–208.

Stapley, Jonathan A. and Kristine Wright. "'They Shall Be Made Whole': A History of Baptism for Health." *Journal of Mormon History*, Fall 2008, 69–112.

Stowers, Robert E. and John M. Ellis, eds. "Charles A. Scott's Diary of the Utah Expedition, 1857–1861." *Utah Historical Quarterly* 28 (1960), 175–176.

Townley, John M. "Stalking Horse for the Pony Express: The Chorpenning Mail Contracts between California and Utah, 1851–1860." *Arizona and the West* 24 (Autumn 1982), 229–252.

Walker, Ronald W. "A Banner is Unfurled: Mormonism's Ensign Peak." *Dialogue: A Journal of Mormon Thought* 26:4 (Winter 1993), 71–91.

———, "Seeking the 'Remnant': The Native American During Joseph Smith's Period." *Journal of Mormon History* 19 (Spring 1993), 1–33.

Warthen, Robert Lee. "The United States v. Howard Egan: The First Murder Trial in Utah Territory." Paper presented at the Sunstone Symposium, Salt Lake City, August 12, 1993.

Watson, Elden J. "The Nauvoo Tabernacle." *BYU Studies* 19 (Spring 1979), 416–421.

Whitney, Helen Mar Kimball. "Our Travels Beyond the Mississippi." *Woman's Exponent* 12 (1884–5), 102–3, 110–11, 117–18, 126–27, 135–36, 161–62, 170, 182, 86; and 13 (1885–6), 2, 10, 18, 49, 50, 58, 65–66, 75, 87, 91.

Woods, Fred E. "The Arrival of Nineteenth-Century Mormon Emigrants in Salt Lake City." In *Salt Lake City: The Place Which God Prepared*, ed. Scott C. Esplin and Kenneth L. Alford. Provo, UT: Religious Studies Center, Brigham Young University; Salt Lake City: Deseret Book, Salt Lake City, 2011.

Wright, Dennis A. and Rebekah E. Westrup. "Ensign Peak: A Historical Review." In *Salt Lake City: The Place Which God Prepared*, ed. Scott C. Esplin and Kenneth L. Alford. Provo, UT: Religious Studies Center, Brigham Young University and Deseret Book, Salt Lake City, 2011, 27–46.

Wright, Norman E. "The Mormon Pioneer Odometers." *BYU Studies* 37:1 (1997–1998), 83–115.

Young, Lorenzo Dow. "Diary of Lorenzo Dow Young." *Utah Historical Quarterly* 14 (1946), 132–170.

Young, S. Dilworth. "The Seventies: A Historical Perspective." *Ensign* 6 (July 1976): 14–21.

Unpublished Manuscripts at LDS Church History Library/Archives Salt Lake City, Utah

Badger, Louisa Adeline Ashby Noble. "A Sketch of the Life of Susan Hammond Ashby Noble," MS 7755.

Ball, William L. Journal. Microfilm of holograph, MS 21264.

Bullock, Thomas. Minutes.

Camp of Israel Manuscript 1848 and First 100, schedule. 1848 July. In Camp of Israel schedules and reports 1845–1849. MS 14290, Box 2, folder 25.

Cumming, Alfred Cumming. Letter, Salt Lake City, Utah, May 12, 1858. MS 14659.

Cummings, James. "James A. Cummings, A journal of the travels by Pres. B Young and Company... to Fort Limhi in Oregon Territory, April 24, 1857." CR 1234 1, Box 73, fd 2, Reel 85.

Clegg, Ann. Autobiographical Sketch of Ann Lewis Clegg" [ca. 1911].

Cummings, James Willard. Diaries, vol. 3. Microfilm of holograph.

Davis, Daniel. Diaries. Available digitally on line.

Egan, Richard E. Correspondence, microfilm copy, MS 14149.
First Council of Seventy. Minutes and Genealogy Book B. Microfilm
Forney, Jacob. Letterbooks, MS 14278.
Hancock, Levi Ward. Journal.
Hancock, Mosiah. "The Life Story of Mosiah Hancock," typescript.
Hansen, Peter Olsen. Diary, 1849 Apr.-Aug.
Hansen, Peter Olsen. "Autobiography of Peter O. Hansen."
_____, Diary, 1849 Apr.-Aug. MS 1437/2. In Journal History Aug. 7, 1849, 1–11.
_____, Journal [ca. 1876].
Mervin Booth Hogan, "The Vital statistics of Nauvoo Lodge," bound typescript, 1976. M230.91 H714v.
Jackman, Levi. Journal, March 1847 to March 1849. MS 12402.
Jacobs, Zebulon. Reminiscences and Diaries, 1861–1877, fd 1, 5–6.
Journal History of the Church. A daily history of The Church of Jesus Christ of Latter-day Saints from 1830 to 2008. It was taken mostly from newspapers but also from minutes and diary entries.
Kimball, Heber C. Journal, March 1846 to Feb. 1847. Kept by Peter Hansen. In Heber C. Kimball Papers.
Kimball, Heber C., Journal, June-Sep. 1848, in Heber C. Kimball, Papers, 1847–1866, reel 2, box 4, fd. 2 and fd. 3. [written by William Thompson]
Kimball, Heber C. Manuscript History of Second Division. 1848. Church Emigration Book. Also in Journal History of the Church, Sept. 24, 1848, 17–54.
Knight, Newel. Autobiography and Journal.
Lee, John D. Diary, 1844–46, typescript.
Miller, Jacob. "Salmon River Mission Journal." Original and typescript.
Monroe, James M. Letter to G. F. Carter, 9 Feb. 1851, in Wilford Woodruff Papers, Correspondence 1851, Box 6, Folder 20, Church History Library, MS 1352.
_____, Letter to Brigham Young. Fort Bridger, Sept. 16. 1851, in Brigham Young Papers. CR 1234/1 Box 69, fd 4. Restricted document, used by permission.
Nauvoo Baptismal Records, Original Record 1.
Nauvoo High Council Minutes.
Nauvoo Freemason Lodge, Minutes.
Nauvoo Relief Society Minutes.
Nauvoo Tax Records, 1842, 1843.

Nauvoo Trustee-in-Trust. Tithing Day Book B, 1842–1844.
Neibaur, Alexander. Journal, 1841–1862, Typescript, microfilm, MS 19986.
Palmer, James. Reminiscences.
Pratt, Orson Journal. "Interesting Items Concerning the Journeying of the Latter-day Saints from the City of Nauvoo, Until Their Location in the Valley of the Great Salt Lake (Extracted from the Private Journal of Orson Pratt)," published serially in the *Millennial Star* between Jan. 15 and June 15, 1850. Posted on the LDS Church Website: "Mormon Pioneer Overland Travel." 1847 Brigham Young Company accounts.
Presiding Bishopric. Minutes of Presiding Bishops Meetings with the Bishops.
Reese, Enoch. Private Journal Commencing June 1, 1849. MS d 7060.
Rich, Charles C. Diary, Vol 8., April 27 to May 6 1850. Microfilm of holograph.
Richards, Willard. Diaries. Typescript.
Rollins, James Henry. Reminiscences.
Salt Lake City Nineteenth Ward Records.
Salt Lake City Nineteenth Ward. Historical Record. LR 6092 2.
Simmons, Ora. "Life Sketch of Howard Egan." Typescript.
Smith, John. Diary Feb. 1846-May 1854. Microfilm of holograph.
Snow, Eliza R. Diary, 1846–48. Typescript.
Taylor, John. "Excerpts from the Journal of John Taylor, 5 June to 5 Aug. 1846." Typescript, 22 pages, in Brigham H. Roberts Papers.
Whitney, Horace K. Journal 1846. Typescript. Digital copy accessible by internet.
Whitaker, George. "The Life of George Whitaker: A Utah Pioneer." Typescript.
Woodward, William. Reminiscent Account. Posted on the LDS Church website, "Mormon Pioneer Overland Travel," for the 1851 John Reese Wagon Train. Published in the *Juvenile Instructor*, 15 July 1896, 415.
Young, Brigham. Letter to Howard Egan, City, Sept. 29, 1859. Brigham Young Letterbook 5, Brigham Young Papers.
Young, Brigham. Papers.

Egan Manuscripts in Western Americana Collection, Beinecke Rare Book and Manuscript Library, Yale University, New Haven, CT.

Egan, Howard. Journals. In Howard Egan Collection.
[Egan, Howard, Daybook]. "Unidentified 1855 Daybook with light pencil notations," Howard Egan Collection.
Egan, William M. Journal. William M. Egan Papers. WA MSS 185 and 160.

———, "Interesting reminiscence of the boyhood life of W. M. Egan in Salt Lake City from 1854–1863." Pencil written manuscript, 24 pp. William M. Egan Papers.

———, "W. M. Egan: Trip from Carson City in 1863." Small handwritten notebook in William M. Egan Papers.

———, "Native Utes of Utah." Typescript, 23 pp and original handwritten.

———, "Publishing 'Pioneering the West,' Letters and Documents."

Monroe, James M. Journal, 1841–1842 and 1845. Also a second version, basically a recopy of the first done by Monroe to make it more attractive. In the Howard Egan Collection. The LDS Church History Library has a microfilm copy, MS 8829, Item 5.

Manuscripts/Documents at Other Repositories

Egan, Byron N. Untitled sketch of his father, Richard Erastus Egan. Typescript, 2 pages. Copy in author's possession.

Byrne, Michael. "Some Members of the Egan Family of the Meelaghans, Tullamore Pioneers and Poets." Typescript, copy in author's file.

Camp of Israel (Iowa) Record of Organization and List of Members, 1846 and Mormon Battalion, Roster of "A" and "B" Companies, 1846, Family History Library. Digital copy of the original handwritten record book.

Clifton Mining District Recorder, Location Notices 1869–1938. Series 24331, reel 1, Utah Division of Archives and Records Service. 300 S. Rio Grande, Salt Lake City, UT.

Clifton District Recorder file Book C. Series 24331, reel 1, 42. Utah Division of Archives and Records Service.

Clifton Mining District (Utah) Recorder. Miners' Meeting Minutes. Series 24163, reel 1, microfilm of holograph notebook. Utah Division of Archives and Records Service.

Dsomhnaill, Eamonn. "The Townlands of Offaly," in *Ireland's Own* (Summer Annual, 1988), photocopy in possession of the author.

Egan, Edward. Letter to Richard Egan. Meelaghans, Tullamore, Ireland, Feb. 19, 1900. Typescript. Copy in author's files.

Egan, Howard. Letter to Brigham Young, 20 Sept. 1845, original in L. Tom Perry Special Collections, Lee Library, Brigham Young University, Vault MSS 192.

Egan, Howard. Trial Records. "1851: People vs. Egan, Series 25011, Box 2, file 9." Utah State Archives.

Egan, Howard. Trial Records. "United States vs. Howard Egan, Murder Case, A True Bill, Daniel Spencer, foreman, Witnesses: G C Robbins, Wm Horner, James Wade, Moore, Utah State Archives #1533, TU-1, 03.18, p. 125–127.

Egan, Howard. Trial Records. "The United States vs. Howard Egan, On Presentment of US Grand Jury for Murder," Utah State Archives, Box A96A1, #61–3, 1533, TJ-1 03.18.

Egan, Tamson. Interrogatory. Photocopy of original, in author's possession. In the Egan Trial Papers at the Utah State Archives.

Gardner, Hamilton. "Pioneer Military Leaders of Utah," 952 typescript, Special Collections Library, University of Utah.

Hascall, Ursula. Letter of Ursula B. Hastings Hascall to Col. Wilson Andrews, April 1847, typescript, Utah State Historical Society, MSS a 290.

Hicks, George A. "History of Spanish Fork,", typescript, Special Collections, Harold B. Lee Library, Brigham Young University. This history was dated by its author June 13, 1913.

Huntington, William. "Diaries of William Huntington," typescript, BYU Library, Provo, Utah.

Kane, Elizabeth W. Journal, June 29, 1857 to Aug 8, 1858. Thomas L. and Elizabeth W. Kane Collection, Box 26, folder 10, L. Tom Perry Special Collections Library, BYU. MSS 792.

Killeigh Parish Records, Diocese of Kildare, King's County (Offaly), Ireland, Baptisms 1808–1823, Marriages 1808–1932, Deaths 1808–1835. LDS Family History Library. Film 990092.

Morgan, Nicolas G., comp. "Pioneer Map of Great Salt Lake City," printed, poster size, no date but sometime in the 1950s. Author's own copy.

Johnson, Mary Jane E. "Short Life Story of David Egan," Typescript, 5 pp., copy in author's files.

Nauvoo Legion. Record of Provo Military 8 District Command, Nauvoo Legion, 1857–1858. Copied 1948–53 by BYU Library. Copy at Utah State Historical Society.

Nauvoo Legion. Record of Orders, Returns, and Court Martial & C of 2nd Brigade, 1st Division, Nauvoo legion, copy BYU April 1946, is record of Nauvoo Legion, Headquarters, 14th Ward, GSLC, July 1857. Utah State Historical Society.

Pace, James. Diary, 1846, photostat. Huntington Library, San Marino, California.

Randall, Sally, to Dear Father and Mother, 3 Oct.1847. Typescript, Iowa State Historical Society, Des Moines, Iowa.

Revolutionary War Rolls. State Papers of New Hampshire, Vol. 1. New Hampshire Revolutionary War Rolls, Vols. 5 and 11.
Robinson, Peter. Report. http://www.geni.com/projects/Irish-Peter-Robinson-Settlers-Canada/2553.
United States. "Certified Contract with Overland Mail Company, March 12, 1861; Senate Executive Document 21, 46th Congress, 3rd Session," pp. 7–8.
United States. Brigadier General's Office to Col. W. B. Pace, August 13, 1857, Military Records, Reel 25. Utah State Archives.
United States. Utah Territory 1850–51 Census, MS 2672, Reel 1, Church History Library.
"United States vs. Howard Egan, Murder Case, A True Bill, Daniel Spencer, foreman, Witnesses: G C Robbins, Wm Horner, James Wade, Moore," Utah State Archives #1533, TU-1, 03.18.
"The United States vs. Howard Egan, On Presentment of US Grand Jury for Murder." Utah State Archives, Box A96A1, #61–3, 1533, TJ-1 03.18.
Whitney, Newel K. Papers. L. Tom Perry Special Collections, Lee Library, BYU. Vault MSS 76 Series 3, Item 2, Box 3, folder 2, on-line accessible.

Newspapers and Periodicals

Black, Susan Easton, ed. *The Best of the Frontier Guardian*. Provo and Salt Lake City: BYU Studies and Univ. of Utah Press, 2009. Includes a DVD-ROM of all 81 issues.
Jenson, Andrew. *Historical Record*. Salt Lake City, LDS Church, 1882–1890.
Davis County Clipper
Deseret Evening News
Journal of Discourses (Liverpool: Albert Carrington, 1875)
Millennial Star
Nauvoo Neighbor
Salem Observer
Times and Seasons

Theses and Dissertations

Baumgarten, James N. "The Role and Function of the Seventies in L.D.S. Church History." Thesis, Brigham Young Univ., 1960.
Bluth, John Frederick. "Confrontation with an Arid Land: The Incursion of Gosiutes and Whites into Utah's Central West Desert, 1800–1978."

Dissertation, Brigham Young Univ., 1978.
Drake, J. Raman, "Howard Egan: Frontiersman, Pioneer and express Rider." Thesis, Brigham Young Univ., 1956.
Hansen, Ralph. "Administrative History of the Nauvoo Legion in Utah." Thesis, Brigham Young Univ., 1954.
Peterson, Paul H. "The Mormon Reformation." Dissertation, Brigham Young Univ., 1981.
Pugh, Byron G. "History of Utah-California Wagon Freighting." Thesis, Univ. of California at Berkeley, 1949, microfilm, Harold B. Lee Library, BYU.
Yurtinus, John Frank George. "A Ram in the Thicket: The Mormon Battalion in the Mexican War." 2 vols. Dissertation, Brigham Young Univ., 1975.

Family Sources

Allebest, Elayne Stanton. "Howard Egan's Irish Heritage." Paper presented at the Howard Egan Symposium, June 12, 2015. Email copy in author's possession dated Oct. 14, 2015.
Billings, Bryce. "Mary Ann Tuttle Egan/Billings/Gardner/Billings." Typescript, 1 page, copy in author's file.
"Mary Jane Egan Johnson, Personal History," Typescript, 9 pp. In Janet Sloan's files.
Mary Jane Egan Johnson, "Howard Egan." Typescript, Egan Family Archives, 6.
Mac Hale, Conor. "The Mac Egan Inheritance." *Annals of the Clan Egan*, Chap. 7, 57.
Hennessy, James to Robert and Janet Sloan, June 6, 1991. Copy in author's file.
Knudson, Adele Newman. "A Brief History of the Family of Howard Egan and Anne Meath of Tullamore, Offaly (formerly Kings), Ireland." Posted at Bushelsofwheat.com
Offaly County Historical Society to Karen Stoddard, Salt Lake City. Undated. In possession of Elayne Allebest.
Simmons, Ora. "Life Sketch of Howard Egan." Typewritten, Salt Lake City, 1956.

Index

A
Adams, Barnabus   176
Adams, Orson B.   97
Adams Express Company   334
adoption, priesthood type   81, 85, 121
Agan, Thomas Howard
alcohol/liquor   20, 47, 70, 80, 120, 126, 143, 241, 472
Alexander, Edmund, Col.   315
Allen, James, Capt.   106–108, 110–111, 117
Allen, John C.   405
Alley, George   42
Anderson, LeRoy   426
Angel, Truman   265
Angel's Camp   235
Antelope Canyon   373
Argenta, NV   409–410
Arkansas River   114–116, 122
Arnold, Josiah   54
Ash Hollow   151, 210–211
Ashby, Nathaniel   37–38
Atchison, KS   377, 379, 387, 393, 395–396, 399
Atchison Co., MO   105, 207
Auburn, CA   234, 244, 247, 293, 295

B
Backenstos, Jacob   73
Badger, Rodney   265
Bagley, Will   xix, 313, 479
Baird, Robert   138, 171
Ball, Lafayette   440, 442, 448
Ball, William L.   448–450
Bankhead, George   192
Bankhead, John H.   192
Bankhead slaves   192
Bannock Indians   310, 320, 367, 374
Baptism   3, 7, 36, 48, 55, 310, 440
Barney, A. H.   xix, 3, 19, 394
Barnstead, NH   28–30, 428
Barrington, NH   29–30
Bartholomew, Willis   186–187
Bateman, Ronald R.   438, 471

Bean, George Washington 296
Bear River Massacre 401–403
Beckwith, Edward G. 296, 298, 302
Beecher, Maureen 134
Beinecke Library, Yale Univ. xviii, 139, 225, 292, 461, 472
Benallack, Henry 20
Benicia, CA 293
Benedict, K. D., Dr. 446
Benson, Ezra T. 96, 164, 168–170, 175, 201–202, 204–205
Bernhisel, John 187–189, 327
"Big Company" 176
Big Mountain 165–167, 175, 198, 213
Big Sandy River 176
Bigler, David 310
Bigler, Henry 218, 235, 244
Billings, George V. 146, 162, 175, 193
Billings, Titus 191, 274, 419, 454–455
Bills, John 232, 236
Bills, William 244
Binley, John 438
Bitter Creek Route 395
Black, Jeremiah S. 339,
Blair, Seth M. 266
Blodgett, Edgar 285–286
Bonaparte, IA 93
Bordeaux, Mr. 155, 178
Boulware's Ferry 206
Bowles, Samuel 398, 407
Boyd Station 381
Brady, Lewis 350–352
Brailey, Jessee 188
Brandebury, Lemuel H. 263
Brannan, Samuel 162
Brocchus, Perry E. 263
Brooklyn, ship 162
Brooks, Juanita 112, 261, 469
Brower, A. C. 265
Brown, Aaron 336, 350
Brown, James, Capt. 120–121, 233–236, 242, 244
Brown, James S. 229, 236–237, 317
Brower, A. C. 489
Bryant, Hyrum K. 37, 44
Buchanan, James (President) 314, 322, 335, 338, 388
buffalo 38, 77, 115, 117, 123, 143, 145–146, 148, 150, 158, 160, 177, 179, 187, 190, 195, 210, 287, 397, 472
Bullock, Thomas 197, 325

Burns' Diggings 237–238, 241
Burr, David 314
Burr, Frederick 310, 312
Burton, Richard 346, 372, 374–376, 390
Burton, Robert T. 310, 317, 321, 425–426, 470, 481
Butte Station 365, 370, 376, 380
Butterfield, John 336
Butterfield Overland Mail 336, 394
Buzby, Joseph 265
Byron, WY 457

C
Cable Creek, NE 206
Cain, Joseph 247, 249, 284
Cajon Pass 222, 226
California Trail xvii, 248–250, 283, 286–288, 291, 295, 301, 333–334, 336–337, 367
Call, Anson 75,
Callao/Willow Springs 299, 363, 365, 374–375, 381, 404–405, 423
Cattle drives to Calif. 284, 290, 312, 477
Cattle brands 413, 475
Camp Creek, IL 71–72
Camp Crittenden 396, 400
Camp Douglas 400–401, 419
Camp Floyd 329–331, 343, 345–346, 348, 350, 358, 363, 365, 367–368, 374, 382, 396, 401
Camp of Israel 79, 85, 89–90, 92, 96–99, 102–103, 115, 132–133, 142, 145, 154–155, 161, 164, 221, 480
Camp Scott 318–320, 322–325, 329
Camp Winfield 318
Cannon, George Q. 220, 227, 235, 244, 246, 320, 447
Cannon, Kenneth, Jr. 268
Carns, Daniel 55
Carrington, Albert 170
Carson City, NV 246, 255, 346, 356–357, 362, 365, 373, 389, 394, 398, 418–420, 423, 476
Carson Pass xviii, 246, 248, 294–295
Carter, Mr., merchant 256, 264
Carthage, IL 60–61, 64, 71–73
Case, James 490
Caverly, Philip 30
Central Overland California and
  Pikes Peak Express Company 355, 377
Central Pacific Railroad 409–410, 433
Central route/trail 292, 295–296, 298, 304, 330–331, 335–336, 338, 348, 352, 354–355, 372, 376–377, 387, 390, 394, 409–410, 431, 469, 476, 480

Chambly, ship   8–10
Chariton River   95
Charles Redd Center for Western Studies   xix, 484
Cherry Creek, NV   483
Chimney Rock   151–152, 179, 191–192, 211, 325
Chisholm, Joseph (ropemaker)   32
Cho-kup, chief   346–347
cholera   20, 207–208, 217, 246, 446
Chorpenning, Frank   337, 341
Chorpenning, George, Jr.   284, 330, 333–334, 336, 339, 349, 352, 423, 467, 478, 480
Cimarron River   21, 117, 122,
City Creek   167, 170, 172, 174, 280
City of Rocks   250, 286
Civil War   257, 313, 331, 376–377, 386–388, 408–409, 445
Clark, Hiram   75, 120, 163, 204, 246
Clawson, Catherine   84
Clawson, Rudger   454
Clawson, Zephaniah   84, 255, 491
Clayton, William   70, 84, 89, 92, 96, 98–99, 138–139, 149, 170, 173, 222, 465, 475, 481
Clifton Mining District   433–434, 438
Cloud, Jeremiah, Major   117, 121
Cloward, Thomas   173
Coe, William Robertson   465
Coe Collection, Yale Univ.   465
Colbourn, Norris   122,
Colfax, Schuyler   407
Coloma, CA   229, 234–235
Commings, A. G., Rev.   36–37
Compromise of 1850   251
Connor, Patrick   401, 423, 432
Conover, Peter   186, 320
Cooke, Philip St. George   118, 120, 319
Coon, Libbeus T.   491
Cosumnes River   294
Cottonwood Springs   226
Council Bluffs, IA   99, 103, 105–107, 110, 201, 203, 325
Council Grove, KS   113–114, 123
Council of Fifty   57, 75, 132
Coward, Dr.   286
coyotes   346, 416–418
Crandall, Jared   337–338, 347, 351
crickets   156, 190, 193, 196, 200, 215, 328
Crosby, Nancy   192

Cumming, Alfred   314, 319, 322–327, 329, 331
Cunningham, Andrew   426, 435
Cushing, James A.   449–450
Cushing, Hosea   138, 148, 151, 174–175

D
Dana, Lewis   76
Davies, J. Kenneth   246
Davis, Daniel   183, 185, 197, 199
Death Valley   220, 222, 226
Deep Creek   21, 250, 279, 295, 298, 344, 347–350, 358, 364–365, 368–371, 373–375, 389, 395–396, 401–406, 411–413, 415–416, 418–424, 428, 430, 432–433, 435–440, 442, 448, 450, 452–453, 455, 457–459, 466, 469, 471, 473–476, 478, 480, 482
Deep Creek ranch described   419–421
Deming, Minor   64
Deseret, state of   251, 257, 263, 268
Deseret News printing press   206
Devil's Gate   158–160, 195
Diamond Springs   294, 364–365, 369, 378, 420, 440
Digby, Lord Edward   3
Dobson, Thomas   358
Doniphan, Alexander, Gen.   119–120
Donner Party   137, 163, 219, 234
Doty, James Duane   406
Douglas, Stephen A.   39, 314
Douglass, Ralph   175
Dowling, James (priest)   7
Drake, J. Raman   xvii, 301
Drummond, W. W.   314
Dugway   343, 363, 365, 419
Dunham, Jonathan   53–55, 64
Dutch Mountain   432–433, 435–436, 438

E
Earl, Jesse   371
Eberstadt, Edward   465
Echo Canyon   164–165, 198, 202, 213, 260, 317–319, 323, 329
Eddy, William H.   234
Edwards, Franklin   205, 234
Egan, Ann   451
Egan, Anne Meath   2–3, 6, 8, 11
Egan, Bernard (Barney)   2, 3, 19, 75, 456
Egan, Catherine (Mrs. Ransom)   20, 418, 335
Egan, Edward   2, 13, 19, 456

Egan, Eliza (Higgins)   3, 19–20
Egan, Emma, wife of Ira Ernest   453, 459
Egan, Evelina   3, 8, 10, 19
Egan, Helen Jeanette   174, 180, 183–184, 200, 202, 204, 208, 213, 215–216
Egan, Horace Adelbert   173, 180–181, 193, 195, 200, 216, 492
Egan, Howard, Jr.   (selected topics shown below; for other topics, see the specific references listed throughout this index)
   barn fire   281–282
   baptism   3, 7, 37–38
   death   448–451
   diary 1847   xviii, 21, 138–139, 148–149, 165–166, 168, 465
   diary 1849–50   xviii, 205, 222, 465
   diary 1855   xviii, 465
   Gosiute mission   441–442
   mining claims   433–437
   murder trial   263–274, 467
   wounded at Elkhorn   186–189
Egan, Howard, Sr.   2, 4, 6, 8–11, 13–14, 17–18
Egan, Howard R. (Ransom)   xix, 20, 32, 38, 42–44, 74, 87, 90, 99–101, 103–104, 127, 134, 136, 178, 180, 185, 188–191, 195, 198–201, 214–216, 246, 252, 273, 275, 277–279, 281–283, 285, 289–291, 298–300, 304–307, 324, 328–329, 335, 341, 352, 354, 358–359, 378–381, 398–400, 403–404, 406, 412–413, 415–416, 418, 423–424, 428, 430, 433–434, 436–437, 452–455, 464, 476–478, 482
Egan, Hyrum William   246, 252, 415, 419, 421–422, 455, 458–459, 492,
Egan, Ira Ernest   411–412, 428, 431, 442, 453, 455, 457, 459
Egan, John   3, 13, 18–20, 45
Egan, Mary Ann   185, 216, 246, 252, 273–274, 279, 384, 412, 415, 419, 454–455, 458
Egan, Mary   20
Egan, Richard   181, 335, 456
Egan, Richard Erastus (Ras)   xix, 25, 37, 252, 290, 309, 354, 358–359, 370–371, 379, 382–385, 406, 411–413, 415, 419, 424, 428–430, 437, 448, 456–457, 459–460
Egan, Tamson   xvii, 26–30, 32, 35, 37, 39–41, 44–47, 49, 52–53, 58–61, 63–64, 69–70, 74, 77–78, 83–85, 87–90, 94–95, 98, 100, 103, 106, 112, 123–127, 130, 133–136, 143–144, 146–147, 172–173, 179–180, 183–186, 189–190, 192, 195, 198–201, 213–216, 246, 251–253, 255–257, 259, 262, 265, 269, 273–276, 279–280, 282, 284, 286, 290–291, 309, 322, 325, 327, 371, 411–412, 419, 428–431, 437, 440, 442, 444, 447, 452–454, 456–461, 468, 471–473, 475–477
Egan, William M.   21, 252, 459, 465
Egan, Vilate Louise   252, 273–274, 449,
Egan Canyon   345, 365, 373–374, 376, 380, 386–387, 399, 420, 432, 482–483
Egan Canyon Mining District   432

Egan Creek   482–483
Egan family reunion   485
Egan homes (Howard/Tamson)   42, 125–126, 442
Egan 100th anniversary   462
Egan 200th anniversary   484
Egan name in western landscape
    Egan Peak   483
    Egan Range   483
    Egan Station   376, 412–413, 483
    Egan Trail   292, 296, 337, 339, 343, 346, 348, 391, 476, 480
Eight Mile Station   403–404, 419, 422
El Camino Real   227, 229, 235
electioneering 1844   56–58
Elmer, Elijah   206
Emigration Canyon   166, 171, 199, 214, 278, 484
Emmet, James   76
Endowment House   384, 454, 457
Enfield, Jack   426
Ensign Peak   169–170, 280
Everett, Addison   138

F
Fairfield, UT   331
Famine of 1856   303, 306
Farmington, IA   93
Fasting, Fast Days   49, 214
Faust, Henry J. "Doc"   494
Faust Station   380, 396, 400, 404
Felt, D. P.   458
Ferril, William   175
Ferris, Cornelia   285
Ferris, H. G.   73, 469
Ferry, ferrying   70, 80, 87, 89, 99, 106, 112–113, 123, 131, 140, 155–158, 162, 178, 185, 187–188, 195, 206, 211, 214, 238, 310
Ficklin, Benjamin F.   319–320, 355–356, 482
Finney, W. W.   355–356
fish, fishing   81, 215, 280, 306, 310
Fish Springs   340, 343–344, 348, 365, 374, 381, 419
Fisher, John   403, 415
Fisher, Mary Ann (Minnie)   370, 384, 411–412, 418, 429–430, 456–457
Fisher, William F. (Billy)   370, 383
Flake, James   227
Flake, James M., company   220
Florence, NE   183, 324–327
Floyd, John B.   331, 374

Follett, King   50
Foot, Mr.   225–226
Ford, Thomas (governor)   65, 73, 86
Forney, Jacob   314, 339, 347, 349, 478
Fort Bridger   162–163, 176, 197–198, 214, 259, 285–286, 316–318, 321, 332, 357, 371, 400–401
Fort Churchill   365, 373, 376
Fort Hall   163, 310, 406, 439
Fort Laramie/Fort John   140, 153–155, 161–162, 175, 178, 193, 211, 315, 321, 324, 386, 395
Fort Leavenworth   107, 111–113, 123, 130, 257, 315
Fort Limhi   303, 309–311, 318, 320, 478, 481
Fort Kearny   207–209, 211, 324, 376, 386, 397
Fort Kearney (Old)   205–207
Fort Supply   317
Forty Mile Desert   248, 300, 341
Fox, Jesse W.   323
Fremont, John C.   75, 81, 150, 286, 314
Frontier Guardian   204, 261
Fuller, Frank   425–426

G
Gamble, James   386
Garden Grove, IA   100–103, 112
Gardner, Walter Elias   455
Georgetown, CA   293, 295
Gheen, John   123
Gheen, Levy   127
Gibbons, Andrew   157, 172, 175
Gold, gold rush   xvii–xviii, 21, 35, 121, 141, 204–207, 209, 211, 213, 215–218, 220–221, 227, 229, 234–235, 237–239, 241–248, 251–252, 255, 259–261, 273, 276, 278, 291, 293–294, 302, 316, 325, 334, 358, 361, 420, 422, 432, 435–438, 469, 471, 474, 476–477, 480–481, 483
gold mining missionaries   220–221, 234, 244
Golding, Robert   279
Goodyear, Miles   164, 219
Goose Creek   250, 286, 298, 334, 459
Gosiute Indians   347, 349, 375, 402–404, 406, 419, 432, 440–441, 467, 471
Gosiute War, Treaty   406
Graham, James   206
Grand Island, NE   208–209
Granger, Fayette   225, 246–247
Grant, George   84, 177
Grant, Jedediah M.   261, 271
Grant, Ulysses S.   445

Grantsville, UT   349, 375, 413, 423, 427, 435, 438, 440
Grass Valley, CA   293
grasshoppers   303–304, 310
Gravelly Ford   250, 288, 297, 337, 348, 390
Great Salt Lake   66, 81, 85, 138, 152–154, 160–161, 164–169, 174, 180–181, 183–184, 193, 198–201, 216, 219, 243, 250, 255, 257, 261, 264, 276, 279, 286, 295, 297, 299, 302, 304, 307, 317, 324, 334, 337, 350, 374, 449, 473–474, 480
Great Salt Lake City   174, 181, 199–200, 216, 219, 250, 255, 261, 276, 279, 299, 324, 374
Great Salt Lake Desert   337
Great Salt Lake Valley   66, 85, 152–154, 160, 165–168, 180–181, 183–184, 193, 198, 201, 219, 243, 307, 317, 449, 473, 480
Greeley, Horace   347, 390–391
Green River   162, 197, 213, 395
Greene, John Y.   335
Groesbeck, Nicholas   325
Gully, Samuel   121–123, 126
Gunnison, John W.   296

H
Hafen, LeRoy R.   222, 388
Hamblin, Jacob   224, 470–471
Hancock, Levi   39, 63–65, 73, 77, 118–119, 121, 469
Handcart companies, emigrants   39, 63–65, 73, 77, 118–119, 121, 469
Hanks, Ephraim   316, 470–471
Hansen, Hans C.   158, 174
Hansen, Peter Olsen   102, 104, 109–110, 127, 205–213, 234, 247
Hambleton, Madison   258, 260
Harmon, Appleton   53, 69, 150, 183
Harold's Club Casino   301
Harper, Charles   141, 143
Harper, Hank   403
Harriman, Henry   192
Harte, Bret   235, 358
Hastings Cutoff   287, 295
Hawley, Charles L.   378
Haws, Peter   97–98, 100, 297, 299
Hendricks, James   279
Hensley (Salt Lake) Cutoff   250
Hernandez Springs   226
Heywood, Joseph L.   263–265
Hickerson, George   241, 244
Hickman, Bill   332
Higbee, Isaac   191

Higbee, John S.   155
Higgins, Adam   20
Higgins, Nelson, Capt.   116
High priests   62–63, 74
Hildreth, Reuben   206
Hill, Walter   455, 460
Hockaday, John M.   338
Hoit/Hoyt, G. H.   206
Holden, Edwin   175
Holister's Mill   183
Holladay, Ben   282, 340, 387, 391, 395–396, 398–400, 406, 408
Holladay Overland Mail Express Co.   408
Holladay and Warner Company   288–289
Holt, Joseph   350
Horner, William (W. G.)   256, 264
Hornets   171–172
Horseshoe Creek   156, 196
Hoover-Gruwell-Derr Company   220
Houston, Isaac   204
Hudson, Wilford   349, 369
Huffaker, Simpson Company   221, 227, 246
Hughes, William   272
Hughes, Bela   394
Humboldt River   249–250, 288, 291, 295–296, 300, 302, 337, 344, 346, 348, 391, 409, 440, 480
Hunt, Jefferson   110–111, 116–117, 219–220, 227–228, 241, 244, 246–247, 337
Hunt-Baxter Company   220
Hunter, Jesse, Capt.   117
Huntington, Dimick   424
Huntington, Lot   338, 340, 344, 358, 400
Huntington, Oliver B.   296, 320
Huntress, Tamsin   27, 30
Hurst, Frederick William   363–364
Hutchinson, Jacob   94, 265

I
Ibapah, UT   349–350, 365, 375, 413, 439–440, 442, 473, 482–483
Independence Rock   158–159, 195, 212, 400
Ingalls, E. S.   249
Ireland   xviii, 1–4, 6–10, 13, 16–18, 22, 26, 29, 52, 388, 405, 456, 459, 466, 473, 475
    Cork   8–9, 226
    Killeigh Parish   3, 7
    Kings County   2, 4, 13
    Meelaghans   1–3, 7–8, 11, 13
    Tullamore   1–4, 6–7, 11, 29, 52, 388, 456

Irish, prejudice against the United States   29
Irvine, John K.   412, 454
Irvine, Marie   288, 297

J
Jack, James   84, 449
Jackman, Levi   146, 158
Jacobs, Zebulon   199
Jarvis, Robert   344, 349
Johnson, Benjamin   66
Johnson, Philo   138
Johnston, Albert Sidney (General)   315, 318, 343, 367
Jones, Frederick   207, 211–212
Jones, Nathaniel V.   212, 321
Jones, Russell, and Company   353
Jones, Samantha   213
Jordan River   279, 305–306, 329
Judah, Jewish   52

K
Kane, Elizabeth Kent   326–327, 466, 473
Kane, Thomas L.   106, 110, 181, 184, 322, 324–325, 332, 481
Kanesville, IA   181–184, 200–206, 209, 218, 221, 254–256, 261, 282, 325, 482
Kanesville post office petition   254
Kay, John   67, 70, 100, 324
Kearny, Stephen Watts   107
Keosauqua   93–94
Kimball, Ellen Sanders   138
Kimball, Heber C.   49, 51, 59, 66, 74, 77, 81, 84–85, 91, 94, 97, 103–104, 109, 112, 125, 127, 131, 138, 144, 169, 185, 189, 200, 208, 214, 251, 255–256, 276, 304–305, 322, 443, 467, 471, 481
Kimball, Helen Mar   67, 468
Kimball, Hiram   335
Kimball, Phineas   246
Kimball, Stanley   186
Kimball, Vilate   85
Kimball, William   126, 132, 186, 197, 256, 266, 321–324
King, William   142, 158, 173, 175–177
Kinkead, John Henry   282, 290, 302
Kinney, John J.   425–426
Klingonsmith, Hannah   212
Knowlton, John Q.   324

L
Lackey's Ferry   131
Las Vegas Springs   224–225

Lathrop, Asahel   219, 245–246, 248, 250
Law, William   36, 49, 54–55, 59
Lawson, Thurston   175
Lee, John D.   21, 53, 85, 104, 109, 111–112, 116, 125, 185, 189, 195, 445, 469, 475, 480–481
Lewis, Tarlton   138
Limhi River   310
Lion House   444–445
Little, Jesse C.   61, 107

Liverton, John   403
Livingston, I. M.   282
Livingston and Kinkead   282–283, 295, 467
Lockhart, John   192
Lockhart, Margaret   192
Locust Creek   98, 100
Los Angeles   219, 222, 227–228, 334, 336, 459, 476
Loup Fork River   144, 189
Lynch, Patrick   426
Lyman, Amasa   49, 59, 76, 124, 138, 172, 218, 220, 222, 235, 242–246, 471
Lytle, Andrew   69

M
Mace, Wandle   67
Macedonia, IA   64, 66–67
Majors, Alexander   355, 361, 387
Malad River, Valley   250, 290, 440
Mandan riverboat   184–185
"Mantle of Joseph"   61
Marcy, Randolph, Capt.   319
Margetts, Richard   279
Mariposa, CA   235, 237–238, 241, 243–244, 247
Markham, Stephen   67, 96, 138, 142, 145, 151, 176
Marks, William   49, 55, 106, 262, 376, 395, 451
Marshall, James   218, 235
Martin, James   xvii, 187, 307, 438, 466
Masonry, Masonic Hall   35–36, 48, 51–52, 74, 67–70, 80
Matthews, Isaac   204
McCulloch, Ben   329
McFarlin, Solen   205
McGraw, William   314, 335
McLane, Lewis   394
MacKinnon, William   322, 331, 469
McKown, Francis   192
McKown, Jane   197

McKune, Theodore, sheriff   444
McLean, Hector   272
Meeks, William   205
Merced River   234, 236–238, 243
Mexican War   106–107, 322
Miles, S.B.   336
Miller, George, bishop   90, 92
Miller's Hollow, IA   180–181, 184
Mississippi River   38–39, 48, 88, 91, 206, 336
Mississippi Saints   115, 170, 191, 197
Missouri River   75–76, 92, 99, 105–107, 109, 112, 123, 125, 127, 130–131, 135,
    180–181, 184, 197, 206, 208, 214, 256, 282, 295, 303, 322, 325, 333,
    335, 392, 406, 409
Monroe, James Madison   53, 252–255, 258, 260–261, 263–265, 273–274,
    276–277, 282, 419, 457–458, 469, 476
Monroe, Rebecca Reese   253
Monroe, Ruth Amelia Rose   255
Monroe, William   254
Montrose, IA   39–41, 75, 87, 93
Moore, George   xix, 264, 266
Morley's Settlement   64, 70, 72
Morrisites, Morrisite War   424–426, 469
Mormon Bar, CA   218, 235, 238, 241, 243
Mormon Battalion   xvii, 21, 109–110, 112, 115, 127, 162, 217–219, 241, 244,
    246, 248, 291, 297, 318, 469, 480
Mormon Gold (book)   218, 245
Monterrey River   233
Montreal   xvii, 8–10, 12, 14–20, 22, 25–26, 29, 32, 37, 297, 456
Mother Lode   234
Mott, Gordon   403
Mt. Pisgah   102–103
Mt. Tambora, East Indies   6
Mountain Meadows   222, 224, 317, 320, 321, 445
Mountain Meadows Massacre   317, 321, 445
"Move South"   323, 328–329
Mulliner, James   265
Mulliner's Mill   328
Murdock, John R.   324
Murdock, Sally   63

N
Napa, CA   294, 302
Napoleonic Wars   6–7, 23, 501
Native American spiritual outpourings   439–440
Nauvoo   xvii–xix, 18, 29, 34–35, 37–56, 58–78, 80, 82–92, 94, 96–98, 100,

102–103, 119, 128–129, 138, 169, 183, 192, 205, 252–255, 257, 259–260, 262, 274–275, 281, 310, 313, 315–317, 321–322, 331–332, 367, 445, 464, 466, 468–469, 471–472, 476, 484
   Charter 60, 65
   City Council 59–60, 67
   constable 53, 65–66
   police 52, 64, 87, 469
   Temple 38, 77, 82–84, 471
   Young Men and Ladies Society 253
Nauvoo Expositor 59–60
Nauvoo Legion, Illinois 50–51, 60, 64, 67, 70, 315
Nauvoo Legion, Utah 280, 310, 313–314, 316–317, 319, 321–322, 331–332, 367, 466, 469,
Needham, John 41, 49
Neibaur, Alexander 261, 271
New Hampshire 28, 30, 32, 37, 57–59, 61, 280, 391, 428–429, 456, 459
Nevada Territory 365
Nez Perce Indians 310
Nicholson, John 439
Nicholls, Ruth 458
Niece, Peter 370
Nineteenth Ward 266, 274, 279, 290, 309, 329, 413, 442–444, 449, 454, 457, 460, 476
Noble, Mary Beatrice 453, 456–457
Nodaway River 183
North Platte River 150, 152
Norton, Eli 54–55

O
odometer 149–150, 173, 236
Omaha Indians 477
Oregon Trail 99, 113, 147, 151, 155–156, 161, 163, 192, 206–208, 210–211, 221, 502
Ospry (riverboat) 58
Our Deseret Home magazine 458
Overland Stage Line 395–396, 398, 408

P
Pace, James, Lt. 111–113, 115
Pacific Express Company 298, 334–335
Pacific Springs 161, 176, 212
Pacheco Pass 235, 336
Pack, John 104, 138, 186, 191, 195, 282
Paiute Indians 364, 367, 502
Palmer, James 48–49, 60

Parshleys   28, 30, 429, 456
    Anna Sloper   30
    Charles   45
    John   30
    Mary Caverly   28, 30
    Paul   28
    Richard, Sr.   30
    Richard, Jr.   28, 30
Patriarchal blessings   29, 52
Pawnee Village, Mission   144, 208
Pearce, James   427
Peart, Jacob   99, 123, 130
Peck, Martin H.   187
Perkins, Delavan Duane, Lt.   368–370, 373
Perkins, George Washington   358
Petite, Richard   265
Phelps, Alva   116
Phelps, Morgan   265
Phelps, William W.   64
Philadelphia   35, 59, 110, 322, 324, 326–327, 332, 467, 469, 473
phrenology   253
Pioneer Fort/Old Fort   173, 199–200, 205–207, 209, 386
Pioneer Stage Line   350
Pioneering the West genesis   275, 452–456
Placerville, CA   234, 246, 293–295, 301, 336–339, 351–352, 365, 393–396, 419
Platte River Road   140, 143, 503
Pleasant Valley   340–341, 344–348
plural marriage, polygamy   50, 84, 280, 309, 314, 425, 471
Polk, James K. (President)   57–58, 76, 107–108
Pomeroy, Ebenezer   213, 220
Pomeroy, Irene Hascall   46
Pomeroy, Thaddeus   213, 220
Pomeroy Company   224
Pony Express   xvii–xviii, 201, 291, 331–332, 338, 352–365, 367, 369–374, 376–379, 381–390, 394–396, 411, 413, 423, 430, 452–453, 461, 466–467, 469, 474–480, 482–484
    stations listed   364
    National Historic Trail   137, 388, 503
Pottawattamie Indians   104, 181, 184
Powell, Lazarus W.   329
Pratt, Addison   228–229, 233
Pratt, Orson, Jr.   280
Pratt, Orson, Sr.   59, 84, 88, 100, 124, 138, 144, 149, 151, 155, 163–164, 166, 172, 280, 441, 449–450, 467
Pratt, Parley P.   59, 96, 170, 176, 196, 272, 457

Preator family   459
Preator, Mary Salome   459
Promontory   290, 410, 431
Provo Utah Industrialist (magazine)   458
Putah Ranch, Berryessa   302
Pyramid Lake Battle   367

Q
Quebec   8–12, 14–16
Quinn, Lt.   404

R
Ragtown, NV   248, 295–297, 300
Raleigh, Alonzo   265–266, 274, 279, 443–444, 454
Ransom, John   20, 32
Redden, George   191, 205
Redden, Nancy   xix, 74, 84, 123, 135, 274, 412, 454
Redden, Return Jackson   xix, 85, 88, 102, 151, 170, 295
Redding, *see* Redden
Reese, Catherine   84, 273, 454
Reese, Enoch   254–255, 282
Reese, John   254–255, 262, 296
Reese, Rebecca   253
Reese, Susannah   254
Reese, J and E, Company   255
Reese Mercantile   255
Reese River   341, 390, 398, 420
Reformation, Mormon   4, 189, 303, 308–309
Relief Society   45
Repsher, Daniel M.   62, 65
Reynolds, George   450
Rhodes, David   388
Rhodes, George   126–127, 133
Rich, Charles C.   26, 68, 71–72, 78, 90, 97, 101, 122, 166–167, 176, 193, 220, 226–229, 233–235, 241–247, 250, 401, 405, 471
Richard, John   325
Richards, Franklin D.   81, 271
Richards, Mary Haskin Parker   134–135
Richards, Willard   49, 61, 66, 84–85, 88, 112, 127, 138, 165, 169, 181, 185, 192, 271
Richmond, UT   455, 458, 461, 464
Ricks, Joel   188
Ricks, Thomas   186–189
Rigdon, Sidney   57, 61, 84
Robbins, George C.   264, 266

Roberts, B. H.   440
Roberts, Bill   356
Roberts, Bolivar   356, 370
Roberts Creek   353, 356, 363, 365, 369–370, 409, 420, 504
Robinson, Peter   8–10, 322
Rockwell, Merritt   133–134
Rockwell, Porter   xvii, 164, 193, 245, 296, 318, 322–323, 332, 358, 400, 470–471
Rockwood, Albert P.   65, 96, 138
"Rocky Mountain Justice," "Mountain Justice"   252, 267, 476
Rocky Mountain Prophecy   138
Rogers, "Uncle Billy"   423
Rollins, Henry   234, 244
Ropemaking   26, 474
Roundy, Capt.   197
Roundy, Shadrack   138
Rowberry, John   440
Ruby Valley Mountains   420
Rumfield, Hiram   395, 402, 404, 418
Rush Valley   323, 358–359, 365, 370–371, 381–383, 396, 400, 418–419
Russell, Majors, and Waddell   315, 340, 353, 355–356, 361, 363, 370, 372, 377–378, 387, 480
Russell, William   355–356
Rydalch, W. C.   438

S
Sacrament   98, 165
Sacramento, CA   xvii, 220, 227, 234, 236, 242, 245–247, 250, 284, 289, 291–295, 297–299, 301–302, 334–335, 341, 355–358, 365, 383, 385, 387, 394, 405, 409, 478
sailor, sailor lifestyle   xvii–xviii, 12–14, 20–26, 29, 32, 53, 104, 113, 145, 157, 170, 205, 209, 276, 389, 421, 466, 468, 476
St. Joseph, MO   99, 112, 123–124, 126, 130–131, 154, 183, 205–206, 208, 338, 355–356, 358, 377, 383, 385
St. Lawrence River   12, 14, 18, 22–23
St. Louis, MO   38, 41–44, 58, 108, 126, 131, 184, 205, 207, 255–256, 314, 326, 336, 338
Salem, MA   xvii–xviii, 18, 21–22, 25–30, 32–33, 35–38, 40, 53, 57, 231, 253, 265, 466, 471
Salem Maritime National Historic Site   26
Salinas/Monterrey River   233
Salt/Saline Creek   207
Salt Lake City   29, 167–168, 173–174, 181, 199–200, 204, 213, 216, 218–221, 246–247, 250–252, 255–256, 258, 261–263, 274–276, 279, 281–286, 295–296, 298–299, 301, 304, 306–307, 309–312, 314, 317, 319–325,

614 ~ Faithful and Fearless

    328–329, 332–338, 340, 343, 345–348, 351–353, 355–359, 363, 365, 370–377, 379, 381–384, 386–387, 389, 393–402, 406–413, 419, 421, 423, 425–428, 430–433, 435, 437, 440–444, 449–450, 453–454, 457–462, 465–466, 474, 476, 480–484
    Cemetery   262, 449, 454, 458
    Temple   214, 281
Salt Lake (Hensley) Cutoff   250
Salt Lake Trading Company   xvii, 221, 241–245, 247–248, 334, 481
Salt Spring, NV   298
San Antonio   233
San Bernardino   226–227, 309, 318, 320, 322
San Buenaventura   229, 231
San Gabriel   228–229
San Joaquin Valley, River   235–236
San Juan Baptista   229, 232–234
San Luis Obispo   229, 232–233
San Miguel   118, 229, 232–233
San Pedro   227–228, 243, 322
Sanderson, George B.   110–111, 116, 121
Santa Barbara   229, 231
Santa Fe, NM   xviii, 107, 115, 117–119, 121–122, 124, 162, 222, 480
Santa Fe Trail   xvii, 111, 113, 122
Santa Inez, Ines   229, 506
Sargent, Abel M.   175
Sarpy, Peter   105
Savannah, MO   130–131, 183
Scott's Bluff   152, 178
scurvy   124, 134, 183
Sessions, Patty   88, 134
Seventies   48, 61–63, 69, 74, 77, 83, 87, 91, 181, 253, 263, 273, 443, 47
Sharp, Albert   175
Shearman, William H.   353, 364, 370, 378, 420, 424, 477
Shell Creek, NV   298, 348, 399
Sherman, William T. (Gen.)   445
Shoshoni Indians   291, 310–311, 320, 346
Shumway, Charles   69, 87
Simpson, James H.   331, 343
Simpson, W. R.   404
Simpson Route   331, 343
Simpson Springs   343–344, 347, 349, 365–366, 371, 378, 381, 405, 419
Sioux Indians   76, 126, 144, 151
Skelton, Robert, Publishing   461–463, 465
Skull Valley   423, 427
Slap Jack Bar   244, 246
slaves   56, 192

Sloughhouse, CA   293–295, 302
Smith, Andrew Jackson   111
Smith, Azariah   218
Smith, Bathsheba   80
Smith, Charles Ferguson   367
Smith, Emma   61, 253
Smith, George   49, 59, 77, 84, 88, 124, 138, 165, 168–169, 201–202, 265–267,
    271, 321, 467
Smith, Hyrum   35–36, 38, 49, 51–52, 54, 84, 186
Smith, John   97, 174, 176
Smith, Joseph, Jr.   xvii, 34–35, 37–40, 42–62, 74–76, 83–85, 91, 119, 137–138,
    161, 169, 174, 176, 192, 257, 267, 467, 469, 471, 484
    Campaign for presidency   56–58
    Martyrdom   38, 58–59, 61, 64
Smith, Joseph F.   462
Smith, Lot   xvii, 318, 321, 400, 470–471
Smith, Mary Fielding   186, 188, 192
Smith, Matthew Hale, Rev.   28
Smith, Orson Kirk, Company
Smith, Sam, Capt.   404
Smith, Thomas S., Col.   310
Snake River   250, 310–311
Snow, Charles   207, 276
Snow, Eliza R.   95, 101
Snow, Erastus   35, 37, 57, 138, 166, 265, 447
Snow, Zerubbabel   263–264, 268–271
Soledad, CA   229, 233
Sons of Utah Pioneers
South Pass   160, 163, 179, 197, 212, 317–318, 386, 395
Southern Trail to California   477
Spencer, Daniel   65, 68, 176, 263, 294
Spring Valley, NV   298, 376
stagecoaches, stagecoaching   xvii, 38–39, 291, 293–295, 327, 330–331, 335, 337–
    340, 343, 346–347, 351, 353–355, 363–364, 372–374, 377, 383–384,
    387, 389–404, 406–413, 415–416, 418–420, 423–424, 426, 428–430,
    432, 450, 452–453, 455, 457, 466–467, 469, 474, 476–477, 480–481
Staines, William C.   87, 323
Standage, Henry   121
Stanislaus River   241
Stanley, Alexander
Stansbury, Howard   257, 295
Stenhouse, T. B. H.   326–327
Stephens, Roswell
Stephens, Wallace
Stephens-Murphy Company

Steptoe, Edmund
Steptoe Valley   344–345, 365, 376, 420
Stewart, John   207
Stewart/Stuart, Maria   20
Stiles, George P.   314
Stockton, CA   235, 241–244, 247, 293, 320, 396, 436
Stone, R. H.
Stout, A. J.   265
Stout, Hosea   xvii, 53, 64, 67–69, 78, 91, 95, 106, 128, 185, 195, 258, 260
Sugar Creek Camp   88–90
Sullivan, Marlene   471
Sulpher Springs   297, 365, 420
Sutter, John   217–218, 235, 237
Sweetwater River   154, 158, 195

T
Tabernacle
        Kanesville   180, 184, 482
        Salt Lake City   44, 280
Tadlock, Edwin   442
tannery   4, 278–279
Taylor, John   49, 61, 64, 76, 85, 87, 105, 176–177, 244, 253, 442, 447, 449
Tecumsee   290–291, 296, 478
telegraph   352, 362, 372, 376–377, 385–387, 389, 391, 395, 398, 400, 403–404, 406, 409, 411, 415–416, 429–430, 453, 459
Thompson, George   207
Thompson, John Albert "Snowshoe"   339
tithing   44, 47–48, 75, 218, 243–244, 283, 320–321, 471
Tooele   298–299, 323, 349, 369, 381, 396, 406, 413, 419, 436, 442, 480
Torbuka, Gosiute chief   439–440
Tracy, Theodore F.   409
Transcontinental Railroad   164, 395, 410, 428–429, 433, 455
Truckee River, Pass   248, 295
Tuttle, Mary Ann (*see* Egan, Mary Ann)
Twain, Mark (Samuel Clemens)   235, 389, 391, 393–394, 398
Twiss, Thomas   314

U
Union Pacific Railroad   395
United Order   443–444
Utah Lake   81, 220, 226, 305–306, 329
"Utah War"   xvii, 110, 313, 319–320, 324, 329, 331–332, 343, 469, 481

V
Van Ettan, W.   324
Van Vliet, Stewart, Capt.   317

Vasquez, Louis   162
Vaughn, John N.   258, 260
Volcano, CA   6–7, 293, 295

W
Wade, James   264, 266
Walker War   281
Warner, Mary   287–289, 424
Weed, Stephen H., Lt.   368–369, 373–374, 376
Wells Fargo   377–378, 391–392, 394, 406–410, 480
Weston, MO   113, 123
Whipple, Edson   138, 150, 163, 170
Whitney, Horace K.   92, 104–105, 125–126, 139, 169, 172, 177
Whitney, Newel K.   81, 89, 112, 126
Whitney, Orson   205
Widtsoe, John A.   465
Wilkes, Charles   75
Williams (Chino) Ranch   226–227, 234, 237
Willow Springs (Callao)   299, 363, 365, 374–375, 381, 404, 423
Wilson, Elijah Nicholas (Nick)   140, 196, 384, 399, 461
Winchester, Benjamin   35
Winchester family   205
Winter Quarters   108–109, 123–129, 131–136, 138–139, 142–144, 146–148, 154, 156, 166–167, 172, 174–176, 179–181, 183–184, 186, 188, 197, 200, 216, 221, 291, 325, 411, 466, 472, 480
Woodward, Absalom, Company   334
Woodward, William   256, 260
Woodruff, Wilford   49, 59, 85, 124, 159, 162, 164–167, 170, 172, 175, 181, 306, 308, 434, 447
Woodson, Samuel   333–334
Word of Wisdom   472
Worthen, Lafayette Shaw   324
Worthington, James   438, 442, 448

Y
Young, Brigham   xvii–xix, 44, 49, 52, 57, 59, 61, 63, 65–67, 69–72, 74, 77–78, 81, 84–92, 94, 96–97, 101, 107, 110–111, 116–117, 120–121, 123, 132, 137–138, 140, 144, 155, 162, 164–166, 168–170, 174, 176–179, 181, 185, 192–193, 196–197, 246, 253, 258–259, 266, 271, 274, 308, 313, 321–324, 326–327, 329, 331–332, 411, 444–449, 454, 467–469, 471, 478, 481, 483–484
    death of   445
Young, Harriet   138
Young, Joseph   87
Young, Lorenzo Dow   164, 170

About the Author

William G. Hartley is a retired Brigham Young University history professor. At BYU he primarily taught Utah History and Writing Family Biography. He grew up in Butte, Montana and the San Francisco Bay Area. He received B.A. and M.A. degrees in history from BYU and completed doctoral course work at Washington State University.

He has authored fifteen books and more than 120 articles and chapters, and is recipient of five best book awards and four best article awards from professional associations. He is co-editor of three *Joseph Smith Papers* volumes, two of which received best documentary awards. He's been a president of the Mormon History Association. As a "trail junkie," he was the founding president of the Mormon Trails Association. He has served on editorial boards for the Journal of Mormon History and Mormon Historical Studies, and is a history consultant for the popular KSL TV weekly documentary program "History of the Saints." In 2012 he received the Mormon History Association's prestigious Leonard J. Arrington Award for a lifetime of distinctive contributions to Mormon history. He and his wife Linda live in Saratoga Springs, Utah, and have six children and fourteen grandchildren.

The Family of
Major Howard Egan

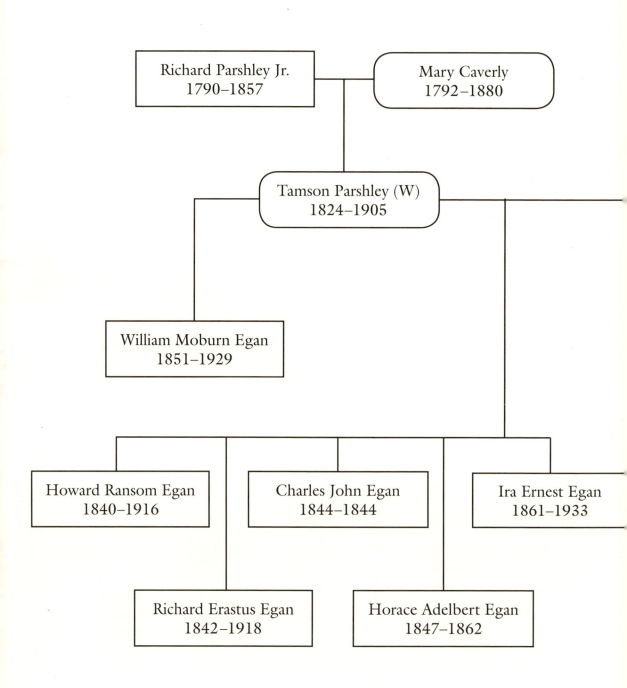